THE VITALITY OF WORSHIP

THE VITALITY
OF WORSHIP

A Commentary on the Book of

Psalms

ROBERT DAVIDSON

WILLIAM B. EERDMANS PUBLISHING COMPANY
GRAND RAPIDS, MICHIGAN / CAMBRIDGE, U.K.

• •

THE HANDSEL PRESS LTD
EDINBURGH

© 1998 Wm. B. Eerdmans Publishing Co.
First published 1998 by Wm. B. Eerdmans Publishing Co.,
255 Jefferson Ave. S.E., Grand Rapids, Michigan 49503 /
P.O. Box 163, Cambridge CB3 9PU U.K.
and
The Handsel Press Limited
The Stables, Carberry, EH21 8PY, Scotland

03 02 01 00 99 98   7 6 5 4 3 2 1

Library of Congress Cataloging-in-Publication Data

Davidson, Robert, 1927-
The vitality of worship: a commentary on the book of Psalms / Robert Davidson.
p.   cm.
Includes bibliographical references and index.
ISBN 0-8028-4246-1 (pbk.: alk. paper)
1. Bible. O.T. Psalms — Commentaries.   I. Title.
BS1430.3.D35   1998
223′.207 — dc21   98-16156
CIP

Handsel Press ISBN 1 871828 46 5

To the Faculty of Divinity, University of Glasgow

*The dedication is an acknowledgement of the privilege I had
of being a member of the Faculty of Divinity
in the University of Glasgow for twenty years.*

*I owe an incalculable debt of gratitude to colleagues
who made these years stimulating and enjoyable
and to generations of students who kept asking questions,
not least about the Psalms.*

CONTENTS

PREFACE

Anyone foolish enough to write a commentary on the Psalms soon realizes that it is a well-nigh impossible task. The Psalms, having been at the center of Jewish and Christian worship and devotion, communal and personal, across the centuries, have given rise to a wealth of spiritual reflection and have been the subject of much contemporary academic debate.

In the context of the series to which this commentary belongs, the emphasis is primarily theological, but it is written in the conviction that theological and academic interests may not only validly coexist, but can enrich one another. The title *The Vitality of Worship* points to where the major theological emphasis lies, namely in the place the Psalms had in the worship of ancient Israel, and in the place they can and ought to have in our understanding of worship today.

There is a considerable amount of repetition and overlap, both linguistic and thematic, in the Psalms. To avoid needless repetition in the commentary, there is normally only one discussion of key words or imagery. Thus "steadfast love" occurs first in Psalm 5:7; thereafter, in most places where it occurs, the only comment is "see 5:7."

My thanks are due to the general editors of the series, Fredrick Carlson Holmgren and George A. F. Knight, whose patience in face of delays in submitting the manuscript was matched only by their encouraging and helpful comments when they received it. I am also indebted to Daniel Harlow, at Eerdmans, for excellent editing work. The Rev. J. Ainslie McIntyre's eagle proofreading eye has led to the correction of many imperfections. Those which remain are my own.

The dedication is an inadequate acknowledgment of the stimulus and the friendship I enjoyed in the university and the faculty in which I spent most of my academic career.

— ROBERT DAVIDSON

INTRODUCTION

It is almost impossible to overestimate the influence of the Psalms on Jewish and Christian tradition, both in terms of the worship of the community and the spiritual experience of countless individuals. Some of the Psalms had a fixed place in the great festivals of the Jewish religious year from an early date. The Gospels tell us that Jesus and his disciples sang "hymns" as they left the upper room in Jerusalem to go out to the Mount of Olives (Mark 14:26). Almost certainly they were singing the hallel psalms, each of them containing the echoing phrase "hallelu-yah," praise the LORD. Psalms 115–118 were normally sung at the end of the Passover meal, Psalms 113–114 at its beginning. Jewish liturgical use of the Psalms has continued across the centuries. In the Daily Morning Service in the Synagogue today there is introductory praise, including Psalms 145–150, since the praise of God should always precede any requests we make to him. The Sabbath Morning Service contains a sequence of psalms culminating in the psalms associated with the Sabbath from an early period, Psalms 92 and 93 (*The Authorised Daily Prayer Book of the United Hebrew Congregations of the Commonwealth*, 1990). Within Christian tradition, worship in many different churches has been nurtured by the Psalms whether spoken or sung in prose or metrical form. Many of the finest Christian hymns are based on the Psalms: witness Luther's "Eine feste Burg ist unser Gott," in its vigorous English rendering by Thomas Carlyle, "A safe stronghold our God is still" (Psalm 46); John Milton's "Let us with a gladsome mind" (Psalm 136); Isaac Watts's "O God our help in ages past" (Psalm 90); Joseph Addison's "The spacious firmament on high" (Psalm 19); and Ian Pitt-Watson's "Thou art before me, Lord, thou art behind" (Psalm 139).

But it is not only in the liturgies of Synagogue and Church that the Psalms have exercised a profound and lasting influence. They have interpreted and are

1

woven into the richly varied experience of countless men and women across the centuries. In the early Church, Theodore of Mopsuestia is on record as saying, "Of other Scriptures most men know nothing. But the Psalms are repeated in private houses, in streets and in market places, by those who have learned them by heart and feel the soothing power of their divine melodies" (quoted in R. E. Prothero, *The Psalms in Human Life* [1903] 14). This is hardly surprising since the Psalms cover the whole gamut of human experience from praise to penitence, from quietly confident faith to agonized perplexity, from joy at the wonder of life in God's world to the struggle to reach out to a God who seems remote or silent, from bowing humbly before the mystery of life to bitter and urgent questioning. It is all there, and because it is all there *we* are there in our ever changing moods and needs. "That is the peculiarity of the Psalter," said Ambrose, "that everyone can use its words as if they were his own" (Prothero, *Psalms in Human Life,* 187). Christians of different persuasions, bitterly divided by theology and politics — Reformers and Scholastics, Roman Catholics and Huguenots, Episcopalians and Covenanters, Royalists and Parliamentarians — have united to face death, often a martyr's death, with the same words on their lips, "Into your hands I commit my spirit" (Ps. 31:5), words which according to Luke were the last words Jesus spoke from the cross (Luke 23:46).

THE HISTORY OF INTERPRETATION

Although the Psalms have spoken in different ways to different people in the varied circumstances of their lives, there have been certain clearly defined ways of understanding the Psalms across the centuries. From an early date many of the Psalms were given a *historical* interpretation. This is clear from the headings attached to some of the Psalms, headings which will be more fully discussed in the commentary. Many of these headings link the Psalms in one way or another with David "singer of Israel's psalms" (2 Sam. 23:1); in certain cases, the headings link the Psalms with specific incidents in the life of David. Thus Psalm 18 claims to be words addressed to the LORD by David "on the day when the LORD delivered him from the hand of all his enemies, and from the hand of Saul"; and indeed Psalm 18 is to be found, with numerous minor variations, in the narrative in 2 Samuel 22 towards the end of David's stormy career. Likewise the heading to Psalm 34 refers to events described in 1 Sam. 21:10-15, when David feigned madness during his spell as a mercenary soldier in the pay of the Philistines, though curiously the psalm heading links the incident with Abimelech, whereas the Samuel narrative says it took place while David was with King Achish of Gath. Psalm 51 is linked with David's penitence "when the prophet Nathan came to him after he had gone in to Bathsheba" (see 2 Sam. 12:1-14). Other such specific historical references are to be found in the headings to Psalms 3, 7, 52,

54, 56, 59, 60, and 63. Even when this traditional link with events in the life of David came increasingly under attack, the attempt was still often made to find other historical contexts in which to place the Psalms. This often entailed dating some of the Psalms to a much later period. Psalm 83, for example, has been assigned to the second century BCE to events described in 1 Maccabees, namely, the expeditions mounted by Judas Maccabaeus in his struggle to achieve and defend Jewish independence.

When the monarchy David founded disappeared and the people of Israel no longer existed as a free and independent nation-state, many of the psalms associated with David were given a new interpretation in the light of the hope of the coming of a future king who would restore the fortunes of his people. It is this future messianic interpretation, already current in early Jewish circles, which we find in the New Testament. Thus in Peter's speeches in Acts 2 and 4, verses from psalms traditionally associated with David are reinterpreted in the light of the life, death, and resurrection of Jesus (e.g., Psalms 2, 16, 110). Even psalms not traditionally linked with David were soon to be given a Christological inter-pretation, as was much else in the Hebrew Scriptures. Augustine, for example, claimed that the blessing in the opening verse of Psalm 1 could only apply to Jesus, and that "the tree planted by the streams of water" (v. 3) is Jesus "who draws in the water, the sinful people as they course along, into the roots of his own moral law." This kind of Christological interpretation has across the centuries been firmly established in Christian tradition — theological, mystical, and litur-gical — and still has many advocates.

A new chapter in the interpretation of the Psalms began with the pioneering work of Hermann Gunkel (1926). Instead of searching for elusive historical events or people in the Psalms, Gunkel adopted a *form-critical* approach, classifying the Psalms into categories or types *(Gattungen)* and seeking to place these types into their appropriate "situation-in-life" *(Sitz im Leben)* in the experience of Israel. Although he identified many "types" of psalms, in the main five predominated and have provided guidelines for the study of the Psalms ever since:

1. The *Hymn,* in which the community gathers to praise God; for example, Psalms 100 and 145-150.
2. *The Communal Lament,* appropriate for a national day of penitence and fasting in response to natural or political disaster; for example, Psalms 44 and 74.
3. *Royal Psalms,* which have as their original reference the position and function of the monarchy in pre-exilic Israel; for example, Psalms 2, 18, 20, 45, and 110.
4. The *Individual Lament,* in which a worshipper in dire straits appeals to God for deliverance, whether it be from sickness, death, or malicious enemies. Within such Psalms — and they are the most common type — the mood

often changes dramatically from the opening cry for deliverance to an assurance that the cry has been heard and answered. Examples are Psalms 3, 5, 7, and 13.

5. *The Individual Song of Thanksgiving,* in which the crisis in the worshipper's life now lies in the past and he comes to give thanks and praise for God's deliverance, sometimes making a vow or offering a thanksgiving sacrifice; for example, Psalms 30, 32, 41, and 116.

Although Gunkel acknowledged that most of these types of psalms had their origin in the worship of the pre-exilic Israelite community, he believed that in their present form they had been loosed from their cultic moorings and had become more personally spiritual in outlook. This belief reflected a Protestant distinction between formal liturgical practice and inner spirituality typical of the nineteenth and twentieth century, a distinction which drew its inspiration from the vigorous attacks which some of the Old Testament prophets made on worship in their day (e.g., Isa. 1:10-17; Jer. 7:1-15).

This Protestant distinction was challenged by Sigmund Mowinckel in a series of important studies on the Psalms (see his *The Psalms in Israel's Worship,* 1962). He emphasized that the Psalms for the most part must still be understood in the light of their place in the cult, many of them in the context of the annual New Year festival in pre-exilic Israel, a festival in which the triumph of Israel's God, Yahweh, in creation and in redemption was celebrated, his kingship over all his foes acknowledged, and the covenant bond between himself and his people renewed. The psalms celebrating Yahweh's kingship, notably Psalms 47, 93, and 95–100, played a pivotal role in Mowinckel's thesis, as did parallels from the Babylonian New Year festival. In the context of this celebration of the kingship of Yahweh, the ruling monarch in Jerusalem played a key role. That the reigning king did have a significant function in worship at the Jerusalem temple seems undoubted, and this has been further developed on the basis of detailed and careful exegesis of some of the Psalms by A. R. Johnson (*Sacral Kingship in Ancient Israel,* 1955), who emphasized the eschatological element in the declaration of Yahweh's kingship.

Whether there ever was in Israel the kind of New Year festival envisaged by Mowinckel, however, is highly debatable. Artur Weiser (*The Psalms,* 1962) argued that the majority of the Psalms have as their *Sitz im Leben* an annual covenant festival in Israel, though he had to admit that the complete liturgy of such a festival never survived. His approach fitted in neatly with the major *Theology of the Old Testament* by Walther Eichrodt, which saw "covenant" as providing the key unifying concept for understanding the Old Testament.

Although Weiser's commentary is theologically stimulating, it must be doubted whether a covenant liturgy was as all-pervasive as he claimed. While Babylonian mythological and liturgical texts deeply influenced the work of

Gunkel and Mowinckel, the impact of the Canaanite Ugaritic texts on the language and thought patterns of the Psalms has been explored, sometimes with surprising results, by Mitchell Dahood (see his three-volume commentary in the Anchor Bible series). Some of his suggestions are highly contentious, but there is little doubt that Canaanite liturgical and mythological tradition has left its mark upon the Psalms.

THE POETRY OF WORSHIP

While a form-critical approach to the Psalms has shown the significant place which the Psalms had in the worship of ancient Israel, there are dangers in merely classifying the Psalms into types, if that encourages us to believe that this is the most important thing to say about them. While each type may have an underlying pattern and contain certain recurring motifs, this must not blind us to the fact that each psalm may contain unique features, which a careful study of the text may reveal and which may have an important bearing on our understanding of the psalm. Moreover, the Psalms are poetry. Poetry is the language of emotion and imagination which, in the context of worship, will seek to explore the mystery of human life as it is touched by God. This is not the place to comment in detail on Hebrew poetry, some of whose features are still a matter of dispute. Many of its characteristics will be noted as we study the texts. The Psalms, however, do not stand alone as examples of Hebrew liturgical poetry. They are part of a tradition whose earliest exemplars are probably the Song of the Sea in Exod. 15:1-18 and the Song of Deborah in Judges 5, a tradition continued in the Prayer of Hannah in 1 Sam. 2:1-10, in Habakkuk 3, and in Jonah 2:2-9.

The authors of most of these liturgical poems are unknown to us. So it is with the Psalms, unless we are prepared to accept uncritically the traditional headings given to some of the Psalms. Even then, the words "to David" are ambiguous. They could mean "composed by David" or "concerning David" or "dedicated to David" or simply "for David." Some of the Psalms may have been specifically composed for worship in the Jerusalem temple by temple singers or musicians prior to the exile; others may reflect the personal experience of otherwise unknown individuals at different periods in Israel's history. Whatever their origin, they became part of Israel's continuing experience in worship because they reflected a common religious pilgrimage and a shared religious heritage with which those who came to worship across the years could readily identify. No religion can have any lasting impact unless it can be handed on, celebrated, remembered, and relived in worship. The Psalms invite us to join Israel in worship and thus come close to the heart of Israel's faith, in all its rich diversity, its confessional certainties, and its perplexities.

In this context, questions concerning the authorship or the original intention of the Psalms become of less importance. Whatever the original meaning and context of a particular psalm, it can be appropriated and given new meaning in new contexts. This is still true of the hymns we use in worship today. Henry Francis Lyte's well-known hymn "Abide with me; fast falls the eventide . . ." was written in the face of increasing physical frailty and in the belief that death was not far distant. This is the original meaning of the "eventide" and the "darkness" of which the hymn speaks. Yet in many hymnals it is classified as an evening hymn. This is where it appears, for example, in the revised edition of the *The Church Hymnary* (1927), among the hymns recommended as suitable for "Worship Evening." In the third edition of *The Church Hymnary* (1973), however, it no longer appears among the evening hymns but among the hymns of "Personal Faith and Devotion," closer to its original intention. Yet for many people it will remain as a favorite evening hymn. It may be wondered whether either classification tells us anything about what it means when sung by 80,000 fans at a football cup final! So it is with some of the Psalms. Whatever pilgrim procession to the Jerusalem temple or liturgical act originally lies behind Ps. 24:7-10, in Scottish Reformed tradition — in its metrical form "Ye gates, lift up your heads on high," sung to the tune St. George's Edinburgh — it is inevitably associated with the celebration of Holy Communion and with the Great Entry when the elements of bread and wine are brought into the church.

This does not mean, however, that the appropriateness of the Psalms for us is always readily accessible. Luther, interpreting the reference to "the garden of nuts" in Song of Songs 6:11 to refer to Scripture, comments: "And the Psalter is properly a garden of nuts, outwardly somewhat hard at first glance, but having a sweet kernel within it" (*First Lectures on the Psalms,* 257). Before we can get to the kernel, however, the outer shell is sometimes harder to crack than at other times.

THE BOOK

Although we talk about the Book of Psalms, or simply the Psalms, we must remember that behind the present book there lies, as there lies in the case of many other Old Testament books, a complex history. Our present book of Psalms contains five collections of psalms: (1) Psalms 1–41, (2) Psalms 42–72, (3) Psalms 73–89, (4) Psalms 90–106, and (5) Psalms 107–150. Each of these collections, with the exception of the last, climaxes in a doxology concluding with the word "Amen."

The relationship between these five collections is far from clear. Two psalms in the first collection, Psalm 14 and part of Psalm 40, occur again with minor variations in the second collection as Psalms 53 and 70. Among the minor variations — and this is characteristic of the first and second collections as a whole — is the tendency in Psalms 14 and 40 to use the Hebrew personal name for God, Yahweh, normally rendered in English translations LORD, whereas Psalms 53 and 70 use the more general name for God, *ĕlōhîm*. In the fifth collection, one psalm, Psalm 108, joins together parts of two psalms from the second collection, Ps. 57:7-11 and Ps. 60:5-12. There are other interesting features of the different collections. In the first collection, all the psalms, with the exception of Psalms 1 and 2, have titles associating them with David, as have more than half of the psalms in the second collection. The second collection then ends with the words, "the prayers of David, the son of Jesse, are ended." Yet one psalm in the third collection is associated with David and others in the fourth collection, while in the fifth collection a quarter of the psalms are Davidic.

In the second collection, a group of psalms are associated with "the sons of Korah," as are four psalms in the third collection, Psalms 84, 85, 87, and 88. The third collection has a group of psalms (Psalms 73–83) associated with "the sons of Asaph," and this group has one forerunner in the second collection, Psalm 50. According to Chronicles, both "the sons of Korah" and "the sons of Asaph" had close links with the temple, "the sons of Asaph" specifically as musicians or temple singers (2 Chron. 5:12).

One psalm is associated with Moses (Psalm 90), one with the shadowy figure of Ethan (Psalm 89), and two with Solomon (Psalms 72 and 127). Some psalms seem to have been grouped together because of their common subject matter; Psalms 93–99, for instance, celebrate the kingship of Yahweh. Others have links with particular festivals; Psalm 92, for instance, is associated with the Sabbath; Psalms 113–118, with Passover; Psalms 120–134, the "Songs of Ascent," with pilgrimage to the Jerusalem temple.

There have been many attempts in recent years to explain how this motley collection of material came into its present shape and form. Links in language and theme between adjacent psalms have been noted, as have the links between the different collections within the book. Whether we can discover one overarching literary or theological purpose linking all the psalms together and accounting for the present order of the book remains uncertain. Like the Torah, the traditional five books of Moses, the five collections which make up the present book of Psalms draw material from many different sources and span many centuries. It is doubtful whether any modern hymnbook editorial committee would be satisfied with the order — or disorder — which lies before us in the present book. That is part of the fascination and the challenge of the Psalms as we now have them.

Unless otherwise indicated, the text followed in the commentary is that of the *New Revised Standard Version* (NRSV), although reference will be made to the *Revised English Bible* (REB), particularly where it differs significantly from the NRSV, and on occasion to the *Good News Bible* (GNB).

BOOK ONE

PSALMS 1–41

We have already noted that Psalms 1 and 2, unlike the other psalms in Book One, have no headings linking them with David. They have other common features. Psalm 1 begins, "Happy the person who . . ."; this is echoed in the closing line of Psalm 2, "Happy are all who. . . ." Psalm 1 speaks of the person who "sits in the seat of the scornful"; Psalm 2 of the God who "sits in the heavens." Psalm 1 commends the person who "meditates on the law of the LORD"; Psalm 2 mocks the nations who are engaged in a different kind of "meditation," namely, plotting — the same Hebrew word being used in Ps. 1:2 and in Ps. 2:1. The closing words of Psalm 1 claim that "the way of the wicked will perish"; Ps. 2:12, addressing those who threaten God's rule, declares "you will perish on the way."

There is some evidence from early Jewish and Christian sources that these two psalms were sometimes regarded as one. Certainly, together Psalms 1 and 2 provide an appropriate overture to the entire Psalter since they introduce themes which are to be heard repeatedly, in infinitely varied form and keys, through the entire book. Since all the psalms in Book One from 3 to 41 are in their present text headings linked to David — assuming that Psalms 9 and 10 are one psalm (see commentary) — Psalm 2, whose theme is the challenge to the LORD and his anointed king on Zion, may originally have provided an introduction to this Davidic collection. Psalm 1 may then have been added to provide an introduction to the psalms in their entirety, once this Davidic collection was placed in a larger setting. Psalm 1 sounds forth the challenge of the two ways, explicit or implicit in every psalm, reminding us that worship and the life of faith confront each one of us with challenge and choice.

Psalm 1
THE CHALLENGE OF THE TWO WAYS

Worship and faith unite, but they also separate. They unite those who appear in the Psalms repeatedly as "the righteous," but they separate the righteous from "the wicked." A rich cluster of descriptive words gather round both "the righteous" and "the wicked" in the Psalms, and the meaning to be assigned to the words will vary according to context. One thing, however, must be said at the outset or many of the Psalms will be misunderstood: "the righteous" are not the self-righteous. Essentially they are those who seek to be in the right with God, often humble folk who find their true home in life within the fellowship of God's people. "The wicked," by contrast, are those who flout the authority of God and who seek in a variety of ways to oppress or to undermine the people of God.

Psalm 1 is carefully structured to draw attention to this contrast. Verses 1-3 describe the way of the righteous and the consequences which flow from following this way, though the word "righteous" does not occur in these verses. Verses 4-5 describe the consequences which follow from walking in the footsteps of the wicked. The psalm then concludes in verse 6 by sharply contrasting the respective fates of the righteous and the wicked.

Some of the characteristic features of Hebrew poetry are well illustrated in this psalm: the same basic thought repeated in parallel lines and phrases (see verses 1, 2, and 5); the neatly stated contrast in verse 6; and the use of chiasm, where the order of words in the first part of a verse is inverted in the second part to give an ABBA pattern (see verse 2). There remains, however, a basic freedom in the poetry with sometimes three pictures in a verse, sometimes two. There is still considerable discussion about Hebrew poetry, concerning how many stresses or accents make up a unit or line and how these stresses are to be calculated. We shall look at this issue only when different ways of dividing the poetry have implications for our understanding of a psalm.

1-3   The psalm is introduced by the Hebrew word *'ašrê,* traditionally translated "blessed." It is the word which in its Greek form *makarios* is central to the Beatitudes in Matt. 5:3-12. If we translate, as most modern versions do, "happy," that leaves us asking what kind of happiness is meant. The word is found most frequently in the wisdom books of the Old Testament. In Proverbs it has close links with that wisdom which leads to responsible and desirable conduct, the fruit of which includes long life, riches, and honor (see Prov. 3:13, 16; 14:21). In the Psalms, however, a strong emphasis is often placed upon the basis for such a happy and rewarding life being in a personal relationship with the living God, a relationship celebrated joyfully in worship since it evokes from people a response of praise and trust (e.g., Ps. 2:11; 65:4; 84:4, 5; 89:15). Here in Psalm 1 the life of a person experiencing such happiness is described both negatively and positively. There is a "no" to be said; "no" to following the advice of the wicked; "no" to conniving with (literally, "standing in the way of") "sinners," those who are well wide of the mark in their attitude towards life; "no" to cultivating the company of "scoffers" or cynics. The word translated "scoffers" occurs only here in the Psalms. Its meaning is well illustrated in Prov. 21:24, "The proud, haughty person, named 'Scoffer,' acts with arrogant pride." This is the insolent "Mr. Know-it-all" who accepts no authority other than his own. The spiritual need to say "No" to such people, and the dangers involved in saying it are well explored in C. S. Lewis, *Reflections on the Psalms.*

Positively, here is a person whose life centers on "the Law of the LORD," on the Torah — the five books of Moses, Genesis to Deuteronomy. The Torah is God's gift to Israel, that story of God's gracious dealings with his people and the people's necessary response enshrined in what was to be forever central to Jewish faith. Forget about harsh legalism. In the Psalms the response to the Torah is not that of trying to climb an impossibly high mountain out of a cold sense of duty. God has placed the Torah in the hearts of his faithful people (Ps. 37:31; 40:8). It is central to their happiness (Ps. 94:12), its richness explored in the symphonic poem which is Psalm 119. It elicits an obedience, a way of life gladly given, rooted in "delight," the fruit of constant meditation. Such meditation probably involved memorizing and reciting the words of the Torah. Such is the basis for human life which is effective and successful. This is spelled out in the picture of the tree planted beside natural flowing streams or an irrigation channel (the Hebrew word in verse 3 can mean either), fruitful and ever green because assured of a constant supply of water. There is a close parallel to this picture in Jer. 17:7-8, where those who trust in the LORD are compared to an ever green, fruitful tree planted beside water. Attempts have been made to draw conclusions about the date of Psalm 1 on the basis of its relation to Jeremiah 17. It is doubtful, however, whether we need assume any link for what is, after all, a fairly natural simile.

But what kind of success in life is implied in the words "In all that they do, they prosper" (v. 3)? Joshua 1:8, which linguistically has many points of contact with Ps. 1:2-3, poses the issue. There Joshua is commanded to meditate on the book of the Law day and night and to act in accordance with its instructions. "For then you shall make your way prosperous, and then you shall be successful." Such success is then spelled out in tangible, this-worldly terms — crossing the Jordan, defeating Israel's enemies, and settling in the promised land. So it is in many of the Psalms. The person who fears the LORD and walks in his ways will, according to Psalm 128, be blessed with a large family, his wife "a fruitful vine" (Ps. 128:3). The author of Psalm 37 declares, "I have been young, and am now old, yet I have not seen the righteous forsaken or their children begging for bread" (Ps. 37:25).

Psalm 144 depicts the happiness which comes to those whose God is the LORD in terms of healthy children, abundant crops and fertile flocks, national security, and "no cry of distress in our streets" (Ps. 144:12-14). Belief in the link between obedience to God and worldly, material prosperity is widespread in the Old Testament both at a national level (see Deuteronomy) and at a personal level (see the arguments of Job's friends). No doubt for some in ancient Israel life did follow this script, and there are those who today claim that it still does. But what of the many others whose experience was and is different? Famine, ethnic cleansing, and bloodshed do not distinguish between the innocent and the guilty, or the God-fearing and the godless.

4-6   The problem is intensified by the contrary description of the wicked in verses 4-5. They are no flourishing tree, fruitful and ever green; "but they are like chaff that the wind drives away" (v. 4). How true is this to experience? When one of Job's friends declares that

> the exulting of the wicked is short,
>   and the joy of the godless is but for a moment (Job 20:5)

Job can only retort:

> Why do the wicked live on,
>   reach old age and grow mighty in power?
> Their children are established in their presence,
>   and their offspring before their eyes.
> Their houses are safe from fear,
>   and no rod of God is upon them. (Job 21:7-9)

Bitterly he asks the question,

> How often are they like straw before the wind,
>   and like chaff that the storm carries away? (Job 21:18)

What then are we to make of the central assertion of Psalm 1, neatly summarized in its concluding words:

> The LORD watches over the way of the righteous,
>   but the way of the wicked perishes?

1. We may argue that what the psalmist is giving us is a confession of faith, not a description of life. The trouble with this is that the more life's experiences call into question statements of faith, the more we need to examine and reexamine what we claim to believe. If indeed the LORD watches over the way of the righteous, then

Why, O LORD, do you stand far off?
  Why do you hide yourself in times of trouble? (Ps. 10:1)

Rouse yourself! Why do you sleep, O LORD?
  Awake, do not cast us off for ever!
Why do you hide your face?
  Why do you forget our affliction and oppression? (Ps. 44:23-24)

If "the way of the wicked perishes," why is it that the wicked sometimes seem to experience that fullness of life which is called *šalôm* in Hebrew? Why are they carefree, successful, popular, flinging defiance in God's face yet amassing wealth (see Psalm 73)? If Psalm 1 provides us with an introductory overture to the entire Psalter, then perhaps it is not surprising that many other psalms seem to enter into dialogue with it, questioning and searching for meaning in the midst of experiences which seem cruelly meaningless. Perhaps it is only those who have struggled with such questions who can fully and honestly join in the great hallelujah chorus in Psalms 148–150.

2. We may argue that the prosperity of the righteous whose life is rooted in the Torah refers not, or not only, to material success but to an inner quality of life which by very definition lies outside the experience of the wicked. Likewise, the judgment which is to befall the wicked points to God's ultimate verdict on their lives. Thus Calvin, commenting on verses 5-6, declares: "We see now how the prophet considers the ungodly to be miserable, because happiness is the inward good of the conscience. He denies not that before driven to the trial all things go well with them, but he denies that they are happy unless they are sustained by solid and steadfast integrity." Calvin is driven to this comment because in terms of his own personal experience he was only too well aware that the true worshippers of God often seemed to get no tangible reward in this life, while those whom he regarded as the enemies of true faith often seemed to flourish. The phrase "the wicked will not stand in the judgment" (v. 5) he then takes to refer to a future beyond this present life when God will sit in judgment and pronounce his final, irrevocable verdict. But this seems unlikely, unless one follows M. Dahood in finding frequent references to eternal life and to the final judgment in the Psalms. Rather, verse 5 means that when called to account either by due legal process in society or spiritually by God in the here and now, the wicked have no valid defense. They have no true part in the worshipping community. If the psalmists had been able to call in the next world to redress the balance of the present, they could have eased their problems. But they couldn't and they didn't. They had to struggle to make sense of the meaning of life both for the righteous and for the wicked in what they believed to be God's world.

Although Psalm 1 has many of the features of the wisdom teaching in the Old Testament (e.g., the doctrine of the two ways and the contrast between righteous and wicked), it is not merely a piece of wisdom teaching. It has its setting in the worship of the Israelite-Jewish community, probably after the return from exile. Like all liturgical material, whether hymns or prayers, it was therefore adaptable to meet the needs of different worshipping communities. Not surprisingly, within Christian tradition it has been given a distinctively Christian interpretation. Thus Augustine argued that the person referred to in verse 1 must be none other than Jesus Christ, since no other person comes near to the human perfection implied in the portrait of that person. A hidden Christian spiritual meaning has often been found in other details of the psalm. Thus, for example, a nineteenth-century commentator claims concerning verse 3: "The green foliage is an emblem of faith which converts the water of life of the divine word into sap and strength, and the fruit an emblem of works which gradually ripen and scatter their blessings around" (F. Delitzsch). While some may find such an approach spiritually helpful, it takes us far beyond the original text and seems to have little organic relationship to it. The central claim of Psalm 1, however, and the way in which it is questioned in other psalms, poses a problem as germane to Christian experience and the often tragic world in which we live, as it was and is to the Jewish community. As Christians we need to reflect upon it in the light of the cross and the two words from the cross which are quotations from the Psalms. According to Luke 23:46 the last words of Jesus were "Father, into your hands I commit my spirit," words taken from Ps. 31:5 and rooted in the conviction that "the LORD watches over the way of the righteous." If these are the words of the only one whom Christians claim to be wholly righteous, then let us remember that according to the other Gospels (Matt. 27:46; Mark 15:34) they were preceded in the agony of crucifixion by the opening words of Psalm 22: "My God, my God, why have you forsaken me?" In the midst of faith's assurance there is often the dark night of the soul, dark precisely because the soul has once known the light of that happiness of which Psalm 1 so confidently speaks. Such happiness has often to be rediscovered and affirmed anew in the midst of what seems to be darkness.

Psalm 2
A FUTILE CHALLENGE

Psalm 1 focused on the continuing choice in life — to identify with the wicked or with the righteous — and on the inevitable consequences of such a choice. But such choice takes place and is only meaningful within the context of a world under the sovereignty of God. Psalm 2 speaks of a challenge, a futile challenge to such sovereignty. This is a royal psalm, probably originally part of the liturgy celebrating the accession to the throne of the king in pre-exilic Jerusalem, and of an annual ceremony reenacting the coronation and confirming the vital place of the king in the life of the community. Verses 1-6 and verses 10-11 were probably spoken by whoever was leading the liturgy, while in verses 7-9 we are hearing the words of the king himself. If, however, we follow the reading of the Greek (LXX) text in verse 6, the whole psalm may have been spoken by the king.

1-3 The psalm begins with an astonished, almost incredulous series of questions, the opening "Why?" applying to the whole of verses 1 and 2. It was not uncommon for subject peoples to make a bid for independence when the throne of their imperial overlord fell vacant. The mettle of the successor to the throne had still to be tested. Now, if any, was the time to throw off the oppressor's yoke. Through echoing phrases in poetic parallelism, the picture of such a rebellion is deftly drawn: "nations" reviewing their position, calculating the odds; "peoples" actively engaged in secret plotting — the verb translated "plot" in verse 1 being the same as the verb translated "meditate" in Psalm 1:2. What these people meditate or contemplate is rebellion." "Kings . . . set themselves," that is, make preparations for war; "rulers," petty princes, sit down together to consider a plan of campaign. They have one aim, to rid themselves of the yoke of the oppressor (v. 3), the "bonds" and "cords" being the strips of leather tying the neck of a domesticated animal to the yoke, and therefore the symbol of subjection. But, claims the psalmist, this is no rebellion against any human overlord; this is rebellion against "the LORD and his anointed" (v. 2).

Anointing with oil as a sign of consecration to some function or office is mentioned frequently in the Old Testament. It applies to things such as the tabernacle, the altar, and all the utensils needed for the worship of God (Lev. 8:10-11); it applies to people such as priests and prophets (Exod. 28:41; 1 Kgs. 19:16; Ps. 105:15). Most frequently, however, "the anointed" (Hebrew *mašiah*, from which we get our English word "messiah") refers to the king (e.g., 1 Sam. 24:6, 10), especially the king from the royal family of David who occupied the throne in Jerusalem.

The language of this opening section of the psalm, and indeed of other parts of the psalm (e.g., vv. 8-9), can hardly be taken as a sober description of any given historical situation. Not even David at the height of his power could claim such world dominion. This is the language of poetry, drawing upon courtly etiquette which we can document from many ancient Near Eastern sources, courtly etiquette which used heavily stylized and conventionally exaggerated language that appealed to royal amour propre. Is the language of this psalm then merely an attempt to massage the ego of a petty Judean king? No, because the psalmist believes that behind this anointed king stands the LORD. Although the rebels may not know it, they are challenging the authority of the God who in the words of another Hebrew poet-prophet is:

> he who sits above the circle of the earth,
>   and its inhabitants are like grasshoppers;
> who stretches out the heavens like a curtain,

and spreads them like a tent to live in;
who brings princes to naught,
and makes the rulers of the earth as nothing. (Isa. 40:22-23)

That is why the opening questions are incredulous. How can anyone, even the most powerful earthly ruler, hope successfully to break free from the constraints of such a God? Instead of trying to throw off what they regard as the yoke of such servitude, they ought to be recognizing that it is only in such servitude that they can find their true freedom (cf. Matt. 11:29-30; Gal. 5:1).

4-6 These verses give God's response. In the dramatic and highly anthropomorphic language of verse 4, such rebellion is regarded not only as futile and misguided but as laughable in the eyes of the divine king who "sits in the heavens," his throne. By the beginning of verse 5 the point of no return has been reached, indicated by the Hebrew word translated "then"; that being the case, the LORD who reacts in anger against any threat to his authority intervenes to speak his decisive word: "It is I [the Hebrew is emphatic] who have set my king on Zion, my holy hill." No other endorsement or validation is needed. The Greek (LXX) translation which reads, "I have been set as your king on Zion," probably arose through a failure to see that within the psalm there is a dialogue between God and the king, a dialogue which means that the "I" who speaks in verse 6 is God, and the "I" who speaks in verse 7 is the king. Hebrew unfortunately does not use inverted commas to introduce different speakers.

In the narrative in 2 Sam. 5:7, "the stronghold of Zion" is the name given to the Jebusite fortress which David captured to make into the capital of his united kingdom. "Zion" then becomes in the Old Testament one of the names of Jerusalem or sometimes, more specifically, of the hill at its center on which stood the temple built by Solomon. City and temple are the focus of the thought of many psalms, the visible and tangible symbols of the people's devotion (see, e.g., Psalms 46; 48; 84; 122). This was not just any city, but "the city of our God . . . the city of the great King" (Ps. 48:1, 2), the city centering upon "the house of the LORD" (Ps. 122:1, 9), where the LORD God of hosts dwells in the midst of his people. It is therefore "holy," different from any other ordinary city however important, since it belongs in a special way to God. The word "holy" in the sense of belonging especially to God or set apart for the service of God is used widely in the Psalms of places (cf. Ps. 11:4, where it refers to the temple) and of people. It is also the word which is used to describe the essential nature of God, that which differentiates him from any human weakness or faults and which evokes from his people a response of awe and praise (Ps. 22:3; Isa. 6:3).

7-9 Now the king speaks. In the coronation ritual in ancient Egypt, the Pharaoh was given a document spelling out his rights and his duties, the power bestowed upon him by the gods and what was expected of him as a wise ruler of the people. Something similar seems to have happened in the coronation service in Jerusalem when the king was given and acknowledged receipt of "the decree of the LORD" (v. 7). What exactly was in this decree we do not know. There may be hints of it in other royal psalms such as Psalms 72, 89, and 110. Whatever its precise content, both the rights and the duties of this king stem from one thing, the special relationship with the LORD into which he enters at his coronation. At that moment he becomes God's son — "You are my son" — by adoption. In 2 Sam. 7:14 the prophet Nathan, speaking in the name of God, declares, "I shall be a father to him [i.e., David's heir], and he shall be a son to me." Other psalms will speak of the same relationship in terms of God's "covenant with David" (e.g., Ps. 89:3-4), the special bond between God and the Davidic royal family.

As son, the king is naturally God's heir, entitled to an inheritance from God (v. 8). This inheritance, which is there for the asking, consists of "the nations . . . the ends of the earth," all those attempting to rise in futile rebellion. The whole of verse 9 is best taken to refer to the powerful, almost effortless way in which the king will crush his enemies. The "rod of iron," a phrase not found elsewhere in the Old Testament, may refer to a royal scepter, symbol of the king's power. With it he will "break" or crush his enemies as easily as a piece of pottery is smashed into bits. Behind this picture there may lie the practice, known to us from Egyptian texts, of inscribing the names of enemies on pieces of pottery, solemnly pronouncing a curse upon them, and then smashing the pottery as a power-charged symbolic act which would guarantee their defeat. Instead of "break," the Greek text (LXX) reads the same Hebrew consonants as "shepherd" or "rule." This is how the passage is quoted in Rev. 2:26-27 (cf. Rev. 12:5; 19:15). The way in which the Greek text is cited in the New Testament, however, cannot be taken to decide the meaning of the Hebrew or used to give it a gentler, more compassionate meaning. The second half of verse 9 continues and reinforces the meaning of the first half. Indeed, even if we follow the New Testament and render "rule," Rev. 19:15 sees this as a majestic, destructive rule and not a gentle shepherding of the people.

10-12   The psalm ends with a warning and an invitation. The warning is to all other rulers not to be so stupid as to take part in a futile rebellion. Instead they must "serve the LORD with fear," acknowledge his power, and bow down in reverence before him. The language of verse 10 and the opening words of verse 11 — "be wise . . . be warned . . . fear the LORD" — have close links with the wisdom tradition as we find it in Proverbs (cf. Prov. 1:7; 2:5, 9, 10). Psalmists and wise men often join hands, with worship providing a context for teaching on how to live the good life. To rebel against God, however, is to court divine retribution.

The text at the end of verse 11 and at the beginning of verse 12 has led to endless discussion. The Hebrew may be translated "and rejoice with trembling, kiss the son"; the word "son" here is not the usual Hebrew word, *ben,* but the Aramaic *bar.* This has been explained on the grounds that it avoids the awkwardness of the Hebrew *ben* being immediately followed by the similar sounding *pen* ("lest, or"). All the early versions and commentators, however, had trouble with the text. Instead of "kiss the son," the Greek (LXX) and the Aramaic render "lay hold of" or "receive instruction," and another early Greek translator, Symmachus, has "worship sincerely." The commonly accepted emendation today — though it is far from certain — is to read "and with trembling kiss his feet." Kissing the feet was a well-known act of humble submission in the ancient world. Isaiah 49:23 looks forward to the day when roles will be reversed and Israel's present oppressors will become humble servants: "With their faces to the ground, they shall bow down to you, and lick the dust of your feet." If this commonly accepted emendation is correct, then all reference to "the son" disappears from verse 12. The obedience which is demanded and expected is obedience to the divine king; to disobey him can only lead to swift disaster.

But warning is not the note on which the psalm ends. There is an alternative to defying God, namely accepting an invitation to "take refuge in him" (v. 12). This is a characteristic phrase in the Psalms to describe the attitude of those who are prepared to put their trust in God, to take shelter under his protection (e.g., Pss. 5:11; 7:1; 11:1). That is the way which leads to "happiness."

We have been looking at this psalm in the light of its setting in the life of ancient Israel, part of the coronation service or of an annual commemoration of the king's accession to the throne. Royal psalms, however, came to take on different meanings in the light of changing circumstances. After the fall of Jerusalem to the Babylonians in 587 BCE, the Jewish people had to live for centuries under foreign overlords — Babylonian, Persian, Greek, and Roman. Except for a brief period, they had no king of their own, no "messiah" crowned and ruling in Jerusalem over a sovereign state. Increasingly hopes centered on the future. One day God would send another king, descendant of the royal family of David, who would crush all his people's enemies and rule in freedom and peace — the king to come. Not surprisingly, when the early Christians came to believe that in Jesus that king *had* come, they read the royal psalms, and in particular Psalm 2, in the light of that belief. Psalm 2, in fact, is quoted or referred to more frequently than any other psalm in the New Testament. According to Mark's Gospel, at the moment of Jesus' baptism the voice from heaven said to Jesus, "You are my son" (Mark 1:11, citing Ps. 2:7). In the story of the transfiguration in Luke 9, the voice from the cloud says, "This is my son" (Luke 9:35). In Acts 4:25-26 Peter in his sermon quotes Ps. 2:1-2, identifying Herod and Pilate with the nations, the peoples plotting against Jesus, God's anointed. Paul in the synagogue at Antioch claims that verse 7 was fulfilled in the resurrection of Jesus (Acts 13:33). Other quotations are to be found in

Hebrews and in Revelation. Many Christians have continued so to read the psalm across the centuries as pointing to Jesus Christ, Christ being simply the Greek form of the Hebrew *mašiaḥ,* "the anointed." Thus, "the Old Testament knows no kingship to which is promised the dominion of the world and to which sonship is ascribed . . . but the Davidic. The events of his own time which influenced the mind of the poet are no longer clear to us. But from them he is carried away into the tumults of the peoples which shall end in all the kingdoms becoming the kingdom of God and his Christ" (F. Delitzsch).

Naturally, Jews do not read the psalm with this Christian slant. But Jew and Christian can join hands in recognizing that this psalm, like Psalm 1, speaks of a stark choice which has ultimate consequences: the choice between believing that what we decide in greed and selfishness, and in our lust for power and security, has the final word to say concerning human life and destiny, or believing that we stand now and forever under the rule of God. It is the choice between believing that naked human power and military hardware decide the history of people and nations, or believing that true security and fullness of life can only be found in the fear of the LORD. The psalm invites us to ponder the consequences of the choices we make and challenges us to decide in what or in whom we are prepared to place our ultimate trust.

Psalm 3
LIGHT IN A DARK HOUR

Psalm 3 is the first of the most common type of psalm, the psalm of lament — striking witness to the fact that for many in Israel faith was no easy passage, but was often severely tested. Like all the following psalms in Book One, Psalm 3 is linked by its heading to David. It is one of several psalms placed in a particular context in David's life, in this case the story of Absalom's revolt as described in 2 Samuel 15. Since the psalm headings are late, this simply tells us how the psalm came to be interpreted in learned Jewish circles, and that is important in the history of the interpretation of the psalm. The crisis in the psalmist's life is described in very general terms. He speaks of "my foes," "many rising against me," "my enemies," "the wicked." A case can be made, therefore, for defending the link with Absalom's revolt. There are other features of the psalm, however — for example, the reference to the LORD's "holy hill" (v. 4) — which make this doubtful and point to a time later than David. Indeed, the psalmist need not be regarded as a king in dire straits. The psalm could mirror the experience of anyone living through a crisis of faith in which he feels isolated and under attack by many enemies. In this crisis he reaches out in trust to the God whom others claim has deserted him. The book of Jeremiah bears eloquent witness to a similar experience in the life of the prophet (cf. Jer. 15:15-18; 17:14-18).

1-2 The psalm begins, typically for such a lament psalm, by describing the situation of crisis in the psalmist's life. Its seriousness is emphasized by the recurring use of the word "many" — "many . . . foes," "many rising against me," "many . . . saying." The many who speak in verse 2 are either his enemies pouring scorn on his faith, saying, "He's had it"; or they could be others still sympathetic to his plight, but sadly shaking their heads since they see no end to his troubles. There is no need to change the "help for him" of the Hebrew text into "help for you," as in the NRSV. The word translated "help" appears in variant form in verse 8, where it is translated "deliverance." The verb from the same root occurs in verse 7, where it is rendered "save." This is the Hebrew root traditionally translated "salvation." It covers a wide range of meanings, indicating deliverance, liberation from any kind of restraint or oppression, physical, mental, or spiritual. It points to a life of wholeness and freedom under God, a life in which people have the space to be what God intended them to be. Whenever it occurs in the Old Testament, context must be our guide as to what kind of help, deliverance, or freedom is appropriate. If others think either gladly or sadly that there is no help, no way out for the psalmist, then his God is being discredited. Personal hatred is hard enough to bear, but it is made the more deadly by the insidious attempt to undermine everything that he believes.

3-6 In the face of this, the psalmist defiantly clings to faith in God, verse 3 beginning emphatically, "But it is you, O LORD. . . ." His enemies may be numerous and powerful, but he draws on his experience of the God who has sustained him in the past, the God who is "a shield around me." Just as the round leather shield gave protection to a warrior in battle, so "shield" becomes a favorite title for God the protector of those who put their trust in him. "The LORD is my strength and my shield, in him my heart trusts; so I am helped" (Ps. 28:7; cf. Pss. 18:2; 33:20).

"But it is you, O LORD. . . my glory." God is the one who is central to all that is important and significant in the psalmist's life, or the one who can be depended upon to defend the psalmist's honor and dignity. The word "glory" (Hebrew *kābôd*, literally, "weight") indicates a person's standing in the community, and when applied to God it points to his standing at the center of life, his supreme power and majesty, awesome and incomparable. God is the one who "lifts up my head" — the God who has vindicated him and seen him through many a difficult situation in the past. In Gen. 40:13 the phrase is used of Pharaoh's cupbearer being released from prison and restored to favor, but when it is applied to the chief baker, it means that he is going to be hanged! The God who "answers me from his holy hill" — here the psalmist is drawing on his experience of answered prayer. Looking back across his life, he knows that it has been enriched and touched at many points and in many ways by God. He has known the healing presence of God in worship in the temple, so he trusts the same God to be with him in his present need. In the same way Paul, on the basis of his past experience of Christ, can triumphantly affirm: "I am convinced that neither death, nor life, nor angels, nor rulers, nor things present, nor things to come, nor powers, nor height, nor depth, nor anything else in all creation, will be able to separate us from the love of God in Christ Jesus our Lord" (Rom. 8:38-39).

In the light of such a faith, the psalmist commits himself to God's care. What might have been a restless, troubled night becomes a night of quiet, restoring sleep with an awakening to a new day, sign of God's continuing protection (v. 5). The crisis remains. There are still those only too eager to attack him, "ten thousands" of them — the Hebrew word contains an echo of the word for "many" in verses 1 and 2. Fear of them, however, has gone (cf. Pss. 27:1, 3; 118:6). In a similar vein, a prophet will say in the name of God over and over again to a people facing a crisis of faith, "Fear not, I will help you" (Isa. 40:13, 14).

7-8   Out of his conviction that his prayers have been answered in the past, the psalmist now prays (v. 7) that God will go into action — "Rise up, O LORD" — to rescue him and to crush the threat of his enemies, whom he identifies with "the wicked." The words "rise up" probably go back to the ark, the early symbol of God's presence with his people and to the old battle cry associated with it. Whenever the ark was carried in the midst of the people, Moses would say, "Arise, O LORD, let your enemies be scattered and your foes flee before you" (Num. 10:35).

"Striking on the cheek" is an act of contemptuous dismissal (cf. 1 Kgs. 22:24; Job 16:10); "breaking the teeth" is a way of taming a wild animal and rendering it powerless (Ps. 58:6; Job 29:17). This is not merely the language of personal vindictiveness. It is the psalmist giving voice to his belief that right, God's right, must prevail, and that all who challenge it do so at their peril.

The psalm ends on a confident note. The "many" have been saying, "There is no help for you in God" (v. 2); the psalmist, on the contrary, declares, "Deliverance belongs to the LORD" (v. 8). For the psalmist such deliverance is not something purely personal. It is there to be shared. He calls for God's "blessing" on "your people," the community in which his life has been nurtured and sustained. Such "blessing" would include all God's providential provision for a full life, all the rich benefits given to the people by God's mighty acts in creation and in redemption, acts which the people are summoned to celebrate and relive as they gather for worship (see Psalm 136). This sharing, this participation by others, in the psalmist's experience is underlined by the use of the liturgical marker "Selah," which occurs three times in the psalm (at the end of verses 2, 4, and 8), frequently elsewhere in the book, and in the psalm attributed to the prophet Habakkuk (Hab. 3:3, 9, 13). It is a word of very uncertain meaning, though it may mean "lifting up." It invites a response from the people gathered for worship, whether a vocal response or some other kind of outward bodily action we are not sure. Thus others were invited to identify with the psalmist in his crisis and share in the healing he found.

Psalm 4
PEACE AND SECURITY — GOD'S GIFT

We must never forget that the Psalms, whatever their origin, found their home in worship and thus came to be sung or chanted with musical accompaniment. The heading to Psalm 4 contains the word "to [or: for] the leader." This leader is in all probability the musical director, responsible for the musical accompaniment, "with stringed instruments" in this psalm and with wind instruments, "flutes," in Psalm 5.

In many ways Psalm 4 follows on naturally from Psalm 3. There are those who regard Psalm 3 as a "Morning Prayer" on the basis of the language in verse 5, and Psalm 4 as an "Evening Prayer" on the basis of verse 8. That is possible, but it unduly narrows the meaning of the two psalms. There are, however, clear linguistic links between them. In both we hear the comments of the "many who say" (3:2; 4:6), and both speak of "lying down and sleeping" (3:5; 4:8). Many of the same critical questions arise. Should we read Psalm 4, for example, as a royal psalm, or is it describing the experience of an otherwise unidentified individual? The latter seems more likely. As in Psalm 3, we are listening to the words of a psalmist who believes he is under attack, this time probably from people who are slandering him or bringing false accusations against him. The psalm, therefore, contains elements of a lament, but the mood throughout is rather one of quiet confidence.

1   The psalm begins with a confident prayer based on past experience of God's goodness. God is described as "the God of my right," the God who has stood by him and vindicated him in the past. The word "right" has a legal background and can mean acquittal, a declaration of innocence, or deliverance, as well as the more general righteousness and justice. Here is the God, says the psalmist, who "gave me room when I was in distress," the God who, as it were, gave him breathing space when life was getting on top of him, rescued him when he was being hemmed in by enemies. It is also possible that we should treat the second line of this opening verse as a plea and translate "Give me room when I am in distress." But if this is a plea, like all the other pleas in this psalm it is backed up by past experience (see v. 3). The psalmist's appeal to God to "answer" him and to "be gracious" to him, to look with favor upon him, is made not because he deserves to be so treated, but because he knows that this is the way a gracious God responds to those in need (cf. Ps. 6:2).

2-5 The cry "How long?" (v. 2) is a cry we often hear, particularly in the psalms of lament (cf. Ps. 13:1, 2). It joins hands with the word "why" as a natural, puzzled, and often painful response to situations in life which seem meaningless. The psalmist is trapped in a situation which screams out to be resolved, a situation where his "honor" (*kābôd;* cf. 3:3), his standing in the community, is under threat. He is being subjected to "shame," humiliation at the hands of those who "love vain words and seek after lies." While the Hebrew words translated "vain words" and "lies" are sometimes used satirically in the Old Testament to refer to idols, it is more likely that they point here to the unfounded accusations, the character assassination from which the psalmist is suffering. But at the hands of whom? The Hebrew says simply "sons of man," which the NEB renders "O mortal men," as if to emphasize that these attacks, however dangerous, are merely the attacks of fellow mortals as opposed to the eternal God who is the psalmist's defense. It is more likely, however, that the reference is to people of influence (REB: "men of rank") who are prepared to use their power to bring false charges against the psalmist, charges which could lead to the death penalty. Exodus 23:1-3 issues a stern warning against such conduct. The corruption of justice by those in positions of influence, particularly those too long in positions of influence, is a common occurrence. The weak are vulnerable — truth sacrificed on the altar of power. The sleaze factor is all too common.

The psalmist challenges these slanders by affirming his faith in the LORD, who "has set apart the faithful for himself." The word translated "faithful" (Hebrew *ḥāsîd*) denotes those who remain loyal to God. It is the adjective related to one of the key words which the Old Testament uses to describe the nature of God, the word *ḥesed,* which occurs as an insistent refrain in every second line of Psalm 136. It describes an enduring quality of God, his tenacious commitment to his people even in face of their lack of commitment to him. It is a word almost impossible to translate adequately into English; perhaps "steadfast love" is the least inadequate rendering. Certainly the traditional translation "mercy" falls far short of conveying its meaning. Our keeping faith with God is always but a pale shadow of the way in which God keeps faith with us. The text in verse 3a is slightly awkward and with minor variations can be read as "The LORD has wonderfully shown his steadfast love to me" (cf. Ps. 31:21). Even without this rendering, however, it is because the psalmist knows that God is dependable that he can trust that his prayer will be heard and answered. (A fuller discussion of *ḥesed* will be found at Ps. 5:7.)

In verses 4-5 the psalmist continues to address those who are slandering him. The verb translated "disturbed" or "be angry" (v. 4), when used in a psychological sense, indicates people who are in the grip of powerful emotions, often emotions which override rational conduct, such as hatred, jealousy, and bitterness. Artur Weiser's translation "tremble" (with fear) and the REB's "Let

awe restrain you" do not really fit the context, in spite of the theological insights
to which they may give rise. To people so "disturbed" the psalmist can only say,
"You may not be able to prevent such emotions from gripping you, but do not
allow them to destroy you, to lead you into sin. Cool it. Sleep on it. And then be
silent; cease to bring your slanderous accusations." Ephesians 4:26 quotes this
verse and takes its logic one step further by insisting that far from "pondering it
on your beds" you should not allow the sun to go down on your anger. To be in
the grip of such powerful, irrational emotions can never be the basis of wise
conduct.

It is not enough, however, for the psalmist to advise such people to cease
their slanders. He calls upon them publicly to make amends, to make amends to
God. "Offer right sacrifices" (v. 5) means either to offer sacrifices according to
the appropriate ritual or to offer sacrifices in the correct frame of mind; or it may
mean both, since the appropriate sacrificial ritual to be acceptable must be the
outward sign of true inward motivation. Such motivation must come from putting
"trust in the LORD." The phrases "to put your trust in the LORD" or "to trust to
the LORD" echo across the Psalms. The verb "to trust," followed as here by the
preposition usually translated "to," occurs again in Pss. 31:6; 56:4; and 86:2.
Much more commonly it is followed by the preposition "in" (e.g., Pss. 9:10;
21:7; 22:4, 5). It comes close to what we normally mean by having faith in God,
a faith which implies not merely intellectual assent but a willingness to commit
the whole of life confidently to God's hands.

6 Who are the "many" whose words we now hear in verse 6? Are they still the
people who have been attacking the psalmist? In that case, they respond to the
psalmist's appeal by saying or thinking, "Yes, indeed, it would be good to be
assured of God's gracious presence and to discover for ourselves what it means
to share in the great priestly blessing of Num. 6:24." But behind the words there
lies not only a longing but an unwillingness to take the step which would convert
that longing into reality, the step of personally trusting in the Lord and thus allying
themselves with, instead of attacking, his people. This interpretation is strengthened if we read the last line of verse 6 as, "The light of your presence has fled
from us, O LORD" (NEB). Here, then, are people claiming to want God, aware
of something amiss in their lives, but unwilling to take the step which would
bring them into the light of God's presence. There have always been, and still
are, many people caught in this dilemma; often good people are frightened to
become God-filled people.

It is equally possible, however, that the "many" are not the psalmist's
attackers, but other people sympathetic to the psalmist, people of faith who long
for a deeper faith but who find it difficult to share the psalmist's confidence. In
this case, in the second half of verse 6, the psalmist allies himself with them in
their uncertainty and shares with them a prayer based on the priestly blessing.

7-8 However we interpret verse 6, the psalm ends on the twin notes of joy and peace as the psalmist shares with us his experience of God. In spite of the difficulties he faces, there is a God-given "gladness in my heart" (v. 7), a great gladness surpassing that with which the people naturally celebrate the gathering of an abundant harvest (cf. Ps. 126; Isa. 9:3). In spite of the jarring words directed against him, he is not troubled by sleepless nights. He knows "peace" (Hebrew *šalôm*), again one of these Hebrew words rich in meaning for which no one English word can ever be adequate (see comment on Ps. 29:11). Here it points to a fullness of life and an unshakable confidence, independent of external circumstances. This psalmist does not suffer from insomnia, nor is his sleep troubled by nightmares. He lies down unafraid, trusting in the LORD; the last word of the psalm, usually translated "securely" or "in safety," echoes the verb "to trust" in verse 5.

This is a story which has been repeated across the centuries and one to which people today bear eloquent witness. On Christmas eve 1981 Vera Chirwa, together with her son and husband Orton, were arrested by the Malawian Security Police. Orton, the first President of the Malawi Congress Party, had dared to criticize the actions of what was becoming an increasingly dictatorial and brutal regime led by Hastings Banda. She was to spend the next twelve years in harsh detention, unable to communicate with her husband or with friends. When Orton died in mysterious circumstances in prison in October 1992, she was not even allowed to attend his funeral. Sustained international pressure led to her release in January 1993. She emerged with a quiet dignity and an unshakable faith in God which invited pity not for herself or for her husband, but for the regime which had so brutally ill treated them and many other prisoners of conscience. There is in this psalm the same implicit sense of pity for those who victimized the psalmist. Whatever influence or power may be at their disposal, such people lack the one thing which can give lasting security and richness of life, a trust in the LORD.

Psalm 5
MY HOPE IS IN GOD

Psalm 5 is the lament of an individual in which, as in Psalm 4, the psalmist feels under threat from enemies who are bringing false accusations against him or are publicly slandering him. The structure of this psalm, however, is much more tightly shaped. It falls into five clearly defined sections. Three of them (vv. 1-3, 7-8, and 11-12) are directed towards God and express the psalmist's need for and faith in God; the other two (vv. 4-6 and 9-10) focus on the activity and the fate of the psalmist's enemies. As in the case of certain other psalms (e.g., Psalms 15 and 24:3-6), the question is raised as to who is fit to be a guest in God's house, to share in worship in the temple. For the heading to the psalm, see the comment on Psalm 4.

1-3 The psalm begins with an urgent and reiterated plea to God — "Give ear . . . give heed . . . listen." It is as if the psalmist is knocking repeatedly on God's door. He is in trouble; he needs to share his distress, his anxious thoughts, with one whom he describes as "my King and my God" (v. 2). Just as the king in Jerusalem was the final court of appeal for those seeking redress for wrongs done, so the psalmist appeals to the divine King whom he knows he can approach, because this is no distant autocrat, but one who is "my" King and "my" God. There are many psalms which celebrate the kingship of Israel's God (e.g., Psalms 93, 95–99), his majesty and power seen in the world of his creating, his rule over all nations and all human history, a God whom no human words can ever adequately describe. Yet this is a King who listens, who cares for his people, who responds to the needs of those who come seeking his help. This King is the "LORD" (best taken as the last word in verse 2 rather than the first word in verse 3), Yahweh in whose name is enshrined the promise "I will be with you" (Exod. 3:12). The same twofold emphasis on awesome majesty and gracious presence is enshrined in the Lord's prayer (Matt. 6:9-13) and lies at the heart of all true prayer. Otherwise, we are in danger of treating God with the overfamiliarity of a next-door neighbor or of banishing him to a majestic remoteness.

The interpretation of verse 3 hinges upon the meaning we give to the Hebrew verb *'ārak,* translated in the RSV as "I prepare a sacrifice for thee," but in the NRSV as "I plead my case." The word can be used in different contexts for arranging or setting something in order. Thus in Ps. 23:5 "you prepare a table [i.e., a banquet] before me in the presence of my enemies." It is certainly used in cultic contexts to describe the preparation of a sacrifice, the placing of the offering on the altar (Lev. 1:8, 12; 6:10). This is the justification for the RSV and the REB supplying the word "sacrifice." In this case, the psalmist makes his approach to God in the context of offering a morning sacrifice. Equally — and this seems better in context — the word can be used in the legal sense of preparing a case to bring before a judge. Thus in Job 23:4, "I would lay my case before him, and fill my mouth with arguments" (cf. Ps. 50:21). This is the justification for the NRSV's rendering, "I plead my case." The psalm may, then, be thought of as a morning prayer, though that would not exclude the possibility that it would go hand in hand with the morning offering in the temple. Having presented his case, the psalmist can only "watch," just as the prophet Habakkuk, wrestling with his unanswered questions, had to stand at his outpost to "keep watch to see what he [i.e., God] will say to me, and what he will answer concerning my complaint" (Hab. 2:1). The answer is not yet. The psalmist must watch and wait for some sign from God, some new assurance that his prayer is being answered.

4-6   The spotlight is now turned on those who constitute a threat to the psalmist. They are described in verse 6 as "the boastful," the arrogant who in Ps. 73:3 are closely associated with the wicked, and as "evildoers." Such "evildoers" (literally, "workers of evil, iniquity") appear frequently in the Psalms (cf. Pss. 6:8; 28:3). There is no one interpretation which will fit all the occurrences of this phrase. The kind of evil in which such people are actively involved depends on context. Here they are further defined as "those who speak lies" (see comment on 4:2); the "bloodthirsty," those prepared to commit any kind of violent deeds to achieve what they want, people ready to resort to any form of "deceit." But the psalmist is not concerned merely to describe those who are out to destroy him. What is at stake for him is the character of God, a God who can take no pleasure in such wickedness. If God is to be seen as the final court of appeal, then he must be a judge who will make plain his hatred, his abhorrence, of such conduct, and must seek its elimination. Inevitably, therefore, such people cannot be guests in God's house; they cannot enjoy the hospitality that Eastern custom would naturally extend to guests. Such people have no place in God's presence (v. 5).

7-8   But the psalmist does enjoy the hospitality of God's house — it is better to treat the verbs in verse 7 as present tenses rather than future tenses. He is there in the temple court, facing towards God's "holy temple" (see comment on 2:6), bowing down, praying, waiting in the spirit of humble reverence and awe (v. 8). He is not there because he considers himself good enough to be in God's presence. His whole attitude is the exact opposite of self-righteousness. He is there because into his life there has flooded the *hesed* of God. Unless we accept the textual alteration in Ps. 4:2, this is the first occurrence in the Psalms of a word which encapsulates much that undergirds Israel's faith, God's "steadfast love." Often closely associated with the idea of the covenant, it describes that attitude which guarantees that a person will remain faithful to a commitment freely undertaken. The Old Testament has no illusions about Israel in this respect. The prophet Hosea complains that the people's *hesed* "is like a morning cloud, like the dew that goes away early" (Hos. 6:4) — there one moment but quickly disappearing. Not so is God's *hesed*. It remains steadfast, constant in the midst of all human frailty and fickleness, the bedrock of Israel's faith. So Psalm 136 in every second line unwearyingly celebrates its presence in creation (vv. 1-9), throughout Israel's history (vv. 10-22), and in present experience (vv. 23-25). The New Testament witness underlines the truth of this by reminding us that, "In this is love, not that we loved God but that he loved us and sent his Son" (1 John 4:10). The psalmist believes in a God who has reached out for him and will never let go. Therein lies his hope. He would have said a resounding amen to Joachim Neander's great hymn:

> All my hope on God is founded,
> he doth still my trust renew.

Me through change and chance he guideth,
only good and only true.

But such a faith demands a response of commitment, an attitude to life which is the exact opposite of that displayed by the arrogant self-confidence of his enemies. A way of life is under threat by these enemies, so he prays, "Lead me, O LORD, in your righteousness" (v. 8). He needs to be challenged and sustained by what he knows to be true of God's nature and of the way in which God acts. Only thus can he be given insight into and the strength to walk along the road God has mapped out for him.

9-10   The reference to the enemies in verse 8 leads into a graphic description of their devious conduct and the fate which awaits them. They have been well described as "mealy mouthed characters" (Dahood). The lack of honesty and firmness in what they say reflects the vicious, destructive thoughts they harbor. The smooth, oily words they utter are an invitation to take a shortcut to death and destruction. There is in the Hebrew a play on the word translated "their hearts" and on the word translated "graves" in verse 9, a play impossible to render into English. A similar dramatic description of such people is to be found in Ps. 52:2-4.

The psalmist is in no doubt as to what their fate ought to be. Such arrogance and deceit are incompatible with God's nature. He asks God to pronounce upon them a verdict of guilty, a verdict they have brought upon themselves by their devious counsels. It remains only that they should be cast out, exiled from God's presence, barred from the temple, because they have displayed an attitude which is tantamount to rebellion against God (v. 10). Even if it is understandable, there is a cold harshness about the psalmist's "cast them out." It is a very human response, echoed in other psalms (e.g., Pss. 109:8-20; 137:7-9), a harshness found elsewhere in the Old Testament. It is there, for example, in the way in which Jeremiah reacted to those who slandered and persecuted him, the bitter words in Jer. 18:21-23 climaxing in, "Do not forgive their iniquity, do not blot out their sin from your sight" (Jer. 18:23; cf. Jer. 17:17-18; 20:11-12).

There is an inevitable tension between such a response and the words of Jesus from the cross, "Father, forgive them; for they do not know what they are doing" (Luke 23:34). There have been many attempts to reconcile such conflicting attitudes. None is needed unless we insist on believing that there must be throughout the Bible from beginning to end one seamless theology, one consistent response to God. You won't find that even within the Psalms.

11-12   The dark, threatening clouds, however, disappear before the radiance of the psalmist's confidence in God. He invites all who "take refuge" in God (see Ps. 2:11) to join him in a confident hymn of joy. Such people are further described as "those who love your name," those who seek to respond to what they know of the character of God as revealed to them — a name in the Old Testament often being the outward sign of a person's character or destiny (see the significance of the names Isaac, Jacob/Israel in Gen. 21:3-6; 25:26; 32:28). Such people are also described as "the righteous" (see Ps. 1:6), those who belong to the company of God's faithful people. It is such people who can be sure of God's protection and blessing (see Ps. 3:8). The "shield" of verse 12 is not the round shield of Ps. 3:3, but a much larger, rectangular shield which gave protection to most of the body. So God graciously protects those who take refuge in him. In Ps. 91:4 God's faithfulness is described as "shield and buckler."

In face of the hate-filled, destructive attacks of his enemies, the psalmist has been grasped anew by the gracious, steadfast love of God. That was cause for rejoicing and for calling upon others to share in his joy. It still is.

Psalm 6
A PRAYER FOR HEALING

In the heading to the psalm, the word "Sheminith" is best left untranslated. It literally means "an eighth," and if we knew more about musical notation in ancient Israel it might refer to the pitch of a tune, an octave, or to the string of the lyre on which the tune was to be played. This, however, is little more than guesswork. The word also occurs in the heading of Psalm 12 and in 1 Chron. 15:21.

In Christian tradition Psalm 6 is the first of seven penitential psalms, the others being Psalms 32, 38, 51, 102, 130, and 143. But there is no specific note of penitence or confession in this psalm. To interpret it as a penitential psalm, we must assume that God's anger and the psalmist's suffering are the consequence of sins he has committed. Since the psalmist in the extremity of his anguish does not protest his innocence, this may be so. In that case, he is passively accepting the view that there is a causal link between sin and suffering, a view widely held in the Old Testament on both a community and personal level. It is openly accepted in some of the other penitential psalms (e.g., Psalms 32, 38, and 51).

But what kind of experience lies behind this psalm? If the language of verses 2-3 and 6-8 is to be taken literally, then here is a man severely depressed, a prey to fears and uncontrollable grief. The last words of verse 7, however, speak of "all my foes," and this leads into references to "workers of evil" (v. 8) and "enemies" (v. 10). Unless we are content to interpret much of the language in the Psalms as highly metaphorical and conventional, there would seem to be two ways of linking the psalmist's dire condition with such enemies. We could assume that the influence of such enemies and the attacks they make upon him are the source of his illness. The terror they inspire have weakened him both physically and psychologically. This would certainly be the case if we were to regard such "workers of evil" as sorcerers (so S. Mowinckel) whose spells or curses were draining away the life of the psalmist, just as the power of the witch doctor can do in certain African societies. The other possibility is that the psalmist was suffering from what today we would diagnose as a case of clinical depression. He would then view with suspicion and as enemies many people around him, including relatives and those previously his friends. Whatever its origin, the psalmist's condition provides a mirror into which many troubled people have looked, have seen their own life-threatening situation, and have found hope. Within the psalm there is a spiritual pilgrimage, as the psalmist moves from a negative plea to God, "do not rebuke me" (v. 1), through a positive plea, "save my life" (v. 4), to the assurance that his plea has been heard and answered, "The LORD has heard" (v. 9).

1-3 With a minor linguistic variation, the opening words of the psalm occur again at the beginning of Psalm 38, another of the penitential psalms. The psalmist is sure that the origin of his plight lies in the "anger" and "wrath" of the LORD (v. 1). The Old Testament has no hesitation in attributing a wide range of human emotions to God. What other language is appropriate if we believe that God is personal? The Old Testament never forgets, however, that there are constraints on the use of such anthropomorphic language, "for I am God and not man, the Holy One in your midst" (Hos. 11:9). Our anger and wrath can often be irrational and unjustifiable, the product of our all too human weakness. Put us in certain situations and we often have a short fuse, liable to blow up at any minute. Not so with God; his anger is a reflection of his care for the world of his creating, of his inevitable response to the mess we so often make of our own lives and the lives of others by our failure to follow his directives (cf. Rom. 1:18-22). The purpose of his anger is to "rebuke" and to "discipline" (v. 1). As Prov. 3:11-12 points out, a father will say "no" and will discipline his children precisely because he loves them. In such circumstances, anger, not indifference, is the true expression of concern. The words "rebuke" and "discipline" are commonly found in parental instruction in Proverbs. Hating or ignoring rebuke leads to ruin (Prov. 5:12-14); discipline is the true basis for life (Prov. 4:13; 5:23). There is a "no" which God must continually say to us. But because this "no" is an expression not of irresponsible anger but of concern, the psalmist turns naturally to God with his plea, "Be gracious to me" (v. 2, see comment on 4:1) and "heal me," the basis for such a plea being his weakness and need.

He is "languishing" (v. 2), his vitality draining away. The same verb is used elsewhere in the Psalms and in Job of the wicked being doomed to wither away like grass burnt up under the merciless heat of the sun (Ps. 37:2; Job 18:16; 24:24) In Ps. 90:6 it is used of human life in its brevity and mortality. The psalmist's whole being — "bones" and "soul" (Hebrew *nepeš;* see v. 4) — is undermined, in the grip of terror. The repetition of the same Hebrew verb translated "shaking with terror" (v. 2) and "struck with terror" (v. 3, this time qualified with the adverb "very") indicates the extremity of his condition. Now for the fourth time in these first three verses, the word "LORD" is on his lips, this time prefaced by the words "but you" (v. 3). Then he seems to hesitate as if not knowing what to say. All that forms in his mind is the question so characteristic of the psalms of lament, "How long?" — the cry which gives voice to urgent appeal in the midst of crisis and at the same time holds on to the conviction that present suffering cannot be God's final word.

4-5 The basis of the psalmist's plea has been his weakness and need. It can be answered because he believes God's true nature is "steadfast love" (v. 4; see comment on 5:7). There is, therefore, nothing surprising in his calling upon God to "turn" (Hebrew *šûb*). This word is often used in the Old Testament of people called upon to do an about-face in life, to change their whole attitude, to repent. Here, because God's anger is not irrational but an expression of his loving concern, the psalmist believes that God's attitude will and must change into one which will ensure that the terror which now crushes him will be replaced by a restoration to full life and health. So he prays "save my life" . . . "deliver me" (see note at 5:7). The word translated "life" is the Hebrew *nepeš*, traditionally rendered "soul" as in verse 2. It does not, however, mean the soul as opposed to the body, that spiritual, immortal part of our makeup. Rather, it is the vital spark which makes us what we are. In the creation narrative in Gen. 2:7, God fashions man out of the dust of the ground, breathes the gift of life into him, and he becomes a "living being" *(nepeš). Nepeš* is very close to our concept of personality, personality which expresses itself through body, mind, and spirit. In many cases in the Psalms "my soul" is simply an emphatic, poetic way of indicating the personal pronoun "I" — I with all that I am (cf. Pss. 103:1, 2, 22; 104:1, 35).

There is another reason for the psalmist's plea. If death is to be his lot, then that means for him the end of any meaningful relationship with God. To die means to go down to *šě'ôl,* the Hebrew word for the abode of the dead, a place from which there is no return. Sheol has, in the Old Testament, a chill, negative connotation. In Job 10:21 it is described as "the land of gloom and darkness, the land of gloom and chaos, where light is like darkness." It is a place where hope and faith no longer have any meaning (Job 17:15-16). It is an insatiable monster (Isa. 5:16), a bottomless pit (Ezek. 32:18-21; Ps. 16:10) — such are some of the other grim pictures of Sheol. No wonder Ecclesiastes protests: ". . . a living dog is better than a dead lion. The living know that they will die, but the dead know nothing. . . . Their love and their hate and their envy have already perished; never again will they have any share in all that happens under the sun" (Eccl. 9:4-6). To be afflicted with a serious illness is to be taken to the very gates of Sheol. According to Isaiah 38, King Hezekiah thanks God for his recovery from such an illness on the grounds that "Sheol cannot thank you, death cannot praise you;

those who go down to the Pit cannot hope for your faithfulness. The living, the living, they thank you, as I do this day" (Isa. 38:18-19).

This is the prevailing attitude in the Psalms, with Psalm 88, for example, denying that there is any access to God's steadfast love or faithfulness, his wonders or his saving help in Sheol. Sheol is a place devoid of any praise of God (see Pss. 30:9; 88:10-12; 115:17). There are hints of another attitude in some psalms (see comment on Psalms 49; 73; and 139). But there is no firm belief in life hereafter in the Old Testament until a belief in the resurrection of the dead emerges in later apocalyptic circles (e.g., Dan. 12:2). The psalmist's thoughts are limited to this world. As has been well said, "The psalms conceived on the sickbed are marked by a profound pathos, for although they contain the words of the living, they are haunted by the shadow of dying" (Craigie). For this psalmist, beyond this life lies the great unknown, where he will be able neither to worship God — "remembrance" in verse 5 means reliving, celebrating, God's presence with his people — nor to give his witness to God's goodness by praising him.

6-7   Unlike other psalmists (cf. 3:6; 4:8), he finds no respite in sleep (vv. 6-7). In highly graphic language he describes wearisome nights spent in "moaning." Floods of tears soak his bed. He can no longer see clearly. His eyes "waste away" (cf. 31:9) and "grow weak," sign of the general weakness which has him in its grip.

8-10   In verse 8 the mood changes because something has convinced the psalmist that "the LORD has heard" (vv. 8, 9) . . . "the LORD accepts my prayer" (v. 9). What has led to this change? It is sometimes claimed that behind these words there lies an "oracle of salvation," words spoken by a priest or temple prophet in God's name, words which declare that his prayer has been heard and is answered. This is possible, but hardly necessary. It could be that simply by bringing his suffering to God, by sharing in worship, the psalmist is lifted out of his terror and despondency and is enabled to feel God's healing touch in his life. We should never underestimate the way in which worship can meet the needs, the widely different needs, of those who come together to share their lives with God. His need met, the psalmist can now call upon his enemies to "depart" (v. 8). Unlike the previous psalm, however, this one has no note of bitterness, no demand that God should make them bear their guilt, no accusation that having rebelled against God they must now be cast out of his presence. His prayer answered, the psalmist knows that the tables have been turned. Those who opposed him "shall be put to shame" (v. 10), experiencing now the humiliation he has suffered; they will know something of the "terror" which has gripped him. The words "they shall turn" (v. 10) probably look back to the psalmist's plea to God to turn (v. 4). God's turning to answer the psalmist's plea has made the turning of his oppressors inevitable. They will now recognize that their hostility to the psalmist has been mistaken. The psalmist's rehabilitation must mark a turning point in other people's relationship with him.

We live in a different world from the psalmist. Such a desperate plea from the sickbed is not normally considered part of our corporate worship, though we are beginning to rediscover the power of prayer and the reality of healing through services of healing. Our thinking is also inevitably colored by our belief in the life everlasting. But if we cannot hold on to God, like the psalmist, and know his healing touch in this life, why should such healing be a reality for us in any other life hereafter?

Psalm 7
A DESPERATE CRY

The heading to this psalm poses some unanswerable questions. "Shiggaion" is a word of unknown meaning which occurs only here in the Psalms, though a related form appears in the heading to the psalm in Habakkuk 3. We are equally in the dark concerning "Cush, a Benjaminite," even if we do know that the tribe of Benjamin, from which Saul came, caused David trouble more than once (e.g., 2 Samuel 20). It hardly helps the interpretation of the psalm to try to link it with an otherwise unknown incident in the career of David.

The tension between a psalmist and those who threaten his life is nowhere more acute than in this psalm. It is possible that we should see in the background a situation similar to that described in 1 Kgs. 8:31-32: "If someone sins against a neighbor and is given an oath to swear, and comes and swears before your altar in this house, then hear in heaven, and act, and judge your servants, condemning the guilty by bringing their conduct on their own head, and vindicating the righteous by rewarding them according to their righteousness." The difference is that this psalmist is not conscious of sinning against a neighbor. Convinced that he is being unjustly accused by enemies out to destroy him, he goes to the temple, takes an oath in which he solemnly protests his innocence, and calls upon God, the divine judge, to vindicate him and bring vengeance upon those who are attacking him. Certain that he will be vindicated, his last words are words of confident faith expressed in a vow of thanksgiving to God.

1-2 The opening section of the psalm describes a person in desperate straits being pursued and savaged by enemies. The graphic simile of being mauled by a lion occurs in other psalms (e.g., Pss. 10:9; 17:12; 22:13, 21). Despairing of any human protection, his sole hope lies in taking "refuge" in the LORD, words which are echoed at the beginning of other psalms (e.g., Psalms 11, 16, 31, 57). He calls upon God to "save" and "deliver" him (see comment on 3:8). He believes such confidence is well founded since it is rooted in a spiritual relation-

ship which is already central to his life. On each of the first two occasions he
addresses God, his appeal is to "O LORD my God" (vv. 1, 3). This is not someone
previously indifferent to God desperately turning to God because his life has fallen
apart; he is drawing on resources which he has already tested. The LORD is no
stranger to him; he is already "my God."

3-5 The psalmist is so sure of his innocence that he is willing to take a solemn
oath (vv. 3-5), which will have dire consequences for him, if he is lying — if I
have done X, then let Y follow. For a similar form of oath, compare the bold, yet
sensitive defense Job offers of his past life in Job 31. It is possible that the
psalmist's words were accompanied by some ritual act such as is described in Ps.
26:6-7: "I wash my hands in innocence and go round your altar, O LORD, singing
aloud a song of thanksgiving, and telling all your wondrous deeds." We may
compare the action of the elders in Deut. 21:6-9 and Pilate's washing of his hands
in Matt. 27:24. The psalmist has been the victim of a smear campaign. He is being
accused of being corrupt and crooked in his actions (v. 3), of indulging in unjustified personal vindictiveness against those he regards as his enemies (v. 4b).

The meaning of verse 4a, however, is not wholly clear. It may refer to the
unwarranted way in which the psalmist has been treating his friends or partners
(NRSV and REB), or it may be taken along with the rest of the verse to refer to
the people who have unexpectedly played him false (so Anderson). What is clear
is that it is in the light of his protestation of innocence that we must interpret his
claim to "righteousness" and "integrity" in verse 8, and his certainty that he is
to be included among the "righteous" and "the upright in heart" in verses 9 and
10. This is not an arrogant claim to moral perfection. It is a declaration that, as
far as the charges laid against him are concerned, he is "in the right," innocent
of that crookedness with which people are slandering him (see comment on Psalm
1). In this conviction, he is willing to jeopardize his future. If the charges against
him can be sustained, then he is willing to pay the penalty — to be handed over
to those who are out to get him; to hazard "my *nepeš*" (v. 5a, simply translated
"me" in the NRSV; see comment on Ps. 6:4), "my life," and "my honor" (*kābôd;*
see comment on Ps. 3:3) or reputation and standing in the community. As many
have found out to their cost, there is nothing more likely to ruin a person's
reputation than a malicious smear campaign.

6-8 The psalmist now makes his appeal to the one true judge and ruler to "rise up"
(see comment on 3:7). The attitude of his enemies is characterized by an excessive
and unjustified "fury," a word which in Hebrew points to something which goes
beyond any reasonable bounds. It must be countered by the justifiable "anger" of
God (see comment on 6:1), the God who acts in defense of the innocent.

More is at stake here than the psalmist's fate. He may address the judge as
"O my God" (v. 6), but that does not mean that he expects this judge to act

towards him in any way different from how he would act towards others in similar circumstances. Here is no small hole in the corner district or provincial court, but the Supreme Court over which God presides ("take your seat" in verse 7 translates the Hebrew verb which normally means to turn; but here it takes the meaning of the somewhat similar-sounding verb meaning "to sit"). To this court are summoned "the assembly of the peoples" (v. 8); here the "nations" are arraigned before a judge whose decisions reflect a commitment to righteousness. So the psalmist sees his fate as a pointer to larger questions. Is this a world in which right prevails, or do the destructive forces of evil have the last word? Whose writ runs in human affairs? If this psalmist confidently affirms, "The LORD judges the nations" (v. 8), we must not assume that this is a statement spoken with glib assurance, born out of a faith which has never seriously wrestled with the challenge of evil in the world. Far from it. Many of the Psalms and other books in the Old Testament (e.g., Job) speak to us of the struggle to maintain faith and of the perplexity born of the apparent powerlessness or absence of God. Psalm 121:4 may declare, "He who keeps Israel will neither slumber nor sleep"; but other psalmists, caught in the agony of what seem meaningless events and suffering, can only cry out:

> Rouse yourself! Why do you sleep, O LORD?
>   Awake, do not cast us off for ever!
> Why do you hide your face?
>   Why do you forget our affliction and oppression?
>
> (Ps. 44:23-24)

So here the psalmist cries out to God, "awake" (v. 6). It was precisely because psalmists had to take evil seriously in their personal experience and in the world at large that they had to take God seriously. That is why they were forced to ask so many questions. There were no easy answers, but there was a faith to be lived, often painfully lived, even in the midst of their questions (see Davidson, *The Courage to Doubt*).

9-11 The essence of the psalmist's faith is to be found in the plea he makes (v. 9), a plea rooted in his conviction concerning the character of the God to whom he bears witness (vv. 10-11). "I believe," he says, "in the God who is 'my shield' (v. 10; cf. 3:5), 'a righteous judge' (v. 11), who can be depended upon to vindicate the innocent, a God who must, therefore, react in 'indignation' against evil in any form." This is a judge who passes sentence not only on the basis of external facts, but by his scrutiny of the intentions, "the minds," and the inmost emotions, "the hearts" (v. 9) — the word translated "hearts" is in Hebrew the kidneys, often regarded as the seat of the emotions. In the light of this faith, the psalmist does not hesitate to make his plea for an end to the evil which threatens him.

12-16   Verses 12-13 may be interpreted in two different ways. In the previous verse, verse 11, God is the subject; in verse 14 the subject is clearly the psalmist's enemies. But who is the "he" who "will whet his sword" in verse 12? Many English translations assume that the subject is God (NRSV, GNB), in which case verses 12 and 13 depict God as a warrior going into battle to destroy his enemies. It is possible that the opening words of verse 12, "If he does not repent (turn)," deliberately echo the use of the same verb in verse 7 to indicate God taking his seat as a righteous judge. His attitude in so presiding is clear and unchanging; those who attack the psalmist must change, or they will experience retribution such as befalls all evil. It is more likely, however, that the "he" of these verses is the psalmist's enemy (REB). Unrepentant, he is determined to continue his vicious and deadly attacks against the psalmist. Graphically, the growth of the evil such enemies devise is depicted in verse 14 in terms of conception, pregnancy, and birth; but this is evil which at birth signs its own death certificate. This truth is noted in imagery similar to that of verse 15 in several wisdom sayings: "Whoever digs a pit will fall into it, and a stone will come back on the one who starts it rolling" (Prov. 26:27; cf. Eccl. 10:9-10).

17-18   Evil having pressed a self-destruct button, the psalmist turns in thankfulness and in joy to renew his commitment to the LORD who has vindicated him — this is what the LORD's "righteousness" means. His praise is directed to "the name of the LORD," because the LORD has revealed his true character as defender of the oppressed (for "name," see comment on 5:11).

In the final word of the psalm, the LORD is described as "Most High" (Hebrew 'elyôn), a liturgical title which has its roots in Canaanite religion, where it is one of the titles of El, the supreme god of the pantheon. Associated in early tradition with Jerusalem (cf. Gen. 14:18-20), it is found frequently in the Psalms (e.g., 9:2; 47:2; 83:18), notably in contexts where stress is being laid on the power of God over all the forces which seek to challenge his rule. Having assigned all other gods to the theological wastepaper basket, the psalmist has no hesitation in using titles associated with such gods for his own purposes. It is in the one all-powerful God, the LORD, that the psalmist has taken his refuge.

Psalm 8
THE MAJESTY OF GOD
AND HUMAN DIGNITY

In this psalm the congregation of God's people celebrates the awesome majesty of God the creator and acknowledges that it is in this context that human dignity finds its true meaning. The relationship between this psalm and the hymn of creation in Genesis 1 has been much and inconclusively discussed. The view taken here is that Psalm 8 is best understood as a series of liturgical variations on the basic theme of Genesis 1.

In the heading of the psalm, the meaning of "according to The Gittith" is far from certain. "Gittith" probably has links with Gath, well known in the Old Testament as one of the Philistine towns. Is the reference then to some particular type of local instrument (cf. Scottish bagpipes) or tune (cf. metrical psalm tunes such as Kilmarnock) or to a religious festival associated with the district? We don't know.

Within the psalm there is a neatly structured and carefully balanced thought pattern. It moves from earth to heaven (v. 1), and from the heavens (v. 3) back to earth (vv. 4-8); from the LORD (v. 1) to the human race (v. 2); and from the human race (vv. 4-8) back to the LORD (v. 9). It ends where it begins with the people confessing the sovereignty of the LORD over all life and bowing down before the God whose nature (for "name" in verses 1, 9, see comment on 5:11) is majestic and awesomely powerful.

1-2 Although the general meaning is not in serious doubt, the text in verses 1b and 2 presents certain difficulties, as may be seen in the different English translations, all of which in verse 1b involve some alteration to either the vowels or the consonants of the Hebrew text.

> You have set your glory above the heavens. (NRSV)
> Your majesty is praised as high as the heavens. (REB)
> I will adore your majesty above the heavens. (Dahood)

There is the further question as to whether verse 1b is best taken with the first half of verse 1, the "heavens" thus providing the counterpoint to the "earth"; or whether it should be taken with verse 2, God's majesty above the heavens providing the counterpoint to the babes of the human race. The latter seems preferable; otherwise, we might have expected verse 1b to occur again at the end of verse 9. Whatever translation or linkage we adopt, the central theme of these opening verses is the "glory" of the God known to Israel. This word "glory" (Hebrew *hôd*) is often associated with the majesty or splendor of an earthly king (e.g., Ps. 21:5). Hence it is appropriately used in the description of one who is the divine king, whose "glory" outshines that of any earthly king, since his rule is universal, embracing both earth and heaven. Psalm 148, another joyful psalm celebrating the king of creation, closely parallels the thought of Psalm 8: "Let them praise the name of the LORD, for his name alone is exalted; his glory is above earth and heaven" (Ps. 148:13).

The phrase in verse 2, "you have founded a bulwark," has also caused difficulty. There is no reason why the Hebrew word *'ōz,* translated "bulwark," should not, like a related word from the same root (see Ps. 27:1), mean stronghold or fortress. It is also on occasion closely associated with the ark, the symbol of God's powerful, protecting presence in the midst of his people (Ps. 132:8). More commonly, however, it simply means "strength," the strength which goes hand in hand with God's majesty (see Pss. 29:1; 96:6), the strength which he demonstrates against anyone or anything opposing him (see Pss. 74:3; 77:15). The psalmist is here drawing our attention to a strange paradox, that it is on those who, humanly speaking, are regarded as weak and helpless, "babes and infants," that God lays the foundation of a strength which can defy all his enemies. The "enemies" in this case are probably the forces of chaos, defeated by God at creation, but ever threatening revenge, a revenge which would turn the world back into disorder (cf. Ps. 93:3-4).

3-4 It is one of the marks of young children that they respond to the world around them with a natural sense of wonder and awe, with delight in ever new discoveries. Because of this they are often the strongest witnesses to the God whose majesty is writ large in creation. Sadly we can too easily lose this sense of wonder as the world, in another sense of that word, closes in around us:

> The world is too much with us; late and soon,
> Getting and spending we lay waste our powers:
> Little we see in nature that is ours:
> We have given our hearts away, a sordid love!
> . . . .
> It moves us not. (Wordsworth)

Yet even the most sophisticated among us have been known to catch our breath as we gaze up into a clear night sky. The fact that the text refers only to "the moon and the stars" (v. 3), and not to the sun, hardly implies that this psalm comes out of a cultic act performed at night. We may have left our footprints on the moon, but the further we probe through radio telescope and orbiting satellite, the more awesome becomes the immensity of space and the whirling galaxies. The big bang, black holes, millions of light-years — these become the stuff out of which we construct our understanding of the universe. At this point we need to recognize the gulf which separates us from the psalmist. We gaze into the mysterious universe and are left asking questions about God, if there be a God. Who or what is God? Is there any need for a God to account for the world around us? The psalmist begins from the other end. Accepting the universe as the handiwork of a creator God, he asks questions about us, about human life. The "how" of God's majesty (v. 1) for him leads into the "how" or "what" (it is the same Hebrew word) of the significance of our existence (v. 4). Two words are used to describe our human life: *'ĕnôš* ("human beings," NRSV; "frail mortal," REB) and *ben 'ādām* (literally, "son of man"; "mortals," NRSV; "a human being,"

REB). Whatever the words "son of man" may have come to mean in later Jewish thought or Christian theology, both expressions are used here in parallelism to refer to our human life. Sometimes the words are used in the Psalms to point to human frailty and mortality: "You turn us *('ĕnôš)* back to dust, and say, 'Turn back, you mortals *(bĕnê 'ādām)'* " (Ps. 90:3). The same question — "What are human beings?" — is found in a very similar context in Ps. 144:3 and in a very different context that reads like a bitter parody of this psalm in Job 7:17.

5-8 To look at ourselves today in the light of the vastness of the universe is to have our insignificance forcefully brought home to us. We are but tiny specks living on one of the smallest planets. Yet it is this frail, insignificant human race that God "remembers" and "visits" (v. 4), words which in context point to a God who keeps us in mind and cares for us. We have been given a special status, crowned with "glory" (see 3:3) and "honor," a word frequently associated with royalty in the Old Testament (cf. Pss. 21:6; 45:4). This status is spelled out in the words "you have made them a little lower than God."

We could read the word translated "God" as "gods," that is, divine beings (v. 5a). The reference could be to the members of the heavenly council surrounding the one supreme God. They are described elsewhere in the Old Testament as "the host of heaven" (1 Kgs. 22:19), the "sons of God" (Job 1:6), or simply "gods" (Ps. 82:1). This is the justification for many of the versions, including the Greek (LXX), to translate "angels." Against the translation "a little lower than God," it has been argued that this would contradict verses 3-4, which stress the awesome distinction between God the creator and us, his frail creatures. It could, however, be the psalmist's way of saying what the hymn of creation in Genesis 1 affirms when it speaks of the human race as made in the image and likeness of God (Gen. 1:26-27). The Greek (LXX) not only translates "angels" but takes the expression "a little" in a temporal sense, "for a little while." This is how the passage is quoted in Heb. 2:6-8, where the author is arguing for the superiority of Jesus over angels. Jesus was "for a little while" made lower than the angels in his incarnation, yet through suffering and death he was crowned with honor to become the one true representative of the human race, the one to whom all things are ultimately subject (cf. Eph. 1:22).

As in Genesis 1, what is distinctive about us in our relationship with God is immediately followed by a statement concerning our relationship with the rest of creation. We are entrusted with "dominion" over everything on land, in the air, and in the sea. The word translated "dominion" (NRSV) in verse 6 is a different word from that used in Gen. 1:28 and is widely used to indicate any kind of mastery or rule. Not infrequently it is used in the Psalms of God's rule: "for dominion belongs to the Lord, and he rules over the nations" (Ps. 22:28; cf. 103:19). It is important to note that this is mastery entrusted to us, not power snatched defiantly from God in an assertion of proud independence. This is no cry of "glory to man in the highest." That is the path which leads to disaster, as the tower of Babel story in Gen. 11:1-9 graphically illustrates. This is delegated authority, a point hammered home in verses 6-7, in which there are four verbs whose subject in each case is God — "you have made them . . . and crowned them . . . you have given them . . . you have put all things." For the use of this given mastery, we are accountable to God. This is an inescapable contemporary issue as we become ever more aware of the rape of the earth and its resources, the threat to so many species of wildlife, and the pollution of the atmosphere. A new sense of stewardship, replacing human greed and irresponsible exploitation, has become a matter of life and death for the human race. Is such a stewardship possible unless we are prepared to accept an authority higher than ourselves? We saw how the author of Hebrews takes the Greek translation of verse 5 and applies it to Jesus, the one perfect representative of the human race. In 1 Cor. 15:27-29 Paul likewise takes the concluding words of verse 6, "you have put all things under his feet," as looking forward to the time when everything, even death the last enemy, will come under the rule of Christ, and God will once again be all in all. For Christians, the glory and honor of human life only come truly into focus in Jesus.

9   The psalm ends where it began, with the people of Israel acknowledging the awesome majesty and mystery of the God whom they know to be their God. That in biblical thought is where all true understanding of life begins, continues, and ends.

Psalms 9 and 10
CONFIDENCE AND PERPLEXITY

In spite of their apparently contradictory moods, Psalms 9 and 10 are best taken as one psalm. This has the support of a few Hebrew manuscripts, the Greek (LXX), and the Latin Vulgate translations. Following the Vulgate, they appear as one psalm in all Roman Catholic translations and more recently in some non-Roman Catholic translations, for example, the REB. Aside from the support of some of the versions, there are three reasons for treating the two psalms as one. First, alone among the Psalms in Book One from Psalms 3–41, Psalm 10 has no heading of its own.

Second, taken together the two psalms exhibit some of the features of an acrostic poem, that is, a poem which ranges through the twenty-two letters of the Hebrew alphabet, with each line or verse beginning with the appropriate letter in sequence. Thus Psalm 9 features ten out of the first eleven letters of the Hebrew alphabet — the letter corresponding to "d" being missing — while Psalm 10 begins with the twelfth letter, with seven of the remaining letters appearing in sequence in the rest of the psalm. Other, and more complete, acrostic poems are to be found in Psalms 15, 34, 37, 111, 112, and 119, and elsewhere in the Old Testament (e.g., in Lamentations and in Proverbs 31:10-31, that golden ABC of the capable wife). Why this acrostic form was used we do not know. There have been many guesses, ranging all the way from an aid to memory, a belief in the magical properties inherent in the alphabet, to an attempt to express the totality of emotion. Whatever its origin, the acrostic poem became an accepted literary form just as the fourteen-line sonnet became a recognized form in English literature.

Third, there are echoing words and phrases which link the two psalms. For example, the verb to "seek" is used in a variety of senses in 9:10, 10:4, and 10:13, where the NRSV translates "call . . . to account." Likewise, the Hebrew phrase translated "in times of trouble" is found in 9:9 and in 10:1 but nowhere else in the Old Testament in this precise form.

How then do we account for the sharply contrasting mood in the two psalms? Psalm 9 is seemingly a confident psalm of thanksgiving, whereas Psalm 10 has the characteristics of a psalm of lament. There have been many attempts to bridge the contradiction, for example by taking the verbs in 9:3-6, 15-17 to refer not to the past (as in the NRSV) but as expressing a wish. This has the effect of bringing Psalm 9 much closer to a lament. Theologically this is unnecessary. The Psalms present not a contradiction, but a tension to which an honest, living faith can hardly fail to bear witness. Precisely because the psalmist believes that he has good reason to thank God in terms of his past experience (9:1-6), he is thrown into turmoil by the strange absence of God from his present life (10:1). Precisely because he believes that God must be a righteous judge (9:7-8; see comment on Psalm 5), he is deeply distressed by the apparent prosperity of the wicked who challenge everything that God holds dear (10:3-11). Confidence and perplexity go hand in hand. Had he not believed certain things so confidently, he would not have been so agonizingly perplexed. Had he not faced so honestly the urgent questions posed by the rampant evil in his world, he would not have been driven to make such urgent pleas to God (9:19; 10:12). It is not that through questioning there must come renewed confidence, as in some of the psalms of lament (e.g., Psalm 4). Equally, confidence must sometimes lead to questioning. The polarity of faith and doubt, confidence and questioning is, as we have seen, characteristic of many of the Psalms and is indeed found elsewhere in the Old Testament (see Davidson, *The Courage to Doubt*). The polarity is an authentic part of spiritual experience for many sensitive people today. Faith does not provide easy answers to the meaningless absurdity or the vicious cruelty and harshness which are part of life. Faith forces us to wrestle at a deeper level with the questions such things raise. To accept this, however, does not mean that we solve all the difficulties in the interpretation of this psalm. Psalm 10 in particular poses many problems, both of text and interpretation. Read Psalm 10 in the NRSV and in

M. Dahood's translation in the Anchor Bible, and you might be forgiven for thinking that you were reading two different psalms!

The heading to Psalm 9 contains its own mystery in the phrase "Muth-labben," a phrase which occurs only here in the headings of the Psalms. Literally it could mean "death for the son," but it has caused all kinds of difficulty for the early versions from the Greek (LXX) onwards. If we take this hyphenated word as one word, what does it mean? Is it the title of a tune, or the description of certain voices (boy soprano?). We do not know.

Step by step we are led into the psalmist's world of confidence and perplexity. It is possible that sharing with others in one of the great annual festivals at the Jerusalem temple provided the psalmist with the framework within which he explored his own personal experience. This would help to explain the way in which the psalm moves back and forward from God's dealings with the nations which challenge his rule (see 9:5-6, 15-16, 19-20; 10:16) to the psalmist's own dilemma as he identifies through suffering with the weak and the oppressed. Just so, a liturgy designed to enable the Christian community to celebrate the Easter event often provides the individual within the congregation with an opportunity to reflect upon his or her own experience of death and resurrection.

Psalm 7 ends on the note of thanksgiving, and this is where Psalm 9, like many another psalm, begins (cf. Psalms 75; 105; 107; 136; 138). Thanksgiving is rooted in a tradition of faith which believes that God has made known his true character and nature (for "name," see Ps. 5:1; for the title "Most High," see Ps. 7:17) through "all your wonderful deeds." The word translated "wonderful deeds" echoes across the Psalms (e.g., Pss. 26:7; 40:5; 75:1). It is used to describe what happened at the Exodus (Exod. 3:20) and the events which led to the settlement in the promised land (Exod. 34:10), events which, remembered and celebrated in worship, called forth from God's people a sense of wonder. It is this sense of wonder, rooted in what God has done, which is at the heart of biblical faith, both Old Testament and New Testament. The psalmist therefore looks forward in faith (vv. 3-4) to a time when present troubles will be over. He knows himself to be in the hands of a judge who must and will vindicate his "just cause," a translation of two Hebrew words which occur again in verses 7-8, words which have a strongly legal flavor (for the picture of God as the just judge, see comment on Ps. 7:6-8).

The verbs in verses 5-6 are often taken as "prophetic perfects," describing coming events as if they had already happened and so are translated in English with the present or future tense. The view taken here is that they are best taken as past-tense verbs, as in the NRSV. It is the past, the story of God's wonderful deeds celebrated in worship, which is the source of the psalmist's present confidence in the midst of perplexity. Here and in verse 17 the "wicked" are identified with the nations who oppose God's purposes. However powerful such nations may have been, however impressive the "cities" they may have built (v. 6), they have nothing to celebrate or remember; "the very memory of them has perished"

(v. 6). Three times in verses 3-6 forms of the Hebrew verb "to perish" occur — "enemies perish before you" (v. 3) . . . "you destroyed (caused to perish) the wicked (v. 5) . . . "the very memory of them has perished" (v. 6). Past and future, all who challenge the authority of this divine king and judge, whether nations or individuals, meet a deserved fate. Perspectives on history may vary. We can so easily have our outlook distorted by what seem to be unassailable, often demonic, contemporary power structures. It is salutary to remember that while ancient Egypt and Canaan, Assyria, and Babylon may rightly fascinate scholars and archaeologists, for most people they are but footnotes to the history of a people who rivaled them neither in military power nor in cultural significance, but who as the people of God have handed on a living faith (cf. Deut. 7:7-26).

But there is another side to this divine king and judge. He may speak a decisive "no" to those who in human arrogance challenge his authority, but he has another word for those who put "their trust" in him (see comment on 4:5). He has a "yes," a compassionate "yes" to say to "the oppressed," those who are the victims of injustice or the abuse of power. For such people he is "a stronghold," a word which indicates a fortress built on a commanding, easily defensible height. God is often so described in the Psalms, particularly in situations where his people are under threat by ruthless and powerful enemies; witness Psalm 46 with its refrain in verses 7 and 11, "The Lord of Hosts is with us, the God of Jacob is our refuge (fortress)" (cf. 48:3), and Psalm 59, where three times the psalmist describes God as "my fortress" (vv. 9, 16, 17). This is the God who is a tower of strength to those who trust him, who never abandons those who "seek" him, the first of five occurrences in the psalm of a verb variously translated. The verb's different uses highlight the dilemmas in the psalm and in human experience. It underlines varied responses to life. People who commit themselves in faith to God are described as "those who seek you" (vv. 9 and 10). Others regard God as an irrelevance, who has no place in their life; their attitude is summed up in the words "God will not seek it out" (10:4) and "You will not call us to account" (literally, "you will not seek") in 10:13.

We live in a different world from that of the psalmist. Belief in God is today an intellectual option which many, for various reasons, refuse to take. Atheism, in this sense, was not a live option in the world of the psalmist. There were always, however, those who based their life on a practical atheism, banishing God to the sidelines of the universe, refusing to believe that he controlled the game. They played the game according to their own rules to suit their own greed and lust for power, and if other people got hurt in the process that was not their problem. It is such people who are repeatedly described as the "wicked" in Psalm 10 (see vv. 2, 3, 4, 7, 10, 15). Over against such people the psalmist places a God who "avenges [literally, "seeks"] blood" (9:12), who holds people responsible for what they do to others (cf. Gen. 4:10; 9:5), a God who "seeks out the wickedness" of such people (10:15) until it is no more than a bad memory.

Believing in such a God, the psalmist invites all the "afflicted" (9:12) to join with him in the praise of this God who dwells in the midst of his people (for "Zion," see comment on 2:6). Here the psalmist is identifying himself with those described in the rest of the psalm by four Hebrew words which occur with great frequency throughout the Psalms and are often variously translated in the NRSV. They are:

1. "the oppressed" (9:9) or "the needy" (10:18), Hebrew *dāk*.
2. "the afflicted" (9:12) or "the poor" (10: 2, 9) or "the oppressed" (10:12), Hebrew *'ănāyîm*.
3. "the needy" (9:18), Hebrew *'ebyôn*.
4. "the poor" (9:18) or "the meek" (10:17), Hebrew *'ănāwîm*.

The fact that the NRSV translates the same Hebrew word differently or uses the same translation for different words indicates that we are dealing here with a cluster of words whose precise meaning is often difficult to define. Do the words have an economic or social meaning, or are they essentially religious terms indicating the godly who humbly recognize their need for God and bow down before him, or do they include all of these things? Compare the form of the beatitude in Matthew's Gospel, "Blessed are the poor in spirit, for theirs is the kingdom of heaven" (Matt. 5:3) with the Lucan form, "Blessed are you poor, for yours is the kingdom of God" (Luke 6:20). Whatever the precise circumstances, these words point to those who feel crushed by life, who recognize their own need, and who seek refuge in God. They are the opposite of and often the victims of the arrogant wicked. One other word of uncertain meaning describes such people in the psalm; it occurs in Ps. 10:8, 10, 14 and is translated "the helpless" in the NRSV and in the REB as "some unfortunate wretch" (v. 8), "unfortunate wretch" (v. 10) and "the hapless victim" (v. 14).

In the midst of his suffering, the psalmist appeals to God to be "gracious" (9:13; see comment on 4:2) and to bring him "deliverance" (see comment on 3:8) from a life-threatening situation so that he may continue to bear witness to the goodness of God among the people gathered for worship in Jerusalem. The "gates of daughter Zion" (9:14) — a name for Jerusalem found only here in the Psalms but common enough in Isaiah (e.g., Isa. 10:33; 16:1) — are deliberately contrasted with the "gates of death" (9:13), which would close the door on any further relationship with God (see comment on 6:5). Richly deserved retribution, however, is the fate of all who challenge God's authority (vv. 15-16; cf. 7:5).

The word "Higgaion" (9:16) occurs only here as a technical term alongside "Selah." In Ps. 92:3 it refers to the melody of the lyre, and the related verb is found in Ps. 1:2 referring to meditating on the Law. Its meaning here is far from certain, but it may indicate some kind of musical interlude designed to help the worshipper to assimilate the full implication of what has just been affirmed.

The thought of verses 15-16, however, is quickly resumed. The wicked/nations go off to Sheol (see Ps. 6:5), not to be punished, but to find their natural habitat. Since they "forget God" (v. 17) in this world, presumably they will feel perfectly at home in Sheol, where no meaningful relationship with God is possible. "Forget" is another key word in the psalm. The wicked "forget God" (vv. 9, 17); they rule God out of any part in their lives. The wicked in 10:11 claim "God has forgotten," that is, he takes no part in their lives; he does not know what they are up to. On the contrary, "the needy will not always be forgotten" (9:18); God has a part to play in their lives, and the psalmist can appeal to God, "Do not forget the oppressed" (10:12).

"Rise up, O Lord" (v. 19; see comment on 3:7). This is an appeal rooted in the fact that however powerful the nations who challenge God may seem to be, they are in the last analysis no more than *'ĕnôš*, translated "mortals" in verse 19 and "only human" in verse 20 (see comment on 8:4). The fear they seek to inflict on others is a fear that they themselves must and will share.

Much of the language and thought of the second part of the psalm, which is now Psalm 10, we have already anticipated. It remains to explore more fully the attitude of the wicked on the one hand and the psalmist on the other. We have already noted how the comments of the wicked point to a practical atheism which has ruled out any interference by God in their lives. Their own ambitions and greed control their thoughts and actions. They "curse and renounce [or: revile] the Lord" (10:3), conduct that is strictly forbidden in the Torah and regarded as a capital offense (1 Kgs. 21:10-14). They ride roughshod over other people, wounding them by the malicious, hurting words to which they are only too ready to give voice (v. 7) and by their brutal actions against those powerless to protect themselves. Their actions are vividly portrayed in two metaphors and a simile in verses 8 and 9; they are brigands or outlaws ambushing their unsuspecting victims, like a lion pouncing on its prey (cf. 7:2), and they are hunters trapping prey in their nets. It seems clear that in the psalmist's eyes it is the refusal of such people to accept the authority of God which leads to their refusal to recognize the rights of other people. This is a theme which runs right through the Bible from beginning to end. Rebellion against God in the garden of Eden (Genesis 2–3) is followed immediately by the first murder (Genesis 4). The wrong in human relationships is rooted in alienation from God. It is not surprising that the sensitive social conscience of Deuteronomy is set within the framework of the basic command to "love the Lord your God with all your heart, with all your soul, and with all your might" (Deut. 6:5), and that in the Gospels Jesus joins this commandment with the injunction from Lev. 19:18, "You shall love your neighbor as yourself" (Mark 12:30; Matt. 22:37; Luke 10:27). There is, however, another feature of the life of the wicked which adds to the psalmist's perplexity. Psalm 1 may have claimed that the wicked, unlike the righteous, do not prosper but are like chaff driven away by the wind. This is not the picture drawn in verses 5 and 6. On the contrary, "their ways prosper [or: "endure"] at all times" (this in context seems better than taking the verb as coming from a root meaning to be twisted or devious, as does the REB). Apparently exempt from divine judgment and immune from human retribution, they claim to be secure, untouched by any misfortune or disaster (for a fuller discussion of this issue, see the comments on 1:3).

It is against this background of the brutality of enemies — the success and the seeming stability of enemies whom he can only characterize as "the wicked" — that we find the psalmist giving voice to his perplexity. "Why?" — that persistent and haunting three-letter word which life forces us all to ask sooner or later — is on his lips (10:1), as it is on that of many another psalmist (e.g., Pss. 22:2; 44:24; 74:1, 11; 88:14). His "why?" is prompted by his sense of isolation. Why is God so remote? Why does the God, in whose gracious presence the psalmist rejoiced (9:2), seem now to be absent when most needed "in times of trouble"? The complaint that God "hides" himself, or more commonly "hides his face," is heard again and again in the psalms of lament: "O LORD, why do you cast me off? Why do you hide your face far from me?" (Ps. 88:14; cf. 13:1; 27:9; 44:24; 102:2). In such psalms there is no sense of a quiet, uncomplaining acceptance of the "slings and arrows of outrageous fortune." There is protest. There are questions. The Psalms challenge us to see that such protest and questions have a legitimate place in worship.

In the midst of his protest and questions, the psalmist makes his urgent plea to God (10:12) in the conviction that what he is now experiencing cannot be the last word. God does "see" (v. 14); he does know what is going on, and he is on the side of the helpless and the vulnerable. He can be trusted to break the stranglehold of the wicked (v. 15) and give new strength to the needy (v. 17). So the psalm ends on a note of confident faith. The LORD is in control, "king for ever and ever" (cf. 5:2). He will take up the cause of "the orphan and the oppressed" (v. 18). With such a protector, why should they fear those who are merely earth-bound humans (cf. 9:19-20)? The Old Testament is never in any doubt that God is particularly concerned to uphold the rights of those most at risk in society — orphans, widows, aliens. God is described as "father of orphans and widows" in Ps. 68:5 (cf. Deut. 10:18; 26:12-13). The psalm thus moves from confidence (9:1-2) to perplexity (10:1) and from perplexity to confidence. It offers both to God.

Psalm 11
DARING TO TRUST

Like the previous psalm, this psalm describes a situation of crisis in the life of the psalmist. But there is a difference. Here there is no protest or questioning, no urgent plea to God. Instead we are given an analysis of the crisis and the dilemma in which the psalmist finds himself (vv. 1-3), followed by a ringing statement of faith which enables the psalmist to put the crisis in its true perspective (vv. 4-7) — a reminder, if reminder be needed, that people of strong religious belief may react to crisis situations in different ways.

1-3 The psalmist begins by putting his cards on the table. It is "in the LORD" — the first emphatic word in the psalm — he says, that "I take refuge" (see 2:11). How we interpret the crisis situation in the rest of verses 1-3 depends upon who we think is speaking in the different verses. There are three possibilities:

1. In verse 1b, and in 1b alone, we are listening to advice which the psalmist is receiving from friends or colleagues. "Flee like a bird to the mountains." Verses 2 and 3 may then be read as the psalmist's response. "Yes indeed," he says, "I am only too well aware of the gravity of the situation, and I don't know how to deal with it."
2. In verses 1b and 2 we are listening to the words of friends. They point to the gravity of the situation. Only in verse 3 do we begin to hear the psalmist's response.
3. Throughout verses 1-3 we are listening to what the psalmist's friends have been saying to him. His response only begins in verse 4.

Whatever view we take, one thing is clear. What is being described is a situation where the fabric of society and presumably the religious life of the community are being undermined. It is best to take verse 3, not as an "if" clause (NRSV), nor as a circumstantial clause introduced by "when" (REB), but as an emphatic statement — "The foundations are indeed being destroyed." Moral and spiritual values are at stake. The "upright in heart" (v. 2; cf. 7:10) and all that they stand for are under attack by the wicked. We would probably replace the picture of the wicked as archers doing their deadly work under the cover of darkness with that of well-concealed snipers and the deadly carnage they can cause. What defense is there in such a situation? "What can the righteous do?" (v. 3). Such despair is a tempting response and one which has a powerful appeal for many people today in the midst of the moral confusion and chaos of our time. Witness the growth of communes, deeply influenced by Eastern, otherworldly mysticism. But how much poorer the world would be if opting out had been the response of heroes of the faith. Suppose Jeremiah had opted out of the moral and political corruption of his day, out of the agony of being a prophet, instead of staying to share in his people's tragedy. Suppose Mother Teresa had opted out of the destitution and poverty of the streets of Calcutta. Suppose Jesus, in the face of opposition and misunderstanding, had opted out instead of setting his face steadfastly to go to Jerusalem. For this psalmist, to opt out would have been the denial of what, in spite of difficulties, he continued to believe about God.

4-7   The faith which is expressed in the second half of the psalm revolves around three unshakable convictions about God.

1. The psalmist believes in a God who is both transcendent and immanent. On the one hand, this is a God who is in "his holy temple," his "throne in heaven" (v. 4). Although in the Psalms "his holy temple" often refers to the temple in Jerusalem (cf. 5:7), it is likely that here it is used in parallelism to God's heavenly throne. Here is a God whose majesty and greatness lie beyond our human ken, a God who cannot be merely at our beck and call, there to be used by us. Yet at the same time, this is a God who is present, who is au fait with what is happening in our world, a God who not only has his gaze fixed on our life, but who "tests" humankind. The word translated "tests" is used frequently to refer to the process of refining metal by fire, and hence is a suitable symbol of God's testing, refining judgment.

2. Such testing means that God is committed to action involving a clear distinction between the "righteous" and the "wicked" (see Psalm 1). Inevitably he reacts against, "hates," those committed to "violence," to that which threatens social stability and wounds other people. The reference to "coals of fire and sulfur" raining upon the wicked recalls the story of the destruction of Sodom and Gomorrah in Genesis 19; while "the scorching wind" is the hot, sand-laden wind which blows in from the desert, making life extremely uncomfortable.

The metaphor of the "cup" is frequently found in the Old Testament. The sharing, the passing of a cup within the family and with a guest is a sign of acceptance, friendship, and hospitality. So Ps. 16:5 declares "the LORD is my portion and my cup," while Ps. 116:13 speaks of the worshipper responding to God's goodness by taking in his hand "the cup of salvation." But "cup" can also be used as a symbol of God's anger and judgment, a poisoned chalice, as it were, from which the wicked must drink to their own destruction (e.g., Ps. 75:8; Jer. 25:15-38; Hab. 2:16). To be, as the wicked person is, "the lover of violence" (v. 5) is to drink of that fatal, self-destructive poison.

3. God is committed to this kind of reaction and response because that alone is consistent with his own character. He is "righteous" (see 7:11), and that is no mere cold, abstract theological statement. He is a God who "loves righteous deeds," who not only acts in a way consistent with his own nature, but also expects a similar response from those who profess their loyalty to him. His "no" to those who love violence finds its counterpart in his "yes" to those who mirror his concern for what is right. So 1 John insists that if Christian faith is rooted in a God who loves, then the only conduct consistent with such a faith is the showing forth of such a love in our relationships with others (1 John 4:7-21).

It is God's "yes" of acceptance which is affirmed in the closing words of the psalm. "His face is turned towards the upright" (REB). This seems more appropriate in context than the NRSV's rendering, "the upright shall behold his face." The "upright" or the "upright in heart" (Ps. 7:11) is a favorite expression in the Psalms for those who are truly committed to God, not only in word but also in deed. It is often found, as here, used in parallelism with "the righteous"; compare the closing words of Psalms 32 and 64. The opening word of this psalm is "the LORD"; the closing word is "his [i.e., the LORD's] face." Within this framework the psalmist faces a potentially deadly crisis and dares to continue to trust.

> Who would true valour see,
> Let him come hither;
> One here will constant be,
> Come wind, come weather;
> There's no discouragement
> Shall make him once relent
> His first avowed intent
>   To be a pilgrim.

Psalm 12
THE ABUSE OF WORDS AND THE PROTECTING WORD

The psalm begins with a dramatic plea, "Help, O LORD," the word translated "help" being the same word which is often translated "save" or "deliver" (see comment on Ps. 3:8). As the psalmist looks at what is happening in society around him, he is profoundly pessimistic. The "godly" person (Hebrew *ḥāsîd,* one loyal to God; see Ps. 4:3) and the "faithful" (Hebrew *'ĕmûnîm*) are conspicuous by their absence (v. 1). These are not, however, the words of a bitterly disillusioned old man, nor of someone claiming, Elijah-like, to be the sole survivor of the faithful (1 Kgs. 18:22). The psalmist goes on to speak of the poor and the needy to whom the LORD listens (v. 5), and he refers to "us" whom the LORD protects. Sweeping general denunciations of society are as old as the hills. There are examples from ancient Egypt long before the psalmist wrote. We hear them on the lips of Old Testament prophets: "The faithful have disappeared from the land, and there is no one left who is upright" (Mic. 7:2; cf. Jer. 5:1). Such denunciations are not unknown on the lips of preachers, evangelists, and politicians today. Such statements can hardly be taken as literally true. How could the psalmist have known that there was not a single godly person left in the land? Had he vetted all its inhabitants? They are, rather, an attempt to read the signs of the times, and the signs of the times brought the psalmist no comfort.

He was conscious of living in a society in which human relationships were being undermined by the misuse of that precious gift which should cement and deepen such relationships, the gift of speech. Instead of dealing with each other honestly, people "utter lies" (v. 2). They indulge in smooth, flattering words and that doublespeak which has its roots in a corrupt and divided mind — what verse 2 describes in the Hebrew as "a heart and a heart." Not only so, but they are arrogant, talking big, assuming that they will never be called to account (v. 4). We don't need to look far to see parallels today, where deceit too often undermines family and business life, where politicians are economical with the truth, and where those who control the media further their own interests through manipulation and slanting of news and comment and deliberate disinformation. On a purely human level, this can be damaging enough, but the psalmist is convinced that God is also involved. Such flattering, arrogant tongues are anathema to God, a theme developed at length in the wisdom literature in the Old Testament (e.g., Prov. 6:16-19; 10:31-32) and in the letter of James in the New Testament (e.g., James 3:1-12).

The abuse of power means that the "poor" and the "needy" suffer (see comment on 10:12). It is in response to their plight and their cry for help that we hear another word, the word of the LORD (v. 5), the God who throughout the Bible hears the cry of those in distress (e.g., Exod. 2:24; Judg. 2:18; Ps. 102:18, 22). This word comes in verse 5 in the form of a brief oracle in which God speaks in the first person: "I will rise up. . . . I will place them. . . ." It is now customary to regard such oracles as having been spoken to the congregation in the name of God by a temple prophet or priest as part of the liturgy. This is possible, indeed probable. Since, however, there is much that we do not know about worship at the temple in Old Testament times, we cannot know for certain. The use of direct speech is a well-known literary device. The previous verse, verse 4, has put words on the lips of those who were making life difficult for the psalmist. Why not then put appropriate words on the lips of God in verse 5? The same issue arises with similar passages in other psalms (e.g., Psalms 50, 60, 81, and 91).

The LORD's word is a promise to go into action (for "rise up," see comment on 9:19), to place those in need in "safety" (a word from the same root as "help" in verse 1), the "safety for which they long." This translation is, however, far from certain; some of the early versions read a text which may be translated "I will shine forth" (i.e., for them), be gracious to them.

Verses 6-7 say "Amen" to this word, affirming what God says. "His promises" are "pure" and thus wholly dependable like silver refined "in a furnace on the ground" (v. 6). The words "on the ground" are not entirely clear in context, and a slight alteration of the Hebrew text leads to the REB translation, which makes a good deal of sense: "like silver refined in a crucible, like gold purified seven times over." Compared with this pure promise, the words of those who utter lies are no more than dross.

The psalmist, however, has no illusions. The LORD has spoken, but this does not mean that the situation in which he finds himself suddenly changes. The "wicked" are still there all around him, successfully peddling their "vileness," if this is the correct translation of a word found only here in the Old Testament, though it comes from a root meaning "to be worthless." The cheap hurting comments do not cease. The psalmist knows that he still belongs to a scorned minority. But he has one assurance. As John Calvin well puts it in his commentary, "However small may be the number of the good, let this persuasion be firmly fixed in our minds, that God will be their protector and that for ever."

Psalm 13
HOW LONG, O LORD?

In many ways this brief psalm is a classic example of the individual lament. It begins (vv. 1-2) with the psalmist urgently describing the crisis in his life with a fourfold repetition of the cry "how long?" (see comment on 4:2). Against this background, he makes his petition to God (vv. 3-4). The psalm then ends on the notes of joy and praise, grateful and renewed trust in God (vv. 5-6).

1-2 But what is the nature of the crisis described in verses 1-2? The psalmist's relationship with God is in the melting pot. How long is he going to feel utterly abandoned? The same sense of numb despair which is found in the words "Will you forget me forever [or: utterly]," is expressed by the poet in Lam. 5:20, when in the aftermath of the pillage and rape of Jerusalem and the destruction of the temple, he cries out: "Why have you forgotten us completely? Why have you forsaken us these many days?" Here is a psalmist who had probably often listened to the words of the priestly blessing: "The LORD bless you and keep you; the Lord make his face to shine upon you and be gracious to you" (Num. 6:24). Now he can only say, "How long will you hide your face from me?" It is as if God had turned away from him, and, instead of being gracious to him, had now despised him and rejected him (cf. Isa. 53:3).

Here is a man experiencing "pain" and "grief," whose mind is in turmoil, knowing that he is face to face with an "enemy" (v. 2) who is gloating over his miserable condition. Much of the interpretation of the psalm depends on the identity of this enemy. It has been argued that the enemy here and in verse 4 is death. In this case the psalmist is suffering from some serious illness which he fears may be fatal. This would certainly account for the language of verse 3, where he talks about sleeping "the sleep of death," and for the sense of continuing and increasing alienation from God, since for most Hebrews death meant the end of any meaningful relationship with God (see 6:4). The god Mot, Death, appears as a powerful enemy in Canaanite literature, of which there are many echoes in the Psalms.

On the other hand, "my enemy" (vv. 2, 4) and "my foes" (v. 4) may be otherwise unidentified people who for personal reasons have their knife into the psalmist, and who mockingly see in his present pain and suffering the sign that he has been abandoned by God (cf. Job 30:9-23). Suppose they are right? How long, O LORD, can this last?

3-4 The petition or prayer for deliverance picks up the themes of the crisis and seeks to respond to them: "Consider and answer" . . . instead of forgetting. "Give light to my eyes" . . . instead of hiding your face. The request "Give light to my eyes" asks for the sparkle to return to eyes dimmed by grief and pain, the sparkle of health and healing which could only come through the restoration of the psalmist's relationship with God.

It is a measure of the psalmist's defiance and desperation that, whatever his own pain and confusion, whatever others may be saying, he addresses his prayer to "O LORD, my God." Here is his only source of hope. It is part of his prayer that if he remains unanswered his enemies will triumph and take delight in a life lying before them, "shaken" (v. 4), shattered and in pieces. It is interesting, however, that there is no call to God to pour out his anger upon these enemies or to crush them, as in Pss. 7:9 and 10:15. This suggests that these enemies are not actively persecuting the psalmist, but that he is fighting what is essentially an inner, spiritual battle which he alone, with the help of God, must resolve.

5-6 The petition ends with the words "I am shaken," my life shattered and in pieces, much to the delight of my foes. The concluding section of the psalm begins with an emphatic, "But I . . ." (v. 5), pointing to a different verdict, a verdict based on "trust" (see 4:17) in God's "steadfast love" (*hesed;* see 5:7), and on the way God "has dealt bountifully with me" (v. 6). We listen to the psalmist rejoicing in the "salvation" God brings (see 3:8) and singing a song of praise to God. The Greek (LXX) text underlines this by adding to the end of the psalm the concluding words of Psalm 7, "and I will sing praise to the name of the LORD, the Most High."

Why the apparent change of mood, a change which occurs in many of the psalms of lament? How do we reconcile the psalmist's "How long?" in verses 1-2 with the joy and praise of verses 6-7? Has the psalmist heard some words of reassurance, an oracle of salvation spoken to him by a priest or temple prophet, declaring that his prayer has been answered? This is possible and indeed likely if we imagine this troubled soul taking his complaint to God at the temple, there to be given words which bring him new hope (cf. Psalm 22). But there is a theological and spiritual issue which needs to be explored further. Is the storm now over, with the psalmist sailing again on a placid sea? There is no reason to believe so. The storm may still be raging, but in the midst of the storm there is a reassuring presence. Protest and trust, pain and joy, may coexist. Indeed, it was probably because the psalmist believed in the steadfast love of God that he was driven to protest and to question when his experience of life seemed to be pointing in another direction. It was in the midst of his continuing pain that he discovered that he could still rejoice. As has been well said, "There is nothing to suggest that the psalmist has dropped his protest against God's adverse disposition. . . . Simultaneously with the psalmist's confession of present trust is his complaint of

God's hiddenness. A God lament need not signal lack of trust, nor does trust obviate lament" (Broyles, "The Conflict of Faith and Experience in the Psalms," 186). This tension receives memorable Christian expression in the words of George Matheson's hymn, written as he faced his own personal crisis:

> O Love that will not let me go,
>   I rest my weary soul in thee;
> I give thee back the life I owe,
> That in thine ocean depths its flow
>   May richer, fuller be.
>
> O Joy that seekest me through pain,
>   I cannot close my heart to thee;
> I trace the rainbow through the rain,
> And feel the promise is not vain,
>   That morn shall tearless be.

Steadfast love and debilitating weariness, pain and joy, strange bedfellows, yet from them hope may be born.

Psalm 14
THE WRONG CONCLUSION

This psalm, which four times uses the Hebrew personal name for God, Yahweh (LORD), in verses 2, 4, 6, 7, appears again in Book Two of the Psalms as Psalm 53. In Psalm 53 the name Yahweh is replaced with the generic "God" (Hebrew *ĕlōhîm*). There is a more substantial difference in the textually difficult verses 5-6, which in Psalm 53 read:

> There they shall be in great terror,
> in terror such as has not been.
> For God will scatter the bones of the ungodly;
> they will be put to shame, for God has rejected them.

The psalm thus circulated in varied forms — perhaps one (Psalm 53) in northern circles in Israel, the other (Psalm 14) in southern circles in Jerusalem — and was adapted to different circumstances and to different liturgical usage. The version in Psalm 53, with its reference in verse 5 to "the ungodly" or "those who encamp against you" (see NRSV footnote), may have been used in a time of national crisis. This would fit in with the use of the word "fool," translated "the impious" (NRSV) in Ps. 74:18, 22. It is tempting to identify the perverse, morally clueless fool of the psalm with the nation's enemies who worship other gods, but this is not the thrust of Psalm 14. It is no monument to nationalistic religious prejudice but is rather an attack on those within Israel who believed that they could live as if God were irrelevant and who drew the wrong conclusions concerning the God-ordained moral fabric of society.

The "fool" (Hebrew *nābāl*) is not a simpleton. He may be highly intelligent, but in the eyes of the psalmist he is a person who hasn't a clue as to what life is really about. In his thinking he has banished God to the sidelines of the universe — "There is no God" being the expression of a practical rather than an intellectual atheism (see comment on 10:4). He consequently accepts no moral restraints. In prophetic literature the "fool" is described as someone who is godless, who ignores or oppresses the poor and the needy, and who amasses wealth unjustly (e.g., Isa. 32:6; Jer. 17:11). Deuteronomy speaks of a foolish and senseless people who profess belief in a God of justice and faithfulness, but who ignore such justice and faithfulness in their lives (Deut. 32:6). Such a "fool" stands in marked contrast to "the wise" (v. 2, Hebrew *maśkîl*) or shrewd who place God at the center of life and who therefore, as Ps. 41:1 puts it, have a concern for the weak. Twice we listen to the bleak comment, "There is no one who does good" (vv. 1 and 3), a sweeping generalization similar to that which we found in 12:1.

Whatever the fool thinks, however he acts, the psalmist is convinced that God is not a disinterested spectator. This is the LORD "who looks down from heaven on humankind to see" (v. 2; cf. 102:19), just as in the tower of Babel story in Genesis the writer, using equally anthropomorphic language, speaks of God coming down to see and to pass judgment on an unacceptable scenario. It is possible that in verses 3 and 4 we are listening to God's verdict on what is happening and that these verses should be put into quotation marks. If so, this verdict is totally in line with what the psalmist has already declared in verse 1. Here are people who have "gone astray" (v. 3) or are "rebellious" (the Hebrew can mean either), who are "perverse" or "corrupt" (REB), a rare word found only in this psalm and in Job 15:16, where Eliphaz attacks "one who is abominable and corrupt, and who drinks iniquity like water." Here are clueless "evildoers" (see comment on 5:5) who devour people as nonchalantly as they eat bread and totally ignore God.

Although verses 5 and 6 are textually difficult, their general sense is clear. Such fools, lacking a social conscience, will end up panic stricken. God's presence is with the "righteous," to be their "refuge," a common description of God in the Psalms (e.g., 46:1; 61:3; for the use of the corresponding verb "to take refuge in God," see comment on 2:11).

Throughout the psalm there are many indications of the influence of wisdom teachers and prophetic preachers, but this psalm is not merely a piece of instruction. It finds its true place in the life of the worshipping community and so ends with a prayer celebrating what God is going to do for his faithful people. "Salvation" (see comment on 3:8), associated with God's presence in the midst of his people on Mt. Zion (see 2:6), will surely come when the LORD will right what is wrong in the life of the nation and "restore the fortunes of his people" (v. 7). This phrase frequently refers to the return of the people from exile in Babylon (see Jeremiah 30 and 31), as does a similar phrase in Ps. 126:1. But the phrase can be used in a much wider sense to refer to any reversal of fortune, any rehabilitation of the people from oppressive circumstances. Its use here is no indication of a late exilic or post-exilic date for the psalm. So the psalm ends, as did Psalm 13, on a note of joy, the only truly meaningful response to God's presence with and deliverance of his people. It is perhaps best to take the last line of the psalm as an invitation: "Let Jacob rejoice, let Israel be glad."

Jacob/Israel — both names are probably used here to indicate the whole people of God who traced their ancestry back to Jacob who became Israel (Gen. 35:10), though in other contexts Jacob and Israel are used in parallelism to indicate in political terms the northern kingdom of Israel as opposed to the southern kingdom of Judah.

In Rom. 3:10-11 Paul quotes verses 2-3 of this psalm following the Greek (LXX) text and adds to these verses quotations from other psalms and from Isaiah 59, which then appear in later Greek manuscripts of Psalm 14. Paul, in fact, is using the psalm in a way which takes us far beyond its original reference. It is part of his argument that all people, irrespective of religious or cultural background, Jews and Gentiles, are under the power of sin. If we accept that Paul is pointing the way towards a contemporary Christian interpretation, then we can say, "The fool is not a rare sub species within human nature; all human beings are fools apart from the wisdom of God" (Craigie). This may be true, but it is hardly what the psalm says. It can hardly be anything other than a sub species within the history of interpretation of a psalm which from early times has appeared in varied form and has spoken to different people in different ways. Early Jewish interpreters argued that it referred to the suffering of Israel in a pagan, hostile world. Calvin finds in it references to Church leaders who oppress instead of tending like a true shepherd the flock of God. Many modern commentators identify the fools and the evildoers with the corrupt, self-seeking ruling class in Israel. We can only bring ourselves to the text and seek to allow it to speak responsibly to us, wherever we are in our life and spiritual experience.

Psalm 15
A SEARCHING QUESTION

The structure of this psalm is clear. It begins with a question that receives an answer in verses 2-5b. This answer, which comes from a priest or Levite at the temple, then leads into a concluding promise or a blessing. Like Ps. 24:3-6, this psalm has been described as an entrance liturgy, the initial question being asked by a pilgrim as he arrives at the gate into the temple courts to share in one of the great annual religious festivals. There are examples of similar liturgies from other Near Eastern religions. The liturgical color of Psalm 15, however, is not so clear as that of Psalm 24. This may be no more than the result of its brevity, but equally it opens up the possibility that the psalm may simply be a piece of wisdom teaching used to instruct the young as to the requirements needed if they are to participate meaningfully in the worship of God, just as instruction is given today to those who seek the privilege and the responsibility of membership in the Church. Once gathered into the hymnbook of Israel, however, it posed searching questions to everyone who claims to belong to the worshipping community. If God, in the words of Ps. 14:5, is "with the company of the righteous," then who may rightly belong to this company and thus be welcomed as a guest, the LORD's guest, in his tent (i.e., temple)? It is not a question designed to provoke general religious discussion; it calls for self-examination.

It is possible to find in the answer given in verses 2-5b ten separate injunctions, five positive in verses 2 and 4, five negative in verses 3 and 5 (for a recent clear statement of this interpretation, see Craigie). This would have provided a useful aid to memory, but it is not typical of entrance liturgies elsewhere in the Old Testament. Psalm 24 has only four injunctions, and Isa. 33:14-16, often cited as such a liturgy, has six. What is significant about the answer is not only what it says, but what it does not say. There is no reference to the devotional life, to prayer either private or public, and no mention of sacrifice or offerings. That is not to say these things were unimportant. The people, after all, were going into the courtyard of the temple on Mt. Zion where they celebrated God's presence with them in worship, which would include all these things. The psalmist, however, joins hands with prophets (e.g., Isa. 1:12-17; Mic. 6:6-8) and with wisdom teachers (e.g., Prov. 15:8) in insisting that worship is meaningless unless it goes hand in hand with an inner moral integrity which expresses itself in responsible living. The sermon which Jeremiah preached to people entering the gate of the temple to worship God contains a searing attack on those who lack such moral integrity and play fast and loose with human relationships (Jer. 7:1-15).

Verse 2 spells out the basis of such living in terms of those who "walk blamelessly" (cf. Ps. 101:2, 6), those characterized by a wholesome integrity. The word translated "blamelessly" is the word used in Deut. 18:13 to describe what is expected of Israel in its relationship with God and is there translated in the NRSV as "completely loyal." Such integrity will express itself in action, in doing "what is right," the antithesis of the conduct of the "evildoers" of Ps. 14:4, and in speech which comes from the heart, from people who mean what they say and say what they mean.

Verses 3-4 give specific examples. Avoid slander, harming friend and neighbor, and malicious gossip; say "no" to the wicked and "yes" to those who revere God (see Psalm 1), and be prepared to stand up for your principles even when that is costly.

Verse 5 points to two activities which can seriously undermine the fabric of society — usury and bribery: "Do not lend money at interest." Elsewhere the Old Testament draws a clear distinction. Interest can be charged on loans to foreigners, presumably as part of normal business transactions (Deut. 23:19-20), but interest must not be charged on any loans given to a fellow Israelite who has fallen on hard times. To do so would not only add to his difficulties, but would be acting in a way contrary to the compassionate way God responds to his needy people (cf. Exod. 22:25; Lev. 25:35-37). In other words, you have no right to profit from the poor and those most at risk in society.

"Do not take a bribe against the innocent." The demand here is for justice and only justice (Deut. 16:20), being unable to be manipulated in the interests of the rich and the powerful (cf. Exod. 23:6-8; Deut. 16:18-20). To connive at the perversion of justice, to make it impossible for the poor and the innocent to get redress through the legal system, how can that be consistent with the worship of the God who is a "righteous judge" (7:11; cf. 9:7-12)? If, as has been well said, "truth and justice are the foundation pillars on which rest the social ethic which governs community life, the administration of justice and man's behaviour in the economic sphere" (Weiser), then to be a worshipper of a God who is concerned with truth and justice, and not to be committed to such community and social concerns, is a contradiction in terms.

But does this not create a barrier to worship, a barrier which becomes greater, the greater the honesty of the worshipper? No. As the Psalms make clear over and again, the heart of worship for Israel is the celebration of the wonderful deeds of God, deeds which are the expression of a divine steadfast love which Israel can neither explain nor deserve (see Psalm 136). To live in the light of this steadfast love is to accept a discipline, the discipline to demonstrate the same steadfast love in daily relationships with other people. The Old Testament uses marriage as one way of describing the relationship between God and Israel (e.g., Hosea; Isa. 54:5), as does the New Testament in speaking about the relationship between Christ and the Church (Eph. 5:25-33). This may help us here. In the marriage service we speak of marriage as "a gift of God and a means of grace." That brings with it the need for commitment. Those who accept the gift take their vows: "I promise to love you, to be faithful and loyal to you, for as long as we live" (*Book of Common Order,* 1994). Without that commitment and without the daily attempt to work out that commitment, the marriage, even if it continues in name, is meaningless. So this psalm brings those who come to worship God face to face with the day-to-day implications of their commitment to God, a commitment which worship will illuminate and which must lead to self-examination. If worship does not lead us to ask searching questions about ourselves, then it is little more than a harmless hobby.

The psalm ends with what is best taken as a promise, that "those who do these things shall never be moved" or shaken. This does not mean that life shall always be plain sailing, that they will never experience difficulties nor have to live with agonizing questions. The psalmist in Psalm 13 was very much moved or shaken — Ps. 13:4 uses the same word as 15:5. But, as in Psalm 13, the unshakable security which is there for the worshipper to receive is the privilege of being in God's presence (v. 1) and there experiencing his steadfast love.

Psalm 16
A JOYFUL CONFESSION OF FAITH

Although the joyful and confident mood of this psalm is clear, textual difficulties in verses 2-4 make it difficult to be sure of the detailed interpretation. Also difficult is the elusive word "Miktam" in the heading, a word which occurs here and in Psalms 56–60. Guesses as to its meaning abound, but none seems more convincing than that offered by the Greek (LXX), an "inscription"; but what kind of inscription we do not know. Psalm 60 links it with "instruction," which can cover a multitude of different teaching situations and experiences. The psalm begins (v. 1) with words of quiet confidence; "in you I take refuge" (see comment on 2:11). It does not need a personal crisis in the psalmist's life, nor a crisis recently resolved, to account for these words. As one commentator has said: "True religious experience inevitably compels man again and again to take refuge in the arms of God and brings about man's dialogue with God" (Weiser). These are the words of an authentic spirituality which recognizes human vulnerability and reaches out for the security which God alone can give. So in confidence the psalmist can say, "Protect me, O God."

The precise interpretation of the psalm, then, depends to a large extent not only on the way we handle certain textual problems, but also on the related issue as to who we think is speaking in verses 2-4. Is it, as some have argued, the king or a priest? Is it a convert from paganism, confessing his newfound loyalty to Yahweh alone and expressing his delight in belonging to the people of Yahweh, "the holy ones" (v. 3), and firmly closing the door on his pagan background (v. 4)? Or should we read the opening words of verse 2, following a Hebrew textual tradition, as "You have said." This opens up the possibility that the psalmist is engaging in a dialogue with some friend or acquaintance who wishes to hedge his religious bets, confessing his loyalty to Yahweh (v. 2), but at the same time indicating his involvement with other gods — "the holy ones" and "the noble" or majestic ones of verse 3. To this the psalmist then responds that such religious syncretism can only lead to ruin.

The view taken here is that verses 2-3 unpack the meaning of the quiet confidence which the psalmist has expressed in verse 1. The psalmist acknowledges that Yahweh, the LORD, is his lord and master and the source of all that makes life good or enjoyable for him (v. 2). He bears witness to the delight that he experiences in being a member of the people of God, "the holy ones" (see comment on 2:6), "the noble" (compare Judg. 5:13, where this word is used in parallelism with the people of God).

This leads him inevitably to a negative verdict on those involved with any other gods and to an adamant refusal to be involved in any practices associated with the cult of such gods. Libations "of blood" (v. 4) need not point to any particularly repulsive practices such as human sacrifice. The blood of the animal sacrificed, the symbol of life, was regularly offered to God in the Old Testament sacrificial ritual. It is "their" drink offerings of blood, offered not to the LORD but to other gods, which is the point at issue. These verses, in fact, reflect the provisions of the Decalogue (Exod. 20:1-17) — the LORD as Israel's God, the prohibition on the worship of any other gods, and the community as the people of God living in the light of God's demands.

Verses 5-8 spell out why the worship of other gods is no real temptation to the psalmist. He has found security and self-fulfillment in his relationship with the LORD. Behind the picture of the LORD as my "chosen [or: allotted] portion" there probably lies the story in Joshua 13–21 of how the promised land was parceled out and allotted to the different tribes as their inheritance. The psalmist has an even greater inheritance, the LORD himself, "my cup," the source of all that makes life joyful (cf. Ps. 23:5). Although verse 6 is often used by people to indicate that they are well satisfied with the place or the country in which they reside, their "lines . . . fallen . . . in pleasant places," the psalmist is probably thinking in spiritual terms. His allotted portion is not a place or a country but the LORD. That is why life is rich and his inheritance deeply satisfying. Yes, no doubt the land, the place, the temple were important to the psalmist, as they were for many other psalmists (see comment on Psalm 48), but they were meaningless apart from the grace and presence of God.

This inheritance is one which respects the psalmist's freedom. The LORD "gives counsel," or advice, which lodges in the psalmist's heart (literally, "kidneys," for the Hebrews the seat of emotions). He "instructs" him "in the night" (or: "every night"; or: "in the darkest night" — the Hebrew word for night being plural), but advice may be ignored and instruction may be disobeyed. Out of this freedom comes the great divide between the "righteous" and the "wicked" (see Psalm 1). The psalmist does respond positively; he puts the LORD always before him. Thus the LORD becomes the focus of his life and his security (for "moved" or "shaken" in verse 8, see comment on 5:5). It is not surprising that the psalmist uses his freedom to "bless the LORD." We have already noted God's blessing of his people (see 3:8), but this is the first time we have heard the psalmist blessing

God. To bless God means to respond in gratitude to all the blessings that God has bestowed upon his people; it is to acknowledge all that God has done to enrich the life of the community or the individual. An illuminating example of this is Psalm 103, which begins and ends with a call to "Bless the LORD" and in between celebrates "all his benefits," all the good things he has given.

The closing section of the psalm is dominated by the twin notes of joy and gladness (cf. 5:11; 12:5), but what does the psalmist mean when he locates his joy in the fact that "you do not give me up to Sheol, or let your faithful one see the Pit"?

The Pit is a synonym for Sheol (see 49:9), the Greek (LXX) often rendering it by "corruption." If the bleak negative picture of Sheol which we have seen in Ps. 6:5 is in the psalmist's mind and if death means the end of any meaningful relationship with God, then in these words the psalmist is rejoicing in the vitality and richness of life he now enjoys, a vitality which God is safeguarding by keeping him out of the clutches of Sheol. The path he now walks is life fulfilling; he expects it to last joyfully "forevermore," that is, during his whole life. Any thought of what may or may not lie beyond this present life does not come over his horizon.

On the other hand, there is no reason why in the Psalms, far less in the Old Testament as a whole, there must be only one attitude towards death. Hymnbooks are not always noted for their theological consistency; nor are worshipping congregations. I have heard a congregation begin worship by singing "O God of Bethel," with its description of life as "this weary pilgrimage" and then sing a hymn of gratitude and thanksgiving in which the thought of life as a weary pilgrimage has been firmly booted out of court. It is thus possible that the psalmist is here conquering his fear of death by affirming that the life he now experiences, rooted in communion with God, is a life which by very definition not even death can destroy. He may not know what form life beyond the present may take, but he believes God will be there, a God who has never abandoned him in this life and will never abandon him in Sheol. The path he now walks is the path of everlasting life. The same issue is to be found in other psalms, notably Psalms 49 and 73.

Peter quotes verses 8-11 in his sermon on the day of Pentecost (Acts 2:25-28), and Paul quotes v. 10 in his homily in the synagogue at Antioch. In each case, they apply the passage to Jesus and his resurrection from the dead, as if to say that not only is this passage to be given a future messianic interpretation, but the answer to the bleak negativity of the Hebrew concept of Sheol and death is to be found in the resurrection of Jesus as the firstfruits of those who have died (cf. 1 Corinthians 15). The very fact, however, that the New Testament bases its hope for eternal life firmly on the resurrection of Jesus means that it goes far beyond the psalmist's experience. The psalmist, however, in the joyful confidence of faith looked the grim reaper in the face and said, "Yes, but God . . ."

Psalm 17
AN URGENT CRY FOR JUSTICE

A comparison of the NRSV and the REB translations of this psalm shows that it presents many difficulties of interpretation rooted in textual problems, notably in verses 3 and 14. Its heading, "A Prayer of David," gives us few clues since the word translated "prayer" is a very general word, found in the opening verse of the psalm ("my prayer") and occurring again in the heading of four others (Psalms 86, 90, 92, and 142) as well as in the heading of the hymn in Habakkuk 3. It is also used in the plural in the concluding words of Book Two of the Psalms, which inform us, "The prayers of David, the son of Jesse, are ended" (72:20).

The psalm has been linked traditionally with that period in the life of David when he was on the run from Saul (e.g., 1 Samuel 23). What we hear in this psalm is an urgent cry for justice from someone who knows himself to be under threat from enemies who are out to destroy him. The basis of his cry is not only his belief that he is innocent of the charges being brought against him — though he vehemently protests his innocence in verses 3-5 — but also his convictions about the character of the God whom he worships and to whom he now appeals. He makes his appeal in confidence because of the way in which the LORD has revealed himself to his people in the past, as a God who in the words of v. 7 does wonders (see 9:2) and whose nature is summed up as "steadfast love" (see 4:3). This is the God whose "right hand" is ready to go into action against those who oppose his purposes, language which echoes the Song of Moses celebrating the deliverance of the Israelites from enslavement in Egypt (Exod. 15:11-13). This is the God who has been and is the "savior of those who seek refuge" (cf. 2:11; 3:8).

In spite of the terseness of the language and the problems it raises, the psalm is carefully crafted, displaying what we call a chiastic pattern, AB followed by BA.

A. verses 1-7, the psalmist's plea based on a declaration of innocence and his belief in God.
B. verses 8-12, a description of the wicked who threaten him.
B. verses 13-14, the call to God to destroy these wicked enemies.
A. verse 15, an expression of confidence that his plea will be answered.

The beginning and the end of the psalm are also characterized by clear linguistic links — the word translated "just cause" in verse 1 occurs again as "righteousness" in verse 15; the word translated "see" in verse 2 reappears as "I shall behold" in verse 15. The literary craftsmanship, however, is at the service of a theology many of whose features we have already met in previous psalms.

In verses 1-5 the psalmist presents to God what he believes is a "just cause"

(v. 1); in respect of the charges being brought against him, he is "in the right," innocent (see comment on Psalm 1). He therefore expects a decision to be given in his favor, especially since he speaks with "lips free from deceit." In terms of our legal process, he claims to be telling "the truth, the whole truth, and nothing but the truth." In verses 3-5 — which may be taken as either a stated fact, "You have tested my heart" (REB), or as expressing a condition, "If you try my heart" (NRSV) — the psalmist declares his integrity. As Calvin puts it, "he submits himself to an impartial examination, seeing God whose prerogative is to search the secret recesses of the heart cannot be deceived by external appearances." Although the details and even the verse division in what follows are uncertain (cf. the NRSV and the REB), the psalmist denies that either in deed or in word has he followed in the footsteps of others engaged in rapacious conduct; instead, he has walked firmly in the way of the LORD (see 1:5)

Confident not only in his own integrity but in the God of "steadfast love" (v. 7), he then asks for protection, describing himself, in language reminiscent of the Song of Moses in Deut. 32:10-11, as "the apple of the eye" (v. 8; cf. 7:2), literally, "the pupil of the eye," the most sensitive part of the eye which regulates the passage of light and needs careful protection. He also asks for God to hide him "in the shadow of your wings," a phrase which may originate in the picture of a mother bird protecting her young, but becomes a common picture in the Psalms and elsewhere in the Old Testament for God's care for and protection of his people (e.g., Pss. 36:7; 57:1; Ruth 2:12). In liturgical contexts, the image would undoubtedly have been strengthened by the twin cherubim whose wings stretched out over the cover of the ark in the holy of holies in the temple, the symbol of God's presence in the midst of his people (cf. Exod. 25:18-20). The psalmist pleads that he needs such protection from the "wicked" (see comment on Psalm 1), from enemies, pitiless and arrogant, ruthlessly hunting him down like a lion waiting to pounce on its prey (cf. 10:9). The first line of verse 10, translated in the NRSV as "They close their hearts to pity" and in the REB as "They have stifled all compassion," might equally well be translated "They are rebellious." The Hebrew is literally "they have closed their fat." (Compare Isa. 6:10, where "make the mind of this people fat" means "dull their conscience so that they fail to understand or respond to God's message.") Faced with such deadly encircling hatred, the psalmist in verse 13 appeals to God to act to redress the situation: "Rise up, O LORD" (cf. 3:7; 9:19-20). That God is being asked to confront these enemies, rescue the psalmist from their clutches, and deal trenchantly with them is clear, but the second half of verse 14 is capable of two very different interpretations.

There are those who believe that there is a "gruesome irony" (Weiser) in the words of verse 14. The good things that these enemies of the psalmist enjoy in their present life they expect to hand on to their children and grandchildren. They will never be in want. They lack nothing except the one thing which makes life truly meaningful. Here are people who "store up treasure for themselves but are not rich towards God" (Luke 12:21). They invest, as it were, in the treasures this passing "world" offers — the word translated "world" is found again in the Psalms only in 49:1. What they are storing up for themselves in abundance can in the end only lead to their downfall. This line of thought, which is reflected in the NRSV, is to be more deeply explored in Psalm 73.

The word translated in the NRSV as "what you have stored up for them" may also, however, be a description of the people of God, "your treasured ones"; hence the REB's rendering, "those whom you cherish." In this case the second half of verse 14 is pointing to God's abundant provision for the people who, in contrast to the wicked, truly acknowledge him. The emphatic "I" at the beginning of verse 15 is then the psalmist's way of saying, "And I belong with such people."

Whatever view we take, the psalm ends on a triumphant note. The psalmist, who has laid his just cause before God, will be vindicated. "I shall behold your face in righteousness" (v. 15). Just as Ps. 13:1 speaks of the sense of alienation from God in the words "How long shall you hide your face from me?", so here both the psalmist's sense of acceptance by the God who vindicates him and his awareness of God's presence are in the words "I shall see your face" (cf. 11:7). "I shall be satisfied," have more than enough (the same verb is used in verse 14), he declares, when I "see your likeness" or form, words which probably point to the psalmist experiencing a vision of the presence of God. But what do the words "when I awake" mean? Do they point forward to some experience of resurrection from death similar to that described in Dan.12:2? Some commentators, ancient and modern, have thought so. It has, however, become common to lay emphasis on the psalmist spending a night in the temple (v. 3) and experiencing some kind of theophany or self-revelation of God which comes to him in the cult the following morning (cf. Weiser). It is equally possible that the psalmist is simply referring to his experience of waking up from the nightmare through which he has been forced to live. Calvin may well be right when he claims that the psalmist "compares his perturbation of mind to sleep. But when the favour of God shall again have arisen and shone brightly on him, he declares that then he will recover spiritual strength and enjoy tranquillity of mind."

Certainly the psalmist, having given voice to his urgent cry for justice, is convinced that this cry will be answered by the God whose steadfast love supports him through all the crises of life. So Jesus encourages us to ask, to search, and to knock in confidence because of who God is. "Is there anyone among you who, if your child asks for bread, will give a stone? Or if the child asks for fish, will give a snake? If you then, who are evil, know how to give good gifts to your children, how much more will your Father in heaven give good things to those who ask him" (Matt. 7:9-11)!

Psalm 18
THE THANKSGIVING
OF A WARRIOR-KING

Psalm 18 appears with minor variations in 2 Samuel 22. Its setting in 2 Samuel indicates that it is intended as a crowning celebration of David's exploits. It looks back across a life which in military terms had dealt with external enemies and crushed internal revolts, including one by his own son Absalom. The language of the poem is consistent with its originating in the time of David. It could come from David himself or from a court poet for use by David (cf. the REB heading). Once incorporated into the worship of the community, it found a new and broader meaning as a royal psalm applicable to any king who came to the throne as "the servant of the LORD," a phrase which occurs in the heading to Psalm 18 but not in the corresponding heading in 2 Samuel 22. It may have found a natural liturgical setting in one of the great festivals of the religious year, perhaps the Feast of Tabernacles, in which the king would have played a leading role. Although it is only quoted once in the New Testament — v. 49 in Rom. 10:9 — the psalm as a whole, like Psalm 2, has been given a distinctive Christological interpretation by many Christian commentators, ancient and modern. Thus Calvin concludes his comments on the psalm by declaring, "We shall only duly profit in the study of the psalm, when we are led by the contemplation of the shadow and the type to Him who is the substance." A modern commentator notes, ". . . from the NT perspective Psalm 18 has a latent messianic meaning, and the deliverance of God's anointed from 'the cords of death' (vv. 5-6) finds deeper significance in the deliverance of Jesus from death itself" (Craigie).

There has been, however, no single Christian approach to the psalm. Few today would feel comfortable with Luther's comments on the opening words of verse 11, "The hiding place of God is darkness." He reads into these words five meanings:

1. the riddle and darkness of faith;
2. God's dwelling in unapproachable light; hence we must ascend to him by way of denials or "analogical darkness";
3. the mystery of the Incarnation, God hidden in humanity, which is his darkness;
4. the Church or the Virgin Mary, in both of whom God is concealed;
5. the sacrament of the Eucharist, in which God is most completely concealed.

Such an approach simply ignores the context of the words of the psalm. Any darkness associated with God in any context in any book could have led to the same speculation. We must first try to understand the text as it lies before us in the Old Testament, before we ask whether there are any theological insights in the text which point us beyond that context.

Psalm 18 is a lengthy poem, and it will help us to understand it if we think of it as containing four stanzas, introduced by a prologue and rounded off by an epilogue.

1-6 The prologue sets the scene by describing a relationship and by placing side by side the power and resources of God and the crisis which threatens to engulf the psalmist. The opening words of verse 1, "I love you, O LORD, my strength," are not found in 2 Samuel 22. The verb translated "love" — related to the Hebrew word for "womb" — occurs nowhere else in this form in the Old Testament; nor is it elsewhere used of human love for God. The more usual form is found in Ps. 103:3, where a father's tender love or compassion for his children becomes an image of God's love for his people. In Isa. 49:5 the word is used of the bond which unites mother and child, a bond of compassion whose strength does not match the bond which unites God and his people. Other words for love are used both for God's love and for human love in the Old Testament, however, and there is no reason why the same should not be true of this word. It is possibly here used to describe the depths of the relationship which unites the psalmist with the God who strengthens and upholds him.

The strength of that relationship is underlined in verse 2 in a series of titles of God, all of them pointing to his protecting power. Most of the titles are drawn from the natural world: "crag" (cf. 31:3); "fortress," the rocky outcrop which in Job 39:28 is the home of the eagle; "rock" (cf. v. 46; Pss. 19:14; 28:1), used as a title for the LORD and other gods in Deut. 32:30-31. Other titles are drawn from the battlefield: "shield" (cf. v. 30 and Ps. 3:3); and "stronghold" (see 9:9). The title "horn of my salvation" occurs only here in the Old Testament and in 2 Sam. 22:3. It could have its origin in the powerful horns of an animal, a symbol of strength, or it could indicate the trumpet blown to signal victory in battle (cf. Josh. 6:5). Each title has the pronoun "my" attached to it. Here is "my deliverer," the one who rescues me, the one in whom I find refuge (cf. 2:1), a God worthy to be praised (v. 3).

The crisis in the psalmist's life is now described in language which probably draws upon Canaanite mythology to underline the extremity of the situation he faces (vv. 4-5). The "cords of death" could mean simply deadly or terrible pains, but more likely there is a reference to the Canaanite deity Mot, Death, who was thought to drag people to destruction. 2 Sam. 22:5 reads "waves" instead of "cords," as if Death were being described as an engulfing sea. There may, however, be a deliberate, ominous repetition in the "cords of death" (v. 4) and the "cords of Sheol" (v. 5; for Sheol, see 6:5). Likewise, although "the torrents of perdition" may mean simply "the destructive torrents" (REB), the word trans-lated "perdition," *bĕlîyaʿal* (used in 1 Kgs. 21:9, 13 to describe the scoundrels whom Jezebel suborned to ensure Naboth's death) is more likely to be another title of Death, the Swallower, closely allied with the waters of chaos. The psalmist is caught in a trap, face to face with destructive powers which threaten to sign his death warrant. He has only one possibility of escape, to invoke the strong help of the LORD, a cry answered "from his temple" (v. 6). This need not imply the temple in Jerusalem (see 5:7) or any other earthly temple; it could refer to God's heavenly palace.

7-19 The first section in this stanza, verses 7-15, draws upon language and imagery traditionally associated with the warrior storm god in ancient Near Eastern mythology. It was adapted and used in Old Testament tradition to describe in awe and wonder the momentous events central to Israel's encounter with God, the escape through the Reed Sea and the giving of the Torah at Mt. Sinai (e.g., Exod. 15:8; 19:18; 20:18; Deut. 4:11; 5:23). It finds its natural setting in poems celebrating God's coming to the help of his people (e.g., the Song of Deborah in Judg. 5:2-3) and in hymns (e.g., Psalm 29; 97:1-5; Habakkuk 3). To attempt to analyze such language is to destroy its rich cadences and to violate its appeal to the imagination. It seeks at one and the same time to witness to, yet to keep wrapped in mystery, the awesome glory and power of God. It is for congregational singing, not for grammatical dissection! The whole universe, earth and heaven, is depicted as responding to God's coming to destroy the forces which oppose him (vv. 8-9). He comes "riding on a cherub" (v. 10), one of those half human, half animal creatures who are depicted in many roles in the Old Testament, from forming a divine security guard banning the way back to the tree of life (Gen. 3:24) to covering the ark in the holy of holies with their wings (Exod. 25:17-22). In Ezekiel 10 they are closely associated with the glory of God departing from the temple. Here they probably signify the moving clouds — the chariot, as it were — of the divine king, driven on the wings of the wind (v. 10). Thunder and lightning herald his coming (vv. 12-13; the REB probably rightly follows 2 Sam. 22:14 in omitting the words "hailstone and coals of fire" from v. 12). All that threatens God's rule, the channels of the sea (or: water; so REB), symbolizing the powers of chaos (cf. vv. 5-6 and v. 16), lie under his feet awaiting his rebuke. Yet as this resplendent cosmic vision comes to its climax, the scene suddenly changes. A God awesome in glory and majesty, yes, but this is the God who reaches down to rescue his servant from the enemies who seek to destroy him, enemies whom the psalmist himself is powerless to defeat (v. 17).

"He brought me out into a broad place" — giving the psalmist space to be himself, room to breathe, freed from the troubles which had hemmed him in, or, as we might say, cramped his style. Such new-found freedom is seen to be the sign of God's approval.

How brilliantly this stanza weaves together a theology which witnesses to a God whose awesome greatness and power we can never fully comprehend and a theology which insists, "Are not five sparrows sold for two pennies? Yet not one of them is forgotten in God's sight. But even the hairs of your head are all counted. Do not be afraid, you are of more value than many sparrows" (Luke 12:6-7).

20-31 It would be easy to dismiss this stanza as a piece of self-righteous justification, the psalmist giving himself a moral and spiritual pat on the back. But this would be to misunderstand the words, "The LORD rewarded me according to my righteousness" (v. 20). The psalmist is not so much congratulating himself as he is affirming that God acts favorably toward those who obey him. The psalmist has taken to heart the prophetic call to repentance, "If you return to me . . . I will bless you." So the point is that God's actions are related to the way his people respond to him. This is something we know to be true in human relationships. Fathers and mothers will react to their children according to what these children do or don't do. This does not mean that the fathers' and mothers' characters change. It simply means that the love which they have for their children will express itself in different ways, ways which will range from commendation and approval to disapproval and anger. So it is here with God and his servant. In this divine-human pas de deux, there are three significant steps.

In the first step, contained within the circle of the echoing verses 20 and 24, the psalmist speaks of the rightness of his relationship with God in terms of his "loyalty" (v. 21), his obedience to God's laws (v. 22), and his singleness of purpose (v. 23) — very similar to the picture of the righteous in Psalm 1. It is this integrity which is given the stamp of God's approval.

In the second step, verses 25-27, the psalmist sets his experience within the context of how God deals with his people as a whole. The same principle is at work. It is the loyal or faithful (*ḥāsîd;* see comment on 4:3) who experience God's loyalty or faithfulness; it is those who show integrity in their relationship with God who experience God's integrity. The "pure" (see 15:2) experience God's purity, but the twisted, the perverse, find God's ways tortuous. The "humble" (see 9:12) experience "deliverance" (see 3:8), but the proud experience humiliation.

In the third step, the psalmist comes back to his own personal situation (vv. 28-30). The contrast between light and darkness (v. 28) runs right through the Bible; darkness is associated with chaos, death, distress, and all the forces which oppose God (e.g., Gen. 1:2), and light is associated with order, life, prosperity, and all that expresses God's purposes. The early Jewish group that produced the Dead Sea Scrolls believed that they belonged to the true Israel, and so they called themselves "the children of light" and everyone else "the children of darkness." The contrast is also found in many New Testament passages, particularly in the

Johannine literature (e.g., John 1:5; 12:35; 1 John 2:8). So into the psalmist's darkness comes "you who light my lamp" (v. 28). In another royal psalm God declares, "I have prepared a lamp for my anointed one" (132:17). This royal association is underlined in 2 Sam. 21:17, where David is described as "the lamp of Israel." On the king's relationship with God and on his God-given vitality depends the well-being of the whole nation. As a warrior, the king can, with God's help, successfully lead his army into battle. He can storm ramparts (REB, better than NRSV's rendering "crush a troop" in v. 29) and, taking his enemies by surprise, leap over a defensive wall.

The psalmist's reflections lead into a celebration of the uniqueness and the incomparable greatness of the LORD (v. 31). This God's way is "perfect," the same word translated as "blameless" in verse 25. This is a God of unquestionable integrity, a God whose word "proves true," or rather who "has stood the test" (REB), the Hebrew word indicating something which has been tested, refined like silver or gold in a crucible to remove from it any alien substance (cf. 12:6).

32-42 The theme of stanza one was God in action; stanza three now looks at the same events from the human perspective as the warrior-king goes into action. He goes equipped with God's strength (vv. 32, 39) and integrity — the words "my way safe" echo the phrase used of God in verse 32, "safe" being another rendering of the word translated "blameless" in verse 25. Sure and swift of foot (v. 33), trained in the skillful use of weapons (v. 34), he achieves a stunning victory. His enemies, deprived of any help from the LORD, are totally humiliated (vv. 41-42). Ephesians employs much of the same imagery when it calls upon Christians to put on the whole armor of God in the battle against the spiritual forces of evil (Eph. 6:10-17).

43-45 With the conflict over, the king now reigns secure, his enemies external and internal acknowledging his supremacy. The "strife with the peoples" (v. 43) is probably better rendered in the REB as "the people who challenge me." The corresponding verse in 2 Sam. 22:24 has "my people." If the psalm has a Davidic origin, this could refer to David's domestic troubles which came to a head in the rebellions of Absalom (2 Samuel 15–18) and Sheba (2 Samuel 20). Nor were later kings unfamiliar with palace intrigue and internal dissension. The second half of verse 43 and verse 44 could then refer to David's success in expanding his empire. In the light of the coronation promise in Ps. 2:8-9, however, and the advice there given to "the rulers of the earth," we may be listening to liturgical language and hopes expressed in worship, hopes which transcend any particular incidents (cf. Psalm 72).

46-50 The epilogue is in the form of a doxology which puts the king's triumph in context. The initial joy-filled cry, "The LORD lives!" (v. 46), sums up the witness of the whole psalm. This is no more a philosophical defense of the existence of God than the attitude of the fool in Ps. 14:1 is an expression of intellectual atheism. It is an assertion of the dynamic presence of the LORD, active in the world, in the history of his people, and in the experience of his servant king. All is of God, the fruit of God's grace. The psalmist focuses his gratitude in the words "Blessed be my rock" (i.e., God). Many other psalms come to the point where the only fully meaningful thing to say is "Blessed be the LORD" (e.g., 28:6; 31:21; 41:13), and many other people in the Old Testament join in this acclamation (see, e.g., Gen. 24:7; Ruth 4:14).

A series of descriptive phrases in verses 47-48, all of which have God as their subject, recapitulate in hymnic style the main themes of the psalm. They praise "the God who gave me vengeance . . . subdued peoples . . . rescued me . . . exalted me . . . delivered me." These phrases hammer home that the king's success is not the fruit of his own skills or the reward for his own achievements. There is no place for human pride. So Deuteronomy warns the people when they have successfully settled in the land and prospered, not to yield to the temptation to say, " 'My power and the might of my own hand have gotten me this wealth.' But remember the LORD your God, for it is he who gives you power to get wealth" (Deut. 8:17-18). Since it is the LORD who gave, what can the psalmist's response be but joyful "songs of praise" proclaiming to all the world the wonder of this God (v. 49). This lies at the heart of all true witness to God — not fear, not stern duty, but thanksgiving for what God has done and the desire to share this good news with others. Paul in Rom. 15:9 cites verse 49 as the first in a series of passages from the Old Testament calling upon the Gentiles as well as the Jews to rejoice in the gospel.

All that God has done for the king is now summed up in the words, "Great triumphs [or: victories] he gives," victories being one of the meanings of the word we have already noted as meaning "salvation" (see comment on 3:8). Such victories are rooted in the "steadfast love" (see 4:3) God shows to "his anointed" (see 2:2), words which echo the relationship between God and David and the promises made to the Davidic royal family in the oracle of Nathan in 2 Sam. 7:8-17. Another way of referring to this relationship is to talk about God's covenant with David, a theme explored in other psalms, notably Psalm 89.

Psalm 19
THE WORLD UNVEILED

Is it one or is it two? That is the first question this psalm poses. There is a clear break both in style and in subject matter after verse 6. The theme of verses 1-6 is the glory of God in creation, while verses 7-14 speak of the place of the Torah of the LORD in Israel's life. In verses 1-6 the word "God" appears only once, in the form of the generic name for deity *('ēl),* while in verses 7-14 the personal name for God known to Israel, Yahweh, the LORD, occurs seven times. In the language of verses 1-6 we sense echoes of mythological themes familiar from other ancient Near Eastern religions — for example, the sun god as bridegroom and hero. It is likely that in verses 1-6 the Hebrew poet is using and adapting for his own purposes an earlier religious text. But the way he adapts it springs out of his own faith. This has two important consequences:

1. We can see in verses 1-6 a process at work similar to that which we find in the hymn of creation in Genesis 1. In other ancient Near Eastern religions, the ordered universe we know comes into being out of a titanic struggle between gods and goddesses representing the natural forces of order and chaos, life and death. Genesis 1 will have none of this. There is only one God. The created world is the result of his word and his alone: "God said . . . and it was so." The forces of nature, including the sun, may be deities in the cultures surrounding Israel, but there is no hint of this in verses 1-6. The sun is merely the handiwork of the one God. It witnesses to his glory.

2. It is a mistake to assume that verses 1-6 present us with an approach to faith in terms of natural theology, the argument that from the existence of the ordered universe around us we are inevitably led to belief in God. Joseph Addison's hymn version of this psalm seems to say so in its final verse:

> What though in solemn silence all
> Move round the dark terrestrial ball?
> What though no real voice nor sound
> Amidst their radiant orbs be found?
> In reason's ear they all rejoice,
> And utter forth a glorious voice,
> For ever singing, as they shine,
> The hand that made us is divine.

The words "In reason's ear" suggest that any rational person may draw this conclusion. But there is no inevitability about such an argument. Many different voices speak to us from the world around us — the wonder of the night sky, the beauty of the setting sun shimmering over water, but equally the terror of earthquake, volcano, and hurricane. We may be left asking whether there is any meaning in all this and, if so, what that meaning might be. But the psalmist is not arguing from the world to God. He is looking at the world through the eyes of a faith born of Israel's encounter with and response to God, the faith which he confesses in verses 7-14. The writer of the epistle to the Hebrews makes the same point when he says, "By faith we understand that the universe was formed by God's command, so that the visible came forth from the invisible" (Heb. 11:3). A modern hymn writer strikes the same chord:

O Lord of every shining constellation
    That wheels in splendour through the midnight sky;
Grant us thy Spirit's true illumination
    To read the secrets of thy work on high.

                        (Albert Frederick Bayly)

Without such illumination we may read a different tale.

1-6 The "heavens," arching like a great dome or vault ("firmament"; see Gen. 1:6) over the earth, proclaim "the glory of God" (see 3:3), the way in which God manifests his awesome power and majesty in creation. Time, the recurring pattern of day and night, instead of merely slipping by, becomes in the words of a modern poet "an endless song." The NRSV translation of verses 3-4 hardly catches the rich variety of words used in the original; neither "voice" nor "words" occur twice. The REB in verse 4 translates "their sign" (the text here is problematic; "tune" is also possible) and "their message," a message which echoes across the universe, but only for those who have learned to tune in to it. Otherwise it remains inaudible. Paul in Rom. 10:18 quotes verse 4b, following the Greek (LXX) text to refer to the fact that the gospel message is being heard across the world.

    Verses 4b-6 focus on the sun, arguably that element in the heavens which has the most powerful effect on human life. The sun here is no deity, but it is vividly personified. It has been provided with a "tent" in which it spends the night. In the morning it rises "like a bridegroom from his wedding canopy" (v. 5). Although the word translated "canopy" means a covering — and in a Jewish wedding the ceremony takes place under such a canopy — the reference here and in Joel 2:16 is probably to the room in which the marriage is consummated. The sun rises like a "strong man" or hero, intent on demonstrating his prowess and vitality. The sun each day displays its vigor, completing its circuit from east to west. A very similar picture is drawn in Eccl. 1:5, "The sun rises and the sun goes down, and hurries to the place where it rises." Interestingly for the author of Ecclesiastes the sun, like the veering winds and the rivers which flow into the sea yet never fill it, are examples of the monotonous regularity of nature which brings no satisfaction. His attitude to the world of creation is very different from that of the psalmist, probably because his belief in God is very different. The psalmist's picture climaxes in the words "nothing is hid from its heat." The sun which brings life, light, and warmth to the earth can also be penetrating and terrifying in its relentless heat. It has been claimed that this final phrase in verse 6 is a key phrase which provides a bridge to the second half of the psalm, which focuses on Torah, the Law of the LORD. From verse 7 the psalmist "is talking of something else which hardly seems to be something else because it is so like the all-piercing, all-detecting sunshine" (C. S. Lewis, *Reflections on the Psalms*).

7-11 Precisely what the "Law (Hebrew *tôrâ*) of the LORD" means in this psalm depends to some extent on whether the psalm is early or late. Torah can mean teaching or instruction of any kind, or it can mean God's definitive self-revelation to Israel in story and in demand enshrined in Genesis to Deuteronomy, the Torah *par excellence*. The view taken here is that it is close to this latter meaning, there being many similarities between this section of the psalm and the great Torah anthem which is Psalm 119. The second half of verse 7 and verses 8-9 attempt to spell out comprehensively what the Torah means for God's people, following a pattern clearly outlined in the opening words of verse 7.

"The law of the LORD is perfect, reviving the soul." "Perfect" (the same word translated "blameless" in Ps. 18:23, 25) in this context probably means without blemish, free from all defect, like the animals offered in the sacrificial cult (Lev. 3:1). As such, countering all negative tendencies in life, it can "revive" the soul, bringing a new fullness of life to all who seek to obey.

This general statement is now fleshed out. The "decrees of the LORD" (v. 7b) are associated with the Torah elsewhere in the Old Testament and point to what is demanded of Israel in terms of its covenant relationship with God (e.g., Ps. 132:12). Such "decrees" (the Hebrew word is singular; the REB translates "instruction") are "sure," that is, dependable, reliable, capable of bringing wisdom to the "simple," a word frequently found in Proverbs (e.g., Prov. 1:4; 3:2). The simple are those who otherwise wouldn't have a clue as to the right way to take in life.

Behind the "precepts" of the LORD" (v. 8) is a word associated with the covenant in Ps. 103:18 and found frequently in Psalm 119 (e.g., vv. 4, 15, 27). To say that the precepts of the LORD are "right" (the same word is used in 11:7 to indicate the upright, people of integrity) is to say that they are characterized by integrity and are therefore a source of joy since in them lies the secret of life as God intended it to be.

The "commandment of the LORD" is "clear" or pure, the same word being used to describe the true servant of God in 24:4 and 73:1, and the flawless, radiant girl in Cant. 6:9, 10. This leads to "enlightening the eyes," that is, a true understanding of what life is all about (cf. Ps. 119:30).

The "fear of the LORD" (v. 9) is a very common expression in the wisdom literature, notably Proverbs (e.g., Prov. 1:7), indicating that reverence towards God which for Proverbs is the beginning and the true goal of wisdom — a reverence which springs out of the recognition that God is "awesome" (cf. 47:2), a word which comes from the same basic root "to fear." The fear of the LORD is "pure" (REB: "unsullied"); this, again, is a word used of animals ceremonially acceptable for sacrifice, for precious metal refined and freed from all dross (cf. 12:6), and for people (Ps. 51:10; Prov. 30:12). It is probably used here of that attitude towards the LORD, uncontaminated by any compromise with paganism, which lasts, an unshakable foundation for a wholesome life.

The "ordinances of the LORD" reflect the decisions of a judge, here the divine judge, and hence that justice which is the basis of true community life. To say they are "true" is to claim that they are trustworthy, dependable (cf. 25:10; 138:20), "righteous altogether," and as such they can never lead anyone astray. Notice how in each case "of the LORD" qualifies the subject of these sentences, as if to emphasize the psalmist's own commitment and to claim that no other source can provide the quality and fullness of life here being offered.

Life, therefore, can have nothing more precious or attractive to offer (v. 10; for a similar comparison with gold, see Ps. 119:72, 127, and with honey, Ps. 119:103; Prov. 24:13-14). We have already looked at the success factor involved in being in the right with God (see comment on Psalm 1), and Prov. 22:4 declares, "The reward for humility and the fear of the LORD is riches and honor and life." But this psalm seems to speak of a different kind of reward, the reward which comes simply through obedience, the reward of a quality of life rooted in a relationship with God which accepts the role of being the "servant" of the LORD.

The psalm ends (vv. 12-14) with a prayer in which the psalmist, in the light of his vision of the Torah of the LORD and what it can give, sees his own weakness. Two things may spoil his life: hidden, inadvertent sins (for such unintentional sins and the sacrifices appropriate for them, see Lev. 4:1–5:13); and the example of the "insolent," arrogant, presumptuous people whose attitude to life may undermine his own good intentions. The RSV's rendering, "presumptuous sins," and the REB's translation, "wilful sins," assume that the reference here is to deliberate violation of the Law rather than to insolent people, but this is hardly borne out by the use of this word elsewhere (e.g., 86:14; 119:51, 69, where the word in question means "arrogant people"). From the weakness within him, which he does not even recognize, and from the potentially powerful and misleading example of others, the psalmist seeks deliverance. Yielding to either or to both would soon undermine his commitment to God. He longs for the integrity which will keep him innocent of "great transgression" or rebellion against God. There seems little need to try to specify what this "great transgression" means — idolatry or adultery has been suggested. It is possible we should interpret this phrase in the light of that defiant disobedience to God which lies at the center of the story of the garden of Eden and from which the writers of Genesis trace all that is wrong in divine and human relationships.

The final words (v. 14) bring the psalmist back to his relationship with the LORD, a relationship which must be reflected in what he says and in what he thinks, a relationship with one whom he describes as "my rock" (see 18:2) and "my redeemer" (gô'ēl). Like many of the great theological words in the Bible, the word gô'ēl has its roots in everyday life in Hebrew society. The gô'ēl was a person's nearest next of kin, usually a brother, who had to accept certain responsibilities. If a piece of family land or property was in danger of being lost, it was the responsibility of the gô'ēl to purchase it (cf. Jer. 32:6-15; Lev. 25:25-28). If a member of the family was forced through poverty or debt to sell himself into slavery, the *gô'ēl* had the responsibility to purchase his freedom. Marrying a brother's childless widow (Deut. 25:5-10; Ruth 4) and seeking revenge for the killing of a member of the family were also his legal duties. The word was then used to describe the God who accepts responsibility for his people, who brings them out of slavery in Egypt (Exod. 6:6; Pss. 77:15; 106:10) and in Babylon (Isa. 43:1; 44:22-23), a God who delivers from all that threatens life, including death itself (Job 19:25; 33:28; Ps. 103:4). Thus launched on its theological journey, it was to become a key word in Christian thought to describe what God in Christ has done (e.g., Gal. 4:1-7).

The last word in the psalm is thus the key to its beginning. Because the psalmist rejoices in an intimate relationship with God, a relationship based on God's acceptance of him, he can look out on a world which he believes to be God's world and sing his song of praise: "The heavens are telling the glory of God." Perhaps the depth of the majesty and wonder of these words can only be truly appreciated when they are sung, as in Haydn's great oratorio, *The Creation*.

Psalm 20
INTO BATTLE

There is little doubt that the last verse of this psalm, "Give victory to the king, O LORD," and the earlier references to "his anointed" (v. 6) point to this being a royal psalm. Although the same liturgical setting as we noted for Psalm 2 is possible, it is more likely that the psalm was part of a special service that took place on the eve of the king's setting out for battle. The narrative in 2 Chronicles 20 provides an interesting parallel. King Jehoshaphat, faced with invasion from the East by what seem overwhelming forces, proclaims a fast, gathers the people in the temple area, and there offers prayers which stress the nation's powerlessness against its enemies. "We do not know what to do, but our eyes are on you" (2 Chron. 20:12). His prayer is answered by an oracle which comes through a Levite. "Thus says the LORD to you: do not fear or be dismayed at this great multitude; for the battle is not yours but God's" (2 Chron. 20:15).

The structure of the psalm lends itself to the interplay of different voices. In verses 1-4, we listen to a priest offering intercessory prayer on behalf of the king, which is echoed by the assembled congregation in verse 5. In verse 6, a Levite, if we follow the analogy of Chronicles, steps forth with a ringing declaration that the prayer is answered. In response, the assembled congregation confidently reaffirms its faith in God in verses 7-9. The psalm reflects a spirituality which commits the whole of life in quiet confidence to God in the face of a world which often bases its assumptions on a different set of values. It is just such a spirituality which leads Paul to affirm triumphantly, "If God is for us, who is against us?" (Rom. 8:31).

It is a short psalm, but one in which skillful use is made of the repetition of words and ideas. Three of the key words in the opening verse, "LORD . . . answer . . . in the day of" are echoed in the closing verse, where the phrase translated "when we call" is literally "in the day of our calling." Three times there is reference to the "name" of God (vv. 1, 5, 7). Three times there occur forms of the noun or verb indicating "victory" or salvation (vv. 5, 6, 9; see comment on 3:8). Throughout the first half of the psalm, verses 1-5, the element of petition is overwhelming on the lips of priest and congregation. Eleven times in these five verses a verb occurs expressing a wish, "May he [i.e., the LORD]," and once "May we." Nor is there any doubt as to the person for whom the petitions are being offered. Eleven times the word "you" (i.e., the king) or "your" occurs.

The king in whom so many of the hopes of the nation are centered (cf. Psalm 2) is facing a crisis (v. 1) which he cannot meet in his own strength. His only security (the word translated "protect" probably means "to set on high"; hence the REB translates, "a tower of strength") is in "the name [see comment on 5:11] of the God of Jacob." According to the traditions in Genesis 32 and 35, Jacob was renamed Israel and thus became the ancestor of all the tribes who made up Israel, the people of God. The God of Jacob is, therefore, the God of the whole community, "our God" (v. 5), "the LORD our God" (v. 7). To look for security in the name of the God of Jacob, to pray for help and support from the God worshipped in the sanctuary on Zion (cf. 2:6), raises an important theological issue which lurks behind much of the language of the rest of the psalm and, indeed, that of many other psalms. Can such help and hoped-for victory be achieved at any cost or by any means, or does invoking the name of the LORD imply certain restraints? The "offerings" — the word used here means simply a gift, usually of cereal (see Lev. 2:1-16) and "burnt offerings" (Lev. 1:3-17; see comment on Ps. 40:6) — were probably accompanied by prayers, but what is meant by God "remembering" or "looking with favor" (literally, "regarding as fat") on such sacrifices? Does this mean that God, in return for such gifts, will grant the king's "heart's desire" (v. 4) and fulfill his plans, whatever these desires or plans may be? Or is it being tacitly acknowledged that such desires and plans must conform to God's will and be consistent with God's character? When the people look forward to unfurling their victory banners (v. 5), will they always signify the victory of the kingship of God?

Verse 7 acknowledges that God's people must not boast in naked power, chariots and horses, the latest in military hardware, the equivalent to our nuclear and chemical weapons; "our pride [or: "our boast"] is in the name of the LORD our God." "Two different worlds here confront one another" (A. Weiser). Is the distinction, however, always clear or easy to draw? Were not the people of Israel, or elements within Israel, tempted to use the name of God to justify their own ambitions? History is littered with examples of religious institutions and individuals using God to protect their own life or to justify their own often questionable actions. Christianity has been just as prone to this as any other religion. And the greater the piety, the greater the danger. To take pride in the name of the LORD our God can be the seedbed of a dangerous religious nationalism or exclusiveness, unless Amos's words of warning are continually heeded: "You only have I known of all the families of the earth; therefore, I will punish you for all your iniquities" (Amos 3:2).

The voice of certainty which speaks in verse 6, "Now I know," marks the turning point in the Psalm. The LORD's help is assured; victory is at hand. God's answer will come from "his holy heaven." This is a recognition that the God who dwells with his people in his sanctuary on Zion is a God who is not bound by an earthly temple. He sits enthroned in the heavens, judging the world with righteousness and with equity (see 9:7-8). He ensures that all who challenge his sovereignty by relying on human power will "collapse and fall" (v. 8).

The confident opening words of verse 9, "Give victory to the king, O LORD" or "LORD, save the king" (so REB, following the LXX), provide the foundation of the British National Anthem, "God, save our gracious Queen." Indeed, every line in that national anthem finds its prototype in the royal psalms (cf. Psalm 72). Yet we need constantly to be reminded that behind the earthly monarch there stands another king, apart from whom all exercise of human power is futile. The closing words of the psalm, "answer us when we call," therefore need to be set in the context of another answer by another king, facing his own desperate crisis: "yet not what I want, but what you want" (Mark 14:36).

Psalm 21
GOD SAVE THE KING

It is tantalizing how little we know, though there has been no lack of speculation, about the background to some of the Psalms. This psalm is a good case in point. Some have argued that just as Psalm 20 contains prayers for the king as he prepared to go into battle, so Psalm 21 celebrates his victorious return (cf. the heading in the NRSV). The language of the psalm, however, suggests that we are sharing in part of the liturgy of the coronation service or an annual service celebrating the king's accession to the throne (cf. Psalm 2). But at what point are we entering the liturgy? Is this the moment when the king, already crowned and having taken or renewed his coronation vows, appears robed in all his royal splendor to receive the acclamation of the people? We don't know. We are not even sure who is speaking or singing in the different parts of the psalm. What is clear, however, is that this Psalm is not merely about the glorification of the king; it is about a relationship between God and the king which undergirds all that the king has achieved, all that he is, and all that he may ever hope to be. It is this relationship which is affirmed by the congregation in verse 7, the midpoint of the psalm. It marks the transition from verses 1-6, probably a priestly thanksgiving for all that God had already given to the king, to verses 8-12, in which a prophet or priest addresses the king and gives voice to what is yet to be. The opening word of verse 7 is best taken as introducing an emphatic statement, "Yes, indeed," rather than the "for" of most English translations. This "Yes, indeed" points to the relationship which on the human side is characterized by "trust" (see 4:5). Such trust, however, is no more than a response to the "steadfast love" (see comment on 5:7) of "the Most High" (cf. 7:17 for this title of God). It is this steadfast love alone which guarantees that the king's status and function are secure.

The book of Deuteronomy, which explains the meaning of the covenant between God and Israel, promises that obedience to the commands of God will bring blessings, enrichment of life (Deut. 28:1-14). It is such blessings given freely by God to the king which are celebrated in the song of thanksgiving in verses 1-6. They include:

(a) joy in the "help" already received from God, the word "help" in verses 1 and 5 being the word translated elsewhere as "salvation" or "deliverance" (see 3:8). This is a joy which finds its deepest fulfillment not in what God gives, but in God himself, in "the joy of your presence" (v. 6).

(b) answered prayer, his "heart's desire," the "request of his lips" (v. 2), assuming that such innermost ambitions and spoken requests are consistent with trust in the LORD (see comment on Psalm 20).

(c) royal status, symbolized by the "crown of fine gold" (v. 3) and "glory" and "splendor" and "majesty" (v. 5), words often used in the Psalms to describe God (e.g., Psalm 8) and here conferred upon the king by God. These words underline the fact that responsible human kingship can be nothing other than a reflection of God's kingship.

(d) "life . . . length of days forever and ever" (v. 4), not immortality, nor a mere extension of existence, but a quality of life, a vitality which will reach into the future and characterize everything that the king is or does (see comment on 16:11) and perhaps embrace his successor to the throne. The words find their echo in the prayer attributed to David in 2 Sam. 7:29, "May it please you to bless the house of your servant, so that it may continue forever before you; for you, O LORD God, have spoken, and with your blessing will the house of your servant be blessed forever." All of this is God's gift to the king. The words "you meet him" (REB: "welcome him") sound as if God, of his own initiative, had gone out of his way to come to the king with presents of "rich blessings" (the Hebrew is literally "blessings of goodness"). This is what the good life means for the king.

In verses 8-12 a prophet or priest addresses the king with words of promise which are, in effect, a curse on all those who oppose him (cf. the curses paralleling the blessings in Deuteronomy 28). All who threaten his authority — and the enemies referred to in verse 8 could be either external or internal — are doomed to be crushed. Their devious plans will come to nothing (v. 11), with dire consequences to themselves and their descendants (v. 10). The imagery used is graphic. "You will make them like a fiery furnace" or oven (v. 9). The word translated "furnace" normally means a portable stove or oven used for cooking purposes. As the REB translation implies, the picture is probably that of the king's enemies being fed like fuel to stoke the fire which heats the oven and thus being consumed. The picture of the burning oven is used as a description of the coming day of God's judgment in Mal. 4:1, and graphically as a description of the devastating impact of famine in Lam. 5:10, "our skins black as an oven from the scorching heat of famine."

As v. 9b stresses, however, the king crushes his enemies not through his own prowess. He is but the channel of God's consuming "wrath" (on the anger of God, see 6:1). To challenge or to plot against the king who is the recipient of God's blessing is to challenge God's authority and to provoke an inevitable response. The picture of "the LORD swallowing them up in his wrath" occurs again in Lamentations 2, where it describes God's anger destructively turned against his own sinful people (Lam. 2:5, 8), against Jerusalem, against the sanctuary on Zion, and against the king and people who had forgotten what it meant to trust in the LORD. God's enemies are not always those whom we identify as his enemies!

Elsewhere the military metaphor predominates, the warrior king routing those who dare openly to oppose him (v. 12). Behind this warrior king stands God the warrior — a well-known picture of deity in the ancient world — wielding his awesome power and fighting on behalf of his people.

The psalm ends where it began, with the words "O LORD, in your strength" echoing the opening words of the psalm. But now it is no longer the king who rejoices, but the community which reaffirms its joyful and strong faith in God. The king may hold high office in the life of the community, but it is ultimately God in whom alone the nation finds its security. It is God who must be lifted high, "exalted," in the thought and praise of his people. Just so the psalmist in Psalm 57, in the face of ruthless persecution, expresses his confidence in the refrain "Be exalted, O God, above the heavens. Let your glory be over all the earth" (57:5, 100). God is exalted, but he is not distant or remote because God's "power," which the community celebrates, is a power which shows itself in his awesome deeds against all the forces which challenge his authority, whether in creation (65:7; 89:12), in the history of his people (66:5; 106:8), or in the person of those who seek to undermine the authority of his servant-king.

Psalm 22
DARKNESS AND LIGHT

This Psalm is indelibly woven into the fabric of Christian thought and spirituality since its opening words "My God, my God, why have you forsaken me" were, according to the Gospels of Mark and Matthew, the last words on the lips of Jesus in the agony of the crucifixion. The words in the heading to the psalm, "according to the Deer of the Dawn," may refer to the tune to which the psalm was set (cf. REB). Some of the early versions, however, including the Greek (LXX), interpret the word translated "dawn" to mean "help." This might refer to the theme of the psalm, "the help of dawn," light like the morning dawn, breaking into the darkness of the psalmist's experience.

The psalm falls into two parts: part one (vv. 1-21) is a lament in which, in dialogue with God, the psalmist gives voice to the grim depths of his agony; part two (vv. 22-31) is a thanksgiving in which the psalmist praises God that the darkness is now over and calls upon the congregation, and indeed the whole world, to share with him in his witness to the goodness and power of God.

1-21 Prayer often involves an inner dialogue in which we place side by side ourselves, where we are in our lives, and what we know to be true of God. Out of this dialogue are shaped our fears and requests. This pattern is clearly seen in this section of the psalm. Thus in verses 1-2, 6-8, 14-18 we listen to the psalmist sharing his agony; the key words are "I . . . me . . . mine." In verses 3-5, 9-11, 19-21 the focus is on God, and the the key word is "you," the emphatic opening word in each of these sections, leading into the plea in verses 11 and 19, "don't be far away."

Verses 1-2 unveil the almost unbearable tension tearing the psalmist apart. Three times we hear the cry "My God, my God . . . O my God." This is supposed to be the very same God who, another psalmist declares, does not forsake those who seek him (Ps. 9/10). But this psalmist feels that he has been forsaken, denied "help" (see 3:8). "The LORD answer you in the day of trouble. . . . he will answer," claims Ps. 20:1, 6; but he doesn't, claims this psalmist; my prayers fall on deaf ears. This is not the collapse of faith. It is someone being torn apart because he cannot deny the reality of faith, nor can he reconcile it with the savage reality of life as he now experiences it.

In verses 3-5, the focus of the psalmist's faith centers on a God who is "holy" (see comment on 2:6), "enthroned on the praises of Israel," a phrase unparalleled elsewhere in the Old Testament — hence the alternative translation involving a slight textual change in the REB. The phrase, however, is perfectly intelligible, since praise and prayer have been the people's characteristic response to God, their divine king. The witness of the past clearly vindicated such a response. Past generations, "our ancestors," had good reason to know this. Trust had been justified; prayers had been answered. God had never let them down. Three times in verses 4-5 we hear the words "they trusted," and we can almost sense the desperation of the psalmist as he repeats the words; they trusted, but what of me? Why is the witness of the past seemingly irrelevant to the agony of the present? Why does God not act now in the same way as he acted then? The same tensions lie at the heart of the national lament in Psalm 44: "Our ancestors have told us, what deeds you performed in their days, in the days of old. . . . Yet you have rejected us and abased us" (Ps. 44:1, 9).

Verses 6-8 provide the first insight into the nature of the problems which led to the psalmist's spiritual agony. He describes himself as "a worm, not a human." The word "worm" is flung derisively at Job by one of his so-called friends (Job 25:6) and is used in Isa. 41:14 as a description of Israel trampled underfoot by more powerful empires. The psalmist feels crushed and helpless, surrounded by mockery and derision which seek to undermine his faith by insidiously suggesting that the claims he once made about God were groundless. Often such sneering mockery can be a far more dangerous enemy of faith than outright opposition, since it can sow the seeds of doubt.

As verses 9-11 indicate, the witness of the past generations had its counterpart in the psalmist's experience. He had known what it meant to trust. The words "you kept me safe" (v. 9) are a translation of a form of the verb "to trust" (cf. v. 5). Life had come to him as God's gift. He had known the security of a mother's breast (v. 9), which pointed to a greater security summed up in the words, "You have been my God" (v. 10). These words are a translation of two very simple Hebrew words, "to me . . . you." Sometimes the most profound theology finds such simple expression. Much of the theology of Isaiah 40–55 is contained in the words addressed to Israel by God in Isa. 43:1 — "to me . . . you" — you are mine, you belong to me. So the center of the psalmist's experience had been, you are mine — you, my God. Yes, but where are you now in my moment of deepest need? Trouble is near, but you are apparently far off when your presence is most needed. The psalmist can only plead, "Do not be far from me" (v. 11).

Verses 12-21 provide the most graphic description of the psalmist's plight. He is at the mercy of those whom he describes in verse 16 as "a company of evildoers" (REB: "a band of ruffians"). Three images from the animal world add color to the description. They are "strong bulls of Bashan" (v. 12). Bashan is a fertile plateau east of the Jordan, embracing what is now the northern part of the Golan Heights; it was rich farming land which produced wheat and pasture to nourish prime cattle. Amos sardonically describes the pampered society belles of Samaria as "cows of Bashan" (Amos 4:1). The power and vitality of these evildoers are thus being underlined. They are like "a ravening and roaring lion" (v. 13), a lion ready to satisfy its hunger by pouncing on its prey (cf. 7:3; 10:9; 17:12). So they are eager to maul him. They are "dogs," not the pet poodles, but the scavengers, living off scraps and human carcasses. Here we may compare Elijah's words of judgment to Ahab and Jezebel, "The dogs shall eat Jezebel within the bounds of Jezreel. Anyone belonging to Ahab who dies in the city the dogs shall eat" (1 Kgs. 21:23-24). So they are waiting to be at the death of the psalmist.

The psalmist's condition at the mercy of such enemies is described in verses

14-17. Although many attempts have been made to identify the physical and debilitating illness from which he is suffering, it is better to take these verses as describing his psychological condition, which the Hebrews would naturally describe as being expressed through various parts of the body. It adds up to the picture of someone who is at the end of his tether, disoriented, a prey to fears he cannot control, a person whose vitality is ebbing away so that he feels as good as dead. He knows that there are those for whom his death cannot come quickly enough. They are waiting to pick up the spoils. With ever increasing urgency, he repeats in verses 19-21 his plea to God, "Do not be far from me." Help is needed, and needed soon, or it will be too late.

The verse division and the text at the end of verse 21 are far from clear (compare the different renderings in the NRSV and the REB). It is possible that the closing words of verse 21 should be rendered "you have answered me," a word of reassurance having come perhaps through priest or temple prophet. Certainly the change in mood from verse 22 onwards is dramatic and remarkable.

22-31 The agonizing questions in verses 1-2 have found their answer. God is no longer far away, abandoning or shunning someone in deep trouble. His face is no longer hidden; he is present. He has answered the psalmist's cry for help (v. 24). The seemingly impassable gulf separating the psalmist from God has been bridged, and bridged by God. This is indeed good news, and good news is there to be shared. All who truly reverence God (for the fear of the LORD, see 19:9), who stand in awe of him, the whole congregation of the people of God are invited to join the psalmist in the hallelujah chorus, "Praise him!" (v. 23). It may indeed have been through sharing in worship with the "great congregation" (v. 25) at one of the major religious festivals in the religious year that the psalmist found healing, his own troubled faith renewed and sustained by the faith of others. This is the context in which, with thanksgiving, he makes his "vows," such vows often being closely associated with the offerings and sacrifices (cf. 50:14) which in the form of a sacrificial meal can be shared with the "poor" or the afflicted (see comment on 9:17). Out of his own experience of affliction, he is sensitive to the needs of others who are vulnerable; out of his own seeking for the God who seemed far away, he is at one with those who "seek the LORD."

It is tempting to see in the closing words of verse 26, "May your hearts live forever!" the psalmist's toast to his fellow diners, the toast of one who had been at the threshold of death (see Craigie).

Verses 27-28 are best taken as a congregational anthem, universalizing the psalmist's experience. In the psalmist's weakness, God's strength had come. The mockery and vindictive cruelty of his persecutors had received their answer. Ultimate power and dominion lie in the hands of the LORD. All nations are summoned to acknowledge his kingship (vv. 27-28; cf. Isa. 45:22). To believe in God is to accept that no barriers of space or time can be erected around God, though sadly religious communities across the ages have often tried to erect them and take refuge in a narrow exclusiveness. "My God" becomes a selfish God.

The psalm ends in verses 29-31 with the psalmist summarizing and reflecting on his pilgrimage. Verse 29, however, poses difficult textual problems. The traditional Hebrew text reads "all the fat ones of the earth eat and bow down." This has been taken to mean that the rich as well as the poor of verse 26 share in the banquet, but in context this seems unlikely. The NRSV translation assumes a simple division of the Hebrew word for "they eat," to become "surely to him"; and an alteration of one letter changes "the fat ones of the earth" into "those who sleep [or: "are going to sleep"] in the earth." Likewise the ending of verse 29, "and I shall live for him," presupposes an alteration to the Hebrew text which can claim support from the early versions. If we accept these changes, then the Psalm ends on a note of challenge and commitment. God's kingship will be recognized by all who go through such shattering experiences in life that they feel they have been taken to the very threshold of death. That had been the psalmist's experience, and he lives to bear witness to its truth. He has shared his experience with the congregation and invited them to join with him in thanksgiving, but he has a story to tell which must be told not only to his contemporaries but to generations yet unborn. His faith must be handed on, a faith rooted in God's "deliverance" (literally, "righteousness"; see comment on 7:11 and 11:7), a faith which is summed up in one final statement: "he has done it" (REB: "the LORD has acted"), a ringing affirmation that nothing, not even the most bitter, seemingly soul-destroying experiences can thwart God's purposes.

The opening words of the psalm on the lips of Jesus on the cross point us, therefore, to the almost unbearable tension tearing apart one wrestling with both the closeness of his relationship with his heavenly Father and the grim darkness of evil, suffering, and alienation. We may never be able fully to understand the intensity of that darkness, but the psalm in its entirety was surely there. Through the darkness and through death, God's purposes were to be fulfilled. It is possible that the last words John's Gospel attributes to Jesus, "It is finished" (John 19:30), echo the closing words of the psalm, "he has done it."

It is not surprising, therefore, that in the light of Jesus' use of this psalm the Gospel writers, and Matthew in particular, use other verses from Psalm 22 as a running commentary on the crucifixion, citing verses 7, 8, and 18. Later Christian writers have further developed this approach, arguing, for example, that the doubtful Greek reading, "they have pierced my hands and feet," in verse 16 ought to be retained since it fits the crucifixion scene. This is to adopt a very mechanical view of the relationship between the Old and New Testaments and may lead us to neglect one vital difference between Psalm 22 and its New Testament counterpart. There is nothing in Psalm 22 to indicate that the psalmist experienced death. Mockery, derision, persecution — someone at the end of his tether both physically and psychologically, yes — but his thanksgiving arises out of the experience of being rescued from that final alienation from God which death would have brought him. For Jesus there was no fulfillment of God's purposes except through death and a resurrection life which lay on the other side of death.

Psalm 23
CONFIDENT TRUST

No other psalm has such a central place in the hearts of people of both sure and uncertain faith. Even those who seldom darken the door of a church or a synagogue have found this psalm speaking to them on occasions as varied as a wedding or a funeral. Its appeal lies both in its simplicity and in its profundity. The picture of the shepherd and his flock still strikes a chord with most people, even those brought up in a heavily industrialized or nonagrarian society. Throughout, the psalm speaks of confidence and trust in a gracious, caring, and generous God. Yet as soon as we examine the psalm in detail and raise questions about its original meaning and its setting in the life of Israel, difficult questions arise.

Verses 1-4 speak of "my shepherd," but in verse 5 the scene seems to switch to that of a generous host, perhaps a royal host giving a banquet. What relationship is there, if any, between these two pictures? Some scholars have argued that the shepherd picture continues into verse 5, the "table" being a grassy turf and the "overflowing cup," an ample supply of water provided for tired sheep. It is equally possible that royal imagery dominates the psalm from beginning to end. "Shepherd" is a traditional title in the ancient world not only for God (cf. Ps. 80:1; Isa. 40:11) but also for a king. The great Babylonian king Hammurapi was called "the shepherd of the people," and it is a recurring royal title in the poems of Homer. In Ezekiel 34, God, bitterly condemning the false "shepherds" who do not feed or care for the sheep, declares "I myself will be the shepherd of my sheep" (v. 15) and looks forward to the time when there will come a true king from the Davidic family who will be the one "shepherd" of the people (v. 23). Royal imagery also provides the framework for the hymnal version of Psalm 23, "The King of Love my Shepherd is, Whose goodness faileth never."

Is verse 5, then, the picture of a guest invited to share in a royal banquet, or should we take it closely with verse 6 and place it in the setting of an act of worship involving a sacrificial meal? For M. Dahood Psalm 23 is one of the psalms which most clearly show a doctrine of life hereafter, verses 2-3 being interpreted as referring to the Elysian fields, with the final verse looking forward to eternal happiness in God's celestial abode. This, however, is hardly a natural interpretation of the psalm.

Attempts have also been made to show that the language of the psalm has been deeply influenced by the story of the Exodus and the subsequent wilderness wandering, the theological centerpiece of Israel's experience as the people of God.

Thus, for example, the phrase "I shall not want" (v. 1) is said to echo Deut. 2:7, "The LORD your God has been with you; you have lacked nothing," and the question "Can God spread a table in the wilderness?" is taken as the cry of those rebelling against God according to Ps. 78:19. Likewise, the expression "for his name's sake" is used in the context of the Exodus event in Ps. 106:8 (cf. Ezekiel 20). All such phrases and words, however, are found in other contexts in the Old Testament. Undoubtedly there is a close link between the faith of the community in which someone is nurtured and the faith of that person, but the emphasis in Psalm 23 is strongly on the personal faith of the psalmist, a faith which draws upon a rich treasury of personal experience.

The psalmist is in no doubt as to where his life finds its center. It centers upon the LORD, the opening word of the psalm, and "the house of the LORD" (v. 6). Whatever life may have brought him or might yet bring him, worship provides the setting which illuminates its meaning. There he meets the one whom he describes as "my shepherd." Here is the caring shepherd who tends to all the needs of his flock. The shepherd provides him with "green pastures," succulent grass on which to graze, and "still waters" (literally, "waters of rest"), most likely a gently flowing stream or a placid pool which makes for easy drinking, though it could also mean "waters where I may rest" (REB). The words "he restores my soul" (v. 3) could be a picture of the shepherd going out in search of and bringing back sheep which have strayed (cf. the use made of this picture in Matt. 18:10-14), or it could mean simply "he revives my spirit" (REB) by bringing new life to one who is weary and exhausted. "He leads me in right paths" (literally, "paths of righteousness") suggests a shepherd who leads his sheep along suitable paths, where they will be safe, protected even in "the darkest valley." The word translated "darkest" (literally, "shadow of death") may very well be a compound noun meaning "the deepest darkness" and describe life-threatening situations in precarious terrain where the flock would be exposed to attack. Even there the shepherd is present, equipped to defend the flock with his "rod" or club, and keeping the flock together with his "staff" or shepherd's crook. The flock finds security under the care of a protecting shepherd.

In simple words, and drawing on images familiar to his contemporaries, the psalmist thus states his faith in the God who meets all his needs and whose protecting presence has been with him even in the darkest situations. Psalm 49:14 speaks of death as a shepherd leading those who are foolish enough to trust in riches down into the grave, the grim world of Sheol. The psalmist knows and trusts in a different shepherd who leads along another way, the way of a secure and satisfying life, a way protected by the "comfort" or renewing strength (cf. Isa. 40:1) of an ever present LORD.

The traditional link between shepherd and king makes the transition to verse 5 much less abrupt than it may seem at first. The picture is now of the psalmist invited as an honored guest to a banquet, which for him is a joyous occasion and a sign of God's generosity to him. We have already noted how "anointing" with oil is a sign of consecration to a particular office or function, including kingship (cf. 2:2), but oil was also used more generally on head and face as a sign of joy on festive occasions. Psalm 104:15 speaks of God providing "wine to gladden the human heart, oil to make the face shine, and bread to strengthen the human heart" (cf. 2 Sam. 14:2). The wine is here as well, in the "cup which overflows."

The fact that this banquet is being held "in the presence of my enemies" should not be taken as a expression of vindictiveness; rather, it is a sign that all those who have threatened the psalmist have now been proved to be wrong. This point would be underlined even more strongly if this banquet were a thanksgiving sacrifice in the temple. Such a sacrificial meal, and God's sharing in it, would be proof, if proof be needed, that the psalmist was accepted by God. Again, the familiar imagery of the banquet invites us to explore deeper spiritual truths. In spite of all that might have marred his life, the psalmist is declaring that in the presence of God he experiences a richly satisfying and joy-filled life.

From the present he looks forward confidently to the future. He has two certainties:

1. "Goodness and mercy will follow me." The verb translated "follow" most frequently in the Old Testament means "to pursue with hostile intent," and this may have been the psalmist's experience at the hands of those he refers to as his enemies (v. 5). But now he is pursued by "goodness and steadfast love" (Hebrew *hesed;* cf. 4:3), by that firm, unfailing friendship of God which is the guarantee of the good life.
2. "I shall dwell in the house of the LORD my whole life long." The traditional Hebrew text reads, "I shall return in the house of the LORD," which may be a compressed way of saying, "I shall come back again and again to be present in the house of the LORD." Whatever translation we follow, there is no reason to believe that the psalmist was a Levite present daily in the temple courts, or that he had any desire to be one. The words are those of one who knows that there can be no continuing satisfying life for him unless it is centered on worship. To the house of the LORD, to God's dwelling place in the midst of his people, he shall return again and again to renew his vitality through joining in worship and sharing a vision with the people of God. Theology divorced from worship is arid; life devoid of worship has limited horizons.

As we have seen, the picture of the shepherd and the flock has a rich and varied religious usage in the Old Testament. It is not surprising, then, that it is picked up in the Gospels in parables (e.g., Matt. 18:10-14; Luke 15:3-7) and in John's Gospel in the claim of Jesus, "I am the good shepherd" (John 10). It finds echoes in early Christian liturgical language, for example in the benediction in

Heb. 13:20, where Jesus is described as "the great shepherd of the sheep" (cf. 1 Pet. 2:25; 5:4). Christians, therefore, will read this psalm in the light of worship and spirituality rooted in the life, death, and resurrection of Jesus, and with a new and lively hope will face the "deepest darkness," including the valley of the shadow of death.

Psalm 24
KING OMNIPOTENT

Psalm 24 divides neatly into three sections: verses 1-2, a brief hymn celebrating God the creator; verses 3-6, an entrance liturgy similar to what we have seen in Psalm 15; verses 7-10, a liturgical poem celebrating the warrior God coming in triumph to the temple. The common theme which holds these sections together is that of the kingship of God, a theme central to the faith of Israel.

1-2 In two brief verses and against the background of mythology widely current in the ancient Near East, the psalm affirms the sovereignty of Israel's God, the LORD, over all that exists — both "the earth," the natural world and its teeming life, and the inhabited "world" and all its peoples. In other ancient Near Eastern religions, creation, involving the triumph of order over chaos, emerges out of a titanic struggle between the gods of order and the divine forces of chaos often associated with water, the sea, and the swirling currents, a struggle which leads to the acknowledgment of the triumphant god as divine king. Just as in Genesis 1, where God has but to speak "and it was so," so in this psalm there is no hint of any such conflict. There is only the LORD, whose sovereignty over all threatening forces is unchallengeable. But creation is not merely a past cosmic event; it is an ever present reality. Nor is it morally neutral. Order and chaos find their counterpart in the forces of good and evil which shape our lives. To celebrate the power of God is to accept responsibility for the way in which God-given life must be used.

3-6 The demands of the King therefore follow on naturally, with searching questions being asked of those who seek to come into the presence of this King (see comment on Psalm 15). Here the demands of the King are couched in more general terms than in Psalm 15. Behind the phrase "clean hands," a phrase which occurs only here in the Old Testament, there may lie the washing of hands as a ritual act of purification (cf. Ps. 26:6; Exod. 30:17-21). "Clean hands and pure hearts," however, as Calvin claims, "comprehend all religion and denote a well-ordered life," a life which will express in outward actions the inner motivation which controls the will and the conscience, an inner motivation which is rooted in total allegiance to the one God. The words "who do not lift up their souls"

(REB: "who has not set his mind on") imply an attitude of worship which must not be given to "what is false" or empty of significance and which in the end can only be "deceit." It is possible that the words "false" and "deceit" here refer to idols and the worship of other gods, the whole verse echoing the words of the Decalogue, "You shall have no other gods before me" (Exod. 20:3); "You shall not make wrongful use of the name of the LORD your God" (Exod. 20:7), where the phrase translated "wrongful use" is the same as that here translated "what is false."

Such an attitude and commitment lead to "blessing" (see 3:8) and "vindication" from the God who can be depended upon to acquit the innocent (see 7:11 and 11:7) and give them "salvation" (see 3:8). Together such words point to that rich fullness of life which is, or should be, the experience and the mark of those who give their loyalty to God. To this the worshipper now says amen in verse 6. He claims to belong to those who "seek" the Lord (see comment on 9:10). This word "seek" often refers to the act of going to the temple to worship God. Another Hebrew word, really a synonym, is used in the phrase "seek the face [i.e., the presence] of the God of Jacob." Although attempts have been made to defend the Hebrew reading at the end of verse 6, "who seek your face, O Jacob," with Jacob being taken to mean the true worshipper of God, or by treating the "Presence of Jacob" as a divine title, it seems better to follow, as most modern translations do, the reading of the Greek and Syriac and find here a reference to "the God of Jacob."

7-10 Here we seem to be eavesdropping on a dialogue between people coming to worship and those on duty at the gates of the temple. In verse 7 we hear the request of those who come seeking admission to the temple courts in the name of the King of Glory. In the first line of verse 8 the gatekeepers pose their question, to which the worshippers respond and repeat their request in the rest of verses 8 and 9. In the first line of verse 10 the gatekeepers' question is heard again. The psalm then concludes with the worshippers' response, identifying the God in whose name they come as "The LORD of hosts . . . the King of Glory."

What lies behind this dialogue? It is often argued that its origins go back to the story in 2 Samuel 6 of David bringing up to Jerusalem the ark, which was associated in early tradition with the description of God as "the LORD of hosts" (e.g., 2 Sam. 6:2). It is further claimed that annually, in association with one of the major festivals of the religious year, the ark was central to a procession which went up to the temple, there to place the ark, symbol of God's presence, in the midst of his people. Whether such a procession involving the ark is needed to account for the dialogue in verses 7-10 is debatable. It does, however, seem likely that we are listening to part of a liturgy associated with the temple.

The language in these verses is highly poetical. There is little use trying to speculate what part of the gates or ancient doors were supposed to "lift up your heads." To "lift up your head," when applied to people, means to carry your head high with pride, or in a negative sense defiantly (cf. 83:2). So the gates and doors are here personified and asked proudly to open up and welcome the coming of the King of Glory (see 3:3).

The key phrase which describes this majestic divine King is "the LORD of hosts," a title which in various forms appears in other psalms (e.g., 46:7, 11; 59:5; 89:8). Early usage links it closely with the ark of the covenant, the visible sign of God's presence among his people, and in this context the "hosts" referred to are the armies of Israel. David faces Goliath "in the name of the LORD of hosts, the God of the armies of Israel" (1 Sam. 17:45), a nuance of the phrase still celebrated in Kipling's Recessional:

> God of our fathers, known of old,
>   Lord of our far-flung battle-line,
> Beneath whose awful Hand we hold
>   Dominion over palm and pine.
> Lord God of hosts, be with us yet,
>   Lest we forget — lest we forget.

From this military base, however, the title moves out into ever widening meaning. There are a series of hymn fragments in the book of Amos with which the words "the LORD of hosts" are closely associated (cf. Amos 4:13; 9:5). In these God is not the God of the armies of Israel, but the God who controls all the forces in the natural world, which will be unleashed in judgment against a people who believed that they owned God and could use him for their own nationalistic purposes. One of the ways in which the Greek (LXX) translators render the phrase is to use a Greek word meaning "ruler of all." The psalm, therefore, ends where it began, celebrating a God majestic in power, a King in whose hands lie all the forces in the universe of his creating (cf. Psalm 29). Yet this awesome, all-powerful God comes to his temple home not in thunder or in lightning bolt, but in the midst of his worshipping people, who acknowledge the demands he makes upon them and celebrate his presence among them.

Whatever its origin, in both Jewish and Christian tradition this psalm has found its place in the liturgy of the community. The heading to the psalm in the LXX links it with the first day of the week and thus with the celebration of creation. In modern Synagogue usage, it is sung while the Torah scroll is being returned to the ark and on festivals which occur on weekdays (cf. Authorised Daily Prayer Book). In Christian tradition it has often been linked with Ascension Day, the day which sets the seal on the victory of Jesus in his death and resurrection and points forward to his ultimate triumph. In Reformed tradition, verses 7-10 in particular are associated with the great entry during the communion service when the elements of bread and wine, signs of God's presence in Christ, are brought to the table. Thus the words of the psalm have echoed in many hearts across the centuries, as people have gathered to worship the God who is awesomely great yet ever graciously present.

Psalm 25
TRUST AND PENITENCE

This is an acrostic poem (see comment on Psalms 9 and 10) which utilizes twenty-one of the twenty-two letters of the Hebrew alphabet, assuming a slight alteration to the first word in verse 18. In language and thought it contains many echoes of the wisdom teaching that we find in Proverbs. It points to the way in which such teaching could find a natural home in worship and be part of a deeply spiritual experience. If Psalm 1 uses such teaching to present "The Challenge of the Two Ways," this psalm provides a traveler's guide for the person who has set out on God's road. The difficulties encountered are clearly indicated — the lurking "enemies," the false steps which may be taken. But there is an unshakable confidence that this traveler is not on his own. He has a trustworthy divine traveling companion. The psalm falls neatly into three sections: verses 1-7, a prayer of confidence; verses 8-14, a celebration of the dependable friendship of the LORD; verses 15-21, a plea for help. The psalm ends with a verse outside the acrostic pattern, in which the community identifies with the psalmist's journey. The "LORD . . . my God" at the beginning of the psalm becomes the God of Israel at its end.

1-7 The keynote of the psalm is sounded in this opening verse, best translated with the REB, "LORD my God, to you I lift my heart." This implies "trust" in God (v. 2; see comment on 4:5) that expects to be vindicated rather than to endure shame (cf. 22:5). Three times in verses 2-3 the verb "to put to shame" occurs. Such shame, claims the psalmist, should be the lot of those who are "wantonly treacherous" (NRSV) or, perhaps better, "break faith without cause" (REB). These are people who seem to delight in being perverse. Such should not be the experience of those "who wait for you" (v. 3), people with whom the psalmist personally identifies in verse 5.

"For you I wait" (v. 5). This waiting is not a grim or stoical sense of resignation; rather, it is an eager hopefulness, which looks forward expectantly for God to act (cf. 27:14). Its meaning is well illustrated in Isa. 40:31, "Those who wait upon the LORD shall renew their strength, they shall mount up with wings like eagles, they shall run and not be weary, they shall walk and not faint." Such trust and waiting do not mean blind obedience. The psalmist acknowledges his need for instruction, for teaching in the "ways," "the paths of the LORD." Notice the twofold occurrence of "teach me" (vv. 4 and 5); the verb translated "teach" in verse 5 comes from the same root as the word for "ways" in verse 4. This is the typical language of wisdom instruction; the word translated "paths," for example, appears four times in Proverbs 2 (vv. 8, 13, 19, 20). But it is not blind obedience, nor is it response to a cold moral imperative. The God whose instruction he seeks is "the God of my salvation" (see 3:8). He prays, "Lead me in your truth" (NRSV) or, perhaps better, "Lead me by your faithfulness" (REB). The word translated "truth" or "faithfulness" (Hebrew 'emet) is related to the word "Amen." Although it can mean truth, the idea of firmness, stability, and faithfulness is implied in this word, and when used of God it often has this flavor, particularly when used alongside the word for "steadfast love," as in verse 10 of this psalm. The fact that the psalmist appeals to "the God of my salvation" means that he expects to receive instruction upon which he can depend, instruction rooted in God's faithfulness. This is the God who in the words of an ancient confession of faith is:

> The LORD, the LORD,
> a God merciful and gracious, slow to anger,
> and abounding in steadfast love and faithfulness,
> keeping steadfast love for the thousandth generation,
> forgiving iniquity and transgression and sin. (Exod. 34:6-7)

Three times in verses 6-7 the psalmist, in the light of this confession of faith, calls on God to "remember." "Remember your mercy" (v. 6) or compassion — the adjective from the same word is translated "merciful" in Exod 34:6. It is a word related to the word for the womb and conveys a mother's compassion for the child she carries.

"Do not remember the sins of my youth or my transgressions" (v. 7). It is unnecessary to see in these words a middle-aged man regretting the wild oats he had sown in his adolescent days. He may be looking back with regrets, but he is also conscious of present shortcomings in his life (see vv. 11 and 18). It is not only for the past but also for the present that he needs to be forgiven.

To live in the light of God's steadfast love is to become all too conscious of the lack of such love and steadfastness in our own response to God. Hence our continuing need to recognize our failures, to confess them, and to seek forgiveness. That alone is the way to spiritual health. As Calvin puts it, unless we confess, "We shall follow the example of unskillful physicians who overlooking the disease only seek to alleviate the pain, and apply mere adventitious remedies for the cure."

8-14 The psalmist now spells out more fully the nature of the relationship with God in the light of which he has been offering his prayer. The previous section ended in an appeal based on God's "goodness." This section begins by describing

God as "good" and "upright"; this means that God is straight and above board in all his dealings. He is therefore a God who instructs those who go astray to redirect their ways, a God who leads and teaches the "humble" (v. 9; see 9:17). The true way of life is available for anyone who is prepared "to fear the LORD" (vv. 12, 14; see 19:9). This God is bound to his people and they to him by "his covenant" (vv. 10, 14). This is the first occurrence in the Psalms of one of the key theological words in the Old Testament, "covenant" (Hebrew *bĕrît*), the word which, via its Latin form, gives us the word "testament." Covenant was a common, everyday concept in the life of Israel. It referred to any kind of pact or agreement between two parties, be they individuals, groups, or nations. So treaties, pledges of friendship, and marriage contracts were covenants. This familiar word was then used to describe the relationship between God and his people, but with a difference. This was a relationship which owed everything to the initiative of one party; it was God who made the covenant with the people. In a sense it was God's gift to them, though the gift brought with it responsibility. This was to be a relationship summed up in the words, "I will be your God, and you shall be my people" (Exod. 19:5; Lev. 26:12).

It was God who had brought his people out of slavery in Egypt (Exod. 20:2); it was God whose steadfast love meant that he would never break the relationship which bound him to his people. So in a situation of national crisis, the people appeal to God to have regard for his covenant (Ps. 74:20). There might be serious doubts about the people's commitment to that relationship (cf. 78:37), but there was never any doubt about God's commitment. Side by side with this covenant relationship the psalmist places "the friendship of the LORD" (v. 14). The word translated "friendship" (Hebrew *sôd*) can refer to the close friendship which exists between people (Ps. 55:14) or to the intimate knowledge that friendship brings, someone's "secrets" (Prov. 25:9). For Jeremiah, a true prophet is someone who has stood in the "council" *(sôd)* of the LORD. He bitterly complains that some of the prophets of his own day would not have dared speak as they did if they had been intimate with God (Jer. 23:18, 22). The REB thus translates the first line of verse 14 "The LORD confides his purposes to those who fear him."

It is to the God who has held out his hand in friendship that the psalmist makes his personal plea for forgiveness. He offers no excuses. He admits the greatness of his errors but implores, "For your name's sake, O LORD" (v. 11) — that is, because you are what you are (see 5:11) — "pardon my guilt" (NRSV) or "forgive my wickedness" (REB). To those who fear the LORD, the promise is that they will "abide in prosperity" (v. 13). Prosperity could be a misleading translation of a word which refers to that "goodness" (cf. vv. 7, 8) or richness of life which is open to those who share in the covenant relationship with God. The same word is used towards the end of Psalm 23, "Goodness and steadfast love shall follow me all the days of my life" (see comment on 23:6).

The words "their children shall possess the land" (v. 13) are probably influenced by another of the promises made by God to his covenant people. "So now, Israel, give heed . . . so that you may live to enter and occupy the land that the God of your ancestors is giving to you" (Deut. 4:1). In view of the political and religious use which has been made of this and similar promises to justify the state of Israel today and its possession of the land, it is important to notice that neither in the Psalms nor in Deuteronomy is this an unconditional promise. It is for those who fear the LORD and are prepared to receive instruction in "the way they should choose" (v. 12).

15-21   With his gaze firmly fixed on this covenant God (v. 15) and with an eager hopefulness (v. 21), the psalmist now makes his plea for help. He feels trapped in a situation which has two troubling aspects. First, he has a feeling of loneliness and inner turmoil, which he links to the need to be forgiven (vv. 16-18). There is a bleakness in his life which only a renewed experience of the friendship of God can counter. Second, he is surrounded by enemies. The brief reference to "my enemies" in verse 2 is now clarified. He is aware of being on the receiving end of "violent hatred." How such violent hatred is expressed we are not told, but it must have taken a specific form, perhaps that of maliciously undermining the psalmist's reputation (cf. the renewed reference to "shame" in v. 20). In face of this, the psalmist "takes refuge in God" (see 2:11) and pleads his own "integrity and uprightness." It is highly unlikely that "integrity and uprightness" are here to be taken as attributes of God. The word translated "integrity" (Hebrew *tōm;* see comment on 15:2) is never used of God in the Old Testament. In Psalm 26 it occurs twice (vv. 1 and 11) with reference to the psalmist's way of life. Such "integrity and uprightness" do not constitute a claim to moral perfection. How could they when the note of forgiveness is so central to the psalm? They do, however, indicate the values which are central to the psalmist's life, in contrast to those which motivate his enemies. Within the context of his continuing relationship with God, he is committed to a life which seeks to be wholesome and blameless, which will be characterized by doing what is right in the eyes of the LORD.

The postscript in verse 22, which lies outside the acrostic form, takes the psalmist's experience and makes it something with which the worshipping community identifies. "Redeem Israel, O God." The Hebrew word translated "redeem" normally involves some kind of quid pro quo, often the payment of a fixed sum of money. We may compare Num. 3:46-51 and 18:15-17, where payment has to be made to release the firstborn of people and animals, regarded as belonging by right to God. Or we may look to Exod. 21:30, where the owner of an ox which has a history of goring has to pay whatever damages the owner decides as a ransom for the victim's life. Hence, the traditional translation of this word is "ransom." Like many other words of common usage, however, it is caught up in the framework of Israel's faith and is used to describe what God did in setting his people free from slavery in Egypt (e.g., Deut. 7:8; 13:6; Ps. 78:42). No payment is specified. Redemption is an expression of God's gracious concern for his people. It is on this central evangelical theme, illustrated by the psalmist's experience and applicable to all God's people, that the psalm ends. That such gracious concern and love is costly, costly to God, is revealed in all its challenging poignancy on the cross.

Psalm 26
TEST ME

This is the first of three psalms (26–28) in which the temple and God's presence in the temple dominate the psalmist's thought. In Psalm 26, the psalmist is living under the strain of false accusations being leveled against him by devious people who are prepared to resort to bribery to see their charges stick (v. 10; for warnings against bribery, see Exod. 23:8; Amos 5:12). Despairing of receiving justice from the courts and knowing that the accusations are false, he takes his appeal to the one Judge he can trust. We do not know what the accusations were, but they were probably serious enough to raise doubts about his fitness to come to worship in the temple precincts (cf. Psalms 15 and 24). He submits his case to God and probably participates in a ritual of purification designed to affirm his innocence (v. 6; see comment on 24:4).

1-3 The opening word of the psalm, "judge me," is rightly rendered "Vindicate me" (NRSV) or "Uphold my cause" (REB), since the psalmist is convinced that he is innocent of the charges being brought against him. This is what he means by "my integrity" (see 25:21), past (v. 1) and present (v. 11). The grounds for that integrity lie in an unwavering "trust" in the LORD (see 25:1) whose "steadfast love" (*hesed,* 5:7) and "faithfulness" (see 25:5) are part and parcel of his daily life (v. 3). At the end of verse 3 it is better to read with the NRSV footnote "I walk in [REB: "live by"] your faithfulness," than "I walk in faithfulness to you." Because this is a God whom he can trust, he confidently makes his appeal, "Prove me, O LORD, and try me; test my heart and mind" (cf. 11:4-5).

4-5 These verses recall Psalm 1 and the "No" that the true worshipper of God must say over and over again. He must say "No" to the company of those here described as "worthless" (cf. 24:4, where the same word is translated "what is false") and "hypocrites," those who conceal their true thoughts and motives; "No" to associating with "evildoers" and the "wicked" (cf. 22:17). This "No," however, is simply the corollary of the "Yes" the psalmist wishes to affirm. The words "I hate" of verse 5 find their counterpoint in the words "I love the house in which you dwell" (v. 8).

6-8 Washing the hands, as a ritual act, is a declaration of innocence (cf. Deut. 21:6 and Pilate's action in Matt. 27:24), but it is a declaration of innocence which here leads into celebration of God's "wondrous deeds" (see 9:2). These inevitably evoke a response of thanksgiving, which expresses itself in that "Yes" which pulses through the psalmist's life. There, in the house which he loves, he comes face to face with the "glory" (see 3:3) of God. There is an obvious danger in locating the awesome power and majesty of God in a building, even a building as holy as the temple. Domesticate God even in the most awesome setting and you run the danger of becoming locked into a limited vision which often seeks to use God for your own purposes. Religions across the centuries have done this, and still do it. Israel was no exception. Jerusalem and the temple, instead of being a means of grace, became the foster mother of religious complacency. So Ezekiel comes to speak of the glory of God leaving temple and city (Ezekiel 10). Yet places and things — as well as people — can be means of grace. The psalmist is here affirming on the basis of personal experience that there is a genuine encounter with God in that temple where the glory of God graciously "dwells" and "abides" with his people. The word translated "abides" (Hebrew *miškan*) is from the same root as the word "Shekinah," which in later Jewish thought indicates the presence of God among his people. A rabbinic saying states "Where two sit together and are occupied in the words of the Law, the Shekinah is among them" (*Aboth* 3:8), a saying which seems to be echoed in the words of Jesus in Matthew's Gospel, "For where two or three are gathered together in my name, I am there among them" (Matt. 18:20). Such words can be either the justification for a narrow religious arrogance or the launching pad for an authentic, outgoing religious commitment.

9-10 This first part of the psalm's concluding plea begins with a negative request: "Do not sweep me away with sinners." The psalmist does not want to be gathered up and consigned to the religious rubbish heap together with those to whom he has already said "No" in verses 4-5 and who are now described as "sinners" and "the bloodthirsty," bent on "evil devices." This last word (Hebrew *zimmah*) can refer to sexual promiscuity (cf. Lev. 19:29, where it is translated "depravity") and, along with other sexual terms, to the worship of other gods (Jer. 13:27). It is more natural, however, in this context to see in it a reference to that brutal deviousness which leads to false accusations and the resort to bribery.

11-12 Now comes the positive plea, backed up by a reaffirmation of "integrity" (see comment on v. 1). "Redeem me [see 25:22] and be gracious to me [see 4:2]." Just as God's steadfast love and faithfulness have been and are part of the psalmist's experience (v. 3), so the costly concern and grace which flow from them will ensure a future where the ground is "level" or "firm" (REB) beneath his feet. He will join the "great congregation" in blessing the LORD (see 16:7). The word translated "great congregation" (REB: "full assembly") occurs only twice in the Old Testament, here and in Ps. 68:26. It is a plural form related to the Hebrew word *qāhal,* which can mean any gathering of people (in verse 5 it is translated "company"). It is the word which is rendered *ekklēsia* in the Greek (LXX) and gives us our word "church." The plural form here may refer to the different groups of people who gathered for worship in the temple precincts at different times, or it may be, as both the NRSV and REB translations assume, a "plural of intensity" (hence the adjective "great" or "full").

The psalm ends on a note which, in a variety of different ways, appears in many psalms. Worship owes much of its vitality to the fact that it is a corporate experience, shared with others, drawing on a common tradition. It owes its richness to the fact that we each, however hesitantly or diffidently, bring our own contribution to that shared experience.

Psalm 27
CONFIDENCE IN THE FACE OF THREATS

Like many other psalms, this is a psalm of changing moods. The change is so marked at verse 7 that some scholars have argued that the psalm was originally two psalms: verses 1-6, a joyful psalm of confidence; verses 7-14, a lament of someone unjustly accused. This, however, is to underestimate the extent to which confidence and perplexity, faith and questioning, may lie side by side in the psalmist's experience (see comment on Psalms 9 and 10). Other scholars treat this as a royal psalm. The Greek text adds in its heading the words "before he was anointed." An interesting approach to the psalm as a royal liturgy related to the Davidic covenant tradition is to be found in the Word Bible Commentary on Psalms by P. C. Craigie. There is, however, nothing in the psalm which demands that the person who speaks must be the king. Nor are attempts to defend the Davidic authorship and to relate the language of the psalm to the crisis in his life prompted by Absalom's rebellion convincing. We are listening to the words of someone who has been and still is in the grip of a life-threatening situation and who finds that, in reaching out to God, light breaks into his darkness. Ultimately this is a psalm of confidence which has been tested and not found wanting.

1 It is this confidence which shines through verse 1 and in the titles which the psalmist uses to describe his relationship with the LORD. The LORD is "my light." In the Old Testament it is common for light to function as a symbol of all that is positive and creative in the goodness of God. Yet only here is the word used as a title. The nearest parallel is in Isa. 10:17, where God is described as "the light of Israel." In Isa. 2:5 the people are invited to "walk in the light of the LORD." What is true of the nation's pilgrimage has become for the psalmist intensely personal, as he has learned to cope with the darkness (cf. 43:3). For the title "my salvation," see the comment on 3:8. As "the stronghold of my life," God is the fortress which guarantees security in face of every attack (cf. 31:3). This intensely personal relationship with God enables the psalmist to face life even in its most threatening forms without fear.

2-3 It is hard to know whether verse 2 contains a snapshot of the psalmist's past experience or of his present difficulties. It is possible to translate "they stumbled and fell" or "they stumble and fall" or "they shall stumble and fall." There is no denying, however, that the psalmist has faced or is facing a crisis in his life. Enemies are closing in "to devour my flesh" (v. 2), that is, to undermine his life. Ironically it is "they" (the "they" is emphatic in Hebrew) who are being undermined themselves by their attacks on the psalmist.

The language of "an army" and "war" (or perhaps "warriors") in verse 3 need not be taken literally. The imagery indicates the seriousness and strength of the attacks to which the psalmist is being subjected. Yet, in spite of this, he does not give way to panic; he "will be confident" or continue to trust (cf. 4:5; 25:1). There is no suggestion of brash self-confidence here. There is no claim that he will not have to walk in darkness, but he trusts that in the darkness he will find light — the light of the God who will be with him to strengthen him. Faith does not sidestep the darkness, whether self-inflicted or the result of circumstances beyond our control. It affirms God's presence in the darkness, and as Paul declares, "If God is on our side, who is against us?" (Rom. 8:31).

4 Not surprisingly, therefore, the all-important thing for the psalmist is worship, the foundation on which he builds his life. For the meaning of the expression "to live in the house of the LORD," see the comment on Ps. 23:6. Worship is for him the key which opens the door to an enriching life:

"To behold [REB: "to gaze upon"] the beauty of the LORD." The word translated "beauty" (Hebrew *nōʿam*) can indicate graciousness, loveliness, or attractiveness. It is used again of God in Ps. 90:17, and the corresponding adjective occurs in Ps. 135:3. The reference here is probably to the temple building itself, to the symbolism attached to it, and to the ritual celebrated there. To be in such a place can be a means of grace, whether it is the beauty of a great cathedral on which famous architects and artists have lavished their gifts, or the beauty which can be present in a simple country church. The Reformation has often been accused of being iconoclastic, but it was John Calvin who declared, "Temples still have their beauty which deservedly ought to draw the affections and desires of the faithful."

"And to inquire in his temple." The meaning of this phrase has been much discussed. It has been argued that the word "inquire" can mean to meditate or to say prayers. It is more likely that it conveys the meaning of "seeking," probably for answers to the difficulties which face him. Whether we imagine such answers being given in oracular form by a priest or as the result of some form of divination is uncertain. Worship was not merely an occasion for adoration or meditating on the wonders of God; it also provided the opportunity for bringing questions, often urgent questions, to God in the conviction that there were answers to be found in his presence.

5-6 Now the psalmist spells out what God will do for him and what his response will be. The words "shelter" and "tent," often associated with Israel's early life before they settled down in the land, are used here to decribe the temple. Perhaps the reference is to the temple as a place of asylum where the worshipper is under God's protection, just as any traveler would expect to find welcome and protection in his host's tent. The temple is, therefore, a place of refuge when danger threatens. It is also a source of the kind of strength he would have if he were to look down triumphantly on enemies from a rock fortress (cf. 18:2).

The psalmist's response is one of "offering sacrifices with shouts of joy." Although the word translated "shouts of joy" can indicate a battle cry, it is used most frequently in the context of worship. In Ezra 3:13 it describes the shouts of joy with which some of the people greeted the laying of the foundation stone of the new temple after the return from exile. Worship which has no place for joy and songs of praise can hardly be the worship of the God of Israel, who is the Father of our Lord Jesus Christ.

7-10 The second part of the psalm begins with a plea very similar to that which occurs at the beginning of Psalm 4. In verse 8 the psalmist seems to be debating with himself what he should do in response to the crisis in which he finds himself. Almost any meaningful translation involves some alteration to the Hebrew text. If we follow the Greek (LXX) we can read, "My heart said to you, 'I have sought your face.'" In this case the psalmist's past piety becomes the basis of his present appeal to God. The translation of the NRSV and the REB, however, makes good sense. Inner meditation and reflection have led him to turn to God, to seek his presence (for "face," see 17:15). He makes his appeal to the God whom he has known in the past as "my help" (cf. 40:17; 46:2) and "my salvation" (cf. 3:8). His plea is that God will not withdraw such help now by hiding his face (see comment on 10:1 and 13:1), by angrily refusing to take up his case ("turn away" in v. 9 probably has a legal background), by deserting him in his time of need. The confidence which he has in God shines through verse 10. Even if the most basic and dependable of human relationships fail to stay the course, the LORD can be depended upon to pick him up. So to a people feeling forsaken by God, the prophet says:

"Can a woman forget her nursing child, or show no compassion for the child of her womb? Even these may forget, yet I will not forget you" (Isa. 49:15).

11-12 Two specific requests follow: "Teach me . . . lead me" (cf. 25:9). Although it is possible that "level path" could mean the way that is right in God's sight, it is more likely that it refers to a firm and secure way cleared of obstacles. The psalmist needs to be guided by and to walk in the company of a trustworthy companion, because there are others watching to take advantage of any false move he may make. The word translated "enemies" (v. 11) comes from a root meaning "to watch"; so these are people who, as it were, have him in their sights ready to shoot. Guidance, therefore, must inevitably involve protection against those who are maliciously bringing false accusations against him, witnesses prepared to perjure themselves to ensure that he will meet a violent end.

13-14 The psalm ends, as it began, on a note of confidence: "I believe that I shall see the goodness of the LORD." Verse 13 begins with the Hebrew word usually translated "unless" or "if not," which introduces the first half of a statement in the form, "unless I do X, Y will follow." But the second part of the statement is missing here, unless it is to be assumed from what has been said in the previous verse. If so, the sense would then be "Unless I see the goodness of the LORD, I shall be at the mercy of my enemies." A few Hebrew manuscripts omit the word, but here it may be pointing to a very emphatic statement. Thus the REB translates, "Well I know." The verb "believe" might better be rendered "I firmly believe," particularly since it is related to the word "faithfulness" (see comment on 25:5). Confidently the psalmist is expecting to experience God's goodness during his lifetime. He expects to be able to share in the words of the prayer attributed to King Hezekiah: "The living, the living, they thank you, as I do this day" (Isa. 38:19).

The timing of God's goodness, however, remains in God's hands. "Wait for the LORD" (v. 14) — there is need for that eager hopefulness which looks forward expectantly for God to act (cf. 25:3). Verse 14 can be taken as words of a priest spoken to the psalmist assuring him that there is no need to panic since God's help will come and his prayers will be answered. It is just as likely that they are the words of the psalmist himself sharing with others his confidence that the great truths which Israel's religious traditions celebrated were confirmed in his own experience.

Throughout the psalm we hear echoes of Moses' words to Joshua in Deut. 31:7-8, "Be strong and bold. . . . It is the LORD who goes before you. He will be with you; he will not fail you or forsake you. Do not fear or be dismayed." In worship, we listen to the witness of the past. We make it our own as, in the company of God's people, we seek to live our lives by its sustaining and challenging vision.

Psalm 28
SILENCE BROKEN

This is a psalm of sharply contrasting moods. Verses 1-5 form a lament; verses
6-9, a song of confident thanksgiving (see comment on Psalm 13). Attempts have
been made to find a specific context for the psalm in the liturgy of the Jerusalem
temple and to reconstruct a dialogue between the worshipper and a priest or other
spokesman for God. Thus verses 1-4, the urgent prayer of the psalmist, are said
to evoke in verse 5 the priestly response declaring the judgment of God. The
psalmist's thanksgiving in verses 6-7 is then capped by the priest declaring the
relevance of the blessing the psalmist has received for the entire community. We
move here into the realm of speculation, whether we are invited to think of a
pre-exilic national covenant festival (Weiser), an individual defending himself
against false accusations of breach of contract (Craigie), or of this being a royal
psalm, because of the reference to "his anointed" in verse 8. It is more important
to clarify the spiritual experience enshrined in the psalm, an experience with
which people across the centuries have identified and can still identify.

1-2 The psalm begins with an urgent cry to the God in whom the psalmist has
trusted for protection, "my rock" (cf. 18:3), but who now seems to be deaf to
what is happening to him. God's continued silence would signal indifference or
powerlessness in a life-threatening situation (for the "Pit" as a synonym for
death, see 6:5). The psalmist has nothing to offer God but "the voice of
supplication" (cf. 31:28; 86:6), a plea that God's mercy and favor may be
extended to him. This cry for help is accompanied by a common religious
gesture: "I lift up my hands" (v. 2). Lifting up the hands can sometimes be an
expression of praise or joyful thanksgiving (63:4; 134:2), but often in the Old
Testament it indicates a reaching out to God in an urgent plea for help. Witness
the words of the poet in Lam. 2:19:

> Arise, cry out in the night,
>   at the beginning of the watches!
> Pour out your heart like water
>   before the presence of the LORD!
> Lift your hands to him
>   for the lives of your children,
> who faint for hunger
>   at the head of every street.

Uplifted hands are directed towards the God who is in heaven or, as here, towards
the place where God is present among his people, "your most holy sanctuary."
The word used here (Hebrew *děbîr*) indicates the innermost part of the temple,

"the holy of holies," the most holy place, in which the ark, the symbol of God's presence, was placed. By this outward gesture, the worshipper acknowledges to himself and to his fellow worshippers that his inmost thoughts are directed towards God.

Verses 3-5 spell out the crisis from which the psalmist wishes to be protected. It centers on "the wicked" (cf. Psalm 1), "the evildoers" (cf. Ps. 5:5), people who are concealing their destructive intentions behind smooth reassuring words (for "peace," *šalôm,* see 4:9; 29:11). The wisdom literature, notably Proverbs, has a lot to say about the gap which often exists between people's words and their real intentions. For example, "The words of the wicked are a deadly ambush" (Prov. 12:6). The psalmist believes that he is in danger of being caught in just such an ambush. In asking God to deal with such people according to what they do (v. 4), the psalmist is not merely being vindictive. He is convinced that what they plan to do is a challenge to the moral order rooted in God, a challenge which must inevitably lead to judgment. They are to get their "reward," a word which can be used in a good sense to mean "benefits" (103:2), but which here carries the negative meaning "deserved punishment." The "work of their hands" (v. 4) is facing a head-on collision with "the work of the LORD's hands" (v. 5), and this must lead to disaster. There is, however, a stern harshness about the closing words of verse 5, as if the psalmist were firmly closing the door on any hope for such people. By way of contrast, we are reminded of the ministry of Jeremiah, described in Jer. 1:10 as "to pluck up and to pull down, to destroy and to overthrow, to build and to plant." Jeremiah's job is to demolish and to clear away the rubbish, as it were, so that rebuilding can then take place. The psalmist, though, cannot see any such rebuilding for the people who seek to destroy him. He would certainly have happily gone along with the attitude of James and John who, when faced with a Samaritan village refusing to provide Jesus with hospitality, said, "Lord, do you want us to call down fire from heaven to consume them?" (Luke 9:54) — only to be rebuked.

6-7 The song of thanksgiving begins, acknowledging that whatever hope the psalmist now enjoys comes from God: "Blessed be the LORD." These verses look back to the beginning of the psalm. The psalmist now knows that his plea has been heard. The phrase translated "the sound of my pleadings" in verse 6 is exactly the same as that translated "the voice of my supplication" in verse 2. The REB catches this more helpfully when in verse 2 it renders "Hear my voice as I plead for mercy," with the echoing "for he has heard my voice as I plead for mercy" in verse 6. God has proved to be dependable. The one whom the psalmist believed to be "my rock" has proved to be "strength" and "shield" (cf. 3:3), one who can be trusted. The cry for help (v. 2) has turned into joyful exultation (v. 7). The psalmist can say a glad amen to the words of Psalm 149:5, "Let the faithful exult . . . let them sing for joy."

8-9 While these verses are often regarded as a liturgical postscript spoken by a priest or other temple official, it is equally possible that it is the psalmist himself who continues to speak, seeing his own experience as one to be shared with the rest of the community (cf. the ending of Psalm 3). Others can know the strength he has found in the LORD. The king, "his anointed" — the one in whom so many of the hopes and expectations of the community are centered — will find in the LORD a "saving refuge" (literally, "a refuge of salvation"), just as the people as a whole will experience God's salvation and blessing (see 3:8).

The psalm concludes with the image of God as a shepherd, carrying his people forever (see Psalm 23). The image stresses the tender care and protection God offers to his distraught people facing the crisis of exile: "He will feed his flock like a shepherd, he will gather the lambs in his arms and carry them in his bosom, and gently lead the mother sheep" (Isa. 40:11).

Is there perhaps a hint of irony in the concluding words of the psalm? As we have seen, shepherd is frequently a royal title (e.g., Psalm 23). The king, "his anointed," is the shepherd of the people. But suppose this shepherd turns out to be no true shepherd — a verdict that could apply to most of the kings of Judah (cf. Ezekiel 34)? There still remains one true shepherd, God himself. The people learned through painful experience the wisdom contained in the words of Psalm 146:3, "Do not put your trust in princes, in mortals, in whom there is no help." There is only one shepherd who never fails to carry his people through life.

Psalm 29
GLORY TO THE GOD OF ISRAEL

This is probably one of the earliest hymns in the Psalms. It has long been recognized that the language and imagery of this psalm owe much to Canaanite mythology, in particular that associated with the storm and warrior god Baal/Hadad (for a balanced discussion of this issue, see Craigie). The analogy has been drawn with General Booth's insistence that the devil should not have all the best tunes! Whatever the Hebrews took over, however, they were able to adapt and modify to become the vehicle of their own distinctive faith. This is a hymn to the glory of the LORD, the God of Israel. It not only replaces, but in some respects mocks, the claims made by Israel's neighbors. Canaanite religion tells the story of gods and goddesses locked in conflict. For example, there is the myth of Baal emerging victorious and being acclaimed as king after doing battle with Yam, Sea, the god of the threatening waters of chaos, "the mighty waters" (v. 3). Here in Psalm 29, however, there is no such conflict. Other gods are reduced to "the sons of god," heavenly beings (NRSV) or angelic powers (REB), members of the heavenly court surrounding the one true God (cf. Job 1:6-7; Psalm 82; 89:5-7). One of their functions is to acknowledge the supremacy of the LORD and to glorify him.

The Greek (LXX) heading links the psalm with the final days of the Feast of Tabernacles. While this may reflect later Jewish usage, the rubric for that feast in Deuteronomy ends with the words "the LORD your God will bless you in all your produce and in all your undertakings, and you shall surely celebrate" (Deut. 16:15; cf. Lev. 23:39-41). This is a psalm of celebration of the awesome power and majesty of the LORD who protects and blesses his people (v. 11).

Within the eleven verses of the hymn, the name the LORD, Yahweh, occurs no less than eighteen times. The psalm has also been carefully structured to hammer home the same point. Verses 1-2 constitute the introduction, in which the LORD is mentioned four times, on each occasion the object of the adoration of the heavenly choir; verses 3-9 are the central core, which depicts in graphic language the power and majesty of the LORD, with a sevenfold occurrence of the phrase "the voice of the LORD"; verses 10-11 form the conclusion, which looks back to the introduction and makes, again, a fourfold mention of the LORD. But now the LORD is the subject of a series of statements which focus upon what he has done and can be depended upon to do for his people.

1-2 The introduction to the hymn is closely paralleled in Ps. 96:7-8 and in 1 Chron. 16:28-29, with this difference: there it is "the families of the earth" who are called upon to ascribe glory and strength to the LORD, whereas here it is the "heavenly beings" (literally, "sons of god"). This anthem begins in heaven — *gloria in excelsis*. The LORD is being worshipped by the heavenly choir arrayed "in holy splendor" or "in holy attire" (REB), which is probably the heavenly equivalent of the vestments considered appropriate for the priests who led worship in the temple. For "glory," "the glory of his name," that is, the glory appropriate to God's revealed nature and character, see Ps. 3:3 and Psalm 24; for "strength" as a characteristic of God, see Ps. 28:7, 8.

Only after the LORD's supremacy in heaven is acknowledged will the psalm move to earth. There can be no conceivable forces outside human control and impinging on human life which fail to recognize the supremacy of the LORD. This is the bedrock of confident faith.

3-9 In this central section, the Hebrew poet utilizes traditional Canaanite themes to draw a graphic picture of the majesty and unchallengeable power of the LORD. The "voice of the LORD" is a thunderstorm (cf. Ps. 18:13), but a thunderstorm which in its awesome ferocity transcends any natural storm, to point to the incomparable God who evokes from his people a response summed up in one awestruck cry, "Glory!" (v. 9).

The thunderstorm begins echoing over the waters (v. 3), probably those sweeping in from the Mediterranean, even if the language of "the mighty waters" may have rolling in its background hints of the forces of chaos threatening the divinely created world order. It breaks over Lebanon's forests (v. 5), uprooting its tallest and strongest trees, the cedars, used extensively by Solomon in his building of the Jerusalem temple (1 Kgs. 5:6, 10; cf. Ps. 92:12; 104:16). The towering Lebanese mountain massif dominated by Sirion (i.e., Mt. Hermon; see Deut. 3:9) is reduced to impotence, forced to skip and play, as it were, to the LORD's tune, frolicking like a playful calf or a young wild ox (v. 6). Lightning and thunder make the wilderness dance or "writhe"; the verb translated "shake" is used of the pains of childbirth (e.g., Ps. 90:2).

The reference to the "wilderness of Kadesh" (v. 8) raises problems. Kadesh appears elsewhere in the Old Testament as one of the staging posts in the journey of the Israelites from Egypt to the promised land (Deut. 1:2; Num. 32:8). If this is correct, the scene suddenly switches from the northern Lebanese mountains to the southern desert. It has been argued that this is deliberate, the poet bringing into his picture one of the central themes of Israel's faith, the Exodus/Sinai events. This, however, is doubtful. The reference may be to another Kadesh in Syria. We could eliminate all reference to a place name by reading "the holy wilderness," but it is hard to see what "holy" in this context means. All specific geographical references disappear in verse 9. We are left with the picture of hinds frightened into giving premature birth (see the annotations in the REB and the NRSV) and of forests stripped bare. The NRSV translation, "causes the oaks to whirl," involves an alteration of the vowels of the traditional Hebrew text, its justification being that "oaks" provides a neat parallel to forests. The text, however, may be referring not only to the forest, but to all the animals who live in it.

The climax to the central section comes in the concluding words of verse 9, "and in his temple all say, 'Glory!'" If the temple in this verse is God's heavenly temple, then the all who cry "glory" are the mighty waters, the hills, the desert, the forest and its animal life, echoing the anthem of the heavenly choir. The scene, however, has switched from heaven to earth. The heavenly choir is now replaced by the temple singers. They echo the heavenly anthem, picking up the one word which encapsulates the incomparable greatness of God, "Glory." They are bowing in adoration before the one whom Psalm 24 celebrates as "The LORD of hosts . . . the King of glory" (24:10). This is where all true worship begins, a theme picked up in the words of a traditional hymn associated with Holy Week: "The company of angels are praising thee on high, and mortal men and all things created make reply."

10-11 It is on this theme of the kingship of the LORD that the psalm ends. This is the God who sits enthroned over the "flood." The word translated "flood" (Hebrew *mabbûl*) is found elsewhere in the Old Testament only in Genesis 6–11, the Noah story and its aftermath. That flood was devastating in its judgment on all that was evil, yet it ended in the rainbow of hope, with God renewing his relationship with the world he created and promising "never again" (Gen. 9:8-16). This is the God whose awesome strength is his people's guarantee (cf. 28:8), the

God of "shalom," that full, satisfying, secure existence in which his people enjoy all the good things which enrich life, unblighted by evil in any form. As in Beethoven's *Pastoral Symphony,* the titanic power of the thunderstorm dies away to lead into the chords of a "shepherd's song," the song of Israel's Shepherd-King (cf. Ps. 28:8-9).

Psalm 30
A FRESH START

Simple and vivid though the language of this psalm may be, it poses some puzzling questions. The first concerns the heading, "A Song at the dedication of the temple" (literally, "house"). In Jewish tradition, the psalm has become firmly associated with the festival of Hanukkah, commemorating the joyful rededication of the temple in Jerusalem in 164 BCE, after its desecration by the megalomaniac Antiochus Epiphanes (see 1 Maccabees 4). Older commentators, assuming a link with David, tend to see a reference to David's palace in Jerusalem (cf. 2 Sam. 5:11). It is more likely that the psalm springs out of the experience of an otherwise unknown individual and was later considered appropriate for a great communal occasion.

But what kind of experience? The notes of "praise" and "thanksgiving" are dominant in the psalm; compare verse 4 and verse 12. But praise and thanksgiving for what? The NRSV heading suggests "the psalmist's recovery" (from illness). This is the common understanding of the psalm, and as such it is often compared with Hezekiah's prayer in Isa. 38:10-20. This interpretation depends to a large extent on verses 2 and 3, particularly the words "you have healed me (v. 2) and "you have restored me to life" (v. 3), in the context of references to Sheol, the Pit, and death (vv. 3, 8). But this is not a necessary interpretation of the language. The verb "heal" can refer to restoration from any situation of crisis (cf. 147:3). The psalmist undoubtedly faced a life-threatening situation, but it need not be illness. Whatever that crisis was, it called into question much that he had taken for granted in life. But now it is over. God has turned his mourning into joy (v. 11). With praise and thanksgiving he is ready for a fresh start.

1-3 The psalm begins with a joyful expression of thanksgiving. "I will extol you, O LORD" (cf. 145:1). Such extolling means that God is being lifted up to his rightful place at the center of life, where his awesome greatness and majesty are acknowledged in a response which involves worship (99:5, 9) and thanksgiving (18:48). The reason for the psalmist's thanksgiving is immediately spelled out: "you have drawn me up," like water drawn up in a bucket from a deep well (cf. Exod. 2:16, 19). The deep well from which the psalmist has been drawn up is "Sheol" (v. 3), the "Pit" (v. 4), the abode of the dead (see comment on 6:5; the word "Pit" is also the Hebrew word for "well"). The NRSV translation at the end of verse 3, "from among those gone down to the Pit," assumes a slight and traditional alteration to the Hebrew text. The REB retains the standard Hebrew text and translates "as I was sinking into the abyss" (cf. NRSV footnote). Both translations are possible. Either way, the psalmist has been led to the very edge of despair. He has faced a crisis in his life which gave enormous satisfaction to those whom he describes as "my foes" in verse 1. No doubt only too anxious, for reasons unknown to us, to stick the knife into him, they were rubbing their hands with glee, arguing that the psalmist was only receiving what he deserved. It was the mark of God's judgment upon him, an attitude well illustrated in the reaction of Job's friends to the tragedy which had engulfed him. Note Eliphaz's words in Job 22:5, 10-11:

> Is not your wickedness great?
>   There is no end to your iniquities.
> . . . .
> Therefore snares are around you,
> and sudden terror overwhelms you,
>   or darkness so that you cannot see;
>   a flood of water covers you.

Restoration by God, however, has meant that such an attitude was unjustified. Their rejoicing has been nipped in the bud.

4-5 Joy must be shared. The psalmist calls upon God's "faithful ones" (see 6:5) to join him in praising God and giving thanks to "his holy name" (literally, "the remembrance of his holiness"). God can be depended upon to act in ways consistent with his own nature and character. That is why people can be assured that although "his anger" (see 6:1) must be treated seriously, it cannot be his last word. That word is a word of grace. His anger is "but for a moment," but his favor is lifelong. Thus to the people in exile, afraid that God in his anger had totally abandoned them, this word came:

> For a brief moment I abandoned you,
>   but with great compassion I will gather you.
> In overflowing wrath for a moment
>   I hid my face from you,
> but with everlasting love I will have compassion on you,
>   says the LORD, your Redeemer. (Isa. 54:7-8)

Just as nighttime tears can turn into morning joy, so God's people know that the harsh reality of God's anger will be replaced by a grace which will call forth from them a response of joy.

6-12 The psalmist now dots the "i"s and crosses the "t"s of his experience, recapitulating what he has had to live through and the steps which led him out of his crisis. The recapitulation takes the form of a dialogue between the psalmist and God. The psalmist begins by admitting the fatal mistake he had made. He had taken all that God had given him for granted. He felt "secure" (REB), as secure as a mountain fortress, or at ease (v. 6). This is better than the NRSV's rendering, "in my prosperity." The same word is used of the God-defying wicked in Ps. 73:12, "always at ease." His piety rested not on God who gave, but on the good things he had received. His own sense of security, his own status, was all-important. The warnings to the people in Deut. 8:11-20 not to forget God in times of prosperity were ignored. He had been so busy enjoying the good things of life that he had forgotten that, in the words of the Westminster Shorter Catechism, the chief end of man was "to glorify God and to enjoy him forever." It is only too easy to confuse God with what we believe to be God's gifts to us. This is especially true when these gifts are what we take to be essential religious gifts, such as a particular view of the Bible, or a particular form of church authority, or a particular pattern of Christian living.

Then it all fell apart: "you hid your face" (cf. 10:1; 13:1). The psalmist was left "dismayed" (v. 7), though perhaps a stronger word would be more appropriate. The same verb is used in Job 22:10 of being "overwhelmed by terror" and is translated in Ps. 6:2 as "shaking with terror." The foundations of his life were shaken. The props of his piety having been taken away, he was left only with the God to whom he now turns in urgent prayer (v. 8). He is at the end of his tether. Death calls. "What profit is there in my death?" (v. 7). That can only mean the end of any relationship with God, with no opportunity of praising God or of witnessing to his "faithfulness." But profit for whom? Is the psalmist challenging God, arguing that there is no point in God condemning him to death, since God has nothing to gain from it — only the loss of one who, however imperfectly, did worship him? Or is the psalmist admitting that he has nothing to gain by continuing along the self-centered road which can only lead to death? Either way, the chill, bleak face of death haunts the psalmist. He can only appeal to God, not on the grounds of any claim on God or any merit of his own, but solely on God's grace. "Hear . . . be gracious to me . . . be my helper" (cf. 4:2; 27:7). He has obviously reacted positively to the crisis he has faced. He has learned his lesson. He no longer looks for any other security than that to be found in God.

Freed from the chains of his own self-esteem and self-importance, his life now takes on a new dimension. "Mourning" is replaced by "dancing," one of the signs of rejoicing in Israel (e.g., 1 Sam. 18:6) that had a recognized place in joyful worship (149:3; 150:4). "Sackcloth," a coarse cloth usually made from goat's hair and worn customarily as a sign of mourning (Gen. 37:34; Pss. 35:13; 69:11), is replaced by festive garments. This is a joy which cannot be contained.

The psalmist breaks forth into songs of praise and thanksgiving, because he has discovered that God's grace has proved sufficient for all his needs. Here is the God who can truly be addressed as "O LORD, my God," the God to whom now he will "give thanks . . . forever." The road back to spiritual health may have been hard, but he is now at home with God.

Psalm 31
SAFEKEEPING

Although this psalm may be described in general terms as an individual lament, there is little agreement on the precise structure of the psalm. Many of the building blocks out of which it is constructed are identical with those in other psalms and indeed in other books in the Bible, notably Jeremiah, Lamentations, and Jonah. Verses 1-3a are found again in Ps. 71:1-3 (for details of the many similarities, see Craigie). This mixture means that the language of the psalm is so general that the precise situation of distress out of which the psalmist speaks is difficult to define. Much depends on whether we are prepared to take some of the language literally or metaphorically. The logical connection between the various parts of the psalm is far from certain. The approach adopted here represents only one of several possibilities.

1-8 The psalm begins with the psalmist entrusting himself for safekeeping into the hands of the one person he can trust, namely the LORD. He is in danger of being "put to shame" or humiliated (cf. v. 17). He has one sure defense, the God of "righteousness," who can be depended upon to vindicate the innocent who seek refuge in him (see comment on 7:9-11). In language familiar from earlier psalms, his confidence is affirmed: "rock of refuge for me . . . a strong fortress [v. 2] . . . my rock . . . my fortress [v. 3] . . . my refuge [v. 4]" (see comment on 18:2-3). Aware of hidden dangers (for "net," see 10:9), he needs someone who can lead and guide him (cf. Ps. 23:2-3). For the meaning of "for your name's sake," see 25:11.

"Into your hands I commit my spirit" (v. 5), the last words of Jesus from the cross according to Luke 23:46, are words which have been on the lips of many subsequent martyrs for the faith. In the context of the psalm, however, they are not the words of a man facing death and entrusting himself and what lies beyond death into the hands of God. They are the words of a man committing his life (Hebrew *ruah*, often translated "spirit," here means simply "life") into God's safekeeping. He does so in confidence because all that he knows of God from past experience points him in this direction. This is the God who "has redeemed me" (cf. 25:22), a "faithful" (cf. 25:5), trustworthy God (v. 5).

He is aware that there are people around him who do not share his trust.

He "hates" or repudiates those who worship "worthless idols" (v. 6) or false gods (see 24:4, where "what is false" translates the word here rendered "idols"). Such gods are powerless to help. The psalmist, however, has grounds for rejoicing in a God of "steadfast love" (cf. 4:2) who is aware of what is happening and who has never and will never abandon him to his enemies. He rejoices in a God who has set his feet in "a broad place," where he is not cramped or subject to deadly attack lurking around the next corner (cf. the REB: "but you have set me where I have untrammelled liberty"). Danger is real. It threatens, but it can never gain the upper hand. Paul shares the same confidence when he talks of the extraordinary power of God working through him and his fellow apostles: "We are afflicted in every way, but not crushed; perplexed, but not driven to despair; persecuted, but not forsaken; struck down, but not destroyed" (2 Cor. 4:8-9).

9-13 In these verses the psalmist laments his wretched condition. Physical weakness and mental turmoil sap his strength (vv. 9-10). Although the Hebrew text in verse 10 links this with his sense of guilt (see the annotation in the NRSV), context favors the reference to his "misery," the reading of the early versions. He faces the agonizing loneliness of pain, mocked by enemies, shunned by neighbors and relatives (v. 11). He is conscious of "terror all around," a favorite expression in the book of Jeremiah (cf. Jer. 6:25; 20:10; 46:5). He feels as good as dead, forgotten, useless as a piece of broken pottery, fit only to be thrown away (v. 12). His misery centers upon the activities of those variously described as "my adversaries" (v. 11), "conspirators" (v. 13), "my enemies and persecutors" (v. 15), and "the wicked" (v. 17). It is difficult, however, to know the precise activities of these people. The extremity of the psalmist's plight is clear, but as always in such laments, his response assumes that there is a God whose compassion reaches out to embrace those in distress. To this God he now turns.

14-18 In two simple words the basic theology of the entire psalm is laid bare: "you . . . my God" (cf. Isa. 40:1, "my people . . . your God"). Here is the unbreakable relationship which sustains him. The whole of life, past, present, and future — its ups and its downs — is in God's care. "My times are in your hands" (v. 15). The prayer he had already offered in verse 1, "deliver me," is now repeated, pinpointing those from whom he wishes to be delivered, "my enemies and my persecutors," those who relentlessly pursue him (cf. 7:1, 5).

His prayer has two foci. First, he wishes to prove in terms of his own experience what was promised to Israel in the priestly prayer in Num. 6:24-26, "The LORD bless you and keep you; the LORD make his face to shine upon you and be gracious to you; the LORD lift up his countenance upon you and give you peace." Circumstances have brought him to the point where a prayer he may often have heard as he worshipped in the temple now becomes relevant to his life in a new way. God's "steadfast love" is no longer merely religious language but a desperate personal need.

Second, he prays that the wicked may be frustrated, that the "shame" they wish to heap on him may rebound on themselves, that their arrogant, derisive tongues may be silenced on the stage of this world. They will make their exit into the silence of Sheol (cf. 6:5), the abode of the dead.

19-22   Answered prayer leads into thanksgiving. It could be that the dramatic change in mood between verses 18 and 19 presupposes some cultic act containing words of reassurance. Equally, it may be that the psalmist, with the thought of God's steadfast love firmly in his mind, is looking forward in faith anticipating that his prayer will be answered. Whatever the reason, he breaks forth into a paean of praise: "O how abundant is your goodness" (cf. 27:13). He celebrates a goodness set aside for those who entrust themselves humbly to God, "those who fear you" (cf. 19:9), a goodness which means "shelter" and "protection" from all the outrageous attacks, verbal or otherwise, which threaten the psalmist's life (vv. 19-20).

The opening words of verse 21 and the concluding words of verse 22 closely parallel Ps. 28:6, but here the wonder of God's steadfast love provides the context in which the psalmist admits that he had panicked, fearing he had been "driven far" or "shut out" (REB; this verb occurs only here in the Old Testament) from the presence of God. If we did not have this line, we might have concluded that the psalmist had never wavered in his trust in God. But he obviously had. Often behind the certainty of faith people show to the world are moments that many are afraid to share with others. Yet why should we be so eager to share our certainties and so unwilling to share our doubts?

23-24   The psalm ends with a summons to the congregation, "all you his saints" (*ḥăsîdîm,* "loyal people"; cf. 4:3), to "love the LORD." The verb "to love" (Hebrew *'āhab*), which covers a wide range of human relationships, is not common in the Psalms with God as the object (but compare 69:36; 116:1; and the frequent use of it in Psalm 119 with reference to God's Torah, e.g., vv. 47, 48, 97, 113, 127). It is more commonly used with God as subject to indicate what he chooses to value (e.g., 11:7; 33:5; 37:28; 47:4). Here it probably echoes the words of the Shema: "Hear, O Israel; the LORD is our God, the LORD alone. You shall love the LORD with all your heart, and with all your soul, and with all your might" (Deut. 6:4-5). This is the God who takes the side of the "faithful" against those who act with proud arrogance (v. 18). The worshippers are, therefore, summoned to be courageous in the face of whatever life holds in store for them. The language of verse 24 is closely akin to that of the appeal with which Psalm 27 ends. The security of faith always brings with it the daily challenge of staking everything on the conviction that what faith affirms is trustworthy.

Psalm 32
THE WISE PATH OF FORGIVENESS

This is the first of thirteen psalms which have in their heading the word "Maskil." The others are Psalms 42, 44, 45, 52-55, 74, 78, 88, 89, 142. It is a word of very uncertain meaning. The verb from the same root occurs in verse 8, meaning "instruct" or "teach." But "instruction," though appropriate for some of these psalms, is not an obvious title for others. Some kind of skill or expertise is usually indicated by the verb, but what kind of skill? Does it refer to the content of the psalm, the musical accompaniment, the officiating priest, or the worshipper? We do not know.

The psalm has had a significant place in Christian spirituality. Its opening verses are quoted by Paul in Rom. 4:7-8. It was one of Augustine's and Luther's favorite psalms. Traditionally it has been regarded as one of the seven penitential psalms (cf. Psalm 6), though penitence is not a dominant note within it. Like Psalm 1, this psalm reveals the influence of wisdom teaching and shows how the teaching of the wise in Israel found a natural place in worship. It begins with the twice-repeated expression, "Happy are those" (see comment on Ps. 1:1). It includes a typical piece of wisdom instruction based on personal experience, verses 8-9. It stresses the contrast between the fate of the wicked and those whose life is centered on God (v. 10).

1-2 The psalm begins with the two "Happy are those" sayings, which seek to draw conclusions based on the psalmist's experience and observation of life. They are, however, unusual in that they are the only such sayings in the Old Testament in which the people so described are on the receiving end of something done to them. Elsewhere such happiness is ascribed to people who do certain things, such as those who do not follow "the advice of the wicked" (Ps. 1:1), those who "walk in the way of the LORD" (Ps. 119:1), and those who "fear the LORD" (Ps. 128:1). Here they are people to whom something has happened; they are on the receiving end of "forgiveness," which can only come from God as a gift. Three words commonly used in the Old Testament to indicate human sinfulness occur in these verses — "transgression" (Hebrew *pešaʿ*), a rebellion against God's authority (v. 1); "sin" (Hebrew *ḥāṭʾāh*), a missing of the mark (v. 1); and "iniquity" (Hebrew *ʿāwōn*), a distortion or the guilt and punishment it deserves (v. 2). They find their counterpart in three words indicating forgiveness — "forgiven" (Hebrew *nāśaʾ*), having a burden lifted; "covered" (Hebrew *kāsāh*), having a regretted action concealed; and "impute no iniquity" (Hebrew *ḥāšab*), render a verdict of innocent (cf. Gen. 15:6).

It is not surprising that Paul (Rom. 4:7-8) uses these verses side by side with an argument based on the Abraham story in Genesis 15. He emphasizes that our standing with God does not depend on any human action or achievement, but solely on God's grace in Christ, which can only be accepted in faith as a gift. This is a gift, however, which must be accepted without any equivocation by someone whose attitude to life is characterized by "no deceit. " Only this kind of person can honestly come to terms with what forgiveness means and implies.

3-5 These verses describe the struggle in the psalmist's life which brought him to this point. It took him a long time to admit his need for forgiveness. He bottled things up inside him ("I kept silent") and found himself in an increasingly desperate condition, graphically described in the words "my body [literally, "my bones"] wasted away" (v. 3). In verse 4 his condition is described in a phrase which is uncertain but which may indicate "the sap in me dried up" (REB). Such an image would picture his life having drained away from him as when a plant shrivels up in the relentless summer sun. There is no clear indication of the nature of the psalmist's condition; either a physical or a psychological ailment may be in view, perhaps with a strong sense of guilt attached to it. Release only came through acknowledging to God the wrong within him, verse 5 repeating the same three words for sin that occur in verses 1 and 2. Now it is all out in the open; God's forgiveness becomes a reality.

6-7 A glad release has now to be shared, since it is an experience open to all the "faithful" (cf. 4:3), who "offer prayer to you" (v. 6). This is followed in the Hebrew text by the words "at a time of finding." If taken closely with the injunction to pray, these words could be pointing to the truth emphasized in Jeremiah's letter to the exiles in Jeremiah 29, "Then when you call upon me and come and pray to me, I will hear you. When you search for me, you will find me; if you seek me with all your heart . . ." (Jer. 29:12-13; cf. Isa. 55:6). In this case, the word "only," which comes immediately after "finding," must be taken as emphatic, introducing what follows, "surely the rush of mighty waters. . . ." Most modern versions, however, accept a slight alteration to the Hebrew and read for the entire phrase "at a time of distress." If "the mighty waters" retains an echo of the threatening powers of chaos (see 29:3), then we might paraphrase "the rush of mighty waters" by "when all hell breaks loose." The picture, however, may simply be that of a flash flood pouring down a wadi, destroying everything in its path while people in the danger zone can only watch helplessly, hoping that it will not reach them. Even in such a dire situation, the faithful express their confidence in the protection God offers and the joyful deliverance they shall experience (v. 7).

8-10 Who is the "I" who speaks in verse 8? Many argue that this is one of the passages spoken in the name of God by a priest or temple prophet. The Good News Bible inserts as an introduction to these words, "The LORD says." Yet what follows is a piece of instruction that in terms of imagery and vocabulary could have been taken from the book of Proverbs or any other piece of wisdom teaching. The view taken here is that it is the psalmist speaking and arguing that forgiveness is not an end in itself but a learning experience which ought to lead to a new attitude toward life. This attitude he describes as "the way of the righteous" (see Ps. 1:6). For it, he is prepared to offer personal counseling. It means giving up the stubborn, self-centered foolishness which refuses to accept the need for forgiveness or for instruction. We may compare Prov. 26:3, "A whip for a horse, a bridle for a donkey, and a rod for the back of fools." Horse and mule cannot be kept under control and close at hand except by the use of bit and bridle, but those "who trust the LORD" (cf. 4:5) know a different control which keeps them close to God, namely, his "steadfast love" (see 5:7).

11 Small wonder, then, that the call goes out to the congregation of God's people — "the righteous" and "the upright in heart" (cf. 7:9, 10) — to "rejoice" and "to shout for joy" (cf. 68:3). The psalmist issues the call not because life is easy or free from problems, but because he wants to witness to what God has done for him and can do for anyone. So Paul, in the light of what God has done for him in Christ, sums up the life to which he and all who share his faith are called: "Rejoice in the Lord always; again I will say, rejoice" (Phil. 4:4).

Psalm 33
CREATOR OF THE WORLD,
DEFENDER OF HIS PEOPLE

This is a hymn of praise which imitates the acrostic form (see Psalm 9) by having twenty-two verses. Attempts have been made to link it with specific incidents in Israel's history or with one of the great religious festivals in the year. They are neither convincing nor necessary. The psalm fashions into one seamless robe some of the great themes of Israel's faith. It focuses upon the sure and dependable word of the LORD, evident in creation, in his lordship over all human history, and in his loving concern for his people (cf. Psalm 136). What other response can this evoke but a glad *Te Deum?*

1-3 The psalm begins where Psalm 32 ends. It may indeed have been regarded as a continuation of Psalm 32 since in the Hebrew text it has no heading of its own, though the Greek (LXX), not surprisingly, adds "to David." Voices are lifted up in praise, blending with the music of "lyre" and "ten stringed harp" because that "befits" (REB: "comes well from") people who live in God's world and experience his grace (for a fuller discussion of the temple orchestra, see Psalm 150).

The call to "sing a new song to the LORD" (v. 3) does not necessarily imply a song never before sung that celebrates some new act of God, though it is used in this sense in Revelation in an eschatological setting (5:9; 14:3). The phrase is a standard formula in the Psalms (cf. 96:1; 98:1; 149:1). It calls upon the congregation to express in their singing the sense of being gripped anew by the majesty and the wonder of the God they worship. To lapse into dull familiarity or boring routine would be, and often is, the death of a living faith.

4-5 What the congregation is summoned to celebrate is the nature of the LORD revealed through his "word" (v. 4; cf. v. 6). That "word" is no mere matter of words, but the demonstration of his dynamic activity, the Hebrew *dābār* means both "word" and "deed" (cf. Isa. 55:11). The picture is filled out by images which appear in earlier psalms. His word is "upright" (cf. 25:8); all that he does is characterized by "faithfulness" (cf. 25:10). This is the God who loves "righteousness and justice" (cf. 7:8-11), a God whose "steadfast love" (cf. 5:7) fills the earth, a God who reveals himself to be not only dependable but gracious.

6-9 These verses focus on the God of creation. The language at many points has links with the hymn of creation in Genesis 1 — the making of "the heavens" (cf. Gen. 1:1); the "host" of heaven, planets, and stars (cf. Gen. 1:14-16; Isa. 40.26); the God who "spoke and it came to be" (cf. the repeated refrain "let there be . . . and it was so" in Genesis 1). In the background there are echoes of the creation conflict language that we find in Mesopotamian and Canaanite mythology (cf. Psalm 29), language which an earlier Hebrew poet in Exodus 15 used to describe God's victory over the Egyptians: "At the blast of your nostrils the waters piled up, the floods stood in a heap, the deeps congealed in the heart of the sea" (Exod. 15:8). In the light of this, it is unwise and unnecessary with the NRSV to change the Hebrew "heap" in verse 7 into "bottle." The delightful poetic imagery of God's "storehouses" or secret treasury in which he holds the forces of nature occurs again in Ps. 135:7, where God brings out the wind from his storehouses, and in Job 38:22, where they are the repository of snow and hail.

The whole world of nature came into being at God's word. All its forces, even the most threatening, are at his beck and call. Small wonder, then, that the whole world and its inhabitants are summoned to respond "in fear" (cf. 19:9) and "in awe" or dread (cf. 22:23).

10-15 This God of creation is the God whose writ runs large in the affairs of the nations. Nations may scheme and plan, but if what they propose is contrary to "the counsel of the LORD" (v. 11), it will come to naught. It is God's purpose and his alone, "the thoughts of his heart" (REB: "the plans he has in mind"), that last in the rapidly changing kaleidoscope of human history. Heaven is not some remote, distant realm, but the vantage point from which God can view what the human race is up to. His eagle eye misses nothing. A daunting, terrifying prospect? Yes, were it not for the fact that this God who "sees all humankind" is the God who has revealed himself to Israel as the LORD and has "chosen" them as "his heritage," to be his own (v. 12). At the heart of Israel's self-understanding there lies the mystery of election (cf. Deut. 7:7-8), easily and often perverted into a blind religious nationalism. As such it comes in for heavy criticism from the prophets (e.g., Amos 3:2; 9:7). Yet when truly understood as a gift of God's grace, Israel's election can be the source of the nation's true happiness and orientation (v. 12).

16-19   In view of this picture of the omniscient God, the question of where lasting security lies is raised. Three times in verses 13-15 the word "all" is heard: "all humankind" (v. 13), "all the inhabitants of the earth" (v. 14), and "all their deeds" (v. 15). Three times in verses 16-17 the word "great" is heard: "great armies" and "great strength" (v. 16), and "great might" (v. 17). All such human power, however impressive, is dismissed as "a vain hope," a "lie" (v. 17), something which promises much but delivers nothing. This is a hard word for those who believe that military might can guarantee security. The psalmist — and he has many allies in the Bible (cf. Isa. 31:1-3; Zech. 4:6) — believes otherwise. "Truly" (v. 18) — this is the NRSV translation of the Hebrew word often trans- lated "behold" — introduces a strong declaration of faith or indicates surprise that people should have such foolish beliefs. The only security lies with those who put their trust in the providential care of the LORD. Only thus can the threatening realities of life, symbolized by "death" and "famine," be faced with confidence.

20-22   To this the congregation now says amen: "Our soul [i.e., "we"] waits for the LORD" (v. 20). The verb here translated "wait" occurs only once again in the Psalms (106:13), where it is said that the people did not have the patience to wait for the counsel of the LORD. Patience, however, will discover that the LORD is "help" (cf. 20:6) and "shield" (cf. 3:3). So the psalm ends in a heartfelt congregational prayer which echoes the psalmist's confident assurance in verse 18.
     From creation through history, the psalm has moved to the faith of God's worshipping people, a faith which faces the future with confidence because it is convinced that life in its wholeness reflects the "steadfast love" of God.

Psalm 34
A TEACHER'S INVITATION

The heading to this psalm links it with the incident in 1 Sam. 21:13 in which David, finding himself in a dangerously compromising situation, feigns madness at the court of Achish of Gath. The wording of the heading is odd, however, unless Abimelech is a recognized title of a Philistine king (cf. Genesis 20 and 26), like Pharaoh in Egypt and Caesar in Rome. Yet the content and language do not give much credence to this linkage. The language of the psalm raises interesting problems, since there are many words and expressions in it which are found nowhere else in the Psalms (e.g., the word translated "be radiant" in verse 5; the word "taste" used in a metaphorical religious sense in verse 9; and the phrase "crushed in spirit" in verse 18). All of this gives the psalm its own distinctive flavor and makes any dating difficult.

The psalm is in the form of an acrostic poem (see Psalm 9) with one letter of the Hebrew alphabet missing, but with an additional verse at the end introduced by the word "redeem" (cf. Psalm 25). It is usual to see two elements in the psalm, a psalm of thanksgiving (vv. 1-10) followed by a piece of wisdom teaching (vv. 11-22). Yet it is better to see the whole psalm as the product of a wisdom teacher who finds in worship a convenient context for his teaching. There is no direct address to God in the entire psalm. Instead, from verses 4-10 the psalmist tells the story which prompted his thanksgiving, a story of answered prayer, of deliverance from all the fears and terrors which threatened him. Throughout this section, however, the psalmist repeatedly moves from his own experience to summoning others to share it. Thus "I sought the LORD, and he answered me" (v. 4) leads into "Look to him and be radiant" (v. 5). "This poor man cried, and was heard by the LORD" (v. 6) leads into "O taste and see that the LORD is good" (v. 8) and "O fear the LORD, you his holy ones" (v. 9). While we have seen this kind of invitation in other psalms (e.g., Psalms 27 and 31), it is also a familiar stylistic feature of the wisdom literature, the appeal to personal experience prefacing an invitation to share the same attitude to life (cf. Prov. 4:1-9; Job 22:15-22). Further marks of a wisdom teacher are to be found in the use of the expression "Happy are those who . . ." (v. 8b; see comment on Psalm 1), and three times we hear the phrase "the fear of the LORD" (vv. 7 and 9; cf. 19:9). We should never underestimate the extent to which worship can and should be a teaching and learning experience.

1-3 The teacher's experience and the way he uses it are anticipated in this hymn-like introduction. The cry "My soul makes its boast" leads into the invitation "let the humble hear and be glad" (v. 2). The call "O magnify the LORD with me" leads into the exhortation "let us exalt his name" (v. 3). In his opening words, "I will bless the LORD at all times," the psalmist gladly acknowledges all that the LORD has done for him (cf. 16:7). He is forever in God's debt, a debt he can only try to repay by praising God and "boasting" (REB: "glorying") in the LORD. When followed by the preposition "in," the same verb that gives us the reiterated "Hallelujah" or "Praise the LORD" is translated "boast." It is a boasting about God and therefore glorying in him.

The psalmist can claim no credit for life being rich and meaningful again; all is of God. The psalmist as a wise teacher is agreeing with the words of Jer. 9:23-24,

> Do not let the wise boast in their wisdom, do not let the mighty boast in their might, do not let the wealthy boast in their wealth; but let those who boast, boast in this, that they understand and know me, that I am the LORD. I act with steadfast love, justice, and righteousness in the earth, for in these things I delight, says the LORD.

Since he himself has known what it means to be one of the "humble" or "afflicted" (see 9:12), he invites his hearers to share his newfound joy. The mood of verse 3 is very much that of the Magnificat, Mary's song of praise in Luke 1:46-55, and the opening words of Timothy Dudley Smith's hymnic version of it, "Tell out, my soul, the greatness of the Lord."

4-10   The story this teacher seeks to share is one of need and answered prayer (vv. 4, 6). It is a story of release from "fears" (v. 4) — a strong word indicating something approaching terrors (cf. Jer. 6:25; 20:3) — and from the "trouble" that dogged him (v. 6). He invites others to share his experiece and "be radiant," their faces, as it were, aglow with the joy they have found. In Isa. 60:5 the same verb is used of Jerusalem, like a mother excitedly and joyfully welcoming back her long-lost children. What a rich vocabulary he uses to describe those who belong with him in the company of God's people. They are "those who fear God" (vv. 7, 9; cf. 19:9); "those who take refuge in him" (v. 8; cf. v. 22; see comment on 2:11); "his holy ones" (v. 9; cf. 2:6); and "those who seek the LORD" (v. 10; cf. 9:10). To this vocabulary there is added in the second half of the psalm the titles "the righteous" (vv. 15, 17) and "his servants" (v. 22; cf. 69:35; 90:13, 16). The very richness of the psalmist's vocabulary reflects a diversity and catholicity of religious experience.

"The angel of the LORD" (v. 7), although mentioned in the Psalms again only in 35:5, 6, is a common Old Testament way of speaking about God's presence with his people (e.g., Gen. 16:7; Exod. 3:2; Num. 22:22). The word translated "angel" can, however, mean simply "messenger," anyone sent on a mission. So in Gen. 32:1 the word is translated "angels," while in 32:2 it is used of the "messenger" whom Jacob sends to his brother Esau, the only difference being that in the one case the sender is God, in the other a man. The story in Genesis 32 goes on to tell how Jacob, confronted with the "angels of God," called the place where he met them "God's camp"; it was a place where he felt safe in the surrounding presence of God. The psalmist uses the same picture here and invites his fellow worshippers to test the truth of this for themselves, "O taste and see that the LORD is good." The verb translated "taste" is used of the industrious wife in Prov. 31:18 when, by her personal involvement, she "sees to it" (NRSV: "perceives") that her merchandise is profitable. There are several references to this psalm in 1 Peter, and the words of v. 8 are echoed in 1 Pet. 2:3, where the writer pleads for his fellow Christians to work out the implications of their personal commitment.

In verse 10, there is no need to change the reading "the young lions," even though the REB's reading, "princes," has some support in early versions. Lions appear in various roles in the Old Testament. Sometimes in the Psalms they represent the "enemies" (cf. 17:2; 35:12) about to pounce upon and savage their prey. But even for some young lions, claims the psalmist, the hunt at times may prove fruitless and leave them hungry. Not so "those who seek the LORD"; they experience "no want" (v. 9); they "lack no good thing" (v. 10). Here everything depends on what we mean by the affirmation "the LORD is good" (v. 8) and the statement that his people "lack no good thing" (v. 10). Within the context of the whole psalm, it is clear that this does not mean that such people will have a life of ease and luxury, untroubled by the difficulties and suffering which come to other people. The psalmist himself speaks from a background of terror and troubles. He speaks to people who may be "brokenhearted" and "crushed in spirit" (v. 18). He recognizes that the "righteous" experience "many difficulties" or misfortunes (v. 19).

The LORD's goodness lies in the fact that he is "near" (v. 18), present with his people, whatever life may bring. He does not save them *from* but *in* the harsh realities of life, a theme developed with rare honesty and spiritual sensitivity in Psalm 73.

11-22 These verses bear all the marks of a wisdom teacher. The opening address, "Come, O children, listen to me," is common in Proverbs and in Egyptian wisdom literature (e.g., Prov. 1:8, 10; 2:1; 3:1; 8:32). The invitation introduces teaching that may have begun as parental instruction, but it became typical of a teacher's admonition of a pupil. The central theme of such teaching is "the fear of the LORD" (cf. Prov. 1:7; 9:10). The question in verse 12 assumes that everyone desires a long and prosperous life (Prov. 3:16-18). It insists that there are moral issues involved in such a search, and that words can be dangerous weapons (v. 13). To this we may compare Prov. 1:16-19, where two out of the seven things the LORD hates are "a lying tongue" and "a lying witness" (cf. Prov. 18:21-22; Jas. 3:1-12). In moral issues there is a double challenge. There is the need to say "no" to evil; but that in itself is not enough. You cannot leave a moral vacuum. There must be a "yes" to what is good, to the pursuit of that rich, full life which is indicated by the Hebrew word "shalom" (v. 14; cf. Amos 5:14, 15 and the parable of the unclean spirits in Luke 11:24-26)

The closing section develops at length the contrast between the "righteous" and the "wicked" and their respective fates (see comment on Psalm 10), a contrast which is also central to much of the wisdom teaching (cf. Prov. 4:18-19; 10:11, 29-31; 11:30-31). Verses 12-16 are quoted in their Greek form in 1 Pet. 3:10-12. The writer of 1 Peter, however, ignores the original setting of these verses — the wisdom teacher's question — and instead uses them to illustrate the appropriate Christian response to suffering.

If the psalmist draws on a rich vocabulary to describe the people of God, no less striking is his portrait of the LORD in verses 11-22. Briefly in two verses, 16 and 21, the LORD says his "no" to "evildoers" and to the "wicked." He sets his face against them; they have no future. "Evil" or "disaster" (v. 21) — the Hebrew word can mean both — seals their fate. They end up "condemned."

But how much more is said about a God who is gracious and caring, the God whose "eyes . . . are on the righteous," watching over them, protecting them (v. 15), whose "ears are open to their cry" (v. 17; cf. Ps. 18:6), who "hears," who "rescues" (vv. 17, 19; cf. 17:2), who is "near" (v. 18), who "saves" (v. 18; cf. 3:8), who "redeems" (v. 22; cf. 25:22). A confidence in the LORD's caring concern for his people shines through these verses. They testify to the glowing faith of someone who knows that the people of God, unlike the wicked, will not be "condemned" (v. 22).

Although the heading to the psalm locates it in a specific historical incident in the life of David, Christian liturgical tradition has found a variety of settings for it. The language of verses 17 and 18, and in particular verse 20 (to which John 19:34 may allude), made this an appropriate psalm for Holy Week. The words "O taste and see that the LORD is good" gave it a place in the sacrament of Holy Communion. Christian faith has naturally taken the confident insights of the psalmist and seen in them a new depth in the light of the life, death, and resurrection of Jesus. This is what leads Paul confidently to say: "If God is for us, who is against us? He who did not withhold his own Son, but gave him up for all of us, will he not with him also give us everything else? Who will bring any charge against God's elect? It is God who justifies. Who is to condemn?" (Rom. 8:31-34).

Psalm 35
ON TRIAL

This has sometimes been regarded as a royal psalm, with the military imagery in verses 2-3 pointing to an international crisis in which the king is being accused falsely of breaking his treaty obligations by former allies looking for an excuse to attack him. The view taken here is that this is a personal lament of someone facing false accusations brought by malicious enemies. The dominant language is that of the law court; the psalmist's plea is for a verdict of not guilty with respect to the charges brought against him. The trial is depicted in three scenes:

scene one, verses 1-10, the initial pleadings; scene two, verses 11-18, the case for the defense; scene three, verses 19-28, the final appeal.

1-10   The opening words of the psalm, "Contend, O LORD, with those who contend with me," center on the Hebrew word *rîb,* which has a strongly legal background. In verse 23 it is translated "my cause." Deut. 19:16-17 provides an instructive parallel: "If a malicious witness comes forward to accuse someone of wrongdoing, then both parties to the dispute *(rîb)* shall appear before the LORD, before the priests and judges who are in office in those days." In Job 23:2-7 we find Job, facing the mounting charges of his erstwhile friends, determined to lay his case before a trustworthy divine judge. So the psalmist brings his case to the LORD, the divine judge who, he believes, will fight the case for him. He is well aware that there are people only too ready to "rise up" to provide evidence against him; he can but appeal to God to "rise up" to help him.

Verses 2-3 use the traditional picture of God the warrior (cf. Exod. 15:3; Isa. 42:13), to whom the psalmist appeals to do battle on his behalf. The imagery is poetic. No one would carry at one and the same time "shield" (cf. 3:3) and "buckler" (cf. 5:12). The word translated "javelin" in v. 3 (REB: "axe") is far from certain. The early versions read a verb here, but a second offensive weapon seems more likely. This is a battle in which the psalmist appeals not only for help, but also for a guarantee of victory: "say to my soul [i.e., to me], 'I am your salvation' " (v. 3; cf. 3:7).

The psalmist has already described his accusers as "those who fight against me" (v. 1) and "my pursuers" (v. 3). These descriptions are developed in fairly general terms in verses 4-8, where they appear as "those who seek after my life" (v. 4) and "those who devise evil against me" (v. 4; REB: "those who plan my downfall"), people whose accusations are unprovoked, "without cause," a word repeated twice in verse 7. But verses 4-8 are concerned in the main with the justified nemesis which the psalmist believes ought to be the lot of such people. The very things they seek to inflict upon the psalmist, "shame" and "dishonor" (v. 4; cf. v. 26), are to boomerang back upon themselves. Whisked away like chaff (v. 5; cf. Ps. 1:4), they are pursued along dark and slippery paths (cf. Jer. 23:12) by the "angel of the LORD" (see 34:7). "Net" and "pit" (vv. 7-8) are the hunter's weapons; but the hunters are to be ensnared in their own net (cf. 7:15). What is at stake here is not the personal vindictiveness of the psalmist, but the character of the divine judge to whom he brings his case (vv. 9-10), a judge who is not susceptible to bribes from the powerful in society. This is the God who guarantees deliverance to those who need protection. This is the God who defies human logic — hence the grateful, surprised question in verse 10, "O LORD, who is like you?"

This is the God who uses his unchallengeable power to "deliver the weak from those too strong for them, the weak and the needy from those who despoil them" (v. 10; see 9:12). This is that divine "bias towards the poor" which calls into question the policies of governments — not to mention churches — today and challenges us to share that bias.

11-18 The case for the defense hinges upon two factors, the character of the defendant and the character of his accusers. The psalmist pleads total ignorance of the charges being brought against him. They concern, he says, "things I do not know" (v. 11), given backing by the brutal conduct of people "I did not know" (v. 15). Such charges, breathtaking in their unexpectedness, can often be difficult to counter. Ignorance and utter astonishment are his response to people who repay "evil for good," people whom he describes in v. 12 as "lying in wait to take my life" (REB), a translation which assumes an alteration to the Hebrew text doubt-fully rendered in the NRSV as "my soul is forlorn." His astonishment is rooted in the fact that when these people were themselves in need, the victims of some kind of illness, he had shared their grief with all the customary rites associated with penitence and grief, "sackcloth" and "fasting" (cf. Jon. 3:6-8). When his prayers for them returned to him unanswered (v. 13, REB), he mourned for them as if they were close friends or near relatives. What then could possibly motivate such people to repay good with evil? For the psalmist, "This was the most unkindest cut of all. . . . Ingratitude, more strong than traitors' arms, Quite van-quished him" (*Julius Caesar,* act 3, lines 188, 190).

The accusers are described as "malicious witnesses" (cf. Deut. 19:17), prepared to pervert justice to destroy him. They are erstwhile friends gleefully watching his "stumbling" (cf. Jer. 20:10) and the difficulties he has encountered. "Ruffians" or "assailants" (NRSV; the Hebrew word is uncertain, and some scholars emend to "strangers") tear him to pieces (v. 15), "gnashing" or grinding their teeth at him (v. 16; see 37:12 and 112:10, where this is an expression of the anger of the wicked).

The intensity and savagery of their attacks lead him into an urgent appeal to God. "How long" (cf. 13:1, though the word translated "how long" here is different) are you going to "look on" — a spectator, as it were, seeing but doing nothing to remedy the situation. Only once God has acted can the psalmist be expected to make his witness of praise and thanksgiving to the "great congrega-tion" and the "mighty throng" (v. 18), both phrases describing the people gathered for worship. It is as if the psalmist refuses to witness to something which he has not proved for himself in his own life. Words, even the greatest theological words, must be capable of being transformed into personal experience, or they remain empty symbols, however eloquently they are proclaimed.

19-28 This section opens with a graphic description of the way in which the accusers are gloating, no doubt believing that their case against the psalmist is as good as won. They are described as "treacherous enemies," prepared to perjure themselves by giving false witness in court (cf. 27:12), people filled with hatred who "wink the eye" (v. 19), giving each other a knowing, conspiratorial wink, as if to say, "He's had it!" To this we may compare the vivid picture in Prov. 6:12-14,

A scoundrel and a villain
   goes around with crooked speech,
winking the eyes, shuffling the feet,
   pointing the fingers,
with perverted mind devising evil,
   continually sowing discord.

They speak words designed to cause trouble and friction, instead of "peace" (*šalôm;* cf. 4:9) among "the quiet of the land," a phrase found only here in the Old Testament, but pointing to the pious and the faithful in the community. That their mouths "open wide" (v. 21) is usually taken to be a sign of contempt or mockery (REB: "Hurrah"). Perhaps it rather indicates satisfied surprise.

The use of the verb "see" pinpoints significant steps in the thought of the psalm. The second scene raised the question, "How long, O LORD, will you look on?" The psalmist's accusers now "see" the trouble he is in. But immediately the confident counterstatement of faith comes: "You have seen, O LORD" (v. 22), and God's seeing must evoke a very different response from that of the psalmist's accusers, for as a prophet declares, "My thoughts are not your thoughts, nor are my ways your ways, says the LORD" (Isa. 55:8). This seeing of the LORD now means that he has something to say about the situation. He will break his silence to reassure the psalmist that he is near, not distant or aloof (v. 22). So the psalmist makes his appeal to the divine judge, "Wake up! Bestir yourself for my defense" (see comment on 7:6-8; 44:23). Give your verdict, says the psalmist, confident that the case will be decided in his favor, for this is a judge who is "my God and my LORD . . . O LORD, my God" (vv. 23, 24), a God who can be depended upon to give a right judgment, much to the chagrin of those who delight in the psalmist's plight.

The scene ends with the contrasting responses to the verdict (vv. 26-28). On the one hand, those who have taken delight in the psalmist's troubles will end up in shame, confusion, and darkness; on the other hand, those who have been supporters of the psalmist will rejoice in the verdict, acclaiming the goodness of the LORD, whose purpose embraces "the welfare *(šalôm)* of his servant" (v. 27). His accusers may have had no word of shalom to speak to the psalmist (v. 20), but the LORD surely has. The psalmist has appealed for help, and his appeal has been sustained, so he ends with a song of praise on his lips (see comment on 7:9-11 and 31:1).

The words of verse 19, "they hated me without cause" (or the similar words from Ps. 69:4), are quoted in John 15:25 as being fulfilled in the hatred which sent Jesus to the cross. There is, however, a difference. The psalmist did not accept such hatred. He rejected it and reacted — and expected God to react — violently against it. Jesus, however, accepted hatred as an inevitable part of his ministry and the ministry of those who seek to follow in his footsteps. Popularity can never be the foundation of the Christian faith nor the hallmark of Christian living. That foundation and hallmark have their roots in this psalm, as Paul reminds us when he argues, in the legal language of the psalm, that "the righteousness of God" is the basis of the gospel. God's righteousness means that our justification — our acquittal — comes to us as a gift from God through the life, death, and resurrection of Jesus, his Son (Rom. 4:21). So the judge's bench becomes the throne of grace.

Psalm 36
LIFE WITHOUT GOD
AND LIFE WITH GOD

Needless difficulties have arisen for the interpretation of this psalm by the failure to recognize the extent to which worship provided a congenial setting for wisdom teaching in ancient Israel (see comment on Psalm 32). Verses 1-4, in wisdom style and imagery, graphically depict life without God. Verses 5-9 describe in hymnic style what life with a gracious God means. The psalm then ends in verses 10-12 with a prayer which springs out of the tension between these two attitudes to life. The description of David as "the servant of the LORD" occurs in the headings to the Psalms only here and in Psalm 18. Its appropriateness here may owe something to the reference to "his servant" in 35:27.

1-4 Any translation of the opening words of the psalm must be tentative. The first word (Hebrew *nĕ'um*), usually translated "oracle" elsewhere in the Old Testament, is most commonly followed by the divine name and refers to a message received by a prophet from God (e.g., Amos 1:5, where the NRSV renders "says the LORD"). Occasionally it is linked to another name (e.g., Balaam in Num. 24:3, 15; David in 2 Sam. 23:1). There is, however, no parallel to it being linked with "transgression" or rebellion, to yield "oracle of transgression" (NRSV: "Transgression speaks"). Is the phrase perhaps being deliberately ironical, as if the only source of inspiration that the wicked have is their own rebellious nature? If any emendation of the text is needed, the most reasonable is to read, "Rebellion is pleasant (Hebrew *na'em*) to the wicked."

"Transgression" (NRSV) and "sin" (REB) are rather colorless translations of a word which means rebellion against lawful authority (see comment on 32:1). The picture drawn in this opening section is of people who accept no higher authority than that of their own desires and plans. As the story in Genesis 2–3 reminds us, this is a recipe for disaster. Put self at the center of life instead of

God and trouble ensues not only for self but for other people. Here are people who want to call the tune. They are utterly devoid of any "fear of God." The word translated "fear" here usually has a sense of dread or terror (cf. Ps. 105:38). Here are people who have dismissed God as totally irrelevant, who have talked themselves into believing that they will never be called to account, or who have become so insensitive that they fail to recognize, far less to hate, the corruption in which they are involved (verse 2 can be interpreted in several different ways; compare NRSV and REB). In word and in deed they lack that wisdom or proper understanding (cf. Prov. 1:3) which leads to the good life (cf. Ps. 14:1-3). Even on their beds they are plotting "mischief" (v. 4; cf. 7:14) which will cause trouble to others. They are prepared to stand on its head the injunction "Depart from evil and do good" (34:14) and to walk along a "no-good" way, happy to be in the company of "evil" (v. 4).

It is hardly surprising that Paul in Rom. 3:18 takes the words of the second half of verse 1, "there is no fear of God before their eyes," and uses them, along with a series of other quotations from the Old Testament, many of them from the Psalms, to underline the universality of human sinfulness. The psalmist, however, is not spinning any theological theories; he is pointing to what often happens in life and insisting that here are facts, facts which any theology must take seriously. To turn a blind eye to the existence of evil is the denial of true faith.

5-9 The psalmist has another story to tell or perhaps to sing. It is the story of the God whose "steadfast love" (cf. 5:7) and "faithfulness" (cf. 26:3) are immeasurable, stretching beyond our earthbound human horizons, and whose "righteousness" (cf. 7:9-11) and "judgments" or decisions encompass the whole of human experience. The "mighty mountains" and "the great deep" symbolize the awesome boundaries within which human life is placed. All of this does not point to a remote God but to one who comes to "save" (cf. 3:2). His steadfast love is there as a "precious" gift for "all people" prepared to take refuge in "the shadow of your wings" (see comment on 17:8).

What is on offer, however, is not merely protection but life in all its fullness. It is sad when religious people assume that what faith offers them is simply their own personal haven to which they can retreat to ride out the storms of life, rather than a life which can provide riches of joy and challenge beyond what anything or anyone else can give.

It is difficult to be sure of the precise allusion in the language of verse 8. The words "the abundance of your house" may refer to the temple with its sacrificial meals, sharing in which became a symbol of the lavishness of all God's grace and goodness. There may be in the words "river of your delights" a hint of the Garden of Eden (Eden being the Hebrew word for "delight") with its river (Gen. 2:10), where life was once as God meant it to be. Or is the whole picture simply that of the world of God's creating in which rich provision has been made to sustain human life? The section ends on a note of quiet confidence. The "fountain of life" (v. 9) describes God as the unfailing source of true life. Jeremiah uses a similar picture in Jer. 2:13 when he describes the God of Israel as the "fountain of living water," in contrast to all other gods, dismissed as "cracked cisterns that can hold no water." "Your light" (v. 9) probably refers to the light of God's face (see comment on 4:6). It is in God's presence that we see light and discover what life really means.

10-12   The celebration of God's graciousness and dependability leads the psalmist into a prayer in which, identifying himself with God's people ("those who know you . . . the upright in heart," v. 10; cf. 7:10), he asks for the continuance of God's "steadfast love" and "salvation." The prayer then returns in verses 11-12 to the wicked in all their arrogant self-confidence. If they were to triumph, the psalmist's faith would be called into question. He therefore prays that they will not be allowed to "tread upon him" like a victorious king putting his foot upon the neck of his defeated enemies, a scene with which we are familiar from ancient Near Eastern pictography. They are to be reduced to impotence, like that of the dead over whom a funeral dirge must be sung (compare the funeral dirge in Amos 5:2, "Fallen, no more to rise, is maiden Israel: forsaken on her land, with no one to raise her up").

It is not characteristic of the Psalms to engage, as we often do, in theological or philosophical explanations of evil in a world believed to be God's world. Rather, the Psalms turn to a faith nurtured in worship. Celebrating in word and action the "steadfast love" and the "faithfulness" of God, they find the bridge between God and this often ungodly world. There is a faith to be lived. The psalmist cannot turn a blind eye to the human perversity which threatens life. He cannot deny the God who comes to him in worship. He lives and prays in the tension which this creates.

Psalm 37
COPING WITH A PUZZLING WORLD

Psalm 37 is an acrostic psalm (see Psalm 9). It is the work of a wisdom teacher whose personal experience is voiced in verses 25 and 35. Nowhere is God addressed directly in the psalm. The content of the psalm has many similarities with the wisdom tradition found in Proverbs. Although a logical connection between the various sections and verses within the psalm is not always clear, running throughout it is one basic theme: What does faith in God mean in a world where wickedness sometimes seems to pay handsome dividends? The central teaching of the psalm is spelled out in verses 1-4, with the rest of the psalm providing a series of variations on the theme. Instead of doing a section-by-section commentary — much of the language is familiar from other psalms — we shall concentrate on certain key elements in the teaching.

1. For those who believe in God, life raises troubling questions, which cannot be ignored. Success often seems to come to the "wicked" or "wrong-doers," people who act perversely. It is such people who "prosper in their way" (v. 7) and successfully carry through what they plan. The word translated "evil devices" in verse 7 (NRSV) may simply mean plans, though often there is an undercurrent of evil in them (cf. 10:2, 4; 21:11). Such plans involve plotting against "the righteous," gnashing their teeth at them (v. 12), mocking them or venting their anger against them (cf. 35:16). They attack "the poor and the needy" (v. 14; cf. 9:12). The goods of life are theirs in abundance (v. 16), yet they are unwilling to pay their debts (v. 21). They use their success to inspire terror (v. 35), dominating the landscape like gigantic trees. The NRSV's rendering "towering like a cedar of Lebanon" (v. 35b; cf. 29:5) assumes the Greek (LXX) text; the Hebrew may be rendered as in the REB, "flourishing as a spreading tree in its native soil," or, as we might say, like oaks which have stood for centuries. This is the world with which we are only too sadly familiar, a world in which, through unscrupulous abuse of power, fortunes are made and the poor go to the wall.

2. All this has a powerful effect on those who seek to remain loyal to God. Three times we hear the words "Do not fret" (vv. 1, 7, 8); the Hebrew verb can mean to be hot with anger. In other words, "Don't get into a tizzy" or "Don't get hot under the collar." That, it is claimed, is entirely the wrong response. Giving way to anger, possibly anger against God for allowing such things to happen, can only lead to evil (v. 8), especially if envy is involved (v. 1). It is often hard not to feel envious of those who have made it to the top, perhaps because of their ruthless selfishness and their willingness to sacrifice everything and everyone standing in their way. The psalmist in Psalm 73 is honest enough to admit, "I was envious of the arrogant; I saw the prosperity of the wicked" (Ps. 73:3). Envy can gnaw away at the vitals of true faith.

3. What then should the response of faith be? However secure and impressive the prosperity of the wicked may seem to be, it is but transitory: "For they will soon fade like the grass and wither like the green herb" (v. 2). This is a picture commonly applied to everything human in the Old Testament (Pss. 90:5; 103:15; Isa. 40:6), but here it is specifically applied to the wicked, as it is in the Aramaic version of Isa. 40:6 (cf. Jas. 1:9, 11, where it is applied to the rich). Repeatedly the psalmist returns to this theme. The wicked will be "cut off" (vv. 9, 11, 38); their day is coming (v. 13), when God will laugh at them (cf. 2:4) and bring them to judgment. Their attacks on the poor and the needy will boomerang (v. 15). Their "arms [i.e., power] shall be broken" (v. 17). They will "perish" and "vanish" (v. 20). Verse 20 is capable of several different interpretations. It may refer to the choicest pastures being burned up in a grass fire, or it may refer to the best of the lambs destined to end up as a sacrificial offering. With a slightly

altered text, it may be comparing the enemies of the LORD to fuel in a furnace going up in smoke (REB). The verdict on the wicked is, in a nutshell, "Here today, but gone tomorrow." The teacher claims that this is a verdict verified by his own experience.

But what of those struggling to hold on to faith? Their response should be that of joyful trust in God (vv. 3-4), which will be gloriously vindicated (vv. 4, 6), especially if it goes hand in hand with a quality of life consistent with such a trust (vv. 3, 27; cf. 34:15). Such a life will be characterized by generosity (vv. 21, 26) backed up with words which respect the rights of other people — words of wisdom based on experience (v. 30). Such a life will be nurtured on "the law of their God," not as some stern call to duty, but as a guide at the very center of life, "in their hearts" (cf. Ps. 1:2; Prov. 10:31).

The language here needs teasing out. What does trusting in the LORD mean for this teacher? It certainly does not mean grim resignation. It means taking "delight" in the LORD (cf. Isa. 58:14), the kind of delight that Job insists is not open to the godless (Job 27:10), the kind of delight which in Isa. 66:11 is compared to what a child receives at its mother's breast. It is the kind of delight that people naturally have when things are going well and they are enjoying abundant "prosperity" (šalôm; cf. 4:9). Trusting in the LORD means "Commit your way to the LORD" (v. 5) — literally, "roll your way upon the LORD," that is, let God take the strain; don't try to go it alone. These words provided the framework for Paul Gerhardt's great hymn, "Put thou thy trust in God." Trusting means "Be still before the LORD" (v. 7), literally "Be silent" — not the silence of blind resignation but the stillness which refuses to become a prey to the fretting and the envy noted in the opening words of the psalm. "Be still . . . and wait patiently for him." The verb translated "wait patiently" is not found elsewhere in the Old Testament with this meaning, but in context it probably means "bide your time," for God will act.

The words used to describe those who seek to keep faith with God are familiar from other psalms: "the righteous" (vv. 12, 16, 21, 25, 30, 39), "the upright" (vv. 14, 37), and "the blameless" (vv. 18, 37). What are they promised? One phrase keeps echoing across the psalm: "you will live in the land" (v. 3); they "shall inherit the land" (vv. 9, 11, 22, 29, 34). What does this mean? The word translated "land" is the word we have already met in other psalms meaning "the earth," the world. Here it has a more restricted sense. The "land" is the land of Canaan, the land promised by God to Abraham (Gen. 12:4; Deut. 1:8), a goodly land where a people obedient to God were to live under God's protection (see 25:13). The land is central to much of the Old Testament and is a symbol of the promises of God and the hopes centering on those promises. Associated with the land, therefore, is "security" (v. 3), the people's rightful "heritage" (v. 18), the place where the people will live out their lives in obedience or disobedience and experience either blessing or curse (Deuteronomy 28). The "land," therefore, is like a divinely organized theater in which a drama is being played out. "The righteous" belong to the resident company who are at home on this stage, but "the wicked" never feel at home there. This feeling of being at home, of belonging to the resident company of the kingdom of God, is expressed in the third Beatitude: "Blessed are the meek, for they shall inherit the earth" (Matt. 5:5; cf. v. 11). The psalm operates throughout on an essentially practical level. It points to an attitude of faith which can face life, recognize its anomalies, yet retain a lively hope based on the conviction that whatever may happen the LORD does deliver. He does provide "refuge" (v. 39) or a stronghold (cf. 27:1) for those prepared to entrust themselves to his protection. This, the language of the last two verses, is the answer to the fretting and envy registered in verse 1.

Yet the psalm does leave us with some unanswered questions, highlighted by the teacher's personal testimony in verse 25, "I have been young, and am now old, yet I have not seen the righteous forsaken or their children begging bread." In context this could be the psalmist's graphic way of underlining the traditional belief that the righteous are never permanently forsaken by God. They may face difficulties; they may stumble; but underneath there is always a steadying hand (v. 24). They remain generous, kindhearted, and their children, instead of having to beg from others, are a source of blessing to others (v. 26). If, however, this is intended to be a literal statement of fact, then either this psalmist moved in very elite circles or was astonishingly blind to what was going on around him. The New English Bible had such a problem with this verse that it transferred the begging children from the righteous in verse 25 to the wicked in verse 20! There are theological issues here which this psalmist does not even begin to explore. He would have been happy with the theology of Job's friends. He has never been where Job has been, nor asked his questions about life out of the raw agony of someone whom bitter experience has led to angry protest to God, instead of being still before God.

Psalm 38
A PRAYER BORN OF SUFFERING

Although this is not an acrostic psalm, it shadows Psalm 37 and the alphabetic structure by having twenty-two verses (cf. Psalm 33). It is not clear what is intended by the word in the heading translated "for the memorial offering" by the NRSV and "for commemoration" by the REB. The NRSV assumes a link with the grain offerings in which a "token [or: "memorial"] portion" was offered to God (cf. Lev. 2:2; 24:7). Equally this might be a psalm designed to help the worshipper to "remember" and to relive in God's presence the suffering he has been enduring. Psalm 70 is the only other psalm with this word in its heading.

The psalm begins (v. 1) and ends (vv. 21-22) in prayer directed to God. The central section of the psalm, however, is in the form of a lament, which in verses 2-10 describes the psalmist's suffering and in verses 11-20 outlines how he coped with the hostile reaction to it from other people, both friends and enemies. The psalm's causal link of suffering with sin (vv. 3-4) and its confession of sin (v. 18) have won it a place in Christian tradition among the penitential psalms (see comment on Psalm 6).

1-2 Verse 1 is a repetition with minor variations of Ps. 6:1. The attribution of the psalmist's suffering to the "anger" of God is developed in the striking imagery of verse 2. The picture of God's arrows sinking into the psalmist's flesh may bear the influence of imagery associated with the Canaanite god Resheph, the plague-bringing god of the arrow. In similar fashion Job bitterly complains, "The arrows of the Almighty are in me" (Job 6:4). It is not surprising that the psalmist feels that God's hand has come down heavily upon him (cf. 32:4).

3-10 These verses describe the psalmist's dire condition. There have been many attempts to diagnose precisely what disease or diseases were wracking the psalmist's body, with guesses ranging all the way from leprosy to syphilis to gonorrhea. The picture is of a man in the grip of a life-threatening illness which is rampaging through his body and evidenced by outward and inward symptoms. The words "no sound-ness in my flesh" occur twice (vv. 3 and 7). The condition is manifested in foul and festering "wounds" or weals (v. 5), in burning loins wracked with fever (v. 7), in ever increasing physical weakness, in failing eyesight (v. 10), and in a throbbing heart (v. 10). This has been taken to point to a serious heart condition. The word translated "throbs" means more literally "traveling to and fro." If, however, the heart means, as it often does in Hebrew, the mind or the will, the picture may be of someone who can no longer concentrate, whose mind keeps wandering. Certainly he is in mental as well as physical pain (vv. 6, 8); thus he is "spent" or numb, bruised and battered, screaming out in pain. The word translated "sighing" in verse 9 is nowhere else in the Old Testament used of a cry of human distress. It usually describes the "roaring" of a lion. "Sighing" seems too mild to do justice to this word. The "longing" (v. 9) is a cry to be free from the suffering. Small wonder the psalmist declares that there is "no health *(šalôm)* in his bones" (v. 3).

 Where this psalm parts company from Psalm 6 is in the psalmist's conviction that what he is suffering is the direct result of his "sin" and "iniquities" (see 32:1). They are compared to waves breaking over his head and threatening to drown him and to a burden too heavy for him to carry (v. 4). What these sins are, we are not told, and there is no use in speculating. Yet for the psalmist they are real, the reason for his alienation from God expressed in his suffering.

11-20 The psalmist is conscious of alienation not only from God but also from his fellow human beings, among them those who were once his "friends and companions" and his "neighbors" (v. 11). They are now shunning him in his "affliction" (REB: "sickness"; the word can mean leprosy, but it probably has a wider meaning here). It is not merely revulsion which makes them "stand far off" (v. 11). Like Job's friends, they are sure that his present condition must be the result of serious moral defects. They no longer have any sympathy for him but are out to destroy him (cf. Job 30:9-15). The alienation is so acute that the psalmist is past listening to their cruel and provocative comments, and he knows that no words of his can alter the situation. As far as they are concerned, he can only play the deaf mute (vv. 13-14).

Yet the psalmist believes that there is still one to whom he can speak, the God whose anger he is experiencing, the God from whom he feels alienated, the God who yet knows what his true needs and longings are (v. 9). He is prepared to "wait in hope" (cf. 42:5, 11) till an answer comes. While he waits, the first thought that fills his mind is that those who are trying to make capital out of his plight should not get that satisfaction (v. 16). ("I pray" is the NRSV's interpretation of the Hebrew word meaning "to speak," but which can also mean "to think.")

Who are these people? And who are those described in verses 19 and 20 as "my foes . . . who hate me . . . who render me evil . . . my adversaries"? ("Adversaries" may also be rendered "accusers"; cf. 71:13; 109:4, 20, 29; the word is from the same root as "the Satan," who appears among the divine beings of God's heavenly court as a prosecuting attorney in Job 1:6-11.) They are still the "friends and companions" of verse 11, but their attitude towards him has radically changed. They have now become his "mortal foes," or — with a slight textual change — his foes "without cause" (cf. 35:7), since he has never done them any harm but only good (cf. 35:12). Indeed, they seem to be down on him because he has been intent on treating them generously and fairly. Suffering can lead to this breakdown in human relationships. It can bring with it a sense of isolation and misunderstanding. That is all too common in certain types of mental illness and in the case of people with severe physical defects. It has reared its ugly head in religious circles concerning the AIDS epidemic, where fears and the glib understanding of AIDS as the judgment of God on homosexuality have led to ostracizing those suffering from AIDS.

The sin which the psalmist is prepared to confess (v. 18), the iniquity which "troubles" him (REB) or causes him anxiety has, therefore, nothing to do with these friends, now turned enemies. He protests that he has never done them any harm, but only good. What he confesses must be something else — we know not what — that he must bring out into the open and get out of his system.

21-22 In closing the psalmist turns again to prayer. He does not ask specifically for healing. In words which recall the agonized cries in Psalm 22, he prays, "Do not forsake me, O LORD . . . do not be far from me . . . make haste to help me." He does not pray for pain and suffering to disappear. What he does pray for is that the one whom he describes as "my God" and "my salvation" will now be present with him even in the midst of his pain and agony, giving him the help he needs. In the very act of reaching out to the God from whom nothing can ever finally alienate him, he is in touch with healing which can speak to his deepest needs.

There is no one approach to suffering in the Bible, not even within the Psalms. Whereas Psalm 6 makes no attempt to link it with sin, Psalm 38 does. Whatever the explanation offered, whatever the questions and the doubts it brings (see Psalm 22), there is the quiet yet defiant conviction that suffering can never have the last word. Those who hold on in hope, even in the midst of continuing pain, point us forward to that vision of the new heaven and the new earth:

"See, the home of God is among mortals.
He will dwell with them;
they will be his peoples,
and God himself will be with them;
he will wipe every tear from their eyes.
Death will be no more;
mourning and crying and pain will be no more,
for the first things have passed away." (Rev. 21:3-4)

Psalm 39
A TROUBLED LIFE

This is one of the psalms which have in their heading "to Jeduthun." The others are Psalms 62 and 77, which read "according to Jeduthun." Although other interpretations have been proposed, it is likely that Jeduthun should be taken as a personal name. 1 Chronicles lists Jeduthun among the temple Levites and links him specifically with the musical accompaniment for sacred songs (1 Chron. 16:42).

From beginning to end a troubled soul speaks to us in this psalm, a man reaching out for assurance in face of unanswered questions. But what has brought the psalmist to the end of his tether? It is hard to be sure. Verse 10 would be consistent with severe suffering, though there is really no clue what kind of suffering. Is it physical or mental or both? We hear echoes of Job in the psalm, especially Job 7:16-21:

"I loathe my life; I would not live forever.
Let me alone, for my days are a breath." (Job 7:16; cf. v. 5)

"Will you not look away from me for a while.
Let me alone. . . ." (Job 7:19; cf. v. 13a)

"Why do you not pardon my transgression
and take away my iniquity?
For now I shall lie in the earth;
you will seek me, but I shall not be."

(Job 7:21; cf. vv. 8 and 13b)

But on the lips of Job these are words of protest, desperately challenging the simplistic assumptions of his friends on the causal link between sin and suffering. The psalmist's standpoint is much more one of puzzlement.

1-3 The psalm springs out of a situation where the psalmist has decided to face the crisis in his life with silent acceptance, "as long as the wicked are in my presence" (v. 1). It is as if he has concluded that any angry, bitter, and impatient outburst would be misunderstood, especially by people who were only too anxious to have their negative thoughts about God confirmed. He has no intention of accepting an invitation to join the club of "the wicked." An outwardly quiet, dignified silence would be his response (v. 2). The translation "to no avail" (v. 2) is questionable. Literally, the word means "from good" or "without good" (GNB: "about anything good"). The REB's rendering, "I refrained from speech," assumes another root. It could be translated "concerning good things," as if the psalmist could not trust himself to speak even about good things lest an undercurrent of bitterness come through his words. Outwardly he was silent, but inwardly he was in turmoil. Silence offered no solace. The more he tried to bottle up his feelings, the greater his distress, "my heart became hot within me . . . the fire burned" (v. 3). In different circumstances, Jeremiah found himself facing the same tension. Having decided to renounce his prophetic ministry, which seemed to be going nowhere, and having decided to speak no more for God, he discovered, "within me there is something like a burning fire shut up in my bones; I am weary with holding it in, and I cannot" (Jer. 20:9). Something had to give. The psalmist's silence is replaced by an emotional outburst.

4-6 He wants some explanation from God concerning the brevity and transitoriness of human life. He wants to know "the measure [or: "number"] of my days," how "fleeting" or "short" (REB) life is to be (v. 4). God has set the length of his life at a few "handbreadths," the measurement across the base of the four fingers (cf. Exod. 25:25), virtually "nothing" in the sight of God. Human life, in spite of its apparent stability, is "a mere breath" (REB: "a puff of wind"; Hebrew *hebel,* the word often translated "vanity" or "futility" in Ecclesiastes). Life is as insubstantial as a "shadow" (cf. 62:9; 73:20). The same verdict applies to all human endeavor and its fruits, including wealth and possessions; it is all "for nothing" (v. 6). This is not morbidity. It is a healthy, albeit troubling, recognition that the one certain fact in life is death. In recognizing this, the psalmist parts company from "the wicked," who in their arrogant self-confidence banish such thoughts (cf. 73:3-12). Longfellow in his "Psalm of Life" echoes what troubles the psalmist: "Time is fleeting. And our hearts, though stout and brave, still like muffled dreams are beating funeral marches to the grave."

7-11 The psalmist, accepting that the verdict on all human life must be *hebel*, "a mere breath" (v. 11), now turns to God as the only possible source of hope (for the meaning of "wait" in v. 7, see 25:3; 37:34). Since this transitory life with all its perplexities is God's doing, there is no obvious way in which he can talk his way through to easy answers (v. 9). He is back in silent acceptance, asking only for deliverance from the way in which he has affronted God's authority (for "transgressions" in v. 8, see comment on 32:1) and protection from those who foolishly try to exploit his plight. He prays for healing, for the removal of what he can only regard as the deliberately heavy hand which God has laid upon him (v. 10). He recognizes that any human verdict on life may be wide of the mark. What people desire in life may be consumed "like a moth" (v. 11). The picture here is not entirely clear. The image of the moth may be used because of the brevity of its life or, as in other passages in the Old Testament, because it silently eats away and destroys (cf. Job 13:28, where Job likens his fragile life to "a garment which is moth-eaten"). If there is hope expressed in these verses, it is hope hanging by a slender thread. The tensions and the pain in the psalmist's life remain; his questions are unanswered.

Nor do the concluding verses take us much further. As in many other psalms, there is the appeal to God to listen to the psalmist's cry (cf. 4:1), but it is a cry born of tears, by someone who is conscious that he is merely a "passing guest" or "a resident alien" in this world — here for a few years, then destined to depart and cease to be. The "passing guest" or the stranger had a recognized place in Hebrew society, with rights which had to be safeguarded. Deut. 10:19 bases the treatment of the stranger on the remembrance that the Hebrews themselves had once been strangers in Egypt. Similarly, Lev. 25:23 reminds the people that they were once only "resident aliens" in the land. Both "passing guest" and "alien" are here used to underline the transitoriness of life in this world.

What do the opening words of verse 13 mean? "Turn your gaze away from me, that I may smile again." Many psalmists express the desire to see God's face or to have God's face turned towards them (see comment on 11:7). Here we have the stark opposite. It finds its parallel in several passages in Job (e.g., Job 7:19; 14:6). It is as if the psalmist, holding God responsible for what has happened to him (v. 9), says to God, "Get off my back, leave me alone. Stop fixing your eye on me. Leave me to enjoy the few years which are left to me before I pass into the nothingness of Sheol" (cf. 6:5).

Whatever these words mean, they are not words of submissive, untroubled faith. Sometimes in the Psalms the dialogue with God ends far short of unquestioning trust. That is why a psalm like this one can speak so powerfully to many today who find themselves in a similar situation, unable to eliminate God from their life, yet unable to find in God answers to their deepest perplexities.

Psalm 40
THANKSGIVING FOR AN ANSWERED CRY

Many scholars believe that Psalm 40 in its present form is the result of the merging of two originally independent psalms: verses 1-10, a typical psalm of thanksgiving; verses 11-17, a psalm of supplication or lament. It is often argued in support of this that the order of the two parts of the psalm is illogical; the supplication (vv. 11-17) ought to lead into thanksgiving, not vice versa. We have, however, already explored in our comments on Psalms 9 and 10 the polarity of confidence and perplexity. Very often it is faith which leads to questioning as surely as questioning leads to faith. There is no reason why thanksgiving for what God has done in the past should not be the basis of a cry for help in the present.

But who is this "I" who once waited, received God's help (v. 1), and now pleads for God to help him again (v. 13)? A case can be made for seeing this as a royal psalm, with the "I" as the king, leading his people in worship, witnessing to them concerning the great things God has done for him and, through him, for the nation. It is, however, far from clear that we must give the psalm this interpretation. The "I" may be an otherwise unidentified individual who has survived a serious illness or some other traumatic experience which took him to death's door and who once again seeks help in an hour of crisis. He gladly witnesses to what God has done for him in the past (v. 10), and this encourages him to commit his present troubles in confidence to God.

1-5 The psalmist begins by describing the experience upon which everything else in the psalm turns. "I waited patiently" is a questionable translation of the opening words, especially if it conveys a picture of quiet resignation. The Hebrew idiom "waiting I waited" strongly emphasizes the act of waiting, hence the NEB translates, "I waited, waited." Such waiting often has the idea of an eager hopefulness built into it (cf. 25:3), and it was this hopefulness, claims the psalmist, which was triumphantly vindicated. His cry was heard. Instead of being trapped in "the desolate [or: "roaring"] pit" and "miry bog" (v. 2), both of which may be images of the underworld of the dead (cf. 6:5), he has been rescued and now has firm ground beneath his feet ("rock" or "crag" in v. 2 is a common description of God and the security he offers; cf. 18:2). This experience overflows into gratitude, in the praise of God celebrated in "a new song" (cf. 33:3) "to our God" (v. 3). So we move from "my feet," "my steps," and "my mouth" to "our God" and a faith to be shared, open to "many" (v. 3b); and in verse 5 from "O LORD, my God" to "your thoughts towards us." This is a faith which calls forth that "fear" which is reverence (cf. 19:9; 34:7), faith which is based on "trust" (cf. 4:5), a faith which is exclusively focused on the LORD. It never compromises with "the proud" or with those "who go astray after false gods" (REB: "the treacherous"), literally "those who turn aside to falsehood." "Falsehood," however, is one of the words the Old Testament uses to describe other gods, hence the NRSV rendering. Whether verse 4 points to open apostasy from the LORD or simply to a type of conduct which is equally a denial of his claim on the lives of his people, it indicates the road along which people must not travel if they wish to find true happiness (see 1:1). Instead they must live acknowledging the incomparable generosity of God, whose "wondrous deeds" (cf. 9:1) and purposes cannot be contained within the inadequate parameters of human speech. Participating in an act of worship in which the community celebrates its rich tradition of faith, the psalmist knows that he is surrounded by amazing grace. So the author of Ephesians will look back to all that God has given in Christ and respond in a prayer which asks for "the power to comprehend, with all the saints, what is the breadth and length and height and depth, and to know the love of Christ that surpasses knowledge" (Eph. 3:18-19). True faith must never lose a sense of abiding wonder.

6-8 The essential message of these verses, God's preference for obedience over animal sacrifice, corresponds to what we find frequently in prophetic teaching (e.g., Amos 5:21-24; Mic. 6:6-8; Jer. 7:21-28; cf. 1 Sam. 15:22) and in other Psalms (cf. Psalms 50, 51) . It would be a mistake to read such passages as a denial of the value or importance of the sacrificial cult. The different types of sacrifice were expressions of different spiritual needs. The "sacrifice" *(zebaḥ)* involved an animal offering and took the form of a shared meal, uniting God, the priests, and the worshippers in a sacramental relationship. The "offering" *(minḥâ)* was a gift, often of cereal, which could express gratitude for favors received or simply be a recognition of the worshippers' status before God. The "burnt offering" *(ʿōlâ)*, the sacrifice which went up *(ʿālâ)* to God as the whole of the animal was burnt on the altar, was an expression of the worshippers' self-offering to God. The "sin offering" *(ḥaṭṭāʾt)* was designed to neutralize any accidental or unintentional offenses against God. The detailed regulations for the different kinds of sacrifice are found in Leviticus 1–7.

Worship in Israel, as in the ancient world in general, always involved such sacrifices. They were a God-given means of grace, but, as these verses insist, they were valueless unless they went hand in hand with an inner dedication to God which expresses itself in joyful obedience. If the worshipper lacked such obedience, the sacrifices were a meaningless charade. For precisely the same reason, Isaiah passes a similar verdict on prayer (Isa. 1:15). It is this obedience which is indicated in verse 6b in the words "you have given me an open ear," literally, "ears you have dug for me." This expression is found nowhere else in the Old

Testament. Some have linked it with Exod. 21:6, where a Hebrew slave, who for personal reasons declines the freedom which is his by right at the end of six years, is brought to a door or doorpost "and his master shall pierce his ear with an awl; and he shall serve him for life." Is this, then, the picture of someone who is committed to be God's willing slave or servant for life? The language in the Exodus passage, however, is very different from that in verse 6, and it is wiser to assume that we are here dealing with an otherwise unattested Hebrew idiom which means "you have given me receptive ears" (REB), that is, made me able to listen and obey. The phrase early caused difficulties. The Greek (LXX) has "a body you have prepared for me," and this is how it is quoted in Heb. 10:5.

The words "Here I am" or "Here I come" have been taken to indicate that the psalmist is offering himself as a sacrifice in place of an animal, but they more likely indicate that the psalmist is placing himself at God's disposal (cf. Isa. 6:8), with a pledge to take upon himself what is written "in the scroll of the book" (v. 7). What book and what passage are far from clear. If the psalmist is the king, then the passage concerning kingship in Deut. 17:14-20 springs to mind. However, if, as we have argued, this is not a royal psalm, then the Shema in Deut. 6:4-5 would be appropriate, demanding as it does exclusive loyalty to the LORD (cf. v. 4) and daily obedience spelled out in the words "You shall love the LORD your God with all your heart, and with all your soul, and with all your mind."

Heb. 10:5-7 quotes these verses following the Greek (LXX) text. It provides them with a new context in which they refer to the incarnation of Christ who through his perfect obedience to God offered the one, eternal sacrifice which supersedes all other sacrifices and makes them irrelevant. Hebrews as a whole provides an interesting example of the way in which the coinage of the Old Testament can be reminted with the image of Christ stamped upon it.

9-10 Joyful obedience, based upon an experience of God's grace, is something which must be shared with others, with the whole company of God's people, "the great congregation" (vv. 9, 10; cf. 35:18). The words "faithfulness" (see 25:5), "salvation" (see 3:8), and "steadfast love" (see 5:7) come pouring out of the psalmist. These are the great, God-given realities which now underpin his life. Not to share this "glad news" is for him unthinkable. Behind the translation "glad news" there is a Hebrew verb (cf. Isa. 40:9) which in its Greek form indicates the proclamation of the good news or the gospel in the New Testament (cf. Mark 1.14), good news which Jesus came to share in word and in deed, good news which from the beginning the followers of Jesus were under obligation to share wherever they went (cf. Acts 8:25). Wherever people nurtured in the biblical tradition gather for worship, there is good news to be shared.

11-12 We now reach the turning point in the psalm, the change in mood which has puzzled so many commentators. From joyful thanksgiving the psalmist now turns to urgent petition. He cannot live in the past. He faces present difficulties, which are partly the result of things over which he has no control. They are "evils" or "misfortunes" (REB) which threaten to engulf him (cf. 18:5) but are partly the result of his own "iniquities," a word which can either mean perversity or the guilt which is its consequence (cf. 25:11). The words "until I cannot see" (v. 12) could refer to fading eyesight, as in 38:10; but it is more likely that both they and the words "my heart fails me" point to a person who doesn't know where to turn in face of the problems which surround him. The phrase "more than the hairs of my head" occurs again in Ps. 69:4, where it indicates the countless enemies who are out to destroy the psalmist.

There is only one place to which he can turn, to the "mercy" or compassion (see 25:6), to the "steadfast love" and "faithfulness" which are in his own and in his people's past. They alone can and must provide him with protection and security in the midst of his present difficulties, otherwise there would be a yawning gap between what he professed to believe and what life now means. Unless we can cash the credit God has freely placed at our disposal, we remain spiritually bankrupt.

13-17   These verses appear again, with minor linguistic variations, as Psalm 70. Twice Psalm 70 uses the word "God" (*ĕlōhîm*) where these verses have "LORD" (Yahweh). Psalm 70 omits the initial word of verse 13, "Be pleased," and reads "hasten to me, O God," instead of "the LORD takes thought for me" in verse 17. Psalm 40 has "be appalled" in verse 15, while Psalm 70 has "turn back."

It is possible that the author of Psalm 40 was using a psalm with which he was already familiar, Psalm 70, and adapting it to his own use, just as certain words used in prayers or hymns may trigger off in our minds the recollection of other prayers or hymns. Nor is the link solely with Psalm 70; verse 15 recalls 35:21, and verse 16 has echoes of 35:27. However much a psalm may reflect personal experience, it finds its context within a shared liturgical tradition.

Verse 13 begins with an urgent plea which finds its counterpart in the closing verse of the psalm. The God with whom the psalmist pleads to "make haste to help me" (v. 13) is the God who in verse 17 is described as "You are my help." The words "to deliver me" are picked up in the description of God in verse 17 as "my deliverer" or "rescuer," with a different but synonymous word. In between, the psalmist turns his thoughts to two different categories of people. First are those who are out to destroy or to hurt him. He prays that the shame and dishonor they seek to inflict upon him may boomerang, becoming their "shame" (vv. 15-16). Second are those who share the psalmist's faith in the goodness and greatness of God, "all who seek you" (see 24:6). He prays that they may share the joy and gladness which such a faith engenders (see 35:27).

The psalm ends where it began, in personal experience, with the psalmist in his human frailty and need — "I am poor and needy" (see 9:12) — reaching out to the one whom he has good reason to know as "my God."

Psalm 41
A HEALING LITURGY

This is a psalm which cries out for a liturgical context to bring it to life and hold together the different elements within it. The different headings given to it by commentators highlight the problem: "Blessed Are the Merciful" (Knight, Anderson), focusing on the opening section with its links with the wisdom tradition (see Psalm 1); "Complaint of a Sufferer" (Delitzsch), or "When a Man Is Down" (Kidner), focusing on the lament element in verses 4-10; "Cured from Illness . . . Rescued from Enemies" (Weiser), focusing on the element of thanksgiving for answered prayer in verses 11-12.

All these elements come together most naturally if we view the psalm as "A Liturgy for the Sick" (Craigie), in which a sick person comes to the temple for healing. It is, therefore, a psalm which may very appropriately be used in contemporary services of healing.

1-3 The worshipper who comes seeking healing is first reminded by the priest, using the characteristic wisdom formula "Happy are" (see Psalm 1), that God's healing power and renewal come to "those who consider the poor." We have already met the word translated "consider," both in the heading and in the body of Psalm 32. Here it points to the person who has acted wisely in his dealings with the "poor," or rather with "the weak, the helpless." This Hebrew word *(dal)* is not one of the words noted in Psalm 9, though it is often used in parallelism with words indicating the poor and the needy (cf. 82:3, 4; 113:7). What the worshipper expects from God, he must be prepared to extend to others. Help from God in his "day of trouble" (v. 1) means holding out a helping hand to others in their days of trouble. To ask anything from God is to be left asking questions about ourselves and our attitude to others. This is what the sick person is asked to remember as he comes in his weakness to the LORD who protects, who is the source of a "happy" or "secure" (REB) life (v. 2). The Hebrew in verse 2 may refer either to the God who is on the side of those who are under attack by enemies or the God who is always reassuringly there in time of trouble. The last line of verse 3 — in Hebrew "you change all his bed in his illness" — may mean, as both the NRSV and REB translations indicate, that God transforms the sick person's illness into health. On the other hand, it may evoke the picture of a kindly relative or nurse changing the bed clothes to make the sufferer more comfortable. Whatever the picture, it is an invitation to the sick person to place himself in his weakness in the hands of a caring God.

4-10 This section begins (v. 4) and ends (v. 10) with a prayer at the heart of which is an appeal to the LORD to "be gracious to me" (see 4:1), the prayer of one who in the face of illness confesses "I have sinned against you" (cf. 38:3, 4,

18). In between, in verses 5-9, the psalmist tells the story of his plight, not by describing the symptoms of his serious illness (contrast Psalm 38), but by focusing upon the response of other people to what has happened to him. If those who consider the weak are indeed happy, then the psalmist knows too many people who will never know this happiness. The vultures surround him. On his sickbed he is visited by those whom he can only describe as "my enemies" (v. 5), people maliciously looking forward to his death — people who no doubt mouth conventionally comforting words in his presence but then go out to gossip and to whisper. They are convinced that he is in the grip of a "deadly thing" (Hebrew *běliya'al*, v. 8; see comment on 18:4). There is always an ominous or menacing overtone to this word. It might mean a devilish disease, a lethal poison, or as the REB suggests, "An evil spell." Perhaps he is regarded as being under a curse which is irrevocably working out its deadly effect in his life. His death is assured. The unkindest cut of all was that among these enemies was "my bosom friend" (literally, "a friend of my shalom"), once a trusted and welcome guest who had shared his hospitality. This is the man who now "has lifted his heel against me," an expression not found elsewhere, but which in context probably indicates someone who, in spite of past friendship, was now prepared to crush the psalmist under foot. John 13:18 quotes verse 9b and sees its fulfillment in the act of betrayal by Judas Iscariot, one of many instances in which the psalms are woven into the passion narrative in the Gospels.

The psalmist's prayer after restoration to health in verse 10 ends with the words "that I may repay them." Here the psalmist in his bitterness wishes to do what other psalmists ask God to do. It is futile to try to justify this attitude as anything other than a very human response which falls far short of the words from the cross, "Father, forgive them; for they do not know what they are doing" (for a fuller discussion of this, see 5:9-10).

11-12 The psalm concludes with a ringing statement of confidence (vv. 11-12), which may have followed words in the liturgy which assured the sick person that his prayer had been heard and healing granted, or may, as the REB translation implies, simply anticipate that his prayer will be answered. Any such answer means God saying "No" to the attacks and hopes of his enemies, and "Yes" to the psalmist's "integrity" (see 25:21). His future is assured in the presence of God.

13 This is the final psalm in the collection we know as Book One. It forms a natural closure to the book, since it echoes at many points the language of the opening psalm, Psalm 1. Compare, for example, Pss. 1:1 and 41:1; 1:5 and 41:8; 1:6 and 41:5; 1:2 and 41:11. Psalm 41 ends (v. 13), as do all the psalms which close the different collections, with a doxology — a prayer of thanksgiving for all that the LORD is and does for his people.

The words "Blessed be the LORD" introduce the concluding doxologies in 72:18; 89:52; and 106:48 and are swallowed up in the great song of praise which is Psalm 150. The twofold "Amen" here and in 72:19 and 89:52, together with the "Amen" and the "Hallelujah" of 106:48, indicates the congregation's firm and committed response to what they have heard. It is a far cry from the sugary and resigned choral amens to which many a congregation listens today. It is a ringing affirmation, a response which declares "I'll stake my life on that" and sends the worshippers out into the world to prove the truth of the One whom they worship, "the God of Israel."

BOOK TWO

PSALMS 42–72

About half the psalms in Book Two (Psalms 42–72) have in their headings the association with David, and the book ends at Ps. 72:20 with the words "The prayers of David, the son of Jesse, are ended." Psalm 72, however, is linked with Solomon, and Psalm 50 is associated with Asaph. There is a major collection of psalms, Psalms 42–49, linked with the Korahites, and there are other such Korahite psalms in Book Three, Psalms 84–85 and 87–88. According to Chronicles, the "sons of Korah" were Levites who served as "guardians of the thresholds of the tabernacle, as their ancestors had been in charge of the camp of the LORD, the guardians of the entrance" (1 Chron. 9:19). Their place in the postexilic Jerusalem temple, therefore, is clear. What is not clear is what lies behind this. Numbers 16 recounts a story of Korah's challenge to the authority of Moses. This may point to inner tensions within the priesthood, but it is difficult to trace their history. M. D. Goulder has traced the history of the sons of Korah back to the northern shrine of Dan. He sees the psalms attributed to them as having their origin in an eight-day autumnal festival at Dan in the ninth and eighth centuries BCE. Much of this is highly speculative, as must be any account of this collection of Korahite psalms. Ultimately, of course, the origin of these psalms does not necessarily tell us much about how they spoke to those who gathered for worship in the Jerusalem temple in postexilic times. Nor does it tell us much about how they have been used in Christian worship or may be used today.

Psalms 42 and 43
LIGHT IN THE DARKNESS

Psalm 43 is one of two psalms in Book Two without a heading, the other being Psalm 71. This, along with other features, suggests that Psalm 43 was originally

141

a continuation of Psalm 42. Three times we hear the same refrain: "Why are you cast down, O my soul" (42:5; 42:11; 43:5), with the psalmist's complaint and plight described in very similar language in 42:9 and 43:2. At the heart of this lament is the experience of someone prevented by circumstances not wholly clear to us from joining fellow worshippers in a joyful religious festival in "the house of God" (v. 4), probably the Jerusalem temple. The worshipper's sense of deprivation, his longing for the restoration of a lost privilege, finds moving expression throughout the psalm. As in other psalms of lament, there is movement back and forth between complaint and trust (see Psalms 9 and 10), with complaint finding expression in urgent questions — "When?" (42:2), "Why?" (42:5, 9, 11; 43:2, 5) — and in the sarcastic comment of other people, "Where is your God?" (42:3, 10). For "maskil" in the heading of Psalm 42, see the comment on Psalm 32.

1-3   The vivid simile with which the psalm begins underlines the desperate nature of the psalmist's plight. As a doe or hind roams across a parched landscape (cf. Jer. 14:1-6) and longs, or perhaps "cries out," for running water, so this psalmist longs or cries out for God, whose name is on his lips four times in the first two verses. The expression "the living God" is found again in the Psalms only in 84:2 (but see comment on 36:9; cf. Jer. 2:13). The psalmist knows that there is only one person who can satisfy his spiritual thirst. For the moment, however, he lives among people who mock his faith, sarcastically asking "Where is your God?" (v. 3). This question is found elsewhere in the Old Testament (e.g., Ps. 79:10; 115:2; Joel 2:17), usually on the lips of pagans making a mockery of the people of Israel facing national disaster. Here, however, it is simply "they" who so speak, identified in the repetition of the question in verse 10 as the psalmist's "adversaries" or foes. They might be foreigners if, as some think, the psalmist is in exile; equally they may be fellow Israelites who no longer share the psalmist's faith. Faced with this hostile environment, the psalmist can only ask, "When shall I come and behold the face of God?" Instead of "behold" or see, the traditional Hebrew text reads with different vowels "appear" in the presence of God (cf. REB). This may be an attempt to tone down the original reading in the light of the conviction expressed elsewhere, "You cannot see my face; for no one shall see me and live" (Exod. 33:20). But just as in daily life "to see someone's face" is to be admitted to that person's presence, so here the psalmist wishes to be admitted to God's presence at the temple (cf. 17:15).

4-5   The tension which is so evident in the psalmist's life is now further explained. His pent-up feelings come pouring out. The "things" he remembers (v. 40) are his past joyful experiences of sharing in worship. Although the language of verse 4, particularly the word translated "throng" and the verb which goes with it, is far from certain (cf. REB), the general picture is clear. Here is a person who once joyfully participated with his fellow worshippers in one of the great religious festivals centering on the temple (cf. Psalm 24). What that meant to him is indelibly imprinted on his memory. It is there, part of his life, to be placed over against the bleakness of his present plight. Neither can be ignored. Both appear in the refrain which we hear for the first time in verse 5; on the one hand, he is "cast down," despairing, "disquieted," or in turmoil; on the other hand, he must still "hope" (cf. 38:15) that one day he will again join in the praise of God whose acts of deliverance are celebrated in worship. It is because both these things are part of his life that the refrain begins with "Why?" They stand in irreconcilable tension. It is this tension — not, as some have thought, a rebuke — which is signaled by "Why?"

6-10   The continuing lament picks up the terms of the refrain — "cast down" yet "remembering you" (v. 6). The center of this remembering is the LORD (v. 8), whose true and unchallengeable nature is "steadfast love" (see 5:7), the "God of my life." Some manuscripts read here, as in verse 2, "the living God," but this living God is the God who has been active in the psalmist's life. At night he remembers the songs of thanksgiving he used to sing, and he prays (v. 8), but the troubling present is inescapable. Verses 6b-7 have been the subject of much debate. If the geographical references to "the land of Jordan and of Hermon" and "Mount Mizar" (Mt. "Tiny") are correct — though Mizar is otherwise unknown — the picture may be of a man exiled from Jerusalem to the northern foothills of the Hermon peaks (the Hebrew reads the plural of the word "Hermon"), the source of the river Jordan. He might have been exiled because of a clash within the Jerusalem establishment or because he had been taken there as a hostage. Verse 7 may then be taken as a picture of the sources of the river Jordan cascading down over the rocks into deep pools. Water indeed, but not the "flowing streams" from which he longed to slake his thirst (vv. 1-2); instead, it is water which reminded him only too vividly that he was in exile, in a strange land. In Near Eastern mythology, however, the "deep" has echoes of the forces of chaos which threaten orderly life (see 29:3; Gen. 1:2), and the whole verse may be no more than a highly poetic way of saying that the psalmist now feels overwhelmed by the chaotic forces of despair threatening to destroy him.

Clinging for dear life to the God whom he describes as "my rock" (see 18:2), he has two urgent questions on his lips: "Why have you forgotten me?" (cf. 13:1); "Why must I walk about mournfully?" His life is drained of all vitality, and he is at the mercy of "the enemy," on the receiving end of the mocking taunts of those who seek to ridicule his faith (v. 10).

The phrase "As with a deadly wound in my body" (literally, "in the slaying of my bones") may mean that he goes around, as we would say, like death warmed over, or it may be taken metaphorically, as in the REB, to refer to the deadly "crushing insults" to which he is being subjected. The repetition of the refrain in verse 11 underlines the continuing tension he faces.

Whereas Psalm 42 contains a lament in which the psalmist is in dialogue with himself, Psalm 43 contains a prayer for God's intervention.

1 Verse 1 uses the language of the law court (see Psalm 35) as the psalmist pleads for God to be both judge and defense counsel against "an ungodly people" who do not belong to the "faithful" (see 4:3) who seek to live in the light of God's covenant demands. A gang of crooks and perverts would probably be a modern paraphrase of the description of them in verse 1b.

2 Verse 2 parallels 42:9, with "my rock" becoming "the God in whom I take refuge" (see 27:1) and "forgotten" being replaced by "cast off" or rejected (REB), a word which we are to hear twice again in Ps. 44:9, 23.

3-5 Verses 3-4 look forward by looking back to what was once central to his life, worship in God's dwelling place on his "holy hill" (cf. 2:6). There is little need to see even in the background of verse 3 the picture of two attendant deities. There is a rich symbolism surrounding "your light and your truth." Trapped in the dark chaos of despair, his sole hope lies in God leading him out of the darkness by sending his "light" (cf. 27:1). This would be particularly appropriate if the worship he remembered included the celebration of creation in which the darkness covering the face of the deep was shattered by the first creative word "Let there be light!" (Gen. 1:2-3). Equally his appeal for God's "truth" or faithfulness (see 25:5) is the necessary antidote to the insidious taunts and deceit which surround him.

In verse 4, the words "I will go . . . I will praise you" anticipate the hope expressed in the twice-repeated refrain, about to be heard again: "for I shall praise him." This is where life can be rebuilt on the foundation of access through worship to the one whom he addresses as "O God, my God," the equivalent in Book Two of the Psalms of the address we have heard often in Book One: "O LORD, my God" (e.g., 7:1, 3; 13:3; 18:28).

All faith finds its natural expression in worship. Through worship the human longing for God finds a fulfillment that, whatever else it brings, conveys the reality of God's presence. This is what the psalmist describes as "my exceeding joy" (v. 4; REB: "my joy and my delight"). However deeply personal worship is, it is also a corporate experience. Part of the psalmist's problem was his sense of isolation in an alien environment. This drove him to introspection in which his sense of isolation was compounded by his previous experience of belonging to "the throng," whose songs and thanksgiving he had once shared as he went to worship (v. 4). To return to God's dwelling, therefore, was to return to belonging to the congregation of God's people, to be taken out of isolation back into communion with God. In this context, the balance in the refrain (v. 5) shifts from the fear and despair which had been so dominant in his lonely isolation, to that hope and praise of God which he now shares with others. Thus Ps. 43:3-5, in its Scottish metrical version, finds a natural and continuing liturgical setting in the sacrament of Holy Communion.

Psalm 44
AN UNANSWERABLE PROTEST

This psalm is a striking example of a national lament in which the community pours out its protest and bewilderment to God, in the aftermath of military defeat and national humiliation (cf. Psalms 74 and 80). Any attempt to define the precise historical circumstances which gave birth to this psalm runs into difficulties. Guesses have ranged all the way from the time of David, through the events which led to the collapse of the northern kingdom of Israel in the eighth century BCE and the events in the early sixth century which led to the collapse of Judah, down to the time of the Maccabees in the second century BCE. Whatever its original historical context, the psalm had continuing relevance in any situation where the religious community found itself facing events which it was powerless to prevent and for which it could find no rational or satisfactory theological explanation.

Although in most of the Psalms we are listening to the words of the community "we," "us," and "our," in verses 4, 6, and 15-16 there is a switch to "I," "me," and "mine." Unless this is a purely literary device, it is likely that in these verses we are listening to the words of a leader or representative of the community, be it the king or a priestly spokesman.

The psalm naturally falls into three sections: verses 1-8, a recital of God's mighty deeds in the past (vv. 1-3) leading into a confident expression of faith (vv. 4-8); verses 9-22, a lament describing the present crisis in the nation's life (vv. 9-16), leading into an expression of puzzled bewilderment over why this should have happened; verses 23-26, a concluding urgent and dramatic plea to God.

1-8 Verses 1-3 recall the tradition of faith in which the community had been nurtured, perhaps through teaching in the home, through storytellers, and through the celebration of the past in worship. This faith had its roots in what God had done, particularly the settlement in the land of Canaan. The ground, as it were, had to be cleared by dispossessing the "nations," crushing the people already settled there, so that Israel could be planted. The words in verse 2 translated "but them you set free" (NRSV) or "to settle them" (REB) may be a continuation of the metaphor of the plant establishing itself and sending out roots. Ps. 80:8-11 speaks of Israel as a vine taken out of Egypt, planted on cleared ground, taking deep roots and sending out spreading branches. All of this was God's doing. The words "you with your own hand," which should probably come at the end of verse 1 rather than at the beginning of verse 2, speak symbolically of God's power in action. The words "by your right hand and your arm" (v. 3) do likewise. The words "the light of your countenance" (v. 3) speak of God's gracious favor extended to his people. It is the mighty acts of God, not merely the military exploits of the people under Joshua, which are being celebrated. Thus the temptation to say, in the words of Deut. 8:17, "My power and the might of my own hand have gotten me this wealth" is ruled out. The same emphasis is to be found in the credal statement in Josh. 24:1-13, a passage with which this psalm has several links. All this is summed up in the words of the representative of the community in verse 4 celebrating the kingship of God (cf. Psalms 93; 95–99). God is the King who ordains "victories" for Jacob (cf. 14:7). Both the word "victories" here and "victory" in verse 3 are translations of the word traditionally rendered "salvation" (see 3:8).

Out of this retrospective glance to the past, there springs in verses 5-8 a confident faith, which in different language parallels and underlines the thought of verses 2-3. Behind verse 5 there is the picture of the wild ox goring and trampling under foot anyone who gets in its way (cf. Deut. 33:17). The interplay of divine and human power is well illustrated in these verses: "through you we push down (v. 5) . . . you have saved us (or: "given us victory," v. 7) . . . through your name we tread down our assailants (v. 5) . . . you have put to confusion" (v. 7). But this interplay takes place within the context of the representative of the community reaffirming the theme of verses 1-3, that trust in naked power and military hardware alone — "my bow . . . my sword" (v. 6) — can only be a misplaced trust which can never guarantee victory. Not surprisingly, then, this section ends with a ringing affirmation of faith, embracing past, present, and future (v. 8), a faith which has "boasted" (see 34:2) in all that God has done and which confidently expects to give thanks for all that he will do in the future.

9-22   The turning point in the psalm comes at verse 9, with the word "Yet" drawing attention to something else which becomes the basis for the lament. How is it possible to square such a faith with the traumatic experience the nation has gone through? The nation has been "rejected" (cf. 43:2), humiliated by the LORD of hosts who had obviously stayed at home while the armies took to the field to suffer disastrous defeat. They had been easy meat for their enemies, "like sheep for slaughter" (vv. 11, 22; cf. Jer. 11:19); "scattered," uprooted from the land in which they had been planted; "sold," probably like a slave for next to nothing — no haggling, no reserved price (for the metaphor of God selling his people cf. Deut. 32:30). Disastrous defeat was bad enough, but with it went shame and the hurtful taunts (vv. 13, 16) of all who witnessed their plight (cf. 22:7). How hurtful such "taunts" can be is underlined in Psalm 69, where the same words occur again and again, translated "reproach" in verse 7 and "insults" in verses 9, 10, 19, and 20. God's people have become a "byword" (Hebrew *māšāl*), an object lesson of what a nation ought not to be, and "a laughingstock" (literally, "a shaking or tossing of the head," an indication of contempt or mockery).

Such a plight would be bad enough if there were some explanation for it. But there is none. The passage in Deuteronomy 8, quoted above, goes on to declare, "If you forget the LORD your God and follow other gods to serve and worship them, I solemnly warn you today that you shall surely perish" (Deut. 8:19). But the community is adamant that this cannot be the explanation of what has happened. They had not "forgotten" (vv. 17, 20); they had not betrayed their loyalty to the covenant. They had not rebelled or deliberately fallen out of step with God. They had not raised their hands in worship to other gods (v. 20). And God must know this, since he knows "the secrets of the heart" (v. 21), the things that might have been kept hidden from other people. This is neither arrogance nor a claim to sinless perfection. It is an assertion that there is a difference between loyalty and disloyalty. They are totally rejecting a theology which claims that it is their disloyalty to God which has led to disaster, a disaster so dire that it can only be depicted in terms of "deep darkness" (v. 19; cf. 23:4). Their once busy and lively country has been turned into a "haunt of jackals" (cf. Jer. 9:11; Isa. 34:13, in both of which passages this is a sign of the justifiable judgment of God).

If the psalmist in Psalm 42 had to listen to the mocking comments of others saying "Where is your God?" here is a community wrestling with the question, "Where is our God, the God we once trusted?" There is no easy answer. If there is any hint to be followed, it may be in the opening word of verse 22, translated "Because of you" (REB: "For your sake"). Is this simply a statement that the people hold God responsible for what has happened to them, even when they have no clue why he acts in this way? Or is it saying that what has happened to them is the result of their being God's people, the result of their loyalty to him in a hostile world? Across the ages, many have found that a high price has had to be paid for loyalty to God. The roll call of martyrs for the Christian faith is more extensive in the twentieth century than in any other century, and millions of Jews have perished for no other reason than that they were Jews. It is in this sense that Paul quotes verse 22 in Rom. 8:35, applying it to the harsh treatment which was the lot of the followers of Christ in his day. But he can face this in the context of a faith which claims that nothing "will be able to separate us from the love of God in Christ Jesus our Lord" (Rom. 8:39). The psalmist has no such assurance. He is left facing a mystery he can neither explain nor reconcile with a theology which sees disaster as the inevitable punishment for sin. This problem becomes even more acute when in Job it moves from the national to the personal level, with the psalmist's protestation of loyalty finding its parallel in Job's declaration of innocence in chapters 30 and 31.

23-26   Behind the mystery facing the psalmist there still stands a God to whom the psalmist believes he must appeal in prayer. Many would dismiss the prayer as a denial of the true attitude of prayer, but it is no more than the most dramatic example of what we find elsewhere in the psalms of lament (cf. 7:6-8; 35:23). The words "Why do you sleep, O LORD? Awake, do not cast us off forever" (v. 23) recall the mocking words of Elijah to the prophets of Baal on Mt. Carmel, as they whipped themselves up into an ecstatic frenzy, seeking to make the power of their god flow through them. Among the reasons Elijah suggests for the futility of their actions is "perhaps he is asleep and must be awakened" (1 Kgs. 18:27). Like Elijah, the psalmist can do nothing except bring his urgent prayer to the God who apparently "hides his face" (cf. 10:1; 13:1), who had forgotten his people as they lay crushed, trampled into the ground, unless verse 25, which is far from clear, indicates the attitude of worshippers lying prostrate in their grief.

For the closing words of the appeal "Rise," see the comment on 3:7, and for "Redeem," see the comment on 25:22. Ultimately the community is calling into question what it believes to be the key to God's character, his "steadfast love" (v. 26; see 5:7)

As James Cone in *A Black Theology of Liberation* has put it: "God doesn't do theology. Human beings do theology." Since theology is a human activity and therefore at its best still flawed, there are times when we are forced to appeal to the God to whom that theology claims to bear witness. Sometimes we are better left facing a God whose ways we do not fully understand than working with a theology which claims to provide us with all the answers. "Everything in this Psalm is easy," said Luther — everything except the experience to which it bears witness.

Psalm 45
AN ODE TO THE KING AND HIS BRIDE

In the heading to this psalm there are two phrases we have not yet met. The one, "according to Lilies," which appears again in the headings of Psalms 69 and 80 and in varied form in Psalm 60, is of uncertain meaning. It may indicate a setting or a tune to which the psalm was to be sung. The other, "A love song," gives us the clue to the content of the psalm. It is a song celebrating a royal wedding. We find echoes within it of the Song of Solomon, though there are no close parallels. All attempts to identify the king and his bride who feature in the psalm run into difficulties. Solomon and his Egyptian bride (1 Kgs. 3:1), Ahab and Jezebel (1 Kgs. 16:31), Jehoram and Athaliah (2 Kgs. 8:18) have all had their advocates. Whoever the original couple were, the psalm was suitable for the splendor associated with any royal wedding.

1-2 The psalm is the work of what we would call today the poet laureate, a court poet who introduces himself and his theme in verses 1-2, the only example of such an introduction in the entire Psalter. His heart "overflows," bubbles over (the verb is found only here in the Old Testament) with "a goodly theme" or perhaps "a happy event," since the Hebrew *dābār* can mean either "word" or "event." My "verses," he says (REB: "the song I have composed"; literally, "my work") are addressed to the king and display a facility matching the skill of a "ready" (REB: "expert") scribe (cf. Ezra 7:6). He begins by complimenting the king in typical, fulsome court language, describing him as "the most handsome of men," words which need no more be taken literally than the language which courtiers used to address the far from stunningly beautiful Elizabeth I of England, "A daughter of the gods, divinely tall and most devoutly fair" (Tennyson). Physical charm is matched by the graciousness of everything he says, fruit of God's blessing which is continually with him (see 3:8).

3-9 In verses 3-9 the poet addresses the king, calling upon him to demonstrate military prowess consistent with his "glory," or pomp, and "majesty" (see 8:1, 6), which will crush his enemies. This is power not to be used for self-glorification, but in defense of "truth" (cf. 25:5), meekness, and righteousness (cf. 11:7; literally, "the meekness of righteousness"). Both the NRSV and the REB translations in verse 4b assume a slight alteration to the text which is not strictly necessary. Such are the "dread [REB: "awesome"] deeds" which he must cultivate.

The opening words of verse 6, "Your throne, O God, endures forever" have provoked much discussion. In the traditional texts, both Hebrew and Greek, the king seems to be addressed as god *(ĕlōhîm)*. Is this possible, even within the contours of excessive court language, in a culture which sharply differentiated between God and even the greatest and most powerful of human beings? Certainly kings in Israel were not deified, as they were in certain other cultures, notably Egypt. Yet Isaiah can bestow upon a child born into the royal family the title "Mighty God" (Isa. 9:6), and we have already noted in Psalm 2 the special relationship between God and the king indicated in the words "son of God" (2:7). It is, therefore, not outside the bounds of possibility that the king should here be addressed as "god," a divine king. This would link with his status being guaranteed by his anointing (cf. 2:2) by "God, your God" in verse 7. Many minor alterations to the text have been suggested. The REB assumes one of the most convincing, "God has enthroned you for all eternity."

Whatever view we take, this is kingship characterized by "equity" or fairness (cf. 67:4). It is kingship that says "Yes" to righteousness and "No" to wickedness (see Psalm 1) in a community in which all will feel protected by a responsible use of power. Such a king bears all the outward marks of success and wealth. God has anointed the king with "the oil of gladness beyond your companions" (v. 7), which could refer to the other members of the ancient Near Eastern royal club, or simply to the king's friends within the community. God has decked the king in impressive royal robes (v. 8), fragrant with "myrrh and aloes," which in Song of Sol. 4:14 appear among the girl's perfumes. Cassia, related to cinnamon, occurs only here in the Old Testament, though Job gave this delightful name to his second daughter (Job 42:14). The king holds court in "ivory palaces" (v. 8), whose interiors were decorated with ivory inlays and no doubt adorned with many ivory objects (cf. Amos 3:15; 6:4). Princesses are "among your ladies of honor" (v. 9), probably in the harem. The word translated "ladies of honor," however, could equally well be translated "precious things." Above all, there is the "queen," standing in the place of honor at the king's right hand, decked in gold of Ophir. The exact location of Ophir is uncertain. It could be in the Arabian peninsula or on the east coast of Africa. Its gold was obviously of superior quality and highly valued (cf. Job 28:16; Isa. 13:12).

In verses 10-12 the poet has advice to give to the queen. Cut your links with the country and the family from which you have come. You are the object of the king's desire. He is your "lord," your husband; bow down before him, "daughter of Tyre." (It is better, with the REB, to take "daughter of Tyre" as a description of the queen at the end of verse 11, rather than to see, with the NRSV, a reference to the "people of Tyre" at the beginning of verse 12.) Accept your new status, and lavish gifts will be bestowed upon you by the wealthiest in the land (v. 12).

This is advice which would hardly be accepted in modern feminist circles, but it reflects both the politics of the age, when dynastic marriages reflected political needs, and the structure of society in ancient Israel. Life, however, did not always follow the social script. Jezebel, Ahab's wife, was hardly a meek, obedient queen (see 1 Kings 19 and 22).

In an interlude in verses 13-15, the poet describes the queen's coming to the king. Dressed in her boudoir in cloth of gold (REB) and costly finery, she is led to the king (or rather "carried," probably in a sedan). Surrounded by her ladies in waiting, amid revelry and rejoicing, she is brought so that the marriage could be consummated. In verses 16-17, which echo the opening verses, the poet turns to address the king, promising him royal progeny and a "name" (see 5:11) or reputation that will be forever remembered, since his people will have good cause to praise him "forever and ever."

Why, we may ask, did an ode celebrating a royal wedding find a place among the Psalms? What was its religious or theological significance? From an early age, following the pattern of the Davidic kingship, the psalm was given a future messianic interpretation in both Jewish and Christian circles. Thus the Aramaic Targum paraphrases verse 2, "Thy beauty, O King messiah, is greater than that of the children of men." Hebrews quotes verse 6, "Your throne, O God, endures forever and ever," as part of its thesis concerning the superiority of Jesus over angels (Heb. 1:8). The picture of the king riding on victoriously in the cause of truth and righteousness in verse 4 may have influenced the imagery of the rider on the white horse in Rev. 19:11-16, on whose robe and thigh is inscribed "King of kings and Lord of lords." There is, moreover, the use which the Old Testament makes of the marriage relationship to describe the relationship between God and Israel (e.g., Hosea 1–2; Ezekiel 16) and the parallel New Testament usage in terms of Christ and the Church.

How far, though, do we take this interpretive approach? Is it right to superimpose upon the psalm, as many commentators through the centuries have done, an allegorical interpretation which reads Christian theology into every detail of the psalm? Thus, for example, F. Delitzsch, commenting on verse 9, wrote "Who are the daughters of the king and who is the queen standing in closest relationship to the king? The former are the heathen nations converted to Christ, and the latter is Israel which is remarried to Christ after the fullness of the heathen is come in." A wise reticence is needed here, or the comments will tell us little or nothing about the psalm and a great deal about the ingenuity of the interpreter. The Song of Solomon has similarly suffered at the hands of over-eager theological commentators. However much we may sense the language of Psalm 45 pointing beyond itself in the wider context of Scripture, why should the Psalms not contain an ode to marriage with its joyful celebration of sexuality, which is one of God's gifts to his people?

Psalm 46
OUR SAFE STRONGHOLD

The phrase "According to Alamoth" occurs only here in the psalm headings (but cf. 1 Chron. 15:20). "Alamoth" can mean "girls" (Ps. 68:25), so the reference could be to girls' voices, to a high setting of a tune, or to high-pitched instruments. As in the case of other indicators in the psalm headings, there is little certainty. Nor is this the only uncertainty surrounding one of the most familiar of all the Psalms, especially in its Scottish Metrical Version or in Luther's vigorous rendering, translated by Thomas Carlyle, "A safe stronghold our God is still." Traditionally there have been two assumptions about this psalm. One is that it springs out of a dramatic historical incident, with the disappearance of the Assyrian army, when it seemed to have Jerusalem in its grasp (2 Kgs. 19:35-37). The other is that the city referred to in verses 4 and 5 is Jerusalem. Increasingly the first assumption has been questioned. The origin of the psalm has been sought in the great autumnal festival in which the community celebrated the mighty acts of God, embracing creation and all human history — past, present, and future. Even against this background, however, the second assumption, the identification of the city with Jersualem, has often remained unchallenged. The psalm is then classified alongside Psalm 48 as one of the Songs of Zion (cf. Psalms 76; 84; 87).

A comparison with Psalm 48 is, however, instructive. The city runs through Psalm 48 from beginning to end, and Jerusalem is clearly in view, with its reference to Mt. Zion (vv. 1, 11) and to the temple (v. 9), and with its closing invitation to walk around the towers and ramparts of Zion (v. 12). Not so Psalm 46. It clearly divides into three sections, indicated by the liturgical rubric "Selah" (see Psalm 3), with the second and third sections ending in the refrain: "The Lord of hosts is with us; the God of Jacob is our refuge." This refrain may have been accidentally omitted after verse 3 as the psalm was copied. There is no mention of any city in verses 1-3, which focus on creation, or in verses 8-11, which look forward in hope to an age of peace. In verses 4-7 a city appears, but it is not specifically identified with Jerusalem or Zion, and there are many features in this section which suggest a mythological background rather than the streets of Jerusalem. Indeed, if there is one key word holding the psalm together in all its sections, it is not city, but "earth" (vv. 2, 6, 8, 9, 10). We need not doubt that the fundamental religious ideas which pulsate through the psalm could be, and in specific circumstances were, relevant to Jerusalem and the crises it faced. Yet the psalm need not have originated there and in the Jerusalem temple worship. It would have been equally appropriate in some other shrine, perhaps a northern one, long before Jerusalem achieved its preeminence in the religious life of the people.

1-3   God rules in creation. The picture in verse 2 of the earth changing or moving to and fro, the solid mountains shaking and trembling, may well suggest a violent earthquake, but there is more to it than that. The "heart [REB: "depth"] of the sea" and "the waters" roaring and foaming recall the mythological theme of the forces of chaos (see comment on Psalm 29), conquered in the beginning to make way for the orderly created world, yet ever threatening to engulf the world. Even if the whole fabric of the created world were in danger of collapsing, the community defiantly affirms its faith in the God who is "our refuge" and "strength," a "help" always there in any time of trouble (v. 1). Here is witness to a faith which remains unshakable, while the very foundations of the world are being shaken. The core of this faith is spelled out in the refrain of verses 7 and 11, but it would be equally appropriate here after verse 3: "The Lord of hosts" (see comment on 24:10), the ruler of all, the "God of Jacob" (see comment on 20:1). This is no distant despot, but the God who is "with us" (cf. Isa. 7:14), our "refuge" or fortress (a different word from that translated "refuge" in verse 1; see 18:2).

4-7   God rules in the maelstrom of history. Like us, the people of Israel lived in a world often at the mercy of the use and abuse of human power. "Nations" are in "uproar" (v. 6; cf. v. 3, where the same verb refers to the roaring of the waters), either through internal divisions or attack from without. "Kingdoms totter" or are overthrown, as many of the kingdoms in the ancient world found out. If that were all, then history is little more than a chancy mess. But at its heart, claims the psalm, stands "the city of God." Attempts to identify this with Jerusalem run into all kinds of trouble. The "river whose streams make glad" this city (v. 4) can hardly be the Gihon spring or the Siloam tunnel. This is the language of mythology, which has its roots in the picture of the garden in Gen. 2:10 with its river dividing into four streams, and in the Canaanite picture of El, the supreme god, whose abode and throne is at the head of two streams. For the description of the city as "the habitation of the Most High," see the comment on 7:17. This is the heavenly city which will "not be moved," even when kingdoms totter or move (the same verb is used in vv. 5 and 6). God is its "help" (cf. v. 1) as surely as dawn breaks each day. Before him the world "melts" as if it were wax in his hands; all the forces in it are helpless.

To identify this "city of God" with any place on the map, even Jerusalem, or any human institution, including any religious institution, is to court misunderstanding and ultimate disaster. Such an identification would convert the God who "is with us" into the God who is on our side, who exists to prop up our human power structures. The "city of God" stands over against all such earthly power as a rock in the midst of the shifting sands of human history.

8-11 The third section contains an invitation and a challenge to acknowledge God's rule. The invitation "Come" (v. 8) is an invitation to see the devastating things God has done, to experience them as they are recited and relived in worship reaching back to creation and embracing all human history. The battles are over; victory is won. The weapons of war are shattered; the "shields" burned. The Hebrew text reads not shields but "wagons," which has been taken to mean chariots. There is, however, no other evidence for the word "wagons" meaning chariots, though the burning of the chariots of a defeated enemy is vouched for in Josh. 11:6, 9. Most modern translations read "shields," which follows the reading of the early versions. This battle theme could embrace both the conflict between the God of creation and the powers of chaos and the events in Israel's history, including the fighting which led to the settlement in Canaan (cf. Joshua 1–12).

The invitation then becomes a challenge directed to the people who gather for worship and to all the forces seeking to undermine God's rule. The challenge "Be still, and know that I am God!" (v. 10) is not the challenge heard in Ps. 37:7, the stillness which waits for God. The Hebrew word here means, as the REB translates, "Let be then," that is, let go, step back from looking for security in anyone other than the God who is "exalted among the nations," the God who in the overwhelming vision comes to Isaiah as "sitting on a throne, high and lofty" (Isa. 6:1).

So we come full circle to Luther's version of the psalm, which makes an identification with any human city impossible but flings defiance in the face of all the oppressive human and demonic forces in the world. It sees faith in "the LORD of hosts" confirmed in Jesus, "Immanuel," God with us (Matt. 1:23). Nor should we forget the way in which the language of this psalm points forward to the vision which crowns the book of Revelation in chapters 20 and 21, the vision of a new heaven and a new earth, with a new Jerusalem at its heart. Through that city flows a river, "the water of life," and in it stands the tree of life, its leaves for the healing of the nations (Rev. 21:2). Thus ancient mythological themes, which provided the psalmist with the imagery to encapsulate his robust faith, are transformed to become the vehicles of an ultimate hope. It is a vision of God "exalted among the nations," with all the forces of destruction marring our world today finally conquered.

Psalm 47
HAIL TO THE KING OF KINGS

This brief psalm is a two-verse hymn calling upon people to celebrate the God who is "king of all the earth" (v. 7). Although the traditional text indicates a break at the end of verse 4 where "Selah" occurs, it is better to divide it after verse 5. We then have two sections, each beginning with a joyful summons, "Clap . . . shout" (v. 1), and "Sing praises," five times in verses 6 and 7. The description of God as "a great king over all the earth" (v. 2) finds its counterpart in the refrain "For God is the king of all the earth" (v. 7). The "peoples" and the "nations" in verse 3 are echoed in the "nations" and the "peoples" in verses 8 and 9, while God "has gone up" (v. 5) appears again in the closing word of the psalm as "exalted," which comes from the verb "go up."

What lies behind the language of the kingship of God in this and similar psalms such as Psalms 93 and 96–99? Does it presuppose an annual New Year festival in the Jerusalem temple, in which the king played an important symbolic role, a festival which celebrated the enthronement of the LORD and his victory over all the forces which challenged his rule? The analogy for this is the Babylonian New Year festival celebrating the kingship of Marduk. Did the ark, the symbol of the LORD's presence among his people, have a prominent role in the celebration, reflecting the story of David's bringing the ark to Jerusalem in 2 Sam. 6:15, where the ark is "brought up" (same verb as "go up" in Psalm 47), with "shouting" (cf. v. 1) and "with the sound of trumpet" (cf. v. 5)? This is possible, though it is important to stress that such a festival can only be reconstructed on the basis of the language of these psalms, read in the light of the corresponding Babylonian festival. Whether we need such liturgical moorings for this psalm, or even, as A. Weiser suggests, an annual festival of covenant renewal, is open to debate. It would not be difficult to reconstruct a similar festival from the language of some of our Easter hymns.

The New Year associations of the psalm have been preserved in Jewish liturgy, while Christian tradition has tended to see it as an Ascension Sunday psalm. What is not in doubt is that, regardless of its original liturgical context, the psalm speaks to the faith and imagination of worshippers in language which calls forth a glad response of praise.

1-5 The opening recalls the coronation of a king. According to 2 Kgs. 11:12, after the king was crowned in the temple, the people "proclaimed him king . . . they clapped their hands and shouted, 'Long live the king!' " After this ceremony, the king was escorted to the palace and "took his seat on the throne of the kings. So all the people of the land rejoiced" (2 Kgs. 11:19, 20). But this is no human king whose coronation is being acclaimed; it is the LORD, "the Most High" (see 7:17). The title "Most High" is singularly appropriate here, since it echoes the verb translated "gone up" in verse 5 and "highly exalted" in verse 9. He is "awesome" (v. 2; cf. 76:7), one who can be approached only with reverence. He is "a great king," a title which the kings of the great empires of the ancient world, notably Assyrian kings, applied to themselves. Esarhaddon, for example, described himself as "great king, legitimate king, king of the world." Here is the divine king whose dominion extends "over all the earth" (v. 2). Although the word translated "earth" can mean land — the country occupied by the people of Israel — here, as in Psalm 46, it has a wider reference to include the whole world. It is this universal divine king who has "gone up" and taken his seat on his throne amid the acclamation of his people (v. 1).

It is characteristic of the Old Testament that it sees nothing incongruous in making this claim and at the same time celebrating God's particular concern for his own people (cf. Psalm 29). So verses 3-4 recall the theme of the entry into the promised land of Canaan and the brushing aside of everyone in the land destined to be "our heritage" (cf. 2:8), "the pride of Jacob." Although the word translated "pride" often refers to human arrogance (cf. 10:2; 36:11), here it is simply a description of the land of which Jacob (i.e., the nation; cf. 14:7) is rightly proud, the gift of God's "love" (see comment on 31:23; cf. 44:2-3).

6-9 Five times in verses 6 and 7 we hear the summons "Sing praises." Let there be no doubt that this is a king who rightly deserves the acclamation of his people, the God who is both "our King . . . and king of all the earth." The word translated "with a psalm" in verse 7 is the word *maśkîl*, which elsewhere in the Psalms occurs only in the headings (see comment on Psalm 32). Does it indicate a particular kind of psalm, perhaps designed to teach the people about the great things God has done for them? The REB has "with all your skill," assuming that the word is being used adverbially.

The king has now taken "his seat," enthroned on his "holy throne," a phrase which is found nowhere else in the Old Testament (but see comment on 2:6). Who are those who gather round to acknowledge his kingship? Everything depends on how we interpret verse 9. The NRSV seems to assume by its insertion of the word "as" that the "princes of the peoples," that is, the nations other than Israel, are now regarded as "the people of the God of Abraham," incorporated equally with the descendants of Abraham in the kingdom of God. Is this pointing to a universal hope found in other Old Testament passages (e.g., Isa. 2:2-4; Mic. 4:1-3), a hope rooted in the promise made to Abraham in Gen. 12:3, "In you all the families of the earth shall be blessed"? This is a hope which the New Testament sees fulfilled in Christ (compare Gal. 2:3 and Eph. 3:6). It could also, however, be translated "with the people of the God of Abraham," in which case "the princes of the peoples" represent subject peoples, forced to be present to witness the kingship of God. This would be in line with the more nationalistic tone of verse 3. These two views need not be mutually exclusive. It is possible to live for a while with a limited, exclusive vision — and the Church can be as guilty of this as certain strands in the Old Testament. But the vision we seek to imprison will ultimately break out, and sometimes it will break us. To speak of God as "a great king over all the earth" must in the end lead to a God who cannot be "our God" in a narrow, exclusive sense. The words we use, the visions we have, can often be far more all embracing than we care to admit.

Psalm 48
THE CITY OF OUR GOD

In many ways the theology of this psalm is similar to that of Psalm 46, and some of the same critical questions arise. For example, is its origin to be sought in some specific historical event or in the cult? In another respect, however, it is different. It is clearly focused on Jerusalem, on Mt. Zion (vv. 2, 11, 12), on the temple (v. 9), and on the surrounding Judean towns (v. 11). Thus it may more truly be described as one of the Songs of Zion.

1-3 The psalm begins with a cry of adoration which we hear in other liturgical contexts: "Great is the LORD and greatly [or: "highly"] to be praised." Elsewhere these words are immediately followed by "he is to be revered above all gods" (Ps. 96:4; 145:3; 1 Chron. 16:25). Here they lead into a loving description of "the city of our God" (v. 1), "the city of the great king" (v. 2; cf. 47:2), God's "holy mountain" (see comment on 2:6). Some of the language used here, "beautiful in elevation . . . the joy of all the earth" (v. 2), could find a place in any glossy tourist brochure. In Lam. 2:15 those who view the devastation of Jerusalem say sneeringly, "Is this the city that was called the perfection of beauty, the joy of all the earth?" (cf. Isa. 60:14-15). The description of Mt. Zion as "in the far north" or "in the recesses of Zaphon," however, raises a different issue. This can hardly be a geographical description. Although Zaphon does mean north, it is also the name of the northern mountain which, in Canaanite mythology, is the abode of the gods. According to Isa. 14:13, the king of Babylon in his arrogance boasted: "I will ascend to heaven; I will raise my throne above the stars of God; I will sit on the mount of assembly, on the heights of Zaphon." Using traditional mythological language, the psalmist is saying that if there is one place on earth which is the abode of God, it is Mt. Zion in Jerusalem. Thus the security of the city and its splendid buildings ("citadels") is guaranteed by the God who is known to be present as its "sure defense" or fortress (cf. 46:7, 11).

4-8   These verses depict the futility of any attack on the city. Who are the kings who assembled and who together "came on" or crossed over into someone else's territory? Is it the king of Assyria and his allies (cf. Isa. 10:8), or is it a coalition of the kings of smaller neighboring states (as in 2 Chronicles 20)? The problem is that there is no specific historical situation known to us which fits neatly all the language of this section. It is therefore possible that we are dealing with language at home in worship, with the "kings" representing all those who have ever, or will ever, threaten the power of the "great king" in Jerusalem.

Calvin quotes Caesar's comment on his invasion of Egypt, "I came, I saw, I conquered." Enemies came against this city; they came, they saw, but they did not conquer. They were "astounded" (v. 5), surely not because of the defensive walls of Jerusalem, which were far from impregnable, but because they sensed that this was "the city of God." They fled in panic, shuddering like "a woman in labor" (v. 6), a simile which Jeremiah ironically uses to describe the disaster coming upon his own people (Jer. 4:31; 6:24). They were like a fleet of ships in the Mediterranean, caught and shattered by a gale blowing from the east. It is questionable whether in the phrase "the ships of Tarshish" Tarshish refers to a place name, be it in Spain or Sardinia, or to a type of ship. Certainly such ships were used by the Phoenicians in their trading along the Mediterranean (Ezek. 27:25; Isa. 23:1), probably bringing in ore (Jer. 10:9) and exporting merchandise. Our modern equivalent would be a huge oil tanker, a monument to human technical and maritime engineering skill, yet known to have foundered at the mercy of hurricane winds and mountainous seas.

What the "kings" saw and the effect it had on them have their counterpart in v. 8 in what the pilgrims and worshippers "have heard . . . and have seen" as they shared in one of the great festivals in the temple. The pilgrims to Jerusalem have seen "in the city of the LORD of hosts" (cf. 24:10; 46:7, 11), "the city of our God, which God establishes forever," as solid and secure as the earth which the LORD established (Ps. 24:1).

9-11   Verses 9-11 shed further light on the thoughts of those who gather for worship in the temple. They are pondering "your steadfast love" (see 5:7). They are acknowledging "your name," that is, God's true character (see 5:11), which, like his praise (v. 1), is not confined to the city but spreads out into all the world.

Yet it is a particular source of joy to Zion and to the towns (literally, "daughters") of Judah, because the power God exercises guarantees "victory" (see 4:1), the vindication of his people in face of all that threatens to destroy them.

12-14   The psalm ends with a procession around Zion which may have been part of the religious festival. On the other hand, the invitation to take part in this procession may be no more than an appeal to the imagination of those who gather for worship. The "towers" (v. 12), the impressive "citadels" or buildings (v. 13), and the "ramparts" or defensive walls linking the towers are the outward, visible sign of a message to be handed on to the next generation. To those who as yet have never had the privilege of being there, the message is that the eternal God is here in the midst of his people; he is the God who will "guide" or lead us, the verb used of Moses leading his flock in Exod. 3:1 (cf. Gen. 31:8).

The translation of the last word of the psalm, "forever," is doubtful. The traditional Hebrew text has two words, 'al mût, "until/over/against death." This has been the subject of different interpretations from an early period. The translation "forever" reflects the Greek (LXX), which seems to run the two Hebrew words together. Others have followed those Hebrew manuscripts that read the two words as one, ălāmôt, and argue that this word should be taken as part of the heading of the next psalm. Perhaps the words mean exactly what they say, "against death" — against all the forces which threaten to destroy the life of God's people. If we follow the historical interpretation of the psalm, the words may mean "against death in battle"; if we follow the cultic interpretation they may mean "against all the forces of chaos symbolized by death."

The danger of identifying the city of God with a place on a map, we have already discussed with reference to Psalm 46. Equally, however, the strong, steadying faith which shines through the language of this psalm needs to be clothed in visible symbols. A great medieval cathedral like Chartres, hundreds of years in the building, or a modern cathedral like Coventry, can convey some sense of the unchanging power of God in the midst of the challenging changes of life, provided we remember that they too share in the transitoriness of everything human and are but pointers to a reality which transcends everything human.

When Babylonian armies were laying siege to Jerusalem, there were no doubt many sincere people manning its ramparts, their faith probably nurtured on the singing of this psalm. They were convinced that this was "the city of God," divinely protected forever. Meanwhile, Jeremiah was in prison, accused of heresy and high treason for openly proclaiming a message advocating that its citizens desert to the enemy. God himself, he declared, had decreed the destruction of the city (Jer. 38:1-5). Jeremiah believed that the same pains, as of "a woman in labor," which the psalmist claimed gripped all who attacked the city would also grip those who lived in it. They too, and their religion, could be a threat to God. To believe that the judgment of God falls only on others is to expose ourselves to the same judgment.

Psalm 49
THE DECEITFUL FACE OF RICHES

1-4 The introduction to this psalm in verses 1-4 makes it clear that we are listening to the words of a wisdom teacher. Worship provided such teachers in Israel with a forum for instruction. The opening invitation, "Hear . . . give ear," is usually in the Psalms addressed to God (cf. 17:1); here it is extended to "all you peoples . . . all inhabitants of the world" (cf. 17:4), to those whom verse 2 calls "the sons of Adam and the sons of man," usually rendered "both low and high" (NRSV), but which may mean nothing more than "every Tom, Dick, and Harry," including both "rich and poor."

The psalmist claims, therefore, to be dealing with a basic human problem, relevant to all people everywhere. This is typical of wisdom teaching. The book of Job, for example, is not even located in Israel. Wisdom teachers were interested in what made people tick, the values they held for good and for ill. What this psalmist has to say is described as "wisdom" and "understanding," both key words in wisdom teaching (cf. Prov. 1:2; 2:2-3). Both words are plural in Hebrew, and this may signal "deep wisdom and profound insight." Such wisdom and understanding are seldom speculative. They are concerned to teach people how to live responsibly and successfully in the face of the issues life raises.

Two other words from the vocabulary of wisdom appear in verse 4, "a proverb" (Hebrew *māšāl*) and "a riddle" (Hebrew *ḥîdāh*). The word *māšāl* appears in the heading of several collections of proverbs in the book of Proverbs (Prov. 1:1; 10:1; 25:1). It covers a wide variety of comment and teaching. In Ps. 44:14 it means a "byword," an object of derision. In Ezek. 17:2 it introduces a lengthy poem in the form of an allegory. In Numbers 23 and 24 it introduces what Balaam has to say and is usually translated "oracle." The word *ḥîdāh* is used alongside *māšāl* in Ezek. 17:2. It usually indicates some kind of puzzle or enigma which demands deep thought from those who hear it. We may compare Samson's riddle in Judg. 14:12 and the queen of Sheba's "hard questions" in 1 Kgs. 10:1. What is being laid before the worshippers in this psalm, then, is something which will make them stop and think, and think hard.

There are no other examples in the Old Testament of such wisdom teaching being given with a musical accompaniment (v. 4), but ballad singers have used this technique across the centuries. There is no reason why it should not be appropriate to teaching in a worship setting, just as guitars feature prominently in this role today.

If the introduction clearly sets the scene, the rest of the psalm is at points far from clear. Even the NRSV, which is not given to overestimating difficulties, has seven footnotes, six of them suggesting readings which depart from the traditional Hebrew text. The psalm itself, therefore, is something of an enigma.

The interpretation which follows is only one of several possibilities. The psalm divides into two main sections: verses 5-12 and verses 13-20, each section capped by a refrain which appears in slightly varied form in verses 12 and 20.

5-12 These verses expose the problem. The teacher begins by identifying himself with those who fear the iniquity of "persecutors" (v. 5). This word comes from the same root as the name Jacob — "the heel" — the twister who supplanted his brother Esau in his father's favor (Gen. 25:26). These persecutors throw their weight around, they "trust in their wealth [or: "power"; the Hebrew can mean either] and boast of the abundance of their riches" (v. 6).

That such trust and boasting should be reserved for the LORD alone is a prominent theme in the Psalms (cf. 34:2; 44:8). The people whom this psalmist is describing obviously have a distorted and fatally flawed sense of values. Using the language of "ransom" (see 25:22), the teacher insists that there is no payment which can ever be made to God to ensure escape from life's one certainty, namely, death. In spite of the NRSV and REB translations, the Hebrew text in verse 7 — "no man can ransom a brother" — makes perfectly good sense once we recognize that "a man — his brother" is good Hebrew idiom meaning "each other." Death, says the psalmist, is not under human control. Life is God's gift to us (Gen. 2:7), a temporary gift. No one can write a check to convert this temporary lease into a permanent possession, no matter how rich he may be. Verse 9 is the natural continuation of verse 7. It is best to take verse 8 as an aside — and such ransom would be costly, so costly that it is better to have nothing to do with it. Verse 10 follows on neatly from verse 9 when we recognize that the Hebrew text can be rendered, "Surely he [i.e., the rich man] will see." Two things, says the teacher, should be obvious to the rich. First, they cannot purchase a ticket to everlasting life; they cannot avoid the "Pit" (v. 9; see 4:9), one of the synonyms for Sheol, the abode of the dead. Second, they must recognize that death is a basic human experience. All must die, the wise as well as the "fool" who despises instruction and the "dolt" who has no clue what life is all about (cf. Ps. 73:22; 92:6). They not only die, but they can take nothing with them (cf. v. 17). They "leave their wealth to others" (v. 10), a fact which causes Ecclesiastes much heart searching, part of the "vanity" (Hebrew *hebel*) of life which leads him to despair (cf. Eccl. 2:18-21). This reality is highlighted in the parable of the rich fool in Luke 12:13-21.

While the opening of verse 11 — "their graves," which is the reading of many of the early versions — makes sense, the Hebrew is not impossible. In Ps. 64:6 the same Hebrew word occurs meaning "inmost thoughts." We could take verse 11 as the opposite of verses 10 and 12. Yes, they must die, but in the sanctuary of their own thoughts the rich are very far from accepting this fact. They have secure "homes"; they have landed property, signed and sealed as their own (v. 11). To have your name called over anything is equivalent to staking a claim to possess it (cf.

2 Sam. 12:28). Into this reverie there breaks the refrain, "Mortals cannot abide in their pomp; they are like animals that perish" (v. 12; cf. v. 20). In spite of wealth or "pomp" (in Esth. 1:4 this word refers to royal splendor), mortals have no secure lodging in this world. Like animals they must die.

One of the most memorable statements of this truth is to be found in Eccl. 3:19 where, drawing on the language of Gen. 2:7 and 3:19, the teacher declares:

> For the fate of humans and the fate of animals is the same; as one dies, so dies the other. They all have the same breath, and humans have no advantage over the animals; for all is vanity. All go to one place; all are from the dust, and all turn to dust again.

This casts a shadow over Ecclesiastes' thinking, since it raises a question mark against all human endeavor and achievement. The teacher in this psalm is driving home the same point, but for a different purpose: to bring comfort to those who are on the receiving end of persecution at the hands of the rich and the powerful.

13-20   The text of verse 13 is extremely difficult. The versions had a tough time with it. The Hebrew seems to be picking up the theme of verse 12 and saying, "There are some people who never learn; yes, that's their way, the way of folly [or: "self-confidence"; the word translated "foolhardy" may mean either], and those who follow them delight in what they say." The "Selah" then invites the congregation to pause for a moment and reflect on this strange attitude.

Lest there be any doubt that such self-confidence is misplaced, verse 14 depicts Death as a shepherd leading such people into Sheol. This is a very different use of the shepherd imagery that we saw in Psalm 23. There the shepherd protects the flock from danger, even when they have to go through "the darkest valley"; here Death, the shepherd, drives them irrevocably into the dark valley (cf. the picture of Death as the grim reaper in Jer. 9:21-22). What the second half of verse 14 means is anyone's guess. The Hebrew reads "the upright shall have dominion over them in the morning," the upright presumably identified with those who have been on the receiving end of persecution. This might mean that their nightmare is soon to pass. The rest of the verse then reverts to the fate of the arrogant rich. Sheol, their true home, is going to consume all that they cherish. The NRSV and most modern translations, however, accept a series of textual alterations which make the whole verse apply to the inexorable and destructive end awaiting the rich in Sheol (for Sheol, see 6:5).

In some ways, the crux of the psalm comes in verse 15 with the words "But God." What does the teacher envisage God doing and to whom? It has been argued that in verse 15 we are listening to the thoughts of the rich and privileged. Enough of this gloomy talk about death! Surely God will ransom us from Sheol. Just as riches during a lifetime were regarded as a sign of God's favor, so that same favor will be with the rich when they come to face death. This, however, seems to be an unlikely interpretation. The words are best taken as words of hope, spoken over against the fate of the rich and the powerful. But hope for what? Do these words point, however dimly, to some hope of life beyond death, coming as God's gift to his faithful people? In support of this it is often pointed out that the words "for he will receive me" (or: "take me") echo the stories of Enoch, who was believed to have been mysteriously "taken" by God from this present life (Gen. 5:24), and of Elijah, who was "taken" to heaven in the whirlwind (2 Kgs. 2:11). On the other hand, verse 15 may read, "But God will ransom my life, from the clutches of Sheol he will surely deliver me." This need mean no more than that God will be his protector against all the deadly forces which threaten his life. Some may put their trust in riches, but the psalmist looks to God to do things for him which even riches can never do — to provide a God-centered security which will carry him through all the ups and downs of this life.

This confident faith in an indestructible relationship with God in this life (cf. Ps. 73:23-24) eventually raised questions whether this relationship could be destroyed even by death. There are hints of an answer to this question in the latest writings of the Old Testament. In Dan. 12:2, for instance, we have one of the few Old Testament passages which envision resurrection from the dead. For the New Testament, the answer comes with an overpowering certainty in the resurrection of Jesus as the firstfruits of the general resurrection of the dead (cf. 1 Corinthians 15). We must not, however, assume that such a hope finds expression in this psalm. Indeed, it is part of the greatness of the wisdom teaching that it wrestles with some of the sharpest issues in life without calling in such an answer. Witness Job and Ecclesiastes.

In the light of the psalmist's certainty, the question "Why should I fear?" of verse 5 receives its answer in verse 16, "Do not be afraid." Riches and wealth are transitory. Self-congratulation and the plaudits of others may be the lot of the rich and the successful in this life, but that life will come to an end in the tomb (cf. Gen. 49:29), in that realm devoid of light which is Sheol, "the land of gloom and deep darkness, the land of gloom and chaos, where light is like darkness" (Job 10:21-22; cf. Ps. 88:12). Although the NRSV and the REB translations conceal this, the closing refrain in verse 20 is significantly different from that in verse 12. Instead of "cannot abide," verse 20 in the Hebrew reads "do not understand." The difference may be deliberate. Mortals caught up in their pomp just do not understand that one day they must bite the dust. They do not understand that, as Shakespeare put it, "sad mortality o'ersways their power" (Sonnet 65).

The psalm began with a plea for understanding (v. 3). It ends by underlining that there is no true understanding of life which does not reckon with its frailty and its transitoriness. This is a lesson desperately needing to be taken to heart today in Western society, which tends to idolize wealth and evaluate life in terms of material possessions.

Psalm 50
TRUE WORSHIP

Psalm 50 is the first of twelve psalms associated with "Asaph," the others occurring in a block, Psalms 73–83, in Book Three. Ezra 2:41 notes that the temple singers were the descendants of Asaph, while 2 Chron. 29:30 lists Asaph the seer along with David as being responsible for some of the words of the temple songs (cf. Neh. 12:46). Although the Psalms never use the phrase "the sons of Asaph" (cf. "the sons of Korah") in their headings, it seems likely that the Asaph psalms come from a collection associated with a group of temple singers who traced their ancestry back to Asaph. Beyond that we may speculate, but certainty is hard to achieve.

1-6   This opening section of the psalm likely describes or summarizes what has been happening in the temple liturgy. Precisely what and when is uncertain. Does the language of verses 1-2 imply a liturgy celebrated at dawn, with God's shining forth associated with "the rising of the sun" (v. 1)? Only two other psalms speak of God "shining forth" (Pss. 80:1; 94:2), and they hardly support this conclusion. The verb "shine forth" seems to denote the dazzling splendor of God's coming to his people. At the outset we are being reminded of what lies at the heart of all true worship. Such worship is not merely our coming to God, but God's coming to us.

The psalm begins by placing side by side three words for God: *'ēl*, an old Semitic term for deity and the name of the supreme god in the Canaanite pantheon (translated by the NRSV as "The mighty one"); *'ĕlōhîm*, the generic word for deity in Hebrew; and "Yahweh," the personal name of the God of Israel, rendered in English translations as "the LORD" (cf. Josh. 22:22). The early versions tended to take the first two words together, translating "God of gods." The bringing together of these three divine names, however, probably serves to underline the awesome majesty of the God who comes to his people. This is the God whose authority extends from one end of the earth to the other, "from the rising of the sun to its setting" (v. 1). He is the God whose coming is marked by a "devouring fire" and a raging storm which sweeps away everything in its path (see Psalm 29 and the language associated with Mt. Sinai in Exod. 19:16-18; Deut. 4:11-12). He is the God who summons "heaven and earth" (v. 4) as witnesses to what he is about to do. Such a summons is characteristic of the lawsuit that God is about to bring against his people (cf. Isa. 1:2; Jer. 2:12; Deut. 32:1).

This awesome God is no distant or unknown God. His people meet him in Zion (cf. 2:6), described as "the perfection of beauty" (cf. Ps. 48:2; Lam. 2:15). He not only comes to his people, but he also has something to say to them. He is a "righteous" judge (cf. 7:11; 11:4-7) who has a charge to lay against his people (v. 4), his "faithful ones" (see 4:3), those "who made [or: "are making"] a covenant with me by sacrifice" (v. 5; for covenant, see comment on 25:10). The reference may be either to the covenant once made at Mt. Sinai which bound the people to God (Exod. 24:5-8) or to the renewing of that covenant taking place in worship. The phrase "to make a covenant" is literally "to cut a covenant." The phrase possibly originated in the ritual described in Gen. 15:9-10, in which the contracting parties place themselves under an oath, which would become a curse if ever they violated the terms of the covenant. They would become like the severed pieces of the sacrificed animal between which they had walked when entering into the covenant (cf. Jer. 34:18-20). Thus sacrifice has a key role to play in Israel's religious experience, but it was capable of being misunderstood (cf. 40:6-8), and one such misunderstanding is the basis of the charge leveled against the people in verses 7-15.

7-15 In other psalms we have listened to the psalmists calling upon God to "hear" (cf. 5:1; 17:1); here the roles are reversed. It is the people who must "hear" what their covenant God has to say to them. The summons "O my people . . . I am God your God" (v. 7) echoes the key provision of the covenant, "I will be your God, and you shall be my people" (Lev. 26:12). The charge God lays against them is not concerned with sacrifice as such (v. 8; for sacrifice and burnt offering, see 40:6) but with the attitude which lies behind the people's bringing of sacrifices. They seem to think that God needs their sacrifices, that if he did not get his daily allotment of "bulls" and "goats" (v. 9) he would suffer from malnutrition. What nonsense! With irony and not a little amusement, God points out that he has his own well-stocked larder to draw from. The wild animals in the forests, the cattle who roam the hills in their thousands (cf. REB), all the birds in the air (here the NRSV follows the early versions, reading "air" or heavens for "mountains"), the teeming life in the fields — all belong to me, says God. In any case, if I were hungry, do you think I would tell you? We are reminded of Deut. 32:37-38, which contains a satirical attack upon the gods of other nations "who ate the fat of their sacrifices, and drank the wine of their libations" and were powerless. In the sacrificial ritual of Israel, either the whole sacrifice or the choice parts of it were offered to God on the altar. Some of the language used to describe this — for example, "food offered to the LORD" (Lev. 3:11) — could lead to misunderstanding. This very psalm is evidence that such misunderstanding happened. Over against this, the psalm stresses one vital point which, in its broadest terms, we may put as follows: God does not need our worship, but we need to worship God. God would still be God if we offered him nothing, but we would not be truly human if we did not make an offering. Sacrifice should have been food for thought, not food for God. That is why the essence of true worship is spelled out in terms of a "sacrifice of thanksgiving" and the paying of "vows" (v. 14). Both "thanksgiving" and "vows" are recognized sacrifices (cf. 22:25), but such sacrifices are meaningless unless they are the expression of inner thanksgiving for the way God has enriched life and of the vows or promises made to God which must be kept. The life committed to God, springing out of thankfulness, is all important. There is a relationship out of which springs deliverance in time of trouble (cf. 3:8), and there are further opportunities to witness to the greatness and goodness of God and to acknowledge that he is the source of all that is significant and important in life (cf. 3:3).

16-23 From the people in general with their misunderstanding of sacrifice, God now turns to address others who are in more serious trouble, "the wicked" (v. 16). Their whole attitude toward life is out of line with what they formally profess when they recite God's "statutes" (v. 16). These statutes enshrine the demands made upon them by their belonging to the people of the covenant. The conduct of the wicked is then spelled out.

"You hate discipline" (v. 17). The word translated "discipline" occurs only here in the Psalms, but it is common in Proverbs, where it indicates a responsible attitude toward life which is the fruit of a willingness to receive instruction. In Proverbs it is normally translated "instruction" (e.g., Prov. 1:2, 3, 7). Only a fool despises such instruction (cf. Prov. 15:5, 32).

"You cast my words behind you" (v. 17). That is, they totally ignore them or pay no attention to them. If "my statutes" refers, as is likely, to the Decalogue, then verses 18-20 are pointing to the deliberate violation of some of these commands.

"You shall not steal" (Exod. 20:15), but "you make friends with a thief" (v. 18) or, following early versions which read different vowels, "you run with a thief," that is, you join him in his thieving exploits.

"You shall not commit adultery" (Exod. 20:14), but "you keep company with adulterers" (literally, "your portion is with adulterers"), that is, you have opted to throw in your lot with adulterers.

"You shall not bear false witness" (Exod. 20:16), but you exercise no control over your tongue; the only bit in your mouth is deceit (v. 19). Even relatives and the members of your own family are regarded as fair game for your slander (cf. 15:3; 38:11).

All such activities, of course, are destructive of the trust and respect for others which are the basis for a stable and thriving community. Not only did the wicked do such things, but they assumed that they would not be called to account for them. God had been silent. They could only conclude that he was as little troubled by what was going on as they were (v. 21a, b). But the time for silence is now over. They may think that they can pull the wool over God's eyes, but not forever. They are face to face with the God who "rebukes" them and who lays his indictment before them (v. 21c).

The psalm then ends, as did Psalm 2, with a warning and a promise. The warning must be heeded by those who "forget God," who ignore the demands he makes upon them. They are on a dangerous path which can only lead to destruction (v. 22; cf. Deut. 8:19; Job 8:11-19). But there is another way, the way of true thanksgiving which glorifies God, the way for those who are set on being loyal to their covenant obligations, the way which will lead to their enjoying God's salvation (see 3:8).

True worship, therefore, is not only glad and obedient response to all that God has done for us. It holds out the promise of an ever deepening experience of that life of wholeness and freedom which God alone can give.

Psalm 51
PENITENCE AND RENEWAL

This is the fourth, and perhaps the best known, of the penitential psalms (see Psalm 6). It has some distinctive and puzzling features. First, it is the first of the Davidic psalms in Book Two. Its heading links it with a memorable incident in David's career, the stinging rebuke he received from the court prophet Nathan for his adultery with Bathsheba and his callous murder of her husband, Uriah the Hittite, one of his own mercenary troops (2 Samuel 11–12). Like all such specific headings, this one raises as many questions as it answers. There are elements in the psalm which can hardly go back to David. For example, only a very forced interpretation of verse 18 ("rebuild the walls of Jerusalem") could link it with David. Even among those who wish to defend the Davidic reference for most of the psalm, there is a tendency to attribute the last two verses to a later age and a different community context. Others have taken the heading and certain phrases in the psalm to be clear indications that this is a royal psalm, with the "I" throughout being the king or someone speaking on his behalf. Whoever added the heading clearly saw that the psalm could have links with the narrative in 2 Samuel 11–12. Equally the psalm may reflect the experience of an unidentified individual. Many people have been here, and still are here, in their experience.

A second noteworthy feature of the psalm is the urgency and intensity of the language, which at times seems to interrupt the natural flow of ideas. The plea for forgiveness in verses 1-2, for example, is repeated in verses 7-9. Yet this is surely evidence of the depth of the psalmist's mind, as his thoughts move back and forward, exploring despair and shame, self-questioning and the need for forgiveness and renewal. It ill becomes those who have never been torn apart by such emotions to question the logical sequence of the psalmist's thought.

Third, there are verses in the psalm (e.g., vv. 10 and 17) which have achieved a firm place in liturgical traditions across the centuries because of their luminous spirituality. There are other verses which have provoked a great deal of theological discussion and controversy, notably the second half of verse 4 and verse 5. Of these Luther is on record as saying, with pardonable exaggeration, "Almost as many interpretations have been offered as there are interpreters."

1-2 The psalm begins with an urgent appeal: "Have mercy on me" or be gracious
to me (see 4:1). This is an appeal which has its roots not in anything the psalmist
can offer in self-justification, but solely in what he believes to be the essential
character of God, summed up in the words "steadfast love" (see 5:7) and "abundant mercy" or compassion, the kind of love that a mother has for the child she
bears (see 25:6). As in the opening of Psalm 32, three words pointing to what has
gone wrong in his life find their counterpart in three words which are an appeal
for the wrong to be righted. Thus in verses 1-2 the words "my transgressions . . .
my iniquity . . . my sin" have their counterpart in the words "blot out . . . wash
me . . . cleanse me."

The verb "blot out" may have in its background the thought of a tablet or
book in which the divine judge keeps a tally of all that people do. The psalmist
is pleading that the debit account be erased. Wipe the slate clean!

The verb "wash me" is commonly used of washing clothes, sometimes to
rid them of any dirt or stain which would make an approach to God inappropriate
(e.g., Exod. 19:10; Lev. 11:25). It is also used metaphorically in Jeremiah, "O
Jerusalem, wash your heart clean of wickedness" (Jer. 4:14; cf. 2:22). Sin is
pictured as ingrained dirt which has to be washed out of his system.

The verb "cleanse me" occurs frequently in cultic contexts. In Numbers 8
it is used of the Levites, who by being cleansed are consecrated to and for the
service of God (Num. 8:7, 15). In Leviticus 13, a person infected with any disease,
such as leprosy, or any clothing in touch with such a disease, must be declared
clean by a priest or the person is barred from worship as "unclean."

3-5 The psalmist, haunted by the fact that there is in his life much that is wrong,
declares his belief that the righting of such wrong can only come from God. His
urgent appeal thus leads naturally, in verses 3-5, into confession. This confession
has three facets. First, it has an honesty rooted in self-awareness. "I know my
transgressions." He has long ceased pulling the wool over his own eyes. He has
faced up to the wrong he has done. The statement "my sin is ever before me"
(v. 3) indicates that it is an inescapable reality which creates the tension in his
life.

The second facet of the confession is the recognition that God is involved.
When the psalmist confesses, "Against you, you alone, have I sinned" (v. 4), this
does not mean that he has committed an offense that is purely cultic or religious,
in the narrow sense of that word. When Nathan accuses David of murdering Uriah
and committing adultery with Bathsheba, David's response is, "I have sinned
against the LORD" (2 Sam. 12:13). For the biblical tradition, any wrong done
against another human being is a wrong done to God. This lies at the heart of
prophetic teaching. Jeremiah underlines the total incongruity of believing that
sins against other human beings — oppression of the alien, the widow, and the
orphan; stealing; murdering; and committing adultery — are consistent with wor-

shipping the LORD in his temple (Jeremiah 7). The parable of the judgment on the nations in Matt. 25:31-46 makes the same point with its declaration "just as you did/did not do it to the least of these, you did/did not do it to me" (Matt. 25:40, 45). The ultimate victim of our inhumanity to each other is God.

The second half of verse 4 raises difficult problems. The Hebrew word translated "so that" normally indicates purpose, and the words of 4b are quoted, following the Greek text, in Rom. 3:4, as part of Paul's argument that human faithlessness exists to underline the faithfulness of God. The logical corollary seems to be "Let us do evil so that good may come," an argument which Paul seeks to counter (Rom. 3:8). There are places, however, in the Old Testament where "so that" introduces a consequence or result. In this case, the psalmist is saying that since he has sinned against God, God is right to pass sentence upon him. The REB leaves out "so that" altogether and is probably correct in putting the two halves of 4b side by side and translating "you are right when you accuse me, and justified in passing sentence."

The third facet of the confession is its awareness that the psalmist himself is powerless to remedy the situation. Much debated has been verse 5, with the psalmist's confession, "Indeed, I was born guilty, a sinner when my mother conceived me." Although childbirth, like menstruation, temporarily renders a woman ceremonially unclean in Levitical law (Lev. 12:2-5), verse 5 can hardly be claiming that sexual intercourse and conception are sinful. How could they be when life is God's gift and numerous children are a sign of God's blessing (cf. Psalms 127, 128)? Nor are these words an indication that the psalmist regarded his birth as the result of sexual impropriety on the part of his mother. He is not trying to make excuses for himself by blaming his conduct on heredity. Nor is the verse to be taken as a statement of the doctrine of original sin, as it has sometimes been misunderstood. This is rather the psalmist's dramatic way of saying that he cannot by himself escape from the web of evil in which he is entrapped and has been entrapped from his birth. Such was the world into which be was born. The word translated "guilty" is the same word translated "iniquity" in verse 2 (cf. REB). He is therefore caught in an evil from which he cannot extricate himself. This thought leads him back to where the psalm begins. There is something which only God can do for him, which he must be open to receive.

6-13   These verses deal with what God demands and what God alone can give. God desires "truth" (v. 6) or, better, "faithfulness" (see 25:5). This lies at the heart of the psalmist's problem. Sin is not simply the individual immoral act, however heinous. It is the gap which exists between God and ourselves, and the closer we come to God the more we are conscious of that gap. It is always the most deeply religious people, those who in the delightful Scottish phrase are "furthest ben with God," who are most conscious of their sinfulness. The "faithfulness" which is characteristic of God makes the psalmist ever more conscious of the lack of such faithfulness in his own life. Both the words translated "inward being" and "secret heart" (v. 6) are unusual words, the first pointing to what is not visible on the surface, the second to what is there at the very core of someone's life. Faced with what is humanly speaking an impossible demand, the psalmist can only plead with God to do what he himself cannot do: "teach me . . . purge me . . . wash me" (vv. 6-7). There can be no self-achieved piety or forgiveness. We are dealing here with what has been called the "paradox of grace," well summed up in the nineteenth-century hymn, "And every virtue we possess, and every victory won, and every thought of holiness are his alone."

The psalmist implores, "Teach me wisdom" (v. 6), that wisdom which is rooted in the fear of the LORD (cf. Prov. 1:7). He asks, "Purge me with hyssop." Hyssop is a plant which because of its bushy head could be used to sprinkle liquid. Thus it was used to smear the blood on the lintel and doorposts of the Hebrew homes in Egypt (Exod. 12:22) and in various acts of ritual cleansing (cf. Leviticus 14; Numbers 19). But this psalmist is looking for something deeper than ritual cleansing. The sin which he has confessed needs to be "de-sinned," which is what the word translated "purge" really means. The request "wash me and I shall be whiter than snow" involves an image that might at first seem foreign for someone in Israel. Snow, however, does fall heavily at times in Palestine. The peak of Mt. Hermon is often snowcapped, and in the dazzling sun it becomes a brilliant image of purity (cf. Isa. 1:18).

As in Ps. 6:2 and 22:14, the "crushed" bones (v. 8) may indicate the psychological condition of tension and despair within the psalmist. He longs for the return of that joy and gladness which would be the sign of his acceptance by God (cf. 16:11), an acceptance that would mean that God's penetrating gaze was no longer focused on his sins. The slate would be wiped clean (cf. v. 1).

The theme reaches its climax in verses 10-12. The psalmist is looking for a miracle, something which God alone can do. The verb "create" (v. 10) is found predominantly in the creation hymn in Genesis 1 and in Isaiah 40–55, always with God as its subject. In the Psalms it is found only here and in Ps. 89:12, 47. The need for God's gift of a "new and steadfast [rather than "right," NRSV] spirit" (v. 10), a spirit which is "willing" or generous (v. 12), echoes the way in which the prophets stress the need for such renewal to guarantee that the nation's future will not be a rerun of its shameful past (Ezek. 12:17-29; 36:26-28; Jer. 31:31-34). The word translated "spirit" (Hebrew rûaḥ) is the word translated "wind" in Ps. 1:4. When used of God, it indicates his powerful activity; when used of people, it points to God-given vitality and gifts. Here the psalmist is looking for a renewed inner life, which will be the product of God's "holy spirit" (v. 11), an expression which occurs only here and in Isa. 63:10, 11 in the Old Testament. In view of the meaning of the word "holy," however (see 2:6), this is simply another way of talking about the spirit of God, the vitality which is the essence of God's character. As such it is God's to give, to become part of the psalmist's life and experience.

From this will flow again "the joy of your salvation" (cf. v. 14; see 3:8) and a life characterized by a "willing" and noble spirit. It is of the essence of such a renewed life that it must be shared (v. 13) with others caught in the same destructive grip of "transgressions" and "sin." They need to be taught that there is an answer to their dilemma. The inevitable corollary of salvation is evangelism. According to Acts 4, the attempt by the authorities to silence Peter and John was met with the response, "We cannot keep from speaking about what we have seen and heard" (Acts 4:20). The student in the school of faith becomes the teacher, who shares not textbook theology, but personal experience of God.

14-19   Such experience also leads to worship, which can never be merely expressed in outward forms, in "sacrifice," and in "burnt offering" (v. 16; see 40:6). Worship will find joyful expression in witnessing to deliverance from "bloodshed." The plural form of the word "blood" used here is capable of different interpretations. It could refer simply to the violent deeds the psalmist has committed, and this would fit with a Davidic reference. In this case, "deliver" means "Save me from the consequences of my bloody deeds and the havoc they have caused in my life." On the other hand, the psalmist may feel that what he has done deserves the death penalty (cf. Ezek. 3:18-20; 18:10-13), a death penalty from which there is no escape, certainly not through the sacrificial rituals. He therefore throws himself on the mercy of God, the only person who can deliver him from the death penalty he carries. All that he has to offer to God and all that can be acceptable to God are "a broken spirit . . . a broken and a contrite [REB: "chastened"] heart." There is something to be said for reading at the beginning of verse 17, "My sacrifice, O God, is . . ." (cf. REB). The experience through which the psalmist has lived has destroyed all self-confidence and self-reliance. All he can offer to God are the broken fragments of his life. All hope for the future depends upon a God who never spurns or "despises" (cf. 22:26) those who in their moment of need turn to him.

As do many other psalms (see 3:8), this intensely personal psalm ends on a community note: "Do good to Zion [cf. 2:6] . . . and rebuild the walls of Jerusalem" (v. 18). These are hardly words which make sense in the time of David. They would be appropriate in the late exilic or the early postexilic situation implied in the book of Haggai, or over a century later in the time of Nehemiah (cf. Nehemiah 2), and may have been added then by an editor. The psalmist's experience becomes the basis for a mood of penitence and the hope for renewal for the entire community.

It has sometimes been wrongly claimed that verse 19, with its emphasis upon sacrifice, represents a total misunderstanding of the substance of the psalm, which is said to reject sacrifice completely and replace it with spiritual worship. But this is to misunderstand the critical attitude toward sacrifice in this and other psalms (see discussion at 40:6). The postexilic community was well aware of the biting criticism of sacrifice in prophetic literature. But that community was responsible for preserving and editing the teaching of the prophets, and it saw nothing wrong in resuming the sacrificial cult in the temple. Given the proper attitude in the hearts and minds of the worshippers, an inner spirituality could be genuinely expressed through "right sacrifices," a phrase which can mean either sacrifices offered according to the right ritual, or sacrifices offered by people who are right with God. When these two things come together, there can be that true worship of God which is the theme of Psalm 50. The outward form, of course, was always easier to control and to criticize than the inner motivation. It still is.

Psalm 52
FALSE AND TRUE VALUES

This and the next three psalms have in their heading the words "A Maskil of David" (see Psalm 32). The rest of the heading links the psalm with the events in 1 Samuel 21–22, where Doeg the Edomite, one of Saul's servants, informs Saul of the help given to David by the priests at Nob. This act leads to their being arraigned before Saul and massacred by Doeg. The content of the psalm, however, hardly supports this linkage. The language in verses 1-3 and 7 says nothing of any massacre; nor is Doeg's part truly described in 1 Samuel as "lying." We are dealing here with accusations directed against someone whose life is characterized by a false set of values, who believes that money guarantees all that is important in life and provides power which can be used for purely selfish ends.

Although the psalm is difficult to classify, it has the feel of a trial scene. It begins with an accusing question, "Why are you boastful, O mighty one." Boasting may not always be wrong, but there is something wrong when a "a big shot" boasts about "mischief" or evil. The word translated "mighty one" (Hebrew *gibbôr*) indicates someone who has power and knows how to use it. Both the NRSV and REB translations of the second half of verse 1 assume an alteration to the Hebrew text which is vouched for in the Syriac translation. The Hebrew text could be translated, "The steadfast love of God is [i.e., lasts] every day," thus placing the false boasting of this big shot in the context of the one thing which is a valid reason for boasting (cf. 49:6). There is much to be said for retaining the Hebrew text.

In verses 2-4, the accusing question leads into a description of the false values which dominate this person's life. Here is a person who is "plotting destruction" (v. 2), doing a demolition job on other people. He uses his razor sharp tongue to deadly effect (cf. Psalm 12) and is a "worker of treachery," someone who practices deceit (Ps. 101:7 is the only other occurrence of this phrase in the Old Testament). Here is someone whose sense of values is so awry that he "loves evil more than good," lying and falsehood more than the truth. He is the archetypal con man (v. 3). The Hebrew word translated "truth" in verse 3 is the word often rendered "righteousness" (see 7:8), but being in the right over against lies means speaking the truth.

After the pause in the psalm, indicated by "Selah" (see Psalm 3), the perversity of this man is underlined by the repetition of the words "You love" (v. 4), as if to say, Yes, indeed, that is the kind of person you are, a person who loves "words that devour." The expression "words that devour" refers either to "malicious talk" (REB) involving character assassination, or perhaps to accusations which destroy (literally, "swallow up") other people. Such words are the product of a tongue steeped in deceit, cheating, and misleading rather than in respect and honesty. Such conduct inevitably leads to judgment. God's judgment is graphically described in verse 5 with four verbs: "break down," a verb often used of demolishing a house; "snatch," denoting a quick and perhaps unexpected act; "tear you from your tent," that is, forcibly eject you from your home; and "uproot you from the land of the living," a poetic way of describing the death penalty. A way strewn with false values can only lead to the ultimate penalty. Such is the verdict of the divine judge.

Verses 6-7 then describe the reaction of those who share other values, "the righteous" (see Psalm 1). They will "see and fear," a phrase which neatly plays on the similarity in sound of these two verbs (yir'û and yîrā'û). Fear in this context is probably the fear or reverence of the LORD (cf. 19:9), rooted in this case in what the righteous see God doing to those who challenge his values.

The righteous will "laugh at the evildoer" (v. 6), not maliciously or with any sense of personal animosity, but, as the words which follow clearly indicate, because they realize what a ridiculous challenge is being made to God's sense of values (cf. God's laughter in Ps. 2:4). The righteous will see a person who, instead of seeking "refuge" in God (cf. 27:1), "trusted" (cf. 4:5) and "sought refuge" in what could ultimately provide no lasting security, "abundant riches" and "wealth" (cf. Psalm 49). "Guaranteed security" is one of the favorite slogans of insurance companies and investment firms. There is no such thing, says the psalmist, except in God.

In the last two verses the psalmist lays his own cards on the table. He compares himself to a "green" or flourishing "olive tree." Since the olive is an evergreen, the word refers not to its color but to its vigorous growth (REB: "spreading"). The olive tree, which can have a life span of hundreds of years, was basic to the economy of the land. It provided food; its oil was widely used for domestic, medicinal, and cultic purposes; and its wood was suitable for carving (cf. 1 Kgs. 6:21). Olive trees may well have grown in the courtyards of the temple area. For the psalmist they are the sign of all that is needed for life, there "in the house of God" (v. 8). There he expresses his trust in the "steadfast love" of God (cf. 5:7) and thanks God for what he has done for him. The man with perverted values may prefer evil to good, but the psalmist knows what is good — to be together with the "faithful" (see comment on 4:3), looking forward expectantly for God to act in accordance with his true character. There is no need to change the Hebrew "I will wait for your name," at the end of verse 9, into "I will proclaim" (NRSV) or "glorify" (REB) your name, once we recognize what kind of waiting this is (see comment on 25:3), an eager looking forward. A living faith, rooted in the steadfast love of God and centered on true and lasting values, ought always to have this eager expectation.

Psalm 53

This psalm is virtually identical with Psalm 14, except that here the name Elohim (God) substitutes for the personal divine name Yahweh (LORD). See the comment on Psalm 14. For "Mahalath" in the heading, see Psalm 88.

Psalm 54
GOD IS MY HELPER

As well as providing liturgical indicators (cf. 4:1), the heading of this psalm links it with a specific incident in David's life, when some of the inhabitants of Ziph, not far south of Hebron, betrayed his whereabouts to Saul (1 Sam. 23:19-24; 26:1-25). This link, however, which is not the unanimous voice of tradition, does little to help our understanding of the psalm. It is a psalm of lament reflecting a crisis situation in life and the discovery of a sustaining truth: "God is my helper" (v. 4). The psalm falls into two sections; the break between them is marked by "Selah" at the end of verse 3.

Verses 1-2 contain an urgent prayer, both verses beginning in Hebrew with the word "God." It is as if the psalmist is facing a situation where he knows that human help is unavailable or futile. His sole hope lies in God. The psalmist implores God, "Save me [see 3:2] . . . vindicate me [see 7:9]," because it is God's nature (for "name," see comment on 5:11) to save. He is a God who intervenes to deliver and who, as a true judge, can be depended upon to acquit those who live under unjust threats (see 4:1; 43:1).

Verse 3 describes the crisis situation which the psalmist has been facing. He is under attack by "the insolent." This translation assumes a minor change to the Hebrew text, which instead of "insolent" reads "stranger," a word which normally indicates those who do not belong to the people of God (cf. 44:20). But "strangers" may well indicate those within the community who by their attitude and conduct have alienated themselves from God (cf. Isa. 1:4, where, unless we change the text, the words "utterly estranged" are a description of a sinful people). A member of a Christian congregation can be as far away from God as a card-carrying member of the Communist party! The psalmist describes such "strangers" as "the ruthless," people who throw their weight about, prepared unscrupulously to use the power and influence they have to destroy anyone who stands in their way. They "seek my life." Such conduct is rooted in one basic error: "they do not set God before them," that is, they have eliminated God from their lives and thus thrown overboard the moral values and restraints that faith in God should bring (cf. Psalms 15 and 24).

Over against this threat to his life, the psalmist in verses 4-5 gives voice to words of confidence and trust, which lie behind his urgent prayer in verses 1-2. "O God . . . O God . . . "(vv. 1, 2) leads into "But surely God. . . ." The words "but surely" are the NRSV translation of the Hebrew word often translated "behold" (see 33:18). The psalmist goes on to affirm, "God is my helper" (cf. 30:2); "the Lord," the one who is master of the situation, is "the upholder of my life." The Hebrew text reads "with [or: "among"] the upholders of my life," which in context probably means that God can be counted upon to be his "upholder" (REB: "sustainer") par excellence (cf. 3:5). So for the psalmist God is the unseen presence countering the all-too-visible presence of his human enemies.

To these enemies the psalmist now turns in verse 5. The first half of the verse is capable of two interpretations. The traditional Hebrew text is consistent with the rendering of the REB: "May their own malice recoil on the foes who beset me" (see 3:14-16). The NRSV assumes an alteration which makes God the subject of the verb: "He will repay my enemies for their evil," and this fits in with the second half of the verse with its appeal to God's "faithfulness" (cf. 25:5) to "put an end to" or to destroy them. Here we meet again something of that cold harshness which we noted in Ps. 5:10, an understandable harshness given that for the psalmist God's justice had to be displayed in this world or it would not be displayed at all. Such a harshness is understandable still on the lips of those who have most reason to gaze into the unspeakable evil that human beings can perpetrate. On the fiftieth anniversary of the liberation of Auschwitz, Elie Wiesel, himself a survivor of the horror, could only pray, "O God of mercy, do not be merciful to those who perpetrated such horrors." This may not be the theology of the cross, but it does take evil seriously. It believes that God must react against evil, and it leaves it to God so to act. At least in the psalm we are spared the picture of a knight in shining armor riding forth in all the arrogance of self-righteousness to slaughter such enemy "strangers" in the name of God, a picture which has sadly besmirched the pages of Christian history.

The psalm ends on a note of thanksgiving (vv. 6-7), which finds expression through the accepted cultic channels. The essence of the "freewill offering" (cf. Lev. 7:16; Num. 29:39) is a spontaneous expression of thanksgiving for what has been received from God. It is not the fulfillment of a vow previously made, as if a deal had been made with God — "I'll offer you a sacrifice if you do this for me." Rather, the offering expresses gratitude for unexpected and undeserved grace. The offering recognizes that if good has conquered or come out of evil, then that good is of God (v. 6; cf. 52:9). God has "delivered me" (cf. 7:1; 31:1) from every kind of trouble, affirms the psalmist. The closing words of the psalm say simply "my eye has looked on my enemies." Does the Hebrew mean "looked in triumph" (NRSV) or "look with delight on the downfall of" (REB)? Or does it mean that his enemies are now "a sight for sore eyes"? We need not read into these words an element of gloating (see 52:6). The psalm ends on a note of role reversal. The psalmist, once under threat, is now delivered; the enemies, who were once out to get him, have got their comeuppance. The time scale of such role reversal may not be our time scale; the way of its happening may not be our chosen way, but in a world where evil often seems rampant and destructive of everything that makes human life meaningful, faith insists that the last word is not with evil but with God.

Psalm 55
AN UNEXPECTED STAB IN THE BACK

Although the heading classifies this as a Davidic psalm, it makes no attempt to link it with any specific incident in David's life. Commentators have not been so reticent. As in many another psalm of individual lament, we listen to an appeal to God in a crisis situation (verses 1-2), at the heart of which there are "the enemy" (v. 3) and "the wicked." This lament, though, has two distinguishing features. First, the psalmist's problems are closely related to life in a city, which has its own seven deadly sins, violence and strife, iniquity and trouble, ruin, oppression and fraud (vv. 9-11). But what city? It fits the Jerusalem of Isaiah's or Jeremiah's day. Equally it could be Samaria, especially if we assume a northern origin for much of the material in Book Two of the Psalms. Some have argued that this is the story of a Jew living in an alien pagan city in the postexilic period. Since there are no clear markers of the date or setting of this psalm, the identity of the city must take its place alongside other unresolved issues in the psalm. Second, central to the psalmist's agony is a stab in the back by someone whom he describes as "my companion, my familiar friend" (v. 13). Those who seek a link with David have tended to identify this Old Testament Brutus with Ahithophel, who became the evil genius behind Absalom's rebellion (2 Samuel 15). Ahithophel's role, however, hardly fits the language of the psalm. The familiar friend must remain in the lengthy list of unidentified persons in the Old Testament.

As in Psalm 51, the intensity of the psalmist's feelings disrupts the logical sequence of thought, with two separate sections on his treacherous companion (vv. 12-14 and 20-21) and several verses dealing with God's judgment upon his enemies (vv. 9, 15, 23).

1-2 The psalm begins with an urgent appeal to God, its opening words very similar to Ps. 54:2. With the words "do not hide yourself" the psalmist is asking God not to look the other way or be indifferent (cf. Isa. 58:7; Deut. 22:3) to his "supplication" (cf. 6.9) or plea for help. Help is urgently needed since "I am troubled in my complaint" (v. 2; REB: "for my cares leave me no peace"). Both these translations assume that the verb translated "troubled" (NRSV) comes from a word meaning to wander to and fro. The picture is of someone who is restless and at his wits' end. So he turns to "complaint," a word common on the lips of Job (e.g., Job 7:13; 9:27; 10:1), the outward verbal expression of inner anxiety.

3-5 With the words "I am distraught," best taken as the opening words of verse 3, we are told of the nature of the crisis in the psalmist's life. He is surrounded by vociferous attacks from people he can only describe as "the enemy" and "the wicked" (v. 3). The word translated "clamor" occurs only here and could equally well be translated "oppression" or "threats." Their words are backed up by their deeds. They "bring" (REB: "heap") "trouble" or evil, the same word being part of the expression "evildoers." They "cherish enmity," though the verb, which means "to hunt down," probably has the sense of bearing a grudge; hence the REB translates "revile." Why these people are active "in anger" is not stated, but from the psalmist's point of view it is totally unjustified and inexplicable. Any inner peace he enjoyed has gone. He is "in anguish" (v. 4), a word associated with childbirth, but used metaphorically by Jeremiah to describe the agony which gripped him as part of his prophetic ministry (Jer. 4:19).

Words are heaped upon words to describe this inner agony: "the terrors of death" (which may mean simply "deadly terrors"), "fear," "trembling," "horror" (perhaps "shuddering"; cf. Job 21:6). Here is a man at the end of his tether, at the mercy of forces and emotions he cannot control and which are tearing him apart.

6-8 It is small wonder that the psalmist dreams of escape, of opting out (see comment on Psalm 11), of finding rest by flying away like a dove (vv. 6-8). Why the dove of all birds? Probably because the dove nests safe and secure on the cliff face on the inaccessible sides of a gorge (Jer. 48:28; Song of Sol. 2:14). So the psalmist wishes to fly away to find safe, temporary refuge in the wilderness, the sparsely populated steppe lands, far from the enemies who threaten him. Like a traveler caught in a sudden storm with its violent winds, he imagines himself hurrying to find shelter. Yet, as we saw in Psalm 11, this kind of escapist dream is futile. In the situation in which he finds himself, with all its hatred and violence, he must find God.

9-11 These verses vividly describe the turbulent city life known to the psalmist. "Violence and strife" are ironically depicted as the city watchmen doing their rounds. The city center, which ought to have been teeming with life and community activities, is being destroyed by mischief and "trouble," a word which, although it can mean hard work (cf. Eccl. 1:2), also means struggle or suffering (Isa. 53:11). The marketplace or public square, where business and legal affairs were transacted, is inhabited by "oppression and deceit" (cf. 10:7). It is not difficult for us to identify with this today — the violence in our cities, both meaningless thuggery and the coldly calculated bomb; the anonymity and lack of community spirit in urban areas, where people rush to work, shop, or lounge about unemployed, finding little time for compassion or caring; the sleaze factor at work in business and public life.

In face of this the psalmist appeals to God. He asks God to "confuse" and "confound" (literally, "divide") their "tongues," which could mean either their "speech" (NRSV) or their "counsels" (REB). There may be an allusion to the Tower of Babel story in Genesis 11, where faced with people proudly attempting to build for themselves a secure and impressive city, God comes down "to confuse their tongues" and to scatter them. Dividing their tongues, however, might mean condemning them out of their own mouths. Luther interestingly drew attention to the story of Susanna, where the elders who have accused Susanna are themselves condemned when interrogated separately and found to be giving conflicting evidence. Strife can only encourage strife. Violence brings its own nemesis. The perpetrator of fraud becomes the victim of fraud.

12-14   To live in such a hostile and destructive environment is bad enough, but it is at least bearable when dealing with people clearly identifiable as "enemies." At least you can always try to keep out of their way (v. 12). The psalmist, however, has received a stab in the back from a totally unexpected quarter, from one who is described (v. 13) as "my equal," which could refer to someone who comes from the same rank or social class, or someone who is regarded as sharing the same set of values, "a man of my own sort" (REB). This figure is described in various ways. He is "my companion," a close friend or buddy. Micah sees as one of the signs of the corruption in society in his day that it was no longer possible to trust such a friend (Mic. 7:5). This the psalmist discovered in his own experience. He is "my familiar friend," one known and therefore trusted. He is one "with whom I kept pleasant company" or enjoyable friendship (for the Hebrew word *sôd,* here translated "company," see comment on 25:14). This was a friendship sealed by their sharing together in the great religious festivals, part of the crowd that thronged to the temple.

15   The description of the corrupt city was prefaced by an appeal to God to destroy those responsible for such corruption. Now the sad description of an erstwhile friend leads into an appeal to God for death to strike such people down swiftly and unexpectedly. The language of the second line of verse 15 suggests a parallel with the fate of Korah and his company who defied Moses (cf. Num. 16:16, 32-33); they went down alive to Sheol (for Sheol, see 6:5). Such must be the response to the evil which is "in their homes and in their hearts," or perhaps better, "the evil which is at home in their hearts," that is, evil which has become second nature to them.

16-19 In contrast to all such devious people, the psalmist puts his own cards on the table, in words which express a confident trust in God. "I call upon God" (v. 16) in the certainty that he will deliver or save (cf. 3:2). Evening, morning, and noon — probably the regular times for prayer in the psalmist's life — he offers God not false piety, but that which is central to his life, complaint and moaning (cf. v. 2), in the certainty that God will hear and respond. He will "redeem me" (see 25:22), "unharmed" (literally, "in shalom"; see 4:9; 29:11) in the battle being waged against the many who surround him and are out to get him.

    This confidence is based on the character of the God to whom he prays, the God "who is enthroned from of old" (cf. 9:7), the God whose authority has never been and cannot be undermined, the God "who will hear and humble them" or "answer" them. To say "Yes" to the psalmist's complaint is to say "No" to his enemies. The second half of verse 19 is very uncertain. The word translated "change" usually means a change of clothing. In Job 14:14, however, it means a change of circumstances, a release or relief. Unless we follow the REB and invoke an Arabic root to give the translation "They have no respect for an oath," we must decide what kind of change is meant here and determine to whom it refers. If it refers to the wicked, it might mean that they have no intention of changing their attitude or that they feel so secure that they cannot imagine any change happening to them. The reference, however, may be to God, the God "who does not change" (cf. Jas. 1:17). In the Hebrew, verse 19 begins "God will hear and will answer them." This could then be followed by two statements describing this God, "the one who is enthroned of old" and "the one who never changes." The last line then further describes the "them," who in spite of this "do not fear God." If the psalmist is a Jew living in an alien city, then those who "do not fear God" are the people of the city, whom he can only regard as pagans. If he is at home, say, in Samaria or Jerusalem, then this is a description of those who in theory share his faith and belong to the community of God's people, yet who by their deeds and their attitude show that this is not where they really belong (cf. Matt. 7:21).

20-21 The description of people who "do not fear God" brings the psalmist sadly and bitterly back to the one who "had laid hands on a friend." The words "My companion" at the beginning of verse 20 are not in the Hebrew but are put there to clarify the reference. "A friend" is literally one who is "in his shalom," one who is at peace with him or who is in a true relationship with him. The friend is one who has a "covenant" with him (see 25:10), and the covenant is "violated" or profaned, that is, regarded as having no sacred or solemn significance at all. Outwardly the friend's speech was smooth as cream, but inwardly he was spoiling for a fight (cf. v. 18); outwardly his words were more soothing than oil, but inwardly they were like daggers drawn (the word translated daggers or "swords" in v. 21 occurs only here in the Old Testament). In these words we are listening to the pent-up bitterness of the psalmist against one whom he once trusted but can no longer trust.

22   Verse 22 raises interesting questions. Who is speaking? Are these the words of a priest or temple prophet encouraging the psalmist to continue his trust in God? "Cast your burden [or, more accurately, "your lot," that is, what you have been given in life] upon the LORD." Since you belong to the "righteous" (see Psalm 1) your trust will be vindicated. Or are these the words of the psalmist's erstwhile friend, mockingly pouring scorn on his faith, saying, "You've got problems? Hand them over to God, surely he won't let you down, will he?" Or are they the words of the psalmist himself, reflecting on his own experience, and saying to anyone prepared to listen (the "you" in verse 22 is singular), "Whatever life may have brought you, share it with God." This seems the most likely interpretation, and it contains within it an important theological truth. The psalmist does not say, "Hand over your life with all its difficulties to God and he will carry it for you." What he does say is, "In the midst of whatever life may bring, God will sustain you; he will give you the resources and the strength to cope." Problems do not necessarily disappear for those who have faith in God. Rather, they become a shared experience, shared with God and drawing upon all the resources he provides. In the context of that shared experience, the righteous shall never be shaken ("moved" is the NRSV's rather colorless translation in verse 22).

23   The psalm ends in verse 23 with a dramatic contrast. Those who have been out to get the psalmist, the "bloodthirsty" and the "treacherous," will come to a divinely decreed and speedy end, cast down into "the lowest pit," a description of Sheol, with their life expectancy unfulfilled. The psalmist, on the contrary, declares his continuing faith in the simple yet profound words, "But I will trust in you" (cf. 4:5). Human disillusionment he has endured, but there is no disillusionment in his attitude toward God.

Psalm 56
TRUST AND COMMITMENT

The text of this psalm poses many problems. It is a psalm of dramatic contrasts: enemies doomed to perish under God's wrath and a psalmist committed to live in God's presence; a God highlighting the frailty of human pretension and a psalmist living in the tension between fear and trust.

The heading to the psalm does not provide us with much help in interpreting it. We are already familiar with "the leader" and a "Miktam" (see Psalm 16), but the words translated "according to The Dove on Far-off Terebinths" (NRSV) or "Set to the Dove of the Distant Oaks" (REB) occur only here. Early translators saw in the "Dove" a reference to Israel, and since then speculation on the meaning of the phrase has abounded. It is perhaps safest to see in the phrase a reference to the tune to which the psalm was to be sung. The historical note links the psalm with David's experience at Gath (1 Sam. 21:10-15). Some features of the psalm would be appropriate on the lips of a king under threat from foreign enemies. The reference to the "peoples" or nations in verse 7 provides one example. Yet one does not need to be royal to identify with the experience enshrined in the psalm.

The psalm divides into two sections of more or less equal length, verses 1-7 and verses 8-13. Central to both sections is a refrain which, with minor variation in language, occurs in verses 4 and 10-11. The theme of the refrain is trust in God, but it is trust which is being challenged by the activity of those described by three Hebrew words: "foes" (v. 1), those who "fight against me" (v. 2), and the most common word, "my enemies" (v. 9). The psalmist graphically describes their activity. They are out to "trample me" underfoot (vv. 1, 2; this is better than the traditional translation "pant after me") and to "oppress me" (v. 1). They "seek to injure my cause" (v. 5; REB: "wound me with words"), a phrase which could also be translated "twist my words." Out to destroy the psalmist, they "watch my steps" (literally, "heels") or "dog my footsteps" (REB).

The influence and the power they use are insidious and demoralizing. However real and threatening, though, this is the activity of those who are no more than mere mortals. The three words which described these dangerous enemies find their counterpart in three words which cut them down to size. They are merely "people" (v. 1; Hebrew ĕnôš, the word translated "human beings" in Ps. 8:4). They represent the threat of "a mere mortal" (v. 11; Hebrew 'ādām; see comment on Ps. 8:4). They are mere "flesh" (v. 3; Hebrew bāśār, a word used in several Old Testament passages to point to the transitoriness and frailty of human life, especially in contrast with God). In Isa. 31:3 the Egyptians with their powerful military machine are described as "human" ('ādām) and not God; their horses are flesh (bāśār), and not spirit (rûaḥ; cf. Isa. 40:6; Jer. 17:5). It is not surprising, then, that the psalmist begins with a plea to the one in whom he believes true security can be found: "Be gracious to me, O God" (cf. 4:1). He appeals to the one who is "Most High," towering above even the most lofty and arrogant of human pretensions. This is the one in whom the psalmist declares, "I put my trust" (v. 3; see 4:5).

Verses 3 and 4 underline the complex relationship between fear and trust.

It is fear, when the whole of life seems vulnerable, which leads to trust: "When I am afraid, I put my trust in you." And it is trust which is the antidote to fear: "In God I trust; I am not afraid; what can flesh do to me?" But this is not trust reaching out desperately into the unknown. It is trust rooted in God, "whose word [or: "promise"] I praise" (v. 4). We are not told what word or promise this is. It may be that the psalmist is anticipating the word of reassurance to be spoken to him in the name of God by the priest or temple prophet (see comment on 12:5). It is also possible that the "word" he praises is the whole tradition of faith in which he has been brought up, the word which is God's revelation of himself to his people. True trust must be rooted in what is known. You can't trust an unknown God; you can't trust a capricious God. You can trust a God whose word of steadfast love came to Israel, the word which became flesh in Jesus (cf. John 1).

If the first half of the psalm begins with the plea "Be gracious to me, O God" (v. 1), it ends with an appeal to God to deal "in wrath" with the people who constitute a threat to all that the psalmist holds dear in the name of God (see 6:1 for a discussion of the anger or wrath of God). Although the first half of verse 7 is open to several different interpretations, it is clear that the psalmist is convinced that the conduct of those who threaten him cannot lead to anything other than their own destruction. They will reap what they sow (cf. Gal. 6:7). The enemies are very much to the fore in verses 1-7, but now they recede into the background in verses 8-13. They are in "retreat" (v. 9), because God — the God who "is for me" (v. 9) — is now central to the psalmist's thought. This is not a claim to any private monopoly of God on either a personal or national level; it is a claim to believe in a God who knows what is happening in life and who in particular cares about what happens to those who are vulnerable and under pressure.

The psalmist believes in a God who "kept count of my tossings" (v. 8). The word "tossings" retains the flavor of the word which means "to move to and fro," but it could equally be translated "my grief" (REB), since grief was expressed through such movement of the body. The translation "grief" moves naturally into the next phrase, in which the psalmist says to God, "You put my tears in your bottle." The word translated "bottle" elsewhere indicates a skin container used for some of the basic necessities of life, wine, milk, and water (Josh. 9:4; Judg. 4:19). The picture is of a God who carefully preserves "the tears" of the psalmist and records them in his book or scroll. The book may be the same book as that called elsewhere "the book of the living" or the book of life (69:28). In it God records the names of, and what has happened to, those who are of his family. Such a book features in several biblical passages from Exod. 32:31-32 to Rev. 20:12 and 21:27. It is one of those colorful images which stress that God knows what is going on here and now and takes note. As Malachi puts it: "The LORD took note and listened, and a book of remembrance was written before him of those who revered the LORD and thought on his name. They shall be mine, says the LORD of hosts, my special possession on the day when I act . . ." (Mal. 3:16-17).

The craft of the Hebrew poet is very much in evidence in verse 8, with the word translated "tossing" similar in sound to the word translated "tears" and "your record" at the end of the verse echoing the earlier verb "kept count."

The refrain of trust in verses 10-11 repeats and expands verse 4, with a conscious repetition of the words, "In God, whose word I praise" by "in the LORD, whose word I praise." The God in whom the psalmist puts his trust is none other than the LORD, Yahweh, with all the rich associations which surround that name (cf. Exod. 3:13-16).

The psalm ends in verses 12-13 with the psalmist accepting an obligation to fulfill vows he has made to God and to express his thanksgiving through an appropriate offering (see comment on 50:14). It is thanksgiving for deliverance from "death," that is, from all the forces which threatened to destroy him. This thanksgiving opens the way to a life which is the negation of death, a life lived out in the presence of God and characterized by "light," not darkness (cf. 27:1). This is God's gift to the psalmist, a gift which commits him to walk in this way. The psalm thus sketches various stages in a spiritual pilgrimage, from faith through crisis to renewed trust in God, and from renewed trust in God to the continuing commitment of faith.

Psalm 57
THE SURGE OF FAITH
AT THE STORM CENTER

Psalms 56 and 57 have much in common in their structure, in the experience they describe, and in their theology. It is interesting, however, to note how different is the language they use. The word "trust" echoes across Psalm 56, but it never occurs in Psalm 57. The words "steadfast love" and "faithfulness" are central to Psalm 57, but we never hear them in Psalm 56. Yet trust is as theologically central to Psalm 57 as it is to Psalm 56, and God's "steadfast love" and "faithfulness" are as basic to Psalm 56 as they are celebrated in Psalm 57. This should remind us that different people will use different language to describe what is basically the same religious experience. Theology can never be cribbed or confined within one set of words, certainly not the words which trip most easily off our own tongue.

The historical note in the heading to Psalm 57 links the psalm with David's precarious situation when he was on the run from Saul, either in the cave of Adullam (1 Samuel 22) or in the cave near En-gedi (1 Samuel 24). It may well be that this was originally a royal psalm, but the experience enshrined in it speaks to anyone struggling to come to terms with dangers which seem to threaten all that makes life meaningful. The only other words in the heading which we have not previously encountered are "Do not destroy" (see also Psalms 58, 59, and 75). The meaning is far from clear, but there is a reference in Isa. 65:8 to a vintage song beginning with these same words, and this may point to the association with a well-known tune.

The psalm is carefully structured in two parts: verses 1-4, leading into the refrain in verse 5; and verses 6-10, leading into the refrain in verse 11. In the first part, the thought moves from God to those who threaten the psalmist; in the second part the thought moves from those who threaten the psalmist back to God, whose "steadfast love" and "faithfulness" are celebrated in verses 3 and 10. Verses 7-11 appear again, along with parts of Psalm 60, as Psalm 108. For the significance of this see the comments on Psalm 60.

The psalm begins with the same plea that begins Psalm 56. It is difficult to understand why the NRSV should change "Be gracious to me" (56:1) into "Be merciful to me" (57:1). The repetition of the plea in verse 1 indicates the depth of the psalmist's need. There is, however, a subtle difference from the opening of Psalm 56. There the psalmist's plea was based on the extremity of the situation in which he found himself; here the plea has its rationale in the psalmist's reaching out to the God who is his "refuge" (cf. 2:12) in face of the storms which threaten him (for "in the shadow of your wings" in v. 1, see comment on 17:8 and 36:7). Such refuge is needed "until the destroying storms pass by." The Hebrew word translated "destroying storms" elsewhere in the Psalms is simply translated "ruin" or "destruction." It is often closely associated with the damage caused by slander and malicious gossip (cf. 38:12; 52:4). Perhaps it is no surprise, then, that when the psalmist goes on to describe the activities of those seeking to undermine his life, he refers to "teeth" and "their tongues" (v. 4). The language in verse 4 is graphic. The translation "greedily devours" conceals a verb which elsewhere in the Psalms is closely associated with destructive fire (cf. 83:14; 97:3). The REB neatly conveys the meaning of "that greedily devours human prey" with "man-eaters."

The psalmist's cry to God "Most High" (see 7:17) in verse 2 is based on three convictions. The first is that this is a God "who fulfills his purpose for me" (v. 2), the God who in the midst of even the most dire circumstances in life still has a purpose for me which can never be thwarted. This same conviction is memorably expressed by Paul in Rom. 8:28, "We know that all things work together for good for those who love God, who are called according to his purpose."

The second conviction is that God "will send from heaven and save me" (v. 3; cf. 3:2, 8). The frequent use of the word "heaven" in this psalm is note-worthy. God will "send from heaven" (v. 3); he is to be "exalted above the heavens" (vv. 5, 11); his steadfast love is "as high as the heavens" (v. 10). Faced with the threat of those who are out to "trample him down" (v. 3) and "devour him" (v. 4), the psalmist reminds himself that such threats are ultimately only the threats of mortals who inhabit the earth. There is a greater reality: the God who is not limited to earth, whose greatness transcends all human might, whose power is not of this world, whose "glory" (vv. 5, 11; see 3:3 and 24:8) not only embraces all that happens in this world, but arches over even the heavens, the ultimate limit of human sight and imagination.

The third conviction is that God can be guaranteed to thwart and "put to shame" (v. 3) all who seek to use their power harmfully. All these convictions spring from the same source. The God whom the psalmist worships is no capricious, uncaring God, but one whose true nature is summed up in the words "steadfast love" (see 5:7) and "faithfulness" (see 25:5). Thus all who seek to challenge or ignore this God meet with richly deserved punishment. The two occurrences of "Selah" in the psalm seem to be inviting the congregation to reflect on this, since in verse 3 it comes immediately after the words "He will put to shame those who trample on me" and in verse 6 after the words "They dug a pit in my path, but they have fallen into it themselves." If we are right in thinking that an element in the attack on the psalmist focuses on slander, malicious gossip, or false charges, then this self-inflicted judgment is readily understandable. Lying and deceit, slander and falsehood, however profitable at the moment, sooner or later get their deserved reward. Truth finds chinks in their armor. Those who traffic in such things come to a sticky end.

Verse 7 marks the change in mood. The urgent plea to God to be gracious (v. 1), the cry to God and the hope expressed in that cry (vv. 2-3) have now been answered. Torn apart by troubled thoughts he may be, but in worship he is in the presence of another reality. It is this which is expressed in the repeated words "my heart is steadfast" in verse 7, echoing the repeated plea in verse 1. This is not a claim to unswerving devotion to God. It is the claim that his mind is fixed on one certainty which nothing can destroy and which calls forth from him joyful celebration. This psalmist finds no need to call upon God to wake up (cf. 7:6; 44:23). He is convinced God is in control. It is his own sense of personal worth and dignity ("my soul" in v. 8 is literally "my glory"; see 3:3) that is crying out to find expression in praise and thanksgiving. Note the threefold use of "awake" in verse 8. Although it has been suggested that "I will awake the dawn" points to some liturgical act in the temple at the break of day, it is doubtful whether this is necessary. A nineteenth-century poet, George Meredith, wrote, "Prose can paint evening and moonlight, but poetry is needed to sing the dawn." This poet is singing the dawn of his liberation from the darkness which has almost overwhelmed him, a liberation symbolized for him in the coming of each new day. The poet in Lamentations expresses the same faith: "The steadfast love of the LORD never ceases, his mercies never come to an end; they are new every morning; great is your faithfulness" (Lam. 3:22-23).

Although the reference to the "people" and the "nations" in verse 9 would be appropriate on the lips of a king celebrating his deliverance from foreign enemies, this may be no more than the psalmist's way of saying that his experience has been so overwhelming that it is something which he must share with the whole world.

The psalm ends in verse 11 with a repetition of the refrain heard first in verse 5. It points the worshipper throughout the psalm to God and to his rightful status, "Be exalted, O God" (see comment on 21:13), a status which is dependent not only on what he has done for the people but also on his position as the creator of the entire universe. The reference to the heavens and the earth reminds us of the opening words of the great hymn of creation in Genesis 1, "In the beginning God created the heavens and the earth." Behind much of the hope and assurance which runs through the Old Testament there is a theology of creation, which the prologue to John's gospel links with the word made flesh in Jesus.

Psalm 58
A QUESTION OF JUSTICE

For the heading of this psalm, see Psalms 56 and 57. The central theme of this psalm is clear. Justice should be done and be visible on earth. When we turn to the detailed interpretation, however, we face two major difficulties. The first is that the text is extremely difficult, if not impossible, to understand at times. All the ancient versions had problems with the Hebrew, particularly in verses 7-9, and most modern translations fare little better, as a comparison of the NRSV and the REB clearly demonstrates. Thus verses 7b-8a are rendered in the NRSV, "like grass let them be trodden down and wither. Let them be like a snail that dissolves into slime." The REB translates the same lines as, "may he aim his arrows, may they perish by them; may they be like an abortive birth which melts away."

The second major difficulty centers on how to interpret verse 1. Although the traditional text could be rendered "Do you really decree what is right silently?" it is generally agreed that this makes little sense. There are two possibilities. On the analogy of Psalm 82, it is argued that those addressed in the opening verse are "gods" distinct from the God of Israel. They are being held responsible for the injustice rampant in the world. This is the implication of the NRSV rendering. In a world where gods and goddesses were numerous and often involved in conflict with each other, the psalmist dismisses as corrupt all such divine powers and any human authority which derives from them. A fuller discussion of this issue will be found at Psalm 82. The other option involves understanding the word translated "gods" in light of its application elsewhere to people in positions of power — "rulers," as the REB translates, or "mighty lords," as the footnote in the NRSV suggests (cf. 2 Kgs. 24:15; Ezek. 17:13). The reference would then be to the supreme judicial authority in ancient Israel, though we must remember that political and judicial power was not so clearly distinguished in the ancient world as it is in modern democracies. This is basically the approach taken here, though I would translate the first verse of the psalm as follows: "Do you rulers [or: "judges"] really decree what is right? Do you mortals really judge with equity?" This translation takes the word "people" in the NRSV not as the object of the verb "to judge," but as another description of those being addressed. There is a note of sarcasm in these opening words. People of power such judges may be, but they are also mere mortals (literally, "sons of man"; see comment on 8:4), sharing the frailty of everything human. What we are listening to in this psalm is a prophetic challenge to the abuse of power in the hands of those who ought to have known better. Such abuse of power, claims the psalmist, is traceable to an inner corruption, hearts that "devise wrongs" leading to acts which "deal out violence," violence which threatens to overthrow that justice and righteousness which guarantee a stable society (v. 2). There is always an awesome responsibility on those in positions of power to think and to act in the interests of society as a whole.

Verses 3-5 give a brief but vivid picture of such people now classified as "the wicked" (see Psalm 1). They are described as being addicted all their life to devious behavior and in particular to lies. They are venomous, as venomous as deadly snakes, and like the "adder" or the cobra deaf to anyone who tries to control them (cf. Eccl. 10:11).

The only remedy against such behavior lies with God, so in verses 6-9 an appeal is made to God, to the one and only LORD, calling upon him to bring curses down on those who challenge or defy his authority. Amid much that is textually uncertain, there seem to be five main pictures:

1. Render them powerless by breaking their teeth; shatter the fangs of these oppressors who are compared to lions or young lions ready to pounce (v. 6).
2. Let their strength dissipate like water in a wadi, quickly drying after rain (v. 7a).
3. Let them prove as ineffective as archers whose arrows miss their target (v. 7b).
4. Let their life turn out to be as futile as that of an aborted fetus (v. 8). (The snail who crawls into the first half of the line in the NRSV is very problematic!)
5. Let them be swept away like twigs on a thornbush, before they are able to heat the pot from which they intend to eat (v. 9).

The psalm ends by focusing on the "righteous," who have been on the receiving end of injustice. The tables are now reversed. Whatever delight the wicked took in abusing power is replaced by the delight the righteous take in their comeuppance. The statement "The righteous will rejoice when they see vengeance done"

(v. 10) is capped by the somewhat lurid picture of them bathing their feet in the blood of the wicked, a picture not unparalleled elsewhere in both the Old and the New Testaments (for similar imagery, see Isa. 63:1-3; for gloating over the destruction of the wicked, see Revelation 18). This desire for and glorying in revenge we have encountered in other psalms (see comment on 5:10). Calvin in his commentary is very anxious to stress that such joy has no element of bad feeling towards the wicked in it, but is simply a holy joy welcoming God's triumph over evil. Whether faith can be as easily disentangled from personal feelings as that is questionable. It is easy to dismiss such a response as sub-Christian, but it not uncommon among those who claim to have studied in the school of Christ, especially against those who are regarded as a threat to the faith. To believe that God, as a righteous judge (cf. 7:8), must say "No" to evil in any form is one thing; to disentangle our own raw and vengeful feelings from this "No" is another. Like many another person, the psalmist does not succeed in doing so.

There is a hidden "Yes" corresponding to this "No," a reward (literally, "fruit") "for the righteous," a reward which is really the vindication of their faith. The closing words of the psalm look back to its beginning. The corrupt power which is questioned in verse 1 finds its answer in the power of God who judges, to defend the righteous. The violence such corrupt people do "on earth" (v. 2) is called to account by the God whose writ runs "on earth" (v. 11). This theology runs through the Old Testament and poses for Hebrew faith some of its most acute problems. The question Abraham poses in Gen. 18:25, "Shall not the judge of all the earth do what is right?" — and do it in this world — demands an answer. How much easier life would have been for many hurt and puzzled people in Israel, including many a psalmist, if they had not been haunted by this question. How much shallower the faith of Israel would have been if there had not been those who wrestled with it, with no easy recourse to a world hereafter.

Psalm 59
THREATENED YET REJOICING

This psalm may originally have been a royal psalm reflecting the experience of a king threatened by enemies, external and internal. So there is a certain appropriateness in the historical note in the heading which links it with David's romantic escape from Saul as described in 1 Sam.19:11-17. As in the case of Psalm 56, though, the psalm speaks to anyone finding cause for rejoicing in the midst of a crisis.

The psalm falls into two main parts: verses 1-10 and verses 11-17. Each part contains an appeal to God (vv. 1-5 and vv. 11-13), a vivid description of the psalmist's enemies as a pack of scavenging dogs (vv. 6-7 and vv. 14-15), and a concluding expression of hope and confidence (vv. 8-10 and vv. 16-17).

1-10   The psalm begins with a fourfold appeal to God: "Deliver . . . protect . . . deliver . . . save" from people variously described as "my enemies . . . those who rise up against me . . . those who work evil [cf. 5:5] . . . the bloodthirsty." For "deliver . . . save," see the comment on 3:2 and 7:2. The verb translated "protect" is used in Deut. 2:36 of a citadel too high for the Israelites to capture; hence, the REB translates "be my strong tower." The psalmist is pleading to be lifted up, to be given security in the face of those who are threatening him. The only security lies in the one whom he calls "my God."

Faced with those waiting to "ambush him" (REB; cf. 10:9), the psalmist protests his innocence, claiming that he has done nothing to justify such attacks. He confidently appeals to God to act, to come to his help, and to "see" (v. 4), that is, to take note of what is happening. For the appeal "Rouse yourself . . . Awake" (vv. 4, 5) see comment on 7:6 and 44:24. The appeal is confident because the God whom he worships, Israel's God, is the "LORD God of hosts," an unusual form of the description of God, which in the Psalms is normally "the LORD of hosts" or "God of hosts" (cf. 24:10). Since Book Two tends to use "God" and Book One "LORD," this may be a fusion of the two. This is the God who controls all the forces in the universe. He therefore reacts in judgment against all who challenge his authority or oppose his people, be they "nations" or "those who treacherously plot evil," a phrase found only here, but giving a more colorful edge to the more usual "workers of evil" (v. 2). Although the reference to the "nations" may point to this being a royal psalm, it need not have this implication. To worship the LORD, God of hosts is to celebrate one whose power embraces the whole world. The personal and the universal join hands in Israel's faith and in all genuine religious experience, a theme well expressed in John White Chadwick's hymn:

> Eternal Ruler of the ceaseless round
> Of circling planets singing on their way,
> Guide of the nations from the night profound
> Into the glory of the perfect day:
> Rule in our hearts, that we may ever be
> Guided and strengthened and upheld by thee.

Verses 6-7 depict those who threaten the psalmist with the vivid image of a prowling pack of howling dogs. Inactive and asleep during the day, they come out at night. The word the NRSV translates as "bellowing" (v. 7) means literally "to gush, bubble up" (cf. Prov. 18:4, where it is used of a fountain). Thus the REB translates: "From their mouths comes a stream of abuse." "Slavering" would probably be a more appropriate word to use of dogs than "bellowing." These treacherous dogs have "sharp words" (literally, "swords") on their lips (cf. 57:4; 55:21), defiantly believing they can get away with their nefarious deeds under cover of darkness when there is no one listening to what they do or say. Although it is difficult from the language of the psalm to identify who these people were, the description would fit the gangs who at night roam the streets of some of our cities. Regardless of what sends these gangs onto the streets — be it mindless violence or social protest — many honest folk are afraid to go out at night.

The Gospels, however, remind us, "There is nothing hidden which will not be made known. Therefore everything you have said in the dark will be known in broad daylight" (Luke 12:2-3). So the defiant words "Who will hear us?" (v. 7) immediately receive a resounding response in v. 8: "But you laugh at them, O LORD"; that is, you treat any challenge to your authority with derision (cf. 2:4). The "mighty" who threaten the psalmist (v. 3) are stymied by the one whom the psalmist, using the same Hebrew root, describes in verse 9 as "O my strength." He has resources at his disposal which they can never have: the God whom he describes as "my fortress" (v. 9; cf. 18:2), a God whose "steadfast love" (cf. 5:7) will "meet me" or will go before me, just as in English the word "prevent" is used in the Latin sense of "go before" in the prayer "Prevent us, O LORD, in all our doings with thy most gracious favor." This could well have been this psalmist's prayer. The corollary is that he will witness the downfall of those who oppose him. The Hebrew verb "see" in verse 10 may be used in the sense of looking "in triumph on" (NRSV) or "gloating over" (REB), in which case we face the same issue as we saw at the end of Psalm 58.

11-17 Part two opens with the psalmist asking God to deal forcibly with those who arrogantly throw their weight around. The opening words of verse 11, "Do not kill them," seem puzzling at first. They have been taken as a question ("Will you not kill them?"). Alternately, the Hebrew word "not" could, with a different vowel, become "O God . . . O God kill them." Yet the NRSV translation may well stand. The psalmist is calling on God not to obliterate his enemies immediately but to make an example of them. They have sown the seeds of their own demise. This must be seen. The very words they thought would wound others prove their downfall. This is a salutary reminder to all that the supreme power over "Jacob" (see 20:1) rests in the hands of God. For the concept of the "anger" or "wrath" of God (v. 13), see comment on 6:1.

Verses 14-15 echo verses 6-7, the picture of the prowling pack of dogs, with verse 15 stressing that as they scavenge for food they "growl" or "whine" until they get their fill. The translation "growl" (v. 15) follows that of the early versions, assuming a verb slightly different from the Hebrew verb, which means "to spend the night." We could retain the Hebrew and translate "unless they are satisfied, they remain all night." Either way, these words underline the perverse character of the psalmist's enemies. They are never satisfied until they have achieved their wicked desires. That is part of the trouble with corruption; it breeds more corruption and its demands become ever more difficult to satisfy.

Whereas the first picture of the prowling pack in verses 6-7 was immediately countered by "But you . . . O LORD," this section finds its immediate response in the words, "But I . . ." (v. 16). The order is surely right. The answer to the abuse of human power is first to set its puny futility in the light of the God who is "my strength" (a title repeated in verse 17), a God who rules, and secondly to celebrate that strength. It is perhaps significant that the word "Selah" occurs twice in the psalm, after verses 5 and 13, in both cases inviting the congregation's response to the power of the God of Israel. At the heart of the faith portrayed in the Bible, both Old and New Testaments, stand the mighty acts of God in creation, in history, and in redemption, acts which culminate in the life, death, and resurrection of Jesus. Life is then a joyful response to who this God is, to what he has done, and to what he is still doing.

The first two lines of verse 17 repeat verse 9, but with one significant difference; the words "I will watch for you" (v. 9) are replaced by "I will sing praises to you." Hope has been replaced by hope fulfilled; expectations give way to exuberant singing. The first word of the psalm was the appeal "Deliver me"; the last word is "his steadfast love" (cf. 5:7). That was the psalmist's assurance, and it is our only assurance — that in the "day of distress" (v. 16) our cries are heard and answered.

Psalm 60
THE VICTORY OF FAITH
IN THE JAWS OF DEFEAT

This is the last of the series of "Miktam" psalms, which run from Psalms 56 to 60 (see comment on Psalm 16). The heading "Lily of the Covenant" (REB: "Testimony") may be a tune title. The historical note seeks to link the psalm with David's campaigns at the height of his career. "Aram-naharaim" is northern Mesopotamia, and "Aram-zobah" is in northern Syria. The "Valley of Salt" is the region south of the Dead Sea. Either the source of this information was careless, or it draws on a tradition different from what we find in 2 Samuel 8. The psalm heading attributes the killing of 12,000 Edomites to Joab, whereas 2 Sam. 8:13 credits David with killing 18,000, and 1 Chron. 18:12 credits the 18,000 to Abishai son of Zeruiah. The heading represents only the earliest of many attempts to provide the psalm with a historical setting. Modern scholarship has variously dated the psalm from the time of the Maccabees in the second century BCE to the aftermath of the fall of Jerusalem in 587 BCE or to the time of Josiah near the end of the seventh century BCE. All such attempts run into difficulties, because the true setting of the psalm is the cult.

In form the psalm is a three-part community lament, the first two parts beginning with the word "God" (vv. 1-5 and 6-8) and the third part with a rhetorical question to which the only satisfactory answer must be "God" (vv. 9-12).

The sense of being "rejected" and on the receiving end of God's anger (v. 1) is typical of such a lament (cf. 44:9; 74:1). The people feel "broken," defenseless (v. 1). Two graphic pictures describe their plight: Their world has collapsed as if the land had been devastated by a severe earthquake, a not uncommon occurrence in the Middle East (v. 2). They have been made to drink a bitter, potent brew which has left them staggering helplessly. The REB translation of the first line of verse 3, "You have made your people drunk with a bitter draught," assumes, probably correctly, that instead of the verb "to see, experience," we should read a form of the similar-sounding verb "to drink deeply" (cf. the use of the similar metaphor in Jer. 25:15-38 and Isa. 51:17).

Yet in the midst of this crisis the people hold on to one thing. We are still "your people" (v. 3), "those who fear you" (v. 4; cf. 19:9), "those whom you love" (v. 5; cf. the use of the same word in Isa. 5:1). So they make their appeal to God: "restore us" (v. 1); "repair the cracks," the fissures left, as it were, by the earthquake (v. 2); use your power, "your right hand," to give us victory (see 3:8); "answer us . . . rescue us" (v. 5).

The meaning of verse 4 has been much discussed. Jer. 4:6 is probably our best guide, where in face of invasion the people are warned to retreat into their fortified cities and in particular to fall back to Zion: "Raise a standard toward Zion, flee for safety, do not delay." So here those who have survived national disaster are called to rally round a banner out of reach of the enemies' archers.

In verses 6-8 we hear God's word of reassurance. It may have been spoken to the congregation by a temple prophet or priest, but equally it may represent the people recalling the God-centered tradition of faith in which they have been nurtured in the sanctuary (v. 6). Enemies may have devastated the country, but it is still God's own country, given by him to be his people's possession. It is God who triumphantly divides up the land (v. 6) and declares his proprietary right to it (vv. 7-8). All the names which appear in the list have a significant place in Israel's historical traditions.

"Shechem" is not far from Samaria, and "Succoth" is east of the Jordan. We may recall the patriarchal traditions associated with Jacob in Gen. 37:12-20. "Gilead," which was east of the Jordan, and "Manasseh," which spanned the land east of the Jordan and the hill country to the west, were part of the conquest assignment of land according to Numbers 32. "Ephraim," destined to be more powerful than Manasseh (cf. Gen. 48:17-21), came to stand for the northern kingdom of Israel, and, together with Judah in the south, is described as part of God's armory, his helmet, and his scepter or general's baton (cf. Gen. 49:10).

"Moab" and "Edom," which are located east of the Jordan and south of Gilead, are depicted as menial slaves. Moab provides the wash basin to wash his master's feet (compare Abigail's response to David's marriage proposal, "Your servant is a slave to wash the feet of the servants of my lord" [1 Sam. 25:41]). Though throwing a shoe has been taken as a symbolic act for taking possession,

Edom is probably here depicted simply as a slave who picks up the shoe his master flings at him when he comes home from a journey.

According to the Hebrew text, the Philistines are ordered by God to "acclaim me with shouts of triumph," to acknowledge God's supremacy. Most English translations, however, follow the parallel passage in Ps. 108:9, which reads "over Philistia I shout in triumph." Either way, the Philistines, who once threatened the very existence of Israel, acknowledge God's claim to the land.

Thus the congregation is reminded that God's promise of the land remains, regardless of the harshness of their present experience. The promise, however, does not immediately resolve the crisis in the nation's life. Who is referred to in verse 9? It may be the king or some other military leader. Who is to deal with the Edomites, the traditional enemies of Israel from the time of Saul onwards (cf. 1 Sam. 14:47), remembered bitterly for stabbing Judah in the back at the time of the Babylonian invasion (cf. Obadiah; Jer. 49:7-22)? Who can lead a successful campaign against their "fortified cities" (probably Petra or, following Ps. 108:10, Bozrah; cf. Amos 1:12)? Ultimately the answer can only be God, but this is the God who no longer goes out with our armies (v. 10; see 44:9).

There is only one way forward — prayer which recognizes that "human help is worthless" (v. 11). Such "help" or salvation (see 3:8) can only come from God. It is unfortunate that the NRSV translates two different Hebrew words by the same English word "help" in verse 11. The REB more aptly translates "help" in the first line and then renders the second line "in vain we look to any mortal for deliverance." This is prayer which opens up the way into a partnership with God, a partnership which makes available resources which can strengthen the feeble arm and ensure victory over the enemy. That partnership enables Paul in Phil. 4:3 to say, "I am able to face anything through him who gives me strength" (REB). The congregation in the psalm is led through lament to listen to God's reaffirming word and thus to find new hope and courage. Having reached the point of knowing that they cannot go it alone, they discover that they need not.

With minor linguistic variations, verses 5-12 appear again as Ps. 108:7-13. There they are prefaced not by a lament but by a song of thanksgiving and praise which occurs in Ps. 57:7-10. The rich treasury and flexibility of Israel's liturgical traditions are well illustrated in the way in which parts of two different psalms can be joined together to form another psalm with its own distinctive ethos.

Psalm 61
FAR . . . YET NEAR

For the musical directive in the heading, "with stringed instruments," see Psalm 4. The word here is singular and may be intended to indicate "to the accompaniment of a stringed instrument."

This brief psalm begins with a lament of an individual, "Hear . . . listen" (cf. Psalm 5). It ends on a note of joyful thanksgiving (v. 8). Its form seems to be broken by a prayer for the king in verses 6-7, where the "I" who speaks elsewhere suddenly becomes "he." Throughout, the speaker may be an exiled or returned king. The switch from the first to the third person in verses 6-7 is not impossible. Parallels are found in other literature from the ancient Near East. Tradition has thus tended to associate the psalm with Absalom's revolt which forced David to seek refuge across the Jordan (2 Samuel 15–17). The psalmist could, however, be an otherwise unknown Israelite who has experienced the bitterness of exile from Jerusalem. Knowing that his own welfare and that of the nation are bound up with the royal family, he offers a prayer for the king.

The psalm opens with a prayer of one whose "heart is faint." The same verb, used in Lam. 2:19 to describe those "who faint with hunger," is found in the heading of Psalm 102. Here is someone who feels his vitality ebbing away. Life has lost all meaning, because he is at "the end of the earth." Although "earth" has been taken to mean the netherworld, with the psalmist near to death, it more probably means that the psalmist is in some remote and distant place, separated from all that once was central to his life. This feeling is poignantly expressed by an exile returned from Babylon in Psalm 137. Separation from roots, not least spiritual roots, can be a devastating experience.

The psalmist turns to God with specific requests (vv. 2b and 4), each of them backed up by a declaration of God's experienced goodness, introduced by "You" or "For you" (vv. 3 and 5). We have already noted how "rock" is used frequently in the Psalms as a title for God (see comment on 18:3). In view, however, of the reference to "your tent" and "the shelter of your wings," both of which point to the temple in Jerusalem (see 27:5; 17:8), the "rock" (v. 2) may indicate Mt. Zion on which the temple was built. In spite of certain modern translations which follow the Greek (LXX) and translate "set me high on a rock" (REB), the Hebrew at the end of verse 2 ought to be retained and translated "that is higher than I." The psalmist recognizes that he needs resources which go far beyond anything that he himself possesses and that these resources are there in the temple.

In verse 3 we listen to the voice of experience. "You are [or: "have been"] my refuge" (cf. 2:11). Because this has been the psalmist's experience, he can pray "let me find refuge" (v. 4). God is "a strong tower against the enemy." The reference is to a stronghold, like the defensive towers which were part of the protecting walls of Jerusalem and which the psalmist in 48:12 notes. This is the only reference to the "enemy" in the whole psalm. Identification, therefore, is impossible. If the psalmist had been forcibly taken into exile, perhaps after the fall of Jerusalem in 587 BCE, then the people among whom he was forced to live would be regarded as "the enemy."

In verse 5 the psalmist expresses his certainty that God has heard his "vows," which have arisen spontaneously out of the crisis in his life and which, if truly meant, point to a continuing commitment to God. God has not only heard but has given "the heritage of those who fear your name." Although a slight alteration of the text yields "grant the desires of those who fear your name," a rendering which is followed by many commentators and translations, the NRSV makes reasonable sense. The land was given to the people as their "heritage" (cf. Josh. 1:15). Once far from his homeland, the psalmist is now back in the land given by God to the people who honor and worship him (for "name," see 5:11). The words "you have heard my vows" (v. 5, NRSV) may also be translated with the REB, "you will hear my vows," but this is a future which in the psalmist's mind is a certainty, since it is guaranteed by God.

The psalm ends on a note of thanksgiving, the psalmist committed to paying his vows "day after day" (v. 8). It is easy for vows made in a situation of crisis to be forgotten when the crisis is over. But if such vows are a recognition of the goodness transforming life, then life should be permanently changed with our response worked out in day-to-day obedience.

The prayer for the king in verses 6-7 recognizes the key role which the monarchy played in the life of the nation (see comments on Psalms 2 and 72), particularly the Davidic dynasty in the southern kingdom of Judah. On its stability, stretching across the generations, depended the nation's stability. The special relationship of the king to God (cf. 2:6) guaranteed the king's authority. God's "steadfast love" and "faithfulness" were his guardian angels, vital for his and the nation's security.

In the postexilic period, when there was no king on the throne of David and no independent Judean state, the words of the prayer in verses 6-7 were taken as pointing to the king who would one day come. This future "messiah" would establish an everlasting kingdom and thus fulfill the promise made to David, "Your house and your kingdom shall be made sure before me; your throne shall be established forever" (2 Sam. 7:16). This is how the Aramaic Targum interpreted verses 6-7, and this, with a specifically Christian slant, is how many Christian commentators have interpreted it across the centuries (see the discussion on Psalm 2).

There is, however, one other aspect of the psalm worth pondering. Separated from his roots, the psalmist knew his sole security for the future lay in the experience of God which worship provides. When the Communist regime clamped down on China, and educational and medical institutions were taken over, the Church pleaded for one thing, the freedom to continue to worship God. When even that was denied during the cultural revolution, groups of Christians continued to meet for worship in each other's homes. Worship kept the Church alive, much to the astonishment of some who had argued that Chinese Communism would ensure the death of the Church in China. The Church can live without many things, but never without the sustaining, renewing, and challenging experience of worship.

Psalm 62
ALL MY HOPE ON GOD IS FOUNDED

For the phrase "according to Jeduthun" in the psalm heading, see Psalm 39. This is the psalm of someone who has known the destructive power of vicious and slanderous attacks upon his character and his standing in the community. In the midst of it all he has discovered he can say, "Yes, but. . . ." The Hebrew word *ak* occurs six times in the psalm, at the beginning of verses 1, 2, 4, 5, 6, and 9. In the NRSV it is rendered "alone" in verses 1, 2, 5 and 6, "only" in verse 4, and "but" in verse 9. It is a word which usually implies that while certain things may be true, there is also something else which we dare not forget. What we hear in this little word is the language of faith tackling head-on the shattering experiences in life and daring to claim that there is still hope.

It is this "Yes, but . . ." which we hear at the beginning of verses 1 and 2, verses which, with minor variations (mostly ignored by the NRSV and the REB), occur again in verses 5 and 6. As the storm rages around him, the psalmist has found "silence" at its epicenter, a silence which looks to God as its source and looks in confidence. "I shall never be shaken," because this is a God who is "my rock" (cf. 18:2), "my salvation" (cf. 3:8), and "my fortress" (cf. 18:2).

In verses 3-4 the psalmist turns to describe those who have been attacking him. The word translated "assail" (v. 3) occurs in the Old Testament only here, but the same root in other languages indicates threatening, often verbal, assaults. He sees himself as a helpless victim, one vulnerable person battered by the many, "all of you," who have ganged up against him. He is in danger of collapsing like a wall that is off plumb, or a "tottering fence," the kind of rampart, usually built of stone, which surrounds a vineyard or an olive grove. Perhaps what we call in Scotland a dry stane dyke, a badly built and neglected dry stane dyke, gives the picture. Although the text is not wholly clear, it seems as if the psalmist was "a person of prominence," whom enemies were out to topple through spreading lies about him, inwardly calling curses down upon him, curses designed to hound and destroy him (cf. 2 Sam. 16:5-14), while outwardly fawning upon him and wishing him well. The "Selah" at the end of verse 4 gives the congregation time to reflect on such dire and devious conduct.

Verses 5-6 look back to verses 1-2, but instead of the psalmist saying there is "silence," he calls upon himself to "be silent," as if admitting that he is in the midst of a crisis with which he still has to wrestle. This is surely a truism of the spiritual life. You don't shelter at ease behind the rampart of faith, the drawbridge pulled up, knowing that no attacks, no doubts or conflicts, will ever again assail you. As Calvin, within the context of accepting the Davidic authorship of the psalm, well says, "It is not without a struggle that the saint can compose his mind: and we can very well understand how David should enjoin more perfect submission upon a spirit that was already in submission, urging upon him further advance in the grace of silence."

God is now described as "my hope" (v. 5), an expression pointing to that eager waiting which looks forward expectantly for God to act (cf. 25:3). Verse 6 ends on a note of unqualified confidence, not as in verse 2 "I shall never be shaken," but simply "I shall not be shaken." Sometimes the less dramatic the claim, the greater the faith.

In verse 7 the psalmist reiterates his faith in God in words with which we are familiar from other psalms: "my deliverance" (cf. 3:8), "my honor" or glory, (cf. 3:3), "my strong rock" (cf. 18:2), "my refuge" (cf. 2:11; 46:1). Then he invites others to share his faith, to show a like trust in God, not only when things are going smoothly and trust seems easy, but "at all times," even when the going is rough, as it has been for the psalmist. To trust means to "pour out your heart" before God (v. 8), even if at times your thoughts can only rise to a puzzled "How long?" and "Why?" (cf. Psalms 13 and 22). Listen again to the wise words of Calvin: to "pour out" is "all the more necessary considering the mischievous tendency which we have naturally to keep our troubles pent up in our hearts till they drive us to despair." The word "Selah" at the end of verse 8 leaves the congregation pondering that open honesty which can lead to the discovery that God is indeed a "refuge for us."

Yes, but isn't there an alternative? No, claims the psalmist, for that would mean putting trust in frail mortals (v. 9) or in the values which they mistakenly allow to control their lives (v. 10). For the translation "those of low estate" and "those of high estate," see 49:2; both phrases here may simply be a way of talking about mere mortals. They are no more than "breath" (Hebrew *hebel;* see 39:5) or a "delusion," the same word translated "falsehood" in verse 4. Place these on a scale and the scale goes up! They may believe that they can throw their weight around, but in fact they are lighter than "breath." The poet prophet in Isaiah 40 passes a similar verdict on the human power structures which seemed so daunting to the people of his day. In God's sight "nations are but drops from a bucket, no more than moisture on the scales; to him coasts and islands weigh as light as a speck of dust" (Isa. 40:15, REB).

It is futile, then, to put one's trust, as some people do, in "extortion," using power for their own personal gain, in "robbery," a word denoting the forceful plundering of something from those too weak to protect themselves (cf. 35:10). This simply fosters "vain hopes" (a verb related to the word for breath). As for "riches" or wealth — the word could equally well mean power — which have an inevitable tendency to increase or bear fruit, such riches can only be a snare, if they take God's place at the center of life (cf. Psalm 49 and 52:7). The author of 1 Tim. 6:17 may well be echoing this verse when he warns those who in the present age are rich not "to set their hopes on the uncertainty of riches, but rather on the God who richly provides us with everything for our enjoyment."

The psalm ends in verses 12-13 by turning from futile human delusions to the dependable consistency which is to be found in God. The form of the statement in verse 11, "Once . . . twice," is the characteristic numerical saying which we find elsewhere in wisdom teaching (e.g., Prov. 6:16-18; 30:15-31) and also in the prophets (Amos 1:3–2:4). Sometimes this type of saying focuses on the higher number, and this has led some interpreters to take the "twice" or the two things heard as the power and the steadfast love of God. It is more likely that here the emphasis is on God's consistency. He speaks, he proclaims his purposes, and he never contradicts himself. "God has spoken" may imply the words of a temple prophet, or the psalmist may simply be recalling the tradition of faith in which he has been nurtured.

The message the psalmist receives is one that many people may regard as self-contradictory. How is it possible to believe at the same time in the "power" and the "steadfast love" of God? Is it not more reasonable to say with the ditty "If God be God, he is not good; if God be good, he is not God"? In other words, talk about the power of God and it is hard to see how that power expresses itself with any loving purpose in the midst of the tragedies and injustices of the world as we know it. Hold on to belief in the love of God and it is hard to avoid the conclusion that this is a weak, powerless love in the face of the brutality which seems to flourish. Yet the Bible insists in holding on to a God who is both a God of power and a God of steadfast love. If we believe only in the power of God and not his steadfast love, why should we trust? Why should God not be a capricious and irresponsible despot? If we believe only in the steadfast love of God, but not his power, does that not cut the feet from any ultimate hope in the triumph of God's purposes? The vision of power and love come together in the Christ hymn in Phil. 2:6-11. It ponders the mystery of the cross and the resurrection of Jesus. Jesus had power, equality with God, yet in love he emptied himself to share our human life, submitting himself to death on a cross. Through that act of self-emptying, he has been given the name that is above every other name, "so that at the name of Jesus every knee should bend, in heaven and on earth and under the earth, and every tongue should confess that Jesus Christ is Lord, to the glory of God the Father" (Phil. 2:10-11). It challenges us as Christians to believe that true power must express itself in steadfast love, and that steadfast love is ultimately the sole powerful answer to the needs and troubles of our world.

Verse 12 marks another interesting stage in the psalmist's thought. For the first time he not only speaks of God, but he addresses God: "steadfast love belongs to you, O LORD. For you repay. . . ." To address God as "you" is to worship, whether in the midst of a congregation or in the solitude and quietness of our own prayers. Ultimately all talk about God, however interesting, is merely an academic exercise unless it is transformed into worship. There we meet with God. There he comes to us to remind us that life involves choice, that in his world all are repaid "according to their work" (cf. Gal. 6:7). A psalm which begins by claiming a God-given silence at the epicenter of the storm, and which offers trust in God as the sole foundation of a hope-filled life, ends by reminding us that such trust involves responsibility, the responsibility of obedience to the God whom we profess to worship.

Psalm 63
SPIRITUAL FOOD FOR EVERY NEED

It is difficult to probe the passionate intensity of this psalm, which has enabled it to be so many different things to different people. The heading linking it with David probably draws upon the linguistic similarities between verse 1 and David's flight from Absalom, which finds him "weary" or "faint" in the wilderness (2 Sam. 16:2, 14). This assumes that the reference in verse 1 is geographical. It is more likely to be a spiritual metaphor. The reference to singing for joy after meditation in the watches of the night (vv. 6-7) made it a suitable introductory psalm for Sunday morning worship in the early, Greek-speaking Church. In other traditions, the satisfying rich feast leading to praise in verse 5 has found it a natural setting in the Eucharist. More recent scholarship has raised other issues. Does the language of verses 1-2 imply that the setting for the psalm is in one of the great festivals in the Jerusalem temple in pre-exilic times, with the worshipper's prayer being offered in the context of some theophany or visionary experience? Does the language of verse 6 imply some night vigil in the temple? What about the reference to the king in the concluding verse? This raises the same question about the identity of the psalmist which we discussed in Psalm 61. The view taken here is that this is not a royal psalm. Even if it were originally, the ardent longing for God in verse 1 could never be merely a royal experience. It has found its echo in many a human heart across the centuries.

Although the movement of thought in the psalm can be approached in different ways, the NRSV is probably right in dividing the psalm into three sections, verses 1-4, verses 5-8, and verses 9-11. Each section is marked by the occurrence of the Hebrew word *nepeš*, traditionally translated "soul" (see 6:4). In verse 1, combined with "flesh," it points to the psalmist's whole being: his personality, its inner vitality, and its outward form. In verse 5 "my soul" is an emphatic way of saying "I," while in verse 9 the NRSV correctly translates "my life."

1-4 It is striking how Old Testament authors have the ability to convey the most profound theology in the simplest of language. Two Hebrew words lie behind the opening description of God, "you are my God." The opposite side of the coin is put equally simply in Isa. 43:1, where God addresses a despondent people and says, "You are mine." Everything else in the psalm hinges on this certainty, "you are my God." It is this which leads the psalmist to respond in a particular way to the crisis in his life, described at the end of the psalm as a crisis in which he is under attack by those whom he brands as "liars" (v. 11), hell-bent on destroying him (v. 9). As a thirsty, exhausted traveler crossing an arid desert desperately seeks to quench his thirst, the psalmist "seeks" and "faints" for God. The word translated "seek" is not the usual word in the Old Testament for seeking God (for that, see 24:6). The REB catches something of the flavor of it by translating "I seek you eagerly." The verb is related to the Hebrew word for dawn. It is as if the psalmist is looking forward eagerly to the dawning of a new day after the darkness which has engulfed him. The word translated "faints" occurs only here and may have something of this same sense of eager longing. This eager search is not merely a reflection of the desperation of the psalmist's plight; it is witness to the fact that he believes that there is an answer. A thirst-crazed traveler may be cheated by a mirage, but the psalmist's God is no mirage. This is the God he has encountered in the sanctuary. The verb translated "looked upon" (v. 2) may, but need not, refer to some kind of visionary experience. In worship he has come face to face with the "power" (cf. 62:11) and "glory" (cf. 3:3) of God. In itself that might have been simply an awesome and terrifying experience, had it not been, as we saw in Psalm 62, that this is power which reaches out and touches our human life in "steadfast love." It is this graciously dependable grasp of God which the psalmist knows is of greater value than life itself. It is the one thing which never changes amid constant changes. It calls forth from him a response of praise (v. 3).

Whatever conclusions we come to about the liturgical setting of the psalm, it is important to recognize that this vision came to the psalmist as he shared worship with the community in the temple. As has been well said, "Public worship draws out the latent life in the human spirit. Those who, when alone, do not, or cannot pray, find an impulse to pray when they worship with others: and some will pray together who cannot pray alone, as many would sing in chorus who would not sing solo. Many who are spiritually weak, find spiritual strength in a common spiritual effort" (*Siddur Lev Chadash,* p. 7). So the psalmist joins in the worshipping chorus, "I will bless you as long as I live" (cf. 16:7), "I will lift up my hands" (cf. 28:2) and "call upon your name," celebrating the true character of God (cf. 5:11).

5-8   These verses contain a series of variations on verses 1-4, the minor chords transformed into the major key, the major chords expanded with joyful creativity.

"My soul thirsts for you" (v. 1) now becomes "my soul is satisfied" (v. 5), satisfied "as with a rich feast." Two Hebrew words for "fat," the choicest parts of a sacrificed animal offered to God according to ritual practice (cf. Lev. 3:14-16), lie behind this translation (cf. 36:8). He now shares in a banquet God has prepared for him, a banquet of very rich food. This is his description of that communion with God which dominates and gives meaning to his life.

"My lips will praise you" (v. 3) becomes "my mouth praises you with joyful lips" (v. 5) and "I sing for joy" (v. 7). It is as if a triumphant cry of joy which he can no longer contain bursts forth from him. This is joy which transforms the hours of darkness when the psalmist was at his lowest ebb, since his anxieties have now been replaced by meditation centering on God (cf. 1:2).

The reference to the sanctuary (v. 2) is picked up in the phrase, "in the shadow of your wings" (see 17:8 and 36:7), almost certainly here a reference to the cherubim whose wings stretched over the cover of the ark, the symbol of God's presence with his people, the God whose protecting power the psalmist now celebrates by addressing him as "my help" (v. 7).

The meaning of "you are my God" (v. 1) is teased out in verse 8. The psalmist "clings" to God, the word used of Ruth clinging to her mother-in-law, refusing to be separated from her (Ruth 1:14) and sticking close to the servants of Boaz (Ruth 2:8, 21, 23). The word is used of a man clinging to his wife so that they become one flesh in Gen. 2:24, and it is used in Deuteronomy to describe the exclusive relationship which Israel is to enjoy with the LORD (Deut. 10:20; 11:22; 30:20). God's strong right hand has a firm grip of the psalmist, a firm grip which will never let go (v. 8). So a prophet speaks God's word to a people in their moment of despondency and doubt in exile: "Do not fear, for I am with you, do not be afraid, for I am your God; I will strengthen you, I will help you, I will uphold you with my victorious right hand" (Isa. 41:10). The psalmist's commitment to God has its roots in God's prior commitment to the psalmist.

9-11 The psalmist now turns his attention to those who threaten to destroy him. They have no future. Death awaits them. The words "depths of the earth" in verse 9 refer to Sheol (see 6:5). Slain, their bodies lie unburied, a prey for scavenging jackals. All that they sought to do is now in total ruin. Their pernicious influence eliminated, the welfare of the community is restored. At its center stands the king who shares the psalmist's God-centered joy. Praises ring forth for "all who swear by him" (v. 11); "him" could refer to either the king or God. Oaths were taken in the name of the king (2 Sam. 11:11) or in the name of God (e.g., Jer. 4:2; 5:2) or in the name of both the king and God (2 Sam. 15:21). Such praise ringing forth is placed in dramatic contrast to the "stopped mouths," the silence which now descends on the liars. Thus the psalm ends by pointing to two ways and their consequences.

Because he, like the psalmist, had been grasped by God, the God who came to him in Jesus, the apostle Paul could say, "it is no longer I who live, but it is Christ who lives in me. And the life I now live in the flesh, I live by faith in the Son of God, who loved me and gave himself for me" (Gal. 2:20).

Psalm 64
VULNERABLE YET CONFIDENT

The text of this psalm poses many difficulties, particularly in verses 6-7, yet the overall picture is clear. The psalmist speaks as one who is vulnerable to insidious attacks from people who are determined to destroy him. Because of his faith in God, he is confident that such attacks will come to naught. Indeed, they contain within themselves the seeds of their own destruction.

1-2 The psalm begins in typical lament style with an appeal to God (cf. 4:1). "Hear . . . my complaint," a word found frequently on the lips of Job (e.g., Job 9:27; 10:1), whose complaint reflects his bitter reaction to the suffering he has endured, the bewilderment of someone who cannot make sense of what has happened to him. The psalmist appeals for protection from the "dread enemy" (REB: "the terror of the enemy"). The word translated "dread" indicates the kind of fear which can have a paralyzing effect. He also asks to be delivered from "the secret plots of the wicked." The word translated "secret plots" is the Hebrew *sōd*, which might equally well indicate a cabal or conclave (see 25:14). Similarly the "scheming" of evildoers points to some kind of disturbance or uproar and could be translated "mob" (REB). The psalmist was probably too vulnerable to worry about drawing fine distinctions between the people who were plotting against him and the intrigues they were devising!

3-6 These verses describe the activity of these "evildoers" (see 5:5) in language which has close parallels to Ps. 10:6-11. The emphasis in verses 3-4 is clearly upon wounding words. Although it has been argued that we are dealing here with magic spells or curses called down upon the psalmist, it is more likely that he has become aware of insidious slander (cf. Psalm 57) or venomous gossip. Their tongues are like sharpened swords (cf. 57:4). They aim bitter words like arrows from their "hideouts," the word translated "ambush" (v. 4) containing a pun on the psalmist's use of the word "Hide me" in verse 2. They work under cover, striking suddenly, unexpectedly, without ever being in danger of being exposed (vv. 5-6). They seek to further their nefarious purposes by laying hidden snares to trap their unsuspecting victim, confident that they will never be caught in the act. "Who can see us?" (cf. 59:7).

The first half of verse 6 is very problematic, partly because the Hebrew seems to play upon different nuances of the word meaning "search." It occurs in different form three times in five words. The NRSV and REB offer only two out of a range of possible renderings. The words seem to convey the impression that their evil scheming against the psalmist has been painstakingly devised and thought through. They are giving no hostages to fortune. This provokes from the psalmist the comment at the end of verse 6. You never can tell what is going on in people's minds; you can never plumb the depths of the deviousness which can control the way people act. Jeremiah, who had more reason than most to explore the mystery of the stubborn evil will which ignored his prophetic message, makes the same point in different language: "The heart is devious above all else; it is perverse — who can understand it?" (Jer. 17:9). Unless we have wrestled with this mystery we have only scratched the surface of that human nature which we all share. There was little room for facile optimism in the psalmist's world; there is little room for it in ours. If we don't take evil seriously, we shall never learn to take God seriously.

7-9   Vulnerable the psalmist may be, but he is also confident. Those who devise plots against him make one crucial mistake: they leave God out of their calculations. But in God's world evil writes its own sordid obituary. The appropriateness of the poetic justice such people face is underlined. They seek to wound the psalmist with their venomous arrows (v. 4); they themselves will be on the receiving end of God's arrows (v. 7). They seek to do it suddenly (v. 4) like a bolt out of the blue; they themselves will be wounded suddenly (v. 7) by a divine bolt out of the blue. The tongues they used as whetted swords (v. 3) will prove their own downfall (v. 8). Defiantly they thought "Who will see us?" (v. 5); now all will see them and "shake with horror" (v. 8), or assuming with the REB a different verb, "flee in horror." Once they acted "without fear" (v. 4); now that punishment has overtaken them, everyone will fear (v. 9). They were "doers of evil" (v. 2); now what they set out to do has been thwarted by what God has done (v. 9).

10   In verse 10 the psalmist invites others to join with him in responding to what God has done. The same stark contrasts are present in this last verse. The psalmist has been the victim of the secret plots of "the wicked"; now "the righteous" (cf. Psalm 1) are called upon to rejoice in the LORD, knowing that they can confidently take refuge in him (cf. 62:7). The wicked illustrated the dark deviousness of the human heart (v. 6); now "the upright of heart" (see 11:7) can exult and sing their praise to God.

This psalm illustrates more clearly than any other the theme of Psalm 1: the two ways, the way of the wicked and the way of the righteous, and the consequences of choosing the one or the other. Is Paul adding his own Christian footnote to verse 10 when he calls upon his fellow Christians to "Rejoice in the LORD always; again I say rejoice" and then spells out the kind of conduct appropriate for those who are upright in heart according to the example of Christ (Phil. 4:4-9)?

Psalm 65
GOD'S EVER-RENEWING BOUNTY

This is the first of a small group of psalms, Psalms 65–68, that all have in their heading the word "Song," alongside the more common word for psalm. There are many links in language and thought uniting these psalms. They are all "songs of praise," fittingly rounded off at the close of Psalm 68 with the exuberant cry, "Blessed be God."

The appropriate setting for this psalm in the life of Israel has been much debated. Both the feast of Unleavened Bread in the spring at the beginning of the barley harvest and the great autumnal harvest thanksgiving festival (cf. Exod. 23:15-16) have been proposed. The view taken here is that in the background there is a situation somewhat similar to that outlined in 1 Kgs. 8:33-36, part of the prayer attributed to Solomon at the dedication of the temple. There four things are stressed: the people's sin against God has led to a crisis situation; the people's sin has been punished with drought; the people therefore need forgiveness from God; the people look to God to "grant rain" to the land given to them as an inheritance. Psalm 65 seems to imply a situation where the long-needed rains have come to renew the earth. The people gather in the temple to praise God, to be assured of forgiveness and to celebrate his "awesome deeds" (v. 5).

1-4   The psalm has many of the marks of a hymn of praise to which verses 1-4 serve as an introit. The traditional English opening, "Praise waits for you in Zion," follows the Hebrew, which uses here the same word that the NRSV translates "waits in silence" in 62:1. Most modern translations follow some of the early versions in assuming that the word comes from a similar Hebrew root meaning "to be like," which certainly in later Hebrew had the meaning of being appropriate or fitting. What God is due, therefore, is praise "in Zion" (see 2:6) and the payment of the vows made in the situation of crisis (cf. 22:25; 61:8). Neither should be given grudgingly, since this is the God who is addressed as "O you who answer prayer" (v. 2). In these words we are close to the heart of all authentic religious experience. God is not some remote, self-contained mystery, but someone who is accessible to anyone — "all flesh" (v. 2) — who not only hears but also answers prayer. As Calvin says, "Could we only impress upon our minds, that it is something peculiar to God and inseparable from him, to hear prayer, it would inspire us with unfailing confidence." If that is not true, then the entire biblical tradition collapses like a pack of cards, and most of the psalms are a study in self-delusion.

In the presence of God we recognize that there are certain things which we cannot deal with on our own, those perverse deeds and rebellious acts which cry out for forgiveness (for the language of verse 3, see 32:1). Only God can forgive. The word translated "forgive" (v. 3, Hebrew *kāpar*) occurs frequently in Leviticus in association with certain sacrifices (e.g., Lev. 4:20; 5:10; 16). It seems to mean either to cover or to wipe off. In the context of the cult, it is often rendered "to make atonement" or "to make expiation." What is clear is that it does not mean to appease an angry God. The people's relationship with God has been broken by their conduct, so that a new "at-one-ment" is needed which depends upon God's willingness to wipe the slate clean.

The praise due to God, who answers prayer and forgives, finds its counterpart in the happiness (v. 4; see 1:1) of those who are privileged to share worship in the courts surrounding God's house, his "holy temple" (see 5:7). They are there, not because they deserve to be there, but at God's invitation. They are people "whom you choose and bring near" (see 33:12). In the temple they can expect to be satisfied "with the goodness [REB: "bounty"] of your house." Although this has been taken to refer to the belief that in worship the deepest spiritual needs of the people are met, there is perhaps more in these words. The people may have been sharing in what the NRSV calls "a sacrifice of well-being" and the REB "a shared sacrifice" (Lev. 3:1-17; 7:11-36). The essence of this sacrifice was its being a shared meal, with part of the animal given to God, part to the priest, and the rest to the worshipper and his family. It was a sacrifice designed to heal broken relationships, to reestablish "shalom" (see 4:9), that is, full communion between God and the worshipper. The sharing of the meal symbolized that the deepest needs and the hunger of the worshipper were met in a renewed relationship with God.

5-8   These verses celebrate the "awesome deeds" (cf. 45:4) of the God who has the whole world in his hands. The description of God in verse 2, "O you who answer prayer," is picked up in verse 5, "you answer us," with deliverance or victory (literally, "right"; see 4:1) and salvation (cf. 3:8). Although the words "deliverance" and "salvation" are often used to refer to God's mighty deeds in history (e.g., the Exodus), in this context the words point forward to God's awesome power in creation, his lordship over nature, which is the theme of the following verses. This is the God who fixes in place the towering "mountains," who calms the great crashing waves of the seas, and who controls nations which challenge his authority (cf. Psalm 46), the God whose "signs" evoke awe from one end of the earth to the other. A "sign" (Hebrew 'ōt) is for the Old Testament something which, whether it be in itself ordinary or extraordinary, points away from itself to something or someone else. So, for example, in the flood story in Genesis the rainbow in the sky is the sign of the covenant between God and the earth (Gen. 9:12). We are not told here what these "signs" are, but presumably they are the things in the world which direct attention to the majesty and greatness of the creator.

The phrase "the gateways [literally, "outgoing"] of the morning and the evening" (v. 8) is a strange one which occurs nowhere else. It may simply be a poetic way of talking about the whole wide world, the distant horizons of east and west from which morning and evening seem to come. For the Hebrew psalmist the world around him is not some cold, closed system of mechanical laws; it is the handiwork of a creator, and to its creator it responds with joy. Just as God's people are again and again summoned to sing for joy (cf. 5:11), so morning and evening join in a hymn of joy celebrating their creator and sustainer. This is a theme explored further in the psalms of the kingship of God, for example Psalms 96 and 98. It is not surprising that the psalmist can here declare "you are the hope of all the ends of the earth and of the farthest seas" (v. 5). The word translated "hope" indicates rather trust (cf. 4:5), hence the REB translates, "in whom all put their trust." There is a strong element of universality in this hymn of joy. It may have been prompted by a particular experience in the life of the community, but the people know that what they are celebrating is the God who holds the entire universe in his hands, the creator of all.

9-13   These verses contain a song of thanksgiving for the renewed fertility which has come to the land through the revitalizing rain. It is a section rich in imagery evoking a series of memorable pictures, even when the detail is not wholly clear. Rain in abundance has come to make the earth fruitful and to enrich it, the expression of God's care (v. 9; for "visit," see 8:4). The "river" or rather "channel" of God may refer to what was believed to be the channel in the heavens through which God sent rain, a notion to which we may compare the picture of the "windows of heaven," opened to send the flood (Gen. 7:11). The words, however, might be translated "the great channel," as if God had provided a massive irrigation system to water the parched earth. It is unlikely that in this context the words have any of the mythological associations of the river in Ps. 46:4.

Although the text of verse 10 is difficult (for example, the word translated "furrows" occurs only here), the picture is clear. The rain softens the earth and makes ploughing possible; the seed sown in the receptive soil germinates and grows.

Instead of what had been feared, a meager harvest, the year has been crowned with God's "bounty" or goodness (v. 11; a similar word is translated "goodness" in v. 4). It may be that the picture of "your wagon tracks overflow with richness" has its origin in the image of God as the "Rider on the Clouds" (cf. 68:5), one of the titles of Baal, the god of fertility in Canaanite religion. On the other hand, it may be simply that of a farm cart, piled high with the produce of the harvest, filled to overflowing and dropping some of its produce as it trundles across the fields and along the tracks (cf. REB).

What was normally dry barren landscape is clothed with lush vegetation, the hillsides joyfully cultivated, meadows covered with flocks, the valleys ripe with grain — and all join with the distant horizons (v. 8) in a hymn of joy (vv. 12-13).

The psalm begins in the temple and ends in the fields and the valleys. It is from beginning to end a joyful *Te Deum* to the God who as creator sustains the world of his creating and counters all the forces which threaten to destroy it.

Psalm 66
A SHARED FAITH

This psalm contains two distinct parts. Verses 1-12 are in the form of a *Te Deum* in which the believing community summons the whole world to join in the praise of God. Verses 13-20 are the song of thanksgiving of an individual who comes to offer sacrifice, to pay his vows, and to give his personal witness to what God has done for him. What is the relationship between these two parts? Attempts to find here two originally separate psalms are not convincing. The reasons alleged for joining two such psalms are equally convincing in arguing for their original unity.

Verses 1-12 are part of the liturgy of one of the great national festivals, in which the people gather to celebrate God's "awesome deeds" (v. 3), not as in Psalm 65 the God of creation, but the God who has been active across the years in the history of his people, with its pivotal event the Exodus, deliverance from Egyptian slavery (v. 6). This community *Te Deum* then provides an opportunity for an otherwise unidentified individual, who might be the king or some other influential member of the community, to step forward and give his own personal witness. Notice the switch from "us" (vv. 8-12) to "I" in verse 13. Thus the faith of the community and the faith of an individual within the community join hands. We have frequently noted how a psalm which begins on an intensely personal note often ends in a community appeal (e.g., Psalm 51). This is the opposite side of the coin, the community *Te Deum* leading into personal thanksgiving. This is surely what happens again and again in worship. When we are present in a great congregation celebrating the Eucharist, praising God for all that he has done for his people in Christ, that act of worship becomes more personally meaningful when, reflecting on our own experience, we find in this the natural setting for our own thanksgiving.

1-12 This *Te Deum* is carefully structured. It falls naturally into three sections. The endings of sections one and two are marked by the liturgical indicator "Selah" (see Psalm 3). Each section begins with an invitation: "Make a joyful noise" (v. 1); "Come and see" (v. 5); and "Bless our God" (v. 8).

1-4 Apart from the use of the different divine name, the opening line of verse 1 appears again as the opening of that great community hymn, Psalm 100, and also in Ps. 98:4. It sounds the universal note we heard in Psalm 65. It summons the whole world, "all the earth," to join in a paean of praise, to celebrate the "glory of God's name" (cf. 19:1; 5:11), to acknowledge his "awesome deeds" (cf. 65:5) and the power before which all who challenge his authority must "cringe" (cf. 18:44; 81:15), recognizing that they are challenging the unchallengeable. This section ends where it began, with verse 4 consciously echoing the central concepts in verse 1, "all the earth . . . praise . . . your name."

5-6 The community recalls all that God has done in its history. The invitation "Come and see" is again directed to the whole world, "mortals," the human race (cf. 11:4), since what God has done is the basis of the community's witness to a wider world. There is no attempt to argue a case for the truth of Israel's faith, simply the invitation, "Come and see," come and see the mighty deeds God has done in the past, deeds which are part of our present experience as we relive them now in worship. In the second part of verse 6 "they passed through the river on foot," there is probably a reference to the crossing of the Jordan to enter the land of promise (cf. Joshua 3), or the whole verse may be celebrating the events recorded in Exodus 14–15, the crossing of the Reed Sea, the words "sea" and "river" sometimes being used interchangeably. This is certainly the event most celebrated in Israel's traditions and poetry (e.g., Isa. 43:15-17). God's identity is most clearly defined for Israel in the words which preface the decalogue, "I am the LORD your God, who brought you out of the land of Egypt, out of the house of slavery" (Exod. 20:2; Deut. 5:6). "There" we rejoiced, but the "there" becomes a "here-and-now" in worship as the community celebrates the God who is forever in control of events, who knows what goes on, and who ensures that any rebellion against his authority is futile (v. 7).

8-12 The inherent universality of Hebrew faith is well exemplified in the opening words "Bless our God, O peoples." What Israel has discovered in her pilgrimage with God is to be gladly acknowledged by other peoples (for "bless," see 16:7). The people of Israel witness to a God who has sustained them across their history. This does not mean that they have had an easy pilgrimage. They have been "tested," as silver needs to be refined in a furnace (see 11:4); they have been trapped, and they often have had to carry heavy burdens (literally, "pressure on our loins," v. 11b). They have been crushed by enemy chariots or horsemen and exposed to "fire" and "water," symbols of extreme danger. But as a prophet in God's name elsewhere reminds the people, "When you pass through the waters, I will be with you; and through the rivers, they shall not overwhelm you; when you walk through fire, you shall not be burned, and the flame shall not consume you" (Isa. 43:2). They have been tested, faced with crisis after crisis, but nevertheless "brought . . . out to a spacious place." This translation at the end of verse 12 assumes a slight alteration to the Hebrew text. The Hebrew text uses the word which in Ps. 23:5 describes the cup which "overflows"; hence, the REB translates, "a place of plenty." In other words, in spite of dangers on the way, Israel's pilgrimage with God has been a deeply satisfying and enriching experience. So Paul, looking back over a stormy Christian pilgrimage, can say: "Therefore I am content with weaknesses, insults, hardships, persecutions, and calamities for the sake of Christ; for whenever I am weak, then I am strong" (2 Cor. 12:10). To that, countless persons, known and unknown, have borne witness across the centuries.

13-20 What particular situation in the life of the psalmist prompted this personal testimony is not clear. He speaks only of "being in trouble" (v. 14) or distress, which led him to cry out to the LORD (cf. 28:1). It is possible that he has been unjustly accused of evil practices; the word translated "iniquity" in verse 18 is the same word which occurs in "evildoers." Whatever prompted it, his cry was heard. God had listened and responded to his prayer, the prayer of one who claimed that he had not "cherished" evil in his heart (v. 18; for such a protestation of innocence, see comment on 7:3-5). The crisis over, he comes to pay the vows he had promised, vows which he acknowledges through the offering of an appropriate sacrifice of "burnt offerings" (see 40:6), the sign of his thanksgiving (cf. Lev. 22:18-19). If we were to take literally all the animals mentioned, "fatlings, choice young rams, bulls and goats," the psalmist must have been extremely wealthy. This may, however, simply be the psalmist's way of saying that he came to offer whatever kind of burnt offering was considered appropriate.

There are many phrases which bind the psalmist's testimony to the community's *Te Deum*. The words "Come and see what God has done" of verse 5 are picked up in verse 16, "Come and hear . . . and I will tell you what God has done for me." The invitation to the peoples to "Bless our God" in verse 8 is turned into the triumphant cry of thanksgiving in verse 20, "Blessed be God." This is the God who has turned aside neither the psalmist's prayer nor his own "steadfast love" (see 5:7), the Hebrew using only the one verb in verse 20, translated by the NRSV as "rejected" and "removed." It is because God has remained true to his steadfast love that he has answered the psalmist's prayer. No spiritual arm twisting was needed. Like the author of Psalm 65, this psalmist knew that to address God as "O you who answer prayer" (65:2) was simply to affirm God's true nature.

Psalm 67
A BLESSING TO BE SHARED

Although there has been much discussion about the original setting of this psalm, both the NRSV and the REB, by their translations of the first line of verse 6, "The earth has yielded its increase [REB: "harvest"]," point correctly to the psalm being used as part of a harvest thanksgiving celebration. If so, then there are two noteworthy features in the psalm.

First, there is the absence throughout the psalm of any other reference to harvest or to the God of the natural world. Instead the key central verse, verse 4, with its refrain on either side in verses 3 and 5, focuses clearly on the God who acts in history, the God who judges the peoples and guides the nations. There is, however, nothing surprising in this. The credal statement in Deut. 26:5-10, whose setting is the offering of firstfruits at harvest time, is a recital of the mighty acts of God in Israel's history, beginning with the patriarchs, leading through Egyptian slavery to the Exodus and the coming to the land flowing with milk and honey, then culminating in the words "So now I bring you the first of the fruit of the ground that you, O LORD, have given me" (Deut. 26:10). The land and its produce were not to be identified with the fertility deities of Canaanite religion. They were the gift of the God who had revealed his true character to his people in the course of their history.

Second, this psalm goes even further. It looks beyond the boundaries of Israel's own experience to declare God's lordship over the whole world, and it invites other nations and peoples to join joyfully in the worship of the LORD. If there was ever a narrow exclusiveness in Israel's understanding of God — and there was at times — then this brief psalm is surely the antidote. The blessing which God's people have received and confidently expect to continue to receive is a blessing to be shared. Here is a faith crying out to be universalized.

The psalm lends itself to antiphonal singing, with whoever was leading the worship responsible for verses 1-2, 4, and 6-7 and a choral or congregational response in the refrain in verses 3 and 5. The psalm begins (v. 1) by echoing the first two lines of the Aaronic priestly blessing in Num. 6:24-26 (see 4:6). Apart from a change in word order, the main difference is that whoever leads the worship identifies himself with the people. It is no longer, "The LORD bless you" but "May God be gracious to us and bless us." In the light of God's gifts in the harvest (v. 6), the community is invited to look forward to being upheld and enriched by God's continuing presence and limitless goodness (for "make his face to shine upon us," see 31:16). While the people ponder this (for "Selah," see Psalm 3), the psalmist's thought takes a decisive and interesting change of direction. In Numbers 6 the purpose of the blessing is to "put my name on the Israelites, and I will bless them" (Num. 6:27). Here the purpose of this blessing is that God's "way," his nature and directions for living and his "saving power" ("his salvation"; see 3:8) may be known "upon earth" and "among all nations." The Hebrew word for nations here, gôyîm, usually indicates nations other than Israel. Lest there be any misunderstanding, from this point onwards we hear the word "peoples" five times in verses 3, 4 and 5. Another word for "nations" occurs twice in verse 4, and the psalm ends by calling upon "all the ends of the earth" to bow in reverence before God.

Nor is this to be a grudging recognition of God's awesome power (cf. Ps. 47:3-4). Verses 3 and 5 speak of the peoples praising "you, O God," the word translated "praise" here meaning to express or to give thanks (cf. 7:17). This, as verse 4 stresses, is thanksgiving rooted in joy, the joy of knowing that they are dealing with a God who judges, or rules (see 7:8), with "equity," fairness, and consideration (see 45:6), a God who guides or leads, the word used of the divine shepherd in Ps. 23:3. What the psalmist pleads for himself in Ps. 27:11 is to become true in the experience of the nations: "Teach me your way, O LORD, and lead me on a level path."

If the first half of verse 6 speaks of the blessing of harvest received, the second half, together with the opening of verse 7, probably expresses a wish for the continuance of God's blessing: "May God, our God, bless us" (REB rather than NRSV). Typical of the whole psalm, however, is the note on which it ends. If this God is "our God," he is not so in any exclusive sense. "Our God" is the one whom all the ends of the earth will "revere" (see 19:9). The confidence Israel had in God, and the God-given enrichment of life they celebrated at harvest, committed them to such goodness being shared with the wider world.

It is perhaps not surprising, then, that in one of the Christian lectionary cycles, Psalm 67 is linked with the Gospel reading from John 5:1-9, the good news of Jesus in action in the healing of the paralytic man at the pool Bethesda, and with Acts 16:9-15 where Paul, in response to a vision of a man from Macedonia, first crosses over to the European mainland "convinced that God had called me to proclaim the good news to them" (Acts 16:10).

Psalm 68
GOD TRIUMPHANT

Any attempt to interpret this psalm runs into serious difficulties. At many points the text itself is far from clear. From the earliest times it has been noted that the psalm contains many words which occur only here in the Old Testament or only rarely elsewhere. To take but one example: in verse 6 does God lead out the prisoners "to prosperity" (NRSV) or "in safety" (REB) or, as some commentators claim, "with music"? All these are attempts to render a Hebrew word which occurs nowhere else. Part of the difficulty may lie in the fact that we are dealing with a psalm which goes back to a very early period and contains archaic language.

Beyond the textual difficulties, however, there lies an even more basic problem. Is there a common thread which holds together the very varied material in the psalm? Some scholars have argued "No." In their view, the psalm is no more than a collection of the opening lines of early Hebrew lyric poems, as if in this psalm we were glancing through the index to a hymnbook! This is a counsel of despair. But if there is a unity, what kind of unity is it? Is it to be sought by seeing the psalm at home in a major religious festival, and if so, what and where? In its present form the natural worship setting would be in the temple in Jerusalem (cf. v. 29), but this may only be a later Jerusalem version of a psalm which was once at home elsewhere, probably further north at Mt. Tabor. Or is the unity purely a literary unity in which a poet draws upon a variety of different sources, including Canaanite religious traditions, which he then seeks to integrate into his own theological understanding? It is no use pretending that the problems do not exist or that there are any easy answers. Any theological interpretation of the psalm must be hesitant rather than assured, tentative rather than dogmatic. What is offered here assumes many decisions which in a fuller, critical commentary would have to be discussed at length.

However we divide the psalm, each section within it seems to focus in a variety of different ways on the triumph of God, past, present, and future. There is something of a watershed in the language used at the end of verse 18. In the first part of the psalm, the dominant note is that of the God who comes, with language such as, "Let God rise up" (v. 1), "God gives . . . leads" (v. 6), "went out . . . marched" (v. 7), "came from Sinai" (v. 17), and "ascended" (v. 18). After verse 18 the emphasis is more on the presence of God with his people, the God "who daily bears us up" (v. 19), the God who is "in his sanctuary" (vv. 24, 35), "in the great congregation" (v. 26), and "in the temple at Jerusalem" (v. 29). It is as if a congregation begins by singing the "Battle Hymn of the Republic":

> Mine eyes have seen the glory of the coming of the Lord:
> He is trampling out the vintage where the grapes of wrath are stored;
> He hath loosed the fatal lightning of his terrible swift sword:
>> His truth is marching on.

and then turns to,

> God reveals his presence:
>> Let us now adore him,
> And with awe appear before him.
>> God is in his temple. . . .

Theology needs to hold together, as this psalm does, these two complementary emphases — the God who is on the march, ever active, going before his people, and the God who stays in their midst, meeting with his people in the beauty of holiness.

1-6   The introit begins by calling upon God in language reminiscent of the traditions centering on the ark, the symbol of God's presence in the midst of his people, and especially the words attributed to Moses in Num. 10:35, "Arise, O LORD, let your enemies be scattered, and your foes flee before you." The capture of the ark by the Philistines led to the saying, "The glory has departed from Israel" (1 Sam. 4:21), but the ark was subsequently brought to Jerusalem by David (2 Samuel 6). Whether these words marked the beginning of a cultic procession in which the ark played a prominent role is debatable. This coming means that all who oppose God will prove to be powerless, as insubstantial as smoke that drifts away or as wax that melts in the fire (v. 2). It also marks a clear point of division between "the wicked," doomed to perish, and "the righteous" (see Psalm 1) who will exult in a hymn of joy (see 5:11). God's coming is the great divider (cf. Matthew 24 and 25).

The introit then moves into a hymn of praise in verses 4-6 to the one who "rides upon the clouds." This title in Canaanite mythology is associated with Baal, the god of the storm and of the life-giving rain. The word translated "clouds" could also mean the desert steppe, in which case there would be a reference to the God who traveled with his people through the wilderness (cf. v. 7). The way, however, in which verse 4 is echoed in verses 32 and 33, which contain the divine title "O rider in the heavens," makes it more likely that the title here anticipates verse 9, with its claim that it is Israel's God who is the source of the revitalizing rain (cf. 65:9-13). This is the God whose true nature is contained in his name the LORD. The Hebrew in verse 4 has "Yah," a shorter form of "Yahweh" found in personal names — for example, Elijah — and in the psalmists' cry "Hallelujah," praise the LORD. We may compare the closing words of Psalms 104–106, the opening call in Psalms 111–113, and its frequent use in the Hallelujah chorus in Psalms 146–150. Typically this LORD, the rider on the clouds, is no distant God but the father of those at risk: orphans and widows, the lonely and the prisoners (see 10:18). Only those who "rebel" against God experience life in an arid wasteland. Although the language of verse 6 is capable of different interpretations, it could be that "the prisoners" refer to the Hebrews in slavery in Egypt, while the "rebellious" are those who rejected God's authority in the wilderness wanderings (cf. Ps. 78:8), never to reach the promised land. It is perhaps not without significance that an introit which begins by echoing Num. 10:35 ends on this note of rebellion of which the immediately following chapter, Numbers 11, provides a classic illustration, the people complaining to the LORD about their hardship in the desert.

7-10 The psalm now turns to celebrate key events in Israel's salvation story in language which is reminiscent of the Song of Deborah in Judges 5, one of the earliest Hebrew poems, and in particular of Judg. 5:4-5 with its picture of God's coming depicted as an earthquake and rain storm, the God who is "the God of Sinai" and the God of Israel. But there is a difference. Judges 5 celebrates a specific historical event; the rainstorm ensures the defeat of a Canaanite army, swept away in the swollen waters of the river Kishon (Judg. 5:21). Here, by contrast, the abundant rain is the sign of that "goodness" or bounty (cf. 65:11) which ensured that the land, God's gift to his people, was ever renewed and sustained with ample provision for the "needy" or the poor (see 9:12). Thus the key events of Israel's story are recalled: the Exodus from Egypt (v. 6), the wilderness wandering (v. 7), the encounter with God at Mt. Sinai (v. 8), and the settlement in the land (vv. 9-10). They are all celebrated as the sign of God's coming to his people and his presence with them.

The phrase translated "the God of Sinai" (v. 8) (REB: "the Lord of Sinai") does not mean that the Hebrews believed that the God they worshipped was simply the God located on Mt. Sinai. The location of Mt. Sinai is uncertain, but from the fourth century CE it has been identified by many with the Jebel Musa at the foot of which stands St. Catherine's monastery. Even its name is uncertain, some traditions referring to it as Horeb (Exod. 3:1 and throughout Deuteronomy), others speaking simply of "the mountain of God" (e.g., Exod. 4:27). Sinai was merely a significant staging post in the journey of a pilgrim-God with his pilgrim-people.

11-14 These verses are plagued with difficulties of translation and interpretation. The section is introduced abruptly by "The Lord gives the command" or "speaks the word," probably to underline that the overwhelming rout of the enemy and the victory celebrations which followed owed everything to the decisive word of the Lord and not to human prowess. There may be an echo of the prophetic word that came through Deborah to Barak, the commander of the Hebrew forces in the battle against Sisera (cf. Judg. 4:6). This would strengthen the case for seeing in verses 11-14 a specific reference to the victory over the Canaanite kings described in prose and in poetry in Judges 4 and 5. The phrase "the kings of the armies" (v. 12), or hosts, may have ironic undertones. Powerful they may be, but confronted by the "LORD of hosts" (see 24:10) they can only flee. It was customary for the women to celebrate the good news of victory with songs and with dancing (cf. Exod. 15:20-21; 1 Sam. 18:6-7). Women also expected to share in the spoils of booty (see Judg. 5:30). The reference to "sheepfolds" (v. 13) may again have its roots in Judg. 5:16, though the specific point is far from clear. The dove with wings "covered with silver, its pinions with green [REB: yellow] gold" remains a mystery. Some have interpreted the dove as a symbol of the Canaanite goddess Astarte, goddess of love, now part of the captured booty; others have argued that the release of doves was a sign of victory, with the silver and gold a poetic description of the vivid marking and coloring on their wings.

The description of God as the "Almighty" (Hebrew *šaddai*) is found only once again in the Psalms, in 91:1. It is also found in the patriarchal narratives in Genesis (e.g., Gen. 17:1; 28:3), and Exod. 6:3 claims that this, and not the LORD, was the name by which God was known to the patriarchs. Elsewhere in the Old Testament it occurs most frequently in the book of Job, both on the lips of Job (e.g., Job 6:4) and of his friends (e.g., Job 5:17). It may have meant originally "the one of the mountain." The Greek (LXX) translates it by a word meaning "ruler of all," and this may be the flavor of it within the context of Hebrew faith. This "ruler of all" speaks a decisive word against any human ruler, no matter how powerful.

"Zalmon," the Dark Mountain, was according to Judg. 9:48 a hill overlooking Shechem, but whether this is the dark mountain of verse 14 is uncertain. What seems to have been regarded as remarkable was the concurrence of victory with snowfall on this mountain, an unusual happening taken as a divine sign. But why is this victory at "Taanach by the waters of Megiddo" (Judg. 5:19) singled out for special mention? The clue may lie in Deborah's words to Barak, "Go take up position at Mt. Tabor, bringing ten thousand from the tribe of Naphtali and the tribe of Zebulun" (Judg. 4:6). Was this psalm originally part of the celebration of God's mighty acts at the local shrine at Mt. Tabor? In this case the memorable local victory over the Canaanites would feature prominently in the liturgy, just as local churches today will give prominence to events in their own history which they see as evident signs of God's presence in their midst.

15-16   Associating the original setting of the psalm with Mt. Tabor would also account for the reference in verse 15 to the mountain range of "Bashan" (see 22:12), described as a "mighty mountain" (literally, "mountain of God"), "many-peaked," if that is the correct translation of a word found only here. The peaks which dominate the Golan and reach as far north as Mt. Hermon were visible from and much higher than Mt. Tabor. Yet, claims the psalmist, they were envious of this smaller hill, because it was there that the LORD made his abode (v. 16). The language of verse 16 is elsewhere applied to Zion in Jerusalem, which, according to Ps. 132:13-14, the LORD "desired . . . for his habitation," saying, "This is my resting place forever; here I will reside, for I have desired it."

17-18   As we noted, the psalm in its present form has its place in the Jerusalem temple, but many rivulets must have fed into the stream of liturgical tradition which eventually centered on the Jerusalem temple. In particular, after the destruction of the northern kingdom by the Assyrians in the eighth century BCE, many northern traditions must have found new and continuing life in Jerusalem, just as many different streams of tradition have fed into the liturgies most of us use today. If the original setting is Mt. Tabor, verses 17-18 describe how the victorious Lord from Sinai, surrounded by his heavenly host (cf. Isa. 66:15; 2 Kgs. 6:17), far outnumbering the ten thousand from the tribes of Naphtali and Zebulun, leads his captives to his mountain abode and receives tribute even from those who rebelled against him. Thus the story of God's triumph, of his past saving acts going back to the Exodus and Sinai, reaches its appropriate climax.

The first half of verse 18 is quoted in Eph. 4:8, but in a form which is found only in the Aramaic Targum, reading "he gave gifts to his people," instead of "he received gifts from people." The common thematic link is the victorious ascension of the LORD in Psalm 68 and of Christ in Ephesians. In the case of Christ's ascension, this is linked with the gifts which he bestows upon the Church. At this point we move into a theological realm which goes far beyond anything which is envisaged in Psalm 68.

19-20   From verse 19 onwards, the presence of God in the sanctuary is uppermost in the minds of the congregation, as they acknowledge that whatever goodness enriches their life and whatever hope they have for the future center on God. This section begins "Blessed be the LORD" (v. 19) and ends "Blessed be God!" (v. 35; cf. 28:6; 66:20). Verses 19-20 celebrate the God who carries the burdens for us.

In a magnificent piece of satire, the poet prophet in Isaiah 46 depicts the gods of Babylon being unceremoniously carried out of the city, "burdens on weary animals," while the God of Israel carries his people across their history: "Even to your old age, I am he, even when you turn gray, I will carry you. I have made and I will bear; I will carry and will save" (Isa. 46:4). Religion should never be a burden we carry around with us; yet it is only too easy for religious people to give that impression with a killjoy attitude to life. Religion should be a liberating, joyful witness to the God who carries us. Here, says the psalmist, is the God whose essential nature is summed up in the word "salvation" (see 3:8), the God who provides "escape from death" (v. 20). The verb translated "escape" is from the verb "to go out," a verb used frequently in the context of God "bringing out" the people from slavery in Egypt (e.g., Exod. 20:2). It would therefore have rich associations in the minds of those who were recalling their salvation story. "Escape from death" might mean rescue from any life-threatening or life-weakening situation, but behind the words may loom the figure of the Canaanite god "Mot," Death, conquered by Baal in Canaanite mythology, but now conquered by the LORD.

21-23 Present confidence leads in verses 21-23 into future certainty that God will deal effectively with all his enemies. The "hairy crown" (v. 21; REB: "flowing locks") may refer to hair allowed to grow as part of a vow, to which we may compare Num. 6:5, where it is part of the Nazarite vow. Samson was the classic example of a Nazarite (see Judges 13–16). No matter what vows the enemies of God take, as long as they persist in their "guilt," in their opposition to the one true God, they are inescapably doomed. "Bashan" (v. 22) probably indicates the far mountain range on the eastern horizon. The "depths of the sea" refers to the Mediterranean marking the western horizon. This is the psalmist's way of saying that there is no corner of the globe in which it is possible to escape from God's judgment (cf. Amos 9:2-4). Wherever they are, they will be brought back, called to account. God's victory is one in which his people will share. The language of verse 23 may be somewhat lurid (see 58:10), but underlying it is the sense of deserved retribution. To it we may compare Elijah's words to Ahab in 1 Kgs. 21:19, "Thus says the LORD: In the place where the dogs licked the blood of Naboth, dogs will also lick your blood."

24-27 These verses describe one of the great festival processions, probably led by the ark, the symbol of God's presence in the midst of his people. It is the procession of the divine king, "my King" (see 5:2), to his abode in the sanctuary, led by the singers, the rear brought up by musicians with stringed instruments. Accompanying them are girls playing tambourines. This is a joyful occasion, an acknowledgment that life's riches come from the God who is "the fountain" of Israel (v. 26; see 36:9). But why the reference to Benjamin, Judah, Zebulun, and

Naphtali in verse 27? If the verse preserves a cultic tradition at home originally at Mt. Tabor, then the reference to Zebulun and Naphtali is understandable (see comment on verses 11-14). Naturalized in Jerusalem, the reference to Judah becomes appropriate, but why Benjamin, and why is little Benjamin said to be "in the lead" or dominating them? It is doubtful that Benjamin features because of the link with Saul (1 Sam. 9:1), since the Jerusalem temple is linked with David and Solomon, not Saul. It may be that in God's procession the natural human order of precedence is deliberately inverted, with traditionally the youngest member of the family given the place of honor (cf. Gen. 43:33).

28-31 From this procession, joyfully celebrating the power of God, the psalmist turns to prayer, a prayer that God's "strength" (v. 28; see 21:1, 13) may again be demonstrated now, as it has been in the past. The temple symbolizes the power of God since to it other kings bring their gifts of homage. Yet not all of the kings of the earth pay homage. It is far from certain whether "the wild animals that live among the reeds" and "the herd of bulls with the calves" can be identified with specific enemies, such as Egypt (cf. v. 31) and Assyria and her allies. The wild animals may simply point to all the powers that threaten the life of God's people, their identity depending upon the specific historical circumstances in which the psalm was sung. The second half of verse 30 poses many problems, though the general meaning in context seems clear. Verse 31 calls upon two specific nations, Egypt and Cush, to recognize God's authority. Cush is normally identified as Ethiopia or Nubia, the territory immediately to the south of Egypt. Although Egypt and Cush featured in a supportive role when Hezekiah faced the Assyrian threat to Jerusalem at the end of the eighth century BCE (2 Kgs. 18:21, 24; 19:9), it is doubtful whether this can be used to date the psalm. Egypt probably signifies the traditional oppressors of God's people, deliverance from Egypt being central to their salvation story. Cush, in the far south, probably stands for people at the far corners of the world. Thus the whole world is being invited to reach out to embrace the God of Israel (cf. Psalm 67).

32-35 The psalm ends with a hymn of praise (verses 32-35) which begins by echoing the hymn in verse 4, but with this difference: no longer is it the worshipping community of God's people who are invited to sing to the LORD; now it is the "kingdoms of the earth" who are invited to sing and to "listen" to what God has to say to them. They are to recognize that Israel's God, who is enthroned not merely in an earthly temple but in the heavens, stands for "strength" or power. Four times in verses 33-35 we hear again the word for "strength," which occurs in verse 28, is translated "mighty" in verse 33, and "power" twice in verse 34 and once in verse 35. The word "majesty" (v. 34), which is often used of human pride or arrogance, is found only once elsewhere in the Hebrew Bible applied to God. That single occurrence, in Deut. 33:26, catches something of the flavor of the closing lines of the psalm: "There is none like God . . . who rides through the heavens to your help, majestic through the skies." Awesome, yes, but no distant despot, for this is the God who "gives power and strength to his people." On this confident note the Songs of Praise, Psalms 65–68, end.

The three occurrences of "Selah" in this psalm are strategically placed to enable the congregation to respond to its basic theology. In verse 7, the word invites the congregation to reflect on the story of Israel's salvation story, beginning with the Exodus. In verse 19, it invites reflection on Israel's experience of God's present goodness. In verse 32, it calls for reflection on a faith which looks forward to becoming a universal faith. Thus through a series of quickly changing pictures, Psalm 68 invites God's people to see past, present, and future as part of God's story and under God's control.

Psalm 69
A CRY OF DESPERATION

This psalm has many of the marks of a typical psalm of lament — urgent pleas, a description of the crisis in the psalmist's life, complaint and bitterness, and finally thanksgiving (see comments on Psalms 3 and 13). It poses the same kind of questions we have faced elsewhere. Who is speaking in the psalm? Is it the king or an otherwise unidentified person? Can we clarify the historical or cultic situation which gave the psalm its present form? Certainly the experience described in the psalm is not peculiar to the king. It finds its counterpart in the experience of Jeremiah, yet it clothes itself in language peculiar to this psalm and invites anyone who shares a similar experience to identify with it.

The urgency of the psalmist's plight is indicated by the repeated pleas for help: "Save me [v. 1; see 3:1] . . . rescue me [v. 14; cf. 7:1] . . . answer me [v. 16] . . . make haste to answer me [v. 17; see 20:1] . . . draw near to me [v. 18; cf. 34:18] . . . redeem me [v. 18; see 19:14] . . . set me free [v. 18; see 25:22] . . . protect me [v. 29]." The urgency of the pleas indicates the depth of the crisis in the psalmist's life, which is described in several sections of the psalm.

1-4 The language describing the psalmist up to his neck in water, sinking inexorably into the bottomless mire, drowning in floods (v. 14), would be consistent with someone being sucked down into Sheol, the world of the dead, particularly when we place it side by side with the way in which the psalmist describes his plight in verse 15, with its reference to the "Pit" (see 6:5 and 16:10). Undoubtedly here is someone *in extremis,* yet there may be a metaphorical element in the language. Compare the way in which we talk about feeling as if we are drowning or in the depths of despair. What is clear is that the psalmist is near the end of his tether, exhausted with crying, his throat "parched" (v. 3) or hoarse, his eyesight failing, the result of exhaustion (cf. Jer. 14:6). He can only "wait" in hope (see 38:15) for one whom he holds on to as "my God" (v. 3).

Verse 4 stresses his general sense of alienation, surrounded by numerous enemies (cf. vv. 14, 18), who hate him "without cause" (cf. 35:7) and who are out to destroy him by bringing false charges against him, including theft. Lev. 6:5 stipulates that in such cases, what has been stolen must be repaid with twenty percent interest and a guilt offering brought to the LORD. But how can I be expected to pay back what I never stole? says the psalmist (v. 4). We get the impression here that he is dealing with people who are seeking to undermine his status in the community by making false innuendoes. However vehement the denials, they leave their mark since people tend to think that there is no smoke without fire.

5-6 Conscious of being unjustly attacked and misunderstood, the psalmist turns to the God who knows him through and through (v. 5), who knows that "folly" and "wrongs" (REB: "guilty deeds") have marred his life. This does not mean that the psalmist is now admitting that there was truth in the charges laid against him (v. 4). The link between sin and suffering was deeply ingrained in much of the thinking we find in the Old Testament (cf. 38:3-5), so the only reason for the extremity of the crisis in which he finds himself must be that there is wrong in his life. What that wrong is, however, only God knows. Such things, he confesses, "are not hidden from you" (v. 5). This leads the psalmist to express concern for those in the community who share his faith, who "hope" or wait expectantly for God (v. 6; see 25:3), those who "seek you" (cf. 9:10). He is concerned that what is happening to him may undermine their faith and cause them to doubt "the LORD God of hosts" (see 24:10). Although he has many enemies, he is not on his own. He still belongs to a community of believers who will react positively or negatively to what is happening to him.

7-12 These verses introduce a further element, when the psalmist claims, "It is for your sake that I have borne reproach" (v. 7); "It is zeal for your house that has consumed me" (v. 9). If "your house" means, as seems likely, "your temple," then we can imagine several possible scenarios. This could be the enthusiasm of a king or leading temple officials to eliminate corruption or the worship of gods other than the LORD which were disfiguring the temple (cf. Josiah's reforms in 2 Kings 22–23). It could be a Jeremiah preaching a blistering sermon against those who thronged to the temple, yet lived as if the moral demands of the LORD were irrelevant (cf. Jeremiah 7). It could be someone in the immediate postexilic period anxious to see the ruined temple restored to something of its former glory (cf. Haggai). Other suggestions are possible.

Whatever this "zeal for your house" was, it was a central element in the crisis in the psalmist's life. It led to alienation from his own kinsfolk and family circle (v. 8). Even when the psalmist resorted to "fasting" and wearing "sackcloth" (vv. 10, 11; see 35:13) he was ridiculed, the subject of gossip in what we would call business circles and in the law courts — "the gate" (v. 12) into a town or village being the place where the elders met to transact business (cf. Ruth 4) and to dispense justice (Josh. 20:4). His name featured prominently in ribald songs sung in the local taverns (v. 12b). The shame, insults, and dishonor he experienced (vv. 7, 9, 19) broke his heart and led him to "despair" (v. 20), a word found only here, but probably pointing to the inward sickness which gripped him. In many respects the classic illustration of this in the Old Testament is Jeremiah. The book bearing his name records the mockery, the insults, and the persecution he received because of his commitment to his prophetic ministry (e.g., Jer. 15:15) and describes his sense of alienation from the community at large (Jer. 15:17) and from his own family (Jer. 12:6).

13-18 In these verses the psalmist interrupts his narrative with a prayer for himself, that God's answer will come "at an acceptable time" (v. 13), that is, acceptable to God. The psalmist does not presume to dictate to God; he is prepared to wait for this "acceptable time." The Hebrew, however, might equally well be rendered "a time of favor," the time when God will demonstrate his favor to his suffering servant (cf. 5:12). The ground for the psalmist's prayer, as always in the Psalms, lies in what the psalmist believes about the character of God. God has "steadfast love" (see 3:8) in abundance; his actions demonstrate "faithful help" (v. 13; REB: "sure deliverance"). The Hebrew here combines the two words which elsewhere speak of "faithfulness" (see 25:50) and "salvation" (see 3:8). This is the God who has abundant "mercy," or compassion (v. 16; cf. 25:6), a God to whom the psalmist can say, "Do not hide your face from your servant" (v. 17; cf. 13:1), "do not reject me in my time of need."

19-21 These verses mark the transition in the psalmist's thought from his prayer for himself, based on God's "steadfast love," to a bitter prayer for retribution on his enemies beginning in verse 22. These verses focus on his enemies, what they have done to the psalmist, all their wounding and destructive activities known to God. If the wrongs done by the psalmist are not hidden from God, neither are the wrongs done to him. In particular he complains of the way in which they have rubbed salt into his wounds.

He looked for "pity" (v. 20; REB: "consolation") or perhaps "sympathy" (the Hebrew word means "to move the head to and fro"; cf. Job 2:11) but got none. He waited for "comforters," but none came. We are reminded of Job's despairing cry, "Have pity on me, have pity on me" (Job 19:21), a cry made to friends described earlier as "miserable comforters" (Job 16:2). Anyone at all moved by compassion might have been expected to invite him to a meal, but all he got was "poison" and "vinegar," a type of sour wine usually regarded as unfit for human consumption (v. 21).

22-28, 29 Faced with such conduct, the psalmist reacts, as do many other psalmists, not with resigned acceptance but with a bitterness which expresses itself in a prayer for retribution (vv. 22-28; see 5:10). The prayer is in the form of a series of curses which contain within them an element of poetic justice. Jeremiah's reaction to those who hounded him is equally if not more bitter (cf. Jer. 17:18; 18:19-23).

Poison and vinegar were all they offered to the psalmist, so he asks God to let their "table" — either the meals in their own homes or the sacrifices they share in the temple — become a trap for them, "a snare for their allies" or their boon companions (v. 22). The Hebrew word here, related to "shalom," is capable of different interpretations. The REB applies it not to friends but to the attitude of the people themselves: "a trap when they feel secure." The psalmist's eyes grow dim (v. 3); now in v. 23 he looks forward to the health of his enemies being undermined, afflicted with blindness, their loins constantly trembling, sign of a physical ailment they cannot control. They have vented their hatred against the psalmist (v. 24; cf. v. 4); let them now be on the receiving end of God's "indignation" (cf. 38:3) and "burning anger" (see 6:1). The psalmist has been alienated from his own family (v. 8), so he prays for a time when their "camps" and "tents," in other words their homes, will be desolate and deserted (v. 25).

If any justification for such curses is needed, the psalmist points out to God that such people have been outdoing God, persecuting those who are already experiencing suffering as a result of their sinfulness (v. 5), adding to the pain of those already suffering enough pain (v. 26). So the psalmist has no hesitation in calling upon God to compound their "guilt" (see 32:1), to make sure that they will never receive from the divine judge a verdict of acquittal (literally, "your righteousness"). He asks God to see to it that their names are erased forever from "the book of the living" (see 56:8) and to give them no place among the righteous (vv. 27, 28).

In dramatic contrast, the psalmist turns from such people who richly deserve all that is coming to them, to himself, "lowly" or afflicted (see 9:12) and "in pain" (v. 29), words which underline his frailty and need and which can be met only by "your salvation, O God" (see 3:8).

30-36 A song of thanksgiving brings the psalm to its conclusion. It begins on a strictly personal note, with the psalmist offering his praise in a song of thanksgiving, its purpose to "magnify," to acknowledge, the greatness of God. Although the word translated "thanksgiving" in verse 30 can mean a thank-offering sacrifice (Lev. 7:12), the psalmist makes clear that such a sacrifice in itself would not be acceptable to God; even the sacrifice of an ox or a mature, ritually acceptable bull (cf. Lev. 1:3) would not be acceptable unless accompanied by the true spirit of thanksgiving (see 40:6-8). Just as earlier the psalmist had expressed his concern that what was happening to him would have an adverse effect on those who shared his faith (v. 6), so now he believes that his song of thanksgiving will give encouragement and new hope to the "oppressed" (cf. 9:12) and "you who seek God" (v. 32). What has happened to him is confirmation that God does respond to the "needy" (cf. 9:12) and does not despise "his own that are in bonds" (v. 33). These last words are a translation of a Hebrew word which can mean simply "prisoners" (68:7), not least prisoners of war (79:11); hence, the REB translates "his captive people." If this verse anticipates verses 35 and 36, which seem to imply a destroyed country with its population exiled, "prisoners" is probably the correct translation. The NRSV assumes that the reference is to any who feel oppressed and who are conscious that what has happened to them must be accepted as God's punishment, as shackles he has placed upon them.

Personal thanksgiving, leading into shared thanksgiving (vv. 30-33), now breaks out into a universal song of praise, in which not merely "all peoples" (cf. Psalm 67) or "the kingdoms of the earth" (68:32) but the whole created world join, praising God because he has demonstrated that his "steadfast love" is dependable in response to the needs of those who seek him (96:11-13) and undergirds the entire universe (see Psalm 19; 136:4-9).

If we press the language of verse 35a, it seems to presuppose a situation in which Zion (cf. 2:6) still survives while other cities in Judah have been devastated. The Assyrian invasion at the end of the eighth century BCE (cf. 2 Kings 18) and the tense situation in Jerusalem following the final revolt against Babylon in 589 BCE are obvious candidates for just such a scenario. It may be, however, that saving Zion points to the renewal of the life of Jerusalem, which like that of the rest of the country now lies in ruin. People are once again to dwell there and repossess the land. The people are described as "the children of his servants," as those who continue truly worshipping and obeying God (see 34:22), and as "those who love his name" (see 34:3).

A lament which begins "Save me" (v. 1) ends on the confident note that "God will save Zion" (v. 35) and all the people of God. The psalmist's personal crisis may have been traumatic and life-threatening, but he recognizes that his own suffering must be placed in the wider context of the suffering and tragedy which have come to other people. He cannot opt out of the world. The intensity of his personal struggle mirrors the struggle of other people. His hope for the future must embrace other people. God is not his personal possession.

Psalm 69 is cited frequently in the New Testament. Verse 4 is quoted in John 15:25 in the context of the hatred Jesus experienced. Verse 21 features in all the Gospel accounts of the crucifixion (Mark 15:36; Luke 23:36; Matt. 27:48; John 19:29). Verses 22 and 23, following the Greek (LXX) text, appear in Rom. 11:9 in the context of Paul's wrestling with the mystery of why most Jews rejected Jesus. The second half of verse 9 is quoted in Rom. 15:3 and applied to Christ as the example of what the true Christian life should be. Perhaps the most interesting citation is in John 2:17, where in the context of the cleansing of the temple, the disciples recollect the opening words of verse 9, "Zeal for your house will consume me." The Johannine narrator immediately takes the word "house," signifying temple, to refer to "the temple of his body." This use of Scripture, claims John, was remembered by the disciples only after the resurrection. New Testament writers do not merely quote texts from the Psalms or elsewhere in the Hebrew Bible, as proof texts. They reflect on the Hebrew Bible in the light of their knowledge of the God who came to them in the life, death, and resurrection of Jesus. This must remain the Christian approach, even if we reject some of the methods which have been used across the centuries to this end, such as an excessively allegorical approach.

Psalm 70

Psalm 70 is, with minor variations, the same as Ps. 40:13-17. For comment, see the discussion on Psalm 40. Psalm 70 has, however, been given a different heading, including the words "for the memorial offering," which occurs elsewhere only in the heading to Psalm 38. Psalm 70, however, is followed by a psalm which has no heading of its own, and it is likely that, in the final editing of the Psalms, Psalms 70 and 71 were regarded as one psalm, as in the case of Psalms 9 and 10.

Psalm 71
A MATURE SPIRITUALITY

The first three verses of this psalm are, with minor variations, the same as Ps. 31:1-3a, and there are frequent echoes of the language and imagery of other psalms (e.g., Ps. 22:9-10 in vv. 5, 6, and 7; Ps. 22:11, 19 in v. 12; Ps. 35:4, 26 in v. 13; and Ps. 36:6 in v. 19). These echoes, however, do not mean that Psalm 71 is simply a pastiche of sections and snippets from other psalms. It has its own distinctive flavor. We are listening to the prayer and the praise of a man who, nurtured in the faith from his earliest days, now in old age reaffirms that faith as he faces a crisis in his life. Here is a mature spirituality which, when tested, draws strength from the language and the tradition of spirituality which have shaped his thinking across many years. The importance of this can hardly be overestimated. We relive the psalmist's experience in almost every act of worship. The call to worship is very often a quotation from a psalm, while the prayers which lead worship will draw on a tradition of spirituality, sometimes echoing the language and imagery of Scripture, sometimes using prayers which have come down to us across the centuries. There are, moreover, many people today, even some whose links with the Church are now somewhat tenuous, who in situations of crisis find their thoughts naturally turning to well-known passages from Scripture, such as Psalm 23 and John 14. This psalmist unashamedly draws on the rich heritage of faith of his people and finds in it a "safe haven" (v. 3; REB: "a rock of refuge") in face of hostility which might otherwise have destroyed him. Since much of the language and thought of the psalm is familiar from other psalms, we shall focus attention solely on what is distinctive in this psalm.

What do we learn about the psalmist? Like the author of Psalm 22, he affirms his belief that God was there sustaining him from the moment of his birth. The Hebrew word translated "took me" (REB: "brought me") in verse 6 may be from a verb meaning "to cut," in which case the psalmist comes close to saying, "You cut my umbilical cord." There never has been a time when God was not present, and God's continuous presence has elicited from him continuous praise, which he believes he will still be able to offer to God now in "old age" and with "gray hairs" (vv. 9, 18), in spite of the difficulties he faces.

He describes himself in verse 7 as having been or having become "like a portent to many." The Hebrew word translated "portent" is often used together with the word "sign" (see 65:8). It usually indicates something extraordinary or striking which cries out for explanation. It is frequently used to describe what God did in Egypt, sending the plagues which paved the way for the Exodus (cf. Ps. 105:27, where it is translated "miracles"). But what kind of "portent" has the psalmist been? There are two possibilities. On the one hand, it may be that throughout his life he has been a striking example of God's providential care, from whose witness others found their faith strengthened, a walking wonder, as it were, of God's grace. In context this makes sense, provided we omit the "but" in verse 7 and translate instead "you indeed are [or: have been] my strong refuge." On the other hand, a portent can also be a warning. If that is the case here, then we may imagine other people are now pointing the finger at the psalmist and saying, "Look, here is a man who trusted in God, but God has quite obviously forsaken him [cf. v. 11]; so much for the faith he professes!" He is an object of scorn, no knight in shining armor, but a walking disaster. That is the kind of argument we hear frequently on the lips of Job's friends and against which Job vehemently protests, while acknowledging the effect that his suffering has had on other people (cf. Job 19:1-22).

But what exactly was the crisis in the psalmist's life? There are references to the "wicked," the "unjust," and the "cruel" in verse 4. He speaks about "my enemies" engaged in a whispering campaign, a conspiracy to destroy him (v. 10). He has "accusers" (v. 13) and "many troubles and calamities" (v. 20). All of this leaves open a wide range of possibilities. Verse 11 is probably a key verse. It seems to presuppose that there are people only too eager to take advantage of some disaster which has befallen him. They are interpreting the disaster as a sign of God's judgment. It may have been a debilitating illness which took him to death's door (v. 20b may be using the language of Sheol; cf. 6:5). It may have been personal misfortune in business or family life. Much depends on how much we read into the words in verse 9, "my strength is spent."

Perhaps the language is deliberately restrained and non-specific, just like his attitude towards those who attack him. Although he is certain that the roles will be reversed and that they will receive the shame and scorn which they now heap on him (cf. vv. 13 and 24), his attitude is much less virulent than that expressed in other psalms (e.g., 69:22-28). The focus throughout is primarily on God, what he has done and will do, what he has been and will still be. Much of the vocabulary he uses is familiar from other psalms. The one key word which is missing is "steadfast love." There are, however, two concepts which echo across the psalm.

The first is the word "righteousness" (vv. 1, 15, 16, 19, 24). The various nuances which hover around this word are illustrated by the translations. In verse 1 we find alternately "righteousness" (NRSV) and "your saving power" (REB); in verse 15, "your righteous acts" (NRSV) and "your saving acts" (REB); in verse 16, "your righteousness" (NRSV) and "your power to vindicate" (REB; cf. v. 19); in verse 24, "your righteous help" (NRSV) and "your vindicating power" (REB). This is the God who, true to his own nature, is in the business of putting right what is wrong.

The second recurring feature of the psalm is a cluster of words which center on praise or joyful thanksgiving. The word "praise" occurs in verses 6, 8, and 14, though not in verse 16 as the NRSV implies (see REB). The verb to "offer thanks" appears in verse 22; the verb to "sing praise" is used in verses 22 and 23; and the verb to "shout for joy" occurs in verse 23. Such is the psalmist's response to the God who rights wrongs, in whose hands are the issues of life and death. The psalmist here joins hands with George Herbert:

> Seven whole days, not one in seven,
>   I will praise thee;
> In my heart, though not in heaven,
>   I can raise thee.
> Small it is, in this poor sort
>   To enrol thee;
> E'en eternity's too short
>   To extol thee.

It may be that the psalmist was one of the professional singers attached to the temple, since he talks of praising God "with the harp" and singing "with the lyre" (v. 22). Whatever he was, his joyful response, even when the going is tough, is rooted in his worship of the "Holy One of Israel," a common title for God in the book of Isaiah (e.g., Isa. 1:4; 5:19, 24), but only twice again in the Psalms (78:41; 89:18). It holds in fruitful tension two aspects of the God to whom the

Old Testament witnesses in a variety of different ways. On the one hand, God is "holy" — wholly different (see 2:6) — and therefore must always be approached with awe and reverence. On the other hand, this same God has chosen to enter into a relationship with his people Israel. He is accessible to Israel, but never at Israel's beck and call; he is to be worshipped but never to be trivialized. Israel learned, often the hard way, the truth of the words in Heb. 10:31, "It is a fearful thing to fall into the hands of the living God." But it would be an even more fearful thing not to be in his hands.

Because he is in the hands of such a God, the psalmist is convinced that he will again experience life in all its fullness (v. 20), that he will be restored to his proper status and standing in the community, and that he will, as in the past, receive the resources needed to cope with the challenges life brings (v. 21; cf. 23:4).

Psalm 72
A TRUE KING

The heading "of Solomon" raises the same kind of issues as "of David." Is it intended to indicate authorship ("by" Solomon)? Is it a dedication "to" or "in honor of" Solomon? Or is it composed "with reference to" Solomon (perhaps meaning something like "with Solomon in mind")? One thing is clear: this is a royal psalm, which like Psalm 2 finds its natural setting in the coronation in the Jerusalem temple or in an annual ceremony commemorating the accession to the throne. In form, it is mainly a prayer for the king, offered in the conviction that the purposes of God and the welfare ("shalom"; see 4:9) of the people are bound up with the person of the king and the way he exercises authority.

1-4 The psalm opens with a scene familiar to us from other cultures in the ancient Near East, the king depicted as receiving from the deity the laws which are to govern the life of the community. Thus Hammurapi, of the eighteenth century BCE, receives the law code from Shamash, the Babylonian god of justice, laws designed, among other things, to "do away with perverse men, so that the strong might not oppress the weak" and "to give justice to the widow and the orphan." Only thus would Hammurapi fulfill his role as the shepherd of his people, ruling over a just and orderly society. So with the king in Israel.

The word translated "justice" in verse 1 is plural in Hebrew. It is the word which in Exodus stands at the head of the law codes, and is translated in Exod. 21:1 as "ordinances" (REB: "laws"). The word refers to laws given as an expression of God's "righteousness" (see Psalm 7) to the king, also referred to as "a king's son," a member of the royal dynasty. The REB translation rightly indicates that the first word in the psalm is "God," just as the psalm closes with a benediction, "Blessed be the LORD, the God of Israel" (vv. 18, 19). This provides the essential framework for the psalm. The justice the king dispenses must reflect God's justice; the decisions he takes must be characterized by the righteousness of God's decisions. This means that he must be responsive to the needs of those most at risk in society, "the oppressed" (v. 2, rather than the "poor"), "the poor," and the "needy" (v. 4; see 9:12). He must restrain the oppressor. Only in the context of this kind of society will the "mountains" and the "hills," the dominant features of the whole land, provide for the people that rich fullness of life and prosperity signified by the words "shalom" and "righteousness." This section thus provides a thematic trailer for much of the rest of the psalm.

5-7   The opening words of verse 5, "May he live," represent a widely accepted emendation to the Hebrew text, following the lead of the Greek version. The opening echoes the language of court protocol, to which we may compare "O king, live forever!" (Dan. 2:4) and the British national anthem, "Long live our noble Queen." Assuming that this is correct, then "May he live" is a prayer for the king or for the royal dynasty to last throughout the generations. A similar picture drawing on the enduring nature of the sun and moon is used with reference to the Davidic dynasty in Ps. 89:36-37, "His line shall continue forever, and his throne endure before me like the sun. It shall be established forever like the moon, an enduring witness in the skies" (cf. 2 Sam. 7:16). The Hebrew text reads "May they fear you." It has been argued that the apparently plural form should be treated as singular; hence the REB translates, "May he fear you," stressing that the king's lengthy and prosperous reign will depend on his attitude toward God, an attitude of reverence and awe summed up in the words "the fear of the LORD" (see 19:9). It is just possible, however, that the Hebrew reading "May they fear you" is correct and that the "they" refers to the people of verses 2 and 4. Similarly, in verse 7 the word translated "righteousness" means "the righteous," which would provide a parallel to "they who fear you." If this is the case, then the section is pointing to the crucial relationship between the people and the king. If both remain steadfastly in step with God, then lasting "peace" *(shalom)* may be expected, with God's blessing on the community channeled through the king. Rain falling on "the mown grass" is hardly a farmer's dream of blessing (v. 6); hence, the REB translates "early crops," fields ready for cutting rather than already cut. For the "showers that water the earth," see 65:9-10.

8-11   True *shalom* involves freedom, security from domination by foreign oppressors. So the prayer is for a king whose dominion will be acknowledged worldwide, a king to whom other rulers bring their tribute. The language of verse 8 may reflect the tradition which in Exod. 23:31 maps out the borders of Israel as being from the "Red Sea" (or "Sea of Reeds") to the sea of the Philistines, that is, the Mediterranean, and from the wilderness to the Euphrates. If so, then there are strong arguments for retaining "those who live in the wilderness" (REB:

"desert tribes"), instead of "his foes" in verse 9. The picture of enemies licking the dust is no more than a standard picture of humble submission, of people groveling before someone whose authority and power they must recognize (cf. Isa. 49:23). "Tarshish" (v. 10) is normally thought to be Tartessos in Spain at the furthest end of the Mediterranean, or in Sardinia (see 48:7); "Sheba" (cf. 1 Kgs. 10:1-13) is southwest Arabia, approximating today's Yemen, while "Seba," associated in Isa. 43:3 with Egypt and Ethiopia, may be somewhere in north Africa or in another part of the Arabian peninsula. The psalmist is here voicing a prayer that the whole world, "all nations" (v. 11), will acknowledge the supremacy of Israel's king (cf. Psalm 2).

12-14 Here the psalm returns to the theme of verses 2 and 4. Yet this is no longer a prayer but a strong affirmation. The word translated "For" at the beginning of verse 12 should be rendered, "Yes, yes indeed." Whether we translate the tenses in these verses as present, "he delivers," or as future, "he will deliver," they express something which admits of no argument. It is the king's duty to answer the cry for help of the "needy" (a word which occurs three times in verses 12 and 13) — the poor and the weak — and to be the helper of those who have no other helper. Power must be exercised with compassion. He "redeems" (see 19:14) the victims of violence and oppression. Their "blood," that is, their life, is to be protected, because it is precious in his sight. Thus the verdict on the responsible use of power depends upon whether it intervenes on behalf of those who need help in society. This is a criterion which still remains valid and bitingly relevant in assessing the activity of governments and politicians today.

15-17 This section is carefully structured. The opening words, "Long may he live!" find their echo in verse 17, "May his name endure forever." The reference to the gold of Sheba (v. 15), symbolizing the tribute other people shall bring, finds its counterpart in the reference to "all nations" in verse 17. The intercession to be offered for the king, "the blessings invoked for him" (v. 15), looks forward to the refrain, "May all nations be blessed in him" (v. 17, NRSV) or "all will pray to be blessed as he was" (REB). Much of the thought of the psalm is a reflection on the promise made to Abram in Gen. 12:2-3: "I will make of you a great nation, and I will bless you and make your name great, so that you will be a blessing. I will bless those who bless you, and the one who curses you I will curse; and in you all the families of the earth shall be blessed." This is hardly surprising since there are close links in tradition between the Abraham stories and the house of David (note the reference to "kings shall come from you" in Gen. 17:6). The blessing in verses 15 and 17 (see 3:8), while focused on the king, does not stop there. It reaches out to all nations, who are destined not merely to be subservient as in verses 8-11, but to share in the rich benefits bestowed by God on the king or to see in the king all that they desire for themselves. Paul takes the vision one stage further when he uses the promise to Abraham as the scriptural basis for his mission to the Gentiles (cf. Gal. 3:8).

Verse 16 focuses on the link between people and nature, a link which for good and for ill is stressed in the biblical tradition (cf. Gen. 3:17-19; Deut. 28:3-4, 8, 11 12, etc.; Isa. 11:6-9). The text of verse 16 is at points uncertain (compare the NRSV and the REB), but the general picture is clear. Through the blessing which comes to the community in the person of the king, the countryside will be clothed with abundant crops, even up to the tops of the highest hills (for Lebanon, see 29:5). This picture is either continued at the end of verse 16 (REB), or there is a switch to the teeming population in the cities (NRSV); in the latter case, the gift of fertility leaves its mark on both countryside and town. King, land, and people are one. The social and moral realms in which people make decisions are inextricably linked with the world of nature. The ecological crises we face today — environmental pollution of land, sea, and air; ozone depletion, the greenhouse effect, and global warming; nuclear testing and decommissioning — are matters of the utmost urgency. We need a theology which will celebrate creation as God's good gift entrusted to us, a gift which will inevitably be abused unless we learn anew to revere the creator and the channels through which his blessing comes to us.

18-19 This is the last psalm in Book Two. Like the last psalm in Book One (Psalm 41), it closes with a benediction acknowledging all that God is and all that he has done. This benediction is longer than any of the other ones, and it continues the universal theme of verses 8-11, 17 by concluding with the words "may his glory fill the whole earth." To this the congregation adds its emphatic response, "Amen and Amen" (see comment on 41:13).

The prayer in Psalm 72 centers on a vision which was often called into question in ancient Israel. The prayer envisions a king ruling in righteousness and compassion, yet often kings in Israel acted as oriental despots, feathering their own nests at the expense of their people (compare Jeremiah's scathing attack on Jehoiakim, accusing him of violating every rule in the royal book, Jer. 22:13-17). The prayer envisions a king whose dominion is recognized by others and who rules over a nation in peace and security, yet often the armies of other imperialist powers were ravaging the land, with the king of Judah paying tribute to an imperial overlord or being shipped off into exile, till there came a day when there was no king and no independent state. The prayer also envisions a countryside blessed with abundant fertility, yet drought and famine were often grim realities (cf. Jer. 14:1-6).

What happened to the vision, so often apparently negated? Unlike Psalm 2, this psalm does not appear in the New Testament with reference to Jesus as the king to come, the long-expected messiah. It was, however, so interpreted early on in the Church, and it had already been given a future messianic interpretation in Jewish circles. The vision looks beyond itself. As we have seen, behind the human king stands God. The king's righteousness is but a mirror of God's righteousness, with the final benediction centering not on the king but on the God whose glory is to fill the earth. So the vision contains within itself seeds of a greater fulfillment in that kingdom of God celebrated by the angelic choir in Revelation (e.g., Rev. 7:9-10), in that final Amen which affirms that this is where all history and human life find their ultimate meaning, not in a whimper or in the triumph of evil, but in that new heaven and new earth, and in that new Jerusalem lit by the presence of God and Christ. "The nations will walk by its light, and the kings of the earth will bring their glory into it" (Rev. 21:24).

The compiler or editor of Book Two appended his comment in verse 20: "The prayers of David, son of Jesse, are ended." Although there are psalms in the later books attributed to David (e.g., Psalms 86; 101; 103; 108), the compiler obviously saw this psalm as bringing to an end the collection of Davidic psalms with which he was familiar. Oddly he uses the word "prayers," not the word "psalms" which appears in most of the headings. Not all psalms are prayers, but in the context of Israel's worship, prayers — often prayers born out of individual experience — became part of the hymns of the community.

BOOK THREE

PSALMS 73–89

Book Three of the Psalter consists of Psalms 73–89. It contains the major collection of psalms associated with Asaph, 73–83 (see comment on Psalm 50); four psalms associated with the sons of Korah, 84, 85, 87, 88, with Heman the Ezrahite joining the sons of Korah in the heading to Psalm 88; one linked with David, 86; and one with Ethan, 89. Attempts to trace the history of this collection and to account for its overall theological impact have not been lacking in recent years, but the element of speculation in all such attempts is high. It is safer to take each psalm as it occurs and attempt to explore its theological significance.

Psalm 73
THE NEED TO QUESTION

This is a psalm with which many people find it easy to identify. With refreshing honesty and on the basis of painful personal experience, it faces the question, "What does it mean to talk about the goodness of God when there is so much in the world which seems to call such goodness into question?" But what kind of psalm is this? Opinion has varied between treating it as a piece of wisdom teaching and looking for a particular cultic context in which it is naturally at home, with the psalmist sometimes identified as the king or a Levitical priest. Since we have argued that worship provided a natural setting for wisdom teaching, there is no need to come down on one side or the other in this debate.

The psalm is carefully and skillfully constructed. The framework within which the problem and the argument are set is indicated in the opening and the closing verses with their association of the word "good" with God (vv. 1 and

28). Three times at key points in the psalm we find the Hebrew word *'ak,* rendered in the NRSV as "Truly" in verses 1 and 18 and by the emphatic "All" in verse 13, and in the REB by "Assuredly" in verse 1 and "Indeed" in verses 13 and 18. There is a "Yes, but" feel about this word. It introduces into the discussion a key factor which flies in the face of what seems to be the case.

Four times a verse is introduced by the emphatic Hebrew "And [or: but] I," translated in the NRSV as "But as for me" (v. 2), "I" (v. 22), "Nevertheless I" (v. 23), and "But for me" (v. 28). Twice this points up the psalmist's problem and spiritual sensitivity (vv. 1 and 22), twice the answer he found in God's sure hold of him (vv. 23 and 28). Six times the Hebrew word *lēbab* occurs, translated as "heart" or "mind" and once as "soul" in the NRSV (vv. 1, 7, 13, 21, and twice in 26).

But what is the psalmist's problem? It is rooted in the same problem which haunts the book of Job (see, e.g., the conflicting arguments of Zophar and Job in chapters 20 and 21). Life didn't seem to be following the script which much traditional theological thinking had handed down. That script is encapsulated in the words of Isa. 48:22: " 'There is no peace,' " (Hebrew *šalôm;* see 4:9), says the LORD " 'for the wicked.' " But, protests this psalmist, "I saw the prosperity *(šalôm)* of the wicked" (v. 3).

1   This provides the setting for the opening words of the psalm. Although most modern translations read, by a small redivision of a word, "Truly God is good to the upright," the traditional text, supported by all the early versions, reads "Truly God is good to Israel." There is little need to change this. Although "the upright" provides a neat parallelism to "the pure in heart," the psalmist is appealing to Israel's experience of God's goodness, a goodness which, so it is claimed, comes most surely to those within the community who are "pure in heart" (see 24:4). It is possible to take this opening verse in three ways:

1. The verse gives the starting point of the psalmist's problem, since it expresses traditional teaching that bitter experience has led the psalmist to question. Yes *('ak),* people may claim that God is good to "the pure in heart," but there is precious little evidence for this in life. It was in vain that I kept my heart pure (v. 13).
2. The verse summarizes the psalmist's certainty born of a bitter pilgrimage. Yes, I have had to struggle, and I am going to tell you about that struggle, but through that struggle I have discovered that God is indeed good.
3. The verse represents both the starting point of the psalmist's spiritual problem and the outcome of a spiritual pilgrimage in the course of which he has been forced to give a new and deeper meaning to what is meant by saying that God is good. It is this third view which is assumed throughout the following interpretation of the psalm.

2-3 These verses lay bare the problem that has taken the psalmist to within an ace of losing his grip on the faith that has hitherto given him security. He is where many people are today, wrestling with real doubts that will not go away. We have seen what sparked off his doubts, "the prosperity of the wicked" (v. 3), but he is honest enough to admit that there is another factor. He begrudges the wicked their success. He was envious of the "arrogant" or the boastful (see 5:5). It was not only what was happening in the world around him, but his reaction to it, that was at stake. It is hard at times not to be envious of those who seem to enjoy in abundance all that society as a whole regards as the trappings of success, be it wealth or popularity. The book of Proverbs may warn: "Do not let your heart envy sinners, but always continue in the fear of the LORD" (Prov. 23:17), but what about when sinners seem to reap handsome dividends and those who fear the LORD seem to gain no tangible rewards?

4-12 These verses vividly describe the "arrogant" and the "wicked." Although the text in places is uncertain, the overall picture is clear. No spare, pinched frames for them, but the Hebrew equivalent of the "fair round belly with good capon lin'd" (*As You Like It*, 2.7.154), sheltered from many of the ailments which afflict the less fortunate. Haughtily they use power to further their own self-interests. Bloated dissipation undermining any moral scruples they might have had (v. 7), they insolently refuse to accept any authority or restraint other than their own malicious purposes (v. 9). They enjoy the popularity which often goes with success (v. 10, textually a difficult verse). They are prepared openly to defy God, assuming that he is some remote distant deity who no doubt has better things to do than to care about what they are doing (v. 11). That is what they are like, claims the psalmist, and their reward is security and an ever more healthy bank balance (v. 12).

13-14 The psalmist's reaction, born of envy (v. 3), is predictable. If that is what life is like, what is the point of being committed to that purity and innocence which he believes to be the corollary of faith in God (for "washed my hands," see 26:6)? His sole reward is "affliction" — the same word is used of the suffering servant in Isa. 53:4 and of Job in Job 1:11 — and "punishment" or reproof (see 39:11). What is intended by these two words is not wholly clear. They are both very general words that could indicate physical suffering, but they might simply point to the mental and spiritual torment which was gripping the psalmist. His faith is on the line, a source not of comfort but of perplexity. Is it therefore pointless? Must doubt lead to denial?

15-16 The full implication of what is happening suddenly comes home to him. He is in danger of being "untrue to the circle of your children." The word translated "circle" can mean a generation, but often in the Psalms it points to a certain class of people (see 14:5). Hence "the circle of your children" means God's faithful people (REB: "your people"). But what does it mean to be untrue or false to God's people? It has been argued that this is the Old Testament equivalent of Rom. 14:1, that is, that the psalmist refrains from giving voice to his doubts lest they make faith more difficult for other people. It is more likely that this is the psalmist acknowledging that to continue along the path his thoughts are taking him would be to become a traitor to the community of faith that had nurtured him. Others must have found life difficult and wrestled with their doubts, but they hadn't given up. They still belonged to the people of God. His own faith may be fragile, but he begins to draw support from the faith of others. That is one very good reason for belonging to the church. There we learn that God never asks us to go it alone. When the going gets tough, we can draw strength from others. In itself, however, this does not solve the psalmist's problem. He found trying to think this through a "wearisome task" (v. 16). The word translated "wearisome task" is the same word translated "trouble" in verse 5. There it was claimed that the wicked did not experience "trouble." Here it is the psalmist's attempt to hold on to faith that causes him "trouble." It is far too easy to think of faith as a problem solver. Sometimes it makes life more difficult as we seek to face up to the issues posed by a world which we believe to be under the control of a just and loving God. The psalmist remained troubled. The answer did not come to him simply by sitting and thinking about it. It seldom does.

17-26 Light came into the psalmist's darkness when he "went into the sanctuary of God" (v. 17). The word translated "sanctuary" is plural in Hebrew, and it has been claimed that it here means "the holy things," the mysteries of God. The psalmist's problem is thus seen to lie in a shallow rationalism that has not probed deeply enough into the mysteries of God. But there is no other place in the Old Testament where the word means mysteries, and it is far more likely that the plural indicates the whole complex of courts and buildings which made up the Jerusalem temple precinct (cf. 68:35). Through worship, probably through sharing in one of the great festivals of the Hebrew religious year, he was gripped by two convictions.

The first, described in verses 17b-20, picks up a theme which we have met in many other Psalms, notably Psalm 37. However secure and successful the wicked may seem to be, there is a "Yes, but" to be placed over against them. Lurking round the corner are "terrors" (REB: "disasters") waiting to destroy them. The wicked are on the slippery slope to ruin. They will prove to be just as insubstantial as a dream that vanishes when sleep is over — here today, gone tomorrow (cf. 37:9-10). We do not know at what religious festival this conviction took hold of the psalmist. A case can be made for Passover or for the New Year festival. To celebrate the kingship of God over all the forces of disorder or evil which challenge his rule from creation on through history (cf. Psalms 93, 95–99) is to confess that evil in whatever shape or form inevitably signs its own death warrant. It can have no lasting or secure future.

The second conviction, described in verses 21-26, comes closer to the heart of the psalmist's spiritual turmoil. He is forced to face the fact that his attitude, that of being envious of the arrogant, is wrong. His bitter reaction to the shalom of the wicked is the reaction of someone who has not yet realized what the essence of true faith is. He admits that his attitude has been no better than that of a "brute beast" (v. 22). Now in worship he discovers that faith depends not on his fragile, often vulnerable grasp of God, but on God's grasp of him: "you hold my right hand" (v. 23), "you guide me" (v. 24), and "God is the rock of my heart" (v. 26). We are here listening to what has been well described as "a note of childlike and profound humility. . . . In marked contrast to the arrogance of the wicked, the certainty of being completely guided and sheltered reflects the supreme form of trust" (A. Weiser). It is certainty well expressed in Joachim Neander's hymn:

> All my hope on God is founded;
>   He doth still my trust renew.
> Me through change and chance he guideth,
>   Only good and only true.
>   God unknown,
>   He alone
> Calls my heart to be his own.

At the center of every facet of experience stands God (v. 25).

What, however, is meant by the much discussed words in the second half of verse 24: "and afterwards you will receive me with honor"? This is a translation of three Hebrew words all of which, in context, are capable of different interpretations: The word "afterwards" is probably a conscious echo of the word translated "end" (REB: "destiny") in verse 17. The psalmist is convinced that God's verdict on his life is going to be different from that on the wicked. But does "afterwards" mean that this verdict will take place at some future time during the psalmist's lifetime, or is it pointing to life after death?

The word "honor" (or "glory"; Hebrew *kābôd;* see 3:3) may refer either to a person's standing or dignity in the community, or it may point to the awesome splendor and majesty of God. Is the psalmist then speaking of a coming reversal of fortune when he, and not the wicked, will experience true shalom and be given his due honor and standing in the community, or is he expressing the belief that after death he will share in the glory that is communion with God?

In the Enoch story in Gen. 5:24 and in the final scene of Elijah's life in 2 Kings 2, the verb "receive" (or: "take") is used in contexts which imply someone being translated from this present life to what lies beyond it (see 49:15). The translation "receive me," however, may simply mean "welcome me" or "accept me." Traditionally many Christian commentators have seen in this verse, as in Ps. 49:15, the hope of the consummation of communion with God after death. It is doubtful, however, whether the words naturally bear this meaning, unless the psalmist was convinced that the nature of God's hold on him was such that even death itself could not loosen that grip, a view questioned in certain other psalms (see 88:10-12). Perhaps Calvin was right in keeping all the options open when he comments "glory . . . I think ought not to be limited to eternal life as some are inclined to do. It comprehends the whole course of our happiness from the commencement, which is seen here upon earth, even to the consummation which we expect to realize in heaven."

That the heart of faith is not our grasp of God but God's sure grasp of us is underlined again and again in the New Testament. Here faith is certainty based, as 1 John puts it, on the fact "not that we loved God but that God loved us and sent his Son . . ." (1 John 4:10). It is a certainty that takes us clearly beyond the psalmist's vision, since this Son is the "Christ who has been raised from the dead, the firstfruits of those who have died" (1 Cor. 15:20), the destroyer of the past enemy death (1 Cor. 15:24). Verse 26 summarizes the new values of one whose attitude to life has been dramatically changed through worship. He accepts his own weakness, but he draws strength from the God whom he knows beyond all shadow of a doubt to be his "portion forever" (see 16:5).

27-28   The psalm ends by summarizing the psalmist's spiritual pilgrimage. By very definition, he claims, the wicked and arrogant are doomed — cut off from God by being "false" or "unfaithful" (REB). The word used here indicates prostitution or infidelity. It is frequently used in the Old Testament to indicate those who play fast and loose with their religious loyalty (e.g., Exod. 34:15-16; Deut. 31:16). The psalmist, on the contrary, now knows what "good" means in a spiritual sense. It means "to be near God," to know that God is his "refuge" (see 14:6). This does not mean that for the psalmist all questions are answered, all struggles over. Rather, he has found that in the midst of his questions God is present. As he struggled, he found God — or, rather, God found him. He never had to go it alone. This is the truth he cannot but share with others.

It is important to notice the role that doubts and questioning play in this psalm. They are not the enemies of faith. It was only by questioning and struggling with the doubts his questions raised that the psalmist broke through to a new understanding of what the goodness of God really meant. Such questions and doubts were the catalyst of a more mature faith. There is need today to learn anew from the Psalms the place which such questions and doubts have in worship.

Psalm 74
UNANSWERED QUESTIONS

For the meaning of the heading "A Maskil of Asaph," see Psalm 32. Although attempts have been made to understand this psalm as a purely cultic drama with its origins in the New Year festival, it seems clear that its background is to be sought in some national catastrophe which involved the pillaging and desecration of the temple. But what historical event gave rise to the agonized questions with which the psalm begins, questions which are never fully answered? While a case can be made for the events in the second century BCE, when Antiochus Epiphanes desecrated the Jerusalem temple in 169 and sparked off the Maccabean revolt, a more natural setting is the aftermath of the Babylonian destruction of temple and city in 587 BCE. The urgency of the questions raised, however, has enabled the psalm to express the religious communities' response to any situation of crisis in which the very future of the community seems to be in jeopardy. It therefore poses questions which both the Jewish and the Christian community have faced, or ought to have faced, in the aftermath of the holocaust.

1-11 The first half of the psalm, which vividly describes the crisis in the life of the community and the response to it, is framed by that haunting and inescapable word "Why?" In Hebrew it is the first word in verse 1 and the first word in verse 11. The question is acute because of the tradition of faith in which the psalmist had been nurtured. Here are "the sheep of your pasture" (v. 1), the flock you are supposed to protect like a caring shepherd (see Psalm 23). Why then have you "cast us off" or spurned us (cf. 43:2; 44:9) "forever" or perhaps "utterly"? Certainly the psalmist can see no end to present misery. It can only be explained in terms of God's "anger" (see 6:1). Perhaps it is the smoke rising from the burning sacred sites throughout the land (cf. v. 8) that gives added poignancy to the metaphorical use of the word "smoke" in the phrase "Why does your anger smoke?" The phrase, however, does appear elsewhere to indicate that God is, as it were, fuming with anger (cf. the REB and 80:4).

The call to God to "Remember" (v. 2) is not an appeal to look back nostalgically, but a cry to God to act, to do something now, to show that his concern for his people which characterized the past is still true in the crisis-laden present. Notice how the words "you" and "your" dominate the psalmist's thinking in the opening verses. The nation's whole existence was rooted in the initiative of God. This is the congregation or assembly "which you acquired long ago" — a phrase which probably points back to the promises made to Abraham (cf. Gen. 12:1-3); it is "your redeemed" (see 19:14), hence "the tribe of your heritage" (see 33:12) — a phrase which goes back to the story of the Exodus and the subsequent settlement in the land of Canaan.

This is a people whose life is centered around the temple in Jerusalem on Mt. Zion (see 2:6), which God has chosen as his dwelling among his people (cf. 132:5, 7). The ball is therefore firmly in God's court to do something to counter the total destruction which has engulfed the sanctuary (v. 3). But to do what? The opening words of verse 3, literally "lift up your steps," are an unusual expression. The early versions all had difficulty with this phrase. The Jewish Midrash, playing upon the ambiguity in the words "steps," which can also mean "times," translates "restore thy times which have long been desolate," meaning the three times in the year when all male members of the community were under obligation to "appear before the LORD your God at the place he will choose" (Deut. 16:16). The REB translation, "Restore now," assumes an alteration to the text. It is possible that "lift up your steps" means, as we would say, "get a move on," come quickly to see "the perpetual ruins," a devastation which seemed so complete that it could never be remedied.

Verses 4-8 graphically describe what happened to the temple. The text in this section, particularly in verses 5 and 6, raises difficult issues, as may be seen by the various translations in our English versions. The general picture, however, is clear. Pagan enemies pour triumphantly into the temple. All signs or symbols of the worship of the LORD are obliterated, replaced by the conquerors' "emblems," which could refer either to military insignia or religious symbols (v. 4). The intricate carvings hacked to pieces, the building is set on fire, razed to the ground, defiled. A similar fate befell all other sacred sites throughout the land, evidence of the enemies' determination to ram home the lesson of who wielded unchallengeable power.

The stunned response of the community is heard in verses 9-11. Although the word "emblems" (v. 9) is the same word translated "emblems" in verse 4, it is used here in a slightly different sense. Here is a community "enveloped in darkness so thick that there does not appear so much as a single ray of light" (Calvin). In the hell through which they are living, they see no signs of the presence of their God. No prophet interprets to them the meaning of this unthinkable tragedy; no one can give them any clue as to when their suffering will end. The reference to there being "no longer any prophet" is interesting. It has been taken to support a late Maccabean date for the psalm, since prophecy is considered to have ceased by that time. After all, was there not a prophet, namely Jeremiah, who lived through the death throes of Jerusalem in 587 BCE and who proclaimed a consistent message about what it meant? This was the judgment of God on a sinful community (cf. Lamentations). Yes, but right to the very end people had listened not to Jeremiah but to other prophets like Hananiah (cf. Jeremiah 28), who had been proclaiming a message of "shalom." It can't happen to us; God is on our side — compare the critique of such prophecy in Jer. 23:9-14. Such prophets had the ear of the people. It was the optimistic message they wanted to hear. Sadly, we often hear what we want to hear and ignore, or even deny, the existence of other, more challenging voices.

"How long, O God. . . ?" (v. 10; see 13:1-3): the questions return, but now the emphasis is upon the challenge to God's power represented by enemies who "scoff" or insult God (cf. 69:9). They "revile" (REB: "pour scorn on") God's "name" (see 5:11), as if daring him to do something to redress the situation. "Why don't you?" says the psalmist. Why do you sit there, as it were twiddling your thumbs? The picture in verse 11 is that of a soldier keeping his right hand inactive across his chest under the folds of his garment, instead of pulling it out to go into action. Both the NRSV and the REB, however, assume an alteration to the final word in verse 11. It is possible to retain the Hebrew text and see in the last word a dramatic cry to God, "End it!" This would provide a neat climax to the first half of the psalm. The urgent questions, the tragic events, and the mockery of the enemy all point to an intolerable situation — end it!

12-17 The mood changes. The questions and pleas give way to a hymnic celebration of the awesome power of God, the God who is "my King . . . from of old" (v. 12). The switch to the first person, "my King" (see 5:2), need not imply that we are listening to another voice speaking on behalf of the community. Any congregation gathered for worship today will sing hymns that use "I" rather than we, as the worshippers personally identify with the faith of the community. At this point in the psalm, the community is probably expressing its faith in the words of a familiar, traditional hymn. It is a carefully structured hymn. Seven times we hear the emphatic "you" in verses 13-17. Throughout there are echoes of mythological language associated with the struggle between the cosmic forces of order and chaos, represented by the gods in other ancient Near Eastern religions (see Psalm 29). The forces of chaos are often associated with the sea or the monsters who inhabit the deep. Thus in the Ugaritic poems the Kingship of Baal is celebrated:

> Have I not slain Sea, beloved of El,
> Have I not slain River, the great god,
> Have I not muzzled the Dragon, holding him in a muzzle,
> The Foul-fanged with Seven Heads?

The emphasis throughout this hymn is on God's awesome power, his saving acts or victories in creation and in taming all the forces of chaos (v. 12; for "salvation," see 3:8; the word is plural here, hence the REB's rendering, "saving acts"). "Leviathan" (v. 14) is described in Isa. 27:1, echoing Ugaritic poetry, as "the fleeing serpent . . . the twisting serpent . . . the dragon that is in the sea" (cf. Job 41:1; Ps. 104:26). The text in the second half of verse 14 has raised problems. Behind the REB translation, "sharks," there lies a redivision of words that has been widely accepted. The NRSV, however, may well be right in sticking with "creatures of the wilderness." The picture, then, is of the sea monster so completely defeated that it ends up as food for the denizens of the desert. God's continuing creative power is underlined in the provision of life-giving water (v. 15), in the pattern of day and night, moon and sun (v. 16), and in the changing seasons — the "bounds of the earth" (v. 17), probably referring to the different temperate zones.

Although the reference throughout in the language is primarily cosmic, there is little doubt that the words "You divided the sea by your might" would inevitably recall for the congregation another dividing of the sea, the way in which God safely delivered his people out of slavery in Egypt (Exodus 14–15). The cosmic power of God celebrated in mythology was the power Israel experienced in her history, in saving acts that made her into a nation and provided the raison d'être of her continuing existence. The celebration of God's saving power in the past, however, does not solve the psalmist's problem. Indeed, there is a sense in which it increases the tension. If that is what faith claims God to be like, why can we see no evident signs of that power at work in the present? That is a question which has been only too real in the bitter experience of many people. Celebration, therefore, leads into renewed urgent prayer.

18-23 The concluding prayer for God's help in verses 18-23 begins by echoing the word "Remember" (v. 2). It is dominated by the thought present in the ending of the opening prayer in vv. 10-11, the intolerable situation created by the way in which enemies have mockingly and defiantly flung down the gauntlet to God. They are described in verse 18 as "an impious people" (REB: "a barbarous nation"), "impious" being an attempt to render the Hebrew word translated in Ps. 14:1 as "the fool." They are people, in other words, who haven't a clue as to what the true values in life really are (see 14:1). The same word appears again in v. 22, where the REB renders "fools." What is at stake is not merely God's honor and power (v. 18; cf. v. 10) but the very future of the people of God, the people of the covenant, still victims of dire brutality (v. 20). They are described in a cluster of words that all point to their vulnerability: "downtrodden . . . poor and needy" (see 9:12). They are compared in v. 19 to a "dove" (a word usually translated "turtledove"; cf. Song of Sol. 2:12), "your dove," gentle and timid and in danger of becoming a prey for other wildlife. The REB translation, "the soul that confesses you" instead of "your dove," involves an alteration of one letter in the Hebrew and has support in some of the early versions. There may, however, be added poignancy in the use of the picture of the dove here. The dove regularly features in the burnt offering to the LORD (cf. Gen. 15:9; Lev. 1:14). Here God's people may be thinking of themselves as being sacrificed, but to whom?

The Psalm, therefore, ends with an urgent appeal, "Rise up, O God [see 3:7] plead your cause" — the language here being that of the law court (see 7:8). Only if God acts can there be any answer to the strident and oppressive clamor, which seems to be unending. If the opening prayer in vv. 1-11 climaxes in the dramatic cry "End it!" the closing prayer assumes that at the moment there is no end in sight.

It is interesting that the questions which dominate verses 1-11 are no longer heard in verses 18-25. Yet they remain unanswered. The Psalm reveals clearly the tension in which faith in the Old Testament sometimes lived, and still has to live today — the tension between the past, which, it is claimed, clearly witnesses to the mighty deeds of God, and the present, in which there seems to be no such witness. It is the tension between the past, which has meaning, and the present, which seems meaningless. There is no attempt in the psalm to resolve the tension by relating present tragedy to the sinfulness of those who experience it. The questions "Why?" and "How long?" receive no answer, except the answer that is implicit in the final plea. Since the psalmist takes God seriously, he must believe that cruelty and violence cannot have the last word. There must be hope for new life beyond what seems unrelieved tragedy. So the word of hope came to women at the garden tomb on the first Easter morning: "I know that you are looking for Jesus who was crucified. He is not here; for he has been raised, as he said" (Matt. 28:6).

Psalm 75
THANKSGIVING BORN OF SECURITY

For "Do Not Destroy" in the psalm heading, see 57:1.

This short psalm raises several difficult questions of interpretation. Perhaps if there had come down to us a Prayer Book or a Book of Common Order from the Jerusalem temple, some of the difficulties would disappear. Many of the hymns we sing only become fully meaningful when we place them in their context in worship. Thus Horatio Bonar's words, "Here, O my Lord, I see thee face to face, here would I touch and handle things unseen. . . ," assume as their setting the sacrament of Holy Communion.

1 The psalm begins with an introit of thanksgiving in verse 1. Do the words of the introit look back to a celebration of the "wondrous deeds" (see 9:2) of God which has already taken place in an act of worship? If so, when and how? We can only guess. "We give thanks. . . . We give thanks," and this thanksgiving is clearly rooted in the fact that God's "name" (see 5:11), his distinctive character and power, have become a new part of his people's experience as they have listened to the recital of these wondrous deeds. It is unnecessary to change "your name is near" to "those who call upon your name" (Kraus), though there is some support for this in the Greek (LXX) version. The REB catches the nuance of the second half of verse 1 very well: "your name is brought very near to us in the account of your wonderful deeds."

2-5 The introit is followed by the word of God, perhaps spoken to the assembled people by a priest or temple prophet. It begins with a word of assurance (vv. 2-3). However threatening or chaotic life may seem to be, the world is still controlled and sustained by the God who is both powerful and concerned "with equity" (see 9:7-8). He will act at the moment of his choosing, "the set time." The word translated "set time" is the same word translated "meeting places" in 74:8. Here it refers not to a fixed place but to a certain time. Elsewhere in the Hebrew Bible it can refer in a temporal sense to the seasons of the year or to the fixed religious festivals. In this context, as in Ps. 102:13, it points to the time when God decides to act. We need not see in the word a reference to the final judgment at the end of time, though the word can have that meaning (cf. Dan. 12:7). God's acting in the midst of human affairs at a time of his choosing is the guarantee of the stability of the created and moral order. The picture in verse 3 of the world as a large edifice supported by pillars is found elsewhere in the Hebrew Bible (cf. Job 9:6). When that building threatens to "totter" (REB: "quake") and to collapse upon its inhabitants — a picture familiar to us from many an earthquake scene — only God's firm grasp of its supporting pillars guarantees security. This, of course, is the language of poetry, not of geology or architecture. It is affirming that the world is not a meaningless, amoral chaos. How can it be if God is both creator, sustainer, and one who judges with equity?

It is not surprising, therefore, that this word of assurance leads into a challenge or a warning to anyone who seeks to challenge this divinely decreed order: whether "the boastful" (see 5:5), pride, as Calvin comments, being "the cause or mother of all rash and audacious enterprises"; or "the wicked," who shamelessly flaunt their power. Twice we hear the words "Do not lift up your horn," the horn of an animal such as an ox or bull being the symbol of its strength (see 18:2). Those who "speak with insolent neck" are those who are full of haughty provocation (cf. 31:18). The REB translation, "who speak arrogantly against the Rock," follows the Greek (LXX) with a minor alteration to the Hebrew text to read, instead of neck, "Rock" as a title for God.

What is at stake in such a challenge is the question as to whose writ runs in the affairs of the world, the writ of human arrogance and perversity or the writ of God — a theme which confronts us again and again in the Hebrew Bible and receives classic expression in the story of the Garden of Eden (Genesis 3).

6-8 It is possible that, instead of being part of the word of God, verse 5 marks the beginning of the congregational response, a response which begins by echoing and expanding the concluding part of the word "Do not lift up your horn" in verse 4. Certainly in verses 6-8 we are listening to just such a response in which the congregation confesses its faith. Where is security to be found? The theme of "lifting up" (vv. 6, 7) suggests the picture of someone in authority indicating his acceptance of a suppliant kneeling before him. If we are to interpret verse 6 in strictly geographical terms, with the "wilderness" indicating the southern desert, then the absence of any reference to the north may be explained by the fact that the north was the region from which the people found the threat to their very existence repeatedly coming (cf. the foe from the north in Jer. 4:6; 6:22-26). It is, however, likely that this verse is simply underlining that no human help will be forthcoming from any quarter. The rising of the sun, "the east," and the setting of the sun, "the west," thus indicate the horizons of the known world, a picture backed up by what would be the last port of call in the search for help, the inhospitable desert. Any search for human power as guarantee of security is, therefore, futile. Lasting security is to be found only in God. This is the God who, uninhibited by the limited and often perverse human criteria of values, uses a freedom consistent with his own character, "putting down one and lifting up another" (v. 7). These words echo the Song of Hannah in 1 Sam. 2:7-8 and point forward to the challenging reversal of human values in the Magnificat, which celebrates the God who "has brought down the powerful from their thrones, and lifted up the lowly; he has filled the hungry with good things, and sent the rich away empty" (Luke 1:52-53). This is the God who guarantees that the wicked, however apparently powerful, will drink of a poisoned chalice (for the cup imagery, see 11:6), a cup of "foaming wine well mixed." Although the noun translated "well mixed" occurs only here in the Hebrew Bible, the verb is used elsewhere of concocting a powerful, intoxicating brew, probably by adding spices and honey. Isaiah attacks those who are "heroes in drinking wine and valiant at mixing drink" (Isa. 5:22). Wickedness, claims verse 8, brings its own inevitable nemesis. Those who indulge in it are forced to swallow the potent brew of God's judgment down to the last dregs.

9-10   The psalmist has a different role to play. Not for him a drunken stupor, but a clearheaded, joyful witness, a song of praise to the "God of Jacob" (see 20:1). The translation "I will rejoice" (v. 9) follows the Greek (LXX) text. The Hebrew reads "I will declare," a word not normally found without an immediately specific object. It is repeatedly used in the Psalms, however, of witnessing to the steadfast love, power, and wisdom of God. In Ps. 9:11 it is used in parallelism to "Sing praises to the LORD." We may very well retain the Hebrew text and render "I will bear my witness forever," the content of that witness then being spelled out in the words that follow.

If the "I" who speaks in verse 9 is the psalmist, who is the "I" who speaks in the concluding verse 10? The difficulty of identifying the "I" of this verse has led many commentators to alter "I will cut off" to "he [God] will cut off," though there is no support for this in any of the early versions. It is better to see in this verse a final word of God, picking up the theme of verses 2-5 and spoken in God's name by the same person. The warning to the wicked in verse 4, "Do not lift up your horn," is underlined. Any such challenge to God's ordering of the world will inevitably end in disaster. The only power which can last and succeed is that of the "righteous" (see Psalm 1), the word translated "shall be exalted" being a form of the same verb translated "lift up" in verse 4.

We live in a world in which we are only too sadly familiar with the ruthless abuse of power both for personal and corporate gain or for national self-interest, abuse which becomes increasingly dangerous in a world of nuclear and biological weapons. Is this not a world in which "the horns of the wicked" often seem to be exalted, while the horns of the righteous are cut off? How then do we respond to this psalm? It is important to remember that the psalmist lived in a world that in its own terms faced the same dilemma. He challenges us to live in hope, hope that finds its justification in a faith which ultimately has at its heart both cross and resurrection (cf. Phil. 2:6-11). Such a faith can and must affirm that the last word never lies with human wickedness, however powerful and triumphant it may momentarily seem. The last word lies with the God who "will judge with equity," a statement which is to be clothed in the rich imagery pulsating through the book of Revelation as it witnesses to the one who is "the Alpha and the Omega, the first and the last, the beginning and the end" (Rev. 22:13).

Psalm 76
THE AWESOME GOD

For the heading, see Psalms 4 and 50.

This is a psalm steeped in the language of battle, "flashing arrows, the shield, the sword, and the weapons of war" (v. 3), "troops . . . horse and rider" (vv. 5-6). Its origin has therefore been sought in some significant national battle in which the enemies of Israel were routed. Ask what event, however, and the guessing begins. David's victory over the Philistines at Baal-perazim (2 Sam. 5:17-21) or over the Arameans and the Edomites (2 Samuel 8), and the fate that befell Sennacherib and the Assyrians before the walls of Jerusalem in 701 BCE (2 Kgs. 19:35) have all had their advocates, the latter supported by the Greek (LXX), which adds to the heading of the psalm "with reference to the Assyrians." There seems little doubt, however, that in its present form the psalm finds its true setting in worship in the Jerusalem temple, worship which, drawing on the tradition of the Holy War, celebrates the awesome power of Israel's God. Here is to be found the answer to the fears and questions that any crisis in the nation's life provoked. This celebration leads the community to look forward in confident and obedient hope to a future that will tell the same story (vv. 10-12). Thus, as so often in the Psalms, worship unites past, present, and future — the whole of history — and celebrates it as God's story.

What is noteworthy about the psalm is the way in which the character of God is underlined in a series of descriptive titles, many of them using the participial form of a verb. This is

- the God who is "known" (v. 1), no remote elusive mystery, but the God who has revealed himself to his people and is present with them in the temple on Mt. Zion (2:6).

- the God who is "glorious" (v. 4) or rather resplendent, bathed in light. The noun from the same root is used to describe God as "my light" in Ps. 27:1 (compare Isa. 10:17, where God is called "the light of Israel"). The association of God with imagery of light runs right through the Bible, from the first word of God in the creation hymn, "Let there be light" (Gen. 1:3), to the words of Jesus in John 8:12, "I am the light of the world."
- the God who is "majestic" (v. 4), a word which points to the sovereignty and glory of God. It is the word used to describe the name of God in the opening and closing lines of Psalm 8 and is a key word in celebrating the kingship of God in Ps. 93:4.
- the God who is "awesome" (v. 7), the same word being translated "who inspires fear" in verse 12, and a related form "awesome" in verse 11. The unique, awe-inspiring nuance in the word is well captured in Deuteronomy: "The LORD your God is God of gods and Lord of lords, the great God, mighty and awesome" (Deut. 10:17; cf. Deut. 7:21). The same point is being underlined here in verse 7, which begins literally "you awesome you."

Following the liturgical rubric "Selah" (see Psalm 3), the psalm may be divided into three sections, though most modern translations, including the NRSV and the REB, divide it into four sections.

1-3 The God who is known, and known in all his greatness (for "name," see 5:11), is here depicted as a lion whose den or lair is in "Salem" and Zion (see 2:6). The words translated "abode" and "dwelling place" are both words normally used to describe the lair of a wild animal. Amos uses the same lion imagery when he says "The LORD roars from Zion, and utters his voice from Jerusalem" (Amos 1:2; cf. 3:8). "Salem" is an archaic form of Jerusalem (cf. Gen. 14:18), possibly used here because of its similarity with *shalom*. The Greek (LXX), in fact, misunderstood it as *shalom*. God's powerful presence is the guarantee that this Salem city will experience *shalom* (see 4:8). The same sense of the city's security guaranteed by God's presence in its midst is the theme of some of the Songs of Zion (see Psalm 48). God's greatness is known by how he has dealt with all threats to his people, shattering all the hostile instruments of war, including "the flashing arrows" (literally, "flames of fire," v. 3), a phrase which probably has in its background the mythology of the Canaanite storm god with lightning described as his arrows.

4-9 The central section of the psalm begins naturally by celebrating the greatness and power of this God who is "glorious" or resplendent (see above) and "more majestic than the everlasting mountains." This translation has its roots in the Greek (LXX) text, the Hebrew reading "more majestic than the mountains of prey." It is possible that the more usual Hebrew word for "prey" has been substituted at some point in the transmission of the Hebrew text for a word which normally means "everlasting" but can also mean "prey" (e.g., Gen. 49:27). Attempts to defend the reading "prey" by continuing the lion image from the previous verse are hardly convincing. "Everlasting" makes good sense. The eternal mountains, symbol of strength and stability (see 46:2), pale into insignificance before the majesty of the eternal God, a theme central to Psalm 90: "Before the mountains were brought forth, or ever you had formed the earth and the world, from everlasting to everlasting you are God" (90:2).

The "stouthearted," the self-confident warriors who looked for spoil, were themselves despoiled (v. 5). They fell into the final sleep of death, impotent to do anything to protect themselves, stunned by the "rebuke" of the God of Jacob (see 20:1), that divine "no" spoken to all who challenge his authority (see 9:5). The language of verse 6 recalls the triumphant Song of Miriam celebrating the deliverance at the Sea of Reeds: "Sing to the LORD, for he has triumphed gloriously; the horse and the rider he has thrown into the sea" (Exod. 15:21). God is "awesome" in his "anger" (see 6:1) when it is provoked, the anger of a divine judge (see 7:8) whose decisions typically "deliver" (see 3:2) "the oppressed" or the afflicted (see 9:12). The response to this awesome God can only be one of "fear" or reverence, which will express itself in being "still" or quiet (v. 8). The verb translated "still" is often used of a land undisturbed by the ravages of war where people live in peace and security (e.g., Judg. 3:11, 30; 18:7, 27). It is a picture of *shalom* that depends on the human acceptance of the just decisions of God.

10-12 If the faith celebrated in verses 4-9 has its roots in past events relived in worship, the concluding section of the psalm reflects upon the continuing meaning of such a faith for the life of the community. The present may have its uncertainties — the future lies beyond all human control — but faith must hold onto one certainty and rise to its challenge. This certainty is expressed in verses 10 and 12 as a theology of hope. Verse 10, however, faces us, as it did the early versions, with difficult problems of text and interpretation. The REB, following widely accepted emendations, renders "Edom, for all his fury, will praise you, and the remnant left in Hamath will dance in worship." Here the place names "Edom" and "Hamath," the southern and northern enemies of Israel, replace the word *'ādām* ("human") in the first line and "wrath" in the second line, while "dance in worship" or "keep your festivals" follows the Greek (LXX). The NRSV seeks to remain close to the Hebrew text, but what does it mean? The first part of verse 10 is clear enough. "Human wrath serves only to praise you." However irresponsible or endemic human evil may be, it can never finally prevail. It meets more than its match when faced with the awesome heavenly king. Its defiance and perversity simply throw into splendid relief his power and glory and therefore redound to his praise. This fits in well with the theme of the previous psalm,

Psalm 75. The second half of verse 10, however, is less clear. Literally the Hebrew is "a remnant of wraths [plural] you will gird on." The NRSV assumes that the word "wraths" refers to God's wrath by inserting the word "your" — "the last bit of your wrath" — as if to say human anger is finally put in its place when God clothes himself in his own intense anger. Equally, however, "the remnant of wrath" could refer to what remains of human anger, in which case the picture may be that of God taking such human anger to himself, girding it on, and thus neutralizing it and transforming it. Thus Joseph can say to his brothers, "You intended to do harm to me, but God intended it for good" (Gen. 50:20). Likewise Peter can speak of the enormity of evil in the crucifixion of Jesus, saying, "This man, handed over to you, according to the definite plan and foreknowledge of God, you crucified and killed. . . . But God raised him up, having freed him from death, since it was impossible for him to be held in its power" (Acts 2:23-24). Thus the concluding words of the psalm celebrate the power of this divine king who can "cut off the spirit" or perhaps "snuff out the life" (for Hebrew *ruah*, meaning "spirit" or "life," see 51:10-12) of any earthly rulers, be they "princes" or "kings of the earth" (v. 12).

But this theology of hope must go hand in hand with a present quality of life. So verse 11 sounds the challenge to those who share such a hope not only to "make vows to the LORD" but also to "perform [or fulfill] them," and to acknowledge in daily life that they stand under the authority of an awesome God to whom they must bring gifts or pay tribute. To live with hope is not a form of escapism. It is a challenge to live day by day responsibly and in obedience to the God who is central to such hope. The more certain the hope, the more demanding the challenge. The epistle to the Hebrews defines faith as "the assurance of things hoped for, the conviction of things not seen" (Heb. 11:1). It goes on to remind us that to live in the light of such a faith, witnessed to by many examples from the past, we face a challenge: "Let us lay aside every weight and the sin that clings so closely, and let us run with patience the race that is set before us, looking to Jesus the pioneer and perfecter of our faith. . . ." (Heb. 12:1-2). Hope without commitment is wishful daydreaming; commitment without hope can end in disillusionment.

Psalm 77
HAS GOD CHANGED?

For the heading "according to Jeduthun," see Psalm 39.

This psalm poses many difficult questions both of text and interpretation. The question of what kind of psalm this is, is posed immediately by the different renderings of verse 1 in the NRSV and the REB. The NRSV's rendering, "I cry aloud . . . that he may hear me," and the present tenses in the following verses, assume that this is an individual lament in which the psalmist is wrestling with an unresolved crisis in his own life. The REB's translation, "I cried aloud . . . he heard me," and the past tenses in the following verses, assume that we are listening to a psalm of thanksgiving on the lips of someone for whom the crisis is now over. The view taken here is that the NRSV approach is essentially correct.

1-3 The psalm begins with an urgent plea. The verb translated "cry" usually indicates a cry for help, a cry to God springing out of a situation of trouble or distress (cf. 107:28). What kind of "trouble" (v. 2) grips the psalmist is not clear. There is no justification for believing that the crisis he faces is the consequence of his own sinfulness, as has sometimes been claimed. Is he facing a purely personal crisis, or is he caught up in a crisis that has overtaken the life of the community to which he belongs? If, as some claim, we are listening to a voice from exile, then it is the latter. Yet it is not always possible to distinguish between these two scenarios. As I write these words, the news has just broken of the massacre of sixteen five-year-old children and their teacher by a crazed gunman in the primary school in the town of Dunblane, Scotland. Clearly for some of the families involved in this horror, it cannot be other than an intensely personal tragedy. But it is also an event which has devastated the whole community of Dunblane and indeed the entire nation. Many people, not immediately involved, share in the grief and horror and are asking questions to which there seem to be no answers, the kind of questions symbolized by a bunch of flowers left at the school gate with one word attached to it — "Why?" This is not the question raised in this psalm. It goes beyond that question to wrestle with profound theological issues in verses 7-10.

The crisis leads the psalmist to "seek the Lord" (v. 2; see 9:10), a seeking which seems to bring him little comfort and indeed deepens his distress. The text in the middle of verse 2 is difficult and capable of different interpretations. The NRSV assumes that the picture is of someone who during the night continues to stretch out his hands in prayer to God. Both the translation "stretch out" and "without wearying" are, however, questionable. Contrast the REB: "My tears ran unceasingly." The picture may be that of the psalmist so tense and distraught that night brings him no respite. Hands remain clenched tight, unable to relax. "I think of [literally, "remember"] God . . . I meditate," the kind of meditation which Psalm 119 claims leads to joy and strengthened faith (cf. 119:15, 23, 27). For the psalmist, however, God is not the answer; he is part of the problem, so his meditation deepens his pain and the blackness that threatens to engulf him. His vitality is at a low ebb (see 51:10).

4-9 Although the REB translates the opening words of verse 4 "My eyelids were tightly closed," it is better to see here with the NRSV a description of someone who finds sleep impossible, his eyelids incapable of closing. Nighttime brings no relief. The psalmist remains distraught — unable to find words to express the dark night of his soul. Once life had been different, but the past simply throws into bitter relief the questions which now haunt him. Most modern translations, including the NRSV and the REB, assume a modification of the Hebrew text and a redivision of the verses at the beginning of verse 6. The Hebrew could be translated "I remember my songs [music] at night." This makes good sense since such songs would include songs of praise celebrating the story of God's gracious dealings with his people in the past. But the more he recalls the story of the past, the more he meditates and searches for understanding, the more stark the questions become. It is as if the whole tradition of faith in which he had been nurtured is being called into question. In Exod. 34:6-7 we listen to the community's confession of faith: "The LORD, the LORD, a God merciful and gracious, slow to anger, and abounding in steadfast love and faithfulness, keeping steadfast love for the thousandth generation." But where is the evidence for such a God now? asks the psalmist. In a series of impassioned questions in verses 7-9, the foundations of this faith are being called into question:

- a God who is gracious? — but now God seems to have irrevocably "spurned" or cast off (cf. 74:1), to have ceased to be gracious.
- a God of steadfast love? — but that steadfast love seems to have completely ceased.
- a steadfast love which would last for the thousandth generation? — but that promise (literally, "word") seems to be at an end "for all time" (literally, "to generation and generation").
- a God who is compassionate, slow to anger? — but that compassion (see 25:6), that tender mother love, seems to have been drowned, "locked up" (REB), in God's anger.

In what kind of God may I still believe? That is the question the psalmist is struggling to answer.

10-15 Verse 10, which marks the transition to the following section and is pivotal to the whole Psalm, has been variously interpreted. The Hebrew word translated "It is my grief" is a verbal form meaning "my sickness [or: "weakness"] is. . . ." The REB needlessly changes the text here. But what kind of sickness or weakness is meant? It has been argued that the verse points to something wrong within the psalmist, and that this, not God, is his real problem. The psalmist, on this view, is suffering from a spiritual illness exemplified by a lament that is unhealthy because it keeps throwing him back on his own distorted thoughts instead of taking him out of himself to God. While there may be an element of truth in this in many a spiritual crisis, it hardly does justice to the psalmist's dilemma. What is undermining his spiritual sanity is the yawning gap between the tradition of faith in which he has been nurtured and the grim present, which seems to call into question every statement in the traditional credo. For him it is the character of God that is at stake. Is it possible that the right hand of the Most High (see 7:17) has changed, that God is no longer the God in whom he had been brought up to trust?

This leads the psalmist into a meditation which seeks to "remember," that is, to recall and relive (see 74:2), the faith handed down within the community. The word "remember" echoes across the psalm: in verse 3, where it is translated "I think of," in verse 5, and twice in verse 11. What he seeks to remember is a God of action, a God of "wonders" (vv. 11 and 14), a word used to describe the Exodus experience in the Song of Moses (Exod. 15:11), a God of "mighty deeds" (v. 12; see 9:11), a God whose way is characterized by the adjective "holy" (see 22:3, though it is just possible we should render this "in the temple"; cf. 73:17), a God of incomparable greatness who in displaying his power "redeemed" (see 19:14) his people, "the descendants of Jacob and Joseph" (v. 15), a phrase found nowhere else in the Old Testament, but which probably here indicates the whole people of God who traced their ancestry back to Jacob/Israel (cf. Gen. 35:10) and whose life had been shaped by the Exodus experience, which was formative for the Joseph tribes.

16-20   The psalm concludes with a hymn that differs stylistically from the rest of the psalm. Each line in the Hebrew, corresponding to each verse in English, contains three elements instead of the more normal two. This hymn likely reflects ancient Canaanite poetic style. It draws heavily upon ancient Near Eastern mythology, which described the conflict between the gods of order and creation, on the one hand, and the forces of chaos represented by water, on the other. Thus verse 16: "When the waters saw you, O God, when the waters saw you, they were afraid [literally, "writhed," REB]; the very deep trembled." The word translated "deep," plural in Hebrew, is the word used in the singular in the creation hymn in Gen. 1:2.

God is then depicted in verse 17-18 in the imagery of the storm god, with his "flashing arrows" (cf. 76:3), his lightning bolts, and his thunder echoing in the "whirlwind" or the storm.

The imagery of cosmic conflict and awesome natural power, however, leads into the Exodus event, where no "sea" or "mighty waters" could thwart God's deliverance of his people. Thus creation and history form for Israel one seamless robe, the work of the one great designer. The fact that the Hebrew Bible uses such mythological themes again and again to elaborate the Exodus story (cf. Isa. 51:9-10) shows that for Israel the Exodus was not merely a passing historical event, but of profound theological significance. Yet this was an event whose meaning could only be grasped in faith, the work of a God whose "footprints were unseen" (v. 19, literally, "were not known"). It is as if at this point the hymn is reminding the people of God that they are faced with the mystery of a God whose ways always remain unrecognized without the commitment of faith. What was true of ancient Israel was equally true of the people of Jesus' day, most of whom failed to recognize in him God's presence in their midst. It remains true today.

The exodus event, however, underlines that cosmic power in itself is never enough. So the psalm ends with the picture of God as the caring shepherd (see Psalm 23), leading his people "by the hand of Moses and Aaron," as God usually shows his care through people prepared to respond to his call.

One major issue remains. What is the relationship between the lament, with its urgent questions in verses 1-9, and the meditation and hymn in verses 11-20? Is the second half of the psalm the answer to the puzzled questions that dominate the first half? Is the psalmist's "trouble" transformed by being placed in the context of the celebration of the praise of God? Does the psalmist's pain find its healing in the picture of the caring shepherd with which the psalm ends? This is possible. Such a movement from lament to praise is characteristic of many Psalms (see, e.g., Psalm 22), and people across the centuries have found such healing coming to them in worship. Perhaps we ought to hesitate, however, before we assume that this is what takes place in this psalm. Are the questions raised on the basis of bitter experience in verses 7-9 ever answered? Is it enough simply to recall an ancient credo if that credo has lost its power to convince? The hymn in Habakkuk 3 begins;

> O Lord, I have heard of your renown,
>   and I stand in awe, O Lord, of your work.
> In our own time revive it;
>   in our own time make it known;
>   in wrath may you remember mercy. (Hab. 3:2)

The psalmist hears again of God's renown, but his own experience is of a God who "in anger shut up his compassion." Can he now confess his faith in a God who in wrath remembers mercy? There is no clear indication in the psalm that he can. When today a congregation rises to confess its faith in the Nicene or Apostles' creed, may there not be those within the congregation who, in terms of their own bitter experience, are left still asking "Has God changed?"

Psalm 78
A TALE IS TOLD

This psalm, which has the same heading as Psalm 74, "A Maskil of Asaph," tells a story that ranges from the time of the people's enslavement in Egypt, through the Exodus, the wilderness wanderings, and the settlement in Canaan down to the establishment of the Davidic dynasty and the temple on Mt. Zion. The earliest possible date for it, therefore, is the tenth century BCE. Does the emphasis upon the rejection of the northern Joseph/Ephraim tribes in verse 67 presuppose the downfall of the northern kingdom of Israel in 721 BCE? Much depends on how we read the closing section of the psalm in verses 67-72 (see below).

This is not, however, a story told as in a history book, but a story told and retold in the context of worship. In its present form it may have been reshaped to take its place in one of the major festivals of the religious year associated with the Jerusalem temple prior to the downfall of the southern kingdom of Judah in 587 BCE. It is, moreover, a story told with a purpose, clearly spelled out in the introduction in verses 1-8.

1-8 In the first two verses we are listening to a characteristic appeal and language typical of a wisdom teacher (see 49:1-4). We are invited to listen to a "parable" (Hebrew *māšal;* REB: "meaningful story") and "dark sayings" (Hebrew *ḥîdôt;* REB: "the riddle"; see 49:4). This is a story designed to make people stop and think, and think hard. It is not dealing with a basic human problem, as Psalm 49 was. It focuses on an issue facing the people of God in the light of their relationship with God, as that has unfolded across their history. It is an old story that in broad outline they knew only too well. Now it needs to get under their skin to make them face certain foundational truths, which they in turn need to communicate to coming generations. There are three central themes in this story:

1. Its foundation lies in "the glorious deeds of the LORD" (v. 4). The word translated "glorious deeds" elsewhere in the Psalms is usually rendered "praise" (e.g., 9:14; 35:28; 79:13), hence the REB's rendering, "praiseworthy acts." Here are events that are demonstrations of the LORD's "might" and his "wonders" (v. 4; see 9:1), events which naturally evoke from his people a response of praise. There is no true faith which does not begin in the joyful celebration of what God has done.
2. This God, however, makes demands upon his people. He "established a decree in Jacob" (v. 5). The word translated "decree" (Hebrew *ʿēdût;* cf. 19:8) is closely associated in priestly tradition with the stone tablets given to Moses by God (cf. Exod. 31:18; 32:15; 34:29, where the NRSV translates "covenant"). It denotes here the obligations laid upon the people in terms of their relationship with the LORD, obligations enshrined in "the law" (*tôrāh;* see 1:2; the same Hebrew word is translated "teaching" in verse 1), obligations which the people have committed themselves to obey.
3. The story is one of failure on the part of the people to honor this obligation.

This is a people who have again and again turned out to be "a stubborn and rebellious generation" (v. 8; cf. Deut. 32:5-6), a people who have proved that they have no fixed purpose or loyalty. The Old Testament never tires of celebrating the steadfast love of the LORD, but it has no illusions about the people of the LORD. The story is being retold so that a lesson may be learned and so that past failure will not characterize the present and the future. It is designed to encourage an obedient people who will put "their hope in God" (v. 7). The word translated "hope" in other contexts can mean stubborn stupidity, foolhardiness (cf. 49:13), and the corresponding adjective invariably describes a fool (cf. 49:10). Here it means a stubborn holding on to God, a meaning perhaps better conveyed in the REB translation "trust" (cf. Job 8:14; 31:24, where the NRSV renders "confidence"). Celebration . . . the call to obey . . . the failure to obey — these are the elements that loom large in the story that now unfolds. The story, however, has been telescoped and shaped to serve a particular purpose, a reminder that history always serves some ideological purpose and that memory, consciously or unconsciously, is selective — a truism illustrated again and again in the contemporary tensions in Israel/Palestine and Northern Ireland.

9-11 The clue to the particular purpose of this story is introduced in verse 9-11 by the recalling of an incident involving "the Ephraimites." This anticipates the verdict in verse 67, which claims that God "rejected the tent of Joseph, he did not choose the tribe of Ephraim." According to Gen. 48:8-22, Ephraim, the younger son of Joseph, received from Jacob a greater blessing than his older brother Manasseh. Certainly Ephraim became the dominant northern tribe, with the central highlands north of Jerusalem known as "the hill country of Ephraim" (Judg. 7:24). It was there in the north at Shechem (cf. Joshua 24) and at the sanctuary at Shiloh (cf. 1 Samuel 1) that the traditions of the Exodus and God's covenant with his people were first celebrated and preserved. After the breakup of the united kingdom on the death of Solomon, it was an Ephraimite, Jeroboam, who established the northern kingdom of Israel, often called Ephraim (cf. Hosea 5). What particular incident, if any, is referred to in verse 9 has been much discussed. Is it the loss of the ark to the Philistines as described in 1 Samuel 4, or the death of Saul and Jonathan on Mt. Gilboa (1 Samuel 31), or the fall of Samaria to the Assyrians in 721 BCE? We do not know. What verses 9-11 affirm, however, is that the Ephraimites were characterized by military power that proved ineffective and illusory because it went hand in hand with a religious apostasy (for "covenant," see 25:10) rooted in ingratitude and forgetfulness (for "miracles," v. 11, see 9:2). It was this that paved the way for God's final verdict of rejection.

The long central section of the psalm, vv. 12-64, focuses upon the past history of the people and contrasts God's wonderful deeds and gracious providence with the people's disobedience and ingratitude. It falls into two parts, verses 12-39 and verses 40-64, which weave variations round the one central theme.

12-39 Verses 12-16 tell the story of God's "marvels" (see 77:11, 14, where the same word is translated "wonders") from the deliverance from slavery in Egypt, through the crossing of the Sea of Reeds, to the subsequent providential care of the people during their period in the wilderness.

"Zoan" (v. 12; cf. v. 43) is not mentioned in the narratives in the book of Exodus. It was an important city in northeast Egypt, built seven years after Hebron (Num. 13:22). It became the capital of the Hyksos invaders, who named it Avaris. It features in prophetic oracles in Isaiah (19:11, 13; 30:4) and Ezekiel (30:14), which stress the futility of God's people placing their trust in Egypt. Verses 13-15 draw heavily on the traditional narratives. The picture of the waters standing in "a heap" (v. 13) echoes the language of the Song of Moses in Exod. 15:8; verse 14 recalls Exod. 14:19-20; and verse 15 echoes Exod. 17:6 and Num. 20:8-13. The seemingly impassable "sea" and "water" of v. 13 find their counterpart in the providentially provided "streams" and "waters" of verse 16. The same Hebrew verb used in 74:15 in a creation context, where the NRSV translates "cut openings," is found twice here in a historical context, translated "divided" in v. 13 and "split open" in v. 15. It is not surprising that in these verses no mention is made of the people's complaints and rebellion, recounted in both Exodus 17 and Numbers 20. The psalm's emphasis is clear. God's grace, and God's grace alone, is the basis of Israel's life. The human response in all its ambiguity and failure can only be truly measured in the light of this grace.

17-20 The ten lines focusing on God's grace in verses 12-16 now find their counterpart in ten lines in verses 17-20 that underscore the people's mystifying response — rebellion in the wilderness. "They sinned still more . . . rebelling [v. 17] . . . they tested [see 11:4] . . . demanding [v. 18] . . . they spoke against God" (v. 19). The word "tested" occurs three times in this psalm, here in verse 18 and later in verses 41 and 56. Together with the unusual verb translated "provoked" in verse 41, it describes pushing God to the limit, seeing as it were how far they could go with him.

Even the miraculous provision of water in the wilderness led not to thanksgiving, but to a "give us more" attitude (v. 20), as if God existed simply to satisfy their cravings or what they considered to be their needs. That is an ever present distortion of religion. Florence Nightingale, at a particularly difficult period in her life, found herself repeatedly telling God what she expected him to do about it. Then she suddenly realized what she was doing and wrote in her diary, "I must remember that God is not my private secretary." The ambiguities in our human response to God are well illustrated by comparing the quietly trusting words of Ps. 23:5, "You spread a table for me in the presence of my enemies" and the almost arrogant, disbelieving words in verse 19, "Can God spread a table in the wilderness?"

21-31 God's response is one of "anger," not the irresponsible, irrational anger that often mars our relationship with other people, but the anger that must say "No" to certain kinds of human activity (see 6:1). The psalmist has no doubts about the reality and justification of this anger. Three times in the psalm there occurs the verb translated in verse 21 as "was full of rage," in verse 59 as "he was full of wrath," and in verse 62 as "he vented his wrath." The God whom other psalms describe as "the God of Jacob" (see 20:1) is the God who has "kindled a fire against Jacob" (cf. v. 21). A people who played with fire are doomed to be burned.

God's anger is the inevitable corollary to the attitude of a people who had "no faith in God," who "did not trust his saving power" (v. 22). For "trust" and "faith," see comment on 4:5 and 25:5, and for the God who has "power to save" (REB), see 3:2. What is at stake here is not merely the lack of intellectual belief, but the lack of a willingness to entrust their lives into God's hands in the conviction that God can meet their every need.

Verses 23-25 recall the tradition of the provision of the "manna" and the "quail" meat in Exodus 16 and Numbers 11. Manna (v. 24) is the honeydew secretion of insects who feed on the tamarisk bush. It is called here poetically

1. "the grain of heaven" (cf. 105:40, "food from heaven"), as if it had miraculously dropped from heaven, rained down by the God who opened "the doors of heaven," a phrase found only here, though Gen. 7:11 speaks of "the windows of heaven."
2. "the bread of angels." This is in fact the Greek (LXX) interpretation of the Hebrew, which reads "the bread of the mighty ones." Compare Ps. 103:20, where "you mighty ones" is used in parallelism to "you his angels."

Both phrases are intended to underline the gracious and supernatural provision of food.

The "flesh" and the "winged birds" of verse 27 are the quails who winter in Arabia and Africa and migrate northwards in March and April. Notice how in both cases the abundance of God's provision for the people is underlined by the use of the words "he rained down on them manna to eat . . . he rained flesh upon them," as if this were all part of his natural providence.

There is, however, an ironic twist in all this. Yes, God lavished his providence upon them. They got what they craved, but in the very act of getting it, "while the food was still in their mouths" (v. 30), they experienced the anger and judgment of God. God gave them what they wanted, but it did nothing to counter that lack of faith and trust which blighted their relationship with him.

32-39 The closing section of this part of the psalm reflects theologically on the story recounted, on a lesson not learned. Nothing changed. The same response noted in verses 17 and 22 continued: "they still sinned . . . they had no faith in his wonders" (v. 32). The harsh brevity of their human life having been forcibly brought home to them — for the meaning of "like a breath" (Hebrew *hebel*), see 39:4-6 — they repented and "sought God earnestly" or perhaps better "they look eagerly for God once more" (REB). They recalled the reassuring titles of God, "their rock [see 18:2] . . . the Most High God [see 7:17] . . . their redeemer [see 19:14]." These are words rich with meaning, but only words, for this was a repentance that was meaningless. It involved no inner change in their attitude to God. Behind their flattering or deceitful words and their lying tongues, there remained the same inconsistency, the same lack of faith that had provoked God's anger. Nothing had changed, but true repentance always means change, a turning away from what is unacceptable. The prophets were only too well aware of this surface, futile repentance in which Israel often indulged (cf. Hos. 5:5-7; 6). God's anger, however, is neither irrational nor his last word. His true nature is to be "compassionate" and forgiving (see 25:6; cf. Exod. 34:6). This is a compassion rooted in the recognition of the brevity and frailty of human life. Human life is "but flesh [see 56:4] . . . a wind that passes." Here "wind" (Hebrew *ruah;* see 51:10) may be pointing to the wind as something over which we have no control, and is therefore a fit symbol of the vulnerability of human existence. It is possible, however, that we should translate "spirit," the vital spark which defines our human existence. In this case the psalmist would be saying that the vital spark of life within us is fleeting, a theme which has been explored in a particular context in Psalm 49 and is to be further examined in Psalm 90.

40-58 Here the traditional story is told again, this time as a story extending from Egypt to the settlement in the promised land. It is set again within the framework of human failure and disobedience. The opening verses, 40-42, develop the theme of rebellion in the wilderness (for "tested" and "provoked," see v. 18). Rebellion is rooted in a failure of memory, a failure above all to remember the time when God "redeemed" them (see 25:22) from the foe in Egypt (v. 42).

Verses 43-51 turn to the plagues that struck Egypt. The plagues are regarded as "signs" and "miracles" (REB: "portents"; Hebrew *môpětîm*). This linking of "signs" and "miracles" is typical of the way in which Deuteronomy describes the events leading up to the deliverance from Egypt (Deut. 4:34; 6:22; 7:19) and is also found in the narrative in Exodus (Exod. 7:3). It is a way of describing events seen and lived through by people who ought to have recognized that they were pointing to the awesome power of God.

The tradition concerning the plagues seems to have been fluid, since neither the number nor the order of the plagues in this psalm is consistent with the sources which have come down to us in the narrative in Exodus 7-12 or in Psalm 105. The differences in detail are hardly of theological significance, and all the traditions climax in the slaying of the Egyptian firstborn. This psalm speaks of rivers turned to blood (v. 44), swarms of flies (v. 45, though the insects are not specified in the Hebrew), frogs (v. 45), caterpillars (or grasshoppers) and locusts (v. 46), hail and frost (or "torrents of rain," so REB v. 47), hail and thunderbolt (v. 48, perhaps better, with the REB, "plague and pestilence"). The final, climactic demonstration of God's fury against the oppressor is that "company of destroying angels" (for angels, see 34:7), that detachment of messengers of death who destroyed the firstborn in Egypt (cf. Exod. 12:29-32), "the first fruits of their strength [or manhood] in the tents of Ham." Ham, according to the genealogical table of the nations in Genesis 10, was one of the sons of Noah and the progenitor of Egypt among other nations. In Ps. 105:23 the land of Ham is used in parallelism with Egypt.

Such signs and miracles, awesome as they were, are but the prelude to that event which was to become central to Israel's religious tradition and definitive for Israel's understanding of God — the Exodus from Egypt. Here it is depicted as a caring shepherd leading his flock, protecting them from all enemies (vv. 52-53; cf. 77:20; and see Psalm 23). Again, this brief description of the Exodus is selective. To say "He led them in safety, so that they were not afraid" (v. 53) hardly squares with the picture in the book of Exodus of the Israelites looking back panic-stricken when they saw the pursuing Egyptians, and crying out "in great fear . . . to the LORD" (Exod. 14:10). But all the human fears and doubts fade into insignificance in the light of what ought to have been the abiding memory of the wonder of God's hand stretched out to save.

Out of Egyptian slavery, the people move across the wilderness to the land God had prepared for his people (vv. 54-55). Although traditionally "his holy hill . . . the mountain his right hand had won" (v. 54) has been identified with Mt. Zion, in context this is unlikely. Mt. Zion only entered Hebrew history in the time of David. If the psalm is talking here of the early period of the settlement in Canaan, with its displacement of the native population, then the reference is probably more generally to the hill country in the north of Canaan where the tribes first settled. These verses stress that the land, just as much as the deliverance out of slavery in Egypt, was God's gift to his people, not their own achievement. How the people would handle this gift was to be one of the recurring dilemmas in Israel's history. A similar dilemma confronts the state of Israel today.

Verses 56-58 return to the theme of rebellion, echoing much of the language in verses 17-20 and 41. The meaning of the phrase "they twisted like a treacherous bow" is well brought out in the REB's translation "unreliable like a bow gone slack," a bow which would not function effectively when needed. Hence God's bitter disappointment with a people from whom he had the right to expect great things. The spiritual root of the people's rebellion is laid bare in verse 58. They ignored what was central to the Decalogue, that for Israel there should be "no other gods" (Deut. 5:7), since the God they worshipped was a jealous God who made an exclusive demand on their loyalty. Participation, therefore, in the worship of other gods — for example, local Canaanite gods at "the high places" with their "idols," images of such gods — was a deliberate challenge to this exclusive loyalty, which could brook no shopping around for a comprehensive religious insurance policy. The verb translated "moved him to jealousy" (v. 58) recalls the description of the LORD as a jealous God in Deut. 5:6. The language of verse 58 is indeed very reminiscent of Deuteronomy and of the Deuteronomic history in Samuel and Kings, where the word here translated "provoked" (not the same word as in v. 41) is repeatedly used of religious apostasy.

59-66   Rebellion brings its inevitable response, verse 59 echoing and taking verse 21 one step farther with its assertion that God "utterly rejected Israel," a phrase which prepares the way for the climactic epilogue to the psalm in verses 67-72. In the early period of Israel's settlement in Canaan, the religious focus of the northern tribes of Israel centered on the sanctuary, the "tent" at Shiloh where God dwelt among his people (cf. Josh. 18:1). Shiloh housed the ark, the visible sign of God's powerful presence in the midst of his people. The reference to "his power" and "his glory" in verse 61 is to the ark captured by the Philistines (cf. 1 Sam. 4:11). Indeed, verses 60-64 read like a poetic version of the narrative in 1 Samuel 4 with its account of the capture of the ark, the death of Eli and his sons the priests at Shiloh, and the death in childbirth of Eli's daughter-in-law, her son's name Ichabod preserving the memory of the disaster in which "the glory has departed from Israel" (1 Sam. 4:21). The normal pattern of community life with its marriages and its funeral rites had come to an end. Such archaeological evidence as we have points to Shiloh having been destroyed in the middle of the eleventh century BCE.

Lest there be any doubt, two dramatic pictures are used in verse 65 to affirm that what happened was the sign of God in action. The picture of the LORD waking up "as from sleep" corresponds to the cries we have already heard in some of the Psalms of lament calling upon the LORD to do just that (see 7:6; 44:23-24). Far from being asleep, he is powerfully in action. The second picture is of the LORD as the Divine Warrior going into battle (cf. Isa. 42:13). The description of this divine warrior going into battle fortified by Dutch courage, however, has caused problems for pious commentators from the early Rabbis to John Calvin. The NRSV's translation, "shouting because of wine," assumes one root for the Hebrew verb. The REB's rendering, "flushed with wine," assumes another. Both remain highly anthropomorphic ways of talking about the vigor and the power unleashed when the LORD goes into action. But who are his "adversaries" destined for "everlasting disgrace" (v. 66)? If we link this verse with what immediately precedes it, then the reference is to the LORD's own people who by their apostasy and rebellion have sealed their own fate. Instead of being their champion, the LORD is their executioner. In context this seems far more likely than to see in these words a pointer forward to David who, after the tragedies under Saul, was finally to crush the Philistines who had wreaked havoc on the LORD's people.

67-72 The concluding verses of the psalm, verses 67-72, speak of a realignment in the LORD's purposes that marks an end and a new beginning. The northern sanctuary of Shiloh, "the tent of Joseph" (v. 67), is replaced by the sanctuary on Mt. Zion in Jerusalem; the tribe of Ephraim is replaced in the LORD's purposes by the tribe of Judah (v. 68). David, the LORD's chosen "servant" (v. 70), takes center stage politically, guaranteeing the future well-being of the whole nation (vv. 71-72). The religious underpinning of this is to be found in the tradition of the LORD's covenant with David and the Davidic dynasty as outlined in 2 Samuel 7.

It is possible to dismiss this entire concluding section as Judean propaganda in the midst of early tribal rivalries, or religious propaganda emanating from the Jerusalem cult with the official imprimatur of the Davidic dynasty. It would be particularly powerful in the aftermath of the destruction of the northern kingdom by the Assyrians in 721 BCE. In the postexilic situation it could also be a useful tool in Jewish hands against the Samaritans. It is, however, dangerous propaganda. Mt. Zion may be the place the LORD "loves," with its sanctuary "founded forever" (vv. 68, 69), but as Jeremiah in his temple sermon forcibly points out, what happened to Shiloh could and would happen to Jerusalem and its temple for precisely the same reasons (Jeremiah 7). David in the closing verses is described as exercising a kingly shepherd role with "upright heart" or integrity (see 25:11) and "with skillful hand," thus ensuring that the true needs of his people would be met. But such integrity and insight were not the obvious characteristics of many of those who sat on the throne of David, nor were they always evident in David's career.

The story of the people of God told in this psalm from the time of the Exodus onwards is the story of divine grace and divine judgment inexorably interwoven, the story of a compassion that was demanding and of a people who, ignoring these demands, rebelled with tragic consequences. It was true of Ephraim with the sanctuary in Shiloh; it was to be equally true of Judah with its Davidic dynasty and Jerusalem temple. It is still true of any religious community, however hallowed its symbols or its places of worship. We cannot truly celebrate the love of God unless we face its demands. As 1 John 1:5-6 puts it, "God is light and in him there is no darkness at all. If we say we have fellowship with him while we are walking in darkness, we lie and do not do what is true." It is, of course, always easier to see the gap between celebration and living in other people than to face it in our own lives. Our failure and rebellion, however, cannot ultimately stymie God's purposes. He is stubbornly compassionate, ever willing to begin anew, to take his people along new and often unexpected roads.

Although there are references, often oblique, to certain verses of this psalm in the New Testament (see, e.g., Matt. 13:15; 1 Cor. 10:8; Acts 8:21), it is more appropriate to see in the New Testament as a whole a commentary on the central theological themes of the psalm. Where else do we find so clearly presented to us that stubborn compassion which will go even to a cross, and which again and again has to break down barriers and challenge the failure to understand of those who claim to belong to the body of Christ?

Psalm 79
WHERE IS GOD?

This psalm, a community lament, has much in common with Psalm 74. It poses the same critical questions of origin and continuing cultic significance. In thought and language it has many links with other community laments, and in turn it has provided the vehicle for facing similar situations of crisis. Verses 2-3 are quoted freely as "the word that was written" in 1 Macc. 7:17, a word of relevance to a particularly bloody incident of internal strife during the Maccabean period.

1-4   Verses 1-4 graphically describe the crisis which has overtaken the community — invasion by the "nations" (Hebrew *gôyîm;* REB: "the heathen"), invasion of "your inheritance," the land given by God to his people (the same words, "your inheritance," describe the people in 74:2). The "holy temple" (see 5:7) has been "defiled" by the very presence in it of non-Jews, though the word probably carries with it the meaning of destruction, as it does in 2 Kings 23:8, where King Josiah, in his reforming zeal, is said to have "defiled" or destroyed all the festering sores of paganism throughout the land. The city of Jerusalem has been reduced to a pile of rubble, its population brutally massacred. All respect for human dignity and worth, expressed through decent burial and the customary mourning rites, are at an end. Verse 2 recalls the words of Deut. 28:25-26, where the nation is described as "an object of horror." This is not merely a human tragedy. It has happened to "your inheritance . . . your holy temple . . . your servants [v. 2; see 34:22] . . . your faithful" (see 4:3). So the opening word of the psalm is the pain-filled, puzzled "O God." It is important to remember the depth of the religious crisis which lies behind this language. If the psalm is initially a response to the destruction of Jerusalem by the Babylonians in 587 BCE, it speaks of a people bereft of much that they considered central to their faith, much indeed that was confidently asserted in the closing verses of the previous psalm. Where now was the free and independent nation living in the land which was God's gift to them, where now the God whose powerful and protecting presence was there in their midst in the temple (see Psalms 46 and 48)? The problem is highlighted by the word "inheritance." It speaks of what ought to have been God's inalienable gift to his people. It has now been wrenched from them. What is in jeopardy, therefore, is the reality of the relationship between God and his people, a relationship which is now an object of mockery and derision to neighboring people (v. 4 occurs again in 44:13).

5-7 Inevitably the cry "How long, O LORD?" — so typical of the Psalms of lament — is heard again (v. 5; see 4:2; 74:10). Not surprisingly, the community believes it is on the receiving end of the LORD's "anger" (see 6:1) and "jealous wrath" (see 78:58). But why should such anger be directed against God's own people, why not against those who have devastated this nation (for "Jacob," v. 7, see 44:4), especially since they are pagans who "do not know you . . . do not call upon your name," both phrases which indicate their lack of true religious commitment and loyalty. The strangeness, the seeming unfairness, of what the Lord has done screams out for redress, and only the LORD can do it — hence the prayer in verse 6 with its apparent xenophobic bitterness.

8-12 A series of appeals to the LORD follows. Some seek the redress of the community's plight and the renewal of its relationship with the LORD (vv. 8-9 and 11). Others give voice to the plea for vengeance upon those responsible for present tragedy (vv. 10 and 12). The appeal for renewal in verses 8-9 is based on the nature of God, his willingness to forgive and to deliver. Three times in Psalm 74 we heard the appeal to God to remember, to act to remedy a tragic situation (74:2, 18, 22). The "do not remember" of verse 8 is equally a call to God to act, to annul the consequences of "the iniquities of our ancestors." This phrase could equally be translated "our past guilt," in which case it parallels "our sins" in verse 9. It is more likely, however, that the thought here is similar to that in Lamentations 5, where the confession "Our ancestors sinned . . . and we bear their iniquities" (Lam. 5:7) leads later in the chapter to "Woe to us, for we have sinned" (Lam. 5:16). The legacy of the past and the sins of the present have led to tragedy. They need to be dealt with — "do not remember" (v. 8), "forgive [see 65:3] our sins" (v. 9). Such forgiveness is rooted in God's "compassion" (see 25:6), that warm, outgoing compassion which quickly responds to those in need whose life is at a low ebb, a compassion which means that, true to himself (for "glory," see 3:3), God is a God of "salvation" (see 3:8) who will rescue his people from their present plight. The repeated emphasis upon the "name" of God in verse 9 stresses that for the community what is at stake in the national crisis is the character and nature of God (see 25:11). It is the depth of the tragedy, "the groans of the prisoners," people "under sentence of death" (REB), which gives added grounds for the appeal in verse 11.

The appeal for vengeance in verse 10 is a response to the derisive cry of the nations, "Where is their God?" (see 42:10), a cry which mockingly casts doubt on the ability of Israel's God to do anything to heal the people's wounds. These words are all the more insidious because they probably echo the doubts and fears which were there in the mind of the people and expressed in the words

"How long, O LORD?" Suppose the answer to that question turned out to be "forever"? What then? The negative comments of others can often destructively reinforce our own questions and doubts, unless we can hold onto the assurance that even in the darkness God is present. The psalmist believes there must come a time when it will be seen to be true, "before our eyes," that the nations have been called to account for the bloody atrocities they have committed. Since the psalmist is convinced that what is at stake is whether God is a powerless spectator of the brutality which destroys human life or a God who can intervene to deliver the victims of oppression, verse 12 appeals to God to act decisively and fully (for "sevenfold," see Gen. 4:15, 24; Ps. 12:6) to call to account those responsible for the horrors of the present. It is in the confidence that this must happen that the psalm closes on the twin notes of "thanksgiving" and "praise," as do many similar psalms (e.g., Psalm 7), unexpected notes perhaps when we look back to the beginning of the psalm, yet appropriate to a people who believed that they were a flock, cared for by a divine shepherd king (see Psalm 23; cf. Isa. 40:10-11).

This is a psalm not for the quietness of the study but for people who have been at breaking point, who have seen much of what they cherished ruthlessly destroyed. Too many people in our own day have been there in the killing fields of Cambodia, in Bosnia and Rwanda. They raise questions demanding an answer, questions born of a raw honesty and bitterness conceived in the womb of human cruelty. There are the cries for vengeance which we have noted in other psalms (e.g., 5:10; 68:21-23), and the cries arise in the Psalms not to a War Crimes Tribunal but to a divine judge. It ill becomes those of us who have lived in sheltered security to criticize such cries of anguish. What is not clear, however, is what kind of deliverance the psalmist anticipated. Was it to be a return to the old securities of people, land, and temple, or had they been irrevocably destroyed? Could there be thanksgiving and praise while there was still no light at the end of the dark tunnel? Could the psalmist have risen to the challenge in Paul's words, "I am content with weakness, insults, hardships, persecutions and calamities for the sake of Christ, for whenever I am weak, then I am strong" (2 Cor. 12:10)? The sole strength the psalmist seems to have had is his holding on in hope that human brutality could not have the last word, because there was still a God of compassion, a God who cared enough for his people to be the God of their salvation. He had to live gripped by this faith. He may not have known what particular form that hope would take; perhaps he did not need to know.

In Jewish liturgical tradition this psalm found its place on the ninth day of Ab, which commemorates the destruction of the temple, not only the temple of 587 BCE, but the second temple destroyed by the Romans in 70 CE. As such, it provides the community with an appropriate vehicle for the corporate expression of penitence and hope. It is not surprising that it is recited today in Jerusalem on Friday afternoon at the Western Wall, all that remains of Herod's temple. In that context it is all too easy for some to equate the blood-stained hands and the taunting neighbors of the psalm with those of another faith who worship at the El Aqsa mosque and whose faith is dramatically symbolized there at the Dome of the Rock. So the cry for vengeance is heard. Whether this is truly to pray for the peace of Jerusalem today or tomorrow is open to question. The trouble is that we can all be selective in identifying our enemies as God's enemies. We assume that those whom we identify as "those who know not God" will suffer retribution from God. That occurs not only in the Old Testament, but also in the New (e.g., 1 Thess. 4:5; Rev. 6:10; 16:6), and it has appeared again and again in the history of the Church. Verse 6 provided John Calvin with an opportunity to make a scathing attack on the Pope and "the blind and devoted votaries of the Man of Sin who have no right knowledge of the God whom they profess to worship." Perhaps we should search our own hearts to see whether we are not in danger of falling into the same mistake.

Psalm 80
AN URGENT PLEA

Why this psalm has such a complex heading is not clear. For the phrase "on Lilies," see the heading to Psalm 45, and for the linking of this phrase with "a Covenant," see Psalm 60. The Greek (LXX) text adds "concerning the Assyrians," an early attempt to fix the precise historical situation which gave rise to the psalm.

The question of the dating of the psalm has been much and inconclusively discussed. Both the liturgical description of God as "enthroned upon the cherubim" (v. 1) and "LORD God of hosts" (v. 4) are associated in the Samuel narrative with the sanctuary at Shiloh (1 Sam. 4:4; cf. 2 Sam. 6:2). Likewise the references to "Joseph" (v. 1), to "Ephraim and Manasseh" (v. 2) and even to "Benjamin" (v. 2), which was very much on the border between north and south, point to northern tradition. Thus the origin of the psalm has been sought in the catastrophic events which led to the final destruction of the northern kingdom of Israel in 721 BCE, and more specifically to the turmoil under Hoshea the last king of Israel from 734 to 721. Links with the book of Jeremiah, however, and the interest of King Josiah in the north, an interest which would have appealed to northern exiles in Judah, have suggested a date in the second half of the seventh century BCE. It has also been argued that postexilic messianic thinking is reflected in the language of verse 17. It is perhaps best to see the origin of the psalm in northern liturgical circles prior to the downfall of the kingdom of Israel, but to recognize that, like many other psalms, it became part of a living stream of tradition adapted and shaped for use in later circumstances and probably did not reach its present form until after the exile.

The psalm is essentially a community lament divided into three parts by a refrain in verses 3, 7, and the concluding verse 19. The refrain varies only in its references to "God" in verse 3, to "God of Hosts" in verse 7, and to "Lᴏʀᴅ God of Hosts" in verse 19. The title is probably deliberately expanded throughout the psalm for the sake of emphasis. A discussion of the meaning of the title "Lᴏʀᴅ God of Hosts" is found in the comment on Ps. 24:10. The plea in the refrain, "Restore us," can mean many different things from "restore us to our former prosperity" before disaster struck, to "bring us back in repentance" to a true relationship with God. It is typical of the Hebrew Bible, however, that what we would call the material and the spiritual cannot be easily separated, so both meanings may be implied in this appeal. Lamentations 5:21, using the same phrase, points in this direction: "Restore us to yourself, O Lᴏʀᴅ, that we may be restored, renew our days as of old. . . ." The second line in the refrain echoes the Aaronic blessing in Num. 6:25 (cf. 31:16) and looks forward to a community experiencing again that shalom which has its roots in the God who comes to "save" (see 3:2).

1-2 The psalm begins with a petition that hinges on three descriptions of God:

1. "Shepherd of Israel," a phrase which somewhat surprisingly occurs only here in the Hebrew Bible, but draws on the familiar imagery with which Psalm 79 closes (see Psalm 23). This naturally leads into the second phrase.
2. "you who lead Joseph like a flock!" — the word translated "lead" here being found in Isa. 49:10 in parallelism with the word translated "lead" in the familiar shepherd imagery of Ps. 23:2.
3. "enthroned [literally, "sit"] upon the cherubim," a phrase which, as we have seen, is closely associated with the ark, the symbol of the Lᴏʀᴅ's presence with his people in the sanctuary at Shiloh (for the meaning of "cherubim," see 18:10).

All these phrases stress the caring closeness of God to his people. The picture of God "sitting upon the cherubim" may be highly anthropomorphic, but as Calvin comments, it is used so "that the faithful might not imagine him to be far from them; and consequently be perplexed with doubts and apprehension in approaching him." Thus in confidence the community makes its plea to God: "Give ear," listen, a word we hear near the beginning of many psalms (see 5:1), "shine forth" (see 50:2), a plea that the majesty of God in all his brilliance should be made visible to his people. In the words "stir up your might," it is as if they are making an appeal to a sleeping warrior to go into action, action which will lead to "salvation" (see 3:8), deliverance from all the oppressive forces which threaten their existence. Thus the way is prepared for the first occurrence of the refrain in verse 3.

4-6 In verses 4-6 we hear the lament, introduced by the characteristic "How long?" (cf. 79:5). It centers on unanswered prayer, unanswered because of God's anger. Literally, verse 4 reads "How long will you smoke against the prayers of your people." Normally the word "anger" is linked with the verb "smoke" in this expression (see 74:1). Here the verb "smoke" stands on its own, hence the REB translation "How long will you fume at your people's prayers?" The language here may be a conscious play upon what normally happened in the liturgy. Incense often accompanied prayer in the sanctuary (cf. 141:2; Ezek. 8:11). The fragrant smoke of the incense rising to God was the sign that God would accept the prayers of the people. But now another kind of smoke is rising, the sign that the people's prayers go unanswered. What had provoked God's rejection of his people's prayers we are not told. Unlike Psalm 79, this psalm has no note of confession or penitence. Were they asking for the wrong things, or was it that their conduct ensured that their prayers would not be answered (cf. Isa. 1:15)? Perhaps the people themselves did not know and were facing the same dilemma which troubles many people today, prayers unanswered for reasons they do not fully understand. All they knew was that life was harsh and painful. Tears were their daily diet, tears to drink "in full measure." This Hebrew word, literally "a third," occurs only here and in Isa. 40:12, where it is translated "a measure." The REB's rendering, "copious tears," catches its meaning here. They had become an object of "scorn" or derision to their neighbors. This translation follows the Syriac text. The Hebrew reads "strife," which might mean that the community had become a "bone of contention" in the eyes of neighbors quarreling over the spoils. Certainly they had become a laughingstock in the eyes of their enemies (v. 6b; cf. 79:4). In the depths of their despair, the refrain sounds again in verse 7.

8-13 Their despair is all the greater when they reflect on the story of Israel's past (vv. 8-13). That past is depicted in terms of Israel as a "vine," an image found elsewhere in the Old Testament (cf. Isa. 5:1-7; Ezek. 15:1-8). This was a vine, transplanted from Egypt into well-tilled soil cleared for that purpose, a vine that flourished, covering the hillsides, towering over the "mighty cedars" (literally, "the cedars of God"). Its branches and shoots reached as far as the "Sea," that is, the Mediterranean, and the "River," the Euphrates, the western and eastern boundaries of the empire of David at its zenith. But now the story is very different. The Midrash comments on verse 12, "Once a vineyard has been breached, everyone goes up into it and plunders it; so also everyone who rises up — Babylon, Media, Greece, Edom — plunders Israel. Come a ruler he plunders it, come a general he plunders it." Sadly, this was Israel's repeated experience. Those who ravage Israel are described in verse 13 as "the boar from the forest," a wild, unclean animal, and "all that move in the field," "all that move" being an attempted translation of a Hebrew word *ziz,* which occurs only here. It could refer to animals, but if it is onomatopoetic it more probably refers to buzzing, stinging insects who make life unbearable. In the Hebrew word for "forest," the middle letter is written above the line of the other letters. Although other suggestions have been offered, the likely reason for this is that given in the Talmud, namely, that this marks the middle letter in the Psalms, it being the custom of scribes to count the letters in a biblical text to check whether the tradition was being handed on accurately.

The unanswered "Why?" of verse 12 leads into the petitions in verses 14-18. The language in verse 14, "Turn again, O God," probably deliberately echoes the refrain, "turn" being a form of the same verb translated "restore" in the refrain. Restoration and the change it will bring to the fortunes of the nation are only possible if there is a change in God's attitude. He has the power; he is the "God of Hosts" (v. 14). Instead of being seemingly distant and uncaring, however, he needs to "look down from heaven and see." Seeing the plight of his ravaged vine (v. 16) will lead him to "have regard for" it. The verb translated "have regard" (REB: "tend") means to visit or confront either threateningly (cf. 59:5, where it is translated "punish") or graciously, as here. Punishment is to be reserved for those who have been cruelly responsible for Israel's plight (v. 16b). This section contains certain difficulties both textually and in interpretation. The word rendered "stock" in verse 15 occurs only here as a noun in the Hebrew Bible. The Greek (LXX) text reads instead a verb, and the line has been rendered "Take care of what your right hand has planted" (Dahood). Both the NRSV and the REB then omit the next line in the Hebrew text, which reads "upon the son you have made strong for yourself," regarding it, as many modern commentators do, as an addition culled from verse 17b. This seems unnecessary. What the line in this context does is to identify "the son" — and hence "the man of your right hand" and "the son of man" in verse 18 — with Israel, the vine. It is natural enough, of course, to read such language as referring to the king — compare Ps. 110:1, where God invites the king to "sit at my right hand," and the royal meaning of "son" in Psalm 2. Then it becomes possible to read this section in a future messianic sense as later Jewish and early Christian tradition did. In context, however, it is wiser to stick to the reference to Israel as the people of God. Calvin has no hesitation in considering the whole body of the Church as comprehended under the expression "the man of God's right hand" and the "son of man," thus continuing the community reference. When in John 15:1 Jesus declares "I am the true vine," he is claiming that he himself is the embodiment of all that is truly Israel, the new people of God which consists of those who are the fruitful branches of this vine.

Before the refrain is heard for the last time in verse 19, petition moves into a vow of renewed commitment (v. 18). The word translated "turn back" or "turn away" in verse 18 points to an attitude of faithlessness, rebellion, or apostasy from God (cf. 44:18; 78:57). Such an attitude is renounced. They are pledging themselvcs to be God's faithful people. As has been well said, the unanswered "Why?" of verse 12 is overcome "by a daring act of faith . . . the people of God renew their life from the hand of God in order to consecrate it anew to God" (A. Weiser). What the refrain in the psalm looks forward to — "that we may be saved" — always brings with it the call to a responsive obedience. Hence in the Decalogue the demanding words spring inevitably out of the prologue: "I am the LORD your God, who brought you out of the land of Egypt, out of the house of slavery" (Exod. 20:1). As 1 John succinctly puts it, "We love because he first loved us" (1 John 4:19).

Psalm 81
CELEBRATE AND OBEY

For "according to The Gittith" in the heading, see Psalm 8.

Like Psalms 50 and 95, this psalm finds its natural setting in the celebration of one of the great festivals of the Hebrew religious year. Although some of the material in it has links with the Exodus story central to the celebration of Passover, Jewish tradition has consistently and correctly associated it with the autumnal harvest thanksgiving festival of Tabernacles or Booths. In this festival the people are summoned to celebrate God's goodness in the abundant fruits of the earth and in the history of his people (cf. Lev. 23:33-44). The psalm was traditionally recited by the Levites in the temple on Thursdays. As the festival is celebrated in synagogue liturgies of the present day, the dominant theological notes are those of gratitude and responsibility.

1-5 The psalm begins with a call for the community to celebrate. The mood is one of unrestrained joy in which both voices and musical instruments have their part to play (see 33:1-3; 68:25). "Tambourines" were usually carried and played by women (see Exod. 15:20). The "trumpet" or ram's horn (v. 3) was not so much a musical instrument as the means which summoned the people to worship at the beginning of the festival, rather like church bells calling people to worship. The trumpet was sounded at the beginning of the seventh lunar month of Tishri, on the day of the "full moon" when the festival of Tabernacles began. This celebration was not something optional for the community. It was God's mandate, his "statute" (REB: "law"), his "ordinance," his "decree" (Hebrew *ʿēdût*, used in parallelism to "Torah" in 19:8). This is something God-given and demanded, to provide yearly shape and meaning to the life of the community. Every community needs to structure its life round such given occasions, be they religious (e.g., Easter and Christmas) or secular (the Fourth of July or Burns' Suppers). For Israel this was a profoundly religious occasion, celebrating the goodness of "the God of Jacob" (vv. 1 and 4; see 20:1), "when he went out over [or: against] the land of Egypt." Although the REB renders this phrase as "at the exodus from Egypt," it probably includes more than that, referring to the whole complex of events, including the plagues, that led up to the Exodus.

The word "Joseph" in verse 5 occurs in a lengthened form, "Jehoseph," found nowhere else in the Hebrew Bible but not uncommon in later Jewish writings. The Midrash saw in this form a reference to the divine name "Jah" and took the decree to refer to God's testifying for Joseph that he had not touched Potiphar's wife (cf. Genesis 39). If that sounds like pious speculation, more recent attempts to explain the form in terms of academic speculation are, on the whole, no more convincing. Although the use of the title "God of Jacob" and the reference to "Joseph" may point to this psalm having its roots in northern tradition, as many of the other Asaph psalms do, in its present form the psalm comes from the later exilic or postexilic period (see Psalm 80).

The closing line of verse 5, "I hear a voice I had not known," has provoked endless discussion across the centuries. The Greek (LXX) text reads "he" instead of "I," presumably making Joseph the subject, with "the voice he had not known" probably a reference to the giving of the Law at Mt. Sinai to Joseph's descendants who had come out of Egypt. The NEB translators were so uncertain what to do with this line that they simply omitted it. Should we link this line with what goes before it in verses 1-5?

In that case, the "I" is presumably Israel, forced to live in Egypt among a people with whom they could hold no communication in language (see Calvin), or Israel who through the Exodus came to a new name and a new understanding of God (cf. Exod. 3:13-15). It is usually assumed today, however, that the link is with the following verses and that the speaker, a Levitical priest, is claiming to be the mouthpiece of God. He is there to proclaim a message which is not his own, but which comes to him from God. This is then often linked, wrongly I believe (see below), with the words at the end of verse 10, "Open your mouth wide and I will fill it" (cf. Jer. 1:9). The "I" of verse 5, however, is most likely the preacher giving the divine warrant for his sermon, the content of which begins in verse 6, where the "I" is now God.

6-10 The sermon in verses 6-10 begins by stressing what God has done and continues to do for his people. There is no need to change the "his" before "shoulder" and "hand" in verse 6 to "your" (NRSV). Past and present join hands in this act of worship. Just as Deuteronomy claims "Not with our ancestors did the LORD make this covenant, but with all of us here alive today" (Deut. 5:3), so those present celebrate the Feast of Tabernacles as part of that Israel which was set free from captivity in Egypt, sharing with them the wonder of that deliverance and being placed under the same responsive obligation. It is this then-and-now which is symbolized by the movement from "his," Israel then, to "your," you who are present now. The same holds true for the use of "him" and "you" in verse 16, where the NRSV needlessly changes "him" to "you," and the REB omits the reference to "you" in the last line. Although the language is different, verse 6 summarizes the oppressive slave labor to which the Hebrews were subjected, as described graphically in Exodus 5.

In verse 7, the cry for help having been heard, deliverance comes through an encounter with God "in the secret place of thunder." This phrase, which occurs only here in the Hebrew Bible, probably points to the awesome, powerful, and mysterious coming of God to his people in the Exodus event and in the giving of the Law at Mt. Sinai (cf. Exod. 19:19; 20:18). The last line of verse 7, "I tested you at the waters of Meribah," has been thought to run counter to the traditions concerning Meribah in Exod. 17:7 and Num. 20:13, which state that it was the people who there tested God, the sign of their lack of trust in his provision for them. The psalm, however, does not necessarily imply a different tradition. In the Exodus narrative, for example, the people test God only after they have been put to the test, thirst-crazed in a waterless wilderness. Faced with this testing, they rebel and put God to the test. The "Selah" at the end of verse 7 (see 3:2) probably provides an opportunity for the worshippers to pause and reflect. It had been easy to trust God when he had been clearly delivering them from oppression, but a very different response had been evident when they were up against it (cf. Psalm 78).

This paves the way for the word of heart-broken rebuke, "Hear, O my people . . . if you would but listen to me!" (v. 8). The language is typical of Deuteronomy, which has close associations with the Levites. In particular it seems to echo Deut. 6:4, 5 — "Hear, O Israel: the LORD is our God, the LORD alone. You shall love the LORD with all your heart, and with all your soul, and with all your might." If only there were such true hearing. Their loyalty to "the LORD our God, the LORD alone" has been compromised. They needed to be reminded of the first demand in the Decalogue, "You shall have no other gods before me." Any other god is a "strange" (cf. 44:20) and "foreign," alien, god (cf. Deut. 34:12). Yet far more they need to be reminded of what lay behind this demand, namely, the gracious faithfulness of the God who had brought them out of Egypt. So the order of the Decalogue is here reversed. The all-important prologue now comes after the demand for exclusive loyalty, to remind them that there were, and are, very good grounds for the exclusive demand made upon them. The pathos is there, pointedly there, when even in the midst of bringing serious charges, God still addresses them as "O my people." The grace of this God shaped their past, and it is in the grace of God alone that their future lies.

"Open your mouth wide" (v. 10) is an unusual construction and hardly one which points to prophetic inspiration (see above). When followed by the preposition "against" (35:21; Isa. 57:4), it means to gloat over someone. Here there is no "against." The picture seems rather to be that of someone, perhaps like a young bird, open-mouthed and waiting to be fed. Place the psalm in the context of the Feast of Tabernacles, where the people would be surrounded by the evident signs of God's bounty at harvest time, and these words are a challenge to the community to put its continuing trust in the God who can provide for all its needs, material and spiritual.

11-16 When attention is focused on the people's response, however, the past is not reassuring. It is the story of a people who "did not listen," who did not "submit" or willingly yield their lives to God (v. 11). Indeed, they used their God-given freedom to follow the dictates of their "stubborn hearts," a phrase which occurs again and again in the book of Jeremiah (e.g., 9:13; 13:10), the prophet who more than any other had to wrestle with that sheer cussedness in human nature which led people to pursue their own ways rather than God's ways. But God's final word is not "If that's the way you want to play it, so be it." No, it is a continuing appeal: "O that my people would listen to me" (v. 13), a continuing appeal which believes that the future can be different. Then all who are bent on making life harsh and difficult for God's people, be they external or internal enemies, will be cut down to size and discover that their time is up. The word translated "doom" in verse 15 normally means "time," but it is time which indicates a crisis point in their life (vv. 14-15). The concluding verse (v. 16) seems to echo the Song of Moses in Deuteronomy 32, which speaks of God feeding Israel with "the produce of the field . . . honey from the crags" (Deut. 32:13), ample food provided from the cultivated land and from the otherwise barren, rocky slopes, home of the wild bees.

What is significant about this psalm in the context of the Feast of Tabernacles is the balance which it keeps between the goodness and the graciousness of God on the one hand, and the need for human response and the questions which the fickleness of that response raises on the other. It speaks of a dynamic relationship between God and his people, a relationship encapsulated in the words "O my people . . . if you would but listen!" Worship is celebration, but celebration should at the same time be an education into a deeper obedience, an education all the more necessary in the light of the failures we dare not forget. To give thanks for our religious heritage is to accept the responsibility of living by it, and to know that only by such living shall we find life in all its fullness.

Psalm 82
THE ULTIMATE TRIBUNAL

This brief Psalm has provoked endless discussion. Much of it has centered on how we should translate the opening verse. What is meant by "the divine council" (REB: "the court of heaven"), and who are the "gods" referred to in the second half of the verse? Traditionally, on the analogy of passages such as Exod. 21:6

and 22:9, the "gods" have been taken to be "judges," those responsible for upholding law and order in society. It is by no means certain, however, that the word "god" or "gods" bears this meaning in such passages. Others have argued that the "gods" refers to the rulers of the nations, kings hedged around with divinity. This has claimed support from the language of the lament over the king of Tyre in Ezek. 28:11-19. It has been used by those who wish to give a late date to the psalm, finding in it a reference to the deified kings of the Hellenistic age. For arguments which would support this identification with "rulers," see Psalm 58.

The language and structure of the psalm, however, seem to point to something more theologically daring. We know from Babylonian and Canaanite sources that in the polytheistic world in which Israel lived the various gods and goddesses met from time to time, often at the New Year, under the presidency of the supreme god — El, in Canaanite sources — to discuss issues of importance and to decide what was to happen on earth. We also know that the existence of such gods and goddesses had a continuing fascination for the people of Israel. Prophet after prophet accuses the people of participating in the worship of such deities (e.g., Hosea 2; Jer. 2:9-11). When Jeremiah was forced to go to Egypt after the downfall of the Judean state, he found himself faced with people who traced all their troubles to the fact that they had ceased worshipping the "queen of heaven" (Jer. 44:15-28). To say "You shall have no other gods before me" (Exod. 20:3) enshrined the demand for an exclusive loyalty to the LORD, but it was often ignored. It left unanswered questions about the very existence and attractiveness of such gods. This psalm seeks to face and answer such questions.

The scene, which has certain similarities with Micaiah's vision in 2 Kings 22 and with Job 1–2, is dramatically sketched in the opening verse. "God," that is, the God of Hebrew faith, is depicted as presiding at a meeting of "the divine council." He presides as supreme judge to bring charges against (v. 2) and finally to pass sentence upon other gods (vv. 6-7). The phrase "How long?" which we have heard frequently in the psalms of lament (e.g., 13:1-2; 74:10), here introduces the charge that such gods "judge unjustly" (v. 2). Over against this stands the description of the LORD in Deut. 32:4 as "a faithful God without deceit, just and upright is he," where the word translated "deceit" is the same word translated "unjustly" in verse 2. The essence of such corrupt judgment is the showing of "partiality to the wicked," something repeatedly condemned in the Hebrew Bible (e.g., Deut. 16:18-19; Lev. 19:15). Responsible justice must be, and must be seen to be, evenhanded. It must not be open to the wicked to pervert the course of justice by using their power or influence to bribe the judiciary.

That is the charge. Over against it, God spells out in verses 3-4 what was supposed to have been the role of the gods, to display that kind of justice and righteousness which has a primary concern to protect "the weak and the needy" (v. 4; see 9:12; cf. 72:4, 12-14; Job 29:12-16), those most at risk in society, "the orphan . . . the lowly and the destitute" (v. 3). It has been argued that verse 5 continues God's speech, further describing the helpless plight of those on the receiving end of such injustice. Unable to understand what is happening to them, they are forced to live "in darkness," their life and their world undermined. It is more likely, however, that God's charge sheet ends at verse 4 and that in verse 5 we are listening to the comment of the narrator who set the scene in verse 1. He now adds his own pointed comment about such gods, claiming that they are clueless, wandering around in darkness as if they had never emerged from chaos into the light which brought order and meaning into the world (cf. Gen. 1:3).

The psalmist is here hacking his way through a theological jungle. The charge against these other gods is not that they fail to fulfill what their worshippers expect from them, for example, the provision of abundant harvests and the protection of their own people against all their enemies. The charge and the comment cut more deeply. No gods are worthy of the name unless they are passionately concerned to maintain that justice and righteousness which seek to respond to all according to their need. Mere power or status is irrelevant; what counts is how such power and status are used. Indeed, the psalm goes further to claim that the gods themselves are to be held responsible for their failure at this point. Since the LORD, the God of Israel, is not responsible for such misuse of power with its consequent evil, it is these other gods who must accept responsibility for the evil on earth. In order to safeguard the character of the one true God, a tentative step is here being taken along the road that in later biblical and postbiblical texts is to lead to the development of the concept of Satan and other demonic powers and that continues in Christian theology in the figure of the devil. Whether this is a convincing approach to the problem of evil in the world is another issue.

The charge having been made in verses 3-4, judgment is now pronounced by God in verses 6-7, which says in effect that these gods are no gods. Stripped of their divine status, they face the stark human fate of death. This runs counter to much mythological thinking in the ancient Near East. The distinction between the human race, even its most powerful people, and the gods is drawn at precisely this point. When in Babylonian mythology the hero Gilgamesh, distraught by the death of his companion Enkidu, goes in search of the secret of eternal life, he is warned by his hostess at an inn that this search is futile: "When the gods created mankind, they set death apart for mankind, life in their own hands retaining." Gods might indeed die in bloody conflict with other gods, but by definition gods did not drink of the cup of mortality. Such gods might be called "sons of the Most High" (v. 6; see 7:17), but here they suffer a most ungodlike fate. They shall "die like mortals" (Hebrew *'ādām;* see 8:4), and "fall," probably go down into Sheol, the abode of the dead (see 6:5), "like any prince" (v. 7). It may be that *'ādām* and "prince" are used in this verse to indicate the whole human race, commoner and potentate alike. The reference to *'ādām,* however, may be pointing us to the story in Genesis 2–3 of *'ādām*'s challenge to the sovereignty of God and his subsequent expulsion from the garden to face inevitable death. If so, then the gods are regarded as no better than *'ādām,* because of their failure to promote justice, and thus share a like fate. Shakespeare's words vividly underline the ultimate frailty of all human power:

> . . . for within the hollow crown
> That rounds the mortal temples of a king
> Keeps Death his court, and there the antick sits,
> Scoffing his state and grinning at his pomp. (*King Richard II,* 3.2.160-63)

The same Death is now to keep court among the gods, scoffing their state and grinning at their pomp.

There is only one exception to this. The psalm ends with a prayer (v. 8) to the one true God to "Rise up" (see 3:7), to go into action to establish his authority over all the earth and to claim all nations as his rightful patrimony.

It is important not to try to make this psalm answer theological questions which do not come within its horizon. We must see it in its context. It may well come from an early period in Israel's life, when the all too seductive attractiveness of the worship of other gods was making inroads into the consciousness of many people in Israel. It is concerned to assert the uniqueness of the LORD, the God of Israel, and to dismiss on ethical grounds the claims, indeed the reality, of other gods. Nor is it concerned solely with what it perceives to be going on in the heavenly realm. What happens on earth is a reflection of what the gods decide. Therefore, the charge against the gods is a charge directed against anyone in a position of power or influence in society, against anyone who indeed claims to worship God. The prophet Micah asks the question, "What does the LORD require?" He cuts through much of what was regarded as important in divine and human terms, to say concerning Israel's God:

> He has told you, O mortal, what is good;
> and what does the LORD require of you
> but to do justice, and to love kindness,
> and to walk humbly with your God? (Mic. 6:8)

Throughout the mythological cast of this psalm, there runs one of the basic convictions of Israel's faith. Although life may be marred by injustice and oppression and may face us with experiences hard to understand, there is at the heart of life a God of righteousness whose purposes must and will triumph. This is a faith to which the New Testament adds its own dimension in the cross and the resurrection, and in that final vision of a new heaven and a new earth to which the book of Revelation bears witness. That vision, like this psalm, ends in prayer, with the words "Come, Lord Jesus" on the believer's lips (Rev. 22:20).

Psalm 83
PRAYER FOR THE HOUR OF CRISIS

This is the last of the Asaph Psalms. It is in many respects a typical community lament. Like certain such laments (e.g., Psalms 44; 74), it attributes the crisis facing the community solely to external forces that threaten to exterminate the people of God.

1 The psalm begins with an urgent cry to God (v. 1), similar in mood to the opening of Psalm 28 (cf. 35:21). It pleads with God no longer to remain aloof, but to take action. Here is a situation crying out for God's intervention, the implication being that if he does not intervene he is either powerless or indifferent.

2-8 Verses 2-8 describe the threat to the community, beginning in very general terms (vv. 2-5) before identifying specific enemies in verses 6-8. The psalmist is in no doubt that the "enemies" are challenging God. They are "your enemies" (v. 2); their attack is against "your people" (v. 3), against "those you protect" (v. 3), or perhaps better "those whom you treasure" (so REB) — cf. Ezek. 7:22, where the word describes the temple as God's "treasured place." Indeed, the attack is "against you" (v. 5). As in 46:7 the enemies are described as being "in uproar" (v. 2, REB), arrogantly defiant (cf. Judg. 8:28 for this meaning of "raised their heads"), plotting, secretly conspiring (v. 3), intent on exterminating Israel (v. 4), making common cause against God (v. 5; for "covenant," see 25:10).

It is when we come to the roll call of those committed to this hostile alliance that problems begin. Some of the names are well known in the Old Testament. From the Gulf of Aqaba northwards, we have in turn, in the territory east of the Jordan, Edom, Moab, and Ammon (vv. 6-7). The "Ishmaelites," the descendants of Abraham through Hagar according to Gen. 25:12-18, never seem to have had well-defined territorial status and were probably nomadic or seminomadic tribes in the northern Arabian peninsula. The "Hagrites," whose name suggests another possible link with Hagar, appear elsewhere in Chronicles as a tribal group east of the Jordan (1 Chron. 5:10-23). "Gebal" has been identified with Byblos north of Beirut, the land of the Gebalites in Josh. 13:5 being linked with Lebanon. Many modern commentators, however, wish to transfer it to the south and link it with Edom and Moab. The Amalekites often constituted a threat to the southern borders of Judah (e.g., 1 Samuel 30). The reference to the Philistines "with the inhabitants of Tyre" takes us up the Mediterranean coastal plain to the important Phoenician trading city of Tyre, which had friendly links with Israel during the time of David and Solomon (e.g., 2 Sam. 5:11; 1 Kgs. 9:10-14), but which later came under the lash of prophetic attack (cf. Amos 1:9; Ezekiel 26–28). The picture so far is of an alliance which threatens Israel from the east, the south, and the west. The circle is closed by the reference to "Assyria" (v. 8), which posed a constant threat from the north to the small states of the Middle East, including Israel and Judah, from early in the ninth century BCE until it was replaced by the neo-Babylonian empire towards the end of the seventh century. Assyria is here described as "the strong arm of the children of Lot," that is, the powerhouse behind Ammon and Moab, sons of Lot through his incestuous relationship with his daughters according to Gen. 19:30-38 (cf. Deut. 2:9, 19). The Assyrians were skilled at playing off some of the small states of the Middle East against each other. The problem with this list of ten names, however, is that there is no known incident in the Hebrew Bible corresponding to such an alliance against Israel. It reads like a composite list of enemies who, on various occasions, threatened the future of the people of God, a list which probably had its origin in pre-exilic times since there is no mention of Babylon. This is not the language of history but of liturgy — or rather of history adapted for liturgical purposes. It enables the congregation to recall many of the traditional enemies of the people and reminds them that the particular crisis situation they now face is nothing new. It was ever thus. Worship relives the past to speak to the present.

9-18 The second half of the psalm, verses 9-18, consists of a series of petitions asking God to act decisively and in judgment against those who threaten the future of his people. There is a harshness and a vengeful bitterness in the language of this section that we have had occasion to note in other laments (see 5:10). The bitterness may have its roots in the fact that nowhere in the psalm is there any sign of the community accepting any personal responsibility for what has happened — no confession, no penitence. All responsibility is laid at the door of the enemies. A prophet, equally convinced that Israel was the people of God, would sound a different note. Amos has no hesitation in pronouncing God's judgment on other nations, but he has a searching word to say to Israel: "You only have I known of all the families of the earth; therefore I will punish you for all your iniquities" (Amos 3:2). It is important, however, to bring to the language of this psalm neither indignant condemnation nor facile acceptance, but understanding. As verses 9-12 clearly indicate, this language and attitude are rooted in a tradition of faith that looks back to the way in which God has dealt with such enemies in the past.

The order of events described in verses 9-11 has led to problems, with many modern scholars accepting a reordering of the text and the alteration of En-dor to En-harod in verse 10 (cf. REB). This seems unnecessary. Verse 9 deals with two crisis situations from the past, one involving the Midianites in the time of Gideon (cf. Judges 7–8) and the other involving a northern coalition under Sisera and Jabin as described in Judges 4–5. Verse 10 then recounts the disaster which befell this Canaanite coalition. Although "En-dor" does not feature in Judges 4–5, it is mentioned alongside Taanach in Josh. 17:11, and Taanach was the site of the decisive battle against the Canaanite alliance according to Judg. 5:19.

En-dor may therefore be regarded as an appropriate scene for rotting corpses lying unburied in the aftermath of the battle. Verse 11 then returns to the fate of the commanders of the Midianite forces (cf. Judg. 7:25; 8:21). Thus verses 9-11 provide us with a neat "a b b a" order. The crime of these past enemies is summarized in verse 12 as the attempt to abrogate to themselves "the pastures of God," that is, the territory given by God to his people.

From the past the psalm now turns to the present, to call upon God to act now as he so evidently had done in the past. Although the opening petition "O my God" of verse 13 is often taken to indicate that we are now listening to the voice of whoever is leading the congregational worship, such a cry would be equally at home on the lips of anyone sharing in the act of worship. The God-decreed fate of the enemies is described in imagery drawn from the destructive forces in nature in verses 13-15 — the violent "whirlwind" (cf. 77:18) carrying everything before it, the wind whisking away the chaff (cf. Isa. 17:13), fire devastating the forest-clad mountainside, the "tempest" and "hurricane" arousing inescapable terror. All of this language is often associated with God's coming in power and judgment.

The psalm then calls upon God to strip these enemies of their arrogant pretensions and to ensure that they themselves experience what they no doubt hoped to inflict upon God's people: shame, humiliation, and a dishonorable end (cf. 40:15; 71:24). But what of the words in verse 16, "so that they may seek your name, O LORD"? Are these words holding out hope that such enemies, duly ashamed, will repent and turn to acknowledge the one true God? In context this seems unlikely. This, says Calvin, means "nothing more than a forced and slavish submission like that of Pharaoh of Egypt," a reluctant recognition that there is a power apparently greater than their own, namely, the LORD who alone is worthy of the title "the Most High" (see 7:17). His authority is not confined to Israel, but embraces the whole world. Thus the psalm ends in celebrating the power and glory of God, demonstrated in the past, embracing the present and any crisis the people may be called upon to face.

Christian commentators across the centuries have sought to counter the harshness of this psalm by spiritualizing it in such a way that the psalmist, surrounded by enemies, becomes a type of Christ on the cross. Given this interpretation, the psalm has found a place in certain Good Friday liturgies. The words "Fill their faces with shame. . . . Let them perish in disgrace" (vv. 16-17), however, issue from a different spirit from that of the words from the cross, "Father, forgive them; for they do not know what they are doing" (Luke 23:34). The psalmist is convinced that those who threatened to exterminate the people of God knew only too well what they were doing, and he has no desire to forgive. There are times when, humanly speaking, such forgiveness seems impossible. At the ceremony commemorating the fiftieth anniversary of the liberation of Auschwitz, symbol of the inconceivable horror of the Holocaust, Elie Wiesel, himself a survivor of Auschwitz, could only offer on behalf of the Jewish community a prayer in which he called upon the God of mercy *not* to forgive those who had perpetrated such bestiality. The psalmist would have understood.

Psalm 84
A PILGRIM'S JOYFUL WITNESS

For the superscription "according to The Gittith," see the heading to Psalm 8, and for "the Korahites," see heading to Psalm 42.

Psalm 84 is one of several psalms that speak movingly of the place which the temple had in the spiritual life of people of faith in ancient Israel. It witnesses to the joy and fulfillment experienced through worship in the temple courts (cf. Psalms 27; 42; 124; 137). Whatever the origin of this psalm — whether, for example, in its original form it can be traced back to some northern shrine (see Psalm 42) — in its present form it speaks of the temple on Mt. Zion in Jerusalem. There are several interesting features in the language of this psalm. Three times God is addressed as "LORD of Hosts" (vv. 1, 3, 12), once as "LORD God of Hosts" (v. 8; for the meaning of this title, see 24:10). This is also the only psalm in which the word "happy" (see 1:1) occurs three times (vv. 4, 5, 12).

1-4 These verses speak of a deep longing. The opening words, "How lovely," are probably better rendered in the REB as "How dearly loved." This is not merely the loveliness of outward appearance or aesthetic charm, but a heartfelt loveliness born out of personal commitment. The word appears in the heading to Psalm 45, the psalm for a royal wedding, and is there translated "a love song" (cf. 60:5). There is a love relationship between the psalmist and the temple. Just as a lover separated from his beloved will give voice to his ardent longing, so the psalmist's longing to be in the temple courts pulsates through every fiber of his being — "my soul" (see 6:3), "my heart and my flesh" (see 73:26) — and leads him to "sing for joy" (v. 2). This is a translation of a verb which means basically "to cry out." In the Psalms it usually means to cry out in praise of God, hence "sing for joy" (cf. 5:11; 64:10), but the corresponding noun can also mean an urgent cry for help (cf. 17:1). Here it expresses a longing which the psalmist can no longer contain, a longing which has to be poured out to "the living God" (see 42:2). Why, he exclaims, even the birds, "sparrow" and "swallow," find a safe place to nest "at [REB: beside] your altars," the altars probably being the large altar for the burnt offerings in front of the temple building (cf. Exod. 27:1-8) and the smaller altar for incense before the holy of holies (cf. Exod. 30:1-10). They are safely at home in the nooks and crannies of the temple courts and its buildings. The psalmist is here envying this privilege they have of being close to the one whom he calls "my King and my God" (v. 3), a phrase which emphasizes both the awesome majesty and gracious presence of God (see 5:2). If the birds are thus privileged, what can be said about the priests and the temple officials? Their life can only be that rewarding and "happy" life cradled in the nearness of God and daily celebrated in joyful worship.

5-7 The next three verses speak of the pilgrim journey to Jerusalem and the happiness which fills the hearts of the pilgrims. The pilgrims are described in verse 5 as those whose "strength" is in God (cf. 46:1), an inner strength focused on "the highways to Zion." The words "to Zion," however, are not in the Hebrew text. The word translated "highways" usually indicates a public road across the country (cf. Isa. 40:3) and therefore here indicates the roads along which the pilgrims traveled from their hometowns and villages as they made their way up to Jerusalem (REB: "pilgrim ways"). The verb related to this noun, however, is used in Ps. 68:4 of lifting up a song. It is therefore possible that the word here means "songs." In this case what we are being given in verse 5 is the picture of singing pilgrims, that "happy band of pilgrims" of John Mason Neale's hymn.

The journey has its difficulties, as does the text of verse 6. The pilgrims have to journey through the "valley of Baca." If "Baca" is a place name, we have no clue as to its identity, since there is no other mention of such a place in the Hebrew Bible. In 2 Sam. 5:23 the word seems to indicate a type of tree, translated "balsam" (NRSV) or "aspen" (REB). The word is similar in sound to the verb "to weep," hence the "vale of weeping," a translation which goes back to the Greek (LXX) rendering. It has also been argued that it means a parched or arid place (REB: "the waterless valley"). Calvin, indeed, took this "vale of weeping" to mean a dry and barren desert. Context suggests a difficult journey through a barren, waterless landscape, which the pilgrims transform in their thoughts into a place of bubbling water (v. 6). Such is the power of their faith. Instead of "they," however, in verse 6 some manuscripts read "he," that is, God; hence the REB translates "the LORD fills it with springs," by sending the early rain to cover it with pools. The traditional reading of the word here translated "pools" is "blessings." There may be a deliberate play on these similar-sounding words, the rain-filled "pools" being the "blessings" needed by the pilgrims as they journey across the arid landscape. What is clear is that, given the expectations and the faith in the hearts of the pilgrims, the difficulties of the journey pale into insignificance as they think of the goal that awaits them. As they approach Jerusalem they go "from strength to strength," their morale and confidence increasing since they know that "the God of gods," the one and only true God, will reveal himself to them in Zion (see 2:6). The word here translated "strength" is a different word from that in verse 1. It can also mean a wall, hence the REB's rendering, "from outer wall to inner." In this case the verse pictures the pilgrims, having reached Jerusalem, making their way from the outer to the inner courts of the temple precincts. Whatever translation we follow, this is a pilgrimage which finds its climax in a deeply spiritual experience, as the pilgrims share in worship and are gripped by the presence of God in the temple on Mt. Zion.

8-9 It is natural enough that on reaching the temple the pilgrim's response is that of prayer (vv. 8-9), prayer not for himself, but for the one whom he describes as "our shield" and "your anointed." Since the setting for this psalm seems to be the Jerusalem temple prior to the exile, the words "your anointed" (see 2:2) must refer to the king, and this suggests that the pilgrimage was to one of the great festivals of the religious year in which the king played a prominent part. But king and people cannot be separated; "your anointed" is "our shield" (see 3:3), the fortunes of the people being intimately bound up with the character of the king (see Psalm 72). The pilgrim is there as part of the congregation. His prayer embraces the entire life of the nation. As a modern Jewish prayer book puts it:

> A community at worship is a society declaring its devotion to God, a community forged by faith in God. Here is an experience which can deepen the society spirit and strengthen the bond of sympathy between men and women. If in public worship I realize that my prayers are also the prayers of the person by my side, it will make us more effectively aware of our common humanity and implant a spirit which will be potent for social good. Those who worship God together bring God into their mutual relations. (*Siddur Lev Chadash*, p. 7)

10-12 The psalm ends by describing a longing fulfilled. In the light of being there in the temple, all else pales into insignificance. A day there is better than a thousand anywhere else. The word "elsewhere" does not occur in the Hebrew text of verse 10. The REB's rendering, "at home," follows a commonly accepted emendation of the word at the beginning of the next line, translated in the NRSV as "I would rather." This makes little difference, however, to the overall meaning of the verse. Being there "at the threshold" of the temple (the REB gives a better translation than the NRSV's "doorkeeper," which usually denotes a position of some status in the temple) is preferable to all that is on offer in "the tents of wickedness," that is, amid the spoils of ill-gotten gains. This psalmist's priorities are rooted in his experience of the LORD, who is "a sun and a shield" (v. 11). This is the only place in the Hebrew Bible where the word "sun" is used to describe God, probably because of its associations with the sun god in Egypt and other ancient Near Eastern cultures. "Sun" here points to all that God freely bestows upon his people, while "shield," echoing verse 9, indicates all the protection he offers. All of this is summed up in the words "favor and honor." The word translated "favor" does not occur frequently in the Psalms, but the related verb "to be gracious" occurs again and again (see 4:2). It points to what is given beyond all deserving, given because of the gracious character of the God who responds to those in need. "Honor" or glory (see 3:3) describes people's standing in the community, that which gives them their true value. Thus, through the grace of God, life for the psalmist finds its true meaning and value. He believes that God gives generously, "withholds no good thing" from those who "walk uprightly" (see 15:2). These words acknowledge that there is a challenge at the heart of all true worship, a challenge underlined in Jer. 5:25, where the prophet stresses that there are good things that God wishes to give to his people, but that his people are not always able to receive: "your sins have deprived you of good things." Jesus takes this one step farther when he invites his disciples to ask, to seek, and to knock, knowing that "If you, bad as you are, know how to give good things to your children, how much more will your heavenly Father give the Holy Spirit to those who ask him" (Luke 11:13). The "good things" which the psalmist believes the LORD gives are not merely quantifiable in material terms. They are the fruit of a relationship with the living God, a relationship which affects all life's values and which is open to all who seek him in worship.

The psalm ends with the longing of verse 1 fulfilled for "everyone who trusts in you" (see 4:5), those who in response to God's grace commit their lives confidently into God's hands. It is appropriate that this psalm finds its place in Jewish liturgy in the Sabbath evening service. It should leave us asking many questions about our own attitude to worship. Where does it come in our priorities in life? What do we expect to receive in and through worship? What does it demand from us? The psalmist knew the answer to these questions, and his answers are worth pondering.

Psalm 85
LIVING WITH HOPE

This psalm falls naturally into three parts: verses 1-3, which recall God's past goodness to his people; verses 4-7, which contain an urgent plea for present help; and verses 8-13, which focus on God's answer to that plea. The relationship between these three sections, and the most natural setting for them, have been much discussed. There are those who argue that the original setting is the liturgy of one of the great preexilic festivals of the Hebrew religious year, probably the Feast of Tabernacles. There the community recalled and relived the story of God's past mighty acts, laid before him present needs, and experienced his saving presence. Others have argued that the psalm is essentially a national lament, springing originally out of a specific set of historical circumstances. Some, including Calvin, have argued that the background is the Maccabean period and the persecution under Antiochus Epiphanes. The most favored setting, however, is that of the postexilic community, which had returned home with high hopes, buoyed by that vision of a new life and a new Jerusalem in Isaiah 40–55, only to find that the reality was very different. Vision gave way to disappointment. God's goodness was swallowed up in the harsh drudgery and the daunting problems of daily life. We can sense some of this in Isaiah 56–66. The arguments are finely balanced, but hardly affect the central theological thrust of the psalm, which has haunted people of faith in all generations. How do we continue to live with hope, trusting in God, in a world in which there is so much that seems cruelly meaningless? Perhaps if we have never felt the cutting edge of such a question, we have still to discover what a lasting and realistic faith means.

1-3 The opening verses look to the past. Here is the story of a gracious God who had looked with favor on the land that was his gift to his people, the God who "restored the fortunes of Jacob" (for "Jacob," see 20:1). The phrase "restored the fortunes" points to any experience of rehabilitation from oppressive circumstances (see 14:7). The editors of the Hebrew text wished to interpret it to mean "restored [or "brought back"] the captivity," a reference to the return from exile. Without any change, the text could in fact mean that. More generally, however, it depicts any set of circumstances in which a bruised and broken community needed healing (cf. Hos. 7:1). The REB translation, "turned the tide of Jacob's fortunes," has the merit of drawing attention to the fact that the phrase contains the first of four occurrences of the Hebrew verb "turn" *(šûb)* in verses 1 6. It is translated "turn" in verse 3, "restore" in verse 4, and "again" in verse 6. Such restoration or healing, however, did not take place purely on a material level. It implied the restoration of the relationship between God and his people, which had been put in jeopardy by the people's failings. Hence the past had to be the story of forgiveness and pardon (for the language of verse 2, see 32:1) and the withdrawal of the "wrath" and burning "anger" of God (see 6:1; 74:1).

4-7 The next set of verses turns the assurance drawn from God's past graciousness into an urgent plea for similar restoration in the crisis of the present (cf. the refrain in Psalm 80). It is a plea that appeals to the known character of God summed up in two of the great recurring theological words in the Psalms, "salvation," which frames this section in verses 4 and 7 (see 3:2), and "steadfast love" (see 5:7), that bedrock upon which the nation's very existence depended. The plea, therefore, is for God to put aside his "indignation," a word used of God only here in the Psalms, though the verb is used in 78:59 to describe how the people "provoked" God to anger. Provocation in plenty there may have been, but how does God's steadfast love respond to it? The prayer in which the plea is couched then takes the form of a series of questions in verses 5-6 that assume that the present crisis cannot be God's final word to his people. The questions in verse 5 are typical of the community laments (cf. 74:1; 79:5). The anger of God has brought the community to the brink of death. They look for their life to be renewed in order that they may again "rejoice" in the restoration of their relationship with God (v. 6). Throughout this section we are listening to that personal dialogue which is of the essence of prayer. Notice how the words "us," "our," "you," and "your" leap out of the text again and again. It is also carefully constructed thematically, with verse 4 sounding the twin notes of "salvation" and "indignation," and verses 5-7 leading from "anger" back to "salvation."

8-13 If the present crisis is not God's final word, what is his word for his oppressed people? It is this we now hear in verses 8-13. It is a message summed up in one word rich in meaning, *shalom,* "peace" (v. 8; see 4:8; 29:11). But when verse 8 begins "Let me hear . . . ," who is speaking, and how does this message of *shalom* come to him? It is often assumed that we are here listening to the words of a temple prophet or priest who claims to be receiving this message through some kind of oracle or revelation. It is, however, equally likely that we are still listening to the psalmist, who now has a word to share with his fellow worshippers based on meditation and reflection on the past, which speaks to him of God's salvation and steadfast love. He believes this word to be equally relevant to the present. It is a message for those who keep holding on to God, "his faithful" (v. 8; see 4:3). Although the NRSV in the closing words of verse 8 follows the Greek (LXX) text and renders "to those who turn to him in their hearts," thus further explaining "his faithful," the REB, rightly I believe, retains the Hebrew text and reads "let them not go back to foolish ways." It was evidently such folly, provoking God's anger, that led to the present crisis in the nation's life. To that there must be no return. This is a warning, neatly placed between the description of the people as "his faithful" (v. 8) and "those who fear him" (v. 9; see 19:9). As Psalm 1 reminds us, life confronts us with continuing choice of saying "Yes" to God and his ways or of flirting with the folly of saying "No."

Psalm 24 celebrated the coming to his people of the God who is "the king of glory" (for "glory," see 3:3). Such "glory," now promised to his faithful people in verse 9, is personified in verse 10 in four familiar words that gather in harmony as attendants round the king of glory — "steadfast love" (see 5:7), "faithfulness" (see 25:5), "righteousness" (see 4:1), and "peace" (*shalom;* see 4:8), ready to act in God's service to fulfill his purposes. "Steadfast love" and "peace" have already made their appearance in the psalm in verses 7 and 8; "faithfulness" and "righteousness" take their second bow, as it were, in verse 11 in language reminiscent of the poetic vision of a new beginning for God's people in Isa. 45:8,

> Shower, O heavens, from above,
>   and let the skies rain down righteousness;
> let the earth open, that salvation may spring up,
>   and let it cause righteousness to sprout up also;
>   I the LORD have created it.

The twin aspects of this vision are summarized in the concluding verses 12 and 13: the land enjoys the God-given goodness of prosperity, symbolized by the fruitful harvest; through the land "righteousness" will go as the herald of God's presence among his people. Although the text in the last line has its difficulties, there is little reason to follow the REB in its reading "and peace on the path he treads."

Such is the hope held out to God's people living in dark and depressing times. It is hope kindled and sustained by worship, which draws on the past, brings its proven certainties into the questioning present, and then points to a future that, like past and present, belongs to God. This is what worship still offers us now; it points us toward the ultimate hope of a new heaven and new earth, where God himself will forever be with his people and "death shall be no more; mourning and crying and pain will be no more" (Rev. 21:4).

Psalm 86
A MODEL PRAYER

It is not clear why this psalm, with its heading "A Prayer of David" (see 17:1), should occur in the middle of a series of psalms all associated with the sons of Korah (Psalms 84–85; 87–88). Throughout the psalm there are many echoes of other psalms and indeed quotations from other parts of the Old Testament, notably the Torah. The psalm seems to be steeped in and drawing upon a common liturgical heritage. Yet this does not mean that it is merely an unthinking copy of earlier material. True spirituality always draws upon the tradition in which it has been nurtured to explore its own faith and needs. Indeed, the psalm displays some distinctive literary characteristics that give it a peculiar nuance all of its own and that encapsulate much of its theology. Here we may mention three such features.

First, in this psalm we hear fourteen times a direct plea to God, beginning with "Incline your ear, O LORD, and answer me" (v. 1) and ending with "Show me a sign of your favor" (v. 17).

Second, throughout the psalm the one to whom the psalmist prays is frequently addressed as "master" or "sovereign" (Hebrew 'adonai), rendered in the NRSV as "O Lord" (vv. 3, 4, 5, 8, 9, 12, 15) and to be clearly distinguished from the divine name rendered "LORD" in verses 1, 6, 11, and 17. It is in keeping with this approach to one who is thought of as master that the psalmist describes himself as "your servant" (vv. 4, 16) and "the child of your serving girl" (v. 16), that is, a child born to a woman already a slave in the household. This is a recognition by the psalmist of his humble status before God, which is the essence of an authentic prayerful attitude.

Third, the Hebrew word *ki,* translated "for," is frequently heard introducing some of the major themes of the psalm. In verses 1 and 2, this word highlights the situation of the psalmist: "for I am poor and needy" (see 9:2); "for I am devoted to you" as one of your faithful people (Hebrew *ḥasîd;* see 4:3). In verses 3 and 4, the words "for to you" point to the source of the psalmist's confidence, the master to whom he makes his appeal. In verses 5, 10, and 13, it underlines the character of God: "For you, O LORD, are good and forgiving" (v. 5); "For you are great and do wondrous things" (v. 10); "For great is your steadfast love toward me" (v. 13), thus stressing what alone makes the psalmist's prayer reasonable and responsible. There is no use praying unless you believe that you are praying to one who has the power to answer and is willing and concerned to answer.

1-7 In typical lament style, the opening section of the psalm makes a repeated appeal for God to hear and answer the cry of one who faces a crisis situation in his life. It is not until we come to the closing section of the psalm in verses 14-17 that we are given any precise indication of the nature of this trouble. The language of this opening section reads almost like a roll call of pleas from other such psalms: "Incline your ear" (v. 1; cf. 17:1), "answer me" (v. 1; cf. 4:1), "save" (v. 3; cf. 3:2), "be gracious" (v. 3; cf. 4:1), "give ear . . . listen" (v. 6; cf. 17:1). What the psalmist prays for is deliverance from a life-threatening situation (v. 2). His prayer has two foci: who he is and who God is. He describes himself as a humble yet faithful servant in need, one who "trusts in you" (see 4:5). He therefore responds to the crisis threatening him by pouring out his concern to God (vv. 4-5) in the hope that the present darkness will be replaced by the dawn of a new, joyful day. The God to whom he makes his plea is "my God" (v. 3), master, yes, but a caring and forgiving master, generous in his "steadfast love" (v. 5; see 5:7), words which echo Exod. 34:6 and Num. 14:18 and which anticipate the quotation from Exod. 34:6 in a similar context in verse 15. Given the character of the two participants in this prayer dialogue, the psalmist has no doubt about its outcome. The plea in verse 1, "answer me," is a plea made in faith and in the conviction with which the section ends, "for you will answer me" (v. 7).

8-10 The certainty expressed in these closing words of verse 7 paves the way for the celebration of the awesome uniqueness and power of God in verses 8-10 (cf. 74:12-17, and for parallels to the language of this section, cf. 22:27-28; 77:13-14). Here again the opening words of the section are echoed in its closing words; "There is none like you among the gods, O Lord" (v. 8) — "you alone are God" (v. 10). There is the same openness here to talk about other gods as in Psalm 82, and to use such talk as a foil to underline the incomparable greatness of Israel's God. This is the God whose power is universal and will, one day, be acknowledged to be so (v. 10). This is the God who does "wondrous things" (see 9:2) that evoke from his people a gasp of amazement since they go beyond all that they expected or believed to be possible. We shall never understand either the Hebrew Bible or the New Testament unless we recognize that surprise and wonder lie close to the heart of the faith to which both bear witness. The Church is called, in Peter's words, to bear continuing witness to "the mighty acts of him who called you out of darkness into his marvelous light" (1 Pet. 2:9).

11-13 The psalmist's response to this celebration is twofold. First, faced with the incomparable majesty of God, he is acutely conscious of his own inadequacy. One of the faithful, trusting in God he may be, but he still needs to be taught (v. 11) to walk in God's way, the way of "your truth" or perhaps "in faithfulness to you," the word translated "truth" (see 25:5) being the same as the word describing God's faithfulness in verse 15. For that he needs "an undivided heart" (literally, "united in heart"), the only occurrence of the verb "to unite" in this form in the Hebrew Bible. The Greek (LXX) reads a similar-sounding word from the verb "to rejoice." He needs the antithesis of what is deplored in Psalm 12, where the faithful have disappeared from the land to be replaced by people who have "duplicity in their heart" (REB, 12:2). Faithfulness and obedience are not once given; they need constantly to be worked out, relived day by day by those here described as "those who revere your name" (see 34:7, 9; 5:11).

Second, celebration also leads to a vow of thanksgiving that expresses itself in the psalmist honoring God with all his heart or will (v. 12). Such thanksgiving springs out of the psalmist's experience of the "steadfast love" of God (see 5:7), which convinces him that God will deliver him "from the depths of Sheol" (see 6:5), that is, from the life-threatening situation he faces. In context it is better to translate in verse 13, "you will deliver my soul," an expression of future certainty, rather than "you have delivered," since the following section describes the still unresolved crisis in the psalmist's life.

14-17 The concluding verses of the psalm echo the opening section in verses 1-7. Verse 14 gives us further insight into the crisis the psalmist faces. He is threatened by people whom he describes as "the insolent" and "a band of ruffians." The "insolent" or the arrogant appear several times in Psalm 119 as people oblivious to God's instruction (e.g., 119:21, 51, 69; cf. 19:13), while the phrase "a band of ruffians" (REB: "ruthless men") describes people who are prepared to use the power they have ruthlessly to destroy those who stand in their way. Both these descriptions are very general and hardly enable us to be precise about the situation the psalmist faced. Such people may ignore God, but over against them stands the compassionate God celebrated in the traditional credal statement in Exod. 34:6. The psalmist, therefore, can in confidence repeat his plea "be gracious to me" (v. 16; cf. v. 3) and ask for "strength" (REB: "protection") to enable him to face his attackers. He craves "a sign of your favor," a sign that all is going to be well (v. 17). What the psalmist envisages here is not wholly clear. Is he looking for a reassuring word to be spoken to him in God's name by a priest, or is he looking for something to happen in his life that would be a clear pointer to the answering of his prayers? Such a "sign" would serve a twofold purpose. It would convince his enemies that their hostility to him was futile, and it would lead them to experience the shame and humiliation (see 35:4) which they no doubt intended to inflict upon him. It would confirm the psalmist in his faith and renew the life which seemed to be ebbing away from him. The word translated "comforted" in verse 17 often has the meaning of giving renewed strength or hope to someone facing a dire threat (see 23:4).

The psalm throws light on many of the elements which make up the life of prayer: it recognizes that in prayer we come to someone infinitely greater than ourselves; it sees our basic human needs as the starting point for many of our prayers; it celebrates in prayer one who is not only all-powerful but uniquely gracious; it stresses the commitment and single-mindedness that provide the context for continuing prayer; it affirms that our prayers are offered to one who can and will answer. It is instructive to ponder how many of these attributes are present in the prayer which Jesus, according to the Gospels, taught his disciples (see Matt. 6:9-13; Luke 11:2-4).

Psalm 87
ZION, MOTHER OF US ALL

This brief psalm comes from the collection attributed to the sons of Korah (see Psalm 42) and is described as a "Song" (see Psalm 65). Its brevity, however, is matched by its difficulty. The language is terse and allusive. Instead of being presented with a logically developed theme, it appears to be a series of snapshots gathered together into a Zion album. The New English Bible claims, "The text of this psalm is disordered and several verses have been rearranged." The REB has decided wisely not to go down this path, and, together with the NRSV, follows the Hebrew text and leaves us to wrestle with its difficulties.

The Psalm divides into three sections, marked by the use of "Selah" (see Psalm 3).

1-3 The first section celebrates Zion, the city of God. The first verse, literally, "His [i.e., God's] foundation on the holy hills," points to a city which claims to owe its foundation to God (cf. Isa. 14:32), a city set on the hills which encircle Jerusalem. Verse 2 speaks of the LORD's special love for or choice of this city, in terms reminiscent of Ps. 78:67-69. The "gates of Zion" probably stand for the whole city, the gates being traditionally the center of the social and business life of the community (cf. Ruth 4:1; Ps. 9:14). This is the city chosen in preference to "the dwellings of Jacob," which may mean either the towns in the north or northern shrines (compare 78:60, which speaks of God's dwelling place at Shiloh). This is "the city of God" (see Psalm 48) about which "glorious things are spoken" (v. 3), words which provide the opening of John Newton's well-known hymn:

> Glorious things of thee are spoken,
>   Zion, city of our God;
> He whose word cannot be broken
>   Formed thee for his own abode.

4-6 The second section explores the question concerning who has the right to claim citizenship in this city of God. In verses 4-5 God speaks to declare that this is a city which has liberal immigration laws, its gates open "to those who know me." "Rahab," the mythical chaos monster, the dragon of the deep in Isa. 51:9, is used here and in Isa. 30:7 to mean Egypt. Egypt, Babylon, Philistia, Tyre, and Ethiopia (REB: Nubians, the Hebrew Cush usually indicating peoples to the south of Egypt) — all of them are either traditional enemies of Israel or distant foreigners. But what is meant by the concluding words in verse 4, "This one was born there," there being no "they say" in the Hebrew text? Does the clause refer to people who come from these countries and are by birth citizens of these countries, just as a Jew born today in Britain would have British citizenship and a Jew born in the United States American citizenship? If so, then verse 5 immediately goes on to say, Yes, but they have another citizenship. "This one and that one," that is, everyone one of them, is also born a citizen of Zion. This is their true spiritual home, the city which the Most High himself established (for "Most High" as a title for God, see 7:17). The Greek (LXX) text reads at the beginning of verse 5, "Zion is mother, a man will say," which involves a not impossible alteration to the Hebrew text, but its rendering may be no more than an attempt to bring out the meaning of the Hebrew. People come from many lands, but their true motherland is in Zion. But who are these people? It has been claimed that they are Jews, the Jews of the Diaspora, living in many different countries from early times, either taken there as captives or going there voluntarily for economic or cultural reasons. They still look to Jerusalem as their spiritual home. The parallel today would be Jews from many different countries — German Jews, Russian Jews, Ethiopian Jews, Moroccan Jews, British Jews, American Jews — all knowing that they have the right to be citizens of Israel, the land which they believe God gave to Abraham their ancestor. It may be that the psalmist saw such Jews from many lands in the temple courts at one of the great festivals and marveled that there were people from all over the world whose spiritual home was Jerusalem. It was just such a crowd of "devout Jews from every nation under heaven," present in Jerusalem at Pentecost, that Peter addressed in his first sermon according to Acts 2:5-11.

It is, however, equally possible that the psalm contains an even wider vision, following on from 86:9, "All the nations you have made shall come and bow down before you, O Lord." This is the vision of other nations, Gentiles as well as Jews, acknowledging Jerusalem as their spiritual home and the God of Israel as the only true God. It is a vision found elsewhere in the Old Testament (cf. Isa. 2:2-4; Mic. 1:1-4; Isa. 19:23-25), a vision struggling against a more narrow and exclusivist theology. It finds moving expression in Isa. 45:22-23 (cf. Zech. 8:20-23; Phil. 2:10):

> Turn to me and be saved,
>> all the ends of the earth!
> For I am God, and there is no other.
> By myself I have sworn,
>> from my mouth has gone forth in righteousness
>> a word that shall not return:
> "To me every knee shall bow,
>> every tongue shall swear."

It used to be said that the sun never set on the British Empire. Is this, then, a vision of a greater worldwide empire on which the sun could never set, an empire embracing peoples of different nationalities, color, and cultural and religious backgrounds? If so, it is part of the seedbed out of which grew Paul's vision of Gentiles, once "aliens from the commonwealth of Israel and strangers to the covenant of promise," coming together with Jews, "no longer strangers and aliens, but citizens with the saints and members of the household of God" (Eph. 2:12, 19). This is a vision which Paul speaks of elsewhere in terms of a new heavenly Jerusalem who is "our mother" (cf. Gal. 4:25-26).

To God's words in verses 4-5 the psalmist now adds his own amen in verse 6. He depicts the LORD noting in a book or register the Jewish citizenship of these people (see 56:8). In the Gospel narratives, Luke speaks of the decree that "went out from the Emperor Augustus that all the world should be registered" (Luke 2:1), a decree that led Joseph to Bethlehem "because he was descended from the house and family of David" (Luke 2:4). The picture drawn in verses 4-6 is one of people from all over the world coming to Jerusalem, there to be registered as members of the household and family of God.

7   The concluding verse of the psalm then depicts Jerusalem as a city of joy, its "singers and dancers" part of the joyful festival procession in the temple courts, a procession which according to 68:26 celebrates the LORD as "the fountain" of Israel. Something of the same meaning is being conveyed in the words, "All my [God's] springs are in you" (cf. Hos. 13:15, where the words "fountain" and "spring" occur in parallel lines). Just as natural springs were essential for the life of many a village

and town, so Jerusalem, the city of God, is here being depicted as the source of all that is essential to the God-centered life, a life bubbling over with all the good things that God gives (cf. REB). In Christian terms the promise held out in these last words is well expressed in the concluding verse of Newton's hymn:

> Savior, if of Zion's city
> I, through grace, a member am,
> Let the world deride or pity,
> I will glory in thy Name.
> Fading is the worldling's pleasure,
> All his boasted pomp and show;
> Solid joys and lasting treasure
> None but Zion's children know.

Psalm 88
THE DARK NIGHT OF THE SOUL

This is the last of the psalms attributed to the sons of Korah. To this there is added the information that it is a "Maskil [see Psalm 32] of Heman the Ezrahite." In 1 Chron. 6:33 Heman appears as one of the singers appointed by David to serve in the house of the LORD. In 1 Chron. 16:41-42 he is given a prominent place in the Jerusalem temple orchestra (cf. 1 Chron. 15:17). In 1 Kings 4:31 he appears alongside Ethan the Ezrahite as one of the sages at Solomon's court. Whether these different passages all refer to the same person may be doubted. The mention of Heman here serves to join this last of the psalms of the sons of Korah to the psalm which follows, Psalm 89, attributed to Ethan the Ezrahite. As far as the phrase "according to Mahalath Leannoth" is concerned, it has been wisely said, "The theories are interesting, but assured conclusions are nonexistent." The phrase may refer to a tune or to a musical instrument appropriate for a lament.

Unlike the meaning of Psalm 87, that of this psalm is clear, too clear for many commentators. It has been described as "unrelieved by a single ray of comfort or hope" (Weiser); "no sadder prayer in the whole Psalter" (Kidner); "one of the most tragic songs in the Psalter" (Anderson). Much of the negative bleakness in such comments is misplaced. It is, in part, the result of the failure of this lament to display some of the elements found in other laments. Here there is no certainty that the psalmist's prayers are answered, no evidence that he finds healing shared with others in thanksgiving (contrast, for example, Psalm 3). We journey here with the psalmist into the dark night of his soul, and the darkness is deep.

1-2 The first two verses of the psalm, however, introduce us to the spiritual tension which underlies the whole lament. The first verse may be more literally translated: "O LORD, God of my salvation, by day I cry out, by night (I cry out) in your presence."

The crisis in the psalmist's life is real, his wounds raw. On his lips are the words "I cry out," the translation of a Hebrew verb which often indicates a cry of anguish or distress (cf. 107:6, 28 and the use of the related noun in 9:12). Yet this anguished cry reaches out to "the God of my salvation." He believes in a God who saves, who delivers, who helps (see 3:8), but who now seems to be of no help — a God who is present, but present now only destructively in the psalmist's experience (cf. vv. 6-7, 15-17). Herein lies the spiritual tension, which remains unresolved and, in the psalmist's mind, unresolvable from the beginning to the end of the psalm. Here is someone who prays and keeps on praying (v. 2; cf. 86:1) while everything in his life seems to scream out against his belief that there is a God who delivers. His prayers (e.g., vv. 9b and 13) provide no answers but only lead to deeper questions and doubts. Yet this is faith, not merely rebellion or gloomy depression. As has been well said, "faith consists in the acceptance of doubt, not, as we generally think, in its repression" (H. A. Williams). For this psalmist such acceptance means the pouring out of all his pain and hurt, his bitterness and unanswered questions, in dialogue with God. If he could have closed the door on God and escaped from this dialogue, he might have settled for stoic bravery or lapsed into depression. For him, however, there was no such escape. Read in this light, the psalm mirrors the experience of countless men and women of faith across the centuries and highlights the spiritual tension with which many people have to grapple today.

3-9   The complaint in verses 3-9 lays bare the crisis in the psalmist's life. Here is someone who has drunk of a bucketful of disasters which have taken him to death's door, "near to Sheol" (v. 3; see 6:5). He thinks of himself as enrolled among those who are about to go "down to the Pit" (for "Pit" as a synonym for "Sheol," see 16:10). The language here would be consistent with the psalmist suffering from some critical illness or facing some other life-threatening situation. He feels helpless, the language in verse 5 pointing to a once strong man who had become a weakling. Whatever strength or status he may once have had, he now feels "like those forsaken among the dead." The word translated "forsaken" more commonly means "free." It is used in Exod. 21:2 of a debt slave to be given his freedom after six years of service. In 2 Kings 15:5 it describes the house apart (NRSV: "separate house") in which King Uzziah, stricken by leprosy, spent his last years. There may be irony in the use of the word in this context. Yes, here is someone who may be described as "free" from all that makes life meaningful and enjoyable, free to be as good as dead. The chill connotation which death has is to be spelled out in verses 10-12, but it is anticipated in the second half of verse 5, where the dead are described as "those whom you remember no more . . . cut off from your hand," as if God were powerless to do anything for them (for "remember," see 74:2).

The psalmist attributes no blame for his condition to other people. He has no complaint to make about enemies. He holds only one person responsible for what has happened — the God to whom he prays: "You have put me [v. 6]. . . . Your wrath lies heavily upon me . . . you overwhelm me" (v. 7). In the dark and bottomless Pit, he feels himself drowning under the waves of God's wrath (see 6:1). The social ties which might have sustained him have been broken. You have made me, he protests, an object of derision, shunned by former friends (v. 8) — a heavy cross to bear, one about which Job complains bitterly (e.g., Job 19:9-15). He faces his pain in agonizing loneliness (see 31:11), a theme to which he returns in verse 18. Imprisoned in an intolerable situation from which there is no escape, he feels his vitality ebbing away (vv. 8-9). Yet he continues to pray (v. 9). Terry Waite describes a similar experience during his years of captivity:

> A battle rages within me and affects every part of me — mind, body and soul. It's the classic conflict between light and darkness, life and death. I continue to pray each day, but I know I am not going to be given a palliative. This battle, which threatens me with total physical and psychological collapse, has to be fought by me as I am. (*Taken on Trust,* p. 379)

10-12 For the psalmist there is no palliative. His prayers only lead to further questions in verses 10-12, rhetorical questions that all expect the answer "No." There is no more chill or negative picture of what lies on the other side of death in the whole of the Hebrew Bible (cf. Isa. 38:17-18; Job 10:21-22). All that is central to a rich, fulfilling, God-centered life is absent. There are no "wonders" (vv. 10, 12; see 77:11), no "praise" of God (v. 10; see 9:4), nothing of God's "steadfast love" (v. 11; see 6:4) or "faithfulness" (v. 11; see 89:1) or "saving help" (v. 12; REB: "victories"). All these are gone in this "land of forgetfulness" (v. 12). It is a land inhabited by those described as "shades" (Hebrew *rĕpā'îm*), a word used elsewhere in the Hebrew Bible to signify the dead (cf. Isa. 14:9; 26:14) and that points to that weak, ghost-like existence from which all real life has been drained. Such is all that remains in "Abaddon" (v. 11). This is the only occurrence in the Psalms of a word which elsewhere in the Hebrew Bible is found as a description of Sheol (e.g., Job 26:6; 28:22). It is related to the Hebrew root meaning "to perish, destroy." It underlines the fact that Sheol is the place in which all that makes life meaningful has come to an end. This is "Destruction" personified. In Rev. 9:11 Abaddon appears in the role of the angel of the bottomless pit.

13-18 We can almost sense the psalmist shuddering as he contemplates a future which is no future. But he is still haunted by God. The battle rages within. The "But I" at the beginning of verse 13 is emphatic: "But I, O LORD, cry out to you." The word translated "cry out" is a different word from that in verse 1 and usually denotes an urgent cry for help in a tense situation (cf. 18:4; 22:24). Here it is a cry for help offered "in the morning," the time of new beginning when God was expected to demonstrate anew his steadfast love for his people (cf. 90:14; 143:8). But the cry remains unanswered. Using typical lament language, the psalmist can only ask why God continues to reject him or cast him off (cf. 43:2; 44:9), and to pay no attention to him in his hour of need (for "hide your face," see 10:1). He describes himself as "desperate" (v. 15), a translation of a Hebrew word which occurs only here in the Hebrew Bible. A minor alteration of the Hebrew text lies behind the REB translation "I am numb," which makes equally good sense in context. Over many years he has been "close to death" (v. 15), battered, he says to God, by "your terrors [v. 15] . . . your wrath . . . your dread assaults" (v. 16). This is language that Job was only too familiar with in the meaningless tragedies that hit his life (cf. Job 6:4, where the word here translated "dread assaults" is rendered "terrors"; Job 9:34; 13:21).

The psalm ends by reverting to the soul-destroying experience of loneliness and isolation (cf. v. 8). The same verb "caused . . . to shun me" is repeated. This time it is "friend" (or "lover") and "neighbor." But what do the two final words in the psalm mean: "my companions" (cf. v. 8) and "darkness"? Does the psalmist mean that darkness, and only darkness, remains as his companion? The friends who once embraced him are gone; only darkness offers its embrace. Thus the REB translates "darkness is now my only companion." It has been argued, however — and it is an attractive suggestion — that we should take "my companions" along with the "friends" and "neighbors" who shun the psalmist, and leave "darkness" as the psalmist's final exclamation, a protest or a sigh that sums up his whole experience in one dramatic word, "Darkness!"

It is, of course, easy to quote other passages from the Psalms and the Bible in general to affirm that this cannot be the final word on God's providence. True, but this psalm is the witness of one who could as yet see no light at the end of his dark tunnel. There are people today, nurtured within the Christian tradition, who, through debilitating illness of body or mind or as the result of personal tragedy, find themselves in the same dark tunnel. They struggle with questions and have no answers. A mother of one of the children killed in the Dunblane school massacre, when asked how she was coping, simply replied, "I am not coping; I never shall." We have no right to stand in condemnation of such darkness, nor to seek to scatter it with glib theological answers. That was where the psalmist was. God was not the answer; he was the problem. But the psalmist could not deny that God was still part of his experience. So he still prayed. He stretched out his hands beseechingly (v. 9); he cried out in his anguish (v. 1); he cried out for help (v. 13). This is not sadness but honesty. This is not the most tragic song, but one which is wrestling with the discordant, jarring notes that shatter the human melody and warning us that for many the resolution is not yet.

Psalm 89
WHERE ARE YOU, GOD?

This is a psalm of sharply contrasting moods. In verses 1-37 we listen to what are believed to be the God-given certainties and promises surrounding the royal family of David. In verses 38-51 we hear a lament describing how all these certainties and promises have been called into question. Another chapter is here added to the story of Psalm 78. That story ended with God's rejection of the northern tribes and all they stood for, but his choice of Judah and of "his servant David" (78:70). Psalm 89 faces a situation where that choice seems to have come to an end. There have been many attempts to trace the various sections and elements in this psalm to different sources or traditions. Much of this can be no more than speculation. All that we now have, and all that the worshipping community in Israel had from early in the postexilic period onwards, is the psalm in its present form. It is this with which we must seek to come to terms.

As in the case of many other psalms, scholars are divided as to whether the origins of this one are to be sought in the cult of ancient Israel, in an annual festival in which the Davidic king played a prominent role, or whether it has in its background a particular, disastrous historical situation in the life of the community. The view taken here is that the latter is more likely. When, however, we ask what particular situation, we are presented with several options. Assuming that the "Ethan the Ezrahite" of the heading is one of the sages in Solomon's court (see Psalm 88), it has been traditionally claimed that the background is the breakup of the united Davidic kingdom after the death of Solomon (cf. 1 Kings 12). The language of verses 38-45, however, hardly supports this view. The tragic death of King Josiah at Megiddo in 609 BCE (2 Kgs. 23:28-30), the deposition and exile of Jehoiachin by the Babylonians in 597 BCE (2 Kgs. 24:10-16), or the aftermath of the fall of Jerusalem in 587 BCE (2 Kings 25) have all had their advocates. Perhaps we should think rather of the situation towards the end of the sixth century, when some at least in the community were harboring longings for the restoration of the Davidic dynasty (cf. Hag. 2:20-23; Zech. 4:6-14). The psalm in this case would originally have been part of a religio-nationalistic manifesto from the frustrated Jewish community still chafing under foreign political oppression. Whatever its origin, though, the psalm has the power to speak to any situation of crisis in the life of the community, when events seem to call into question the promises God had made and force the community to ask, Where are you, God? Thus it parallels on a community level the more intensely personal issues explored in Psalm 88. Like Psalm 88, it comes up with no easy answers.

1-4 In verses 1-4 we listen to an introit praising God in general terms (vv. 1-2), which then focus on God's covenant with David (vv. 3-4). Many of the main theological ideas and themes which we hear again and again in the Psalms appear here for the first time.

There is God's "steadfast love" (see 5:7). The Hebrew word behind this phrase occurs in verses 1, 2, 14, 24, 28, 33, and 49; in verses 1 and 49 it appears in the plural, hence the REB translates it "loving deeds." Verse 49 poignantly or accusingly questions why such "loving deeds" so typical of God's dealings in the past are now conspicuous by their absence.

There is God's "faithfulness." The word used in verses 1, 2, 5, 8, 33, and 49 is a variant form (Hebrew *'ĕmûnāh*) of the more commonly used word in the Psalms, *'emet,* which occurs in verse 14 (see 25:5). It serves to underline that consistent and unshakable dependability of God to which creation and history bore witness, but which now seemed to have lost its power (v. 49).

There is God's "covenant" with David. The words "You said" at the beginning of verse 3 in the NRSV are explanatory and are not in the original text. They are unnecessary provided we recognize that the "I" who now speaks in this verse is not the psalmist, but God. This is the covenant God made (literally, "cut"; see 50:5) with David to be enduring, unchangeable (v. 28), a covenant to which he would never be "false" (v. 34). Yet this is the covenant which he has now "renounced" (v. 39), a word which occurs only once elsewhere in the Old Testament, in Lam. 2:7, where it refers to God "disowning" his sanctuary in Jerusalem. How can a faithful God disown what he himself had initiated and to which he had committed himself "forever" (vv. 1, 2, 4, 29, 36, 37), that covenant with David whom he acknowledges as "my servant" (vv. 3, 20)?

The word "Selah" (see Psalm 3) occurs at the end of the introit, at the end of the hymnic celebration of God's covenant with David (v. 37), and at the end of the descriptive part of the lament (v. 45). In each case it probably gives the congregation time for reflection.

5-18 What has been celebrated in the introit in verses 1-2 is now developed in a hymn in verses 5-14. The hymn focuses upon the "wonders" and "faithfulness" of the LORD (see 77:11) expressed in his unique status among the gods (vv. 5-8). The heavenly council of the gods, which we met in Psalm 82, is here described as "the assembly [or "congregation"] of the holy ones" (v. 5) and "the council of the holy ones" (v. 7; for "council," see 25:14). None of the other "heavenly beings" (v. 6; literally, "sons of gods") can be compared with the LORD, Israel's God, "great and awesome" (v. 7), his supreme power underlined in the title "God of hosts" (v. 8; see 24:10). The text of verse 8 has its difficulties. The REB assumes an alteration to and redivision of the text, but this makes little difference to the overall meaning of the verse. The emphasis upon the LORD as the "God of hosts" leads naturally into his power in creation, his subduing of all the threatening forces of chaos, raging "sea" and "waves" (v. 9) and mythological monsters such as "Rahab" (v. 10; cf. 74:12-14). The whole created universe, which owes its very existence to God, joins in a hymn of praise (v. 11). In verse 12 "The north and the south" may be used to indicate the whole wide world. There is, however, something to be said for seeing in north and south a reference to two mountains. *Zaphon,* "north," is the northern mountain abode of the gods in Canaanite mythology (see 48:1), and, by a slight alteration to the text, *Amanus* is a mountain in southern Turkey. The whole verse would then refer to four mountains, Saphon, Amanus, Tabor, and Hermon (cf. 42:6). All of these mountains had traditional religious associations that long predated the coming of the He- brews, but here they join in joyously praising the LORD, the God who created them. God's kingship rests not on the arbitrary use of power but on qualities that the Psalms never weary of attributing to the LORD: "righteousness and justice" (v. 14a; see 9:7-8), "steadfast love and faithfulness" (v. 14b).

It is small wonder, then, that verses 15-18 affirm that people who share in the festal worship of this God are "Happy" (see 1:1). They know a quality of life and a joy which is not their own. Midway through verse 17, "their" changes to "our," as if in renewed wonder the congregation remind themselves, "That is we!" It is we who by the grace of God "hold our heads high" (REB, v. 17; see 75:4-5), we who know a "strength" which is not our own. Our "shield" (see 3:3) is the LORD, our king "the Holy One of Israel" (see 71:22).

19-37 Verses 19-37 now pick up and develop the theme of verses 3-4 in the introit. Although both the NRSV and the REB in verse 19 change "your faithful ones" (see 4:3) into the singular "your faithful one," that is, David, the change is unnecessary. What is here introduced is a "vision," a word often used to refer to a revelation given to a prophet (cf. Isa. 1:1; Amos 1:1). The vision will affect the whole life of the nation and is therefore communicated to the people, "your faithful ones." What follows has close links with the oracle of Nathan in 2 Sam. 7:4-17, though there are significant points of difference. Psalm 89, for example, makes no reference to the building of the temple (2 Sam. 7:5-8). It could be that both 2 Samuel 7 and this psalm are adapting to their different contexts the underlying tradition of God's covenant with David. Four key claims concerning the Davidic royal family are highlighted in this section.

First, this royal family is based on God's free choice. With the words "I have set the crown on one who is mighty" (v. 19), the NRSV assumes a widely accepted alteration to the text. The REB retains the Hebrew text and translates, "I have granted help to a warrior." It has also been suggested that the Hebrew could be rendered, "I have set a boy [or "young lad"] over warriors." This would fit in with the story in 1 Samuel 16 of the young lad who emerges from the people, "found" and "anointed" by God (v. 20; see 2:2).

Second, the future of David's dynasty is built on God's promises. There is the promise of God-given strength (v. 21), the promise that David will never be outwitted by or be on the receiving end of oppression from enemies (v. 22), and the promise that, on the contrary, he will crush his enemies, whoever they may be (v. 23). There is the promise that under God "his horn shall be exalted" (v. 24; for this use of "horn," see 18:2); he will be strong and victorious, ruling over a kingdom that will stretch from "the sea" to "the rivers" (v. 25), probably from the Mediterranean in the west to the Euphrates in the east and the Nile in the south. It is possible, however, that the language here may be deliberately evocative of verse 9, with David's kingship conceived as the earthly counterpart of God's cosmic kingship.

Third, the Davidic covenant involves a peculiar relationship between God and the Davidic king, a relationship described in terms of adopted sonship (see 2:7; cf. 2 Sam. 7:14), its intimacy stressed in the words "my God, and the Rock of my salvation" (v. 26; see 18:2; 62:2). This is the son who has the status of "the firstborn" (v. 27), who would expect to receive the paternal blessing (cf. Gen. 27:32), and who would be entitled, according to Deut. 21:15-17, to a double portion of the family heritage. As such he becomes a peerless king, of higher status than any other earthly king (v. 27).

Fourth, this is a relationship which can never be broken, a relationship guaranteed by a solemn and irrevocable oath of God (v. 35). It means the establishment of a dynasty which is to be as solid and lasting as the created world itself (vv. 29, 36-37; cf. Jer. 33:17-22, which binds together the Davidic family and the Levitical priesthood in a similar promise). Within this relationship, disobedience will call forth harsh discipline (cf. 2 Sam. 7:14), but it is a relationship which the "steadfast love" and "faithfulness" of God ensure will never be rescinded (v. 33). Here is the covenant which God can never "violate" or profane. To do so would be an offense against God's own nature or "holiness" (v. 35). It would turn God into a liar.

38-51 Yet it happened (v. 38). Events took place that seemed to indicate that God's covenant had been "renounced" (v. 39). It is this, God's apparent disowning of David, which is the theme of the lament in verses 38-51. The typical lament language comes pouring forth: the Davidic king, God's "anointed," has been "spurned" or cast off (cf. 43:2; 44:23; 74:1), "rejected" (cf. 78:59, 67), and put on the receiving end of God's "wrath" or fury (cf. 78:49). His "crown," symbol of royalty, has been defiled; the cities and fortresses throughout the land have been ravaged (v. 40); the taunts of the enemies are only too real. God's powerful right hand (v. 13) has ironically turned out to be "the right hand" of David's foes (v. 42). Defeated in battle, stripped of all insignia of royalty, the Davidic king is reduced to impotence and shame (vv. 43-45).

This descriptive part of the lament now moves into the typical and urgent questions: "How long, O LORD?" (see 4:2). "Will you hide yourself forever?" (v. 46; see 10:1). "How long will your anger burn?" (cf. 74:1). These questions, as verse 49 indicates, throw into jeopardy the much vaunted and celebrated steadfast love and faithfulness of the LORD. But what are we to make of verses 47-48? They touch on the brevity and the "vanity" or purposelessness of human life, which wends inexorably towards death and into the grip of "Sheol." This is a theme with which we are familiar from other psalms (e.g., Psalms 39 and 49). In this psalm, what has been hinted at in verse 45 is here being underlined. The earthly king, however seemingly powerful and secure, is not exempt from the questions raised by the fate that comes to everyone. It has been argued that in the words "how short my time is" (v. 47) the king is now speaking, but equally it may still be the psalmist identifying himself with and applying to himself the fate he sees facing the king. All that remains is to point out to God the intolerable nature of the current situation — the king, "your servant," is the object of the deeply wounding taunts of his enemies, enemies who must be God's enemies since they dog the footsteps of God's "anointed" (vv. 50-51).

No answers are given to the questions that dominate the second half of the psalm. The tension remains between promise and reality, between God's faithfulness and events which seem to scream out that it is a sham. It is interesting to compare the structure of this psalm with that of Psalm 74. Psalm 74 begins with the lament in the form of questions that lead into a dramatic description of the disaster which has struck (74:1-11). This is followed by a hymnic celebration of the awesome power of God (74:12-17), which leads into a concluding prayer to God to do something to redress the situation. It is as if in Psalm 74 the psalmist, in a crisis situation, recalls the community's tradition of faith to sustain belief that the present cannot be God's last word, even if he does not know how God will act. In Psalm 89 this structure is stood on its head. It begins with the celebration of God's awesome power and of his covenant with David, and ends with the plaintive questions that seem to query the whole tradition of faith. In this sense it ends, like Psalm 88, in the darkness of present despair. The celebration of God's steadfast love and faithfulness simply underlines the bleakness of the present. In the darkness of tragedy, does remembered faith provide a basis for hope, or does it merely deepen despair? That is a very personal question to which people today provide different answers. Perhaps it is helpful that, whatever answers they give, they can turn to fellow travelers in the Psalms.

As the last psalm in Book III, Psalm 89 ends, like all the other psalm collections, with a doxology (v. 52; see Psalm 41). It is the briefest of all the concluding doxologies. Book III begins (with Psalms 73 and 74) and ends (with Psalms 88 and 89) by focusing upon fundamental questions being asked, individually and corporately, by people of faith. The response to such questions is varied. Perhaps a brief doxology was all that was needed or possible in the midst of such questions and the varied responses they evoked.

BOOK IV

PSALMS 90–106

Book IV comprises Psalms 90–106, most of which have no specific heading in the Hebrew text. Two are associated with David (Psalms 101 and 103), and two are related to specific occasions for worship (Psalm 91, "A Song for the Sabbath Day," and Psalm 100, "A Psalm of Thanksgiving"). One has a longer heading linking it with a specific experience of affliction (Psalm 102). The opening Psalm 90 is headed, "A Prayer of Moses, the man of God." This is the only psalm in the entire Psalter associated with Moses, though Exodus 15 and Deuteronomy 32 and 33 link Moses with poetic material that has many echoes in the Psalms.

Psalm 90
HUMAN LIFE UNDER
THE DIVINE MICROSCOPE

Although traditionally commentators, including Calvin, have accepted Moses as the author of this psalm, this is highly unlikely. The description of Moses as "the man of God" appears in Deut. 33:1, but it is also used of other people in the Hebrew Bible, particularly of the prophets Elijah and Elisha in 1 and 2 Kings. From early times there was much intriguing speculation as to why this psalm was attributed to Moses. As likely as any is the suggestion that in the whole of the Hebrew Bible only Moses dared to tell God to "change his mind" (Exod. 32:12, which uses the same verb translated, probably wrongly, in verse 13 as "have compassion on"). The psalm in its present form may well come from the postexilic period.

Although the psalm has certain features characteristic of the community laments (e.g., the appeal in verse 13), it addresses no specific crisis in the life of

299

the community. Indeed, it deals with a basic human problem, the universal need for wisdom (v. 12). How such wisdom was integrated into Israel's tradition of worship has been discussed in the comments on Psalms 32–34.

In verses 1-12 we view human life under the divine microscope. It is only from verse 13, which for the first time in the psalm uses the personal Hebrew name for God, LORD (Yahweh), that this universal teaching is applied to the particular circumstances the congregation faces. This should remind us that a basic understanding of what human life means should inform and shape our approach to God. We find the same pattern in the book of Genesis, which moves from the universal, beginning with creation, in chapters 1–11, into the specific experience of Israel, beginning with the call of Abraham in chapter 12.

1-12 The Psalm begins by expressing confidence in the creator of the world (vv. 1-2). He is addressed in verse 1, and in the closing verse 17, as Lord, master, or sovereign (see Psalm 86), but a master who has made gracious provision for his subjects: "you have been our dwelling place" (the REB translation, "refuge," follows the Greek [LXX] rendering). The word "dwelling place" can be used of an animal's den (e.g., Jer. 10:22), but in Ps. 68:5 it is used of the temple as God's dwelling place among his people. Here, however, and in 91:9 it is used of God himself as "the dwelling place" of his people, pointing to the sense of security that God provides and that has never failed across all the generations. That security is rooted in the fact that this is the God who was there before the mountains came into existence, the God "who formed the earth and the world." The word translated "formed" is used of the labor pains of childbirth. The same imagery is used of God giving birth to Wisdom in Prov. 8:25 (cf. Job 38:8). Although the REB, following some commentators, takes "the earth and the world" as the subject of the verb, this is unnecessary. The psalm is using the vivid human analogy of a mother giving birth to a child, to affirm what Genesis 1 claims when it says, "In the beginning God created . . ." (Gen. 1:1). This is the God who is, therefore, the source of all life, the God who embraces all time "from everlasting to everlasting."

No arguments are put forward for belief in such a God. It is simply stated as the sine qua non in the light of which human life must be evaluated. It is to this evaluation that the psalm now turns in verses 3-12. Two words are used in verse 3 to describe human life, 'ĕnôš, translated "us" in the NRSV, and children of 'ādām, translated "mortals." The same words are used in Psalm 8 to underline the frailty and creaturely mortality of our existence (see 8:4.). Although the word translated "dust" simply means something which has been crushed and is not the same word as is used in Genesis 2–3, there seems little doubt that in the background to the words of verse 3 there lies the story of the fate of 'ādām in Gen. 3:19, "you are dust, and to dust you shall return." There may indeed be in verse 4 a side glance at the abnormal life span attributed to some of the pre-flood worthies, Methuselah heading the list with 969 years to his credit. Go beyond that, even to a thousand years, and they still remain insignificant in the eyes of the everlasting God, no more than our yesterday or a brief, four-hour night watch. 2 Peter 3:8 quotes the first part of verse 4 in a different theological context, to counter those within the church who were complaining about the delay in the final establishment of God's kingdom. This, however, is but to stress the same basic theological truth. We dare not assume that God's standards are our standards, not least when we are talking about time.

Two striking images are used in verses 5-6 to stress this theme of human frailty and mortality. First, although the text in the first half of verse 5 is difficult, the picture seems to be that of people caught in an unexpected flash flood and swept to their death (the REB assumes that the word "sleep," translated "dream" in the NRSV, refers to the sleep of death). The second picture is that of grass that sprouts and shoots up in the morning, but under the merciless rays of the sun or the scorching wind has withered by evening. A similar picture is used to good effect in Isa. 40:6-7,

> All people are grass,
> > their constancy is like the flower of the field.
> The grass withers, the flower fades,
> > when the breath of the LORD blows upon it;
> > surely the people are grass.

Longfellow in his *A Psalm of Life* passes a similar verdict:

> . . . Time is fleeting,
> And our hearts, though stout and brave,
> Still, like muffled drums, are beating
> > Funeral marches to the grave.

This is a theme to which the psalm returns in verse 10, where seventy years probably indicates what was regarded as the normal limit of life expectancy. It could hardly be the average in ancient Israel. If abnormal strength takes you beyond that limit, to "perhaps eighty," then "at their best they are but toil and sorrow" (compare the REB, which retains the Hebrew word meaning "pride," with the NRSV, which follows many of the versions in reading "span"). Even then they will soon be gone and "fly away" (cf. Job 20:8). Ben Sirach might well have been reflecting on this psalm when he wrote:

> He who lives forever created the whole universe. . . .
> What are human beings, and of what use are they?
> What is good in them, and what is evil?

> The number of days in their life is great
> > if they reach one hundred years.
> Like a drop of water from the sea and a grain of sand,
> > so are a few years among the days of eternity. (Sir. 18:1, 8-10)

There is, however, another factor in the psalmist's evaluation of human life. We are not only frail and transitory; we are sinners on the receiving end of the justifiable anger of God (vv. 7-9). We are "consumed," "overwhelmed," or spent because of the wrath (see 6:1) of God, who knows not only our obvious way-wardness, but what we seek to hide from him — "our secret sins" (v. 8). Our sorry life comes to a climax like "a sigh" (v. 9). This uncommon word is found in Ezek. 2:10 in a context of mourning or moaning. Does this mean then that life ends in a regretful but resigned whimper, or does it mean that the inevitable end of human life, however long, is the moan of mourning? Whatever view we take, the verdict here on human life is somber.

This leads into the question in verse 11. The meaning of the second half of the verse is debatable. The rendering of the NRSV, "Your wrath is as great as the fear that is due you," seems to imply that we can place no limits on God's justifiable anger at our sinfulness, just as there can be no limits placed on the reverence we owe him. The wording of the REB, "who feels your wrath like those who fear you?" implies that it is only those who reverence God who are truly conscious of the reality of his anger. Others, presumably, simply live for themselves and for the present with no sense of either their transitoriness or sinfulness.

In typical wisdom style, the section ends by drawing a practical conclusion. Teach us "to count our days," or as the REB renders, "make us know how few our days are." To recognize our transitoriness and mortality is to recognize that many of the values which are placed on life — for example, wealth, status, and power — have no ultimate significance. What is needed is that "wisdom" (see Psalm 49) which will enable us to live responsibly in the light of a true, God-given understanding of what our human life really means. Such wisdom points to abandoning any self-reliance or seeking security in merely human values. That security only God can give.

13-17 The psalm ends with a typical plea. The characteristic cry, "How long?" (see 4:2), is now addressed to the LORD, the God of Israel. The God who "turns" frail humanity to dust (v. 3) must now himself "turn" — do a volte-face and change his mind concerning his servants (v. 13). Only such a change can lead to a meaningful and satisfying life here and now. His anger must be replaced by his "steadfast love" (v. 14; see 5:7); the evil days of "toil and trouble" (v. 10) turn into days of joy and gladness (vv. 14-15). God's "deeds," which demonstrate his "glorious power" or majestic splendor, must be made visible to his people (v. 16), probably through their participation in one of the great festivals of the religious year. There the reality which is being celebrated must grip their imagination and become once again part of their life. That is what worship can be, and sadly so often is not — a transcendent wonder that transforms our lives. Only thus do we experience the "favor" or perhaps better "the loveliness" of God; only thus can what we seek to achieve "prosper" or "be established" (v. 17; cf. REB). The repetition in the last words of the psalm is probably deliberate. It points to a situation in which over many years the community has had to face despair and live with frustration, their plans thwarted, their life clouded by what they believe to be "the wrath of God." The twofold plea in v. 13 for God to change — "turn" . . . "change" — finds its counterpart in the twofold plea that the life of his people may now change for the better.

For many people this psalm is best known in Isaac Watts's hymn version:

> O God, our help in ages past,
>   Our hope for years to come,
> Our shelter from the stormy blast,
>   And our eternal home!

While the hymn catches something of the strong sense of confidence that pulsates through the psalm, it fails to give recognition to the element of lament that features in verses 13-17. It has no place for the questioning that goes hand in hand with the confidence.

Psalm 91
THE SECURITY OF FAITH

This psalm has no heading, though the Greek (LXX) and other versions link it with David. It poses critical questions that have no agreed answers. What kind of psalm is this? Who is the "you" addressed in the psalm, and who is speaking? Is this a royal psalm in which the king is being addressed by a court poet or priest, a confession of faith by a convert from paganism, or part of a longer temple liturgy in which different voices speak? There have been countless suggestions. The view taken here is that verses 1-13 contain instruction given in the context of worship and that this instruction receives its divine imprimatur in verses 14-16, an oracle spoken by a priest as the mouthpiece of God.

1-13 In verses 1-2 we are listening to a worshipper's confession of faith, which sets out a theme that is developed in different ways in the rest of the psalm. The translation of the opening words in the NRSV, "You who live," is an attempt to depart from the sexist implications still present in the REB, which has "He who lives." We could achieve the same end by translating "Whoever lives. . . ." Basically the theme of the psalm can be summed up in one word: "security." That security is found through faith in God. The true worshipper is described as one who lives "in the shelter of the Most High" (see 27:5) and "abides" or "lodges" (REB) — the word literally means "to spend the night" — "in the shadow of the Almighty." This language probably anticipates the picture of the protecting mother bird in verse 4 and reflects the common use in the psalms of the phrase "under the shadow of the wings" of God (see 17:8). For the divine title "the Most High," see 7:17, and for "the Almighty," see 68:14. They are both titles which have their origin in pre-Israelite religion and point to the majesty and power of the deity. In the psalm, however, they are immediately identified with the LORD (v. 1).

At the beginning of verse 2 it is better to follow the REB translation, "says of the LORD," rather than the rendering of the NRSV, "will say to the LORD." The privilege of the worshipper, noted in verse 1, leads directly into the description of the Lord as "my God," who is "my refuge" (see 14:6) and "my fortress" (see 18:2), "in whom I trust" (see 4:5). These words express a deeply personal faith and reflect a life entrusted confidently to God. Here faith has found God's protecting care verified in experience.

Confirmation of the security which faith brings is now given to the worshipper by someone who may be either a priest or a wisdom teacher, there being many parallels in thought and imagery between verses 3-12 and Psalm 34. The Hebrew word translated "For" at the beginning of verse 3, and omitted in the REB, may be introducing an emphatic statement, with the underlying implication, "Be assured that. . . ." Be assured that God will protect you from dangers of every kind, real or imagined, dangers unexpected, "the snare of the fowler" (v. 3; cf. Prov. 6:5) and life-threatening "deadly pestilence" (cf. v. 6) or plague. The language of verses 5-6 may be interpreted in terms of demonic forces or could indicate irrational fears or circumstances leading to serious illness. All such threatening forces are robbed of their destructive power because the worshipper is encircled within God's protecting power. This is spelled out in two pictures in verse 4, a mother bird placing protective wings over her young (see 17:8), and the military metaphor of protective "shield and buckler" describing God's "faithfulness" (see 25:5). The word translated "buckler" occurs only here in the Old Testament, but may refer to the small round shield used to ward off missiles. For "shield," see 5:12.

Such God-given protection looks for a response from the worshipper, a response indicated by the words "You will not fear" (v. 5). As has been well said, "The difference between belief and unbelief could not be expressed more clearly than in the simple, positive and firm statement, 'you will not fear,' made in face of the sinister and gruesome forces that existed in popular belief" (A. Weiser). Indeed, it is fear, not doubt, which is the opposite of faith. Again and again the poet-prophet of Isaiah 40–55 seeks to encourage his despairing compatriots and to rekindle their faith with the words, "Do not fear, for I am with you" (Isa. 41:10; cf. 41:14; 43:1, 5; 44:2). Trusting in God grants no exemption from the life-threatening and destructive forces which are part of human experience, but it deprives them of their sting and enables them to be faced without fear.

It is in this light that we must seek to understand verses 7-8, whether the picture is that of slaughter on the field of battle or that of an army or community stricken by plague (cf. 2 Kgs. 19:35). These verses raise serious theological issues. In their background is the conviction, expressed in various psalms, that God's protection is given to the righteous while his judgment rests on the wicked, and the assumption that this can be verified by how life works out in this world. Stories abound in religious tradition of people who believe that because of their faith they have been miraculously protected by God in desperate circumstances where others have perished. Verse 7 is often quoted as the grounds for this belief. But what of those of equal faith who know no such miraculous protection and fall with the thousands around them? There is no answer to this unless we can affirm that even in death God is with us, and can share the faith Paul so challengingly expressed in Romans 8, climaxing in the words, "For I am convinced that neither death, nor life, nor angels, nor rulers, nor things present, nor things to come, nor powers, nor height, nor depth, nor anything else in all creation, will be able to separate us from the love of God in Christ Jesus our Lord" (Rom. 8:38-39). Lacking this certainty, the psalmist can yet defiantly state in verses 9-10 his conviction that, even in the most dire circumstances, he can depend on God's protection, because he believes in the security which comes from entrusting himself to one who is his "refuge" (v. 9; cf. v. 2) and his "dwelling place" (v. 9; cf. 90:1). That is a security which the "wicked" (v. 8) can never know.

The theme of God's caring protection is further developed in verses 11-13 in the picture of God's "angels" (see 34:7) accompanying the worshipper in all the circumstances of life (for "way," see 1:6), supporting and defending from all harm (v. 12) and enabling all dangers encountered to be overcome (v. 13). It is difficult for Christians to read these words without thinking of the temptation narratives in Luke 4:9-12 and Matt. 4:5-7, where the devil, being a good biblical literalist, quotes these words to Jesus in order to tempt him into a dramatic demonstration of his faith in God. To this, Jesus responds in the words of Deut. 6:16, "Do not put the LORD your God to the test." The security which God brings is something to be accepted in humble trust, not something to be used for personal aggrandizement. It is the security which enabled Jesus in the agony of the cross to say "Father, into your hands I commend my spirit" (Luke 23:46), using words from Psalm 31:5.

There has been much discussion concerning the dangerous animals mentioned in verse 13. Some have argued for four members of the snake family, the Greek (LXX) reading the first word "lion" as "asp." Hence the REB translation, "asp and cobra, . . . snake and serpent." It is better, however, with the NRSV to stick with two members of the lion family and two of the snake family, probably representing different kinds of danger. This verse may lie behind the words Jesus spoke to the seventy when they returned from their successful mission, "See, I have given you authority to tread on snakes and scorpions" (Luke 10:19), words immediately followed by a warning against false pride.

14-16   The essence of the security of which the psalm speaks lies in a continuing relationship with God. The character of this relationship is spelled out in the concluding oracle in verses 14-16. As the REB translation indicates, the human partner in this relationship is spoken of in the singular, as is indeed true throughout the psalm. But since this person represents any and every worshipper, the NRSV uses the plural throughout. The two-way nature of this relationship is stressed in verse 14 and in the first line of verse 15. God's assuring words "I will deliver. . . . I will protect [see 20:2]. . . . I will answer" find their counterpart in the words "Those who love me . . . who know my name . . . when they call upon me." The REB's rendering "Because his love holds fast to me" (v. 14) signals that the word translated "love" here is not the common word for love. It often indicates a strong desire, rooted in the attractive qualities of another person (cf. Gen. 34:8; Deut. 21:11). There is a passion implicit in this word, here a passion for God. Those "who know my name" are those who worship God because they are gripped by what God has revealed of himself (see 5:11). This is a divine-human pas de deux which finds its counterpart in the Gospel: "Ask and it will be given you, search and you will find, knock and the door will be opened for you" (Matt. 7:7). It is not, however, a pas de deux between equals. There is a lead dancer, so the concluding words of the psalm focus solely upon what God will do. He will deliver and "honor" them, that is, ensure that they will be given their true status in the community (cf. 1 Sam. 2:30). He will satisfy them "with long life," one of the signs of God's blessing in Israel (cf. Psalm 128; Job 29:18). And he will ensure that his people experience all that is indicated by the word "salvation" (see 3:8).

Precisely because the security of which this psalm speaks is based upon a relationship with God, it finds its New Testament counterpart in the lives of those who are "in Christ." As 1 John 5:4-5 puts it, "And this is the victory that conquers the world, our faith. Who is it that conquers the world but the one who believes that Jesus is the Son of God?" Such belief, of course, is never merely intellectual assent. It involves that commitment and trust to which this psalm bears witness. It offers a security which the world can neither give nor take away.

Psalm 92
THE CALL TO WORSHIP

The opening words of this psalm are still today rightly used as a call to worship. This is hardly surprising since, as the heading indicates, this psalm has from an early age been linked with the Sabbath. The Sabbath comes as the climax to the creation story in Gen. 1–2:4 and, as a modern Jewish prayer book declares, calls on us to "stand in wonder before the mystery of creation." The prayer book then uses this psalm in the Sabbath service, but interestingly only verses 1-5 and 12-15, thus ignoring in this context a key central section of the psalm. There have been many attempts to go back beyond this traditional link with the Sabbath. Was the psalm originally a royal psalm, with the "I" who speaks in it the king, or was it part of a longer liturgy used at one of the annual festivals at the Jerusalem temple? The arguments made to support each view are hardly convincing. It is as well simply to follow the heading. At least we know that, from an early period in Jewish tradition, its natural home was the Sabbath.

1-3 The psalm begins with a resounding call "to give thanks to the LORD" and to praise God. The Sabbath in ancient Israel was intended to be a day on which the whole community was set free to celebrate. As Calvin comments, "the right observance of Sabbath does not consist in idleness, as some absurdly imagine, but in the celebration of the divine name." For the significance of the "name" of God, see 5:11, and for the divine title "Most High," see 7:17. This is the day to celebrate the theological twins who feature so prominently in the Psalms, the LORD's "steadfast love" and "faithfulness" (v. 2; cf. Psalm 89), to celebrate them joyfully with musical accompaniment (v. 3; cf. 33:2). The reference to "in the morning" and "at night" has been linked with the offering of the morning and evening sacrifice, but this may be no more than a way of saying "all day long."

4-6 Verses 4-6 spell out the reason for such joyful celebration in terms of what God has done. In v. 4a "your acts," the rendering of the REB, is better than "your work," the rendering of the NRSV, since we are dealing with a different Hebrew word from that translated "the works of your hands" (v. 4b) and "your works" (v. 5; cf. 90:17). The link with Sabbath might suggest that we should think especially of God's acts of creation in this context, but the language could equally well refer to what he has done in history and providence. Deuteronomy 5:12-15 links the celebration of Sabbath with the deliverance from slavery in Egypt. One thing is clear, claims the psalmist; wherever we turn we are faced with a God, whose purposes are "very deep" (v. 5), not obvious or readily understandable to one and all. In particular, they remain totally incomprehensible to the "dullard" and the "stupid," both fairly weak translations of two Hebrew words we have already met in 49:11. They are not referring to people merely lacking in intellectual ability. The first word is rendered "brute beast" in 73:22, and the second word indicates someone who shows by his attitude that he has no clue as to what life is all about. Sensitivity and commitment are essential in the understanding of God's ways. This is a theme which Paul explores in Christian terms in 1 Cor. 2:6-16.

7-11 The rest of the psalm wrestles with an issue that, in a variety of different ways, confronts us from Psalm 1 onwards, namely, the respective fates of the "wicked" and the "righteous" in a world under the control of God, who is "on high forever" (v. 8). As far as the "wicked" and "evildoers" (see 5:5) are concerned, there is no denying that they seem at times to flourish, but their end is certain. They have no greater stability than "the grass," which shoots up only to wither under the heat of the sun (v. 7; see 37:2). Evildoers are by very definition "enemies" of the LORD, since they challenge everything he regards with approval. They are, therefore, doomed to perish and to disintegrate. The threefold pattern in verse 9 stylistically has its roots in early Canaanite poetry, for example,

> Behold your enemies, Baal,
> > Behold your enemies you will crush,
> > Behold you will crush your foes.

This traditional literary style provides the psalmist with a suitable framework within which to bear witness to his own theology, which centers on the LORD.

The psalmist now clothes this theology in terms of his own experience in verses 10-11. He himself has known security and renewed vitality. The text in these verses is not wholly clear. The "horn . . . of the wild ox" is a symbol of strength and power (see 18:2). The second line of verse 10 in the NRSV assumes a small, and probably correct, alteration to the text to give the picture of fresh oil poured over the psalmist, a sign of joy and gladness (see 23:5). He has witnessed the defeat of his "enemies," the frustration of all those who have planned his downfall. It is impossible to identify clearly who these enemies were, or what precisely they intended to do.

12-15 In the closing verses the psalmist is inviting others to identify with and to learn from his experience. There is a richness of life open only to the "righteous" (see Psalm 1). They flourish "like the palm tree." This is the only mention of the palm tree in the Psalms, but its grace and fruitfulness were well known. In Song of Sol. 7:7-8 the palm tree is used to extol the attractiveness and sexual charm of the girl. The "cedar in Lebanon" is the symbol of majestic size and strength (v. 12; see 29:5). Such grace and strength are rooted in worship (v. 13). Trees may very well have grown in the temple courts, as they still do today, but in the context of the celebration of creation, there may well be in verse 13 a reference back to that paradisal garden in Genesis 2–3, with its tree of life and the tree of the knowledge of good and evil. Even in old age the righteous are characterized by never failing vitality (v. 14), witnessing to the fact that "the LORD is upright" (see 25:8); he is "my rock," says the psalmist (see 18:2), which means that he is utterly devoid of that perversity which so often characterizes human conduct (cf. 37:1). The Jewish prayer book neatly makes this point when it translates the final verse: "Proclaiming that God is just, my Rock in whom there is no flaw."

The psalm affirms that the nature of the God to whom it bears witness makes it impossible for evil to have the last word. Yet it is often hard to discern this in the world as we know it. That is the justification for the comment in the Mishnah which describes the psalm as "a song for the time to come, for the day that shall be all Sabbath and rest in the life everlasting" (*Mishnah Tamid* 7:4). That is but to look forward in hope to the ultimate vindication of what the psalm so confidently affirms.

Psalm 93
THE RIGHT ROYAL KING

The Greek (LXX) text provides this psalm with a heading which links it with David and assigns it to the day before the Sabbath, "when the earth was inhabited." This picks up the Sabbath-creation theme which we noted in Psalm 92, and indeed Psalm 93 at several points echoes the language of the previous psalm.

"The LORD is king": these are the opening words of Psalms 93, 97, and 99. They indicate the theme which dominates a group of psalms, Psalms 93–100. The question as to whether these opening words presuppose an annual New Year enthronement festival in the Jerusalem temple has been discussed in the commentary on Psalm 47 and need not be repeated here. The REB translation, "The LORD has become king," is possible and would fit in with the language appropriate for such an enthronement festival.

Normally in a Hebrew sentence the verb comes before the subject. Here the order of the words — only two in Hebrew — is reversed. The first word is "The LORD," followed by the verb. This provides us with the clue to the central claim of this and similar psalms. It is the LORD who is king, not any other gods, not any other forces in heaven or earth. It is the LORD, and he alone, who rules. There is an unashamed theological imperialism at work here. Even when, as we have frequently seen in the Psalms, people of faith in Israel found it difficult to see how this kingship of the LORD was being demonstrated in the often apparently meaningless events in which they were caught up, they still held tenaciously to this belief. If they had not, the whole fabric of biblical faith would have collapsed.

1-2 Verse 1 depicts the LORD as clothed in royal regalia, "robed in majesty" (cf. Isa. 26:10), girded with the "strength" or might appropriate to a warrior king. But this is the king whose power overshadows all earthly kingship. This is the king who established the world and guarantees its stability and permanence. This is the king who has been enthroned "from of old," the God who is "from everlasting" (v. 2), there from the beginning of time, here in the present, and the one who will be there as time stretches into the still unknown future.

3-4 Verses 3-4 place everything under the authority of the LORD by referring to all the forces which challenge him, and challenge him in vain. Both the structure of verses 3-4, the three-line pattern in both verses (cf. 92:9), and their content show that their roots lie in earlier Canaanite poetry and mythology. The "floods" — "the mighty waters" — "the waves of the sea" (REB: "breakers") all point back to the forces of chaos which had to be conquered in creation, but which ever threaten to break into the ordered universe (see Psalm 29). It is also likely that these forces of chaos were believed to be embodied in all the human forces that arrogantly threatened the life of the people of the LORD. They were powerful and destructive. At the end of verse 3, the REB translates "crashing waves" and catches the flavor of the Hebrew better than the NRSV's rendering, "their roaring," the related verb meaning to crush (cf. 94:5). Such forces, however, more than meet their match in the one who is more "majestic" (see 76:4) — awesomely powerful — since this is the LORD "on high" (cf. 92:8).

5 Though awesomely powerful, this king is trustworthy and accessible to his people (v. 5). He is trustworthy because his "decrees" are "very sure" or "stand firm" (REB), a translation that perhaps catches better the flavor of the Hebrew word, which is related to the word translated "faithfulness" in 89:1. His "decrees" or testimonies probably here mean all that is witnessed to in the Torah, from creation through the LORD's revelation of himself to his people in their history and the demands he makes upon them. It is a word frequently found in Psalm 119.

He is accessible because he is present with his people: "holiness [see 2:6] befits your house." The word translated "befits" occurs only twice again in the Hebrew Bible, in Isa. 52:7, where it is rendered "beautiful," and in Song of Sol. 1:10, where the NRSV translates "comely" and the REB "lovely." It is as if the LORD's holy presence is not only appropriate in the temple, but brings with it a loveliness which should transform the lives of those who come to worship. As the law code in Leviticus 18–26 repeatedly insists, "You shall be holy, for I the LORD your God am holy" (Lev. 19:2; 20:26).

This psalm celebrates the LORD, the right royal king, source and ruler of all that is, powerful beyond all human power, yet trustworthy and accessible "forevermore" (literally, "for length of days"; cf. 23:6, where the same phrase is translated "my whole life long"), in whatever experiences his people may be called upon to face. For Israel that was always a challenge to faith and obedience, just as it continues to be a challenge for discipleship today. This is nowhere more clearly illustrated than in the story in Mark 4:35-41, where Jesus, present with his disciples in the midst of a raging storm on the Sea of Galilee, is asleep.

Awakened by frightened disciples, he demonstrates his awesome yet caring power. To the crashing waves and the violent wind he says, "Peace! Be still"; of the disciples he asks, "Why are you afraid? Have you still no faith?" — the words of a right royal king.

Psalm 94
WHO IS ON THE LORD'S SIDE?

This psalm has no heading in Hebrew, but the Greek (LXX) links it again with David and assigns it as appropriate for "the fourth day of the week." So many different elements have been brought together in this psalm that all attempts to classify it into one of the common types of psalms run into difficulties. Not surprisingly, therefore, it has sometimes been argued that at least two different psalms have been joined together in this one, the division usually located after verse 11. Certainly we can see features of a communal lament in verses 1-7 at the beginning of the psalm; and at the end, in verses 17-23, this moves into thanksgiving. In the middle we listen to teaching material with a strongly wisdom flavor. There is, however, a consistent theme holding together these disparate elements. The whole psalm reads like a commentary on the teaching of Psalm 1 and on the theological issues which that psalm raises. We shall approach the psalm as an example of instruction given by a wisdom teacher in the context of worship, instruction that tackles a general theological problem in verses 1-16, and then authenticates its teaching by an appeal to personal experience in verses 17-23.

Although there is no mention of the LORD as king in the psalm, there are, as we shall see, links in language with Psalms 92 and 93. The psalm, indeed, has as its central theme the dilemma posed by the evident power of the wicked in the world, which faith claims to be under the sovereignty of God. The psalm, therefore, finds an appropriate place among those psalms that affirm belief in the kingship of the LORD. But who are the "wicked" (vv. 3, 16), the "evildoers" (vv. 4, 16; cf. 92:7) who feature so prominently in the psalm to challenge the kingship of the LORD? Undoubtedly we are talking about wickedness in high places. They are people in positions of power, who use their power arrogantly and destructively to oppress those at risk in society (v. 6). Does this mean that, as some have argued, they are foreign governors or overlords? There is little doubt that in the postexilic period, when the Jews had lost their national independence, the psalm could be and probably was interpreted along this line. It is equally possible, however, that the original reference was to internal corruption and abuse of power within the Jewish community. The language used to describe the activities of such people echoes the teaching of the prophets in both the preexilic and the postexilic periods, from Isaiah (e.g., 1:17, 23) in the eighth century to Malachi (e.g., 3:5, 13-15) in the fifth century. Much depends on how we interpret a phrase in verse 20 that literally means "a throne of destruction," in dark contrast to the throne of the everlasting LORD in 93:2. The NRSV translates "wicked rulers," leaving open who these rulers may be. This could be a reference to postexilic oppressors, or it could be an attack on the royal family in preexilic Jerusalem, since that family stood at the apex of the judicial system, the ultimate human court of appeal (cf. 122:5 with its reference to "thrones for judgment" in Jerusalem and "thrones of the house of David"). The REB translates "corrupt justice," which suggests that we may be dealing with venal judges or with people of influence within the community who seek to use the judicial process for their own nefarious purposes (cf. Isa. 59:1-4).

1-3 The psalm begins with an appeal to the "God of vengeance," a phrase which occurs twice in the opening verse. To understand this title we must rid ourselves of the notions of bitterness and rancor which so often surround our understanding of vengeance. This is in effect an appeal to the divine judge and king (see 7:8). In a crisis situation, where the very fabric of society is being undermined by the "wicked," the LORD, claims this psalmist, can still be depended upon, as the "judge [or ruler] of the earth" (v. 2), to redress the situation. The arrogant and the wicked will get their just deserts, and justice will triumph. The psalmist calls on God to "shine forth" (see 50:2), to manifest himself in all his glory to his people, and to "rise up" (see 3:7). In the midst of corruption that has obviously lasted for some time and that seems to be giving the wicked a great deal of personal satisfaction, the cry inevitably goes up: "O LORD, how long?" (v. 3; see 4:2).

4-7 The charge against the wicked is threefold: First, they are brazenly self-confident, "pouring forth" — perhaps, more graphically, "spewing forth" — their arrogance (v. 4; cf. 31:18). Second, they are throwing down the gauntlet to the LORD, since they are crushing and oppressing a people who are "your people . . . your heritage" (v. 5), that is, the people that the LORD has chosen as his own (see 33:12). In particular, they kill and murder those most at risk in society: the widow, the stranger, and the orphan. Deuteronomy clearly lays down the basis for a different attitude. The LORD is the God who "takes no bribe, who executes justice for the orphan and the widow, and who loves the strangers, providing them food and clothing. You shall also love the stranger, for you were strangers in the land of Egypt" (Deut. 10:17-19). The conduct of the wicked is, therefore, a denial of the very basis of Israel's life, which is to be lived in grateful remembrance of all that the LORD has done for them. One of the curses in Deut. 27:19 is directed at those who deny justice to widow, orphan, and stranger. Third, their arrogance, their violation of all that the LORD enjoins, is rooted in one simple belief. They assume that the LORD is some remote deity who neither knows nor cares about what goes on in this world (v. 7; for "the God of Jacob," see 20:1). Though the language is different, this attitude is the same as that castigated in Ps. 73:11.

8-11 All of this just proves how stupid and clueless such people are. In verses 8-11 an appeal is made to such people to think again. They are admonished as "dullards" and "fools" (v. 8), the same words used in 92:6. They are people devoid of any understanding of what life is all about. The REB rightly at the beginning of verse 8 picks up the wordplay present in the Hebrew. Those who have dismissed the God of Jacob as a God who "pays no heed" (NRSV: "does not perceive") are now called upon to "Take heed yourselves. . . ." The God whom they arrogantly defy is in fact the God who is the source of all the faculties they possess, a God who, therefore, does "hear" and "see" all that goes on (v. 9). Moreover, this is a God who hears and sees not with moral indifference, but who "disciplines" (see 6:1), who teaches the human race, and who "chastises" or corrects those who refuse to accept instruction. His verdict on all merely human intentions or thoughts is *hebel*, "empty breath" (REB: "a puff of wind"; see 39:5) — a damning verdict on the futility of the arrogance of the wicked.

12-15 There is, however, another way (vv. 12-15), the way of those prepared to accept the LORD's discipline and to be taught by the LORD's "law" *(torah)*. They are those who are "happy" (see 1:1). They may face difficulties, but even in the midst of difficulties, they know a God-given inner quietness and peace, until the wicked meet inevitable retribution. In verse 13 "respite" is a weak translation. In Isa. 32:17 it indicates the quietness which goes hand in hand with trust in God. For "a pit" dug for the wicked, see 7:15. In this context, it is unlikely that "pit" functions as a synonym for Sheol, the abode of the dead. Verse 14 looks back to and provides the answer to verse 5. The destructive intentions of the wicked will be countered by the protecting power of the LORD. Justice (see 7:6-8) will, therefore, "return to the righteous" (see Psalm 1) and to "the upright in heart" who are committed to God not only in word, but in deed (see 11:7).

16-23 This teaching, with its clear distinction between the arrogant wicked who challenge God and the righteous who are prepared to live in obedience to God, is now backed up by an appeal to personal experience in verses 16-23. The point of the questions with which this section begins, "Who rises up for me. . . . Who stands up for me" (v. 16) is not to invite sympathy or to express personal doubt, but to pave the way for the resounding answer in verse 17: who but the LORD? If such help had not been forthcoming the psalmist would "soon have been in the land of silence" (v. 17), a phrase indicating death (cf. 115:17), hence the REB translation "the silent grave." When the psalmist's faith was in danger of being undermined (cf. 73:2), he found himself supported by the LORD's "steadfast love" (see 5:7). Beset by "anxious thoughts" (REB v. 19), he found joy in the "consolations" of the LORD. The word "consolations" occurs only here in the Psalms, but in Job 15:11 and Isa. 66:11 it is used of the satisfaction and security a child finds at a mother's breast. There is, therefore, total incompatibility between the

LORD and those who seek to crush his people (vv. 20-21). They may conspire against the righteous and seek to pervert the course of justice "by statute," neatly rendered in the REB as "under cover of law," but the LORD can have nothing to do with such conspiracy, this "throne of destruction."

The final two verses point up the contrast which runs through the whole psalm. On the one hand, there is the LORD who is central to the psalmist's life, "my stronghold" or fortress (see 9:9), "my God, the rock of my refuge" (see 2:12 and 18:2). On the other hand, there are the wicked doomed to receive the just reward of their perversity, doomed to be "wiped out." This verb, which occurs twice in verse 23 for the sake of emphasis, is used in 73:27 of the God "who puts an end to" those false to him. There are indeed many parallels between this psalm and Psalm 73, though Psalm 73 explores more deeply the inner crisis in the psalmist's life. The two concluding verses of Psalm 94 summarize the teaching of the psalm in the same way as the two concluding verses of Psalm 73 do, but in reverse order. Psalm 94 moves from the God who is the psalmist's refuge to the fate of the wicked, while Psalm 73 moves from the fate of the wicked to the God who is the psalmist's refuge.

The overall theology of the psalm is familiar from many other psalms. It is worth noting, however, how the psalmist's personal experience is used to back up the theological teaching of the psalm. This is a model which is universally valid. However correct our theology, it remains cold theory unless it is verified in our experience. We have no right to proclaim or to defend what we do not personally know. The opening verse of 1 John underlines the basis for effective proclamation: "We declare to you what was from the beginning, what we have heard, what we have seen with our eyes, what we have looked at and touched with our hands. . . ."

Psalm 95
AN INVITATION AND A WARNING

This psalm, which the Greek (LXX) text again associates with David, is similar to Psalms 50 and 81 in that it clearly has a section, verses 7b to the end, in which a temple priest or prophet, speaking in the name of God, addresses the people gathered for worship. Some of the issues concerning the likely liturgical context of this psalm are discussed in the introduction to Psalm 81.

The Psalm falls into two parts: verses 1-7a, the invitation or call to worship; and verses 7b-11, a serious warning. There have been ingenious attempts to see in the first section of the psalm the movement of a group of worshippers from the outer entrance to the temple complex, through successive gates into the inner court. This is possible. Part of the evidence for it may be concealed in the NRSV translation. Three times (vv. 1, 2, and 6) it uses the word "come," when the

Hebrew text uses three different words. Verse 1 uses a word that is appropriate for an invitation: "Come." Verse 2 says "let us approach his presence," the same verb being used in 88:13, where it is translated "my prayer comes before you." Verse 6 more clearly indicates "enter" (cf. REB). Across the centuries, of course, in both Jewish and Christian tradition, this first section of the psalm has been sung meaningfully by congregations oblivious of any such hypothetical scenario. In Christian liturgy the psalm is called the *Venite,* Latin for "Come."

1-7a The first part of the psalm begins in verses 1-2 with an invitation and a call to uninhibited, joyful worship. The mood is one of acclamation and thanksgiving. The worshippers may be there under the open sky, but in our terms they are being invited to raise the roof! The Hebrew word translated "make a joyful noise" in verses 1 and 2 indicates an unrestrained shout (for similar language, see the opening of Psalm 47). What other mood is appropriate, since they come to acclaim one who is "the rock of our salvation" (see 89:26)?

Verses 3-5, introduced by "For," then spell out the reasons for this joy-filled worship. They come to acclaim the LORD, "a great God, and a great King above all gods" (see Psalm 82), the one who rules supreme, the creator who has the whole world in his hands, from "the depths of the earth" to "the heights of the mountains." Both of these poetic expressions are unusual. "Sea" and "dry land" are also God's handiwork, fashioned by his hands (see 24:1-2).

The pattern of verses 1-5 is now repeated in verses 6-7a. In verse 6 we have the invitation and call to worship, this time focusing on the need to recognize humbly the authority of the God whom they joyfully acclaim. All three verbs in verse 6, "worship . . . bow down . . . kneel," point to the physical act of submission. Joyful acclamation and humble submission before the mystery of God are still essential elements in that adoration where all true worship begins. Now "the rock of our salvation" becomes "our Maker" (v. 6). Verse 7, introduced by "For," spells out the reason for such humble adoration in language which has its roots in the tradition of the covenant between the LORD and his people (see 25:10), a relationship summed up in the words "I will be your God, and you shall be my people" (Lev. 26:12) and developed in the imagery of the caring shepherd who provides for his flock and keeps them under his protection (v. 7; cf. Psalm 23).

Notice how the two sections of this first part of the psalm are held together linguistically. The God who "made" the sea (v. 5) is "our Maker" (v. 6), the God who made us, echoing the hymn of creation in Genesis 1. "In his hands" are the depths of the earth (v. 4) and his people are "the sheep of his hands" (v. 7). The poet-prophet of Isaiah 40–55 makes the same point when he speaks of the God "who created the heavens" (Isa. 42:5; cf. 45:18) and of the God "who created you, O Jacob" (Isa. 43:1). For Israel, creation and God's revelation of himself to his people in and through their history are part of the one theological tapestry, both of them, as Psalm 136 affirms, the expression of God's steadfast love. Neither an all-powerful God who is indifferent to us nor a caring God who is powerless can satisfy our deepest needs or be the object of joyful worship.

7b-11   The word of God to the worshippers is introduced in verse 7b by an urgent appeal. This is a word to which the people must listen. "Today" they must take to heart the lesson of the past. This emphasis upon "today" is typical of the sermonic material in Deuteronomy (e.g., Deut. 4:39; 5:3; 6:6). In verses 8-10 God recalls the story of the rebellion in the wilderness, which featured so prominently in Psalm 78. The reference in verses 8-9 to "Meribah" ("quarrel" or "strife"; cf. 81:7) and "Massah" ("testing" or "tempting") recalls the incident in Exod. 17:1-7, where the people, lacking water, turn on Moses with the complaint summed up in the words of Exod. 17:7, "Is the LORD among us, or not?" The worshippers are, therefore, being warned that they must not succumb to such a hardening of the spiritual arteries that they question whether God is with them now. That would be to deny the whole tradition of faith in which they had been nurtured. God's response to such a hardening was inevitable: "I loathed [REB: abhorred] that generation" (v. 10). This was a response rooted in the fact that God was dealing with people who had deliberately chosen to "go astray" and to ignore his ways (see 25:4, 9). This led to severe judgment, expressed through God's anger (see 6:1).

"They shall not enter into my rest" (v. 11). "My rest" in this context almost certainly means reaching the Promised Land, the land in which the people would find rest from enemies around and would be able to live in safety (cf. Deut. 12:9-10). Here then, says God, is the story of a people on pilgrimage through the wilderness, a rebellious people who never reached their desired goal. Do not be like them, or you will suffer a like fate.

We have noted the similarities to Psalms 50 and 81. There is, however, a significant difference, well illustrated by comparing the ending of this psalm with the ending of Psalm 81. Psalm 81 issues stern warnings, but it ends by holding out the promise of a satisfying future for those who are prepared to listen to God. This psalm leaves the people to ponder for themselves the dire consequences of disobedience. This has led some interpreters to suggest that this psalm was used to precede and prepare the way for a recital of the demands God makes upon his people in the Decalogue. That is possible. There are, however, times when being left to contemplate a stern warning is in itself a necessary step on the road to the restoration to spiritual health. What is clear from this psalm is that there can be no truly joyful celebration of God which does not lead to moral responsibility and urgency.

Contemporary Jewish and Christian service books and hymnals tend to use verses 1-7a as suitable for a worshipful approach to God, ignoring the second half of the psalm. *Siddur Lev Chadash,* however, adds to these verses the words, "Today the world would be redeemed, if only we would listen to your voice."

Interestingly, Heb. 3:7-11, ignoring the first half of the psalm, uses the second half as part of a Christian midrash or meditation (3:1–4:11) designed to warn and encourage those within the Christian community who are in danger of lapsing from the faith. It hammers home the significance of "today" (3:13; 4:7) and collates the "rest" of verse 11 with God's resting on the Sabbath in the creation hymn in Genesis. It speaks of such a "rest" as being available to all who have faith (4:3), yet as something which "still awaits the people of God" (4:9). The meditation then ends with the clarion call, "Let us make every effort to enter that rest, so that no one may fall by following the old example of unbelief" (Heb. 4:11, REB).

These varied uses of the psalm, or different parts of it, underline the way in which the biblical tradition can be used to speak a relevant word in different circumstances. Yet we need constantly to be reminded of the wholeness of the tradition, and not least of the way in which in this psalm the two parts interact. In our spiritual journey, rejoicing divorced from obedience is escapism, and obedience divorced from rejoicing is uninviting.

Psalm 96
THE KING WHO IS COMING

The central theme of this psalm is "The LORD is king," the very words which introduce Psalm 93 and which appear in this psalm in verse 10. This psalm shares many thoughts and idioms with surrounding ones, notably Psalm 98. Its opening words, "O sing to the LORD a new song," are the opening words of Psalm 98; its closing two verses appear with minor variations as the closing verses of that psalm. There are many links with other psalms and other biblical material. Verses 7-9 closely resemble Ps. 29:1-2, and we frequently hear echoes of the poetry of Isaiah 40–55. The entire psalm, with minor variations and in a slightly abbreviated form, appears in 1 Chron. 16:23-33 in the context of the songs of praise which accompanied David's bringing of the ark to Jerusalem. There it is prefaced by Ps. 105:1-15 and followed by the opening and closing words of Psalm 106. We seem, therefore, to be in touch in this psalm with a long-established tradition of praise, since Psalm 29 is usually regarded as one of the earliest Psalms, and Isaiah 40–55 and Chronicles take us down into the postexilic period. The Greek (LXX) provides the psalm with a heading: "When the house was built after the captivity. A song of David." This suggests that the psalm was regarded as appropriate in connection with the rebuilding of the temple after the return from captivity in Babylon. For possible links with the preexilic enthronement festival, see the introduction to Psalm 47.

The psalm has striking stylistic features. Three times in verses 1-2 we hear the summons, "sing to the LORD"; three times in verses 7-8, "ascribe to the LORD." In

each case further injunctions follow: "bless ... tell ... declare" in verses 2-3; "bring
. . . come . . . worship . . . tremble" in verses 8-9. There is also the deliberate
repetition in verse 13 of the words "for he is coming, for he is coming." The overall
structure of the psalm follows basically the same pattern which we noted in Psalm
95. The summons in verses 1-3 leads into the hymnic celebration of the greatness of
the LORD in verses 4-6. The summons in verses 7-9 leads into the hymnic celebration
in verses 10-13. Where it differs from Psalm 95 is that summons and celebration are
not merely the concern of the congregation of God's people, but of "all the earth"
(v. 1) and "the families of the peoples" (v. 7).

1-3   The opening summons in verses 1-3, with its threefold crescendo, "sing,"
invites "all the earth" to "sing a new song to the LORD" (see 33:3; cf. Isa. 42:10),
to "bless his name" (see 16:7) and daily to proclaim good news. The word translated
"tell" in verse 2 is the same verb translated "herald of good tidings" in Isa. 40:9. In
the Greek translation it provides the word for the proclamation of good news, the
evangel of the New Testament. It is good news because it is the witness to God's
"salvation" (see 3:8), "his glory" (see 3:3), and "his marvelous works" (see 9:2).
It is good news which the psalmist believes, with radiant confidence, concerns not
simply Israel, but "all the earth . . . the nations . . . all the peoples."

4-6   This universalistic note is the inevitable corollary of the character of the
LORD, now celebrated in hymnic style in verses 4-6. The LORD is no petty, minor
tribal deity. Verse 4, in slightly different language, echoes the acclamation in 95:3.
Not only is the LORD "more to be revered," more awesome than other gods (see
47:2); other gods are in fact no more than "idols." The word translated "idols"
is a neat pun on the Hebrew word for god. It indicates something which is weak
or worthless. It is one of a series of satirical words which Hebrew writers delight
in using to describe other gods or their visible representations (cf. Isa. 2:8, 18,
20). Compared with the LORD, they are no more than nonentities, mere ciphers.
The LORD alone is the creator (v. 5), surrounded with the dignity of true royalty
(see 8:1, 6). His "sanctuary," which could mean either the temple in Jerusalem
or his heavenly temple, or both, witnesses to his "strength" and "beauty," both
words which have royal associations. The word here translated "beauty" is in
71:8 rendered "glory" in the NRSV and "splendor" in the REB.

7-9   The second summons in verses 7-9, with its threefold "ascribe to the LORD"
has clear similarities to the opening verses of Psalm 29. In Psalm 29 the appeal
is to the heavenly choir; here, as in the previous section, it has a universal earthly
relevance to "families of the peoples" (v. 7), "all the earth" (v. 9). All are invited
to bring an "offering," an appropriate gift (see 40:6) in recognition that they
accept the authority of the LORD, an authority before which they "tremble" (cf.
29:9; 97:4; 114:7).

10-13 This summons leads into the celebration of the kingship of the LORD — for "the LORD is king" (see 93:1). It is one of the eccentricities of Christian exegesis that there is a Greek/Latin version of the psalm which adds the words "from wood" (i.e., the cross) to this phrase. This thought may have been prompted by the reference to the "trees of the forest" in verse 12. There is, of course, no justification for this. It highlights the danger to which Christian thought has often succumbed in its attempt to find references to Christ in the Hebrew Bible. This is the king who is the creator and sustainer of the whole world (cf. 93:1), the king who "will judge the peoples with equity" (see 7:6-8; 9:7-8). In highly poetic language, but which nevertheless has its roots in an all-embracing theology, the whole universe — the heavens, earth, sea, field and trees — is summoned to join in joyful celebration. Much of this language in verses 11-13 is closely paralleled in Isaiah 40–55 (compare, e.g., Isa. 44:23; 49:13; 55:13).

This is a celebration, however, which looks forward in anticipation. The antidote to any dull formality in worship is an expectant faith which looks not only to the past, but to the future, to the good news of a God who comes and will come to his world. This is the LORD who "is coming . . . is coming" (v. 13), to exercise his kingly rule over the world and all its peoples, a rule characterized by "righteousness" (see 7:8) and "truth" (v. 14; see 89:1). He is coming "to judge the earth" (v. 13). This judging does not mean merely condemning the world for its evil and corruption. It means saying "No" to all that threatens to destroy the world of God's creating, but saying "Yes" to all that will lead it to finding its true purpose and peace. It means putting the world to right. Whatever the words "he is coming" may have meant in the context of the liturgy in the temple or in a specific historical context in Israel's life, they inevitably point forward to a more distant horizon beyond which there lies that new age in which all God's gracious purposes will be fulfilled, an age which can only be described in visionary language. In Christian vision, as contained in the book of Revelation, it climaxes in the words of the risen, exalted Jesus: "Surely I am coming soon," to which the response of faith can only be "Amen. Come, Lord Jesus!" (Rev. 22:20).

Psalm 97
RESPONDING TO AWESOME MAJESTY

The Greek (LXX) text links this psalm with David, "when his land was restored." This last phrase probably points to the postexilic period, and this is where most commentators locate the psalm. There is little doubt, however, that the psalm draws extensively upon traditional imagery which had its place in worship in the Jerusalem temple prior to the exile, notably in its description of the awesome coming of the LORD in verses 2-5. Much of the language and imagery of the psalm is shared with the surrounding psalms that celebrate the kingship of the LORD and with other parts of the Old Testament, but this psalm weaves out of this its own distinctive tapestry.

Psalm 95 focused upon God's own people, "let *us* sing" (95:1); Psalm 96 called upon "all the earth" to sing (96:1). Psalm 97 embraces both. At the outset it calls upon "the earth" and "the many coastlands" to rejoice. "Coastlands" or isles is typical of the language of Isaiah 40–55 (e.g., 40:15; 41:1, 5). Perhaps the word originally indicated the islands of the Aegean, but it points to the distant corners of the world, a meaning which often attaches to our use of the word "overseas." In the concluding verses 10-12, the psalm addresses God's "faithful people" and calls upon "the righteous" to rejoice. Thus the world and Israel unite in the one anthem. The psalm falls into two main sections, verses 1-6, which, after an initial call to rejoice, depict the awesome coming of the LORD; and verses 7-11, which focus upon the effect of his coming.

1-6 Verses 1-6 draw upon imagery associated in particular with the decisive coming of the LORD to his people at Mt. Sinai, the imagery of storm and earthquake. Deuteronomy describes the day the people stood there before the LORD, "at the foot of the mountain which was ablaze with fire to the very skies, and there was dark cloud and thick mist" (Deut. 4:11, REB). Exodus 19:16 speaks of "thunder and lightning as well as thick cloud on the mountain." Similar use of storm imagery marks Psalm 29 (cf. Judg. 5:4-5), with storm and earthquake associated with God's coming or presence in Pss. 68:8 and 77:17-18. Such language directs attention to the awesome mystery of a God who must never be trivialized. Awesome mystery, however, is never enough in itself. The Mt. Sinai tradition speaks of a voice announcing the terms of the covenant and the commandments; so here, this is the LORD whose kingly rule is based on "righteousness and justice" (v. 2; cf. 89:14). The "fire" which accompanies him is, therefore, deadly to those who seek to oppose his kingly rule (v. 3). The earth itself "trembles" (cf. 96:9), and "the mountains melt like wax" (cf. 68:2) before the LORD whose awesome power and inescapable moral demands are writ large in all the earth. Not surprisingly, therefore, this opening section of the psalm climaxes in "the heavens" proclaiming the "righteousness" of the LORD, and "all the peoples" witnessing to his "glory" (see 3:3), just as in Psalm 29 the heavenly and temple choirs join in a triumphant *Te Deum*.

7-12 The second half of the psalm deals with the effect of the coming of this divine king. It spells out first in verse 7 the devastating effect on those who erroneously, yet confidently, worship other gods. Their "images" (cf. Exod. 20:4) are no more than "worthless idols" (see 96:5) or nonentities. Indeed, far from being the object of worship, such gods can do no more than bow in worship before the LORD, the one true God. There is in verse 7 a rich vein of satire, which is further developed in many passages in Isaiah 40–55 (e.g., Isa. 40:18-20; 44:9-17; 46:1-7).

Verses 8-9 note the effect on "Zion" (see 2:6) and "the towns of Judah" (literally, "the daughters of Judah," an expression which refers to the towns and villages which surround Jerusalem; cf. 48:11). Here the response is one of jubilation, rejoicing in "your judgments." While we are not told what these "judgments" or decisions of this awesome God are, it is probable that, as in Psalm 48, they point to the way in which the LORD's power is demonstrated in defending his people against all threatening forces. Jubilation is, therefore, rooted in the fact that the LORD, the God they worship, is "most high" (see 7:17), incomparable, exalted above all other gods (cf. 95:3; 96:4-5).

At the beginning of verse 10, the NRSV and the REB assume a slight alteration to the Hebrew text, to make the opening words a further description of the LORD, "The LORD loves. . . ." This makes sense since the subject of the next two lines is obviously the LORD. There is something to be said, however, for retaining the Hebrew text, noted in the footnote "You who love the LORD" (cf. 31:23). This is then followed by the command "hate evil," hate evil because it is contrary to the nature of the LORD you love, the LORD who "guards," or keeps safe, the lives of his "faithful people" (see 4:3), and rescues them from the clutches of the wicked. They can be assured that "Light dawns for the righteous" (v. 11; cf. 112:4), a translation which involves a minor alteration to the Hebrew text and has the support of the Greek (LXX). The Hebrew text reads "is sown" instead of the verb "dawns." The REB tries to retain something of the flavor of this by translating "A harvest of light has arisen for the righteous." This is an idiom, however, for which there is no parallel in the Old Testament. Light dawning to scatter the encircling darkness makes good sense in context. For the "righteous" and "the upright in heart" used in parallelism, compare 94:15.

Having thus addressed a word of challenge and reassurance to his fellow worshippers, the psalmist now invites them, "the righteous," to join in the universal anthem with which the psalm begins, to "rejoice in the LORD" (see 32:11) and "to give thanks to his holy name" (v. 12). The word translated "name" here means a memorial or remembrance. In Ps. 135:13 it is used in parallelism with the usual word for name and is translated "renown" (cf. Exod. 3:15, where it is translated "title"). Since "name" in Hebrew is more than an identity marker and points to all that is known and remembered about the character of a person, the translation "name" here is justified (see 5:11).

Theologically the psalm reminds us how much our response to God is conditioned by who we believe God to be. If we eliminate the awesome mystery of God, we encourage worship which, in its banality and overfamiliarity, breeds contempt. The worst of modern choruses tend to do just this. If we stress only the awesome mystery of God, there is no reason why our response should be one of joy. That can only be evoked by a God who is not only awesomely mysterious but who, in the language of this psalm, is characterized by a righteousness and justice which reach out in caring protection.

In Christian hymnology Charles Wesley holds these two aspects together in the hymn:

> Rejoice, the Lord is King;
>   Your Lord and King adore;
> Mortals, give thanks and sing,
>   and triumph evermore:
> Lift up your heart, life up your voice;
> Rejoice! again I say, "Rejoice!"

This adoration of the awesome King, then immediately leads into verse 2, which begins:

> Jesus, the Saviour reigns,
>   The God of truth and love.

We need verse 2, but perhaps we should not come to it until we have steeped ourselves in the mystery and wonder celebrated in verse 1. In this, we would be but following the structure of Psalm 97.

Psalm 98
THE VICTORIOUS KING

This psalm has a curiously brief heading, "A Psalm," with the Greek (LXX) adding "of David." As we have already noted, it has strong links with Psalm 96. For its opening words and its closing verse, the commentary on Psalm 96 should be consulted. Yet it has its own flavor. Three times in the first three verses the word "victory" is associated with the LORD (vv. 1, 2, 3). This is the same word translated as "salvation" in 96:2 (see also 3:8). The precise content to be given to this word can only be decided by context. "Victory" is appropriate in this psalm because much of the language in the opening verses is drawn from the picture of the LORD as a victorious warrior. The statement "His right hand and his holy arm" (v. 1) is just such language, long part of liturgical tradition in Israel pointing to God's victorious power (cf. Exod. 15:6; Ps. 20:6; 44:3). This is also the justification of the translation "vindication" (v. 2) for the word which is most frequently rendered "righteousness" or "saving help" (88:12; see 7:11). This "victory" consists of the "marvelous things" (cf. 96:3) the LORD has done for his people, "the house of Israel," the expression of his "steadfast love and faithfulness" (cf. Psalm 89). Yet the psalmist is convinced that what has been happening in the life of Israel, what the LORD has done for his people, has no limited audience in view. It has universal significance and is seen by "all the ends of the earth" (v. 3). "All the earth" (v. 4) is, therefore, invited to join in the victory celebrations. What has happened to Israel is something to be shared with the whole world. How can it be otherwise, since the king who is being acclaimed is the creator and sustainer of the universe (cf. 95:1-5)? To forget this was to lapse, as Israel sometimes did, into a narrow religious nationalism.

What is remarkable about this psalm is the way in which it is fixed solely on the LORD and his victory. There is no mention of defeated enemies and no mention of the gods of other peoples, as in Psalms 96 and 97. They have faded into the background. The LORD alone holds center stage. His victory is celebrated with the unrestrained, joyful acclamation appropriate for a king (cf. Psalm 47; 95:2) to the accompaniment of a royal fanfare. The word translated "trumpets" in verse 6 occurs only here in the Psalms. According to Num. 10:2 they were made of silver and used "for summoning the congregation and for breaking camp." They feature in the coronation of Joash in 2 Kgs. 11:14. Together with lyre, harp, and other musical instruments they grace important religious ceremonial occasions in Chronicles (e.g., 1 Chron. 13:8; 15:28). We shall meet with the temple orchestra in its full glory in Psalm 150.

The whole created world is invited to join in this *Cantate Domino,* to give the psalm its common Christian liturgical title, which is the Latin translation of its opening words. The "world" in verse 7 is the dry land and its inhabitants; every ocean and continent is called on to celebrate. In verse 8, "the floods" are better translated "the rivers" (REB). Together with the "hills" they are the dominant natural features of the inhabited world. This joyful universal anthem not only celebrates the past, but it looks forward expectantly: "He is coming" (v. 9; see 96:10-13).

No psalm more neatly or succinctly lays bare the heart of genuine worship. In worship God's people join with the whole creation in celebrating the wonderful deeds of the one who is king and creator of all. In such celebration we open ourselves to the future which, like the past, will be marked by the coming of this king. The New Testament, as it tells the story of "the man born to be king," challenges us to explore anew what this kingship means in the light of the cross and resurrection, and then to place at the center of our faith and worship the acclamation "Jesus is Lord" (1 Cor. 12:3).

Psalm 99
EXALTED AND HOLY

While Psalm 99 begins with the same word of acclamation as Psalms 93 and 97, "The LORD is king," it is in many respects significantly different from these psalms.

The text is far from certain at key points. This has led to much discussion as to how the psalm should be divided into meaningful sections. The approach taken here assumes that we should divide it into three sections, each ending with a refrain in which the key word is "holy": verses 1-3, ending with "holy is he"; verses 4-5, ending with "holy is he"; and verses 6-9, ending with a slightly expanded refrain, "the LORD our God is holy." It is possible that these refrains were sung by a group of temple singers, responding to the invitation to praise and exalt the LORD.

If "holy" is a key word in these three sections, so is the Hebrew word meaning "to be high." It appears in verse 2 in the description of the LORD as "exalted." It reappears in verses 5 and 9 in the repeated call to the congregation to "extol" (REB: "exalt"), to lift up on high the God they worship.

"Holy" (see 2:6) is that word which directs our attention to the essential nature of God as being different from what we are. Something of what that difference means morally was brought searingly home to the prophet Isaiah in his call experience centering on the threefold, "Holy, holy, holy" (see Isa. 6:1-4). The three sections of the psalm focus on separate aspects of this difference.

1-3 This section celebrates the king who sits "enthroned upon the cherubim" (see 18:10), a phrase associated with the ark in the holy of holies, the throne of the invisible God. God is the king in "Zion" (see 2:6), in the temple, the king who is "great" and "exalted" (cf. 96:4) and "awesome" (the same word is translated "revered" in 96:4). His subjects, "the peoples" and "the earth," respond as the subjects of a powerful ruler are wont to do, with a mixture of fearful agitation and praise. The imagery of the earth which "quakes" or trembles is linked with the awesome coming of God in liturgical poetry from an early period in Israel, though the word used in verse 1 is found only here in the Old Testament. Notable is Judg. 5:4-5, where, in the face of the LORD's coming:

> the earth trembled,
>   and the heavens poured,
>   the clouds indeed poured water.
> The mountains quaked before the LORD, the One of Sinai,
>   before the LORD, the God of Israel.

Although this God was "in Zion," Israel knew far better than to reduce the LORD to petty human banality in worship. Always in worship people came to face a mystery, an awesome mystery which must transcend prosaic human language. If there is no mystery, there is no God. That mystery lies close to the heart of what is meant when the psalmist says "Holy is he" (v. 3).

4-5 But this mystery has a human face. This is no irrational, power-crazed despot. Here is one who has the might of a king at his disposal, but who is a "lover of justice" (v. 4). Twice the word "justice" occurs in these two verses, and allied to it are "equity" and "righteousness," words which echo across the Psalms (see 9:7-8, where the same three words occur). This is the LORD who is concerned to see that right is done on earth, that human life and society are ordered in such a way that the needs of all are safeguarded, with oppression and abuse of power eliminated. Only such a God is worthy to be lifted up on high by the people who worship "at his footstool." The "footstool" may be a reference either to the temple (cf. 132:7; Lam. 2:1) or to the ark of the covenant in the holy of holies where the invisible God sits enthroned. The Hebrew Bible as a whole joins hands to affirm that if there is no justice, there is no God (cf. Psalm 82). Such justice is essential to what the psalmist means when he says "Holy is he" (v. 5).

6-9 The closing section of the psalm focuses on Israel's own privilege, that knowledge of God which came in her peculiar history and experience. There in the past was "Moses," forever associated with the foundation events of Israel's life, the Exodus from Egypt and the covenant relationship sealed at Sinai (cf. 77:20; 103:7; 105:25); "Aaron," the prototypical priest; and "Samuel" the prophet. All of them traditionally played their part in interceding with God on behalf of the people (e.g., Exod. 32:31-32; Num. 16:43-47; 1 Sam. 7:8-9). The LORD's presence with his people had been symbolized in "the pillar of cloud" (v. 7) over the tent of meeting, where God spoke to the people through Moses (cf. Exod. 33:7-11). What the LORD had to say to the people was always a reminder that they were a people under obligation of obedience to the "decrees" (see 19:8) and "statutes" (see 81:4) of the LORD. If, as verse 7 affirms, "they kept his decrees," nevertheless such obedience was to prove only too momentary and fickle (see Psalm 78). This leads into verse 8, which has caused needless trouble. Commentators have wondered how we can reconcile the picture of the LORD as "a forgiving God" with that of him as "an avenger of their wrongdoings." Much of the difficulty lies in a misunderstanding of what forgiveness means. Forgiveness does not imply turning the clock back as if nothing had happened. In human terms, forgiveness does not mean that you do not have to face the consequences of the wrong you have done. It means that even in the midst of such consequences, you can be sustained by a relationship which nothing that you have done can ever break or change (cf. Luke 15:11-32). So verse 8 affirms that Israel was held by the LORD in a relationship which nothing that they did could ever break, even when they were reaping an inevitably bitter harvest as the result of their disobedience (cf. Exod. 34:6-7). This sense is well conveyed in the REB translation: "you were a God who forgave them, yet you called them to account for their misdeeds."

Much of the theology of the book of Hosea draws on human experience to explore this issue in terms of God's relationship with his faithless people, and the cost involved both for the one who forgives and the one who needs to be forgiven.

The forgiveness offered by God's grace is never cheap. That is why at the center of the gospel there stands a cross. True worship for the people of God at the temple (for "holy mountain," see 2:6) involved acknowledging a forgiving and demanding God. Grace and obedience and the inevitable consequences of disobedience are, therefore, close to the heart of what the psalmist means when he says, "The LORD our God is holy." The psalm is a call to worship, but it is also a challenging sermon on what we mean when we use the word "holy" when we think of God.

Psalm 100
THANKSGIVING AND PRAISE

"A Psalm of thanksgiving." This is the only time the word "thanksgiving" (Hebrew *tôdāh*) appears in the headings of the Psalms. The word can either refer to a type of sacrifice or to the attitude that gives rise to and accompanies such a sacrifice (see 50:14). It is often linked with the word "praise," as in verse 4, where both the noun "thanksgiving" and the corresponding verb "give thanks" occur together with "praise." In the light of verse 4, it is reasonable to assume that the title here refers more to the attitude of the worshipper than to the sacrifice offered. The whole psalm speaks of that unashamedly joyful response to life which seeks to praise God for all that he has done and for all that he is. It is possible that lurking behind the language of the psalm — though this is not evident to readers of the English text — there is the thought of the LORD as a great king. The opening words, for example, are words suitable for the acclamation of just such a king (see 98:4). The description of the people as "the sheep of his pasture" depicts the LORD as the caring shepherd, a well-known royal title in Israel and in the ancient Near East in general (see Psalm 23). Moreover, the psalm is closely associated with psalms which affirm that it is the LORD who is king (Psalms 93, 97–99). It is hardly necessary, however, to catch such a nuance in the language to appreciate this psalm.

The psalm falls into two neatly balanced sections: (a) verses 1-2 sound the call to joyful worship, with verse 3 then stating the reasons for such worship; (b) verse 4 reiterates the call to worship, with verse 5 then stating the reasons for such worship.

1-3 The mood of unrestrained joy and gladness which pulsates through the first two verses echoes 98:4. The call to "all the earth" to participate in such worship points to the same relationship between Israel's own experience and that of the wider world which was discussed in the context of Psalm 98. "All the earth" may be summoned to join in the celebration, but it is the LORD, the center of Israel's religious pilgrimage, who is being celebrated.

The word translated "worship" in verse 2 might equally well be translated "serve." It is a word used frequently in Deuteronomy of "serving other gods" (e.g., Deut. 7:4; 8:19; 11:16) and of serving the LORD (e.g., Deut. 6:13; 10:12). For Deuteronomy this means far more than worship in a liturgical sense; it means walking in the LORD's ways, loving him, keeping his commandments (cf. Deut. 10:12), demonstrating a quality of life consistent with commitment to the LORD (see Ps. 2:11). "Worship," however, may be defended as a legitimate translation in the context of this psalm. The fact that we sometimes talk about worship as "divine service" should remind us that without the wider life-commitment of which it is an expression, worship comes in for severe criticism throughout the Hebrew Bible (see 40:6-8).

The reason for such worship is now spelled out in verse 3. This is worship based on an appeal to experience. "Know" does not merely imply theoretical or head knowledge. In this context it implies a confession of faith based on two things: First, "the LORD is God." Since in Hebrew the word "he" occurs emphatically after LORD, the true flavor of these words probably requires that we insert the word "alone" — the LORD alone is God. This is a confession of faith which features prominently in the preceding psalms (e.g., 95:3; 96:4-5; 97:9). Second, there is the relationship between the LORD and his people. "It is he that made us, and we are his." This reading follows some Hebrew manuscripts, early scribal notes on the text, and some of the versions. It is in context preferable to the AV reading, "and not we ourselves," and to the reading "without our aid" of the Scottish Metrical Version. The words for "not" and for "his" sound the same in Hebrew. Israel knows herself to be the community made or formed by the LORD, the people he has chosen (cf. Isa. 43:1; 44:2), "the sheep of his pasture" (REB: "the flock he shepherds"; cf. 74:1; 79:13 and the shepherd imagery throughout Psalm 23). It has been said that these words "simultaneously express pride and humility, awe and trust" (A. Weiser). There may also be in them more than a hint of surprised amazement. Imagine . . . we . . . his people! Something goes out of faith when we lose that sense of amazement.

4-5 Verse 4 invites the people to bring with them this mood of thanksgiving and praise as they enter through the gates into the temple courts, there to "bless his name" (see 16:7), to acknowledge all that God is and all that he has done to enrich the life of his people. The reason for this is then spelled out in verse 5 in words which sound like a standard liturgical formula. They occur again at the beginning of Psalms 106, 107, 118, and 136. The statement that the LORD is "good" is rich in meaning. It implies that he is the source of all that gives life its rich positive and creative variety, and that he says "No" to all that is evil and threatens to destroy his creative purposes. The fact that such goodness often seemed to be called into question by the bitter reality of life lies behind the struggle of many of the psalmists, not least the author of Psalm 73, which, as we have seen, is a startlingly honest exploration of what God's goodness means. The LORD's goodness has its roots in those elements in his nature which last unchanged to embrace "all generations," namely, "his steadfast love" (see 5:7) and "his faithfulness" (see 25:5; cf. 89:2; 98:3).

A people's thanksgiving and praise transcend all time. The Midrash claims, "In the time to come all offerings will cease, except the thank offering; this will never cease. All prayers will cease, except the prayer of thanksgiving; this will never cease" (*Midrash on the Psalms,* ed. Braude). Across the centuries Psalm 100 has been the vehicle of the thanksgiving of God's people. The first three hymns in the *Church Hymnary,* third edition of 1973, are versions of this psalm. Hymn 1 is the Scottish Metrical Version, "All people that on earth do dwell," sung to the magnificent sixteenth-century tune "Old Hundredth." Hymn 2 is the Isaac Watts/Charles Wesley paraphrase, "Before Jehovah's awesome throne, Ye nations bow with sacred joy." Hymn 3 is the prose Psalm version, the *Jubilate Deo.* This psalm takes us close to the heart of true worship, with congregations invited to experience this in whatever form of the psalm most appeals to them.

Psalm 101
A ROYAL MANIFESTO

This is a royal psalm. The one who speaks in it has personal and social responsibilities which point clearly to the role of the king in the life of Israel. In Book IV, only this psalm and Psalm 103 have in the Hebrew text a heading linking the psalm with David. When, however, we try to explore what precise situation in the life of the king is presupposed in the psalm, we sail into very uncertain waters. Much depends on what we make of the question which appears in the middle of verse 2, rendered "When shall I attain it?" (NRSV) or "When will you come to me?" (REB). Many think this question is wholly inappropriate in the context of the psalm. It is often either emended to read, for example, "may truth come before me" or tacitly ignored in the overall approach to the psalm. The question, however, presupposes that the psalm springs out of some crisis situation in the life of the king, or out of a moment of challenging commitment in which the king is pleading for help. It may have been a political crisis, though if it had been we might expect a more specific reference to the king's enemies. It has been claimed that the psalm has its background in the New Year festival in which the king went through a process of ritual humiliation before being enthroned anew. The details, however, of such a festival are far from clear (see comment on Psalm 47), and it is questionable whether it is needed to account for the language of this psalm. There is a further issue. What is the relationship between the question in verse 2 and what follows? It has been argued that the verbs which follow should be treated as past tenses in English: "I have walked . . . I have not set." In this case the plea for help from God is being backed up by a protestation of innocence and integrity, as in 18:20-24. The NRSV and REB, however, render "I will walk . . . I will not set." This means that these words are to be taken as a vow or promise. This is the view taken in the comments which follow. Such a vow or promise would have been appropriate at the coronation service or at any reliving of such a service. The plea for help is, therefore, being strengthened by a promise of commitment to the values which are close to the heart of God. Either that, or the thought may be that only if his plea is answered will the king be able to fulfill the promises expected of him.

This royal manifesto falls neatly into two sections: verses 1-4, the king's promise of his own personal integrity; and verses 5-8, which we might call today a citizens' charter, in which the king promises to guarantee that the same integrity will characterize the whole life of the community for which he is responsible. Various key words or phrases bind these two sections together. Thus "the LORD" appears in the opening and the closing verse, providing a theological framework for the whole psalm. The "way that is blameless" appears in verses 2 and 6; "my house" in verses 2 and 7; and "my eyes" in verses 3 and 6, being translated "I will see" in verse 6.

1-4 The psalm opens with the king acknowledging that the integrity to which he is committed is rooted in his relationship with the LORD. He celebrates that "loyalty and justice" which are the bedrock of the LORD's dealings with his people, not least with the royal family in terms of the covenant with David (see Psalm 89). The word translated "loyalty" here is the same word usually rendered in the NRSV by "steadfast love"; to this we may compare the opening words of Psalm 89, "I will sing of your steadfast love, O LORD, forever . . ." (see also 5:7). Because of the LORD's unswerving commitment to the king and because, in the words of 99:4, the LORD is "a lover of justice," the same "loyalty and justice" must characterize the king's own life and be displayed in his dealings with his people.

In verses 2-4, the king makes his pledge of personal integrity. It begins with a general commitment, "I will study the way that is blameless." This Hebrew verb "to study" is very common in the wisdom teaching in Proverbs. It points to a certain type of acquired expertise which will enable the cultivation of a wise and prudent attitude to life (see Ps. 2:10, where it is translated "be wise"). The noun *maśkîl*, which appears in some of the psalm headings, comes from the same root (see Psalm 32). In this context it implies a commitment to follow "the way that is blameless" (see 15:2). The REB translation, "I shall lead a wise and blameless life," catches the meaning. The NRSV translation of the question, "When shall I attain it?" — literally, "When shall it come to me?" — assumes that "it" refers back to the way that is blameless. The REB rendering — "When will you come to me?" — takes the subject to be "you," that is, the LORD. The

Hebrew may be rendered either way. Given the assurance that wisdom will be forthcoming or that God will make his presence known to him, the king then specifies in more detail the kind of life to which he is committed.

It involves personal "integrity of heart," the word "integrity" being the same Hebrew word translated "blameless" in v. 2a. Such integrity is to be displayed "within my house." The word "house" covers a wide range of meanings from family and household to the royal court or the temple or the community at large. Here it may well mean the royal court, the members of the privy council, as it were, who advise the king. He will set a personal example of integrity to them. We need not exclude, however, the possibility that the reference is to all the members of the royal family, who in Israel, as in the modern world, were not always models of propriety.

It involves shunning "anything that is base" (see 41:8, where the same phrase is translated "a deadly thing"). There is always in this word an element of something menacing yet worthless. It is the antithesis of integrity.

It involves saying a final "No" to those who "fall away," a word which occurs only here in the Old Testament but which may very well indicate, as the REB translation implies, apostasy or, more generally, any swerving from acceptable conduct.

It involves renouncing "perverseness of heart," a phrase which indicates a twisted personality (cf. 18:26), the exact opposite of the integrated personality indicated by "integrity of heart." It means closing the door on everything that is "evil" and therefore potentially destructive.

5-8 For the king such personal integrity must also be reflected in the life of the community which he governs. Verses 5-8, therefore, provide us with a citizens' charter, promulgated and guaranteed by royal fiat.

Verse 5 speaks of what can have no place in the king's realm — insidious slander or snide comments which undermine community life, and the overweening haughtiness and arrogance which devalue other people (see Psalm 57).

Verse 6 speaks of those who are acceptable — "the faithful" (see 4:3), the loyalists, those who reflect in their daily life "the way that is blameless" to which the king has committed himself (v. 2). Such are the people who will "minister" to the king. The word "minister" is used frequently in the Old Testament of the priests and Levites functioning in the temple (cf. Deut. 10:8; Num. 3:6), but it can also be used of court officials or of anyone who provides assistance or service to someone superior in status (e.g., Exod. 24:13; 2 Sam. 13:17-18). Probably the king is here indicating that, to further the well-being of the community, he will surround himself only with officials who are prepared to share his integrity and give unswerving loyalty to him. This rules out any sycophants, who practice "deceit" and "utter lies" by telling the king only what he wants to hear, whether it be true or not; or any who spread rumors designed to create friction at court.

The psalm ends with the king promising daily to dispense justice which will eliminate the "wicked" (see 1:1) throughout the land and which will rid "the city of the LORD" (Jerusalem) of all "evildoers" (see 5:5).

What the king is promising in this psalm, then, is that he will take seriously his royal duties and guarantee an administration that will ensure that the country experiences *shalom* (see 4:8; 29:11). It hardly matters whether this is a promise given within the coronation service or in some other cultic act, or whether it is in response to some historical crisis; it remains a promise which was to be repeatedly broken. Israel knew only too well what the abuse of royal power meant. It suffered from maladministration by court and justice officials. Many of the Psalms point to situations where there was no true *shalom* in the community. This psalm reads almost like the kind of promises we expect to hear from politicians in a party manifesto leading up to an election. They are rightly greeted with a fair measure of cynicism, because they are seldom delivered. It is hardly surprising, therefore, that such a royal psalm was given a future messianic interpretation, with the promises understood as a future hope to be fully realized only in an ideal kingdom yet to come. The New Testament bears its own witness to that hope: in the words of Jesus, "The time is fulfilled, and the kingdom of God is upon you: repent and believe the good news" (Mark 1:15); in the picture of the risen Lord who will judge the world in righteousness (e.g., Acts 17:31); and in the vision which throbs through the book of Revelation, with its picture of a new heaven and a new earth and a new city of God (see Revelation 21).

Psalm 102
DESPAIR AND HOPE

Issues which we have had to face in many other psalms abound in the interpretation of this one. The answers to them are almost as numerous as the commentators. Who is the "I" who speaks in this psalm? Is it the king or some other representative of the community, or is it some otherwise unidentified individual sharing with us the nightmare of his own personal experience? Are there any clues in the psalm to the possible historical situation out of which it comes? Do verses 14-15, for example, imply the exilic or immediately postexilic situation with Jerusalem still in ruins and the temple not yet rebuilt? Or are we here in touch with traditional liturgical language, communicating eternal hopes, in much the same way as a struggling congregation today will sing John Newton's hymn, "Glorious things of thee are spoken, Zion, city of our God. . . ." How do we hold together the sharply contrasting elements within the psalm — the lament in verses 3-11 and 23-24 and the hymnic celebration of the LORD in verses 12-22 and 25-28? Such contrasts have led some scholars to argue that the present psalm is an amalgamation of two originally separate psalms.

The view taken here is that, as the extended heading to the psalm implies, we are dealing essentially with an individual lament, in which the psalmist sees, mirrored in his own suffering, the plight of the community. A setting in the exilic or early postexilic period seems most likely. The existence, side by side, of lament and hymnic celebration occasions no surprise; it occurs elsewhere both in the individual and in the community laments (see, e.g., Psalms 22 and 74).

1-2 The opening appeal to the LORD in verses 1-2 uses language with which we are familiar from other laments (cf. 31:2; 39:12; 88:2). The psalmist is facing a crisis in his life, "the day of my distress." God is conspicuous by his absence (for "hide your face," see 10:1; 88:14), an absence all the more disturbing since the psalmist believes that he is appealing to the God who answers the cry of those in distress (cf. 86:7). An answer is needed, and needed urgently: "answer me speedily."

3-11 Verses 3-11 vividly describe the nightmare the psalmist is facing. Two corresponding pictures, coming at the beginning and end of this section, provide the framework within which the detail of the psalmist's plight is sketched:

* "my days pass away like smoke [v. 3] . . . my days are like an evening shadow [v. 11]";
* "my heart . . . withered like grass [v. 4] . . . I wither away like grass [v. 11]."

Life is fragile and transitory. The end is drawing near. In the grip of fever, depressed, pain-wracked, his appetite gone, he is reduced, as we would say, to skin and bones (vv. 3-5). Although the precise identity of the birds in verse 6 is uncertain (both of them are listed among unclean birds in Lev. 11:17-18), the picture is of someone who is desperately lonely, like a solitary bird on a rooftop where we would normally expect to see a flock of birds (v. 7). His loneliness is compounded by the fact that night brings him no relief — he lies awake (vv. 6-7). He is surrounded by enemies taunting him, no doubt with ruthless theological logic, pointing out, as Job's friends did, that his suffering must be the result of his sinfulness. They "use my name for a curse" (v. 8), that is, he becomes a byword for all that is God forsaken (cf. 69:11; 44:14). The REB translation "they conspire against me," however, is equally possible, since the phrase literally means "they have taken an oath with [or: against] me." Nor does the psalmist dissent from this view. He can only attribute what has happened to him as the outworking of the LORD's "indignation and fury," strong words (cf. 38:1, 3) pointing to the heavy hand of God's anger. Unless he regarded such anger as irrational, the psalmist would tend to assume that this was God's response to his sinfulness, even if he were not sure what that sinfulness was. For the psalmist, therefore, all the joy has gone out of life. He speaks as if the only appetite he has left is for a daily diet of "ashes" and "tears," the customary signs of humiliation and mourning (cf. 2 Sam. 13:19; Isa. 61:3).

12-22   Despair abounds, but in the midst of despair there is a source of hope. "But you, O LORD, are enthroned forever" (v. 12). There is a divine king, whose rule and graciousness, there from the beginning of time to its end, have been the theme of many of the preceding psalms (e.g., Psalm 93). In many other laments, the emphatic "But you . . ." leads into a recital of God's mighty acts in the past as the basis for hope (e.g., 22:3-5; 74:12-17), but here the focus is entirely on the future, on what God will do. What is at stake is the continuing future of a relationship, a relationship summed up in two words which echo across verses 12-22 — the "LORD," whose name is invoked or mentioned seven times in these verses, and "Zion," referred to in verses 13, 16, and 21.

It is a relationship which has two interwoven themes. First, "Zion" (see 2:6), central to so many of the hopes and religious affirmations of the past, is no more than a pitiable heap of stones, dust, and rubble (v. 14). Yet it remains central to the prayers of people who are "destitute" (v. 17, a word only found here as an adjective, but probably pointing to a people stripped of all that they once cherished), tormented "prisoners" "under sentence of death" (REB v. 20; literally, "sons of death"). This description would fit the late exilic or early postexilic period, when the temple in Jerusalem was still in ruins and the people either still in exile or struggling to survive in and around Jerusalem, as they face a very uncertain future. In this situation there is expressed the conviction that now is the time for the LORD to "favor" or to be gracious to Zion (see 4:1). He will act, "rise up" (v. 13; see 3:7). He will "have compassion" (v. 13; see 25:6); he will "build up" or rebuild Zion (v. 16). He will respond to the prayers of his despairing people. The word translated "regard" in verse 17 is often used of turning one's face graciously towards someone, the opposite of that hiding of the face (v. 2) which seemed to be the present grim reality.

This leads into the second theme in verses 18-21. The LORD's "will" is no mere hope. It is a certainty, to be recorded for the future, a certainty to which generations "yet unborn" will look back with a song of praise on their lips (v. 18). The God of heaven is concerned with what happens here on earth (v. 19). Zion will arise from the ashes of present despair to become the focus of the nation's celebration of the greatness and the goodness of the LORD (v. 21).

Both themes look out beyond Israel to the whole world joining in the acknowledgment of what God does for his people (see Psalm 98). The "nations," the "kings of the earth" will acknowledge "the name" (see 5:11) and "the glory" (see 3:3) of the LORD (v. 15) and will be part of the universal worshipping congregation which will gather at Zion (v. 22).

This whole section, verses 12-22, is also bound together by the echoing letters *š (sh)* and *m* in Hebrew. They occur in the Hebrew words for "name" (vv. 12, 15, 21), for "heaven" (v. 19), and for "hear" (v. 20). This last word "hear" in verse 20 provides the answer to the plea with which the psalm begins: "Hear my prayer, O LORD." To live in hope, therefore, is to believe that God will step decisively into the crisis of the present to assert anew his kingship and to evoke from his people an anthem of praise.

23-28   The closing section of the psalm reverts in verses 23-28 to the twin themes of lament (vv. 3-11) and celebration (vv. 12-22). It begins with the psalmist lamenting that though he is still "in midcourse" (literally, "on the way"), in what ought to have been the prime of life, his strength and vitality have been shattered, his life expectancy cut short (v. 23). Haunted by the brevity and transitoriness of life, he seeks refuge in the God "whose years endure throughout all generations" (v. 24). Even the apparently secure universe, earth and heaven, shares in that same frailty and transitoriness; they are doomed to "wear out like a garment" (cf. Isa. 51:6). The LORD alone remains unchanging: "you are the same" (v. 27). The Hebrew is literally "you [are] he," a phrase which finds its counterpart in the repeated use in Isaiah 40–55 of the words "I [am] he" on the lips of God (cf. Isa. 43:10, 13; 48:12), where the prophet, in a similar crisis situation, seeks to lift the eyes of his people beyond the fears and troubles which beset them, to the one unchangeable certainty: "Listen to me, O Jacob and Israel whom I called. I am he: I am the first and I am the last" (Isa. 48:12). Thus there is lasting security available to "the children of your servants" (v. 28), those who across the years have committed themselves to the LORD, the security of God's presence (cf. Psalm 73).

In verse 25 the Greek (LXX) text places alongside "you" the word "Lord" *(kyrios)*. This Greek word is applied to Jesus in the New Testament. Verses 25-27 are thus used in Heb. 1:10-12 as one of a series of quotations from the Psalms which seek to illustrate the unique place of Jesus in the revelation of God. This exalts him far above anything or anyone else, particularly "angels," whom Jewish tradition claimed to be agents in the transmission of the Torah to Israel. The particular form which the argument takes in Hebrews may strike us as somewhat strange today, but the theology which gave it birth remains central to Christian faith.

In Christian tradition this psalm is the fifth of the penitential psalms (see comment on Psalm 6). As in the case of some of the other penitential psalms, there is no specific note of penitence or confession in this one. In addition to the references to "ashes" and "tears" in verse 9, however, there is an acceptance that the suffering experienced is justified (see v. 10), and there is throughout the note of submission to God, a reaching out from human frailty to the security which the eternal God alone can give. It is the combination of such elements which makes penitence honest and keeps it from lapsing into morbidity. A modern Jewish prayer succinctly reaches to the heart of the theology of this psalm: "Eternal God, help me to feel your presence when dark shadows fall upon me. When my own weakness and the storms of life hide You from my sight, help me to know that You have not deserted me. Uphold me with the comfort of Your love" (*Siddur Lev Chadash*).

Psalm 103
BLESS THE LORD —
MY GOD AND YOUR GOD

Book IV ends with four psalms that have as their framework the call to bless or praise the LORD. Psalm 103 thus begins and ends with "Bless the LORD, O my soul." Psalm 104 begins and ends with "Bless the LORD, O my soul," with "Praise the LORD" added to the ending. Psalm 105 begins with "O give thanks to the LORD" and ends with "Praise the LORD," unless the "Praise the LORD" at the end of Psalm 104 should be taken as the opening words of Psalm 105, in which case it begins and ends with "Praise the LORD." Psalm 106 begins with "Praise the LORD! O give thanks to the LORD" and ends with "Praise the LORD" appended to the typical doxology which closes a book. Struggle and questioning were part of Israel's pilgrimage, but it was never marked by a joyless or a petty faith. In Psalm 103 we see what has been well described as "one of the finest blossoms on the tree of biblical faith" (A. Weiser), suffused with colors of amazing divine grace and the response it evokes.

There has been much discussion as to whether this is a song of personal thanksgiving, as verses 1-5 seem to indicate, or a community hymn, as verses 6-18 seem to imply. Is the "I" who speaks in verses 1-5 an otherwise unknown individual inviting others to share in his experience of divine grace, or is he a cultic official or some other representative of the community, giving voice to the faith he shares with the community? We have perhaps seen enough in our discussion of other psalms to realize that the distinction between the individual and the community is difficult to make, nor is it important for our understanding of the psalm as it now lies before us. Both the way in which the psalm seems to echo material from a variety of different sources in the Hebrew Bible and the occurrence within it of linguistic features common in Aramaic suggest a postexilic date, though tradition associated it with David. Whatever its date, however, it bears witness to religious experience, and the worship related to it, which were characteristic of Israel's pilgrimage across many centuries.

1-2   An introit in verses 1-2 gives voice to the major theme of the psalm: "Bless the LORD, O my soul." The call to "bless the LORD" is a call to acknowledge all that God has done to enrich life (see 16:7). This call is made not to the congregation or to the people, as it would be in a typical community hymn, but to "my soul," to everything which makes me what I am, my God-given personality (for the Hebrew *nepeš,* translated "soul," see 6:3). It is, therefore, paralleled by "all that is within me" — my mind, my heart, my will. It is as if the psalmist is addressing himself, every fiber of his being, and saying to himself, "Come on, bless the LORD!" Two complementary aspects of the LORD's character come into view as the reason for such blessing: "his holy name" (see 5:11), all that makes God awesomely different from anything or anyone else; and "his benefits," the way in which he deals bountifully with his people (see 13:6, which uses the verb related to the word "benefits"). To "bless the LORD" is to acknowledge that all that makes life richly meaningful comes to us as a gift that we should never take for granted. This is the implication of the words "forget not . . ." (v. 2).

3-5 In a series of descriptive participles, the psalmist acknowledges what God has done for him. The word "your" in these verses points back to "O my soul." This is the God "who forgives" all that has been perverse in the psalmist's life, his "iniquity" (see 25:11). This is the God "who heals all your diseases." The word translated "diseases" occurs only here in the Psalms, though it is found elsewhere in the Hebrew Bible. Since disease and illness were commonly attributed to sin in the ancient world, including Israel, forgiving and healing may be regarded as two aspects of the same experience; healing is the outward sign of the restoration of the inner relationship with God (see the discussion on forgiveness at 99:8). There were, however, sufficient voices raised in Israel to question the necessary link between sin and suffering (e.g., Psalm 73 and Job), to warn us against making this assumption. Disease, whatever its origin, was, however, regarded as a challenge to God's goodness and grace. Therefore, it was appropriate to look to him for healing. This is the God

- "who redeems" (see 19:14), that is, who delivers from everything which is life-threatening. For the "Pit" as a synonym for Sheol or Death, see 16:1.
- "who crowns you," the picture being that of a royal bridegroom prepared for his wedding (see Song of Sol. 3:11), crowns you with "steadfast love," that divine loyalty which never fails (see 5:7), and "compassion" (v. 4), which is to be spelled out more fully in verse 13 with the picture of a father's attitude to his children.
- "who satisfies you," his goodness lavished upon you, "as long as you live." The translation "as long as you live" assumes a minor alteration to a Hebrew text which has puzzled translators and commentators across the centuries. The REB's rendering, "in the prime of life," is based on an Arabic root.

Much needless speculation has centered upon what is meant by youth being renewed like the eagle's (v. 5). The eagle is used here as a symbol of soaring strength, as in Isa. 40:31, where it is claimed: "Those who wait for the LORD shall renew their strength; they shall mount up with wings like eagles." In other words, the psalmist attests that whatever life may have thrown at him, he has found ever renewed strength which has enabled him to cope, and to cope successfully. That is his song of thanksgiving.

6-18 Verses 6-18 now turn to the parallel experience in the history of the people of God. This is a story which hinges on a God who "works vindication" or righteousness (see 98:2), a God who puts right what is wrong (see 7:9-11), a God who guarantees "justice" for those who are on the receiving end of oppression (see 97:8, 10). Verses 7-8 focus attention upon specific incidents within this story. The statement "He made known his ways to Moses" (v. 7) echoes the narrative in Exodus 33 where Moses, disconsolate and weighed down by the burden of leadership of a people who, in his temporary absence, had made a golden calf image, turns to God to say, "Show me your ways, so that I may know you and find favor in your sight" (Exod. 33:13). The subsequent revelation to Moses leads into the classic statement of God's character in Exod. 34:6: "The LORD, the LORD, a God merciful and gracious, slow to anger, and abounding in steadfast love and faithfulness. . . ." These words are virtually quoted in verse 8. Such is the nature of the God who has acted powerfully in the history of his people. The word translated "acts" in verse 7 usually has this idea of power hovering around it, hence the REB translates it as "mighty deeds." In 78:11 it is used in parallelism to the word usually translated "wonders" or miracles.

Verses 9-14 move into a meditation upon the confession of faith in verse 8. God may have to bring charges against his sinful people, but he does not keep on and on in this vein. The word "anger" is not in the Hebrew text of verse 9, though most English translations assume, unnecessarily, that it is implied in context. This is not a God who demands his pound of flesh. In two bold images in verses 11-12, the psalmist stresses that God's steadfast love and forgiveness are infinite. The image in verse 11 is found in several other contexts. After using the same language of a God who is "compassionate," a God who "abundantly pardons," Isa. 55:8-9 declares, "For my thoughts are not your thoughts, nor are my ways your ways, says the LORD. For as the heavens are higher than the earth, so are my ways higher than your ways, and my thoughts than your thoughts." We may find it difficult not to place limits on our compassion, but God doesn't. We may find it impossible to wipe the slate clean, to forgive when others offend us, but God doesn't. There is, however, a human analogy which takes us part of the way — the picture of the father who has compassion on his children, used interestingly in Isa. 49:15 with the mother center stage, as an imperfect analogy of God's unchanging compassion for his people (see 25:6). Over and over again in the Hebrew Bible family imagery is used to make theological statements. The people of Israel are the children of God (e.g., Exod. 4:22; Deut. 14:1; Isa. 45:11).

Thus both the mother and father image may be applied to God. The "father" image is found elsewhere in the Psalms (see 89:26; cf. 68:5). The analogy is used in a variety of ways. In Prov. 3:12 it is used to point to the way in which God disciplines those he loves, "as a father the son in whom he delights." It is developed in the New Testament largely in terms of Jesus' relationship with God, particularly in John's Gospel (e.g., John 1:18; 3:16) and in terms of God's loving care for all his children (e.g., Luke 11:11-13). Here it is used to stress the LORD's compassion for "those who fear him" (v. 13), a phrase which occurs in verses 11, 13, and 17 (see 19:9).

This "fear of the LORD" is spelled out in verse 18 in terms of "those who keep his covenant, and remember to do his commandments" (see 25:10).

The psalm emphasizes that this is a compassion rooted in a recognition of human frailty (v. 14). We are made by God "out of dust" (Gen. 2:7) and are destined to return to dust (Gen. 3:14; Eccl. 3:20). The frailty of "mortals" (Hebrew *ĕnôš;* see 8:4) is then developed in verses 15-16 in terms of an image which depends upon Isa. 40:6-8 (cf. Ps. 90:5-6). As in the Isaiah passage, this picture of human frailty and creatureliness leads into a sharply contrasting statement about God. In Isa. 40:8 it is "the word of our God will stand forever"; here it is "the steadfast love of the LORD is from everlasting to everlasting" (v. 17).

19-22   The psalm ends with a closing hymn which celebrates the one and only heavenly king. Since he "rules over all" (v. 19), all are summoned to bless him — "angels" (see 34:7; cf. 91:11); "mighty ones," literally "warriors of strength," a phrase found only here in the Old Testament; "all his host" (see 24:10); and "his ministers," those who serve him. All these four words in verses 20-21 point to the members of the heavenly court who surround the heavenly king and who are obedient to his every wish and command. From the heavenly host we turn in verse 22 to "all his works," every created thing in every corner of the universe over which he rules. Here is the whole of creation echoing the anthem of the heavenly choir (see Psalm 29). Then, with breath-taking wonder, we are back where we began: "Bless the LORD, O my soul," as if the psalmist's own contribution was a vital element in this anthem. And so it is. When we bring our experience of God's grace with us to worship, we do not come in the loneliness of the long-distance runner. We come in the company of all that exists in heaven and on earth, whether we are with the two or three in a small country church or in a large cathedral congregation. We come with our own contribution until the day comes when the barriers between heaven and earth finally dissolve, and in the words of the vision in Revelation 4 and 5 we hear the anthem of "every creature in heaven and on earth and under the earth and in the sea, and all that is in them singing: " 'To the one seated upon the throne and to the Lamb be blessing and honor and glory and might forever and ever!' " (Rev. 5:13).

Psalm 104
BLESS THE LORD —
THE WORLD IS HIS

Whoever the author of Psalm 104 was, he was a poet of no mean stature. This psalm contains some of the finest lyric poetry in the Old Testament, notably in the central section from verses 5 to 30. Read it through and enjoy it before you begin to ask questions about its meaning. In many respects it may be seen as the twin of Psalm 103. It begins like Psalm 103 with the call "Bless the LORD, O my soul," and it ends on the same note. Both are concerned to meditate on God's providence, but whereas in Psalm 103 it is that divine providence, that steadfast love, in human experience, in Psalm 104 it is God's providence writ large in the world which he created and which he sustains.

Many similarities have been noted between this psalm and an earlier Egyptian *Hymn to the Sun* from the fourteenth century BCE. It is worth reading the two texts side by side, because they point up not only the similarities but also the differences. The major theological difference is that, in the Egyptian hymn, the sun or the solar disk is the divine source of life, while in Psalm 104 the sun receives but a brief entry in God's calendar (v. 19). Like everything else in the world the LORD has created, the sun knows its place and fulfills its God-given role. In this respect Psalm 104 is much closer to the creation hymn in Genesis 1, where the sun is merely "the greater light" set by God in the dome of the sky (cf. Gen. 1:14-18). There are other similarities, as we shall see, between Psalm 104 and Genesis 1, though we are not entitled to assume literary dependence either way. Both may be different expressions of a theological attitude to the created world celebrated in worship in ancient Israel. It has been claimed that Psalm 104 stands in relationship to Genesis 1 "like a coloured picture to the clean lines of a woodcut" (A. Weiser). Certainly we cannot fail to be impressed by the color and the variety of images which leap out from the text of this psalm.

1-4   Like Psalm 103, this psalm begins in verses 1-4 with an introit, but this introit has more in common with the ending of Psalm 103 than with its beginning. The one whom this psalmist addresses as "O LORD my God" (see 7:1) is depicted as "very great" (cf. 95:3), royally clothed (for "honor" and "majesty," see 8:1, 5), dazzlingly resplendent, "wrapped" in a sheen of light, an image which signifies the presence of the invisible God. We may compare this to the hymn in Habakkuk 3, which depicts the coming of the God whose glory fills heaven and earth in the following terms: "The brightness was like the sun; rays came forth from his hand, where his power lay hidden" (Hab. 3:4). The transcendent majesty and effortless power of the LORD are graphically described. The "heavens" are no more difficult for him to put in place than hanging a curtain within a tent. The word translated "tent" in verse 2 is strictly the curtain which acts as a room divider within a tent, though by extension it can apply to the tent itself (cf. Song of Sol. 1:5). The waters above the heavens (cf. Gen. 1:6-7) provide the foundations for the beams of his celestial royal penthouse! For the language of verses 3b-4, with its mythological associations, see comment on the very similar passage in 18:10-14. The Greek (LXX) rendering of verse 4 — "He makes his angels winds and his servants flames of fire" — is cited in Heb. 1:7 in the context of arguing for the superiority of Jesus over angels (compare the use of Ps. 102:25-27 in Heb. 1:10-12). This, however, is an unlikely rendering of the Hebrew of verse 4 in the context of this psalm.

5-13   In the light of this awesome introit, the psalm now turns to depict what this celestial king has done and continues to do. Verses 5-9 draw on the mythological creation theme of conflict between the forces of chaos symbolized by "the deep" and "the waters" (see Psalms 29 and 93), the deep which "covered" the earth "like a cloak" (REB v. 6; cf. Gen. 1:2). Such forces proved powerless to stand in the way of the creative purposes of the LORD who laid the unshakable foundations of the earth (cf. 24:2; 102:25). Rebuked, they fled to become mountain springs and rivers in the valleys, recognizing the boundaries within which they must flow. They had no option. This is the psalmist's way of communicating the theology reflected in the hymn of creation in Genesis 1 — "In the beginning . . . God said . . . and it was so."

Verses 10-13 speak of the taming of the potentially destructive waters and celebrate the life-giving role of water in the world of God's creating — the "springs" in the valleys providing drink for the animals of the wild (vv. 10-11), the "streams" on whose banks grow the trees in which the birds happily build their nests (v. 12), and the rain which teems down on the mountains to enrich the earth (v. 13). It is small wonder that in a land where drought, with consequent famine, was often a grim reality (cf. Jer. 14:1-6), the provision of this life-giving water heads the list of the LORD's providential provision for his people.

14-23   In verses 14-23 we are presented with a kaleidoscope of the daily pattern of life in the world. There is the vegetation which provides fodder for domestic animals, and the cultivated fields which provide people with daily food (vv. 14-15), cheering wine (cf. Eccl. 10:19), and oil (cf. 52:8). There are "the trees of the LORD," the towering forests and the cedars of Lebanon (see 29:5), nesting places for migrating birds, "the stork" which winters in Africa but returns each year to nest (vv. 16-17). There are the "high mountains," home to the wild goat or ibex, their crags safe home for the coney or rock badgers (v. 18; cf. Prov. 30:26). There is the recurring pattern of night and day, moon and sun, the forests alive at night with prowling animals, the lions stalking their prey, retiring at sunrise to sleep in their dens (vv. 19-22). There are people participating in the rhythm of daily work and nightly rest (v. 23). And all of this is the LORD's doing.

24-30   Small wonder, then, that verses 24-30 proceed to celebrate the wondrous activity of this creator God and stress how all life is his gift. If we believe in God we look at the rich variety and order of life all around us and break into a song of praise — "O LORD, how manifold [REB: countless] are your works" (v. 24) — and think of God as a master craftsman skillfully crafting all that exists (cf. Prov. 3:19). The writer of the *Hymn to the Sun* similarly exclaims, "How manifold is that which you have made. . . ."

Earth and sea now come into view. The earth teems with the life God has skillfully created (v. 24b). The sea always had a mysterious and somewhat repelling fascination for the Hebrews. It spoke of vast horizons. Innumerable strange creatures, large and small, swam in its depths. It was home to Leviathan (see 74:14), one of the chaos monsters, but now reduced to being no more than a plaything of the LORD (v. 26). Ships set sail across its uncharted waters. All creatures on earth and in the sea are wholly dependent upon the continuing daily providence of God (vv. 27-29) and indeed only exist because life has come to them as a gift from the LORD, a gift which may be withdrawn at any time. Here again, as in 103:14-18, the psalm draws on the picture in Gen. 2:7 of God breathing into the human being he has created "the breath of life." The Hebrew in this passage, however, uses different language; twice the word *ruaḥ* appears (see 51:10-12), hence the REB translation "their spirit" in v. 29, as well as "your spirit" in v. 30. Since the vital spark of life comes from the living God, when "you hide your face" (see 10:1), that gift is shatteringly withdrawn and there remains only death, that "return to dust" (see 103:14). Renewing of life in all its forms lies entirely in God's hands and depends on his continuing grace.

31-35   The closing stanza of the psalm expresses its continuing confidence in the "glory of the LORD" (v. 31; see 3:3) and in the awesome power of a God who is known to "rejoice in his works," words which take us back to the creation hymn in Genesis with its concluding verdict, "God saw everything that he had made, and indeed it was very good" (Gen. 1:31). What other acceptable response can there be to the wonder of life in God's world than a lifetime characterized by songs of praise (cf. 96:1)? Such songs are but the outward expression of an inner devotion ("meditation," v. 34; cf. 77:6, 12). Yet such joyful celebration is not universal. There are those who challenge the authority of the creator God, "the sinners" and "the wicked" (see Psalm 1). They are the fly in the ointment of creation. They have no proper place in a world which exists to praise God (v. 35). The closing words "Praise the LORD" are not inappropriate, since they but underline the theme of the whole psalm. If, however, following the Greek (LXX) text we transfer them to the beginning of Psalm 105, then every psalm in the group from 103–106 begins and ends with the same words.

The same theological issues discussed in Psalm 19 arise here. It is wrong to believe that people in Israel moved from the contemplation of the world around them, in all its richness and order, to belief in the LORD. The character of the LORD was made known to Israel in other ways, through the revelation in Torah and the events to which it bore witness. Believing in such a God, however, Israel saw writ large in the world in which she lived an ordered mystery and wonder which bore witness to a gracious Creator who held the whole world in his hands. The concept of nature as a closed system following its own laws is not part of biblical thinking. It would be difficult to rejoice personally in cold, immutable laws, if such things exist — and modern science seems far from working with such a model. It is not difficult to rejoice in a gracious Creator. Psalm 104 invites us to share that joy. In a shortened paraphrase of the psalm, Robert Grant's well-known hymn invites us to do that in worship, beginning with the words "O worship the King, all-glorious above, O gratefully sing his power and his love; our Shield and Defender, the Ancient of Days, pavilioned in splendour, and girded with praise."

Psalm 105
GRACE ABOUNDING

Like Psalm 78, this psalm sets out to tell a story. In this psalm the story extends from the patriarchs, beginning with Abraham, through Israel's experience in Egypt, to the settlement in Canaan. Like Psalm 78, it is a story told in the context of worship, as the opening call to worship in verses 1-6 clearly indicates. It is not surprising, then, that verses 1-15 of this psalm, plus most of Psalm 96 and the opening and closing verses of Psalm 106, appear in 1 Chronicles 16 in association with the celebrations which accompanied David's bringing of the ark to Jerusalem. Context, however, vitally affects the way in which the story of the people's past is retold. In Psalm 78 it was the story of God's grace and a people's rebelliousness, climaxing in God's final "No" to the northern tribes and their cult centers, and his choice of the Davidic dynasty with its political and religious center in Jerusalem.

There are three ways in which Psalm 105 is significantly different from Psalm 78. First, this story has nothing to say about David and his dynasty; it ends with Israel's coming out of Egypt to settle in the promised land. Second, the story goes further back, to the promise-filled covenant God made with Abraham. Interestingly, apart from the reference to the God of Abraham in 47:9, this is the only psalm in which Abraham appears, and he appears three times, in verses 6, 9, and 42. Third, this story has nothing to say about the people's sinful ingratitude; it is focused entirely upon God's abounding grace. That sinful ingratitude is to be the theme of Psalm 106.

All of this probably tells us something about the situation to which the psalm originally spoke. The absence of all reference to David points to a time when the monarchy was no longer relevant to the life of the nation. The land, however, certainly is. Assurance is needed that this is the land promised by God to his people. This promise is closely associated in tradition with Abraham (cf. Gen. 12:1; 15:18). Abraham is virtually ignored by the prophets prior to the exile, but he comes to the fore in the theology of Isaiah 40–55, where the people are addressed as "you, Israel, my servant, Jacob, whom I have chosen, the offspring of Abraham, my friend" (Isa. 41:8; cf. 105:6). In their time of uncertainty and doubt the people are told: "Look to Abraham, your father and to Sarah who bore you; for he was but one when I called him, but I blessed him and made him many" (Isa. 51:2). An early postexilic date would account for these features in the psalm. By that time the traditions of Israel's early history, as they now lie before us in Genesis to Deuteronomy, were in existence. The author of the psalm draws freely and, on occasion, selectively, on these traditions.

1-6   The psalm begins with a call to worship, a call repeated over and over again: ". . . give thanks . . . make known [v. 1] . . . sing, sing . . . tell [v. 2], . . . glory in . . . rejoice [v. 3], seek . . . seek [v. 4] . . . remember [v. 5]." This is worship shot through with joyful thanksgiving for all that God has done, "his wonderful works" (vv. 2, 5; see 9:2), his "strength," and his "presence" (v. 4; see Psalm 24 for the traditional link between these words and the ark). Worship means coming to "sing praises" (v. 2; cf. 27:6, where this word is translated "make melody") and to "glory in" (see 34:3) all that is known to be true of God and God alone, "his holy name" (see 5:11). The "judgments" this God uttered (v. 5) are the decisions he took against all who sought to oppress his people, decisions exemplified in his "wonderful works" and "miracles" (see 78:43). This is worship offered by those who believe themselves to be the true descendants of the patriarchs, of Abraham "his servant" (cf. 79:2), the children of Jacob, "his chosen one" (cf. 78:68; see 20:1).

7-11   The essence of what it means to claim to be God's chosen people is now celebrated in verses 7-11. It means that the LORD, the God whose writ runs throughout the world, is "our God" (v. 7), the God who has owned us as his people in that relationship which is conveyed by the word "covenant" (v. 10; see 25:10), a covenant "made with Abraham" (see 50:5) to be an "everlasting covenant." The covenant traditions associated with Abraham are first set out in Genesis 15 and 17. Their promises were solemnly reaffirmed to Isaac (Gen. 26:3-5) and handed on to Isaac's son Jacob (Gen. 28:13-17), who became Israel (Gen. 35:10). Of the various strands of promise associated with this covenant relationship, the gift of "the land of Canaan" (v. 11) here occupies center stage, the land which is "your allotted holding" (REB; cf. 78:55), an expression used of property, usually land, handed down within the family, and of the land divided among the tribes during the settlement in Canaan (cf. Josh. 11:23). We hear the word "forever" twice in these verses, in verses 8 and 10, backed up by "for a thousand generations" (v. 8). This is thus a God-given promise which, it is claimed, neither time nor circumstances can ever annul. The people may need to be summoned to "remember" what God has done, but God needs no such prompting. He "remembers" (translated "he is mindful of," v. 8) and actively upholds this covenant.

12-15 The psalm now moves on to describe various episodes in this gracious commitment of God. Verses 12-15 deal with the story of the patriarchs, "few in number, of little account" (v. 12), thus ruling out that God's commitment to them had anything to do with any greatness or merit in them. Deut. 7:7-8 strikes the same note as it explores the mystery of God's choice of his people: "It was not because you were more numerous than any other people that the LORD set his heart on you and chose you — for you were the fewest of all peoples. It was because the LORD loved you and kept an oath he swore to your ancestors." Although Psalm 105 does not use this language, it is aware that to speak of God's choice of Israel is to speak of a mystery and wonder which can have no other explanation than that it is something in the character of God for which the word "love" is the only adequate word. John's Gospel can only explain Jesus' coming by saying, "God so loved the world that he gave his only Son . . ." (John 3:16). The story of the patriarchs is the story of seminomads, moving around as "strangers," aliens in a land inhabited by and under the control of other people (v. 13). They lack security, yet are providentially safeguarded. Verse 14 probably refers to the potentially dangerous incidents involving Sarah in Gen. 12:14-20 and 20:1-7. Although Abraham is called a "prophet" in Gen. 20:7 (cf. v. 13), there is no parallel in the Genesis narratives to the patriarchs being called "my anointed ones" (v. 15). There may be an interesting undertone in the choice of this word. As we have seen in 2:2, the LORD's "anointed" (Hebrew *mašîaḥ*) is a title commonly used of the Davidic king. It may be that, in a situation where there was no such king, this title is being transferred to the patriarchs and by implication to the people descended from them. There is an interesting parallel in Isa. 55:3, where "an everlasting covenant, my steadfast, sure love for David" is democratized, as it were, by being transferred from the royal family to the people of God. Even if this is not so, the title "my anointed ones" marks out those who have a significant part to play in God's purposes and are under the protection of God.

16-22 Verses 16-22 recall the story of Joseph in Genesis 37–50. Joseph was sold into slavery and thrown into prison in Egypt (vv. 17b-18). He was put through the mill, tested by the LORD, "until what he had said came to pass" (v. 19). This could refer either to Joseph's dream visions of future greatness in Gen. 37:5-7, or to his ability rightly to interpret the dreams of his fellow prisoners or of Pharaoh in Genesis 40–41. Released from prison, he became the grand vizier of Egypt. In verse 22 the translation "to instruct his [Pharaoh's] officials" involves a slight alteration to the Hebrew text. It makes good sense in context and has support in the early versions. The Hebrew "to bind," however, may well be correct, used deliberately to stress the role reversal which has taken place. Joseph, once "bound" or imprisoned (Gen. 39:20), now "binds" Pharaoh's officials, that is, forces them to submit to his authority. The whole Joseph story could be read as an account of how a man rose from dust to destiny, but verses 16-17 stress that this is the story of God's providence. It was God who "sent a man ahead" to ensure that when famine hit Canaan and basic food was unobtainable, there would be help available in Egypt. Compare Joseph's words to his brothers in Gen. 45:5: "And now do not be distressed, or angry with yourselves, because you sold me here; for God sent me before you to preserve life" (cf. Gen. 45:8; 50:20).

23-36 Verses 23-36 describe what happened to the people when they were in Egypt, in "the land of Ham" (vv. 23, 27; see 78:51). This section in outline follows closely the narrative in Exodus 1–12, with initial prosperity leading to the Hebrews becoming "stronger than" (v. 24; REB: "too numerous for") their foes, with consequent Egyptian hatred and double-dealing. When it comes to the plagues, the psalm mentions the ninth plague, but omits plagues five and six of the Exodus tradition. It may be that the darkness "which darkened the land" (v. 28) in the ninth plague (Exod. 10:21) and which prefaced Moses' final interview with Pharaoh was for the psalmist symbolic of all that benighted intransigence which led the Egyptians to disregard God's commands and sealed their fate. Most English versions rightly follow the early versions in omitting "not" before "rebelled" in verse 28b. The alternative is to read "to him" instead of "not" (see 85:8), that is, as far as he was concerned, they rebelled against his words. Their fate reached its climax in the tenth plague, the death of the Egyptian firstborn, "the first issue of all their strength" (or "manhood," as in the REB; cf. 78:51; Gen. 49:3).

37-42 Verses 37-42 cover the period of the Exodus from Egypt and the journey through the wilderness. It is highly selective in its approach. It has nothing to say about the crossing of the sea. It begins by stressing the dramatic role reversal. The people who had been forced to go down to Egypt broken by famine (v. 16) now leave Egypt with all the riches they could desire (cf. Exod. 12:33-36), never putting a foot wrong. The Egyptians who hated them and cruelly used them are now only too glad to be rid of them (v. 38). Verses 39-41 deal with God's guiding and protecting presence and his provision of needed food and water in the wilderness (cf. 78:14-15, 24-28; Exodus 13, 16, 17). All of this is narrated as proof that God was remaining true to the promise he had made to Abraham (Gen. 15:14-16).

43-45 The closing verses look back to the beginning of the psalm with its summons to joyful songs of praise. This is but an echo of the "joy" and "singing"

(v. 43) with which the people left Egypt to settle in the land God gave them, there to possess what others had prepared by their labor. The word translated "wealth" (v. 44) normally means toil or labor (cf. REB), a reference no doubt to the already cultivated land with its settlements and amenities.

From beginning to end this is a story retold as the activity of a gracious God, caring for his chosen people even in situations which seemed grim. There is no allusion to the people's response until we come to the last verse. There it is stressed that grace looks for a response, not merely of joyful worship but of daily obedience, the kind of obedience which tradition associated with Abraham (cf. Gen. 26:5). The psalm thus ends on a note which characterizes the central ethical stance of the Hebrew Bible. Obedience is grateful response to the grace of God. It is no accident that the Decalogue begins not with "you shall" but with "I am the LORD your God, who brought you out of the land of Egypt, out of the house of slavery" (Exod. 20:2; Deut. 5:6). This is the context within which obedience is expected. It may be, as some have suggested, that in the context of the festival liturgy, the closing words of the psalm prepared the way for the recital of the Decalogue.

We find the same pattern in the New Testament. Paul deals at length with the nature of the gospel (Romans 1–8) and the place of Israel in it (Romans 9–11). Only then does he say: "I appeal to you therefore, brothers and sisters, by the mercies of God, to present your bodies as a living sacrifice, holy and acceptable to God, which is your spiritual worship" (Rom. 12:1).

The strong emphasis upon the giving of the land in the promises to Abraham is, as we have seen, related to the situation which the psalm reflects. It is a theme which has struck a powerful contemporary chord in many Jewish minds in the insecurity born of the Holocaust. It poses its own problems when identified with the State of Israel today, with Jews themselves deeply divided on this issue. The New Testament, picking up the theme which was the subject of much discussion in New Testament times — namely, the identity of the true offspring of Abraham — develops different strands in the promises to Abraham, in order to speak about the citizens of a new kingdom that is no longer a geographical location, and about a universal community that is no longer racially or nationally defined but composed of those who are in Christ (cf. Gal. 3:6-4; Romans 4).

Psalm 106
REBELLION — INCOMPREHENSIBLE
BUT ALL TOO REAL

Unless, as we have suggested, the closing word of Psalm 104 is the opening word of Psalm 105, this is the first psalm introduced by the word "Hallelujah," which means, "Praise the LORD!" — the Yah at the end of the word being the short form of Yahweh (see 68:4). Book V of the Psalms contains several other examples of this opening (Psalms 111; 113; 135) as well as the concluding Hallelujah chorus in Psalms 146–150.

The central core of this psalm is the retelling of the story of Israel's past encounter with the LORD, but, unlike Psalm 105, the focus is very much on the people's rebelliousness. We may think of it as the opposite side of the coin to Psalm 105. In that sense it stands much closer to Psalm 78. There is, however, a major difference from Psalm 78, which is highlighted by the way the story is introduced. Psalm 78 was designed to make people stop and think — and think hard. The mood was essentially didactic. Using language familiar in wisdom teaching, it was making an appeal that, learning from the past, the present generation "should not be like their ancestors, a stubborn and rebellious generation" (78:8). Psalm 106, by contrast, uses in its introduction the language of worship (vv. 1-3), and its first words are words of confession (v. 6). Thanksgiving and confession, praise and penitence, still elements central to worship — such is the mood of this psalm. The most natural interpretation of verse 27, which talks about Israel's descendants dispersed "among the nations," and of verse 47, with its appeal "gather us from among the nations," is to place the psalm in the exilic or postexilic period.

1-3 After the initial "hallelujah," verse 1 gives voice to the note of thanksgiving for the goodness of the LORD, his unchanging "steadfast love" (see 5:7). The same words occur at the beginning of Psalms 107 and 136. Worshippers are thus reminded that they are face to face with a mystery, the depth of which inevitably means that any human words are inadequate to explain the "mighty doings of the LORD" (see 21:1, where the singular of this word is translated "strength"). It is important to see that these opening verses provide the proper context for confession. Sin, for the Bible, is not simply a record of moral failings, great or small. Sin is the difference between what we are and what God is and what in his graciousness he calls us to be. Therefore it is the vision of God, the awareness of his "steadfast love" and "mighty doings," which leads inevitably to confession. That is why it is those who are most close to God who are most conscious of their need for confession. That is why the truly "Happy" (v. 3; see 1:1) are those who are committed to that "justice" and "righteousness" which are characteristic of God (see 96:13).

4-6 In verses 4-5 we listen to a personal prayer in which the psalmist identifies himself with, and knows that his future in bound up with, the community which has nurtured him, the community whose "prosperity" (v. 5; literally, "goodness") depends upon its relationship with God, since they are God's "chosen ones" (cf. 78:68-73). The psalmist knows — as surely we all do — that he does not and cannot live on his own. If the future holds gladness for him, it is a gladness which comes to him within the context of the life of the community. As the REB translation rightly sees, "your heritage" in verse 5 is just another way of talking about "your own people." If future joy is shared joy, so is confession, shared not merely with the present community but with Israel throughout her history.

Verse 6 has something of the trademark of a liturgical formula of confession: "Both we and our ancestors have sinned; we have committed iniquity, have done wickedly." The same three Hebrew words, translated slightly differently, appear in such a communal confession in Solomon's prayer in 1 Kgs. 8:47, "We have sinned, and done wrong; we have acted wickedly."

7-12 The story now to be retold in verses 7-46 is one which the worshipping community claims as its own, not simply because it is the story of their own ancestors, but because it corresponds to their own experience. This is the only reason why a religious community keeps retelling a story from the past. The past is the present. The story begins with the Exodus from Egypt, following closely the narrative in Exodus 14. What happened is seen as proof of God's "wonderful works" (see 9:1), his lavish "steadfast love" (see 5:7), and his "mighty power" (cf. v. 2, where the plural of this word is translated "mighty doings"). But the people's response is basically one of unbelief (cf. Exod. 14:10-12). They did not "consider," that is, ponder or take to heart (cf. 64:9) what happened; they did not "remember," that is, they did not allow it to control their actions. They "rebelled against the Most High at the Red Sea" (v. 7). The reference to the "Most High" in this verse involves a minor alteration to the Hebrew text. The REB's translation "on their journey" follows the Greek (LXX) rendering. The "Red Sea" is hardly what we commonly call the Red Sea today. The Hebrew means "the sea of reeds," a marshy stretch of water or a body of water ringed with reeds in the eastern Nile delta area. The translation "Red Sea" goes back to the Greek (LXX). Verses 8-11 succinctly summarize the narrative in Exod. 14:15-31 of the crossing of the sea and the disaster which overtook the pursuing Egyptians. So God "saved them" (see 3:2) and "delivered them" (see 19:14). The immediate response was one of joyful belief or trust (see 27:13) expressed in a song of praise: the Song of Moses (Exod. 15:1-18) and Miriam's Song (Exod. 15:21). But this was a response which did not last; they "forgot," a favorite word of warning in Deuteronomy (e.g., Deut. 4:9, 23; 6:12).

13-18 Verses 13-15 describe the discontent in the wilderness (cf. 78:17-20 and Numbers 11). Having put God to the test, they got what they craved and with it a "wasting disease," a word which occurs only here in the Psalms (cf. Isa. 10:16). The Numbers narrative at this point speaks of a "great plague." There is probably deliberate irony in the word choice here. What the people were looking for was a further demonstration of God's gracious favor (Hebrew *rāṣôn*); what they got was "wasting disease" (Hebrew *rāzôn*). What we crave does not always bring the outcome for which we hope. Verses 16-18 focus upon the rebellion of Dathan and Abiram against the authority of Moses and Aaron. This section differs from the narrative in Numbers 16 by making no reference to the part played in the rebellion by Korah and the Levites. It is possible that the Numbers narrative at this point is dovetailing two different traditions of rebellion in the wilderness. Yet, since the psalm seems to know the narratives in Exodus, Numbers, and Deuteronomy in their present form, it may be that the reference to Korah is omitted in deference to the part the "sons of Korah" play in the collection of the Psalms. The rebellion, rooted in jealousy, is regarded as rebellion against God, Aaron being described as "the holy one of the LORD" (cf. Lev. 21:6; for "holy," see 2:6). Some of the problems of translation are well illustrated in verses 17-18, where the word translated "faction" by the NRSV in verse 17 is the same Hebrew word translated "company" in verse 18. In other contexts it refers to the assembled people of God (e.g., "congregation" in 1:5).

19-23 The story of the golden calf is seen as a supreme example of ingratitude and apostasy in Exodus 32 and Deut. 9:8-21. The use of the word "Horeb" instead of "Sinai" in verse 19 suggests that the psalmist is probably drawing on the Deuteronomic version of the story. There may be heavy irony in the language of verses 19-20. Both Exodus and Deuteronomy speak about an image of a calf, which may have echoes of the "bull" images associated with the worship of El and Baal in Canaanite religion. The further description here of the image as that of "an ox that eats grass" (v. 20) is probably intended to underline the crass stupidity of the entire scenario. Imagine substituting a grass-eating animal for "the glory of God" (see 3:3). The Hebrew text reads "their glory," which the early scribes wished to change to "his glory," but "their glory" is another way of talking about the glory of the God they worship (cf. Jer. 2:11). The incident would have had fatal consequences for the entire community if Moses, as God's "chosen one" (cf. 105:43), had not "stood in the breach" (v. 23) and interceded for them (cf. Deut. 9:25-29; Exod. 32:11-13, 31-32). This is an interesting metaphor which probably originates in the picture of soldiers or citizens rushing to man the breaches in the walls of a city under attack. Moses, of course, offers no defense of the breach which has been created in the relationship between God and the people because of the people's apostasy. He can only appeal to God to "turn away" his justified anger.

24-27 Here we are on the verge of the promised land, noting the jitters which gripped the people, according to Numbers 14, when they contemplated only the dangers and not the opportunities of entry into the land God had promised them. The words in verse 24 "having no faith in his promise" (or: "word") directly recall verse 12, "they believed his words." This is the familiar story of people who swing between faith and lack of faith; when all is going well, they trust in

God, but when faced with what seem at the time to be insurmountable human difficulties, they can no longer trust. While death in the wilderness (v. 26) is the LORD's solemn word to such people in Num. 14:26-35, the dispersing of their descendants among the nations (v. 27) is not mentioned in the Numbers narrative. It does, however, appear as a threat in Lev. 26:33 and Deut. 4:27 and is echoed in Ezek. 20:23 in the context of the exile. To people who were in exile or had just returned from exile or who remained in Judah while most of their compatriots were in exile, this verse would have contextualized this story from the past in a vivid way.

28-31 These verses put us in the plains of Moab on the east side of the Jordan, overlooking the promised land. "Peor," according to Num. 23:28, was a mountain in Moab, a cultic center for the worship of Baal. Numbers 25 recounts how Israelites became involved with Moabites who "invited them to the sacrifices offered to their god" (Num. 25:2). When verse 28 of the psalm says "they ate sacrifices offered to the dead," this may be a reference to their involvement in certain cultic practices associated with the dead that were part of the worship devoted to Baal, a dying and rising god. Such practices are rigorously forbidden elsewhere in the Old Testament (e.g., Deut. 14:1; 26:14). The "dead," however, may be an ironic description of these other gods in contradistinction to the LORD, the living God (see 42:2; 84:2). Although verse 30 claims that in this situation Phinehas of the family of Aaron stood up and "interceded," the REB translation "intervened" makes better sense in the light of the narrative in Numbers 25. We are not here talking about a Moses-like intercession (cf. v. 23). Phinehas stepped in dramatically to run a spear through an Israelite and a Moabite woman caught in the act. His action indicates that not all Israelites approved of what was happening. Numbers 25:12-13 attributes the assured privileged future of the Aaronic priesthood to his act, while the psalm claims that it "has been reckoned to him as righteousness" for all time. This phrase is used of Abraham's act of trust in the LORD in Gen. 15:6. It was to become a key phrase in Paul's use of the Abraham tradition in Galatians 3, to argue for the acceptance of Gentiles as well as Jews into the Church on the common basis of faith in Christ. The plague, the expression of God's anger, "was stopped," but only after 24,000 Israelites had died according to Num. 25:9.

32-33 From the borders of the promised land, we are now taken back to the incident in the wilderness at Meribah (see 81:7). Although the people are said to have angered the LORD at Meribah, the focus in these verses is on Moses. It is not clear what happened at Meribah to make Moses blot his copybook by becoming bitter and speaking rashly. Both in Num. 20:12 and Deut. 32:15, Moses and Aaron are accused by God of failing "to uphold my holiness among the Israelites." Whatever this means precisely, the net result was that both Moses and Aaron were denied the privilege of setting foot in the promised land. This may be why the incident is placed at this point in the psalm, out of chronological order. It comes as the climax to the story of Israel before they entered Canaan. It stresses the seriousness of failure to respond in obedience to God. If Moses, the LORD's chosen one, who interceded successfully on behalf of the people, failed at a crucial point and was denied entry into the promised land, how much more did others need to examine their consciences.

34-39   The story continues into the settlement in Canaan. It is a story of religious apostasy, of the fatal attractiveness of Canaanite religion undermining the exclusive loyalty which the LORD claimed. The story had a certain inevitability about it, since the incoming Hebrews had to settle down side by side with a native agricultural community and saw no harm in opting for a comprehensive religious insurance policy which would embrace the gods who guaranteed fertility to the soil as well as the LORD who had brought them out of Egypt. In theory, according to Deuteronomy, the settlement in Canaan was to involve a holy war, waged in the name and in the power of the LORD. All other people were to be driven out or exterminated (cf. Deuteronomy 7). In practice there had to be compromise, with its inevitable religious spin-off, which involved offering sacrifice to what the psalm calls "the idols of Canaan" (v. 38). There may again be bitter irony in the word used here for idols. It has the same consonants in Hebrew as the word for hurt or pain (cf. 139:24). The worship of Canaanite deities was to be the bane of Israel's life from the period of the early settlement in Canaan right up to the exile (cf. Deut. 32:15-17). Child sacrifice (v. 31) was well known in the ancient world; the more costly the sacrifice, the more likely the deity was to respond to the worshipper's need. In the Hebrew Bible it is often associated with the worship of the god Molech (e.g., 2 Kgs. 23:10), but it also featured in times of crisis in the worship of the LORD (e.g., Jer. 7:31), even though it was rigorously forbidden in the Torah as one of the practices which the Hebrews ought not to adopt from other nations (e.g., Deut. 12:31; Lev. 18:21). The word translated "demons" in verse 37 occurs again only in Deut. 32:17. It is not clear what its meaning is in the psalm. The REB renders "foreign deities." Certainly it points to the worship of deities other than the LORD. The enormity of what is being described in verse 37 is underlined in verse 38, which, referring to the same practices, speaks of pouring out "innocent blood" (cf. Jer. 19:4-5). The consequence was that the land was polluted or defiled by such bloodshed (cf. Num. 35:33) and the people made themselves "unclean," a word with strong cultic overtones indicating that they were unfit to come into any contact with God. Such was the effect of religious apostasy, often referred to in the Old Testament in terms of acting as a prostitute (v. 39; cf. Hosea 2).

40-46   Verses 40-41 hammer home the inevitability of the anger of the LORD as he reacts in horror against his own people. The word translated "abhorred" in verse 40 is related to the noun "abomination," which describes what is wholly unacceptable to the LORD, often the idolatrous practices associated with the worship of other gods (e.g., Deut. 27:15; 2 Kgs. 23:13). It is as if the LORD is saying to his people, "You are no better than the pagans among whom you dwell, and so you will be at their mercy" (vv. 41-42). What follows in verses 43-46 sticks closely to the outline of the story of what happened during the early settlement in Canaan as portrayed in the book of Judges (e.g., Judg. 2:11-23). Disobedience and apostasy led to the people being delivered into the power of their enemies. The cry for help in the crisis situation leads to the LORD sending a deliverer as "judge." The LORD's response was conditioned by the fact that, whatever the people might have done and done repeatedly, he remained true to his covenant commitment (v. 45; cf. 105:9). So his anger, however justified, was swallowed up in a pity which responded to bitter need. In verse 45, the REB's rendering "relented" is in context probably better than the NRSV's "showed compassion," though the Hebrew could mean either. In spite of the NRSV and REB translations of verse 46, it is doubtful whether compassion for the people's plight was roused in the heart of their captives. It is more likely that the LORD enabled his people to experience his compassion, a compassion witnessed by their captives. So into this sorry tale of Israel's apostasy and rebellion there is built a theology of hope based on the character of God, as any lasting theology of hope must be. That is why the theology of hope which pulsates through the New Testament is Christ-centered, with his people summoned to "rejoice in the LORD" (Phil. 3:1).

47   The ray of hope which lit up the darkness of the past thus leads in verse 47 into a renewed appeal to God to act again in the present crisis facing his people. The verse picks up themes heard at the beginning of the psalm. There is an appeal to the LORD to "save" or deliver (see 3:7) since he is "our God"; to gather again his scattered people, so that they may personally know that it is good to give thanks to the LORD for all that he is and for all that he has done (cf. v. 1; for "your holy name," see 5:11; cf. 105:3). His people then may take justifiable pride in singing his "praise" (cf. v. 2). Only personal experience can turn a past story into our story.

48   The doxology which ends the psalm and Book IV is, therefore, thoroughly appropriate in its context, even though it may have been added later (see 41:13).

BOOK V

PSALMS 107–150

Psalm 107
VOICES OF THANKSGIVING

Psalm 107 is the first psalm in Book V, the last collection of psalms. Although some of these psalms have no heading, there are clear indications of several different collections within the book. Two groups, Psalms 108–110 and Psalms 138–145, are associated with David. In early Jewish liturgical tradition, Psalms 113–118 were known as the "Egyptian Hallel" and associated with the celebration of Passover. Fifteen psalms, Psalms 120–134, form a group, each with the heading "A Song of Ascents," while the last five, Psalms 146–150, provide a concluding Hallelujah chorus, each beginning with "Praise the LORD" (Hebrew *halĕlû-yāh*). Book V is also noteworthy for containing the shortest Psalm, Psalm 117, and by far the longest Psalm, the 176-verse acrostic meditation on the Torah, Psalm 119.

To describe Psalm 107 as "Voices of Thanksgiving" is to highlight some of the difficult critical questions it raises. An introduction, verses 1-3, is followed by four carefully crafted sections, each introduced in the NRSV and REB translations by the word "Some. . . ." Each section paints a graphic picture: verses 4-9 — lost travelers; verses 10-16 — hapless prisoners; verses 17-22 — people struggling with ill health; verses 23-32 — those in peril at sea. Each section contains a refrain which echoes the opening words of the psalm, "Let them thank the LORD for his steadfast love, for his wonderful works to humankind" (vv. 8, 15, 21, and 31). In each section this refrain is preceded by a standard cry of distress: "Then they cried to the LORD in their trouble, and he delivered them from their distress" (vv. 6, 13, 19, and, with minor variations, 28), followed, in each case, by a brief description of what deliverance means. The first two sections are capped by an emphatic statement of what the Lord has done or does, verses 9 and 16, while the remaining two sections develop the theme of the refrain, verses 24 and 32.

How are we to interpret these different sections? Are they to be taken as graphic illustrations of the kind of dangers to which different people are exposed? Or are they all metaphors of the experience of the whole community in exile? Or can they be regarded as both? It has been argued that the earliest form of the psalm contained only verses 1 and 4-32, part of a traditional liturgy designed for varied acts of thanksgiving, and going back long before the exile. To this were added verses 2-3 in the light of the people's experience in exile, with the pictures that followed then being reinterpreted in that context. Verses 33-43, which bear some of the formal features of the earlier verses, were then added as a hymn or meditation celebrating the awesome power of God. There is nothing improbable in this. It is of the very essence of liturgical material, and indeed of the Bible as a whole, that it has the vitality to speak, in an ever new way, to different people in different circumstances. If it were not so, it would be merely a fossil. Much of the language does have echoes of writings from the exilic and postexilic period, notably Isaiah 40–55. Contemporary worship, however, suggests that this is not strictly necessary for understanding the psalm. When we gather as a congregation to offer to God our prayers of thanksgiving or intercession, there is nothing strange in including in that setting material which focuses on the needs of specific categories of people, whether it be those rejoicing in the birth of a child, those mourning the loss of a loved one, or those struggling with unemployment or ill health. Thus it is possible to approach the psalm as essentially a community song of thanksgiving, which provides space for more personal thanksgiving.

1-3   After verse 1, which is the same as 106:1 — the first of many echoes of Psalm 106 in this psalm — the introduction uses language which would be at home in a postexilic setting. The picture of God as redeemer is one which has its roots in social and family life in ancient Israel (see 19:14). It is used theologically to point to the meaning of what happened at the Exodus (cf. Exod. 6:6; 15:13). It is, however, a favorite word in Isaiah 40–55, following the paradigm of the Exodus event, to describe what the Lord did for his people in bringing them back from captivity in Babylon (e.g., Isa. 41:14; 43:1, 14; 44:6, 22, 23; cf. Isa. 62:12). Here the people are called "the redeemed of the Lord" (v. 2), "gathered in from the lands" (v. 3; cf. 106:47), from the four points of the compass. The NRSV assumes a slight change to the text in the final word of verse 3 to read "south." It is possible, however, that the Hebrew "sea" is correct. While "sea" often means the Mediterranean Sea, that is, the west, and is so translated in conjunction with "the north" in Isa. 49:12, early Jewish tradition saw here a reference to the southern sea, which could mean the Gulf of 'Aqaba or the Red Sea. Isaiah 49:8-12 is one of several passages in Isaiah 40–55 which speak of the homecoming of the exiled people from all corners of the world.

4-9 In the Hebrew text, this section begins with the words "they wandered," which may mean simply "people wandered" or, continuing verses 2-3, refer to the redeemed of the LORD coming home from distant lands. Although the two words "wilderness" and "desert," translated "desert wastes," often occur in contexts which refer to the post-Exodus wandering through the wilderness (e.g., 106:14), the language is also associated with the homecoming from exile in Babylon (cf. Isa. 40:3; 43:18-20). The return from Babylon, involving a journey across the northern Syrian desert, was long and harsh. It is, therefore, natural to depict exhausted people, sometimes desperately looking for the next "inhabited town" (vv. 4, 7) where they would find rest and refreshment. Yet this was the LORD's way. He was leading them by a direct route, a "straight way" (v. 7). Weary, thirsty, and hungry, they were satisfied by the LORD's providential care and bounty (cf. Isa. 55:1-3; Jer. 31:25). Thus the community celebrates a joyful homecoming, with difficulties overcome because of the "steadfast love" (see 5:7) and the "wonderful works" (see 9:1; cf. 106:7) which embraced "humankind," literally, "the sons of *'ādam*" (see 49:2). Anyone in the community, however, who had gotten lost while traveling across barren terrain would identify with the words in this section in a profoundly personal way.

10-16 The picture of prisoners incarcerated in a dark dungeon is used often in Isaiah 40–55 to describe the plight of the exiles in Babylon (cf. 42:7, 22; 49:9). Likewise, various prophets insist that the exile was the self-inflicted, just punishment for a people who had rebelled against God (cf. Isa. 40:2; Ezek. 2:3), flouting his "counsel" (v. 11), his advice or teaching (for "the Most High" as a title for God, see 7:17). Verse 11 may contain one of these subtle Hebrew plays upon words similar in sound, a play impossible to render in English; the Hebrew for "rebel" and "words" both contain the Hebrew letters corresponding to *m* and *r*: "for they rebelled *(himrû)* against the words *('imrê)* of God." Prison life was brutal. Chained slave gangs were subjected to harsh, unremitting labor. But in response to desperate cries for help, the prisoners were released (v. 13), their chains snapped, the massive enclosing bronze prison door, held in place by iron bars, shattered (v. 16). Isaiah 45:1-2 describes the victorious career of Cyrus which led to liberation for the Judean exiles. It involved God removing all obstacles in his way, opening doors, ensuring that gates would never be shut in his face: "I will break in pieces the doors of bronze, and cut through the bars of iron" (Isa. 45:2; cf. v. 16). Liberation was a cause for thanksgiving. Anyone in the community, however, who had experienced the harshness of imprisonment would identify with the words of this section in a profoundly personal way.

17-22 The NRSV's rendering of the opening words of verse 17, "Some were sick," involves an alteration to the Hebrew text, which reads "fools." The REB rightly retains "Fools," a word found frequently in Proverbs that usually denotes someone who is morally insensitive and incapable of accepting correction or discipline (e.g., Prov. 1:7; 27:22). Verse 17 stresses that the affliction described in this section is self-inflicted, the consequence of the people's "sinful ways" or rebellion (see 32:1) and their "iniquities" or perverseness (see 25:11). With their vitality ebbing away, and all their appetite for food lost, such people are described as drawing near to "the gates of death" (see 9:13). This is a description of debilitating and potentially fatal illness that takes people to the threshold of Sheol (see 6:5). The word translated "destruction" in verse 20 has echoes of the word for "Pit," one of the synonyms of Sheol (see 16:10). The urgent cry for help leads to the LORD's healing touch. It is possible that when verse 20 says "he sent out his word and healed them," the reference is to an oracle of healing delivered by a priest to someone whose illness had led to his temporary exclusion from full participation in worship in the temple courts. Compare Jesus' words to the lepers: "Go and show yourselves to the priests" (Luke 17:14). Their "cleanness" had to be formally verified before they could be readmitted to the full life of the community. The psalmist is here stressing that the initiative in such restoring healing comes from the LORD. Healing is thus cause for thanksgiving and for the joyful offering of "thanksgiving sacrifices" (see 50:14), the public acknowledgment of what the LORD has done. Although this image of debilitating illness is not commonly used to describe the exile, it is central to the picture of Israel as the suffering servant in Isaiah 53. The theology of Isaiah 53, however, is strikingly different. There it is not self-inflicted illness, but suffering borne for the sake of others, so that healing may come to them. Anyone in the community, however, who had experienced debilitating illness and had stared death in the face would identify with the words of this section in a profoundly personal way.

23-32 While Phoenician traders ranged far and wide across the seas, particularly the Mediterranean, the sea with its mythological associations (see Psalms 29 and 46) always had a sinister connotation. With few natural harbors along the coast to which they had access, the Hebrews were essentially landlubbers. You had to be pretty desperate to embark on a sea voyage (cf. Jonah). All seafarers knew only too well the dangers they faced; a sudden hurricane with its tumultuous waves could strike fear into the stoutest hearts and ram home the message that there were forces beyond human control (vv. 25-27). There is a similar vivid picture of the ships of Tarshish caught in a storm in Ezek. 27:25-36. The mountainous waves were not beyond the LORD's control. He sent the storm. He responded to the sailors' cries of distress. He stilled the storm and brought the sailors across calmed seas to their "desired haven" (v. 30) or, as the REB has it, "to the harbor they were making for." The word translated "haven" occurs only here in the Old Testament and is usually linked with an Akkadian word meaning "city." The Greek (LXX), however, translated "harbor," and there is now some support for this in the Ugaritic texts. With the storm stilled and the safe haven reached, there is cause for thanksgiving and for extolling (literally, "lifting up") God in the face of the assembled congregation and the "elders" (v. 32). The "elders" here probably refer to those in positions of influence who are representative of the entire community. Anyone in the community, however, who had had any experience of a violent storm at sea would identify with the words of this section in a profoundly personal way.

The Gospel story of Jesus stilling the storm on the lake (Luke 8:22-25) follows closely this section of the psalm. It describes the sudden storm wind, the panic-stricken disciples, Jesus' rebuke to the wind and waves, and the subsequent calm. The Gospel story, however, puts this in the context of a challenge to the disciples, "Where is your faith?" and implicitly identifies the power which Jesus wielded over the elements with the power of the LORD celebrated in the psalm.

33-43 The rest of the psalm is in the form of a hymn or meditation on the awesome power of the LORD, of which the four sections have provided graphic illustration. This is the God who, in response to human wickedness (v. 34), can act destructively, cutting off needed sources of water and turning fruitful land into a "salty waste" (REB: "salt marsh"). This recalls the story of the destruction of Sodom and Gomorrah (Genesis 19; Deut. 29:23). Equally (vv. 35-38), he responds to human need by providing richly watered land suitable for cultivation (cf. Isa. 41:18), land capable of sustaining a settled and flourishing community experiencing the tangible fruits of his "blessing" (see 3:8). It has been noted, even by early editors of the Hebrew text, that the order of the verses in verses 39-41 is rather odd. Verses 39 and 40 are often transposed, thus making verse 39 continue the description of what happens to the "princes," who may be foreign rulers (cf. 83:11) or irresponsible, power-abusing nobility in Israel. God brings them into contempt, turning them into homeless vagabonds who wander off into "trackless wastes." The word translated "wastes" is one of the words used to describe the formless chaos which existed before God imposed order on the world (cf. Gen. 1:2), but it is also used more generally of empty, desert-like space (Job 12:24; Deut. 32:10). Now stripped of their former power and influence, these potentates experience instead what they had often inflicted upon others — crippling misfortune and sorrow. Verse 41 then goes on to contrast how the LORD lifts the needy (see 9:18) out of their distress and guarantees that they flourish. Without changing the order of the verses, the REB gives basically the same picture by beginning verse 39, "Tyrants lose their strength and are brought low." It is equally possible, however, that the "they" at the beginning of verse 39 looks back to the previous verses and to those who in verse 36 are described as the "hungry." Yes, God's blessing does come to them (v. 38), but when, or if, they experience misfortune

(v. 39), God will then call their oppressors to account (v. 40), since he is a God who constantly acts as a protector of the needy (v. 41). This is hardly, as some have claimed, a senseless text. It has something to commend it, since the last word of verse 38, translated "he does not let . . . decrease," is a form of the same verb translated "they are diminished," the first word of verse 39. Suppose they do "decrease," what then? What does God do? The psalmist knows what the LORD does. It is something which makes "the upright" (see 7:10) glad and reduces to silence all who traffic in evil.

The psalm ends with an appeal in verse 43. To participate in worship, to celebrate the "steadfast love" of the LORD, is not in itself enough. It must lead to something which will remain with those who are "wise," those who have a true grasp of what life is all about. They must continue to ponder the significance of what has come to them in worship, until it permeates their life. This is a wholesome recognition that worship must never be merely a momentary emotional experience. It must be educational for living.

Psalm 108

This psalm takes the concluding verses of Psalm 57, verses 7-11, and adds to them the concluding verses of Psalm 60, verses 5-12, to make of the two a new psalm, in which the lament element in the opening verses of Psalm 60 is replaced by a song of thanksgiving. There is nothing strange in this. Contemporary hymnals provide examples of the same process at work. The *Church Hymnary* (third edition, 1973), for example, has produced a new baptismal hymn in this way, hymn 549. It takes the first two verses of Thomas Haweis's hymn "Our children, Lord, in faith and prayer" and joins them to the last two verses of Reginald Heber's hymn beginning "By cool Siloam's shady rill." The net result is an excellent new baptismal hymn, unembarrassed by the meaningless reference to cool Siloam's shady rill. For detailed comment on Psalm 108, see the comment on the appropriate verses of Psalms 57 and 60.

Psalm 109
THE CASE FOR THE DEFENSE

In some respects this is a typical psalm of lament. It begins with an appeal to God prompted by a crisis situation in the psalmist's life (vv. 1-5). A resolution of the crisis is confidently anticipated in verses 21-29, and the psalm ends on a note of thanksgiving and praise (vv. 30-31). The nature of the crisis is clearly indicated by the recurring use of the word "accuse." It occurs as a verb in verses 4, 20, and 29 and as a noun in verse 6. This is the Hebrew word *śāṭān*, which, though developed into a demonic figure in later Jewish and Christian thought, points in the Hebrew Bible to the activities of a prosecuting counsel whose role is to bring charges against another party (cf. 38:20; Job 1). The psalmist is facing accusers who are bringing against him what he protests are totally false charges. The setting may be a religious court. If the charges are sustained, the penalty could be death. The psalmist is, therefore, fighting for his life.

The key issue for the interpretation of the psalm as a whole, however, is the relationship between the central section, verses 6-20, and the rest of the psalm. It gives voice to and speaks of curses, but by whom and against whom? Traditionally this central section has been read as the words of the psalmist calling down curses upon his accusers. The psalm as a whole has therefore been classed as a psalm of imprecation and taken to be one of the most bitter and uncompromising exemplars of this class. The spiritual issues raised by such psalms have already been discussed (see comment on 5:10; 58:6-9; 69:22-28). They are here in all their starkness. Commentators have often been defensive in their handling of this psalm and have noted that it is difficult or impossible to reconcile its sentiments with the Gospel words, "Love your enemies and pray for those who persecute you" (Matt. 5:44).

The NRSV, however, suggests another approach to this section that has had powerful advocates in recent years. It introduces verse 6 with the words "They say. . . ." These words are not in the Hebrew text, but adding them is intended to indicate that the speaker is no longer the psalmist but his accusers. (The REB also begins verse 6 with these words, but it attributes only verse 6 to the psalmist's accusers, with the psalmist's response beginning in verse 7.) What follows in this case represents the charges that their prosecuting counsel levels against the psalmist. Justification for this is found in the fact that while in verses 1-5 the psalmist speaks of those who are out to get him in the plural, from verse 6 the text switches to the singular ("him . . . his prayer"). Can the reference to "him" and "his" be anything other than a reference to the psalmist who is under attack? In the NRSV, verses 6-20 thus become part of the transcript of the trial, the case made by the prosecuting counsel against the psalmist. The NRSV, through its use of quotation marks, indicates that the whole section from verses 6-19 should be interpreted in this way. While initially this seems to transfer the ugly bitterness from the psalmist to his accusers, it does not in the end change the central spiritual issue raised by the psalm. In verse 20 the psalmist insists that the charges brought against him should rightly fall upon his accusers. There is to be no turning of the other cheek. In the background may be the legal dictum concerning false witnesses in Deut. 19:15-21. If it is proved that "the witness is a false witness having testified against another, then you shall do to the false witness just as the false witness had meant to do to the other" (Deut. 19:18-19). Indeed, it could be argued that the psalmist, convinced that he is innocent and that the LORD was on his side, takes a grim satisfaction in recounting the charges brought against him. He has nothing to lose; his accusers have everything to lose when their accusations are proved to be false.

To transfer the curses which begin in verse 6 to the psalmist's accusers, however, is not the most natural interpretation of the psalm. It would never have been suggested if there had not been the switch from the plural to the singular in verse 6. Such a switch from plural to singular, from a group to an individual within the group or vice versa, is not unparalleled in the Psalms. It is natural enough in this context to think of one of the accusers acting as the prosecuting counsel in the name of the others and being on the receiving end of the psalmist's bitter response. In verse 4b the Hebrew text has a very compressed construction, "and I prayer." A similar construction in 120:7, "and I peace," describes the psalmist as being for peace in opposition to others who are for war. In verse 4, this psalmist, in face of false accusations, resorts to prayer, which would be particularly appropriate in the context of a religious court. It is natural, then, to see in verses 6-20 the content of his prayer. The NRSV in verse 4, "even while I make my prayer for them," gives a false impression if it suggests that the psalmist is interceding for them, or praying positively for their welfare. His prayer is in fact a curse, as verses 6-20 clearly indicate. The psalmist's closing prayer in verses 26-29 has a striking parallel in Jer. 17:14-18: "Heal me . . . save me," capped by

> Let my persecutors be shamed,
>> but do not let me be shamed;
> let them be dismayed,
>> but do not let me be dismayed;
> bring on them the day of disaster,
>> destroy them with double destruction!

1-5 The urgent cry with which the psalm begins, "Do not be silent, O God," finds its parallel in other psalms (see 28:1; 83:1). It is urgent, yet it springs out of a confidence that God will answer. This is the "God of my praise," the God who has been and remains the God to whom the psalmist turns with justifiable praise and thanksgiving (cf. Jer. 17:14, "Heal me . . . save me, you are my praise"; cf. Deut. 10:21). The psalmist then describes his wicked accusers. Their "deceitful mouths" and "lying tongues" are evidence that they are prepared to perjure themselves to ensure that the psalmist is condemned. Such false witness is prohibited in the Decalogue (Exod. 20:16) and condemned elsewhere (cf. Deut. 19:15-21; Ps. 27:12). It is rooted, claims the psalmist, in "hate" (vv. 3, 5), which he dismisses as wholly unjustified. His experience mirrors that described in 35:11-14. The "love" and friendship he has offered, his concern for the good of others, has been spurned. No wonder he has reached breaking point. Facing a potential death sentence as the result of such hate-filled perjury, he turns on his accusers in a prayer which is a curse.

6-20 The psalmist pleads for a role reversal (vv. 6-7) — that his wicked accuser may find himself on the receiving end of the perjury of a "wicked man," an "accuser." Thus he will be found guilty. The pseudopious prayer on his lips is dismissed for what it really is, "sin" (see 32:1), totally irrelevant in God's eyes. He himself prays (vv. 8-12) that his accuser be stripped of all that constitutes *shalom* in Hebrew thinking (see 4:8), a long life, shared by wife and family, enriched by material prosperity and with a recognized status in society. The word translated "position" in verse 8 can in certain contexts mean wealth (REB: "hoarded wealth"), but "position" seems appropriate here. Verse 8 is quoted by Peter in Acts 1:20 in the context of Judas forfeiting his position among the twelve disciples. The accuser's property is to become a deserted ruin, his wife widowed, his children orphaned. Neither he nor his children are to experience any of that "kindness" (v. 12; Hebrew *hesed;* see 5:7) or compassion which sustain community life. "Creditors" are at the door; "strangers" help themselves to all that he had acquired through hard work. The pain and depression which such a reversal of fortune would bring are perhaps best appreciated by reading Job 29–31.

For him there is to be no future (vv. 13-15). Within a generation there will be no posterity to continue the family name (cf. 37:38, where this is considered the just punishment for the wicked). The fatal legacy of the past (cf. Exod. 20:5; 34:7), "the iniquity" of his forefathers (the NRSV's change to "father" is unnecessary) and his mother, is to remain unforgiven, constantly "on the record before the LORD" (REB v. 15), guaranteeing that all that the family stood for, "their memory," will be consigned to oblivion. The psalmist has no hesitation in consigning his accuser to such a fate, because he believes that it is richly deserved (vv. 16-19). This was a man who showed no "kindness" (cf. v. 12), who ruthlessly harried those who were vulnerable and in need (see 9:12). He "loved to curse," so it is but poetic justice that he should now be on the receiving end of a curse. Since he would have no truck with "blessing" others in the past, why should he experience it now? "Let it be observed," says Calvin, "that the machinations of the wicked will recoil on their own heads." Cursing has been part of this man's life, as much part of it as the clothes he daily wore (vv. 18-19). The reference to "water" and "oil" in verse 18 is not wholly clear. It may be no more than a graphic way of stating that his whole life was saturated with cursing. It is possible, however, that the picture of water soaking into his body has in its background the regulations in Num. 5:16-28, where, in the case of suspected adultery, the priest administers to the woman "the waters of bitterness that bring the curse" (Num. 5:18). This leads to miscarriage if the woman is guilty. The psalmist is in no doubt that his accuser is guilty. As the curses he uttered work their way into his own life, he is but receiving the due reward for his malicious and false slanders against the psalmist (v. 20).

The forces arraigned against the psalmist in court are malicious and powerful, but there is a counsel for the defense who can be trusted, "you, O LORD my

Lord" (v. 21). The psalmist's case for the defense is based on two grounds. The first is the nature of the LORD, summed up in the words "steadfast love" (see 5:7), a steadfast love which is characterized by a goodness which is the antithesis of all that his accusers display, a steadfast love which will come to his rescue (v. 21). The second is the psalmist's own frailty and need. Verse 22 echoes the language of verse 16, but it does so in the conviction that while verse 16 describes a situation in which no pity was shown, God can be depended upon to show pity. Vividly verses 23-25 underline the psalmist's desperate plight. The end is near, just as day comes to an end as the shadows lengthen in the evening. He is as vulnerable as a locust which can be shaken off. He is physically weak and gaunt, either because his appetite for food has gone or because he has been fasting in preparation for his coming trial. He is an object of mockery and derision — for the "shaking of the head" as a sign of derision, see 22:7; Lam. 2:15; Mark 15:29.

26-29 The parallels between the words of the psalmist in his closing prayer in verses 26-29 and Jer. 17:14-18 have already been noted. There are, however, also many echoes of images and language found earlier in the psalm: "your steadfast love" (v. 26) recalls verse 21; "you will bless" (v. 28) stands in sharp contrast to the accuser who would have nothing to do with blessing in verse 17; the clothing image in verse 29 echoes verses 18-19.

Again, verses 28-29 strongly stress the reversal of fortune element. The "shame" and "dishonor" his accusers sought to bring upon the psalmist are to redound on their own heads, while the psalmist is to be "glad," no doubt because of what the LORD has done for him, but perhaps also because the curses he has called down upon his accusers are working out in their lives!

It is equally important to the psalmist that his accusers should know that what is happening to them is the LORD's doing, and his alone. Note the emphatic "you" in verse 27b. They may believe that they have the upper hand and that they will succeed in having the psalmist condemned. In fact, the outcome lies not in their hands but in the LORD's. He will ensure acquittal.

30-31 The psalm concludes with a vow of thanksgiving and praise. The God whom he addresses in the opening words of the psalm as "the God of my praise" is the LORD whom he will now publicly thank "in the midst of the throng." The word translated "throng" is in Hebrew "the many" or "the great." The situation described here, however, is the same as in 22:25, where the psalmist publicly offers his prayers for all that God has done for him "in the great congregation." What God had done, and always does, is to aid "the needy" (cf. vv. 16, 22), to act as their defending counsel against all who seek to "bring them to trial" (REB). The NRSV translation of the closing words assumes that the outcome of such a trial is intended to be a death sentence.

The spiritual and theological issues which the bitter curses in this psalm raise have already been discussed. We should neither apologize for such curses nor seek to minimize the way in which they stand in tension with other aspects of the biblical revelation. The psalmist who appeals for pity from the God of steadfast love has no iota of pity for his accusers. Nor is it enough to say they don't deserve it. If we got what we deserved, none of us would ever experience true forgiveness. In the light of the gospel, Paul rightly says, "Bless those who persecute you; bless and do not curse" (Rom. 12:14; cf. Matt. 5:44). The psalmist, though he believed in a God who "will bless" (v. 28), could not contemplate such blessing embracing those who had malevolently brought accusations against him. Yet a confidence based on God runs through the psalm; it is a confidence which remains and to which the psalmist can appeal in the direst circumstances. Paul, using similar legal terminology, witnesses to the ultimate Christian significance of such confidence when he declares:

> What then are we to say about these things? If God is for us, who is against us? He who did not withhold his own Son, but gave him up for all of us, will he not with him also give us everything else? Who will bring any charge against God's elect? It is God who justifies. Who is to condemn? It is Christ Jesus, who died, yes, who was raised, who is at the right hand of God, who indeed intercedes for us. (Rom. 8:31-34)

Psalm 110
PRIEST AND KING

This psalm has been the center of much scholarly argument and discussion in recent years. The voice of tradition, both Jewish and Christian, is virtually unanimous in claiming that this psalm, with its heading linking it with David, points clearly to the king who is to come, the future messiah. Verse 1 is cited or referred to more frequently in the New Testament than any other verse from the Psalter. It is used confidently to affirm the messianic status of Jesus (Mark 12:35-37). Calvin stands within the mainstream of Christian interpretation when he says concerning verse 1, "That the whole of what is stated in this verse cannot be entirely or exclusively applied to David is very obvious from Christ's reply to the Pharisees (Matt. 22:44) . . . there is something in Christ more excellent than his humanity, on account of which he is called the Lord of David his father."

What, then, are the problems we face in the interpretation of this psalm? For one thing, the text is notoriously difficult in places. You have only to read the very different translations of verse 3 in the NRSV and the REB to realize that there are textual problems. If, moreover, you wonder, as many have done, what the closing verse with its reference to drinking from the stream means, then your wonder may deepen when faced with the following translation: "The Bestower of Succession set him on his throne, the Most High Legitimate One lifted up his head" (M. Dahood). Some of the translation problems are related to a more fundamental issue. No one doubts that this is in some sense a royal psalm. As such, there are echoes in it of Psalm 2. Verses 5 and 6, for example, which speak of other kings destroyed by the anger of the LORD, recall 2:2, 5. If in verse 3, instead of "your youth" we follow the Greek (LXX) text and read "I have begotten you," this parallels 2:7. Some of the critical questions discussed in Psalm 2, therefore, apply to this psalm, not least the relationship between the place of such a psalm in the life of Israel and the future messianic interpretation later tradition gave to it. This is a royal psalm, but to what particular aspect of the king's life does it refer? Is it a psalm welcoming the king's victory in battle? Is it linked to his coronation or to his part in an annual enthronement festival, and, if so, can we reconstruct from the psalm certain ritual acts associated with such a festival? It is here that we move into critically turbulent waters. This commentary can only invite you to set sail hopefully, following one of many possible courses.

The psalm is structured around two oracles (vv. 1, 4) in which the LORD addresses a word to the king. Each of these oracles is followed by a commentary in verses 2-3 and 5-6, respectively. If, as seems likely, the subject of verse 7 is the king, then the psalm closes with a promise to the king.

1-3 Verse 1 begins with the Hebrew expression "oracle of the LORD," which is common in prophetic literature, usually as the concluding words of a message (e.g., Amos 1:5, 8, 15 — where the NRSV in each case translates "says the LORD." This is the only occurrence of this phrase in the Psalms, though the word "oracle" (Hebrew *nĕ'um*) occurs in 36:1. The core of the psalm is, therefore, a word spoken by the LORD to the king, a word probably delivered to the king in a worship setting by a priest or temple prophet. It is a word spoken to one whom the psalmist describes as "my lord" or master, a respectful title applied to anyone in a position of authority (cf. 12:4 and 105:21, where it is used of Joseph as "the lord of Pharaoh's household"). This royal master is invited by the LORD to occupy the place of honor at his "right hand." Although attempts have been made to identify a ritual act to which these words refer, they are best treated as metaphorical, rooted in traditional language we find elsewhere in the ancient Near East with a king invited to take his seat beside the appropriate god or goddess. Not only favored status, however, is implied, but power which will ensure that all the king's enemies become subject to him (cf. Psalm 2). The image of the "footstool" has many parallels. In the fourteenth-century Amarna letters, the petty rulers of Canaan and Syria, in the course of diplomatic correspondence with their Egyptian overlord, say "A stool for your feet I am." This first oracle, therefore, spells out clearly the unique status and political role of the Davidic king. It stresses that the power he wields is delegated power, a gift from the LORD.

Verses 2-3 examine more specifically the meaning of the oracle in verse 1.

The LORD, present in Zion (see 2:6), is the source of the king's power. He sends forth "your mighty scepter," the scepter being one of the visible signs of royal power (cf. Jer. 48:17, where "mighty scepter" symbolizes the power of Moab). The people gathered for worship would be familiar with the Exodus story, where the same word translated "scepter" is used for the "staff" carried by Moses and Aaron with miraculous effect. Twice it is called "the staff of God" (Exod. 4:20; 17:9). The king's "mighty scepter" carries with it the power of the LORD, the assurance that the king "will rule in the midst of your foes." This has echoes of another royal psalm, Psalm 72, where the verb translated "rule" here is rendered "May he have dominion" (cf. Gen. 1:26, 28). It is a strong word indicating unchallengeable power. "Enemies" (v. 1) and "foes" (v. 2) the king will encounter, but ultimately they are powerless. The REB translation redivides verse 2 and takes "from Zion," with the second line, "From Zion rule." This seems unnecessary and makes little difference to the sense.

The NRSV and the REB represent two among many different approaches to verse 3. The verse begins with the picture of the people offering themselves willingly for service in the king's army, with all the enthusiasm associated with a crusade. The NRSV translation "on the holy mountains" involves a minor alteration to the Hebrew text, which has some support in the versions. It probably depicts the army being mustered on the hillsides around Jerusalem. The REB, retaining the Hebrew text, translates "Arrayed in holy garments" (cf. 29:2, where a similar phrase is translated "in holy splendor") and takes it to be part of the description of the king robed in festal garments. The phrases which follow are certainly evocative descriptions of the king, some of which may have their roots in traditional mythological concepts. To the phrase "from the womb of the morning" (REB: "child of the dawn") we may compare the description of the king of Babylon in Isa. 14:12, "O Day Star, son of Dawn." The Hebrew word for "Dawn," *šaḥar,* may echo the name of the Canaanite goddess Shahar. The whole phrase, however, may be no more than a poetic way of speaking of hopes centered upon the king symbolized by the dawning light which shatters the darkness of night.

The clause "like dew, your youth will come to you" (REB: "you have the dew of your youth") may be a way of talking about the ever renewed youthful vigor of the king, a vigor which comes from God, since God is regarded as the source of the fertilizing dew of heaven (cf. Gen. 27:28; Hag. 1:10). Many commentators follow the Greek (LXX) and change "your youth" to "I have begotten you." This reading is plausible, since it involves no more than an alteration of the vowels added to the traditional Hebrew text and provides a neat parallel to Ps. 2:7, but it is hardly necessary.

4-7 The second oracle is introduced in verse 4 by a solemn, irrevocable oath of the LORD that is elsewhere associated with the LORD's covenant with and promises to David (cf. 89:35). Here it is concerned not with the king's political or military power, but with his priestly function. That the king in Israel, like kings in other ancient Near Eastern nations, exercised certain priestly functions is clear from many Old Testament texts (e.g., 2 Sam. 6:12-18; 1 Kgs. 8:14, 54-55). The priesthood was not, however, traditionally a royal prerogative in Israel. David did not come from the family of Aaron or Levi. How then could the king legitimately exercise priestly functions without undermining the traditional role of the priesthood? The answer lay in the Abram traditions in Gen. 14:18-19, where Melchizedek, the pre-Israelite king of Salem (probably Jerusalem) appears not only as a king, but as a priest of the Canaanite god El Elyon, "the Most High." The Davidic king in Jerusalem claims to continue this role. He is a priest "according to the order of" or in the manner of Melchizedek. The Epistle to the Hebrews develops basically the same argument in claiming that Jesus, the king who has come, but not from a priestly family, uniquely fulfills the true high-priestly role (cf. Heb. 5:5-10; 6:19–7:28). Three times Hebrews quotes verse 4, linking it with Ps. 2:7. Whether any specific tensions between the Davidic royal family and the priesthood lie behind this claim that the king is a priest "forever according to the order of Melchizedek" we do not know. It would hardly be surprising, however, if there had been such tensions (cf. 1 Samuel 13). Relations between church and state, between royal or secular power and ecclesiastical power, have often been fraught with tension across the centuries.

Verses 5-6 do not develop this priestly theme but instead revert to the content of the first oracle. Indeed, verse 5 deliberately picks up the words of verse 1 in a new way. Here the word "lord" or master, applied to the king in verse 1, is now used as a description of God, a usage which has many parallels in the Hebrew Bible (cf. 8:1, 9, where it is translated "our Sovereign," and 136:3, "Lord of lords"). While this use of the same word to apply to the king in verse 1 and to God in verse 5 may, as some have suggested, underline the close relationship between the king and God, it is more likely that verse 5 is stressing that the king is not his own master. He is in the service of a higher authority, another "lord." While in verse 1 the king was invited to sit at the LORD's right hand, here the divine master is "at your right hand," ready and willing to give assistance whenever needed. In his anger he will "shatter" or crush other kings or nations who oppose the king in Jerusalem (cf. 2:5, 8-10). The second phrase in verse 6, "filling them with corpses," is questionable. The Hebrew reads "filling corpses." Certain versions read the Hebrew word for "valleys" instead of corpses, a word similar in sound in Hebrew. It is possible that the original reading was "filling the valleys with corpses." The REB rendering, "in glorious majesty" (literally, "full of majesty"), implies a modification of the Hebrew text which is possible but hardly necessary.

The subject of the final verse, verse 7, can hardly be God. It must be the king. But what do the words "He will drink from the stream by the path" mean? What stream or spring? In 1 Kgs. 1:38, Solomon is led to Gihon, a spring just outside Jerusalem, as part of the coronation ritual. It was from this spring that Hezekiah constructed his famous aqueduct into the pool of Siloam within the city walls (2 Kgs. 20:20). It is not said in 1 Kgs. 1:38 that Solomon drank from the spring Gihon, but it is possible that some such ritual act was part of the coronation ceremony. On the other hand, verse 7 may simply be a way of saying that, however tired the king may become as the result of his military exploits, there will always be refreshing water at hand wherever he goes, ensuring that he will be victorious (for "lift up his head," see 3:3).

Two general comments may be made about this psalm as a whole. First, the psalm undoubtedly presents us with what has been called "the high theology of Judean kingship." That theology promises political and military success to the Davidic king, but it does so only within the context of affirming that the power the king wields is delegated power, a divine gift. But if it is delegated power, it must be used in ways consistent with the known character of the God who is the king's master. It is this which prevents such a theology from becoming "a partner of national arrogance" (A. Weiser). For this reason a prophet has no hesitation in calling to account a king who seeks to abuse his position in pursuit of personal aggrandizement (see, e.g., Jeremiah's censure of Jehoiakim in Jer. 22:13-19). There is always a danger that God may be degraded to be a partner of national arrogance or, for that matter, a partner of ecclesiastical arrogance. State and church exist to serve God, not vice versa.

Second, Calvin is right when he claims that this psalm speaks of what cannot ultimately be identified with any Judean Davidic king. Such kings often failed God and their people. Yet the vision remained. When there was no longer a Davidic king ruling over an independent Judean state, that vision was projected into the future to speak of a king who would one day come. It is not surprising, therefore, that the New Testament, believing that in Jesus that king had come, makes frequent use of this psalm. According to the Gospels, Jesus himself uses verse 1 in controversy with the Pharisees to argue that the coming king is greater than David (Mark 12:35-37; Matt. 22:41-45; Luke 20:41-44). Acts 2:34 uses the same verse to witness to the risen and exalted Jesus at the right hand of God, and it is referred to in a similar context in Eph. 1:20 and in Heb. 1:13; 8:1; 10:12. Verse 4, as we have seen, becomes part of the scriptural argument for the high priesthood of Jesus in Hebrews. Yet it is important to realize that when Jesus and the New Testament writers use the psalm, they are talking about a kingdom which transcends the political and military power of the Davidic dynasty. They are talking about a king who claims that his kingdom "is not from this world" (John 18:36) and about a kingdom which does not share the kind of power that the world so highly values. We are not asked to see Jesus as the literal fulfillment of the words of this or any psalm. Rather, we are invited to look back at this psalm in the light of what we know of Jesus and to see how the vision of the psalm is transformed in his life, death, and resurrection.

Psalm 111
IN PRAISE OF WHAT GOD HAS DONE

Psalms 111 and 112 form a marching pair. They may indeed come from the same author. After the introductory words "Praise the LORD," they are both acrostic poems, each line beginning with the appropriate letter of the Hebrew alphabet (see Psalms 9–10). Since most of the lines contain only three words in Hebrew, four at the most, the poet has shown considerable skill in employing this form.

Psalm 111 is a thanksgiving hymn of an individual participating in one of the great festivals of the religious year celebrating what God has done for his people. It is noteworthy how often the Hebrew verb "to do" or "to make" (*ʿāśāh*) echoes across the psalm, primarily with reference to what the LORD does or has done. We hear of "the works of the LORD" (v. 2), the "power of his works" (v. 6), "the works of his hands" (v. 7). The same verb appears in the words "he gained renown" (v. 4) and in "to be performed" (v. 8). In the closing verse there is a reference to "all those who practice it," which provides the bridge to Psalm 112, a psalm in praise of the godly life that spells out what God's people are expected to do in response to what he has done for them.

1 The thanksgiving hymn is in response to the call in the liturgy "Praise the LORD." It is a response which is deeply personal, offered by the psalmist "with my whole heart" (v. 1). This may have its roots in the words of Deut. 6:4-5, "Hear, O Israel, the LORD is our God, the LORD alone. You shall love the LORD your God with all your heart. . . ." Deeply personal, it is at the same time something to be shared with the congregation which has gathered for worship, with "the company of the upright" (see 25:14 and 7:9-10). Thus the individual knows that his faith is nurtured in the life of the congregation, and the congregation draws upon the faith and piety of the individual.

2-4 Verses 2-4 celebrate "the works of the LORD." This could refer to what God has done and continues to do in the world of his creating through his providence or in the history of his people. These works are described in terms which are often associated with royalty, "honor and majesty" (see 8:1, 6). They are defined in terms of his "righteousness," his concern to uphold all that is consistent with his nature (see 7:11 and 11:7). His "wonderful deeds" (see 9:1) thus witness to a God who is "gracious and merciful," words which recall the description of the LORD in Exod. 34:6, "The LORD, the LORD, a God merciful and gracious, slow to anger and abounding in steadfast love and faithfulness." No wonder his works are described as "great" (v. 2), broadening the horizons, "studied" or worthy of study, "by all who delight in them." The word translated "studied" comes from a verb which often means to go to a shrine to inquire of God (see 9:10). It has, however, a wide range of meanings. Increasingly, as the core of God's revelation was believed to be in a book, it came to mean to study (cf. 119:45, 94, 155). From it comes the later word "midrash," the detailed investigation into and exposition of the text. But this is no arid, merely academic study. It is the attitude of those who "delight" in the works of the LORD because they see in them the nature of God and, therefore, the clue to what life means.

5-6 Verses 5-6 briefly trace episodes in Israel's history — God's provision of food (literally, "prey"), the key illustration being the provision of manna and quails in the wilderness wandering (see 78:23-24); God's keeping his "covenant" (see 25:10), probably a reference to the Sinai events; and God's demonstration of his power in settling his people in Canaan, their promised heritage (see 78:54-55).

7-9 Verses 7-9 now summarize what gives the community strong grounds for trusting in and obeying God. They can trust because, in what he does and in what he demands, the LORD is "trustworthy" (for the words translated "faithful" and "trustworthy" in verse 7 and "faithfulness" in verse 8, see 25:5). What the LORD does is firmly fixed, "established" for all time, "upright" (see 25:8), devoid of any duplicity or chicanery. In verse 8 it is better to follow the REB's translation "enacted" (by God) rather than the NRSV's "to be performed," which might suggest the people's response. In case such language seems unduly general or abstract, verse 9 roots it firmly in what the LORD has done for his people. He "redeemed" them (see 25:5) and placed at the center of their life his "covenant" (see 25:10). This is the God who is "holy" (see 22:3) and "awesome" (see 47:2), a God, therefore, before whom his people must bow down humbly, yet in adoration. The word translated "awesome," a form of the Hebrew verb "to fear," provides the transition to the concluding verse, which uses language typical of the wisdom tradition. The "fear of the LORD" is not only "the beginning of wisdom" (see 19:9) but is also the basis of a life characterized by "good understanding." This phrase occurs twice in Proverbs. In Prov. 3:4 the NRSV translates "good repute," the REB "success," and in Prov. 13:15 both translations opt for "good sense." The phrase points to people who know what life is all about and who recognize the parameters within which the good life must be lived.

10 But, as if to remind us that this is no mere daunting struggle, the psalmist's closing words take us back to the beginning, to the fact that such a life finds its rationale in the "praise" of the LORD, which his people will gladly give "forever."

Psalm 112
IN PRAISE OF THE GOD-CENTERED LIFE

Psalm 112 shadows Psalm 111 not only in its acrostic form but also in the way it deliberately echoes words and phrases from the earlier psalm. The focus, however, is no longer on the praise of what the LORD has done but on the description of the desirable God-centered life. Here the psalm draws upon the typical wisdom language and ideas found in Psalm 1.

1   After the introductory "Praise the LORD," the tone of the psalm is set by the wisdom formula, "Happy is . . ." (see 1:1). Although the NRSV reasonably translates "Happy are . . ." and uses the plural throughout, thus avoiding what could be construed as sexist language, the REB sticks with the Hebrew in using the masculine singular. The psalm is describing a life rooted in joyful obedience to the LORD. It begins, where Psalm 111 ends, with "those who fear the LORD" (cf. 111:10) and with those "who greatly delight in his commandments" (cf. 111:2). This is no negative dread — a "you better obey God or else" attitude — but a gladly given response which recognizes that here is where the true secret of the fulfilled life is to be found. Thereafter, key words and phrases often used in Psalm 111 to refer to the LORD or to the works of the LORD are now applied to whoever makes such a response. Thus in verses 3 and 9 "their righteousness endures forever" exactly shadows "his righteousness endures forever" in 111:3. In verse 2 their descendants are called "upright," the word associated with the precepts of the LORD in 111:8. In verse 6 the clause "they will be remembered forever" uses the same Hebrew word that refers to the LORD's "renown" in 111:4. In verse 8 the description of their hearts as "steady" uses the same verb which in 111:8 is used to describe the LORD's precepts as "established." Notably in verse 4, the second line, which should probably be translated "the righteous are gracious and merciful," recalls 111:4 — "the LORD is gracious and merciful." Likewise the words translated "forever" echo across this psalm (vv. 3, 6, 9), as they do in Psalm 111 (vv. 3, 5, 8, 10).

2-3   In typical wisdom style the fruits of such a God-centered life are spelled out. Verses 2-3 direct attention, as so often in the Old Testament, to the good fortune which will come to the family. Their descendants will be "mighty" (REB: "powerful") or influential in the community, enjoying the "wealth and riches" which come to the upright. There is little doubt that tangible material prosperity is here intended. That life does not always follow this script raised serious questions for the Psalms and other books in the Old Testament. While such issues need to be honestly faced and explored, this psalm is surely right in stressing that we do not exist as isolated individuals but are bound together in life with others whose lives we influence for good and for ill. There is a sense of community which spans the generations.

4-5, 9a   Verses 4-5 and 9a focus upon the quality of life which reflects the character of a God who is "gracious and merciful" (cf. 37:21). The first half of verse 4 is capable of different interpretations. Context, however, suggests that it is spelling out that "in the darkness" — that is, when life is difficult — those who fear the LORD bring "light" — that is, encouragement and hope — to others, to the "upright," to those who are seeking to remain faithful to the LORD. They can be such a "light," just as the LORD in Isa.10:17 is described as the "light of Israel" (cf. 4:6). Moreover, such people will be generous, lending without exacting interest (cf. Exod. 22:25; Lev. 25:35-37), and conducting all their business affairs with integrity (v. 5). Such generosity and integrity find expression in willingly giving alms to meet the needs of the poor in society (v. 9). There is much that is attractive in this portrait. It reflects a principle which, in various forms, lies close to the heart of Hebrew biblical ethics — as God has acted, so must you. It finds its counterpart in Matt. 5:48, "Be perfect, therefore, as your heavenly Father is perfect." This may be an ultimately impossible ideal, but it is an ever challenging ideal. In the increasingly fragmented and polarized world in which we live, where the weak are becoming weaker, and the "haves" dictate to the "have nots" through crippling debt, this psalm has something to say.

6-8, 9b Verses 6-8 and 9b stress that such a life brings lasting security which can face "evil tidings" or misfortune, because it is a security firmly grounded in trust in the LORD. The word translated "secure" in verse 7 is a form of the verb "trust" (see 4:5). This recognizes that the God-centered life does not guarantee that life will be all plain sailing. There will be difficulties to be faced, but they can be faced with God and with an assurance which those who have no such commitment, described by the psalmist as "his foes," can never know. The God-centered life, therefore, has an inner strength (for "horn," v. 9, see 18:2; 75:4, 5) which will be recognized and honored (see 3:3).

10 The Psalm closes, not on a vindictive note, but by stressing that "the wicked" (see 1:1) will be consumed by helpless envy and anger (for "gnashing of teeth," see 35:16) when they see the fruit of such a God-centered life. They "melt away," gripped by despair (see 22:15), as they realize that their own coveted plans are doomed to come to naught.

It is surely no accident that Psalms 111 and 112 are closely bound together in structure and in language. Biblical faith is grounded in the celebration of what God has done and does, but it never allows us to forget that this places us under an obligation of responsive obedience. The Torah, the Prophets, and the Psalms repeatedly stress that the failure to make such a response is the ultimate betrayal, a denial of the pious words that so often trip off the lips of worshippers. Paul quotes part of verse 9 in 2 Cor. 9:9 in his plea for Christians to give generously. Since God provides every blessing in abundance, we are called to share abundantly in every good work. Debtors to a generous grace are ever called to be gracious and generous.

Psalm 113
INCOMPARABLE IN GREATNESS AND COMPASSION

This is the first in a series of Psalms, 113–118, known in Jewish tradition as "the hallel." The psalms in this series are associated with several of the major festivals and are called "the Egyptian hallel" in the context of Passover. Psalms 113–114 are intoned before the family passover meal, and Psalms 115–118 at the conclusion of the meal. Attempts have been made to identify a precise cultic setting for Psalm 113, involving several different choruses in verses 1-4 and 5-9, but this is highly speculative.

1-3 The psalm begins with a call to "Praise the LORD," a reiterated call to praise, the verb "praise" occurring three times in verse 1 and again in verse 3 and in the closing words of the psalm. Similarly, the phrase "the name of the LORD" occurs three times in verses 1-3 (for "name," see 5:11). Thus, at the outset, the people are being reminded that praise must be central to their worship. The "servants of the LORD" (v. 1) could be the Levites on duty in the temple courts, but it is more likely that they are the whole congregation of God's people gathered for worship (cf. 34:22; 136:22). They are invited to join in an anthem which acknowledges all that God has done to enrich the life of the community (for "blessed," see 16:7). This is an anthem which is to reverberate for all time to come (v. 2) and to embrace the whole world from east to west (v. 3). This is no local or petty deity who is being praised, but the LORD of all time, the king of the universe (see Psalm 96).

4-6 Verses 4-6 speak of the incomparable greatness of the LORD. He is "high above all nations" (cf. 97:9), and his majesty or "glory" (see Psalm 24) transcends the heavens, which, as the psalms celebrating the kingship of God affirm, were made by him (96:5) and rejoice in his kingship (96:11). Yet this is no mere awesomely distant deity; this is "our God," the God who reveals his nature to his people Israel.

"Who is like the LORD our God?" (v. 5) — no one, of course, no one in heaven or on earth (cf. Isa. 40:18-15; Ps. 35:10). The reference to "heaven" and "earth" at the end of verse 6 is best taken closely with the question at the beginning of verse 5. This is stressed in the REB by its reordering of the lines in verses 5 and 6. The incomparable greatness of the LORD is underlined in two descriptive phrases. He is the one who is "seated on high" (cf. 2:4), the king of kings, and he is the one who "looks down," literally, "who humbles himself to look" (REB: "who deigns to look down so low"). This is no disinterested look, a spectator's passing glance, but a look which leads to action and in particular responds to human need.

7-9 This response, the fruit of a caring compassion, is illustrated in verses 7-9 in two pictures: First, God reaches out to take the lowest and the unwanted in society (for "poor" and "needy," see 9:12) out of the "ash heap," the rubbish tip, where they eke out a meager existence, and gives them a place among the elite of society, those of noble birth or rank. Perhaps we can get the sense of this if we imagine the down-and-outs who scavenge in the litter bins and sleep on our city streets being given membership in a country club. Second, in a society which cherished the family and saw children as a sign of God's blessing (cf. Psalms 127 and 128), God heals one of the dread curses on women, the curse of barrenness (cf. Gen. 16:1-4; 1 Sam. 1:5). The woman in a childless house now becomes a joyful mother.

Neither of these illustrations makes explicit reference to the Exodus from Egypt, which is central to the celebration of Passover, but in the context of Passover both of them could strike powerful chords. The "poor and the needy" easily recall the Israelites groaning in slavery in Egypt and raising to God their cry for help (Exod. 2:23), a cry which was answered. The miracle of the childless woman becoming unexpectedly the mother of a large family is also found in Isa. 54:1-3, where it depicts the rebirth of Israel after the barren years of exile, a rebirth spoken of elsewhere in Isaiah 40–55 in terms of a new Exodus (e.g., Isa. 43:15-21; 52:12). The language of verses 7-8 also closely parallels and indeed at times virtually quotes the Song of Hannah in 1 Samuel 2, particularly 2:5b, 7-8. The psalm ends appropriately where it began with "Praise the LORD," though some of the early versions transfer these concluding words to the beginning of the next Psalm.

Throughout this psalm there is a theology of wonder which speaks of a God whose greatness goes hand in hand with his compassion for those most at risk in life. It is a theology which challenges many of our ingrained values, a theology which finds its rightful climax in the incarnation, in the king to come, born not in a palace but in the stable attached to an inn. It finds expression in the early Christian hymn in Phil. 2:6-11 which speaks of the one who emptied himself of his divine status to take the form of a slave, sharing our human life even to the point of death, death on a cross. Out of this weakness and degradation he was "highly exalted," his name above every name, celebrated by the whole of creation to the glory of God. Who indeed is like this LORD, our God? If this cannot move us to praise, nothing will.

Psalm 114
THE PAST COMES ALIVE

The best way to understand this psalm is simply to read it. Read it aloud. Revel in its rich and sometimes startling poetic imagery. Allow it to appeal to your spiritual imagination. Only then will you rejoice in its continuing relevance. That it comes to us out of a cultic setting in ancient Israel seems clear. But what particular setting and at what date are uncertain. The words of the opening verse point up its appropriateness in the celebration of Passover, and in Jewish tradition it found its place on the eighth day of Passover.

1-2 The opening verses fix our attention on the miraculous transformation which was basic to Israel's understanding of her life and history as the people of God. Israel, the house or family of Jacob (see 20:1), came out of Egypt. They exchanged the life of aliens, living among a people "of strange language," for the welcome and acceptance of a new God-given life. The word translated "of strange language" occurs only here in the Hebrew Bible. Its meaning, however, is clear from postbiblical Hebrew and from the Greek (LXX) translation, which uses the Greek word that lies behind our word "barbarian," originally one who speaks a foreign language. The sense of isolation this brings has been the repeated experience of ethnic minorities, particularly the women who, confined to the home, often find it difficult to communicate with the people among whom they have come to live. Language is one of our most precious means of communication, but it can also divide and isolate.

Verse 2 claims that for the people this isolation was overcome when Judah became "God's sanctuary" and Israel "his dominion" or "domain" (REB). This verse raises several difficult questions. "God's sanctuary" is in Hebrew simply "his sanctuary." But there has been no previous reference to explain "his" in the psalm. This is one reason why the closing words of Psalm 113, "Praise the LORD," are sometimes transferred to the beginning of this psalm. Nor is "sanctuary" the only possible translation of a word which is literally "holiness" (see 2:6). That it can mean "sanctuary," often the Jerusalem temple, is undoubted, but it is also used as a description of the people God has claimed as his own (cf. Jer. 2:3; Isa. 62:12). There is much to be said for giving it this meaning here and taking "his own people" as parallel in meaning to "his dominion." There is a further problem. What does "Israel" mean in this verse? When placed side by side with "Judah," it is natural to think of it as the northern kingdom which perished in 721 BCE, as distinct from the southern kingdom of Judah. If so, it is now being used in a different sense from the Israel of verse 1, which refers to the people of God who experienced the deliverance from Egypt. Perhaps in verse 2 Israel and Judah are simply a way of speaking about the whole land in which the people settled, a usage which continued long after they had ceased to exist as separate political entities. Whatever the detail, what is being celebrated in these opening verses is the key role which the Exodus played in the life of the people, that moment when they discovered their true destiny and vocation. They were to be not merely a nation among other nations, but a people claimed by God as his people.

3-4 In kaleidoscopic fashion and with striking poetic embellishment, the past is relived in verses 3-4. Three key incidents come into view. First, there is the crossing of the Reed Sea. The sea "looked [see 77:16] and fled." "Fled" is a poetic embellishment of the tradition in Exod. 14:21, which speaks of the sea, wind driven, turning into dry land. Second, the Jordan, the last barrier before the entry into the land of Canaan, "turned back." This represents a poetic version of the tradition in Josh. 3:16, which speaks of the waters of the Jordan being cut off and the Israelites crossing dry-shod. Third, "the mountain and hills" skip and dance like startled rams or lambs (for a similar simile applied to the natural world, see 29:6). It is customary to see here a reference to the giving of the Law at Mt. Sinai, where, according to Exod. 19:18, the mountain shook violently (cf. 68:8). It is more likely, however, that the reference is to the mountains and hills of Canaan, startled at the coming of the awesome God of Israel. Each description in this section is designed to heighten the miraculous elements in the story and to show that all obstacles which might have stood in the way of God fulfilling his promises to his people were totally powerless to do so.

5-6 The poet now intervenes in verses 5-6 and interrogates sea, Jordan, mountains, and hills with his question "Why?" or perhaps "What's up with you, that you. . . ?" It is doubtful whether there is any hint of irony in this question. Rather, it provides an opportunity to pause and reconsider what lies at the heart of Israel's tradition of faith and to allow the miracle of God's awesome power and concern for his people to become part of the spiritual experience of the worshipping congregation. Liturgics down to the present day know well the value of such repetition and recapitulation.

7-8 Having interrogated sea, Jordan, mountains, and hills, the poet now turns to address the "earth," probably the land given by God to his people, the land of Canaan. The land is called upon to "tremble." Although this word can mean to "dance" (REB; cf. 87:7), in context "tremble" or "writhe" is more likely. Here in the land the presence of the LORD, the "God of Jacob" (see 20:1), is awesomely powerful. Awesome he may be, but as the closing verse underlines he is graciously awesome. The miracle of what happened in the wilderness at Kadesh is recalled (see Num. 20:1-11; cf. 105:41). Water in abundance flowed out of the dry and hardest rocks to meet the needs of the people and their livestock. So the congregation is left contemplating the miracle of God's grace, the foundation of Israel's life in the past and their continuing hope in the present and the future. This is where every act of worship should end, as we bow before the mystery of the God who unites past and present and therefore bathes the future in hope. That is what we are saying every time we pronounce or listen to the benediction, "The grace of the Lord Jesus Christ, the love of God, and the fellowship of the Holy Spirit be with you, now and always."

Psalm 115
IN PRAISE OF THE LIVING GOD

Many of the early versions join this psalm to Psalm 114, but it is clearly different in style and in tone. Although there have been many attempts to be more precise,

Calvin's words still remain true: "It is not certain by whom or at what time this psalm was composed." That it comes out of a crisis situation in the life of the community is clear from verse 2. Other people are pouring scorn on Israel's faith with the mocking words, "Where is their God?" Although the psalm may have roots in an earlier age, this would certainly be a burning issue in the postexilic period, when the Jewish people were increasingly scattered, living in alien environments and in cultures dominated by other faiths and ideologies. Worship provided the community with a context within which to face and to work through this challenge.

The precise liturgical setting for this psalm is unclear. Do verses 1-11, for example, accompany the offering of a sacrifice, with verses 12-18 expressing the priest's and the congregation's joyful conviction that the sacrifice has been accepted? That the psalm has an appropriate word to speak in the context of Passover will become clear. Beyond that, it is hard to go with certainty. It is possible that in the psalm we are listening to different voices with an element of antiphonal singing. The approach taken here assumes the following pattern: verses 1-2, the congregation's plea; verses 3-8, a solo voice, probably that of a priest, answering the plea by ridiculing other gods; verses 9-11, the call to trust, probably sung antiphonally by groups of temple singers; verses 12-15, the priest's words of assurance and blessing; verses 16-18, the congregation's concluding responsive hymn of praise.

1-2   This psalm is unique in its beginning, the repeated "Not to us, O LORD, not to us." The congregation is acknowledging that they are facing issues which go far beyond their own reputation and their own future. What is at stake is the honor of the LORD's "name" (see 5:11) and whether his "steadfast love" and "faithfulness" have any meaning (see Psalm 89). The opening words, "Not to us, O LORD" (Latin: *non nobis, domine*), have echoed across the centuries in words and music, often as a thankful acknowledgment that what has been achieved owes more to God than to any human efforts. In Shakespeare's *Henry V,* the king, contemplating the enormity of the victory at Agincourt, exclaims, "O God! thy arm was here; And not to us, but to thy arm alone, Ascribe we all" (4.8.111-13). And shortly later: "Do we all holy rites: Let there be sung *Non nobis* and *Te Deum*" (4.8.127-28). William Wilberforce meditated thankfully on this psalm when the bill to abolish slavery went through the British parliament. This, however, is hardly what the words mean at the beginning of this psalm. Here we are listening to an urgent plea that God should act decisively to defend himself, his own power and his own authority, which are now under attack. This is a theme which occurs frequently in Ezekiel, who speaks of God having to act for the sake of his holy name (e.g., Ezek. 36:22-23; 39:7). The mocking words of the "nations" (Hebrew *gôyîm,* a word usually denoting foreign nations, Gentiles as opposed to Jews) are calling into question all that the congregation affirms when it addresses God. Is there, they claim, any evidence for the presence and activity of the LORD in the events which shape their lives?

3-8 The answer comes in verses 3-8, which may have been spoken to and in the name of the congregation by a priest. "Our God is in the heavens" (v. 3). This does not mean he is solely in the heavens, remote from what is happening on earth. This is an assertion of the total sovereignty of God over all the forces in the universe, a celebration of the kingship of God, the theme of Psalms 93, 95–99. This is the God who "does whatever he pleases" (v. 3), a statement to which, not surprisingly, Calvin devotes considerable attention. This is not to say that God, being omnipotent, can do anything. The key words are "whatever he pleases" (REB: "whatever he wills"). God does whatever is consistent with his own character and whatever furthers his own purposes. This is an issue which is central to the temptation narrative in the Gospels (Luke 4:1-13; Matt. 4:1-11), where Jesus says "No" to the abuse of power and a quick-fix ministry, since he knows this to be inconsistent with the purposes of his heavenly Father. But our God is in control; he does act, says the priest, which is more than can be said for the gods of other peoples.

Verses 4-8 stand in a tradition of satirical attacks on the idol images of such religions, a tradition which comes to the fore in Isaiah 40–55 (e.g., 40:18-20; 44:9-20; 46:1-7), but is found elsewhere in the Old Testament (e.g., Jer. 10:1-10; Ps. 96:5). This section of the Psalm occurs again in 135:15-18. It is important to see that such passages are not part of a serious argument with exponents of another faith. As such they would be futile. It would be easy to retort, "but we don't worship images, they are merely our icons, aids to devotion." This satire is for home consumption. Look at such images. Costly, well crafted they may be, but in the end of the day they are but lifeless blocks of wood or metal, fit symbols of gods who can do nothing. This is designed to underline the dramatic contrast to the LORD of Israel's faith. Such idols cannot speak, but the LORD speaks (cf. 33:9). They "cannot see," but the LORD "sees" (cf. 113:6). They cannot hear, but the LORD hears (cf. 6:8-9). Their hands cannot even feel, but the LORD's hands are powerful and creative (cf. 102:25). People who put their "trust" in such gods will end up as powerless and as clueless as the gods they make (v. 8). Irony is here being used to confirm the congregation's confidence in the LORD and the LORD alone. Yes, "trust" is justifiable, but only "trust" in the LORD.

9-11 In verses 9-11 the temple singers call for such "trust" (see 4:5), appealing to "Israel" (v. 9), to "the house of Aaron," the priests (v. 10), and to "you who fear the LORD" (v. 11). This last phrase has been taken to mean non-Jews who have attached themselves to the Jewish community. There are examples of this across Israel's history (e.g., Ruth; Naaman in 2 Kings 5). In postexilic times, "God fearers" became a recognized description of proselytes or people attracted to the Jewish faith (e.g., Acts 13:16, 26). In the context of this psalm, however, the phrase may mean no more than all who truly worship the LORD, including the people in general and the priests. Three times in these verses we hear the call "Trust in the LORD!" and on each occasion it is answered by "He is their help and their shield" (see 3:3; 28:7). We might have expected "He is our help and our shield," but the responsive choir is probably providing its own comment on this call to trust.

12-15 Verses 12-15 are in the form of a priestly blessing, echoing the language of verses 9-11. It is based on the assurance, "The LORD has been mindful of us" (v. 12). Crisis there may be, but it is not a crisis in which the LORD has forgotten his people. He is present, caring for them. This whole section is dominated by the verb "bless" (see 3:8). Four times we hear the words "he [i.e. the LORD] will bless" (vv. 12, 13) those mentioned in verses 9-11, "Israel, . . . the house of Aaron . . . those who fear the LORD," in fact "both great and small" (v. 13), everyone in the community. Verse 15 then expresses the wish "May you be blessed by the LORD," a blessing which will take tangible form in the enrichment of life across the generations.

16-18 The concluding words of the blessing, the description of the LORD as the God "who made heaven and earth," provide the theme for the congregation's final words of praise. The blessing uses the key words "heaven" and "earth" to spell out clearly the sphere of human responsibility. It is this life on earth, the here and now, which has been given to "human beings." Beyond this here and now lies the silent world of the dead (cf. 94:17), where the praise of the LORD is no longer possible (see Psalm 88). Now is the time for acknowledging the LORD's goodness. So the congregation pledges itself to "bless the LORD from this time on and forevermore" (v. 18). This "forevermore" looks to the congregation handing on a tradition of lively praise from generation to generation. In personal terms, however, for the psalmist this "forevermore" is bounded by death and can only mean for him, throughout my whole life. We have to travel further along the theological road in Jewish thinking and into the Christian revelation before the silence of death is replaced by the triumphant heavenly chorale on the other side, with the last enemy conquered (e.g., Rev. 7:9-17.)

Although there are no specific references to the Exodus event in this psalm (cf. Psalm 113), its language and imagery are at home in the context of Passover. It celebrates the living, active God, the God who hears the cry of his oppressed people (cf. Exod. 2:23). This is the God against whom the religious and the political might of Egypt, its magicians and its army, were to prove powerless, the God in whom all power in heaven and on earth resides. The familiar concluding words, "Praise the LORD," have no finer illustration than in the triumph song of Miriam: "Sing to the LORD, for he has triumphed gloriously; horse and rider he has thrown into the sea" (Exod. 15:21). Across its history, Israel had good reason to praise this living God. So do we.

Psalm 116
LOVE AND GRATITUDE

Some of the early versions divide this psalm into two after verse 9, prefacing both verses 1 and 10 with *halĕlû-yāh,* which means "praise the LORD." There is, however, little reason to regard the psalm in its entirety as anything other than an intensely personal psalm of thanksgiving. The psalm is usually thought to have been designed for use at one of the great festivals, when opportunity was given for the expression of personal thanksgiving. This fits in well with the closing of the psalm, verses 17-19. It is, however, also possible that in origin this was a purely personal literary composition, in which an otherwise unknown individual expressed his gratitude to the LORD for the resolution of a traumatic crisis in his life and acknowledged his need to share his gratitude publicly. It would then have entered the liturgical riches of the community because it described an experience with which others could identify.

It is not clear precisely what the crisis situation in the psalmist's life had been. The reference to "the snares of death . . . the pangs of Sheol" (v. 3) would fit any situation in which the psalmist felt his vitality was draining away (see 18:4-5). Other references to suffering — "distress and anguish" (v. 3), "greatly afflicted" (v. 10), and "my consternation" (v. 11) — are general words which could apply equally to severe physical illness or to mental depression or to both. Whatever the precise content, the psalmist found himself having to cope with a devastating experience, which thankfully was now in the past.

1-4 The psalmist begins by describing the breakdown which had threatened to destroy him and the rich assurance which had come to him through answered prayer (vv. 1-4). Thanksgiving and prayer for help often lie close together in the Psalms. English translations tend to conceal the more dramatic opening of the psalm, which literally reads "I love because the LORD has heard." Although the assumed object of "I love" may well be the LORD, the emphasis is upon a love which is a response to something which the LORD has done. So 1 John 4:19 declares, "We love, because he first loved us." The LORD has not only listened but answered (for "incline his ear," see 17:6; cf. 88:2) the psalmist's plea for help (cf. 28:2, 6). Such answered prayer provides the psalmist with the motivation to commit himself to the life of prayer as long as he lives (v. 2). This interpretation of verse 2 assumes that "I will call on him" picks up the thought of "my voice and my supplications" in verse 1. Since the verb "call" in verse 2, however, like "love" in verse 1, has no object in the original, it may mean simply "to cry out" or "to proclaim."

3-7   What the psalmist wants to proclaim is then contained in verses 3-7. The one thing he dare not do is to minimize the depth of the crisis he faced and from which he has been delivered. Death, like some dread monster, had threatened to swallow him alive. Sheol had got its claws into him (see 18:5; for "Sheol," see 6:5). The word translated "pangs" (v. 3) is probably a synonym for the "snares" or "cords" of death. In this situation there was only one glimmer of hope, an urgent appeal to the LORD: "save my life!" (v. 4). The Hebrew word *nepeš,* here translated "life," occurs again in the psalm in verses 7 and 8, where it is translated "soul" (see 6:4). The phrase "call on the name of the LORD" (v. 4) is heard twice again in the psalm with a different shade of meaning on each occasion; this is not surprising, since the "name" or the essential character of God (see 5:11) impinges upon the life of the psalmist in different ways. In verse 4 the phrase means to invoke God's help. In verse 13 it is in the context of acknowledging gratefully what the LORD has done, and in verse 17 it goes hand in hand with offering a thanksgiving sacrifice. Why should God answer such a cry for help? Just because that is what the LORD is like: "gracious . . . righteous . . . merciful" (see 111:3-4; 112:4), a God who "protects the simple" (v. 6). The word translated "simple" does not refer to the mentally impaired. It is a word found most frequently in Proverbs to describe people who have "no sense" (Prov. 9:4, 11), people who lack "shrewdness" (Prov. 1:4) or "prudence" (Prov. 8:5), people who are prepared to believe anything (Prov. 14:15). Here it seems to refer to the gullible or the vulnerable. By identifying himself with "the simple," the psalmist is admitting that he was at the end of his tether — "brought low," uncertain of the next step to take. Then in his weakness he discovered that the LORD "saved" (see 3:3). He knew he had found "rest" or security — the same word is used for what Ruth was to find in marriage (see Ruth 3:1) — and found it not in any qualities or resources which he himself possessed, but simply because the LORD "dealt bountifully" with him (see 13:6).

8-11   Verses 8-11 spell out what that divine bounty meant in practical terms. Rescued from death, tears banished, instead of stumbling the psalmist walks again in confidence wherever life takes him, because he walks "before [or "in the presence of"] the LORD" (v. 9). After the reference to tears, verses 8-9 are almost a repetition of 56:13. Verses 10-11 pose more difficult problems. In 2 Cor. 4:13 Paul, in a different context, quotes the Greek (LXX) ending of verse 10, "I believed, and so I spoke." The Hebrew text, however, hardly justifies this rendering. It might just mean, as the NRSV translates, "I kept my faith [I believed] even when I said" — that is, even when things were at their worst, when he had to admit that he was "greatly afflicted," the psalmist held on to God. This would parallel Paul's words in 2 Cor. 1:8-10; after referring to his afflictions in Asia, where "we were so utterly, unbearably crushed," he speaks of having found his faith in God, "who rescued us," confirmed. The construction in verse 10 of the

Hebrew, however, is awkward. This is the justification for the REB, with a slight alteration to the text, translating, "I was sure I should be swept away." The first half of verse 10, in that case, provides a parallel to verse 11, which speaks of the psalmist's "consternation" (REB: "alarm"). The closing words of verse 11, "Everyone is a liar," do not necessarily mean that the psalmist was being subject to false accusations, a common enough situation in other psalms (see Psalm 109). In Ps. 62:9 a word from the same root is translated "a delusion" (REB: "a sham"). The REB catches the flavor of the words by translating, "How faithless are all my fellow creatures." The psalmist had probably been promised support by others, but their promises had come to nothing. He was left to face his crisis alone, alone except for the LORD.

12-19 It is to the LORD that the psalmist turns in gratitude in verses 12-19, a gratitude which he knows can never match what the LORD has done for him, a gratitude which must be expressed not only in words but in action. Three such acts are highlighted in the closing verses of the psalm. First, "I will lift up the cup of salvation" (v. 13). Although the "cup" has many rich associations in the Psalms and throughout the Old Testament (see 11:6), the reference here is probably to the drink offering which accompanied the burnt offering (see Num. 28:7). As the wine was poured out, it became for the psalmist a visible symbol of all that the LORD had done for him, "the cup of salvation." Next, the psalmist resolves to "offer you a thanksgiving sacrifice" (v. 17; see 50:14), the sacrifice offering which gave tangible expression to the inward need to say "thank you" for what had been so generously given, that "thank you" which is to burst forth into "Praise the LORD!" (v. 18). Finally, in verses 14 and 18 the psalmist promises, "I will pay my vows to the LORD." Such "vows" often accompanied the thanksgiving offering. They were a recognition that there could be no true thanksgiving which did not lead to commitment, to vows or promises made to the LORD, vows made to be kept. What the content of such a vow would be depended upon personal circumstances (compare, for example, Jacob's vow at Bethel [Gen. 28:20] and Hannah's vow in 1 Sam. 1:11) and upon the particular gifts of mind and spirit which the worshipper possessed. A Christian counterpart of this is found in 1 Cor. 12:4-31.

All three acts, to be done publicly "in the presence of all his people" (vv. 14, 18) in the temple courts, depended upon the relationship between the LORD and the psalmist, a relationship which is encapsulated in verses 15-16. On the one hand, the LORD is a God who cares about what happens to his "faithful ones" (see 4:3). The untimely death of any of his covenant people is, therefore, something which weighs heavily upon him and leads him to act (v. 15; cf. 72:14). On the other hand, the psalmist recognizes his true status. He is the LORD's "servant" or slave, "the child of your serving [or: slave] girl." Here is someone who has always seen his true destiny to be within the household of God, totally at the service of and under the protection of a divine master who has "loosed my bonds" (v. 16), freeing the psalmist from the constricting tentacles of Death and Sheol.

Put this psalm into the context of Passover, and it is easy to see how it would speak to people who were celebrating the God who had answered their cry born of oppression, who had delivered them from the death of Egyptian slavery, and who had set them free to become a people for whom life was to be lived, through obeying his law, in thankful response for all that God had done for them. It is small wonder that we find the same thoughts in the celebration of Holy Communion, which is the Christian Passover. With its invitation to take "the cup of salvation," Ps. 116:12-14 is one of the key scriptural texts which summon the people to share in the sacrament. The sharing of bread and wine is preceded by prayers of thanksgiving which celebrate all that God has done in Christ, prayers of thanksgiving which lead into a vow of commitment: "here we offer and present to you our very selves, to be a living sacrifice, dedicated and fit for your acceptance, through Jesus Christ our Lord." We do well to remember how the roots of Christian worship were nourished in the soil of Israel.

Psalm 117
PRAISE THE LORD

This is the briefest of all the Psalms. It is not surprising that some Hebrew manuscripts wished to tag it onto the end of Psalm 116, while others wished to join it to Psalm 118. Yet this is a case where small is beautiful. Nothing is said in it which has not been said in other psalms, but in one sentence — if we leave aside the final "Praise the LORD!" — it takes us close to the heart of Israel's faith. It celebrates a faith which could not but burst all narrow nationalist fetters to reach out to the whole world — "all you nations" and "all you peoples" (v. 2; cf. Psalm 96). Because it does so, Paul weaves the first half of the psalm into his argument that the gospel is for the Gentiles as well as for the Jews (Rom. 15:11). The psalm leaves us in no doubt that the essential and unchangeable elements in that faith center on the "steadfast love" (see 5:7) and the "faithfulness" (see 25:5) of the LORD. Since there is no point in worship unless that be true, this psalm is often still used as an authentic call to worship.

Psalm 118
A NATION'S THANKSGIVING

This psalm highlights many of the difficulties facing us as we seek to understand the Psalms, both in their original setting and in their contemporary relevance. Many different elements seem to surface in the psalm. It begins in verses 1-4 and ends in verse 29 with a call to the community to celebrate the "steadfast love" of the LORD. The central section in verses 5-21, however, contains the thanksgiving of an individual, probably the king or some other representative of the community. It also presupposes a festal procession to the Jerusalem temple, with a question and answer session at the gate into the temple courts (vv. 19-20) similar to what we have seen in Psalms 15 and 24. The culmination of the procession seems to involve a ritual beside the altar outside the temple building (v. 29), a ritual which is capable of varied interpretation. It may be linked — as the Mishnah, the second-century C.E. compendium of rabbinic teaching, suggests — with the autumnal Feast of Tabernacles. How do all these elements fit together? There have been and are many different theories. The view taken here is that the psalm comes from a service of national thanksgiving celebrating a decisive military victory. Such a service has always been part of a nation's worship, especially where there is a close link between church and state. Its modern parallel would be a service of thanksgiving to mark the end of the Gulf War. It is not surprising that the king, the focus of the nation's hopes, who led his people into battle, should in such a context play a prominent role, giving his personal testimony to what the LORD has done. Nor would it be inappropriate for such a service to take place within the setting of the Feast of Tabernacles or Booths. Although essentially the great autumnal harvest thanksgiving festival, it is nevertheless linked in Leviticus 23 with the Exodus event, reflecting the fact that the people lived "in booths when I brought them up out of Egypt," the victory which gave birth to the nation. This link is strengthened by the way in which the psalm at various points echoes the language of the victory hymn in Exodus 15. The psalm must, therefore, be preexilic, coming from the period of the monarchy; how early in that period depends on the interpretation we give to certain verses. As in the case of all early psalms, however, its language was capable of being adapted and reminted in a later age. Nowhere is this adaptation more evident than in the New Testament's use of verses 22 and 25. This psalm was Luther's favorite, not surprisingly since, as has been well said, "it is a powerful testimony to the strength of faith which flows from the direct experience of the help of God" (A. Weiser).

1-4 The psalm begins with a call to the whole community to give thanks, the community which embraces "Israel . . . the house of Aaron . . . and those who fear the LORD" (see 115:12-13). It is thanksgiving rooted in the unchanging element in Israel's experience, "the steadfast love" of the LORD (see 117:2). The opening verse seems to reflect standard liturgical usage, since it appears again at the beginning of Psalms 106, 107, and 136, and reappears in the closing verse of this psalm. The opening section displays a feature which is to be characteristic of the psalm: the deliberate, emphatic use of repetition. Each of the first four verses ends with "his steadfast love endures forever," while verses 2, 3, and 4 each begin with, "Let X say. . . ." Verses 6 and 7 each begin with two Hebrew words, "The LORD to [or for] me," that is, "the LORD is on my side"; while verses 8 and 9 each begin with the phrase translated, "it is better to take refuge in the LORD." In verses 10-12 we hear four times the words "they surrounded me" and three times "in the name of the LORD I cut them off." In verses 15 and 16 there is a threefold reference to "the right hand of the LORD."

5-21   In the context of the community thanksgiving, the king gives his personal testimony. Verse 5 describes in brief and general terms the basis for this testimony. It is the testimony of answered prayer. He has been delivered from "distress" and taken to "a broad place" (see 31:8). It is as if, hemmed in, overwhelmed by threatening circumstances, he had been given breathing space. He can, therefore, face whatever life may bring without fear, because "the LORD is on my side" (vv. 6, 7). This is the guarantee that he will triumph over his enemies. They are no more than mere "mortals" (see 56:11). In verses 8-9 he points out the relevance of his experience for the whole community. Anyone looking for security in life ought to realize that it is to be found only in the LORD, and not in any human resources, not even in the apparently powerful "princes." The words "take refuge" and "trust" recur frequently in the Psalms (see 2:12; 4:5). The psalmists are never in doubt that those who put their trust in anyone or anything other than the LORD will be sadly disillusioned (cf. 41:9; 49:6; 115:8).

In verses 10-14 the crisis the king faced is graphically described. He was surrounded on all sides by hostile "nations." They are compared in verse 12 to bees buzzing around and attacking him, a simile used in Deut. 1:44 to describe the way in which the native inhabitants of Canaan chased the incoming Hebrews. The other picture in verse 12 is that of "a fire of thorns" or brushwood, a fire which blazes up quickly and sweeps across the countryside with devastating effect. The translation "blazed" assumes a slight alteration to the Hebrew text and follows the Greek (LXX) interpretation. The Hebrew says "extinguished," which presumably stresses that a fire of thorns, although it burns fiercely, soon dies away. In context this is less likely, since both similes seem to refer to the aggressive ferocity of those who surrounded the king. The verb translated "I cut them off" normally means in Hebrew "to circumcise." If this were its meaning here, it might point to the early wars against the Philistines, who, unlike other people in the region, were uncircumcised. According to 1 Sam. 18:25-29, when David wished to marry Saul's daughter Michal, Saul demanded from David a hundred foreskins as a marriage gift, and David duly obliged after killing one hundred Philistines. The verb, however, may mean simply "ward off," in which case it gives us no clues as to the historical circumstances implied in this section.

One thing, however, the king has no doubts about. Hard pressed though he may have been, the "help" of the LORD was sufficient for all eventualities. The crisis is over. In verse 14 he echoes the traditional victory song formula in Exod. 15:2a, while verse 28 recalls Exod. 15:2b. Although to witness to the LORD as "my strength and my might" (v. 14) is appropriate, the word translated "might" and its related verb usually refer in the Psalms to singing (cf. 81:2). There is no reason why that meaning should not be retained here. The help and the strength the LORD have given are to be celebrated in a song of praise whose theme is the "salvation" (see 3:8) the king has experienced. This prepares the way for "the glad songs of victory," a "victory" — the same word is translated "salvation" in verse 14 — which reverberates across the tents of the victorious troops. They are "righteous," because they have been vindicated by the LORD. They owe their victory to the powerful "right hand of the LORD" (see 20:6). Again we are conscious of the echoes of Exod. 15:6, "Your right hand, O LORD, glorious in power — your right hand, O LORD, shattered the enemy."

Like the LORD's right hand, the word translated "valiantly" (v. 16) has strong associations with the battlefield and the power the LORD there displayed (cf. 59:11); hence, the REB translates "mighty deeds." The king was snatched from the jaws of death to do what the dead can never do, to bear witness to the "deeds of the LORD" (see 88:10-12). He recognizes, however, that his experience has been salutary. He has been disciplined by the LORD (cf. 94:12, where the word here translated "punished" is rendered "disciplined"), chastened yet never finally abandoned. Why he needed to be so disciplined or corrected we are not told, but it is interesting that in this context there is no reference to the anger of the LORD. He did not seem to view the crisis through which he lived as God's just punishment for his sins. Rather, it was an experience which taught him more about what the LORD wanted him to be and to do, a needed corrective to keep him on course. The NRSV translation in verse 18, "The LORD has punished me severely," is too strong; the REB's rendering, "The LORD did indeed chasten me," is nearer the mark.

The king now approaches the gate into the temple precincts, and we listen to the kind of dialogue familiar from Psalms 15 and 24. The king wishes to give thanks to the LORD, so he asks for admittance: "Open to me the gates of righteousness," the gates through which those who have been vindicated by the LORD may rightly enter. Since the king has been so vindicated, he claims the right to enter. In verse 20 the Levites on duty at the gates give their positive response. Yes, this is "the gate of the LORD," the gate which leads into the temple courts where the LORD dwells. Yes, it is open to the "righteous." The word "righteous" is here plural and may refer to the king and his retinue. In the words of the gatekeeper the king hears the LORD's "Yes" to all his requests. With thanksgiving in his heart, he enters the temple courts confessing: "You have answered me and have become my salvation." His entry into the temple courts sets the seal on his relationship with the one who, in the words of 46:1, has proved to be "a very present help in trouble."

22-25 In verse 22-25 the congregation, or perhaps a chorus, like the chorus in a Greek play, reflect upon the king's testimony and its relevance for both the king and the community. Notice the switch to "our," "us," and "we" in verses 23-25. Verse 22 may well be a proverbial saying, a miniature parable describing how something or someone, rejected as useless, comes to be accepted as essential. The foundation "cornerstone" (literally, "the head of the corner") was the block of stone which joined together at right angles the walls of a building. If it were flawed, the whole building would be unsafe. Builders, therefore, chose this corner-stone with care. Anything which did not meet their specifications and quality control would be rejected. Surprise, surprise, then, that just such a rejected stone becomes the cornerstone. Applied to the king, it points to one who had been in distress, surrounded by enemies, in danger of being dismissed as rejected by the LORD. But in the providence of the LORD he had been vindicated and accepted. Since that is a verdict on the king's experience, it is not surprising that it is used in a future messianic context (see comment on Psalm 2). All the Synoptic Gospels put it on the lips of Jesus in the context of the passion narrative, in the story of the wicked tenants who kill the son of the owner of the vineyard (Mark 12:10; Matt. 21:42; Luke 20:17), a use which provokes a violent reaction from the listeners. It becomes in the New Testament documents a key verse in the apolo-getic for Jesus as the long-expected messiah who was yet rejected by his own people (Acts 4:11; 1 Peter 2:7), and in Ephesians Jesus is described as the corner-stone who holds together the whole structure, the church which is the household of God (Eph. 2:20).

The reversal of fortune of the king may be a surprise, but the LORD is a God of surprises, before whom his people can only bow in wonder (for "mar-velous," v. 23, see 9:1). It is not entirely clear what is meant in verse 24 by the claim "This is the day that the LORD has made." The REB rendering, "This is the day on which the LORD has acted," assumes that the day is important because of its association with what the LORD has done for the king. On the other hand, "the day that the LORD has made" may refer to the festival day, part of the celebration of Tabernacles, one of the special days ordained by the LORD as part of the religious calendar. However we interpret it, it is a day which calls forth from the community joyful celebration. In Christian liturgical usage this verse often calls the congregation to joyful worship on Sunday, the day which marks the resurrection of Jesus from the dead — cause indeed for joyful celebration.

The celebration of the LORD's past goodness leads naturally into the appeal that the same goodness will characterize the present and the future: "Save us . . . give us success!" (v. 25). What precisely these words mean depends on the expectations which were in the minds of the congregation as they shared in the national euphoria associated with the king's victory. The word translated "Save us" (Hebrew *hôšî'āh nā'*) appears in abbreviated form in the New Testament as "Hosanna." When joined to the opening word of verse 26, it is heard on the lips of the crowd as Jesus enters Jerusalem on Palm Sunday (Mark 11:9; Matt. 21:9; Luke 19:36). In that context it had probably lost something of its original theological content, to become little more than a cry of joyful welcome and acclamation, just as an original "God be with you" has become for us "Good-bye."

26-29 In verses 26 and 27 we listen to a priestly blessing, the first part of which was probably pronounced by the priests at the gate leading into the temple courts. He "who comes [REB: "enters"] in the name of the LORD" is the king and possibly each one of those who accompany him in the procession, coming to the temple with the LORD's imprimatur. As is clear from the Palm Sunday story and elsewhere in the New Testament, the phrase "who comes" or "is to come" (Matt. 11:3) gathers to itself messianic significance. The reference to the LORD "who has given us light" (v. 27) uses the same verb as is found in the priestly blessing in Num. 6:25, where it is translated "make [his face] shine upon you." This verse is probably a deliberate echo of that blessing, affirming that it has now been authenticated in the experience of the nation. The second half of verse 27 has been variously interpreted, as may be seen from the widely different translations in the NRSV and the REB. The word translated "festal procession" (Hebrew *hag*) usually means a pilgrimage or pilgrim festival (cf. 81:3, where it is translated "our festal day"). The REB assumes that it refers to the pilgrims; others have argued that it refers to the sacrifice offered in the context of the festival. But what picture is implied? This is complicated by the fact that the word translated "branches" can also mean "cords." The REB translation assumes some kind of sacred dance round the altar with cords attached to "the horns of the altar," the projections at the four corners of the altar, to grasp which was to place oneself under the protection of God (cf. 1 Kgs. 2:28). This would give us something like the Israelite equivalent of the sacred dance round the maypole tree. The NRSV translation follows more closely the account of the Feast of Tabernacles as we find it in the Mishnah. There, worshippers process to the altar, carrying the *lulab,* greenery symbolizing the fertility of the land, branches made up of myrtle, willows, palms plus citrus fruits (cf. Lev. 23:40). These branches adorn the altar. This may be what is meant by "up to the horns of the altar." Whatever the precise picture, attention is being drawn to the climax of the procession, approaching the altar in the inner temple court. There expression is given to the unrestrained joy of the community. Fittingly, therefore, the psalm ends with words of thanksgiving and praise on the lips of the king in verse 28 (cf. Exod. 15:2b), words which find their counterpart on the lips of the whole congregation in verse 29, where the opening words of the psalm are heard once more.

Psalm 118 is the last of the "Egyptian Hallel" Psalms (see introduction to Psalm 113). Whatever its original setting, its appropriateness in the context of thanksgiving for deliverance from slavery in Egypt is clear. It is there in the echoes of Exodus 15. The mood throughout is one of thanksgiving for national deliverance. In contemporary Jewish liturgical usage, it finds a place in the celebration of Hanukkah, the Festival of Lights, which commemorates the rededication of the temple after the successful Jewish resistance to Antiochus Epiphanes and his attempt to force the Jews to give up their beliefs and religious customs, in the second century BCE (see 1 Maccabees). One can only guess what was in the minds of the disciples if they were singing this psalm on the way to Gethsemane after their last supper with Jesus. It was to take the Easter event to bring the psalm sharply into focus in Christian thinking. There would have been no victory to celebrate with thanksgiving if the Christian story had ended in the distress of the cross. The psalm, therefore, finds its place as the psalm appropriate for reading on Easter Sunday in contemporary Christian lectionaries.

Psalm 119
THE ABC OF THE GOD-CENTERED LIFE

If Psalm 117 is the briefest of the Psalms, Psalm 119 is by far the longest. It is the most complex acrostic poem (see Psalms 9–10) in the Bible. Its one hundred and seventy-six verses are divided into twenty-two sections, each of eight lines. Each line in verses 1-8 begins with 'alep, the first letter in the Hebrew alphabet; each line in verses 9-16 begins with bêt, the second letter in the alphabet; and so it continues until we have journeyed through the twenty-two letters of the alphabet. Of its ingenuity there is little doubt, but it has evoked the most diverse reactions. It has been dismissed as "a particularly artificial product of religious poetry . . . a many colored mosaic of thoughts which are often repeated in wearisome fashion" (A. Weiser). It has been hailed as a "precursor of the finest flowering of both Judaism and the Christian faith" (L. C. Allen). If we set out to look for an author, then we can hardly do better than recall the comment of Calvin: "it cannot be ascertained, even by probable conjecture, who he was." A young man or an old man, a prisoner whiling away his idle hours, a king, a wisdom teacher, or a priest — all have their advocates, with dates ranging from the seventh to the third century BCE. What seems clear is that the psalm incorporates richly varied material, with many elements of wisdom teaching combined with prayers, often urgent prayers for help, and sections focusing on the praise of God.

What is central to the whole psalm — it occurs in twenty-one of the twenty-two sections — is the word Torah, the word we so often translate as "law," wrongly associating it with legal or legalistic concepts. Torah, which comes from the verb "to teach or instruct," means far more than law (see 1:2; 19:7). It embraces God's revelation of himself to Israel and all that this implies for the God-centered life of obedience. In Judaism, Torah came to refer to Genesis through Deuteronomy, the first five books of the Bible, with their story of creation, the call of Abraham, the Exodus event, and the promise of the land, as well as the commandments which were to define the life of the people of God. Throughout the commentary on this psalm, we shall refer to "Torah" rather than "law," in order to preserve the breadth of meaning in the word.

Psalm 119 is a celebration of Torah. Associated with Torah, there is a cluster of words met repeatedly in the Psalms, some of them in Psalm 19; for example, "decrees" (v. 2), "precepts" (v. 4), "commandments" (v. 6), "ordinances" (v. 7). While "the fear of the LORD" (19:9) does not appear in Psalm 119, there are frequent references to "those who fear the LORD" (e.g., vv. 38, 63, 74, 79, 120). Other frequently occurring words are "way" (v. 1) or "ways" (v. 3), "statutes" (v. 8), and "word" (v. 16). We shall explore this rich vocabulary further as we look briefly at each of the sections in the psalm, giving them the heading which corresponds to the appropriate letter in the Hebrew alphabet.

'Alep

1-8 In this opening section there are two major themes. First, there is the claim that the source of happiness (for "Happy," see 1:1) and of the "blameless" (see 15:2), fulfilled life is to be found in obedience to "the Torah of the LORD" (v. 1). It is noticeable that throughout the psalm the reference is never to "the Torah," but always to "the Torah of the LORD" or "your Torah" (e.g., 18, 29, 34). This is teaching which has its roots in what God has done and what, therefore, God may rightly expect and demand, in the light of the covenant relationship which exists between himself and his people. The emphasis throughout is positive. To live fully means to keep the LORD's "decrees" (v. 2). This word in Deut. 4:45 is used in the context of Torah and, in association with "statutes" (v. 8) and "ordinances" (v. 7), leads into the Decalogue. In Exod. 31:18 it refers to the two tablets of the Law, and the NRSV there translates it as "covenant." Such "decrees" are the witness to the covenant relationship and the demands it makes. To keep them, the people must seek God "with their whole heart" (v. 2) — a typical Deuteronomic expression (see Deut. 6:5) — "walk in his ways" (see 25:9 and 12, where "way" is associated with the covenant), and faithfully keep his "precepts" (v. 4). This word "precepts" is found only in the Psalms, mainly in this psalm; compare 103:18, where it is used in parallel to covenant and translated "commandments." It has about it something of the flavor of what may be rightly demanded by a master. God's ways are to be reflected in the psalmist's ways, "my ways" (v. 5). He is to keep a steady course, in the light of God's "statutes" (cf. 99:7; 103:7), with eyes fixed on God's "commandments" (v. 6). The outcome of such a life is not cringing or fearful obedience, but thanksgiving, "I will praise you with an upright heart" (v. 7). This is praise rooted in the fact that here is life which goes on learning "your righteous ordinances" (v. 7). The word here translated "ordinances" means decisions, the decisions of a judge or ruler. It is frequently used to introduce a series of legal decisions (e.g., Exod. 21:10) or judgments, and this may be its meaning here. But the phrase "the decisions of your righteousness" might also refer to what God had done for the psalmist (see 7:11) and his people. Certainly it is what God has done for his people which rightly calls forth their praise and provides the motivation for their ethical response to God.

The second major theme in this section focuses on a darker side to life, a side which is to come to the fore in other sections of the psalm. The words, "Then I shall not be put to shame" (v. 6) imply that shame and humiliation were a very real possibility (see 4:2), and the closing words of the section, "do not utterly forsake me" (v. 8), contain a heartfelt appeal. This implies that the psalmist may be facing real difficulties and problems which he feels unable to cope with on his own.

Bêt

9-16 This section begins with a question and an answer, a technique typical of a wisdom teacher (see 34:12-13). That the question concerns "young people" (literally, "a young man") does not mean that the psalmist himself is young. How often today do we find older people raising questions about the values young people have or ought to have to carry them through life? The psalmist is quite clear as to the answer. It lies in a "purity" (cf. 73:13) which only comes through holding on to God's "word" (v. 9; cf. v. 16). God's "word" has many meanings in the Bible. Here it probably means what God said to his people, notably in the Ten Words (cf. Deut. 5:5). The psalmist is clear that such desirable purity cannot be self-manufactured. It is the child of obedience, of that wholehearted seeking after and dependence upon God (v. 10; cf. v. 2) which does not go astray by turning aside from God's commandments (v. 10b). But this is not to submit to the voice of a coldly stern deity. The psalmist would hardly have understood what Walt Whitman in his "Song of Myself" was talking about when he envied the placid animals because: "They do not lie awake in the dark and weep for their sins. They do not make me sick discussing their duty to God." On the contrary, the psalmist thrills with joy. He has been given something he "treasures" or takes care of, the LORD's "word" (v. 11) or "promise" (REB). This is a different word from that translated "word" in verses 9 and 16. It may be no more than a synonym, but elsewhere the NRSV recognizes that "promise" is an equally valid rendering (cf. v. 140). This "word" or promise is held out as the antidote to "sin," that attitude which shows that we are well wide of the mark as to what life is really all about (see 32:1). "I have rejoiced" (v. 14, REB), claims the psalmist, in your "decrees" (cf. v. 2), in the life your decrees have mapped out for me; yes, I rejoice in this "as much as" or more than in riches (cf. vv. 72, 127; in Proverbs, the same claim is made for wisdom; see, e.g., Prov. 3:14-15; 8:19). He knows that there are values in life more important than and more satisfying than wealth or material prosperity. "I delight [v. 16, a different word from that used in v. 14] in your statutes." The same verb occurs in verse 70, where the psalmist says, "I delight in your Torah," and the corresponding noun occurs frequently throughout this psalm (e.g., vv. 24, 77, 92, 143, 174). It was not fear that led to obedience, but joy. No wonder he cries out, "Blessed are you, O LORD" (v. 12; see 28:6), an exclamation which is usually followed by a description of what the LORD has done. Here, however, it leads into a request: "teach me your statutes." The psalmist recognizes that such statutes and the teaching enshrined in decrees, precepts, and God's word are the LORD's gift to his people. So his delight finds expression in "meditating" (v. 15; see 1:2) and in ensuring that God's word will actively direct his life. "I will not forget your word" (v. 16); this resolve stands in stark contrast to the story of rebellion in the wilderness, described in Psalm 106 in the words "they forgot his works" (v. 13), "they forgot God their Savior" (v. 21).

Gîmel

17-24 Here we listen to an urgent prayer for help, side by side with a deepening spiritual experience. We are given several clues as to the crisis the psalmist faces.

"I live as an alien in the land" (v. 19). The "alien" (Hebrew *ger*) or stranger, temporarily resident in the land, was often vulnerable to oppression (see 94:6). Psalm 146:9 lists the stranger along with the orphan and the widow as being specially under the LORD's protection; compare Exod. 22:21, where the Israelites are warned not to oppress the aliens in their midst, since they had once themselves known what it was like to be aliens in Egypt. But what do these words in verse 19 mean? The REB translation, "Though I am but a passing stranger here on earth," suggests that the psalmist is recognizing that he is no more than a passing guest in God's world, with no natural rights and dependent entirely upon God's generosity and kindness (see 39:11). His only security lies in an ever deepening knowledge of God's Torah and commandments. This is possible. Equally, however, the psalmist may be giving voice to his belief that he is living in what we would call an alien environment, out of sympathy with so much that was going on "in the land," that is, in society around him. Certainly, other words in this section point to just such a situation.

The psalmist is aware of people whom he describes as "the insolent" (see 86:14). "The insolent" make frequent appearances in this psalm, sometimes rendered as "the arrogant" in the NRSV and once in verse 122 as "the godless."

They scorn the psalmist and plot his downfall with lies and deceit. Rightly, in the psalmist's eyes, they are called "accursed ones" (v. 21), though some of the versions take "accursed" with the following words in verse 21. Thus the REB translates, "cursed are those who turn from your commandments." The word "cursed" is normally used in such an exclamatory sense, like its opposite "blessed," but there is no reason why in this context it should not be an adjective describing the insolent, as in the NRSV. Those who are plotting against the psalmist are called "princes" in verse 23. This need not refer to members of the royal family, but simply to those in positions of influence in society (cf. Jer. 36:12, where the same word is translated "officials"). The psalmist is surrounded by people who have power and influence and are prepared to use them against him.

Surrounded by such hatred and scorn (v. 22), the psalmist appeals to God to "deal bountifully" with him (v. 17: cf. 116:7), to enlarge his vision and to deepen his spiritual and moral commitment. He has traveled so far with God, but he is "consumed with longing" (v. 20). "Consumed" is the translation of a word which occurs only here and in Lam. 3:16, where it has a somewhat different meaning. This is a longing which can only be satisfied by continuing joyfully to meditate on God's "statutes" and "decrees" (cf. vv. 14-15). Amid much that is disturbing and threatening, they are there to be his "counselors" (v. 24), there to give him guidance and advice which he knows he can trust.

Dalet

25-32 These verses closely parallel the previous section. Its opening words describe the psalmist's plight. "My soul [i.e., "I"; see 6:3] clings to the dust." As in 22:15, 19, this may point to a life-threatening situation, "dust" being one of the words associated with Sheol, the realm of the dead. His life is collapsing under the impact of "sorrow" (v. 28), a word found elsewhere only in Proverbs, where it denotes the opposite of joy (cf. Prov. 14:13; 17:21). "Falsehood" (v. 29, REB) and "shame" are words with which he is only too familiar. There is, however, hope of renewed vitality and strength, promised by God. Notice the twofold occurrence in this context of "according to your word" (vv. 25, 28). There is the experience of answered prayer (v. 26). There is further enlightenment to be had from a continuing faithful commitment to God's gracious revelation of his purposes (vv. 29-30). There is an answer to the threatening embrace of Death, namely, to reach out to embrace what can provide him with space and freedom, the LORD, his decrees and his commandments. Twice we hear the word "cling." Once, in verse 25, it describes the psalmist's plight, "my soul clings to the dust," and in verse 31 it points to his continuing hope, "I cling to your decrees, O LORD." It is a word used frequently in Deuteronomy to describe religious loyalty (e.g., Deut. 10:20; 13:4). The closing words of the section are translated in the NRSV "for you enlarge my understanding." This may be too intellectual an interpretation. The verb is the same as that used in 4:1, where it is translated, "you gave me room" in my distress. The psalmist's problem was not primarily intellectual. In face of the distressing circumstances in which he finds himself, he finds space, new vigor, and vitality in God's revelation and word. In terms of his own experience, the psalmist is echoing the words of the Second Collect for Peace in Morning Prayer in the *Book of Common Prayer,* which speaks of God as the one "in knowledge of whom standeth our eternal life, whose service is perfect freedom."

Hē

33-40 These verses follow on naturally from the previous section. They contain a series of requests to God, which seek to confirm and give content to the new vitality which God offers. Each of the first seven verses begins with such a request: "Teach . . . Give . . . Lead . . . etc.," while the closing words of the section are "give me life." "Teach" (v. 33) is the verb from which the word Torah comes. The requests "Teach . . . Give understanding" are not requests merely for intellectual enlightenment. They speak of a commitment which expresses itself in wholehearted obedience and which will have moral and social consequences. The second half of verse 33 is difficult. Although the NRSV translation "to the end" receives support from the Greek (LXX) "always," it is better to follow the REB rendering of this whole line "and in keeping them I shall find my reward" (cf. 19:11). Obedience involves facing choices. It means saying "No" to "selfish gain" (v. 36; cf. Prov. 1:19) and to "vanities," to what is meaningless or false (see 24:4). It means saying "Yes" to life. The phrase rendered "give me life" in verses 37 and 40 is the same Hebrew word translated "revive me" in verse 25. This is life which can only be God-centered — "according to your word" (v. 25), "in your ways" (v. 37). It is the gift of God's "righteousness" (v. 40; see 11:7), of God being true to his own gracious and faithful nature (cf. v. 50).

Verses 38 and 39 contain an interesting play on words which in 33:8 are virtually regarded as synonyms, the verbs translated "fear" and "dread." The psalmist is gripped by a deep-seated "dread" that he may experience "disgrace" (cf. v. 22, where the same word is translated "scorn"). The antidote to that kind of oppressive fear is to be found in belonging to those "who fear you" (see 19:9), that is, those who truly revere and worship the LORD. They will find God's promises being fulfilled, and have moral and spiritual guidelines which are constructive.

Wāw

41-48 Two words which lie close to the heart of Torah, "steadfast love" (see 5:7) and "salvation" (see 3:8), dominate the opening of this section. The experience of their reality in the psalmist's life will enable him both to refute "those who taunt me" (v. 42, a verb related to the word translated "disgrace" in v. 39) and to bear confident witness to what God gives and demands, even to those in positions of authority — "kings" (v. 46), a word probably indicating any people who wield power. He can do so because he "trusts" (see 4:5) in a word which he believes to be "the word of truth" (v. 43; see 25:5), a dependable word. Such trust goes hand in hand with "hope," a word which echoes across the psalm (e.g., vv. 74, 81, 114, 147). It is the word translated "wait for" in 31:24 and points to the challenge of living daily, staking everything on the conviction that what God promises will be verified in experience. What is remarkable about this section are the words used to describe the psalmist's attitude to and response to Torah; "liberty" (REB: "freedom"; see v. 45), "delight" or joy, and the repeated "love" (vv. 47-48). These are not words which you find in the context of a harsh legalism. They are words which the New Testament uses again and again to describe the Christian's relationship with and response to Christ (e.g., John 8:36; Phil. 4:4; 1 John 4:7-12). Regrettably, they do not always characterize the life of the Church in the world.

Zayin

49-56 This section begins with a prayer, "Remember your word," a call to God to continue providing the psalmist with his sole source of comfort in the midst of his troubles, which center on the activities of "the arrogant" (see v. 21) and "the wicked" (see 1:1). They have been seeking to undermine the psalmist's commitment to God. They have no religious convictions. They "forsake your law" (v. 53), "but I do not turn away from your law" (v. 51). When he thinks of such people, the psalmist gets, as we might say, hot under the collar. The word translated "hot indignation" (v. 53) is the word used in 11:6 of the scorching wind blowing in from the desert, a symbol in that psalm of the judgment of God. The phrase "wherever I make my home" in v. 54 contains in Hebrew a noun related to the word translated "alien" or temporary resident in verse 19. It probably means that in whatever changing circumstances he finds himself, he will join in "songs of praise" (v. 54) whose theme is the LORD's "statutes" (cf. v. 5). He holds fast to the LORD — the "I remember" of verse 55 recalling the opening word of the prayer in verse 49 — and remains steadfast in his obedience. Although the NRSV begins the closing verse of this section with "This blessing," there is no word for "blessing" in the Hebrew, just "this." The REB's rendering, "This has been my lot," is perhaps better, though there is something to be said for translating "Such has been my practice," the practice then being spelled out again in the closing words, "I have kept your precepts" (cf. v. 4).

Ḥēṯ

57-64 The opening verse sets the theme for the entire section. It is concerned with the LORD — who he is and what he does — and with the worshipper and his response to the LORD. "The LORD is my portion" (see 16:5), or, following some early manuscripts, "You are my portion, O LORD," a reading which avoids the somewhat awkward switch to "your" and "you" in the rest of the section. This is the LORD who can be approached to "be gracious" (v. 58; see 4:1); a God characterized by "righteous ordinances" (v. 62; cf. v. 7); a God whose "steadfast love" (see 5:7) fills the world (cf. 33:5). On the psalmist's lips are familiar words of commitment (vv. 57, 60, 61, 63), with a recognition of the dangers which threaten him. For the imagery in verse 61, compare 18:4-5, which speaks of the "cords of Sheol" and "the snares of Death."

For all his words of commitment, the psalmist knows he comes to the LORD as a humble suppliant: "I implore your favor [literally, "your face"] with all my heart" (v. 58). The same expression is found in Psalm 45, the coronation hymn, in which the queen to be is commanded to bow before the king and with gifts seek his favor (45:12). The psalmist is recognizing that he has no claim upon the LORD. He can only humbly request the LORD to be gracious to him.

The psalmist also recognizes that his commitment to the LORD is not a lonely commitment. He is the "companion" of others who share his desire truly to reverence the LORD and to obey his precepts (v. 63; cf. 73:15). Although night was often seen as a time of terror or danger (e.g., Exod. 12:29; Job 27:19-20), the reference to "midnight" (v. 62) and "in the night" (v. 55) may refer to what certainly later became accepted practice, the members of a religious community or brotherhood meeting for prayer and meditation at set times during the night.

Ṭēṯ

65-72 Here the psalmist recognizes that he needed to be disciplined. Such discipline was one of the ways in which the LORD "dealt well" with him (v. 65). It almost looks as if in the past he himself had displayed something of the attitude of the "arrogant" who now, he claims, "smear me with lies" (v. 69). Twice on his lips we hear the words "I was humbled" (vv. 67, 71) or "chastened" (REB).

He admits that before he was humbled he "went astray" (v. 67). This is similar to the conduct of the insolent, which he deplores in verse 21. He accepts that such humbling was for his "good" (v. 71), by making him more willing to learn what the LORD demanded. He does not tell us here what form such humbling took. It could have been either physical or mental suffering. Whatever it was, he accepts it as a necessary discipline. It altered his attitude to life. It leads him to confess that the Torah which comes from the mouth of the LORD is more precious to him than any earthly wealth (v. 72; cf. v. 14).

Yōd

73-80   The theme of the psalmist's humbling by the LORD continues in this section. He accepts that it was wholly justified, indeed an expression of the LORD's "faithfulness" (v. 75; see 89:1). The LORD could have done no other to bring him to his senses. The LORD was not only his creator, the one who "made and fashioned" him, but he was concerned that life should be lived responsibly in the light of the commandments (v. 73). It is tempting to wonder whether this is the psalmist's reflection on Genesis 1-3, where, "made in the image of God," man tragically decides to disobey, thus shattering life as God meant it to be. The psalmist's total dependence upon the LORD is underlined in his prayer in verses 76-80, a prayer which stresses that all of life, his security, his delight in Torah, hinges upon the LORD's promised "steadfast love" and "mercy" (REB: "compassion"; see 25:6). His thoughts focus on two groups of people:

First, there are "the arrogant," who seek treacherously to undermine his life. For them, his prayer echoes what we have heard over and over again in the psalms of lament (e.g., 6:10; 7:15-16), namely, that the shame they seek to inflict upon him may rebound upon themselves (vv. 78, 80).

Second, there are those who are his companions in the community of faith, "those who fear you" (cf. v. 63). He knows that they will rejoice in his spiritual growth (v. 74). He believes that they may have something to learn from him about the meaning of discipleship (v. 79).

Kap

81-88   The mood of the psalms of lament comes strongly to the fore in this section. The psalmist is struggling to come to terms with the crisis in his life (see Psalms 6 and 7). The answer is not yet. He is near the end of his tether, exhausted, waiting, uncertain when the LORD's promised comfort will come (v. 82). The vivid simile in verse 83, "I have become like a wineskin in the smoke," probably draws on the picture of an old wineskin, shriveled up, blackened in a smoke-filled house — past its sell-by date, as we might say. He can think of no justification for what has happened to him. He is the LORD's faithful servant "persecuted without cause" (v. 86) by the "arrogant," who think nothing of the LORD's Torah and who are out to trap him (see 57:6; Jer. 18:22). He can only hold on, believing that the "faithfulness" (cf. v. 75) that he associates with the LORD stands in the sharpest contrast to the "falsehood" which characterizes his persecutors (the REB in v. 86 catches this contrast more successfully than the NRSV). That "life" for which he has pleaded in verses 37 and 40 lies in the hands of the "steadfast love" of the LORD — that life which will enable him to continue his commitment to the LORD.

Lāmed

89-96   In the midst of the unanswered questions and uncertainties of life, the psalmist now reaches out for stability. He finds it in the LORD's "word" — following the REB translation of verse 89, "Your word is everlasting, LORD." This "word," the LORD's creative purpose, is seen in the stability of the universe. Words stressing that stability echo across verses 89-91: "firmly fixed . . . established . . . it stands fast . . . they stand." Such stability is the expression of the LORD's unchanging "faithfulness" (cf. v. 75). It finds its counterpart in the LORD's revelation, his Torah, which is an unfailing source of "delight" and life in the midst of the psalmist's "misery" or distress (vv. 92-93).

The opening word of this section in Hebrew is "forever," and this, the LORD's "forever," finds its counterpart in the psalmist's "forever" at the beginning of verse 93, never to forget what the LORD asks of him. All things exist to serve you, claims the psalmist in verse 91. They are "your servants." This finds its personal affirmation in two simple words at the beginning of verse 94, "I (am) yours," words whose inexhaustible depth of meaning can only be explored in a lifetime of discipleship (cf. v. 125, "I am your servant"). The converse is equally succinctly stated in Isa. 43:1, where God reassures his people by saying "You (are) mine." Thus the psalmist, though surrounded by those who are seeking to destroy him, can confidently appeal, "Save me" (see 3:3).

The last verse in this section, verse 96, is open to different interpretations. The word translated "perfection" occurs only here in the Old Testament. "Perfection" is an attempt to convey the meaning "wholeness" associated with related words. The REB translation, "I see that all things have an end," omits the word that the NRSV renders as "limit" and assumes that it has crept into the text in an attempt to convey the sense of the unusual word the NRSV renders as "perfection." The verse would then be saying that everything apart from God is finite or limited. Only the LORD's "commandment" transcends all human limitations. If, with the NRSV, we retain both words and render "I have seen a limit to all perfection," what does this mean? The Hebrew of this verse is simply one line of seven words. Here is one attempt to render it: "Every aspiration I have seen falls short of realization, your command is so wide in its scope" (L. C. Allen). This assumes that the contrast is between our limited understanding and the boundless scope of the LORD's word. Since this last verse, however, probably echoes the beginning of the section, it is unwise to limit these words to human understanding. Rather, it is "all things" — everything in the universe (v. 91) — which, in its finitude, is here being contrasted with the LORD and his word.

Mēm

97-104   It is hardly surprising that the psalmist lavishes his love upon and sings the praises of the LORD's Torah. The words "I love your law" (v. 97) are to be heard twice again in the psalm, in verses 113 and 163, on each occasion in stark contrast to what the psalmist hates or rejects. In this section that contrast is held over until the closing words in verse 104. For the psalmist, the secret of true wisdom and "understanding" (vv. 99, 104) lies not only in study and "meditation" (v. 97; see 1:2), but in obedience. There is a wisdom associated with "my teachers" (v. 99) and "the aged" (v. 100), but it is the LORD who is truly my teacher, says the psalmist: "you have taught me" (v. 102), and that teaching leads to a total commitment to Torah and a shunning of every "evil way" or path (v. 101), every "false way" (v. 104). The use of the word "path" or way to indicate a way of life or an attitude to life is very common in Proverbs (e.g., Prov. 2:9, 13, 19, 20), and we have met with it in earlier psalms (e.g., 16:11; 17:5; 27:11). For the thought of verse 103, see 19:10. While the NRSV, following some of the early versions and a few Hebrew manuscripts, reads "your words" in this verse, the standard Hebrew text reads the singular "your word." It is the singular, moreover, of a word which the NRSV tends elsewhere to translate as "promise" (e.g., v. 41); hence the REB's rendering, "your promise." Since the reference is certainly to Torah, "word" and "promise" in English are both acceptable and point to the rich content of that Torah.

Nûn

105-112   Verse 105 is probably the most frequently quoted verse from this psalm. It is usually applied in general to Scripture, "a lamp to my feet and a light to my path." But it is important to place these words in context. The need for "a lamp" and "a light" imply that the psalmist has some dark paths to tread. This section stresses that the darkness is only too real. The psalmist is "severely afflicted" (v. 107), at a low ebb, desperately in need of new vitality. "I hold my life in my hand continually," he says (v. 109). In other words, he is constantly exposed to danger; compare 1 Sam. 19:5, where the same expression is used of the risk David takes in attacking the Philistines. He is well aware that there are wicked people out to trap him (v. 110; cf. v. 61). The darkness is threatening, but there is light, the light of the LORD's word. To this the psalmist has made a solemn and unbreakable commitment (v. 106), "to observe your righteous ordinances" (cf. v. 7), to stick to the straight and narrow way (v. 110), while recognizing that he needs further instruction (v. 108). However deep the commitment of faith, there is always more to learn. This is memorably expressed by Paul in Phil. 3:12-14, where, putting his past religious experience in context, he stresses the need to press on, "forgetting what lies behind and straining forward to what lies ahead, I press toward the goal for the prize of the heavenly call of God in Christ Jesus." The darkness is threatening, but in the darkness there is also "joy" (v. 111), a joy which leads the psalmist to ask the LORD to accept "offerings of praise" (v. 108), or perhaps better "the willing tribute of my lips" (REB; literally, "the freewill offering of my mouth"). This may be a reference to prayers gladly and willingly offered to the LORD. Such prayers are the expression of a lifelong commitment. Thus "I incline my heart" (v. 112) means "I am resolved" (REB). As in verse 33, it is best to take the word translated "end" in verse 112 as meaning "reward" (REB). The psalmist is responding to the LORD with a joyful commitment which brings its own reward. Faith always does.

Sāmek

113-120 Some of the tensions which characterize the psalmist's life come through clearly in this section. There is the tension created by the challenge posed by those who do not share his wholehearted loyalty to the LORD. There are those whom he describes as "double-minded" (v. 113), a Hebrew word which occurs only here. It is related, however, to the word Elijah uses when challenging the people on Mt. Carmel, where the REB translates, "How long will you sit on the fence?" (1 Kgs. 18:21). In contrast to such sitting on the fence, which he abhors, the psalmist declares, "I love your Torah" (v. 113), echoed by "I love your decrees" (v. 119; see v. 47). The security this offers him is expressed in the description of the LORD as "my hiding place [cf. 32:7] and my shield [see 3:3]" in verse 114; and in an attitude of "hope" (see v. 43). He is threatened by "evildoers" (v. 115). This is not the usual word for "evildoers" in the Psalms, but a word which rather points to people who are intent on doing him harm. He seeks to close the door on their influence in order to safeguard his loyalty to the one whom he describes, for the first and only time in this psalm, as "my God" (v. 115; cf. 3:7). This is the God whose promise he believes will sustain him and carry him through all the difficulties he faces. The same LORD, he believes, will have nothing to do with those who deliberately "go astray" from his statutes (v. 118) The NRSV in the second half of verse 118 translates "for their cunning is in vain." This assumes an alteration to the Hebrew text which claims support from the Greek (LXX) text. The Hebrew may be rendered "their deceitfulness is a pack of lies" (literally, "fraudulent"). Such wicked people are judged to be utterly worthless, like the "dross" removed from precious metal in the process of smelting (v. 119). The REB catches the implications of this when it describes them as the "scum of the earth." Faced with such people, the psalmist repeats his commitment, "I love your decrees" (v. 119).

But the psalmist faces another tension, the tension between his love of the LORD and that "dread" (REB) and fear of the LORD expressed in verse 120. The tension is underlined by the use of two words for fear in this verse, the first of which is never used in the description of the true worshippers as those who fear the LORD. However strange it may seem at first sight to us, "love" and "fear" stand side by side in the Old Testament, not least in Deuteronomy. "So now, O Israel, what does the LORD your God require of you? Only to fear the LORD your God, to walk in all his ways, to love him, to serve the LORD your God with all your heart and all your soul, and to keep the commandments of the LORD your God . . ." (Deut. 10:12-13; cf. 6:5, 13). This is the healthy recognition that to be committed to God brings with it awesome responsibilities which must never be taken lightly. God asks for an exclusive loyalty, a loyalty implied in the description of God as "a jealous God" (Exod. 34:14; Deut. 5:9) who reacts against any breach of that loyalty. As the author of Hebrews reminds those who were wavering in the faith they had once embraced, "It is a fearful thing to fall into the hands of the living God" (Heb. 10:31).

ʿAyin

121-128 Three times in this section the psalmist describes himself as "your servant," culminating in the unequivocal claim in verse 125, "I am your servant" (cf. vv. 122, 124). This is the basis for his plea for protection from "my oppressors" (v. 121), "the godless" (v. 122; see v. 22), protection for a servant who claims to have fulfilled his master's command, "I have done what is just and right." Justice and righteousness are essential characteristics of God, hence they are what he looks for from his people (cf. 33:5; 89:14). The psalmist, therefore, expects the LORD, in legal parlance, to stand surety for him (v. 122; cf. REB). But if "well-being" (literally, "good") is what the psalmist expects, it is not yet a reality (v. 123; cf. v. 82). He is weary with waiting, troubled by hopes still unfilled, hopes of "salvation" (see 3.8) and promised vindication. He pleads for a deepening understanding, and against the background of Torah being broken or violated, he insists that it is time for the LORD to act (v. 126). All the more so since the psalmist's life is centered on "commandments" than which nothing is more precious (v. 127; cf. vv. 14, 72). The text in the first half of verse 128 has its difficulties; witness the different translations. Its general meaning, however, is clear. In contrast to the "false way" or path which he rejects, he is being pointed in the right direction by the LORD. It is tempting to wonder whether the psalmist's closing words "I hate every false way" are not a gentle, implicit reminder to the LORD that he ought equally to hate such ways.

Pē

129-136 Much of the language of this section is familiar from previous sections. The section begins with a warm and enthusiastic appreciation of Torah, "your decrees . . , your words . . . your commandments" (vv. 129-131). The "unfolding" (v. 130) or revealing of God's words gives light to those who otherwise would not know where to turn — the "simple" (v. 130; see 116:6). God's commandments are the object of the psalmist's ardent longing (v. 131). This leads into a prayer in verses 132-135 which contains a series of requests relevant to the crisis situation he faces, a situation caused by the "iniquity" he suffers at the hands of others. Be true to your "gracious" character, especially to those whose attitude to you is one of love (v. 132). Steady me when the going becomes rough (v. 133). Redeem me (see 25:22) when I am up against it (v. 134). Let the traditional word of the priestly blessing in Num. 6:25 be confirmed in my experience; teach me . . . (v. 135). The section ends in "tears," streams or rivers of tears (cf. Lam. 3:48) that stem not from self-pity but from the serious threat to much that the psalmist holds dear: "your Torah is not kept." It is as if other people are tragically indifferent to or openly challenging the one thing which holds the secret of a fulfilled life. Although elsewhere the psalmist gets hot under the collar when he thinks of such godless people (v. 53) and is convinced that they will get what they deserve (vv. 78, 84), here his attitude towards them is not one of bitterness, but rather of sorrow that they seem oblivious to what life is all about.

Ṣāḏē

137-144 The theme of the previous section is further explored. This section begins with a ringing declaration of what the psalmist believes to be the true nature of God,

"You are righteous, O LORD" (v. 137). The word "righteousness" then appears in verses 138 and 142, and associated with it "faithfulness" (v. 138) and "Torah" (v. 142). The section ends by declaring that "Your decrees are righteous forever" and links the essence of life with the understanding of such decrees. Although the psalmist describes himself as "small" or "insignificant" (REB; see 68:27) and "despised" (v. 141), a man experiencing "trouble and anguish" (v. 143), there is no mistaking that he is a man with a burning passion which centers on the LORD's "well tried" or "well tested" (REB; v. 140) promise. To that he clings.

Qōp

145-152 Here we listen to words strongly reminiscent of the psalms of lament. There are the urgent cries to the LORD — "answer me" (see 4:1), "save me" (v. 146), "hear me" (v. 147) — which appeal to the LORD's "steadfast love" (see 5:7) and "justice" (see 97:8). The urgency of the cries stems from the fact that the psalmist believes that godless persecutors are closing in on him, with malicious intent (v. 150). The cries are backed by a promise to be faithful, "I will keep your statutes" (v. 145; cf. Psalm 146), a promise which reflects his present piety and commitment. Prayer, study, meditation — these are what bring him out of his bed before the morning twilight dawns; these are what keep him awake during "each watch of the night" (v. 148; cf. 90:4). It is not wholly clear what this means. The night was divided into three watches, six to ten, ten to two and two to six. Does this mean that the psalmist had a regular pattern of meditation at the beginning of each night watch, or are the references to each watch and the dawn simply the psalmist's way of saying that his whole life revolved round a daily pattern of devotion, rather like the way in which we speak of doing something morning, noon, and night? One certainty sustains the psalmist. His malicious persecutors may have distanced themselves from Torah, but "You are near, O LORD" (v. 151). Indeed, in Hebrew verse 151 is very similar to the structure of verse 137, which begins "You are righteous, O LORD" and expresses the same ringing confidence, based on long experience of the LORD's dependability.

Rēš

153-160 The same twin themes of urgent plea and a declaration of commitment continue in this section. The reiterated appeal "give me life" (vv. 154, 156, translated "preserve my life" in v. 159) emphasizes the extent to which the psalmist feels under threat from those called "the wicked" (v. 155; cf. 1:1), "my persecutors" (v. 157), "my adversaries" (cf. v. 139), and "the faithless" (v. 158), this last word usually having the idea of treachery hovering around it (cf. 73:15). In contrast to such people who ignore or deliberately disobey the LORD's commandments, the psalmist protests his fidelity (vv. 157, 159) and pleads with the LORD to be his advocate and act on his behalf (for "redeem" in v. 154, a different word from that used in v. 134, see 19:14). What he believes to be true of the LORD is the basis of his plea — "your promise" (v. 154), your great "compassion" (v. 156; cf. v. 77), "your justice" (v. 156), and "your steadfast love" (v. 159). His certainty shines through the concluding verse. The essence of the LORD's word is that it is "true" or dependable (see 25:5) and exemplified in his unfailing "righteous ordinances" (cf. v. 7).

Śîn

161-168 After a brief reference to the unjust persecution he is receiving at the hands of the authorities (for "princes," see v. 23), this section focuses on the psalmist's awesome yet joyful response to the LORD, a response which enables him to live eagerly looking for deliverance. The word translated "hope" in verse 166 occurs in 104:27 and 145:15, where in both cases it is rendered "look to you." The praise of the LORD permeates his whole life. "Seven times a day" (v. 164) is not to be taken literally. The word "seven" often has the idea of completeness associated with it (cf. Lev. 26:18; Prov. 24:16). This is a way of saying, "In all I do, I praise you." Twice this commitment is expressed in the words "I love"; in verse 163, "I love your Torah"; in verse 167, "I love your decrees"; and in verse 165, he speaks of the great "peace" (Hebrew *šalôm*; see 4:8) which comes to "those who love your Torah." Life for the psalmist is a life of obedience since he knows that nothing is hidden from the LORD, "for all my ways are before you" (v. 168). Psalm 139 is to explore this thought in depth. Much of what the psalmist is saying in this section finds its parallel in George Herbert's hymn which begins, "King of glory, King of peace, I will love thee," affirms that all life lies open to God, and ends, "Seven whole days, not one in seven, I will praise thee."

Tāw

169-176 Not surprisingly, much that we have heard elsewhere in the psalm is summarized in this closing section. There is the cry for help (vv. 169-170), the appeal to the LORD to act (v. 173), with the familiar words "Let me live" (v. 175).

There is the psalmist's sense that life centered on the Torah of the LORD must be a life of joy and praise (vv. 171-172, 174-175). The concluding verse seems to pose a problem. The picture of the LORD as a caring shepherd going in search of sheep which have wandered off and are lost has an important place in the theology of the Old and New Testaments (see Psalm 23). However, the opening words of the verse, "I have gone astray," seem directly to contradict what the psalmist says in verse 110, "I do not stray from your precepts." The contradiction, however, is more apparent than real. Within the context of a life of commitment, underlined by the last words, "for I do not forget your commandments," which echo what the psalmist has repeatedly claimed (e.g., vv. 61, 93, 141, 153), the psalmist still remains conscious of his own frailty. Faced with the responsibility of discipleship (cf. v. 120), he knows he does at times fail and needs to be picked up again by the LORD. If that were not so, the psalm would be a hideous monument to a self-righteous prig. Always it is those who are closest to God who are most aware of their own need for confession.

The format of the psalm is undoubtedly something of a straightjacket. The need to provide within each section eight lines, each beginning with the same letter of the alphabet, leads to a certain artificiality. The psalmist's ingenuity in working within this format does not, however, detract from his theological sensitivity. The psalm is the precursor of much that is best in the teaching of the Rabbis and in later Judaism. It bears its witness to a warm-hearted, joy-filled obedience to God. It speaks of choices which have to be made, choices which will mark out people of faith from others in the world around them. It stakes everything on a God who reveals himself to his people in his Torah, a God ever gracious who stands by his people, constant amid the changing and sometimes difficult circumstances of life. This provides the basis for a theology of hope. It is not surprising that such themes are picked up and reminted in the New Testament in the light of God's revelation of himself in Jesus Christ.

Psalm 120
LIVING IN AN ALIEN ENVIRONMENT

Psalm 120 is the first in a collection of psalms (Psalms 120–134) that all have in their heading the words "A Song of Ascents," with a slight variation, "A Song for Ascents," in Psalm 121. What does the word "Ascents" or "Going Up" mean in this context? Early Jewish tradition noted the link between the number of these psalms, fifteen, and the number of steps which led from the court of women up to the court of men in the temple complex. This link was gradually embellished until we are told that the Levites sang one of these psalms on each of the steps. Calvin rightly dismissed this as "a silly conjecture," a verdict which applies with equal force to his own view that these were psalms sung in a higher key than other psalms. More plausible is the view, much favored in early Christian circles, that the title refers to the return of the Jews from exile in Babylon. In Ezra 7:9 the same word, "going up," is used in the context of the journey home from Babylon. So these would be psalms sung during that homeward journey. Recently, attention has been drawn to the literary characteristic of most of these psalms, the way in which they display a stairlike structure, through the deliberate repetition of words and phrases, leading up to a climax. Thus, to take Psalm 120, "deceitful tongue" in verse 2 is repeated in verse 3; "live" in verse 5 is echoed in the word translated "dwelling" in verse 6; while "peace" at the end of verse 6 is repeated at the beginning of verse 7. This characteristic, however, is more prominent in some of these psalms than in others, and it is not confined to this group (cf., e.g., Psalm 93). The most likely explanation is that these psalms were a collection of "Pilgrim Songs" that were sung as worshippers prepared to go up, or made their way up, to Jerusalem to celebrate one of the major religious festivals. References to Jerusalem and in particular to Zion occur in most of these psalms, and, even when there is no such reference, worship at the temple on such an occasion provides a meaningful setting. We may then think of these psalms as having been collected to provided a "Pilgrim Song Book." Whether they were all originally associated with such pilgrimage is another question.

1-2 The initial song in this collection, Psalm 120, raises several difficult problems of interpretation. The first is highlighted by the different translation of verse 1 in the NRSV and the REB. The NRSV's wording, ". . . I cry to the LORD, that he may answer me," assumes that this is a lament psalm in which the psalmist is bringing to the LORD an urgent plea for help. The REB's rendering, "I called to the LORD . . . and he answered me," assumes that this is a psalm of thanksgiving for answered prayer. If, as seems likely, the REB approach is correct, what are we to make of the prayer for deliverance in verse 2? Does verse 2 provide us with the content of the psalmist's prayer which he acknowledges has now been answered? The REB makes this assumption by adding the words "I cried" to verse 2: " 'Lord,' I cried, 'save me. . . .' " But there is another possibility. The psalmist, having come to the temple to offer his thanksgiving for answered prayer, is still conscious of difficulties he faces. He uses his thanksgiving as the basis of a plea for continuing help, "Deliver me, O LORD." There is nothing improbable in this. The confidence that past prayers have been answered is a powerful stimulus to continuing prayer. He has much for which to be thankful, but he is still living with difficulties which he believes the LORD can help him face. These difficulties center upon "lying lips" and "a deceitful tongue" (v. 2; cf. Psalms 5 and 64). He is being slandered or is aware that totally false accusations are being brought against him.

3-4 It may be that such slanders or accusations have been made under oath, in which case the psalmist turns in verses 3-4 to remind the "lying lips" and "deceitful tongue" that such perjury and false oaths inevitably rebound in judgment against those who indulge in them (cf. 2 Kgs. 6:31). The reality of such coming judgment is spelled out in terms, first, of "sharp arrows" fired by a powerful warrior. This image of weapons of war, including arrows, is found elsewhere in the Psalms as a description of accusations or bitter words (cf. 64:3), with the inevitable judgment God brings upon them (cf. 7:13). Such a military metaphor is to be developed at length to affirm the Christians' need to fight against evil in all its aspects in Eph. 6:10-17. Update the metaphor, and the psalmist is affirming that such people are doomed to be killed by the bomb they are priming. The coming judgment is also pictured in terms of "glowing coals of the broom tree." The hard wood of the broom tree provided a fierce heat which was used in the production of charcoal. The expression "burning coal" is used in a very similar context in 140:10 (cf. 11:6).

5-6 Who precisely the people are who are threatening the psalmist and signing, as it were, their own death warrant depends to some extent on how we interpret verse 5. Here the psalmist speaks of himself as living as an "alien (see 119:19) in "Meshech" and "among the tents of Kedar." If taken literally as place names, Meshech and Kedar cause a problem, since "Meshech," elsewhere in the Old Testament, lies in the far north, beyond the Black Sea, probably modern Georgia (cf. Ezek. 38:2), while "Kedar" denotes desert Arabian tribes to the south and east (cf. Gen. 25:13; Isa. 21:11-17). Part of the difficulty is that we can only guess at the tone of voice in which verse 5 was spoken. If there was a hint of irony in it, then the psalmist might well be saying, "I am so little at home in the society in which I am living, that I might as well be on the distant northern frontier or living among the fierce desert tribes." It is also possible that "Meshech" and "Kedar" are meant to be taken metaphorically as symbols of threatening alien forces, just as we talk today of "Huns" and "Philistines." Although the words of verse 5 would find an echo in the hearts of Jews living or forced to live in the Diaspora, far from Jerusalem, verse 5 need not mean that the psalmist was such a Jew. There are other kinds of alienation than living in a foreign land.

7 The rest of the psalm indeed suggests that his problems lie nearer home. He lives among "those who hate peace" (*shalom;* see 4:8), those who are "for war," while he is for "peace" (for the compressed construction here — literally, "I peace" — see 109:4). What the "lying lips" and "deceitful tongue" (v. 2) are doing is undermining the fabric of society by fostering hatred and insecurity. When the psalmist speaks, he is concerned to promote *shalom,* a society at peace with itself, a society in which social cohesion replaces divisions, a society which seeks the welfare of all its members instead of tearing itself apart. He seeks to foster caring human relationships, while others sow the seeds of conflict. Nations and communities have paid a heavy price across the centuries for such conflict and divisions. They are still paying it today, not least in Israel/Palestine. Such conflicts have also marred the life of the church from the earliest times. It is arguable that one of the best commentaries on what lies close to the heart of this psalm is the Letter of James. It focuses upon divisions within the Christian community and, not least, upon the dangers of the tongue, "a restless evil, full of deadly poison" (Jas. 3:8).

Answered prayer, with which the psalm begins, does not mean that the way ahead will be free of difficulties and dangers. It does mean that, in the midst of such difficulties and dangers, faith reaches out in hopeful trust and seeks to embody that *shalom* which is God's will for his people (see 29:11). A pilgrim going to Jerusalem would find such thoughts and such a faith strengthened as he celebrated with fellow worshippers one of the great festivals of the religious year in the temple precincts.

Psalm 121
TRUE SECURITY

This psalm has a firm place in Presbyterian tradition in its Scottish Metrical Version: "I to the hills will lift mine eyes, from whence doth come mine aid." These are words which have made hill-loving Scots view their hills as symbols of God's power and protection. Interestingly, the version of the psalm in the *Church Hymnary,* third edition, adds correctly a question mark at the end of the second line.

1-2 The psalm opens with a question in verse 1 which receives its answer in verse 2. It is the LORD, and the LORD alone, who is the true source of help. But what lies behind this question, and why is there a change from the first person, "I . . . my eyes . . . my help" in verses 1-2, to the second person, "you . . . yours," in verses 3-8? We have already studied several psalms which not only presuppose a pilgrimage to the temple in Jerusalem (e.g., Psalm 84) but point to a dialogue taking place between pilgrims and priests at the entrance to the temple area (e.g., Psalms 15; 24). Some have seen in this psalm a similar situation, the pilgrim confessing his faith as he approaches the temple in verses 1-2, with a priest confirming that faith and stressing anew the LORD's promises in verses 3-8. There is, however, another possibility. If words of promise and demand were spoken to the pilgrim coming to the temple (see Psalm 24), did he also receive a benediction as he left on his homeward journey? The psalm would fit into such a context.

The question in verse 1 may express something of the pilgrim's anxiety as he sets off on that homeward journey. If the "hills" are the hills of Judah, they probably symbolize for him not security but danger, the dangers of robbery and attack as he makes his way home through the hills (cf. the parable of the Good Samaritan, Luke 10:29-37). The question which is there in his mind is "From where shall my help come?" Then he remembers the God whom he has been celebrating at the festival, the God of creation, "who made heaven and earth" (cf. 124:8; 134:3), the LORD who has the whole world in his control. Therein lies his true security. Verses 1 and 2 provide a fine example of the stairlike structure which is evident in these psalms. The concluding word of verse 1 in Hebrew is "my help," and the first word in verse 2 is "my help." So we find "slumber" in verses 3 and 4, and the description of the LORD as he who "keeps Israel" as a persistent note in verses 4, 5, 7 (twice), and 8.

3-4 In the rest of the psalm, verses 3-8, the pilgrim, about to set off for home, is being addressed by a priest who reminds him of the LORD's promises. This is the LORD who, whatever dangers lie ahead, "will not let your foot be moved" (v. 3; cf. 66:9). In other words, there are no dangers which cannot be overcome. The LORD is ever on the qui vive. He will never "slumber nor sleep" (v. 4). Since the "hills" had associations with the high places, the shrines of the native fertility gods and goddesses, there may be an underlying apologetic in these words. Such deities died, went to sleep as it were, during the winter season when there was no growth. Compare Elijah's mocking words to the prophets of Baal on Mt. Carmel when they cannot conjure up the power of their god: "Perhaps he is asleep and must be wakened" (1 Kgs. 18:27). The faith that the LORD "never slumbers nor sleeps" — and it was a faith severely tested and questioned at times (see 44:23) — is rooted in three convictions. First, as we have already noted, the LORD is the creator God who has the whole world under his control (v. 2). Second, the LORD is the one who "keeps Israel" (v. 4), the one who has been with his people throughout their history. This would come forcibly home to the pilgrim as he celebrated the mighty acts of the LORD in the festival liturgy he has been sharing. This is the LORD whose covenant promise to his people was "I will be your God, and you shall be my people" (Lev. 26:12). Third, the LORD is "your keeper" (v. 5) — not simply the nation's God, but yours! Nothing is more characteristic of the Psalms than their emphasis upon the intensely personal concern of the LORD for each of his people. Nothing is more celebrated and explored than the personal spirituality this evokes (e.g., Psalms 23; 73). It is a breathtaking assumption that the God who controls the whole universe is interested in and cares for me. Yet it is at the very heart of the biblical witness. It finds moving expression in an Indian hymn which begins:

> One who is all unfit to count
> As scholar in thy school,
> Thou of thy love hast named a friend —
> O kindness wonderful!

and ends:

> If there is aught of worth in me,
> It comes from thee alone;
> Then keep me safe, for so, O Lord,
> Thou keepest but thine own.

5-8 The protection the LORD offers the psalmist is spelled out in verses 5-8. The LORD is "your shade" or shadow (cf. 91:1), a metaphor rich in meaning for those who live under the merciless glare of the Palestinian sun. The LORD is "at your right hand," a powerful protector (cf. 16:8), protector against sunstroke and against the "moon by night" (v. 6). The reference to the moon may be a reference to the bitter cold of the night, but there may be more to it than that. In popular thought in the ancient world and in superstitions down to the present day, the moon is often regarded as having a baneful influence and is associated with particular illnesses and diseases. In Matt. 7:15 the Greek word translated "epileptic" is literally "moonstruck," and this association lingers on in our word "lunatic." This is the LORD who offers protection against all the dangers which threaten life, "evil" in verse 7 referring to disaster rather than to moral perversity. In verse 8 "your going out and your coming in" embraces wherever you go and whatever you do, not only today and tomorrow, but for all time to come.

So the pilgrim, his faith nurtured by sharing in the festival, leaves for home to face the responsibilities and demands of daily life, with the promises of God ringing in his ears. That is what worship ought to mean for all of us. We gather together to celebrate the God who holds in his hands the whole universe and all human history, the God who knows each one of us. Worship then sends us forth with a benediction ringing in our ears, a benediction which reminds us that the promises the pilgrim took with him are ours in Jesus Christ.

Psalm 122
THE CITY OF GOD

1-5 The opening verses of this psalm speak clearly of a pilgrim and his joyful reaction to a journey to Jerusalem. But are they the words of a pilgrim who has just arrived in Jerusalem, overwhelmed by the wonder of the city and all that it means to him and to his people, or are they the words of someone who, having returned home after his visit to Jerusalem, is reminiscing about the wonder of having been there? Although both views are possible, on balance it seems more likely that we are listening to the reaction of someone who has just arrived in Jerusalem. He has come there as one of a pilgrim group. Throughout he thinks of himself as part of such a group and is reflecting a group experience. The words "Let us go to the house of the LORD" (v. 1) are typical of an invitation to join such a pilgrimage (cf. Isa. 2:3; Jer. 31:6). The picture we have is of someone today who sees an advertisement for "Pilgrimage to Lourdes" or "Tour of the Holy Land," decides "That is what I have always wanted to do," and joins the group.

Nor is he disappointed when they reach the city, not any city but "Jerusalem," center of the nation's life and faith. Three times Jerusalem is mentioned in the psalm, in verses 2, 3, and 6 (cf. Psalm 137). It is the last word in verse 2 and the opening word in verse 3, sign again of the stairlike structure of this psalm; and in verses 6-8 the name is echoed in the words for "peace," "prosper," and "security." Similar rhetorical style is evident in "To it" (v. 4; REB: "there"), which is picked up in "there" in verse 5; in "the tribes . . . the tribes of the LORD" (v. 4); in "the thrones for judgment . . . the thrones of the house of David" (v. 5); and in the repetition of "For the sake of" in verses 8 and 9. As he enters the city, he gazes in wonder at such a city "bound firmly together" (REB: "compactly and solidly"). Although it has been argued that these words refer not to the buildings but to the people who thronged together into Jerusalem, it is more likely that the reference is to the buildings huddled closely together within the city walls (cf. Exod. 26:6, 9, where the word here translated "bound" refers to the joining together of the different parts of the tabernacle). If the city of the psalmist's day was anything like the old city of Jerusalem today, then "bound firmly together" is an apt description, particularly on the lips of someone who may have come in from the countryside. To the psalmist, however, Jerusalem was much more than just an impressive city. It stood for all that was central to the life of his people.

Jerusalem was the visible symbol of the unity of the people, the place where the tribes gathered. According to tradition, the nation was founded out of twelve tribes, whose eponymous ancestors were the sons of Jacob (cf. Genesis 49). They lived in separate parts of the country. They had their own traditions. Intertribal rivalry and conflict were not unknown (e.g., Judges 20–21) and found new political expression in the division of the united kingdom after the death of Solomon. But they were "the tribes of the LORD" (v. 4). This is an unusual description. Normally a tribe is given a specific identity, for example the tribe of Benjamin, or collectively they are called "the tribes of Israel" (2 Sam. 5:1; Ps. 78:55). But this phrase, which uses the short form *Yah* for the divine name (see 68:4), is stressing that, with all their diversity and tensions, the tribes have a unity which transcends their separate identities. This unity lies in their common loyalty to the LORD. That was the "decree" (cf. 119:2) or obligation to which they were all called to witness. This loyalty found its focus in earlier times in shrines such as Gilgal (1 Sam. 11:14) and Shiloh (1 Sam. 1:3), but increasingly it centered on Jerusalem and its temple. There the people gathered to recall their common traditions at the great festivals of the religious year and "to give thanks to the name of the LORD" (cf. 7:17 and the comment on "name" at 5:11).

Jerusalem was also the visible symbol of where God-given human power and authority rested, in the Davidic dynasty. The reference to "the house of David" in verse 5 may well be the reason why, exceptionally in the case of the Songs of Ascent, the words "of David" appear in the psalm heading. In 1 Kgs. 7:7 we are informed that among the buildings Solomon erected in Jerusalem was the "Hall of the Throne where he was to pronounce judgment." It would be wrong to think of "the thrones for judgment" in verse 5 as the equivalent of the Supreme Court. Rather, here was the place where the king gave his decisions affecting the whole life of the people, political decisions concerning relations with other peoples as well as internal issues of justice. Here was where power lay. The welfare — the *shalom* (see 4:9) — of the nation depended upon that power being used responsibly.

6-9 It is small wonder, then, that this description of Jerusalem leads into earnest prayer: "Pray for the *shalom* of Jerusalem" (v. 6). This is a translation of three Hebrew words, each of which contains the letters *š (sh)* and *l,* with the same letters appearing in the verb translated "prosper" and the noun "security" in verse 7. *Shalom* is the typical Jewish greeting down to the present day, though it may be doubted whether in daily conversation there is any awareness of its deep religious significance. The words in verse 6 echo the traditional greeting which in Jer. 15:5 is translated "to ask about your welfare," interestingly referring to Jerusalem (cf. Matt. 10:12-13). The prayer is heartfelt, since the future of all God's people — "those who love you" — is bound up with the city whose very name, *Jeru-shalem,* is a pointer to that *shalom* which is essential for its security and prosperity. So the psalmist invites his fellow pilgrims to join him in this prayer for *shalom,* a prayer which he himself offers on behalf of "relatives and friends" unable, no doubt, to join him on the pilgrimage to Jerusalem.

The psalmist's focus, however, is not merely city-centered, but God-centered. He seeks the "good" of the city because in it is "the house of the LORD our God." That is why he came, not as a tourist or a sightseer, but as a pilgrim. If we are tempted to think of the emphasis upon Jerusalem in this psalm as a sign of a limited, nationalistic outlook, let us remind ourselves that for both the Old and New Testaments it is more than that. The invitation to pilgrimage with which the psalm begins becomes in the vision of Isa. 2:3 (cf. Mic. 4:1) an invitation to "many peoples" to come to Zion and Jerusalem in order to receive from the LORD instruction leading to the end of war and conflict between the nations. How sobering that 2,500 years later this vision still seems a distant dream. Today the words "Pray for the peace of Jerusalem" are words urgently on the lips of Jews, Christians, and Moslems. Jerusalem today is a symbol not of unity but of division, not of peace but of violence. But the vision remains, transformed in the book of

Revelation into that "new Jerusalem" in which God dwells among his people and life is stripped of all that causes pain and suffering, even death itself (Revelation 21). Every vision we have, however limited our horizons, should point us towards such an ultimate vision; and every vision should haunt us until we work and pray for its fulfillment, however imperfectly, in God's world.

Psalm 123
LOOKING UPWARDS

As in the previous psalm, this one moves from the individual "I" to "our" and "us" (v. 2). Again we may be listening to a pilgrim identifying himself with the pilgrim group which has come to the temple. Though there is no specific mention of Jerusalem or the temple in this brief psalm, it is in the form of a prayer which a pilgrim might well have offered in the temple court. It is a brief gem of Hebrew poetry, with its clear, stairlike structure. Four times in verses 1-2 we find the word "eyes." Verse 2 ends with "until he has mercy upon us," with verse 3 twice voicing the appeal "Have mercy upon us." The word "contempt" features in both verses 3 and 4, as does the phrase translated "we have had more than enough" in verse 3 and "has had more than its fill" in verse 4.

4 To understand the psalm we have to begin at the end, since it is only in the last verse that we become aware of the situation which prompts the prayer. It comes from the lips of people who feel themselves vulnerable or oppressed, subject to "scorn" and "contempt" (cf. 44:13; 119:22). They have been treated like dirt at the hands of "those who are at ease" and "the proud" or "the arrogant" (REB). It is not clear who these oppressors are. They may be foreign oppressors who pour scorn on the Jewish people and all they stand for. In this case, we may be talking of the immediate postexilic period or later periods of persecution. On the other hand, we may be talking about conflict within Israel, listening to the complaint of the poor and the vulnerable in society as they tell of their suffering at the hands of the rich and the powerful who have no sympathy for other people or their needs. Amos bitingly describes the self-indulgent aristocracy of his day as "those who are at ease in Zion," people heedless of the need for a society which would embrace justice and righteousness for all (Amos 6:1).

1-3 Whatever the precise situation, the psalmist in his opening words is confessing his own powerlessness in the face of such oppression. He is reaching out to the one whose power he believes transcends all human power, the divine king who sits "enthroned in the heavens" (see 2:4), a phrase whose full meaning we only grasp if we go back and read again the psalms celebrating the kingship of God (Psalms 93, 95–99). There has been much discussion as to what aspect of the servant-master, maid-mistress relationship is implied in the homely simile in verse 2. Why the emphasis upon looking "to the hand of" the master/mistress, an expression which occurs nowhere else in the Psalms? Is this just the opposite of the plea the psalmist makes to God in 140:4, "Guard me, O LORD, from the hand of the wicked"? Just as the slaves in the household, having no rights of their own, look for protection to their master/mistress, so the psalmist in his vulnerability looks for protection to the LORD. This makes sense in the context of the psalm. If, however, we link the words closely with what follows, "until he has mercy upon us," then perhaps we should think rather of the way in which a master or mistress would indicate approval or gracious acceptance of something done through a hand signal, or with an open hand make generous provision for the members of the household (cf. 104:28). Whatever the precise meaning of the simile, it stresses total dependence upon the LORD. They have no claim upon the LORD; only his grace can bring light into the surrounding darkness of "scorn" and "contempt." The depth of this dependency is clearly heard in the threefold occurrence of the word "mercy-upon-us" in verses 2 and 3.

There is in this psalm a spirituality which has echoed across the centuries. It is there in the Lord's Prayer, which begins with the words "Our Father in heaven" (Matt. 6:9) and reminds us of a power which transcends all human power and of a kingdom whose values often run counter to what people cherish in this world. It is there in the haunting, thrice-repeated *Kyrie Eleison,* "Lord, have mercy," which has a central place in many Christian liturgies. It is there whenever, in our moments of need, we humbly look upwards to God in recognition that we do not have the resources to go it alone.

Psalm 124
ALL OUR HOPE ON GOD IS FOUNDED

What is remarkable about this psalm, a thanksgiving for national deliverance, is its staccato-like quality. Its place in the liturgy of the Jerusalem temple we can only guess. It is reasonable to assume, however, that it would come after a hymnic celebration of the greatness and goodness of the LORD. Against this background it jumps straight in: "If it had not been" — one word in Hebrew, heard again at the beginning of verse 2 — followed by verses 3-5, each beginning with "then."

1-5 The opening verse, with its conviction that the LORD "was on our side" (cf. 118:6), is abruptly interrupted by the words "let Israel now say." It is possible that the opening words of the verse are spoken by a priest in the presence of the assembled people and that "let Israel now say" is his invitation to them to participate in the thanksgiving by repeating what he has said or sung. The "now" is his call to them to echo his theme. In a more contemporary setting, one might imagine a frustrated choirmaster listening to the opening bars of a hymn and breaking in to say to choir and congregation, "Come on now, you can do better than that! Sing out!" "If it had not been the LORD who was on our side," then the outcome might have been fatal when "our enemies" attacked. "Our enemies" is an interpretation of the Hebrew word *'ādām,* "human being." Verse 2 is stressing the dramatic contrast between the LORD and any human power (cf. 118:6). Such human power was real and threatening enough. It is compared in verse 3 to a ravening monster gulping down its victims, and in verses 4 and 5 to "flood . . . torrent . . . raging waters." It may be that both these pictures have their roots in ancient mythology, where Sheol is a devouring monster and where the powers of chaos are symbolized by the primeval waters (cf. Prov. 1:12; Jonah 2:2-6). But, if so, such forces are embodied in present enemies. Verses 4-5, however, could well be describing a flash flood sweeping down a wadi or riverbed and destroying everything in its path That, says the psalmist, would have been our experience had the LORD not been "on our side" (literally, "for us"). We can almost hear the sense of wonder and humble gratitude which lies behind these words.

6-8   It is not surprising, then, that the psalmist suddenly turns to acknowledge gratefully all that the LORD has done: "Blessed be the LORD" (see 28:6). What he has done is described in two pictures. The LORD has not left them to be savaged by a wild animal. He has sprung the trap set to snare a bird, and the bird has flown free (vv. 6-7; cf. 91:3; 119:110). So the psalm ends with a confession of faith similar to 121:2, finding the nation's security in the conviction that this is God's world, created by him and ever in his hands.

In its Scottish Metrical Version, this psalm — "Now Israel may say and that truly" — is often sung on occasions of thanksgiving for deliverance from national or community disaster. Wrongly understood, it can be the vehicle of a jingoistic piety, with its claim that God is "for us" and therefore against all who endanger us. The psalm, however, is not aggressively jingoistic. It is a psalm of humble thanksgiving, which recognizes the limitations of all human power and grounds faith and hope in the LORD alone. It finds its counterpart in Paul's Jesus-centered cry "If God be for us, who is against us?" (Rom. 8:31).

Psalm 125
TRUST VINDICATED

As in previous psalms, much of our interpretation of this psalm depends on whom we identify as those who are posing a threat to the people of God. They are spoken of in general terms — "the scepter of wickedness" (v. 3), "those who turn aside to their own crooked ways," and "evildoers" (v. 5). A strong case can be made for seeing in "the scepter of wickedness" a reference to foreign occupation, to harsh imperial despots who sought to destroy the distinctive life of Israel; and in "those who turn to their own crooked ways" a reference to Jewish quislings who were prepared to compromise the faith of their fathers and collaborate with such regimes. The natural background to the psalm would then be the postexilic period, possibly as late as the Maccabean period in the second century BCE. On the other hand, the references may simply be to deep internal divisions within Israel, to people who are prepared to use power and influence to further their own ambitions at the expense of others. This could have happened at any time. The very fact that general descriptive terms are used means that, whatever the original circumstances out of which the psalm came, people in any age and in different circumstances can identify with the psalm and see in "the scepter of wickedness" the forces which threaten the life of the people of God in their own day and in their own experience.

1-3 The opening words of the psalm identify the true people of God. They are "those who trust in the LORD" (see 4:5). It is important to realize that other descriptions used in the psalm, "the righteous" (v. 3), "those who are good " (v. 4), and "those who are upright in heart" (v. 4), far from making absolute moral claims are ways of saying the same thing. All of these point to people who are prepared in trust to commit themselves to the LORD. Naturally, such commitment had and has moral implications, but it does not convert such people into self-righteous do-gooders.

Two pictures, familiar to anyone who knew Jerusalem, are used in verses 1-2 to describe the security and protection which come to those who put their trust in the LORD. The first focuses on Mt. Zion, there at the center of the city, the temple mount where God dwells in the midst of his people and, in the words of Psalm 48, makes this place "the city of our God, which God establishes forever" (48:8). Indeed, the best way to catch the full flavor of what this picture conveys is to go back and read Psalms 46 and 48. The second picture reminds the worshipper that, however impressive Jerusalem may be, it is surrounded by higher hills. You have only to stand on the Mount of Olives or Mount Scopus today to realize that you are looking down on the temple mount and the old city of Jerusalem. The surrounding hills, which cradle Jerusalem, are thus used to stress the protective care with which the LORD surrounds his people (v. 2).

The description in verse 3 of the country as "the land allotted to the righteous" goes back to the tradition in Joshua when, after the conquest of Canaan, the land was divided among the tribes by lot (cf. Num. 26:55-56; Josh. 18:6), a reminder that the land was a gift to those who had committed themselves to the LORD. By very definition, therefore, it was land which should not be allotted to the wicked, however powerful. Were that to happen, the faith of the righteous might well be undermined. They might be tempted to compromise, to join the wicked in the pursuit of easy but ill-gotten gains.

4-5 The psalm ends in verses 4 and 5 with a prayer to the LORD which calls upon him to say a resounding "Yes" to those who seek to be faithful to him (v. 4) and a firm "No" to those who "turn aside to their own crooked ways." They are people who, instead of sticking to the broad, God-designated highways, follow their own devious byways (cf. Judg. 5:6, where the word here translated "crooked ways" is rendered "byways"). Such ways can only lead to inevitable, divinely decreed disaster or punishment (v. 5). The final words, "Peace *(shalom)* be upon Israel," occur again at the end of Psalm 128 (cf. Psalm 122) and provide a fitting climax to the psalm. This is what the prayer, and indeed the whole psalm, is seeking: a God-given, richly satisfying life for the community that would make it resistant to attacks from without and tensions within. Journey further along this spiritual road, and among the last words of Jesus to his disciples in John's Gospel we hear: "Peace I leave with you; my peace I give to you. I do not give to you as the world gives. Do not let your hearts be troubled, and do not let them be afraid" (John 14:27; cf. Gal. 6:16).

Psalm 126
JOY — EXPERIENCED AND ANTICIPATED

This psalm falls clearly into two sections, verses 1-3 and verses 4-6. The first section speaks of the past, of joy experienced "when the LORD restored the fortunes of Zion." The second section is a prayer for the present and the future, for joy anticipated. Although the relationship between these two sections has been much discussed, there is nothing strange in finding them side by side. The first section provides some of the motivation for the prayer in verses 4-6. It is a pattern which lies behind many prayers, whose basic thought is "You have been with us in the past, O Lord; be with us now and in the days to come." The reliving of the past becomes the launching pad of urgent prayer for a future in which present troubles will be overcome (cf. Psalm 74).

The meaning of the Hebrew phrase "restored the fortunes" (v. 1) has been discussed in the comment on 85:1. Those who see in this phrase a historical reference to the return from captivity in Babylon tend to regard verses 1-3 as a song of thanksgiving on the lips of those who have come back from exile to Zion, Jerusalem. The prayer in verses 4-6 is then either a prayer for those who were still in exile, or an appeal by those who, having returned, were now living with some of their hopes unfulfilled, facing difficult times (cf. Haggai). Such a precise historical reference, however, is hardly necessary for the understanding of the psalm. There must have been many occasions when worshippers gathered in Jerusalem on festival occasions to celebrate God's past goodness to his people and to plead for continuing help and a change in their present distressing circumstances. It is a mood which often surfaces when we celebrate New Year's Day.

It is well expressed in Henry Downton's hymn that begins "For thy mercy and thy grace, faithful through another year, hear our song of thankfulness" and later moves to an appeal: "In our weakness and distress, rock of strength, be thou our stay." The deliberate echoing of words and phrases is again characteristic of this psalm. Its opening words are picked up in the appeal "Restore our fortunes" in verse 4. Each line in the Hebrew of verse 2 begins with "then," and the closing words of the verse, "The LORD has done great things for us," are repeated at the beginning of verse 3. One Hebrew word translated "shouts of joy" occurs in verses 2, 5, and 6.

1-3 The first part of the psalm expresses an almost childlike delight in what the LORD has done. It has a miraculous quality about it, something unexpected, something for which the people had hardly dared to hope. The REB's rendering, "we were like people restored to health" (v. 1), instead of "like those who dream," is a possible translation, but "like those who dream" makes perfectly good sense. It was as if they had been dreaming, but it was real. The only response had to be one of gratitude, which expressed itself in "laughter" and unrestrained "shouts of joy" (cf. 95:1). What has happened is so awe-inspiring that it must echo across the world (cf. 96:7-9; 100:1). The psalmist imagines the nations bearing their witness — "The LORD has done great things for them," or perhaps more accurately, "The LORD has done great things in his dealings with them," the Hebrew having "with" rather than "for." It would be more than surprising, therefore, if the LORD's own people, who had witnessed the reversal of their fortunes, did not joyfully make this witness their own: "The LORD has indeed done great things in his dealings with us" (v. 3). Sometimes, sadly, familiarity makes us take for granted the great things God has done in his dealings with us, things which, if those outside the community of faith could only believe, would make them shout for joy.

4-6 Two homely illustrations from the world of nature fill out the appeal "Restore our fortunes, O LORD." During the summer, the Negev, the arid region to the south of Judah bordering the Sinai desert, was parched, inhospitable, and apparently lifeless. But the winter rains would come flooding through its "watercourses" (v. 4), its riverbeds and wadis (cf. 42:1, where this word is translated "streams"), transforming the terrain till, in the words of Isa. 35:1, "The wilderness and the dry land shall be glad, the desert shall rejoice and blossom." Both in Isaiah and here, this transformation is a symbol of the transformation which will take place in the life of the people because of what the LORD is going to do. The second picture centers upon the farmer's life of sowing and harvesting. Verse 5 may be a proverbial saying whose roots go back to the fertility rites of Canaan, lamentation and weeping being associated with the annual death of the fertility god, joy with his resurrection to new life. Even without this background, however, the illustration is vivid. The farmer goes out into the plowed but still dry fields carrying with him the seed for sowing. He can only trust that there will be a harvest. Much lies beyond his control. Only when the harvest is safely gathered in can he thankfully rejoice, his exertions over. The unrestrained joy of the welcome harvest is here the symbol of the hoped for renewal of the life of the community and the joy that this will bring (cf. Isa. 9:3). It all depends on the LORD. He alone sends the revitalizing rain which guarantees that there will be a harvest; he alone can answer the prayers of his people and revitalize their lives. Joy experienced in the past is the same joy anticipated in the days to come.

Seedtime and harvest provide the Hebrew Bible with rich theological symbolism. This is continued in the New Testament. Jesus, in John's Gospel, speaks of the need for a grain of wheat to fall into the earth and die before it can bear much fruit (John 12:24), while Paul uses the bare seed sown into the earth and its subsequent transformation as a pointer to the nature of the resurrection life which lies beyond death (1 Cor. 15:37-38).

Psalm 127
FALSE AND TRUE VALUES

This brief and at first sight simple psalm has led to the most varied interpretations. Part of the trouble is that certain key words in the psalm (e.g., "house" in verse 1) are capable of having different meanings. It has further been argued that the psalm has two sections on totally different themes, both reflecting different wisdom sayings, with verses 1-2 highlighting the futility of all human endeavor apart from God, and verses 3-5 celebrating a large family as a gift from the LORD. Certainly there is a strong wisdom flavor about the psalm, for example, in the "Happy" formula in verse 5 (cf. 1:1). The underlying unity of the psalm, however, ought not to be questioned. The wisdom characteristics in the psalm may have led to the link with Solomon in the heading, as may the reference to "his beloved" in verse 2. This was the name the prophet Nathan, at the instigation of the LORD, gave to Solomon at his birth (cf. 2 Sam. 12:25).

1-2 The first two verses of the psalm stress the futility of any human activity undertaken apart from the LORD. What verse 1 implies depends on the meaning we give to the word "house." "House" can mean the temple, "the house of the LORD" (122:1), in which case the reference could be to the building of the temple in Solomon's day or to the rebuilding of the temple after the return from exile (cf. Haggai). "House" can also mean "palace," the royal abode, with reference perhaps to the lavish palace that Solomon and other kings built for their own comfort and prestige. Jeremiah mounts a slashing attack on one such king who "builds his house by unrighteousness" (Jer. 22:13), more concerned to keep up with the imperial

Joneses of his day than to care for the needs of his own people. But "house" can also mean "household" or family, whether it be the royal dynasty (122:5) or the priestly family, "the house of Aaron" (115:10, 12), the community as the LORD's family, "the house of Israel" (115:12), or any ordinary family. In the light of verses 3-5 we ought to interpret it here in its broad "family" sense. This is supported by the fact that there is within the psalm a play in Hebrew on the similarity between the word "builders" in verse 1 and the word for "sons" in verse 3.

Not only family life, but the life of the wider community, "the city," are in jeopardy, claims verse 1, unless they are centered on the LORD. Watchmen may be set to guard the city, but the only true watchman or keeper is the LORD (cf. 121:3-5). Not even the most feverish activity should blind us to this truth. You may be a workaholic, up at the crack of dawn and late home in the evening, but the verdict on it all will be "in vain" — futile, worthless (cf. 24:4; 108:12) — a verdict we hear three times in the first two verses. This is not an attack on work as such but on any human activity which believes it can accomplish everything by its own efforts while ignoring God. This is given additional emphasis in the closing words of verse 2, which are capable of varied interpretation. The NRSV, following the Greek (LXX) text, renders "for he [the LORD] gives sleep to his beloved." The sleep presumably symbolizes the rest, the quietness, the serenity in the midst of the busyness of life which only the LORD can give, a serenity which is the antidote to needless anxiety. The REB omits the word translated "sleep" as unintelligible and renders the rest as "he supplies the need of those he loves." Whatever translation we adopt — and "honor" or "prosperity" have been proposed in place of sleep — these closing words are insisting that there are things in life which we cannot achieve on our own, no matter how hard or how feverishly we try. We must be open to the gifts God wishes to give.

3-5 The reference to the "house" or family in verse 1 is now developed in verses 3-5. These verses are introduced by the Hebrew word conventionally translated "Behold." It is as if the psalmist is saying, "Here is a good illustration of what I mean." The NRSV tries to retain something of the flavor of this by saying, "Sons are indeed. . . ." Childlessness was regarded as a stigma in Israel; compare the stories of Rachel (Gen. 30:23) and Hannah (1 Samuel 1). A large family, particularly sons who would inherit the family property and continue the family name, was regarded as a sign of the LORD's blessing. Just as the land was regarded as the LORD's gift to his people, their inheritance or heritage (see 105:11; cf. 125:3), so within the family sons were such a gift, "a heritage from the LORD" (v. 3), particularly "the sons of one's youth" (v. 4), born in a man's prime, healthy and able to provide lifelong support. Just as a warrior needed to go into battle well equipped with a "quiver full" (v. 5) of arrows, so a man needed sons who, when he was under attack by enemies, would spring to his defense and safeguard his honor within the community (for "gate," see 69:12).

This is a picture of the family which has as its background cultural and social assumptions that are far removed from those of the Western world today. It is a wholly male perspective. There is no mention of daughters or of family responsibility to the mother. Large families are out of fashion today. Indeed, to many they are regarded as irresponsible in a world of population growth and finite resources. The pattern of family life is changing. Yet whatever form the family may take, a society which does not cherish family values and celebrate the family is immeasurably impoverished. The family is part of the gracious gift of the God who said, "It is not good for the man [or for the woman!] to be alone" (Gen. 2:18).

Psalm 128
THE SECRET OF A FULFILLED LIFE

This psalm begins where the previous psalm ended, with the typical wisdom formula "Happy is . . ." (cf. 1:1). The setting for the psalm is almost certainly worship in the Jerusalem temple, probably at the Feast of Tabernacles. There the pilgrim receives a blessing from a priest. The blessing may be part of his welcome, or it may be given to him as he participates in the feast, or it may be a benediction to send him on his homeward way (cf. Psalm 121).

1-4 This is a psalm whose brevity is matched only by the largeness of its vision. It begins in verse 1 with a general statement spelling out the indispensable secret of the truly fulfilled life. It is a life committed to the LORD, the life of "everyone who fears the LORD," a life of faith which finds expression in an obedience to God which shapes daily conduct (see 34:9-12). The psalm then moves, as all effective teaching and preaching must do, to apply this general teaching to the life of the individual — "you" (singular), the pilgrim standing there in the temple courts. This teaching is applied in three specific areas of life.

First, the psalm promises (v. 2) that daily needs will be met by the fruit of honest daily labor. Work done not only provides for daily physical needs, but brings with it contentment and satisfaction: "it shall go well with you." These words underscore the positive value and the important place of daily work within the providence of God. This perspective contrasts sharply with the workaholic attitude condemned in 127:2, where "eating the bread of anxious toil" stands in contrast to "you shall eat the fruit of the labor of your hands" (v. 2).

Second, picking up the theme of 127:3-5, the psalm promises a fulfilling family life. A rich and varied symbolism gathers round the "vine" (v. 3) in the Hebrew Bible. In Ps. 80:8 the vine is Israel. In erotic poetry it has sexual overtones (compare Song of Sol. 7:8, where the girl's breasts are said to be like "clusters of the vine"). Here the "vine" and the "olive," both basic to the economy of the land (see 52:8), are used as symbols of life and fertility. The wife is compared to a "fruitful vine" (v. 3), her children numerous like the many clusters of grapes on a healthy vine. In the words "within your house" — or, better, "within the innermost parts of your house" — there may be emphasis upon the fidelity of the true wife. She finds her role as mother in that inner part of the house, furthest from the street. Certainly this is in sharp contrast to the description of the adulteress in Prov. 7:11-12, "She is loud and wayward; her feet do not stay at home; now in the street, now in the squares, and at every corner she lies in wait." The children are like "olive shoots," the many new green shoots which come from an old olive tree, signs of continuing vigor and life. What binds the family together is underlined in the words "around your table" (v. 3), where the family gathers to share a meal, the visible sign of their acceptance of one another (cf. 23:5). Lest there be any misunderstanding, verse 4 takes us back to the opening words of the psalm to emphasize that such a healthy family life is a gift to the one "who fears the LORD."

5-6 The psalm ends with a benediction (vv. 5-6) which stresses that the family does not exist in isolation. It is part of a wider community. The word translated "prosperity" or well-being in verse 5 echoes the words at the end of verse 2, "it shall go well with you." This statement implies that it must also go well with the community of which you are a part. It is likely that in verse 5 "Zion" and "Jerusalem" are synonyms for the city at the heart of the nation's life, though that would also include the religious life of the nation centering on the temple at Mt. Zion. No one, and no family, has any right to opt out of the community. We receive from the community, and we have a responsibility to contribute to and share in its common life. This is true whether we think of the society in which we live or of the church to which we belong and in which, as Eph. 2:19 reminds us, we are "citizens with the saints and also members of the household of God." To remember this is to be pulled out of our selfishness. Even families at times can become self-centered, with little concern for what is happening beyond their own door. A wise man once defined a Christian family as a family which keeps an ever open door.

But we do not live only for today. Verse 6 includes in the benediction the wish, "May you see your children's children." This is not only a wish for the blessing of a long life, but a recognition that just as life comes to us as a gift, so we hand on life to the future, which will continue long after we have "shuffled off this mortal coil." Not only are we not an island isolated from the world around us, we are not merely a moment in time, but part of a stream of life — past, present, and future. Since Israel was a community conscious of its past, present, and future under God, the psalm ends, as did Psalm 125, with the words "Peace be upon Israel!"

The link between the spirituality of the Psalms and Christian spirituality is surely evident in this psalm. Themes central to this psalm are prominent in the Lord's Prayer (Matt. 6:9-12). The words "hallowed be your name. . . . Your will be done on earth as in heaven" recall "everyone who fears the Lord" and "walks in his ways" (v. 1). The prayer "Give us this day our daily bread" is based on the promise "you shall eat the fruit of your hands" (v. 2). The appeal "Forgive us our debts as we forgive our debtors" reminds us that for good and for ill we live in relationship with other people. The closing words of the psalm find their counterpart in Paul's prayer for his fellow Christian pilgrims: "peace be upon them, and mercy, and upon the Israel of God" (Gal. 6:16).

Psalm 129
TESTED AND VINDICATED

This psalm comes from the lips of people who have been tested almost to the breaking point yet have held on to their faith. It is a psalm which breathes confidence, not the shallow confidence of the starry eyed, but the robust confidence of those who have often had to face the worst that life could throw at them and have responded with a realism rooted in faith in the LORD. It is unnecessary and perhaps futile to try to read this psalm in relationship to a particular historical event (e.g., the Babylonian exile). Its setting is worship in the Jerusalem temple. As the people join in worship, they look backwards in verses 1-4 and seek a word of reassurance for the present in verses 5-8.

1-4 The first two verses recall the opening of Psalm 124, with its echoing verses interrupted by "let Israel now say." There is a difference, however. Where Psalm 124 from the beginning celebrates what the LORD has done for his people, this psalm begins by recalling what has been done to them, the suffering they have experienced. The "I" who speaks in the opening verses is a representative of the community with whom the congregation may immediately identify. The words "from my youth" (v. 1) probably point back to the people's bitter experience in slavery in Egypt. The word translated "youth" here is from the same root as the word translated "child" in Hos. 11:1: "When Israel was a child, I loved him, and out of Egypt I called my son." But that love, which took the people out of suffering in Egypt, did not mean that their future was to be a bed of roses. Right across the nation's history there were bitter days to be faced, harsh experiences to be lived through. Some of them, as the prophets insisted, were self-inflicted, others scarcely understandable (cf. Psalm 44). The reasons for such attacks are not explored in this psalm, nor are those responsible for such attacks identified. It was enough to recall the facts, which repeatedly bruised the life of the people but were incapable of destroying it. The words "yet they have not prevailed against me" (v. 2) are spoken not in the spirit of bravado, but quietly and in a spirit of thankfulness.

The pain of the past and the indelible mark it left are vividly described in verse 3. Just as plowmen cut into the soil as they make their long, straight furrows across the field, so there has been raised on the nation's back, as it were, the weals made by the oppressor's whip. But that is only one part of the story. Even in the midst of pain, "the LORD is righteous" (REB: "victorious"), true to himself, vindicating his people (see 7:11). The exodus experience is ever repeated. Oppression gives way to freedom; pain is replaced by joy. This is the God who "has cut the cords of the wicked" (v. 4). The plowing is ended, the "cords" probably being the ropes which bound the oxen to the plow, though it is possible that the metaphor changes, with the "cords" standing for the yoke which had been imposed upon the people.

5-8 From the past the congregation now turns to the present, which has its own difficulties. What precisely these difficulties are depends on what meaning we give to "all who hate Zion." This is a phrase unparalleled elsewhere in the Hebrew Bible. It may, of course, be a unique description of the "attackers" and the "wicked" of verses 1-4. It would have a special appropriateness if applied to enemies who sacked and desecrated Jerusalem and the temple, as did the Babylonians in 587 BCE and Antiochus Epiphanes in the second century BCE. But there may have been deep-seated divisions within the community. Not all would respond to external pressure in the same way. Not all would necessarily see Zion as the symbol of God's protecting power and presence among his people. Some may have resented the dominance of Jerusalem in the religious life of the community. Some may have willingly cooperated with their foreign masters. Whoever "all who hate Zion" may be, verses 5-8 assert that their plans will be frustrated and that they themselves have no future. These verses may either be taken, as in the NRSV and the REB, as expressing a wish, or as a confident statement, "All who hate Zion will be put to shame" (v. 5); "they will become like the grass . . ." (v. 6). Verse 6 begins on the flat roof of a house, with its beams and its branches held together by impacted earth. Grass seeds itself on such a roof, but because there is no depth of soil, it withers before "it grows up" (REB: "shoots"), a word which elsewhere in the Hebrew Bible means either "to unsheath a sword" (Judg. 8:20; 9:54) or "to pull off sandals" (Ruth 4:7, 8). Quickly withering grass, however, provides a frequent simile of all that is ephemeral, be it evildoers (37:2) or everything or everyone mortal (90:5-6; 103:15; Isa. 40:6). From the rooftop, the scene switches to the fields in verse 7, where the reapers normally take handfuls of the growing grain, cut it, and gather it into sheaves (cf. Gen. 37:7) to be bound and carried to the threshing floor. This is the picture of the harvest safely gathered in. For "all who hate Zion," however, there shall be no such harvest. Nor shall they hear the normal greeting given to those hard at work in the fields. The book of Ruth provides a good example of this when Boaz the landowner says to his reapers, "The LORD is with you," and they respond "The LORD bless you" (Ruth 2:4). Nobody will ever say to these harvesters, "The blessing of the LORD be upon you!" (v. 8). Such people are outside the pale of the LORD's blessing and the powerful influence for good that such a blessing would convey (see 3:8). Both the NRSV and the REB assume that the closing words of the Psalm, "We bless you in the name of the LORD!" are part of the blessing these people will never hear. It is possible, however, that the words of that blessing should finish with the words "upon you." The "we" who speak in the closing words would then be the priests pronouncing a valid blessing upon the assembled congregation who truly trust in the LORD. The second half of the psalm would thus end, where the first half of the psalm ends, with the righteous LORD (v. 4), whose powerful blessing is the sole guarantee of his people's future, as it has been their support in the difficult days of their past. What other spirituality can enable us to face the challenge and the questions which life often brings?

Psalm 130
THE NEED FOR FORGIVENESS

As in other psalms (e.g., Psalm 120), our understanding of this psalm will depend on how we translate some of the verbs in it. If in verse 1 we translate "I cried to you, O LORD" and in verse 6 "my soul waited for the LORD," we are saying that this is essentially a psalm of thanksgiving. The psalmist is bearing witness to the reality of that divine forgiveness he has experienced. On this basis he turns in verses 7-8 to invite the wider community to share his experience. If, however, we translate with the NRSV "I cry to you, O LORD" in verse 1 and "my soul waits for the LORD" in verse 6, then the psalm is closer to being a psalm of lament, with the psalmist facing a crisis in his life and coming to the temple to pour out his soul to the LORD. Such psalms usually go on to describe the crisis in the psalmist's life, but here that is replaced by the psalmist confessing his sins and reaching out for forgiveness. We must assume that his plea is answered, perhaps by a word of forgiveness spoken to him by a priest. He then turns in verses 7-8 to share the wonder of his experience with others. For such a change in mood after verse 6, see the comment on Psalm 22 with its dramatic change in mood after verse 21.

1-6 The crisis in the psalmist's life is described in one word in Hebrew, the opening word of the psalm, translated "Out of the depths." What is meant by "the depths" here we are not told. It could be physical suffering which, in the light of what follows, other people, or the psalmist himself, believed to be the result of his sinfulness. However, the association of "the depths" with Sheol, the abode of the dead (cf. 69:2), may be pointing to a life-threatening situation in which the psalmist felt himself alienated from God. The very fact that the word is not further defined means that across the centuries people facing their own crisis situations have found it easy to identify with the psalmist, as they "cry" to the LORD (cf. 57:2; 66:17) out of their own "depths." Sometimes it is only when we are in "the depths" that we urgently reach out to God. The appeal to the LORD to hear, to give heed or be attentive (v. 2), is a recurring theme in the Psalms. The psalmist knows that he has no claim upon the LORD. All that he has to offer is "the voice of my supplications," words which acknowledge that he is throwing himself upon the mercy of the LORD, pleading with him to be gracious (cf. 4:1, where the verb translated "be gracious" is the verb from which the noun "supplications" comes). In verse 3 the words "who could stand" may indicate that the psalmist is haunted by the fear that he has no right even to be in the LORD's presence in the temple. The entrance liturgy in Psalm 24 asks the question: "Who shall ascend the hill of the LORD? And who shall stand in his holy place?" (24:3). It then spells out that inner moral integrity without which worship is a charade. But this psalmist cannot offer "clean hands" or a "pure heart." All he is conscious of is "iniquities," a life distorted by perversions and their accompanying guilt (see 32:1). Something has to be done, not *by* him but *to* him. He believes that this can happen since "there is forgiveness with you [the LORD]" (v. 4). This is the only occurrence in the Psalms of the word "forgiveness," though the verb "to forgive," always with God as its subject, is common (see 25:11; cf. 103:3). Yet if the word "forgiveness" occurs only here, what it represents is conveyed in a rich cluster of words, no more emphatically than in the credal confession in Exod. 34:6-7, "The LORD, the LORD, a God merciful and gracious, slow to anger, and abounding in steadfast love and faithfulness . . . forgiving iniquity and transgression and sin." But such "forgiveness" must not be trivialized. It does not mean that God says casually "Forget it," with the psalmist happily going off to do his own thing. It must be part of a continuing relationship, cradled in mystery, which demands from the psalmist a response of awe and reverence which will shape his life. Hence the words "so that you may be revered" (v. 4). He must align himself with those who fear the LORD (see 34:9). This sense of reverence, of the mysterious, is fundamental to a true response to life. As has been well said: "The sense of mystery stands also as the cradle of true religion. But then it goes hand in hand with another: the sense of being commanded to act. Reverence combines with love and both together prompt us to enter into God's service, to engage in the struggle of good against evil" (*Siddur Lev Chadash*, p. 186).

The fact that the psalmist is willing to make such a commitment comes through strongly in verses 6-7. The key words "wait" (see 25:3) and "hope" (see 38:15) do not express resignation. They point rather to the psalmist's eager expectation that the LORD will answer his cry with "his word" (v. 5), a forgiving and renewing word. It makes little difference to the meaning of verse 6 whether with early Jewish tradition we regard "those who watch for the morning" as the Levites on night duty at the temple, or think of them as the city watchmen. With emphatic repetition, the psalmist stresses that no watchman on night duty ever more eagerly waits for the coming of dawn than he waits for this word.

7-8 It is easiest to assume that, such a word having come to the psalmist, he now turns to address his fellow worshippers who represent the people as a whole, "Israel." He invites them to share his experience and to live in expectant hope. Such hope, he claims, will be vindicated, since to speak of the LORD is to speak of his "steadfast love" (see 5:7) and of his "great power to redeem" (for "redeem," Hebrew *pādāh,* see 25:22). Although the words "redeem" and "redemption" have found a central place in religious language and experience, verse 8 is, interestingly, the only place in the Hebrew Bible where the word "redeem" is linked with "iniquities" or sin. The Hebrew Bible normally uses the language of "covering" or atoning for sin (see 65:4). It may be that the language here reflects the psalmist's experience. He had been through a liberating experience, taken out of the depths of his despair, freed from the crushing weight of his "iniquities" and his sense of guilt. He believes that such a liberating experience is the gift the LORD offers to all his people. It is almost as if behind the closing words of the psalm we can hear his plea, "Accept this gift."

In Christian tradition this is the sixth of the seven penitential psalms (see introduction to Psalm 6). Not surprisingly, it was to be one of Luther's favorite psalms. It was one of what he called his "Pauline Psalms," since it spoke to him of our human helplessness in the face of sin, and of that justification by faith which for the Christian gives "peace with God through our Lord Jesus Christ, through whom we have obtained access to the grace in which we stand" (Rom. 5:2). Certainly, out of the depths of his experience, the psalmist bears thankful witness to the truth that "where sin abounds, grace abounds all the more" (Rom. 5:20). There is no greater human need and no more relevant evangelical conviction than to be able to say "there is forgiveness" (v. 4), forgiveness which comes to us from the very nature of God, the God of steadfast love.

Psalm 131
SERENITY

This brief psalm has been well described as "one of the neglected gems of the Psalms, expressing a type of piety not always credited to Old Testament religion" (G. W. Anderson). The words "Of David" in the heading and certain phrases found in other royal psalms have suggested that we should think of this psalm as coming from the king. The words "Of David," however, do not appear in all the versions, and indeed they would be more appropriately attached to Psalm 132. There is no reason, of course, why similar words should not be on the lips of king and commoner. It is best to hear in the psalm the words of someone who has come to terms with life and found a quiet serenity.

1-3 The denials which characterize verse 1 suggest that this had not always been the case. Vaulting ambition, pride, and meddling in affairs beyond his ability and comprehension had once shaped his life (cf. Prov. 18:12; Ps. 18:27). But now he has found peace. The "But" which introduces verse 2 has in its background an implied oath, as if the psalmist is saying, "I swear that calm and quietness [or silence; cf. 62:1, 5] have replaced restlessness and needless anxiety." He compares himself to "a weaned child" (v. 2). Although the language in verse 2b is not wholly clear, as the NRSV indicates, the REB translation, "like a weaned child clinging to its mother" or perhaps "carried by its mother," conveys the sense. The picture is of a child weaned, but content simply to be in mother's arms, symbol of the security and serenity which the psalmist has found in his relationship with the LORD. Things "too great" (v. 1) had been replaced by quiet trust, things "too marvelous" (see 9:1), by the wonder of being carried by the LORD (cf. Isa. 46:4). Added color may be given to this picture in the context of the Songs of Ascent, from the way in which later Jewish sources describe children being carried by their parents up to Jerusalem to the great festivals of the religious year. Not surprisingly, this is a serenity the psalmist wishes to share with others. The psalm ends, as did Psalm 130, with an appeal to the congregation, to the whole people of God, to relive his experience. "O Israel, hope in the LORD" (v. 3); fix all your expectations on the LORD. That, and that alone, is the secret of security and serenity which will carry you through all that life may bring, now and in the future. He might well have quoted in support Deuteronomy's description of what happened in the wilderness, "when you saw how the LORD carried you, just as one carries a child, all the way that you traveled until you reached this place" (Deut. 1:31).

Those caught up in the feverish restlessness which features in so much modern life, and the pursuit of personal achievement no matter what the cost, would do well to ponder this psalm. As Jesus reminds his potential disciples, "What will anyone gain by winning the whole world at the cost of his life?" (Matt. 16:26, REB). The mood of this Psalm is well conveyed in the words of John Greenleaf Whittier's hymn:

Drop thy still dews of quietness,
Till all our strivings cease;
Take from our souls the strain and stress,
And let our ordered lives confess
    The beauty of thy peace.

Psalm 132
TEMPLE AND PALACE

This psalm has generated much inconclusive discussion. That we are listening to different voices within the psalm seems clear. What is not always clear is who is speaking and where quotation marks should begin and end. The psalm echoes traditions found elsewhere in the Hebrew Bible, for example, the stories surrounding the ark in 1 and 2 Samuel, and it uses language similar to that in the book of Deuteronomy. This has led to attempts to get behind the present psalm and its literary development. Since this has led to little or no agreed results, it seems doubtful whether such an unscrambling of the present text is at all helpful. 2 Chronicles 6:41-42 puts verses 8-10 on the lips of Solomon as part of his prayer at the dedication of the temple, though they do not appear in the version of that prayer in 1 Kgs. 8:22-40. All that the Chronicler's use of these verses indicates is that he thought them appropriate in such a context. It does not prove that Solomon was responsible for this psalm or for any part of it.

The psalm stands within, and makes its own contribution to, a powerful religious tradition which celebrates the close link between the Davidic monarchy and the temple in Jerusalem (cf. Psalm 110). It is probably part of the Jerusalem temple liturgy, celebrating that link within the context of one of the major religious festivals. In view of the prominent part played in the psalm by the ark which disappeared in 587 BCE, victim of the Babylonian rape of city and temple, the psalm is in all likelihood preexilic. It falls into two parts, parallel in thought and language: verses 1-10, spoken by the king or his representative; verses 11-18, the words of a temple prophet or priestly spokesman.

1-10 In verses 1-10, the king or his representative recalls the tradition which, in religious terms, ensured for the Davidic dynasty a central place in the life of the nation. It begins with a prayer to the LORD to "remember . . . the hardships" David endured. Such "hardships" probably focus not on the difficulties David encountered in the course of his checkered career, but on the troubles he faced in fulfilling his oath to bring the ark, after its long years of comparative obscurity in Kiriath-jearim, up to Jerusalem (cf. 1 Sam. 7:2; 2 Samuel 6). For the LORD to "remember" what David did would ensure that he would act graciously towards David's successors on the throne in Jerusalem. Verse 2 indicates that David's action was the result of a solemn oath and vow. The Samuel narrative, however, simply says that he did it. Whether this indicates that the psalm is drawing on a different tradition from that found in Samuel, or whether it is simply adapting that tradition for liturgical use, we do not know. Twice in this section the LORD is called "the Mighty One of Jacob" (vv. 2 and 5). This title appears in the Blessing of Jacob in Gen. 49:24 and elsewhere only in the book of Isaiah. Its association with the patriarchal traditions and the northern Joseph tribes may indicate that the psalm is stressing that there is unity to be found for all Israel, both north and south, in worshipping the one God in Jerusalem. Calvin noted that the language of verses 3-4 could not be taken literally, but must be hyperbolic. Indeed, verse 4 may well be based on a traditional proverbial saying (cf. Prov. 6:4) that there can be no rest until promises made are fulfilled. What David promised was to find a "place," a "dwelling place" (v. 5; cf. 43:3; 84:1) for the LORD, both words which elsewhere in the Hebrew Bible point to the temple in Jerusalem (cf. Deut. 12:5, 11). Jerusalem, with its temple, was to be the political and religious power base of the Davidic monarchy. This had its roots in the story of David's bringing of the "ark" to Jerusalem. Verse 8 is the only place in the Psalms where the ark is specifically mentioned, though it may be referred to indirectly in several other psalms (see 24:7-10; 68:1). The "ark" — a wooden chest which, according to one tradition, contained the tablets of the Law given to Moses at Mt. Sinai (cf. 1 Kgs. 8:9) — was regarded as the visible sign of the LORD's powerful presence among his people. Its capture by the Philistines was a severe shock to the people and led to the saying "The glory has departed from Israel" (1 Sam. 4:21). Its restoration to a central place in the nation's life was one of David's masterstrokes.

Verse 6 in Hebrew begins with the word usually translated "behold." It is ignored in most modern English translations. It is, however, a pointer to the fact that in verses 6-9 past and present merge as the congregation relives the story of the bringing of the ark to Jerusalem. They may well be reliving it in dramatic form, in an annual procession in Jerusalem in which the ark played a central role. The references to "Ephrathah" and "the fields of Jaar" in verse 6 pose problems. Ephrathah in the Hebrew Bible is normally associated with Bethlehem (cf. Ruth 4:11; Mic. 5:2). It does not appear, however, in any of the traditions surrounding the ark in the Samuel narratives. Perhaps the words "we heard of it" mean that David and some of his entourage were in Bethlehem when the news reached them of the whereabouts of the ark. In 1 Chron. 2:53, moreover, "the families of Kiriath-jearim" are listed among the descendants of Ephrathah, a further link with the Bethlehem area. If, as seems likely, "the fields of Jaar" refers to Kiriath-jearim or its neighborhood — Jaar being the singular form of Jearim — then both Ephrathah and "the fields of Jaar" are pointing us to the neighborhood of Bethlehem and to Kiriath-jearim where the ark languished for some twenty years (1 Sam. 7:2) before it was rediscovered and began its journey to Jerusalem. It was a journey which led to the LORD finding his appropriate "dwelling place" (v. 7; cf. v. 5), the place where his people would worship at his "footstool" (see 99:5), a reference either to the temple or to the ark, which in 1 Chron. 28:2 is described as "the footstool of our God." Such worship assumes that this powerful symbol of the LORD's presence among his people, "the ark of your might" (v. 8), has come to its lasting home in Zion. The traditional cry, attributed to Moses in Num. 10:35 — "Arise, O LORD, let your enemies be scattered, and your foes flee before you" — rang out when the ark of the covenant was carried by the people as they set out on their journey. It was their assurance that the LORD journeyed with them.

When the people rested in their travels, the cry was heard, "Return, O LORD of the ten thousand thousands of Israel" (Num. 10:36). Now traveling days are over, the people securely settled in a state centering on Jerusalem. So it is for the LORD. He has come to his desired "resting place" (v. 14). The traveling God of a traveling people is now at home, there to be joyfully acclaimed in the worship of his "faithful" people (v. 9; cf. 4:3), there to be ministered to by priests "clothed with righteousness" (v. 9), a phrase capable of several different interpretations. It may mean either that they worship the LORD employing the correct ritual or with the right attitude, or that through them there flows what the LORD wishes to give to his people, "righteousness" here being equivalent to "salvation" (v. 16). This first part of the psalm ends, as it began, with a prayer to the LORD, asking that because of what David "your servant" (cf. 89:20) did, the LORD may be gracious to the descendant of David who now occupies the throne, "your anointed one" (v. 10; see 2:2). Thus worship is the bridge which spans the centuries. In it the past is relived, and the present finds its meaning in the light of the past.

11-18   The second part of the psalm shadows the first part. In it we listen to the words of a priest or temple prophet recalling the promises made to David (vv. 11-12), celebrating the LORD's presence in Zion, and stressing the link between temple and monarchy (vv. 13-18).

Verse 11 echoes verses 1-2. David's oath now finds its counterpart in the LORD's oath to David. It is "a sure oath," a phrase containing the word normally rendered "faithfulness" (see 25:5). The content of this oath recalls the prophet Nathan's word to David in 2 Samuel 7, though that appears not as an oath but simply as a word from the LORD (but cf. 89:35 and the comment on v. 2 above). The oath is in the form of a promise, a dependable promise of a Davidic dynasty which would last "forevermore" (v. 12). However, it contains within it a conditional element stressing the need for David's descendants to "keep my covenant" (see Psalm 89) and "my decrees which I shall teach them" (cf. 119:2), that is, the duties and responsibilities which fall upon the king by reason of his relationship with the LORD. The conditional element also appears in 2 Sam. 7:14, where it is depicted in terms of a father's need to discipline a son who goes astray.

Verses 13-16 provide a parallel to verses 8-9. "This is my resting place" (v. 14) echoes "go to your resting place" in verse 8. Verse 16 echoes verse 9, with "righteousness" replaced by what is virtually its synonym, "salvation." However, while the first half of the psalm concentrates on David's oath and David's action, the emphasis here is firmly on the LORD and what he does. It is he who "has chosen Zion" (cf. 78:68). This is what he has "desired" (v. 13) or longed for. This is the only place in the Hebrew Bible where God appears as the subject of the verb "to desire." It is almost as if the psalmist was straining language to stress that David was but the human instrument in something which can only be traced back to what the LORD himself wanted.

It is the LORD's gracious presence among his people which is the guarantee that their needs will be met, needs which are as down-to-earth as what we ask when we pray "Give us today our daily bread" (Matt. 6:11). It means that "provisions" (REB: "food in plenty") will be available and that those most vulnerable in society, "the poor" (see 9:18), will never be in want (v. 15).

The psalm ends in verses 17-18 with a ringing endorsement of the Davidic king, "my anointed one," which answers the prayer for the king in verse 10. There, in Jerusalem, God will "cause a horn to sprout for David," which is a promise of the continuing vigor and power of the dynasty (for "horn," see 18:2; 75:4). The "lamp for my anointed one" probably points to the permanence of the dynasty, a metaphor drawn from the lamp which was to be kept burning regularly in the temple (cf. Lev. 24:2). There was always to be a king like David, who is described by his officers in 2 Sam. 21:17 as "the lamp of Israel." All who challenge his power, "his enemies," "I will clothe with disgrace" (contrast verses 9 and 16), while upon his head there will be a gleaming or shining crown, symbol of royal status and prosperity.

No psalm more clearly celebrates the central religious certainties of the people of Judah during the monarchical period — the presence of the LORD in his temple in Jerusalem, and the Davidic dynasty ordained and guaranteed by the LORD. It is important to realize the depth of the religious crisis the people had to face when the temple became a charred ruin (cf. Psalm 74) and the shining crown of that monarchy was "defiled . . . in the dust" (89:39). It is a measure of the inherent vitality of the faith of the community that the crisis was faced and the hopes which those certainties enshrined were refashioned. For centuries Judaism has survived without a temple, its God-centered spirituality nurtured in the synagogue; without a king, but with hopes fixed on the fulfillment of God's purposes through a king yet to come. Peter's sermon at Pentecost picks up the reference to God's oath to David (v. 11) in Acts 2:30, while Stephen may have had verse 5 in mind in his anti-temple polemic in Acts 7:46. Both are pointing to the Christian refashioning of the tradition, which sees the promise to David as having been fulfilled in Jesus, "the anointed one," with God's presence among his people being affirmed in him. This then looks forward to the ultimate vision in Revelation of a new heaven and a new earth, with a new Jerusalem where "the home of God is among mortals. He will dwell with them as their God" (Rev. 21:3). This is a city with no temple, "for the temple is the LORD God the Almighty and the Lamb" (Rev. 21:22).

Psalm 133
THE FAMILY OF GOD

The key question for our interpretation of this Psalm centers upon the meaning we give to the word "kindred" (REB: "brothers") in verse 1. It can refer to the natural family, that extended family where "brothers reside together" (Deut. 25:5) and accept responsibility for one another. The whole psalm may, therefore, be interpreted in terms of family life and seen as an extended comment on traditional wisdom sayings commending family harmony (e.g., Prov. 17:17; 20:20). Several stories in the Hebrew Bible highlight the bitter consequences of the breakdown of such harmony — Abram and Lot, Jacob and Esau, Joseph and his brothers, and David and his kin. Nor need we look far to see the tragic personal and social consequences of the breakdown of family life today.

This psalm, though, is one of the Songs of Ascents and stands at the center of three Zion psalms (132:13; 133:3; 134:3). Such a context suggests a wider reference. The "kindred" of verse 1 are all who belong to the family of God, the pilgrims who come together to Jerusalem to share in the festival occasions of the religious year. Bring together crowds of people, pushing through narrow gates and jostling each other in narrow streets, and the appeal for harmony needs to be heard loud and clear. Tempers can quickly flare.

1-3 This is the lesson which is being hammered home in the opening words of the psalm, which begins with the Hebrew word usually rendered "behold" (see 127:3). To be together and in harmony is commended as "good and pleasant," something which makes life not only bearable but enjoyable for everyone.

This is backed up in verses 2-3 with two similes, the first one of which probably strikes most of us today as bizarre. No doubt people in ancient Israel would have regarded as equally bizarre a simile drawn from football fans traveling together to a game and expressing their unity by singing ribald songs at the expense of the opposing fans! To understand the simile in verse 2, we have to think our way back into the religious life of Israel, and in particular to the priestly ordination of Aaron as described in Leviticus 8. Anointing oil is poured on Aaron's head as a sign of consecration to the priestly office (Lev. 8:12). After sacrifice some of the oil and blood from the sacrifice are sprinkled on Aaron and his vestments. The oil used is described as "precious oil" (literally, "good oil"). This might equally well be translated, as in the REB, "fragrant oil," specially prepared from the finest spices for use in the priestly ordination ceremony (cf. Exod. 30:22-32). The point of the simile may well lie in the special nature of this oil and its fragrance. So harmony among the pilgrims who belong to the family of God has its own special fragrance.

The second simile in verse 3 draws on the Hermon mountain range which dominates the northern landscape of Israel (cf. 42:6; 89:12). The heavy dew characteristic of the range seems to have become proverbial as a symbol of the life-giving moisture needed in an often arid landscape. It is as if this life-giving northern dew is falling upon the barren "mountains of Zion," turning them into a source of life-giving unity which binds the people together. It is there, in Zion, that the people receive from the LORD the blessing which ensures "life forevermore," a phrase which implies not personal immortality but the ever continuing vitality of the community.

Echoing words are again characteristic of this brief psalm. The word "good" in verse 1 is picked up in the phrase "precious oil" (literally, "oil of good") in verse 2, while the same Hebrew word translated "running down" in verse 2 is translated "falls" in verse 3.

If we consider the wider family of God to which we belong today, whether it be Jewish or Christian, the message of the psalm strikes home. Paul had to make urgent pleas for unity in Christian communities which were in danger of tearing themselves apart (e.g., 1 Corinthians 3; Philippians 2). As Christians we dare not forget the challenge in Jesus' prayer for his disciples, "that they all may be one. As you, Father, are in me and I am in you, may they also be in us, so that the world may believe that you have sent me" (John 17:21). Calvin caught the spirit of the psalm when he commented, "So long as animosities divide us and heart burnings prevail among us, we may be brethren no doubt still by our common relation to God, but cannot be judged as one as long as we present the appearance of a broken and dismembered body."

Psalm 134
A PLACE OF BLESSING

This brief psalm provides a fitting climax to the Songs of Ascents. It sums up two essential elements in worship: what we offer to the God we worship and what we receive from God in worship. Both these aspects center on the use of the verb "bless" in this psalm. The psalm begins with the same Hebrew word which introduced the previous psalm and which is rightly identified here as a call to worship, "Come." Thereafter, verses 1-2 begin and end with the words "bless the Lord," a grateful acknowledgment of all that the Lord is and what he has done to enrich life (see 16:7). There follows in verse 3 a prayer for the Lord to bless his people (see 3:8).

1-3 But who are being addressed in the psalm? It has been claimed that verses 1-2 are the people's words addressed to the priests as they go on night duty at the temple. Verse 3 is then the answering blessing from the priests upon the people. In this case the "servants of the Lord" in verse 1 are the priests, and the phrase "stand by night" (Hebrew "nights") refers to the nightly duties they perform in the temple. Hence the REB translation "who minister night after night in the house of the Lord." While this is possible, it is more likely that we should see in the whole psalm words addressed by the priests to the people who have come to worship. There is certainly evidence from later Jewish sources (e.g., Mishnah *Sukkah* 5:4) for the worshippers at the temple sharing in a night liturgy during the Feast of Tabernacles. That may be the setting here. In this case, the priests in verses 1-2 are calling upon the "servants of the LORD," all the assembled people (cf. 113:1), to acknowledge their dependence upon the LORD: "lift up your hands" towards the sanctuary where the LORD dwells and "bless" him (cf. 63:4 for a similar use of "bless" and "lift up the hands" in a context of praise and thanksgiving). In verse 3 this call to worship is backed up by the pronouncement of a blessing upon the worshippers, a blessing which draws its power from the fact that the LORD who blesses is the "maker of heaven and earth" (cf. 121:1), the creator whose writ runs across the whole world. This is the God who is present with his people "in Zion." The psalm thus speaks of a giving and receiving which is part of all true worship and of the life of faith. It is well expressed in the answer to the question in the *Shorter Catechism*, "What is the chief end of man? To glorify God and to enjoy him forever."

The Songs of Ascents help us to enter into what worship meant for those who journeyed to Jerusalem for the great festivals of the religious year. There is the joyful celebration of Jerusalem/Zion as the place where God dwells among his people — Jerusalem, the center of the nation's religious and political life and thus associated with the Davidic dynasty (Psalms 122; 132). There is the recognition that the LORD, maker of heaven and earth, is a God who is compassionate, the God to whom his people can confidently turn, whatever the difficulties they face (Psalms 120; 123; 129; 132). Worship provides the context for celebrating the joys of family life and affirming the unity which binds together the wider family of God (Psalms 127; 128; 133). Here there is space for eager expectancy (Psalm 130), quiet trust (Psalm 131), joyful thanksgiving, and praise (Psalms 124; 134). If you are ever tempted to dismiss worship in the Jerusalem temple as fear-stricken legalism or sacrificial mumbo jumbo, read again the pilgrim Songs of Ascents.

Psalm 135
A HYMN OF PRAISE

It would be easy to dismiss this psalm as a pastiche of bits and pieces from other psalms and other books in the Hebrew Bible. That would be to do it scant justice. Yes, it does draw heavily upon liturgical material found elsewhere, but what it uses it reshapes into a hymn which has its own distinctive character. There is nothing strange in this. In conducting worship today a minister or priest may draw on liturgical material from a variety of different sources, yet so shape it that it has a new flavor and relevance. The fact that the psalm does draw freely from many sources indicates that this is a late psalm. It lies before us as a carefully constructed hymn of praise. It begins and ends with "Praise the LORD." The "LORD" is named six times in the opening call to praise in verses 1-4, and six times in the concluding call in verses 19-21. Four times in verses 1-3 we hear the word "praise," and four times in verses 19-21 "bless the LORD."

1-4 As in the previous psalm, the opening summons in verses 1-4 is directed to all the people who have gathered for worship, the "servants of the LORD" (cf. 134:1). Verse 1 echoes 113:1 with the order of its phrases inverted to keep the words "servants of the LORD" to the end, since they are to be further identified in verse 2. They are the people who are there in the temple complex with its surrounding courts (cf. Psalm 134, which refers only to "the house of the LORD"). Their worship is to focus on "the name of the LORD" — "Praise the name of the LORD" (v. 1); "sing to his name" (v. 3). His "name" symbolizes the character or nature of God (see 5:11), particularly as that is communicated to his people in the festival liturgy. The language of verse 3 parallels the opening of 147:1 in its use of the words "good" and "gracious," this latter word usually indicating what is beautiful or delightful (cf. 16:6), hence the REB's rendering "pleasing," which it takes to be not a description of the LORD, but of the act of singing. What is central to the people's knowledge of the LORD is that they belong to him: "he has chosen Jacob for himself" (v. 4; for "Jacob," see 14:7; 114:7). Although the word "covenant" is not used, verse 4 is speaking of the covenant relationship between the LORD and his people, a relationship initiated by the LORD, the result of his choice of a people which made them "his own possession." The word translated "possession," found only here in the Psalms, has overtones of something valued by the person who owns it (REB: "treasured possession"). It occurs frequently in Deuteronomy in the context of the LORD's election of his people (cf. Deut. 7:6; 14:2; 26:18; Exod. 19:5), in all of which passages the NRSV translates "treasured possession" or "treasured people." The emphasis is not on Israel's intrinsic value as a great or powerful nation — that is explicitly ruled out in Deut. 7:7 — but on the mystery of a divine graciousness which calls Israel into being as the people of the LORD.

5-12 The call to worship and praise, therefore, leads naturally into the celebration of the LORD's power and greatness in verses 5-12. This section may probably have been spoken by a solo priestly voice addressing the congregation and reminding them of the tradition of faith in which they stand: "For I know . . ." and you too must surely know! In verse 5 the speaker takes as his motto text words attributed to Moses' father-in-law Jethro in Exod. 18:11, "The LORD is greater than all gods" (cf. 95:3; 96:4). This is the God who does "whatever he pleases" (see 115:3). It is the LORD, and the LORD alone, who is in total control of all the forces in the natural world from "heaven" to the "deeps" (v. 6), the "seas" and the "deeps" probably indicating all the forces of chaos which threatened the LORD's sovereignty (see 104:6). The "clouds," or perhaps "the mist [so REB; literally, "what rises"] . . . lightnings . . . rain . . . wind (v. 7), all feature prominently in the storms which sweep across the Palestinian landscape. Verse 7 occurs again in Jer. 10:13 and 51:16, which indicates that it is part of the common stock of liturgical material. For God's "storehouses," see 33:7.

From the world of creation and nature the psalm turns in verses 8-12 to Israel's history, highlighting selectively in verses 8-9 the "signs and wonders" (see 78:43) against Pharaoh and the Egyptians, noting in particular the death of the firstborn (cf. 78:51). Verses 10-11 focus upon the destruction of all who disputed the people's entry into the promised land (for "Sihon" and "Og," see Num. 21:21-35), and verse 12 upon the giving of the land to Israel as a "heritage" (see 78:55). That there is no mention in this historical survey of the crossing of the Reed Sea or the giving of the Law at Mt. Sinai should occasion no surprise; the psalm is simply using selected incidents which would trigger off in the people's minds a larger story. The same episodes appear as part of the larger story in 136:10, 17-22.

13-14   In verses 13-14 the congregation joins in a choral refrain which springs naturally out of this celebration of the LORD's power and of how that power has been used for his people. They celebrate the LORD's "name" (cf. vv. 1, 3) and his "renown" (literally, "remembrance"), his nature and acts which have been relived in the liturgy. They affirm that, far from celebrating momentary past events, they are declaring what is true for all time, "throughout all ages" (v. 13). They worship a God who, to quote the Song of Moses in Deut. 32:36, will "vindicate" or plead the cause of his people — this is legal terminology — and show "compassion" to his people (v. 14).

15-21   It is hardly surprising that, in the light of all this, all other gods and those who worship them are dismissed as powerless nonentities. Verses 15-18 are a direct quotation from 115:4-8. The psalm then ends with a choral antiphon summoning all who belong to Israel — the Aaronic priests, the Levites, and the whole congregation, "you that fear the LORD" (see 118:4) — to "bless the LORD" (cf. Psalm 134). Like many other psalms, including the immediately preceding Songs of Ascents, the psalm affirms that such blessing centers on "Zion" and on the LORD who "resides in Jerusalem" (cf. 132:4).

This is a hymn of praise appropriate for all who believe that by grace and by the mystery of God's election they belong to the people of God (cf. 1 Pet. 2:9). It is triumphalist in the best sense of that word. It sees God at the heart of everything we experience — the universe around us, the living world of nature, human history past present and future, and our own lives. It would have no truck with a faith which confines God to what human rationality and ingenuity have not yet explained or which retreats into a purely personal piety. The psalmist would not have regarded such a "God of the gaps" as worthy to be praised or blessed.

Psalm 136
STEADFAST LOVE

The liturgical pattern of this psalm is clear. Every verse ends with the refrain "for his steadfast love endures forever" — words on the lips of the assembled worshippers responding to the priest's affirmations of who God is, what he has done, and what he does. In Jewish tradition this psalm came to be known as the "Great Hallel" and was associated with the Feast of Passover. In contemporary Jewish liturgy it is recited by the standing congregation at the morning service for Sabbath and Festivals. It may be thought that the constant repetition of the refrain "for his steadfast love endures forever" is wearisome and monotonous. It is worth remembering, however, that such responsive repetition, though not often on this scale, has been a part of liturgical practice across the centuries (compare the *Kyrie Eleison*). This response, in three brief Hebrew words, takes us to the essential core of Israel's experience and understanding of God. The Hebrew word *hesed,* translated "steadfast love" (NRSV) or "love" (REB), is notoriously difficult to render accurately into English. The traditional translation "mercy" is misleading. John Milton's refrain in his hymn version of this psalm comes closer to its meaning when he expands the three words into "For his mercies aye endure, ever faithful, ever sure." The introduction of the word "faithful" is a pointer in the right direction. We have already discussed the meaning of *hesed* in the commentary on 5:7. When applied to God, it speaks of a divine commitment and loving concern which remain unchanging in the face of all human frailty and fickleness. Here is the unchanging certainty which Israel flung defiantly in the face of the ever changing and often testing experiences of life.

1-3 The psalm begins in verses 1-3 with an introductory call to worship, the thrice-repeated "O give thanks to the LORD," words which we have already heard at the beginning of Psalms 106, 107, and 118. It is a call to give thanks to the God whose status and power are unique and unchallengeable. The description of the LORD as "the God of gods" (v. 2) and "the LORD of lords" (v. 3) may well go back to the polytheistic background to Israel's developing faith (cf. Psalm 82). There was no philosophical or theoretical denial of the existence of other gods, but they were reduced to powerless nonentities (cf. 135:15-18). The same words are found in Deut. 10:17 in the context of demanding an exclusive and obedient loyalty to the LORD. For many people in the postexilic period, however, "God of gods" and "LORD of lords" would be a convenient way of describing the one and only God, whose nature is summed up in the words "steadfast love." To believe in such a God is to be committed to a universal faith which cannot be confined within limited boundaries of space or time (cf. the psalms of the kingship of God, Psalms 93, 95–99).

4-9   To speak of this God is to speak of "one who alone does great wonders" (v. 4; see 9:2; cf. 86:10). Verses 5-9 then spell out these wonders in terms of creation, following the basic form of the first half of the creation hymn in Gen. 1:1-19. The words "by understanding" (REB: "in wisdom") he "made the heavens" (v. 5), however, follow the development of the creation tradition in the wisdom literature (e.g., Prov. 3:19). This "by understanding" does not necessarily point merely to intellectual power, but to the practical skills employed in creation (cf. 78:72, where the same word is translated "skillfully"). God is the master craftsman. In contrast to the hymn in Genesis 1, the great lights, defining day and night, are specified in terms of "the sun" and "the moon and stars" (v. 9). The religious associations which these bodies may have had do not trouble the psalmist because the reiterated emphasis upon the steadfast love of the LORD rules out any other religious influences.

10-22   The next section turns to the history of the people of the LORD. These verses cover the same ground as 135:8-11 but expand it with reference to the crossing of the Reed Sea in verses 12-15, in language reminiscent of Deuteronomy (e.g., Deut. 4:34), and to the journey through the wilderness (v. 16). There is little doubt that the story of the LORD's gracious dealings with his people was so well known through its liturgical celebration that, whether in brief or in longer form, it served as a constant reminder of what was central to the very existence and the continuing life of "his servant Israel" (v. 22; cf. 135:14).

23-25   For the first time in the psalm we hear the word "us": "he remembered us . . . rescued us." This may simply point to the way in which the assembled worshippers are identifying with the story just recited: "That is our story, the story which defines our life." So Deuteronomy insists that "The LORD our God made a covenant with us at Horeb. Not with our ancestors did the LORD make this covenant but with us, who are all of us here alive today" (Deut. 5:2-3). Faith never lives in the past. That defining past becomes the present in worship, through word and sacrament, for the Christian congregation. It is equally possible, however, that in the words "he remembered us . . . rescued us" we are listening to the words of people bearing witness to the way in which they had seen the LORD at work in their own experience. In "our low estate," when we were at a low ebb facing humiliation, when we were on the receiving end of hostility, we discovered that what was true in the past was true for us. We could imagine these words being appropriate on the lips of people who had just returned to Jerusalem after the humiliating experience of exile in Babylon, but the words are so open-ended that they would be relevant to any experience of humiliation and oppression in which people were able to affirm that what had been true in Israel's past is true for "us." But not only for us. The psalm begins by affirming a universal faith, and that is the note on which the recital of the steadfast love of the LORD ends in verse 25. This is the God who gives food "to all flesh," whose providence sustains the life of the whole world.

The closing words of the psalm take us back to its beginning with the call to "give thanks." To recall the great wonders of God in creation, in history, and in personal experience leaves us with no option but to "give thanks" to the one who is here described as "the God of heaven." This title occurs in this precise form nowhere else in the Hebrew Bible, though a variant form of it occurs in other postexilic writings. Jonah, for example, says in response to the sailor's questions, "I am a Hebrew. I worship the God of heaven, who made the sea and the dry land" (Jonah 1:9; cf. Ezra 1:2; Neh. 1:4). The title is not intended to convey the remoteness of God — only up there, as it were, in heaven — but to assert his unchallengeable authority and his control over all that happens. "Our Father in heaven" may be the opening words of the LORD's prayer (Matt. 6:9), but the rest of the prayer is centered on the here and now and on the concern for the working out of God's kingship here on earth. To acknowledge the authority of God, however, might be a cause for fear or impotence, if we were dealing, in Thomas Hardy's words, with "The President of the Immortals" who "has ended his sport with Tess" (*Tess of the D'Urbervilles,* chap. 59). But the psalmist's "God of heaven" is not one who plays with us for his own amusement; he is the LORD whose "steadfast love endures forever" — cause indeed for thanks. Since the New Testament claims that we find ourselves face-to-face with that steadfast love in all its costly glory in Jesus Christ, it is not surprising that Colossians defines one of the marks of the Christian life in the words, "With psalms and hymns and spiritual songs, sing from the heart in gratitude to God" (Col. 3:16, REB). What better psalm with which to do this than Psalm 136?

Psalm 137
IN CRISIS . . . AND REACTING

This psalm touches the raw nerve of Israel's faith. In it we seem to be listening to the words of a Jew who had been through the traumatic experience of exile in Babylon. He has returned to Jerusalem, a Jerusalem still struggling to recover from its devastation at the hands of the Babylonians in 587 BCE. The temple probably is still to be rebuilt. It is a psalm which found its appropriate setting in later Jewish liturgical usage on the ninth day of Ab, when the destruction of Jerusalem was commemorated and relived in worship.

1-4 Verses 1-4 reflect on the crisis of faith provoked by the destruction of Jerusalem and the subsequent exile to Babylon. The picture of the exiles in Babylon is vividly drawn. They sit stunned, weeping by "the rivers of Babylon" (v. 1). Although the word translated "rivers" is used elsewhere in the Hebrew

Bible of the rivers Euphrates and Tigris, it is likely that here, as in Exod. 7:19, it refers rather to the network of canals which used the waters of the rivers to irrigate the land. Their banks were lined by "willows" or poplars. The harps which once had been used joyfully in worship at the temple in Jerusalem (cf. 81:2) hang unused on the willows. Being in exile in a foreign land was bad enough, but it was compounded by the memory of what had happened to "Zion" (see 2:6), to Jerusalem and its temple, and, by implication, to the faith which had invested so much in that city of God. The mocking request from their "tormentors" (REB: "captors"; the Hebrew word is of uncertain meaning) to sing "one of the songs of Zion" (v. 3) brought the exiles face-to-face with the depth of their spiritual crisis. To appreciate it we need to recall the certainties which were celebrated in the songs of Zion, such as Psalms 46 and 48: "God is in the midst of the city; it shall not be moved; God will help it when the morning dawns" (46:5). But where is God now? Where was he when the city was devastated and no help was forthcoming? There in Jerusalem — "in the city of the LORD of hosts, in the city of our God, which God establishes forever" (48:8) — they used to celebrate that foes who threatened that city fled in panic. Now it was not these enemies but the people of God who had known what it meant to flee in panic. Once they had been invited to "walk around Zion" to savor its towers, its ramparts, and its citadels — "that you may tell the next generation that this is God, our God forever and ever" (48:12-13) — but now they can only wander disconsolately along the banks of Babylonian canals. What is there left to tell that next generation?

No wonder they found it impossible to "sing the LORD's song in a foreign land" (v. 4). It was a heathen, "unclean" land (cf. Ezek. 4:13-14) in which they were alienated from so much that had hitherto sustained their faith, given them security (cf. Amos 7:17), and shaped their distinctive identity. A "song of Zion" would have been no more than a cruel parody on their lips. The crisis provoked a twofold response.

5-6 The crisis leads in verses 5-6 to a reaffirmation of the centrality of Jerusalem for faith. This is the city which can never be forgotten or regarded as irrelevant. Verse 5 plays on different meanings of the Hebrew verb translated "forget." The second part of the verse reads "let my right hand forget" — forget what? Some of the early versions, including the Greek (LXX), rendered "let my right hand be forgotten." Some English versions have sought to clarify by adding as an object to "forget" such words as "its cunning" (AV) or "its skill" (NIV). Both the NRSV and the REB, however, assume that the verb can also have the meaning "wither," which makes good sense in context. Verses 5 and 6 are in the form of a solemn oath, whose violation will have serious consequences — if I do X, then let Y follow (cf. Job 31). "If I forget" . . . let my power drain away (v. 5b), let me be struck dumb (v. 6). Notice how in verse 6, the words of verse 1 — "we wept when we remembered Zion" — are picked up and transposed into a positive affirmation of the supreme importance of Jerusalem for the psalmist's faith. All else pales into insignificance: "if I do not remember you, if I do not set Jerusalem above my highest joy." Weeping can only be replaced by celebration once Jerusalem is restored. Only then can the harps, which now hang silent on the willows, come to life again as the congregation sings out its praise to God in Zion.

7-9 In verses 7-9 we listen to the bitter response flung in the face of those who are held responsible for what has happened. Here there is a call for a different kind of remembrance, a call to God to "remember," to act in judgment against those who had destroyed the place which he had chosen as his "resting place forever" (132:13, 14).

Verse 7 focuses on the Edomites, blood brothers of the Hebrews according to Gen. 25:30, since they traced their ancestry back to Esau, the brother of Jacob. The book of Obadiah is a bitter diatribe against the Edomites for joining in the looting of Jerusalem and massacring its fleeing survivors (cf. Obadiah 11-14). The words put into the mouth of the Edomites in verse 7, "Tear it down! Tear it down!" is a translation of a verb which means "to lay bare," in this context probably to tear down the walls of the city to lay bare their foundations. The verb, however, often has heavily sexual overtones (cf. Lev. 20:18-19), and the picture could be that of Jerusalem as a woman about to be raped by her conquerors.

Verses 8-9 deal with the Babylonians (for "daughter" as a description of a city, compare "daughter Zion," 9:14). The address to Babylon as "you devastator" assumes a slight alteration to the Hebrew text, which reads "you who are destroyed." There is, however, no hint in the psalm that Babylon has been destroyed, or the language throughout would have been very different. Verses 8-9 pick up the traditional wisdom "Happy" formula (see 1:1) and give it a new twist. Elsewhere in the Psalms we have seen it used of those who avoid the ways of the wicked (1:2), who take refuge in the LORD (2:7), who trust in the LORD (40:4; 84:12), who fear the LORD (112:1), who receive strength or forgiveness from the LORD (32:1-2). "Happy" here has a more savage edge; it is applied to those who bring divine retribution upon the Babylonians for what they did to the people of God (v. 8), and to those who ensure that the Babylonians themselves experience the full horrors and the barbarity which accompanied defeat in war in the ancient world (v. 9). Such barbarity is well described in 2 Kgs. 8:12, where a man of God describes what he expects the conquering Arameans to do to his people: "you will set their fortresses on fire, you will kill their young men with the sword, dash in pieces their little ones, and rip up their pregnant women." Such war was designed to wipe out a conquered people and to ensure that they had no future. We are all too sickeningly familiar with similar barbarities in our own day, from the gas chambers of the Holocaust to ethnic cleansing in the former Yugoslavia and Rwanda.

But how do we reconcile these verses, and in particular the concluding words of verse 9, with the spiritual sensitivity which speaks to us in verses 1-6? Christian liturgical tradition tends to solve the problem by singing verses 1-6 and consigning verses 7-9 to what is considered as pre-Christian oblivion. That, however, is to destroy the psalm and to ignore the challenge it poses. We must face the fact that there is nothing incongruous between the "highest joy" centering on Jerusalem and what seems the vicious barbarity which follows. We have already seen in other psalms how a deep faith in God can exist side by side with bitter curses screamed against those whom the psalmist considers to be his and God's enemies (see Psalm 109). This psalm underlines this tension and points to the unresolved theological problems to which it gives rise. The very fact that the psalmist's faith is centered on what for him were the irreplaceable symbols, Jerusalem and its temple, meant that inevitably he reacted in violent anger against those who destroyed these symbols. We do not need to look far for contemporary parallels. It is often those who are most deeply and narrowly committed to their faith who are most harshly judgmental towards those whom they see as a threat to their stance. It matters not whether the center of their commitment is the Bible or the Koran or a specific issue such as a pro-life stance.

Sometimes the only way out of this tension is to begin to think the unthinkable. Jeremiah wrote a letter to the first group of exiles to Babylon which invited them to do just that. Those who had gone into exile in 597 BCE were being encouraged by nationalistic prophets to believe that what had happened was only a temporary blip; Jerusalem still survived, and soon they would be safely back home again, living in the security of city and temple. Jeremiah will have none of this. He tells them in God's name to settle down, to prepare for a long stay, to "seek the *shalom* of the city where I have sent you into exile and pray to the LORD on its behalf, for in its *shalom* you will find your *shalom*" (Jer. 29:7). Pray for the *shalom* of Babylon — a startling contrast to the words "Happy shall they be who take your little ones and dash them against the rock!" But it is a stark contrast which has its roots in the words which follow: "when you call upon me and come and pray to me, I will hear you. When you search for me, you will find me; if you search for me with all your heart" (Jer. 29:13). It is as if Jeremiah is saying to these people, "You can pray to God; you can seek and find him just as surely by the waters of Babylon as ever you did in the temple in Jerusalem. He is there with you, in what many of you are dismissing as a godless disaster."

Judaism has survived as a living faith across the centuries only because it has taken the path Jeremiah pioneered. With no access to the temple, nor until recently to the city, it has searched and found and continued to bear witness to a God who hears his people's prayers. It is wise to read Jeremiah 29 and Psalm 137 side by side. Together they pose questions to which all of us who are deeply committed to our faith must respond. If you wish justification for this linking of Jeremiah 29 and Psalm 137 from tradition, then the Greek (LXX) text gives the psalm a heading which links it with David, with one textual tradition adding the words "through Jeremiah."

Psalm 138
CAUSE FOR THANKSGIVING

This the first of eight psalms which form a Davidic collection in the Hebrew tradition of Book V. Some of the critical problems which surround these psalms are well illustrated in this one. Who is the "I" who speaks in the psalm? Is it, as some have argued, the king or his representative, thus making this one of the royal psalms, or is it an otherwise unidentified individual? Related to this issue is the question of date. If it is a royal psalm, then it comes originally from the preexilic, monarchical period. There have not been lacking those who have been prepared on linguistic grounds to trace it as far back as the Davidic period (e.g., M. Dahood). Others have argued for a postexilic date, pointing out strong similarities between this psalm and Isaiah 40–55. A postexilic date may claim support from one of the Greek manuscript traditions which adds to the title the name "Zechariah." One thing is clear from the content of the psalm: its setting is the Jerusalem temple, whether the preexilic temple or the rebuilt, postexilic one. With such different conclusions being confidently proposed, it is perhaps wise to keep the question of date open. Nothing in it, however, necessitates it being classified as one of the royal psalms. It is best to treat it as an expression of the faith of an individual who knew on the basis of experience that he had good cause for thanksgiving. The psalm naturally falls into three sections, verses 1-3, verses 4-6, and verses 7-8.

1-3 It is almost as if in the opening section the psalmist is making his own personal response to the summons which opens Psalms 106, 107, and 136, "O give thanks to the LORD." "Yes," says this psalmist, "I give you thanks, O LORD," joyful, heartfelt thanks, which leads him to sing the LORD's praises "before the gods," words which raise the same issues as we have discussed in Psalm 82. Against the background of the traditional picture of the council of the gods, the psalmist is affirming that there is only one God worthy of praise, the LORD. His cause for thanksgiving is rooted in what Psalms 106, 107, and 136 invite the people to celebrate, the LORD's "steadfast love" (see 5:7) and what is often associated with that steadfast love, the LORD's "faithfulness" (see 25:5; cf. 85:11; 115:1). In the temple courts he worships with eyes fixed on "your holy temple" (cf. 2:6). He may indeed have been offering a sacrifice of thanksgiving (see 50:14). The closing words of verse 2 in the NRSV, "for you have exalted your name and your word above everything," assume an alteration of the awkward Hebrew text and make sense in context. It is the LORD's "name," his essential nature (see 5:11), and his "word" or promise which have been the key factors in the psalmist's ability to cope with what life has thrown at him. He has prayed, and his prayers have been answered (v. 3; cf. 3:4; 120:1). The NRSV translation of the second half of verse 3 again assumes a slight alteration of the Hebrew text in its reading "you increased." This gives the picture of new strength and vitality flowing back into the psalmist's life, through answered prayer. The REB translation in verse 3, you "made me bold and strong," assumes that the verb, which is not found elsewhere in the Hebrew Bible, is related to the adjective rendered "proud" in 40:4 and the noun "pride" in 90:10. In this case the psalmist is speaking about a new confidence in his life, perhaps similar to the confidence of which Paul boasts in 2 Cor. 12:9-10.

4-6 These verses contain a hymnic celebration of the LORD which echoes and universalizes the psalmist's personal experience. For this universalizing theme in the Psalms, see the comment on Psalm 96. The psalmist's opening declaration in verse 1, "I give you thanks," finds its counterpart in the opening words of verse 4, "All the kings of the earth shall praise you." "Praise" and "give thanks" are different renderings of the same Hebrew word. Similarly, "the words of your mouth" which these kings heard (v. 4) picks up the reference to "your word" in verse 2. The words "for great is the glory of the LORD" (v. 5) look back to "for you have exalted [literally, "made great"] your name" (v. 2). Likewise, the description of the LORD in verse 6 reflects what has been hinted at in verse 3 and anticipates verses 7-8. The psalmist had prayed in his weakness for new strength or confidence. His prayer had been answered because the LORD, however great and "high" (see 46:10), regards the "lowly," the poor and the vulnerable (see 113:4-9) and is well aware of those who are "haughty" or proud (cf. 101:5). God may be "far away," transcendent, his throne in the heavens, but he is *au fait* with all that goes on in human affairs. Throughout this section "all the kings of the earth" are being reminded that they are responsible for shaping their conduct in the light of one who is truly described as the king of glory (see 3:3; cf. 24:7-10).

7-8 The concluding verses speak of the psalmist's confident continuing trust in the LORD. The God whose strength he has experienced will be protectingly with him "in the midst of trouble" (v. 7). The word translated "trouble" is a very common word in the Psalms (cf. 22:11; 25:17; 120:1). Its specific meaning can only be determined by context. Here it seems to be related to the psalmist's awareness that he is surrounded by people who are out to get him. He speaks of "the wrath of my enemies." In this situation his confidence is rooted in the fact that "you stretch out your hand" (v. 7), a phrase which sometimes is used of God acting decisively against those who oppose him (cf. Exod. 3:20; 24:11) but which here, as in 144:7, points to the God who "delivers" (see 3:2) someone in danger. It must be so, because the psalmist knows on the basis of past experience that the LORD "will fulfill his purpose for me" (v. 8; cf. 57:2). Thus the concluding words "Do not forsake the work of your hands" are not words of near despair, but words of quiet confidence that the LORD who had been at work in and through his life in the past would continue that work whatever the future might bring. The past had given him cause for thanksgiving; the future would tell no other story, since the foundation of that past thanksgiving, the "steadfast love" of the LORD, "endures forever" (see Psalm 136). This is no shallow or unrealistic faith. It bears its witness in the midst of unresolved present difficulties, but it looks to the future with hope, because it believes that God never changes — cause for thanksgiving, indeed!

Psalm 139
"I" AND "YOU"

This is one of the most widely quoted of all the Psalms. Verses 7-12 in particular have found their place in many an anthology of spiritual meditations and have inspired poets and hymn writers. Ian Pitt-Watson's hymn "Thou art before me, Lord, thou art behind," based on the NEB version of verses 5-12 and verses 23-24, is but the latest of many such hymnic interpretations. It has found a ready response in congregational singing. Yet this is a psalm which poses many difficulties. The text at points is far from certain. Some of these difficulties are highlighted in the different translations offered by the NRSV and the REB in verses 14, 16, and 18. Nor is there agreement as to what kind of psalm this is. Any answer to that question must embrace the psalm as a whole, instead of selecting from it, as is often done, verses 7-12 and totally ignoring verses 19-22. It is generally agreed that there is a major break after verse 18. This has led some to argue that the harsh words of verses 19-21 were not originally part of the psalm, since they are totally out of place after the spiritual sensitivity of verses 1-18. In that case we can only wonder why anyone was so insensitive as to add them to verses 1-18. We must seek to understand the psalm as a whole, as it now lies before us.

One approach is to see in the psalm the words of someone who comes to the temple to protest his innocence of charges which have been brought against him. If we translate the word rendered "wicked" in verse 24 as "an idol," then the charge may have been one of dabbling in other cults. Faced with such a charge, the psalmist turns to the LORD who, he believes, knows everything about him, to seek vindication. Psalm 7 provides an interesting example of a similar type of psalm. This approach does take the psalm as a whole seriously and has had many advocates in recent years. Yet for this view to be wholly convincing we might have expected a more explicit protestation of innocence, such as we find in 7:3-5. Some of the language in the psalm suggests a different approach. The word translated "search" in verses 1 and 23 (cf. 44:21) occurs elsewhere most frequently in the wisdom literature — in Proverbs and, in particular, Job (e.g., Prov. 18:17; 25:2; Job 5:27; 13:9; 28:3, 27). The reference to the two ways with which the psalm ends points in the same direction (cf. Psalm 1). It is perhaps best not to attempt to be too precise in defining either the original setting or the form of this psalm. Rather, we should see in it the words of an intelligent, highly sensitive person meditating upon the meaning of life. He looks at himself and the world in which he lives in the light of the one certainty which he can neither deny nor escape, his intimate relationship with the LORD. This relationship is explored in the psalm in five sections.

1-6 The opening words, "O LORD, you have searched me" or "you search me," are the psalmist's acknowledgment that the LORD has "examined" (REB) or scrutinized him in such a way that, even if he wanted to, he could not pull the wool over the LORD's eyes. Using the same verb, Job challenges his unsympathetic friends: "Will it be well with you when he [God] searches you out? Or can you deceive him, as one person deceives another?" (Job 13:9). The psalmist's life and everything he does lie open to the scrutiny of the LORD. It is not only his outward actions — "when I sit down," that is, rest, or "when I rise up," that is, prepare to do something — but even the "thoughts" which he might conceal from those close to him that lie open to the LORD "from far away" (see 138:6). In verse 3, "you search out" translates a verb which usually means "to scatter" or "to winnow." It is here used in the metaphorical sense of sifting (REB: "trace"). The REB's rendering "my journeying" is perhaps better than the NRSV's translation "my path." The LORD has no difficulty in keeping tabs on the psalmist, wherever he goes or beds down. He even knows what the psalmist is going to say, before he says it (v. 4). All of this could be a terrifying experience, as if an evil eye were constantly watching. But this is no evil eye; it is the LORD. The words "You hem me in" (v. 5) could mean "you besiege me with hostile intent," but in context means "you keep close guard" (REB). The statement "Lay your hand upon me" may indicate giving a blessing (cf. Gen. 48:14, 17) or offering protection (cf. Exod. 33:22). In face of "such knowledge," the way in which the LORD knows him through and through, the psalmist can only respond with a sense of wonder which he cannot fathom. It is important to notice the intensely personal framework within which the psalmist speaks. It is characteristic of the whole psalm. A philosopher or theologian might wish to attach to these verses the label "the omniscience of God," just as the following section might be headed "the omni-presence of God," but the psalmist is not interested in that kind of intellectual discussion. He is simply saying, "The LORD knows me through and through, and that is breathtakingly wonderful."

7-12 It is the inevitable corollary of verses 1-6 that the psalmist, even if he wanted to, could never escape from the LORD. "Where can I go. . . ?" (v. 7). Together the words "your spirit" (see 51:10-12) and "your presence" (literally, "your face"; cf. 17:15; 31:16) speak of an ever present LORD in all his power and his graciousness. To be on the run from this God is impossible. There is no place where he is not present. The vertical extremities of the psalmist's worldview are represented in verse 8 by "heaven" and "Sheol," the underworld of the dead (see 6:5). Its horizontal extremities are represented in verse 9 by "the wings of the morning [or dawn]," a fine poetic image for the eastern horizon with its rising sun, and by "the farthest limits of the sea," the western end of the Mediterranean, where the known world stopped. That God would be there in "heaven" occasions no surprise. That after all is where he sits enthroned (see 2:4). But in "Sheol"? That is the place where, according to Psalm 88, people are cut off from the LORD's hand (88:5), where the "steadfast love" and the "faithfulness" of the LORD are unknown (88:11). Much of the Hebrew Bible speaks of Sheol as a place outside the LORD's jurisdiction. The developing faith of Israel, however, began to realize that to confess the LORD as the creator of heaven and earth, king of kings and lord of lords, was to recognize that no one, no experience, and no place could lie outside his domain. So Amos 9:2 affirms that there is no escape from the judgment of the LORD in Sheol; Jonah discovers that there is no escape from obedience to the LORD in Sheol (Jonah 2:2); and this psalmist is confident that there is no escape from the presence of the LORD, even in Sheol. Wherever the psalmist goes, he believes that the LORD "shall lead" him (cf. 77:20) and shall keep a firm grasp of him (v. 10; cf. 73:23). The "darkness" which features so prominently in verses 11-12 may refer to suffering or distress or to the dark night of the soul which the psalmist fears, but there may be ominous overtones of death. Sheol and death are described as "regions dark and deep" and "the darkness" in 88:6, 12. The contrast between darkness and light runs through the biblical literature in many different contexts, from God's first creative word, "Let there be light," shattering the darkness of chaos (Gen. 1:2-3), to the celebration of the incarnation in John's Gospel, "The light shines in the darkness, and the darkness did not overcome it" (John 1:5). The psalmist is a realist. He accepts that there is "darkness," the seemingly negative experiences in life which may very well "cover" or "steal over" (REB) him (v. 11) as if to hide the LORD from him. But there is no escape from the LORD even in the midst of such darkness, since, as the REB neatly renders the closing words of verse 12, "to you both dark and light are one." "Nothing can hide the LORD from me," says the psalmist. There is no escape from his gracious presence, and that for him is the basis of a quietly confident faith.

13-18   There is no escape because the LORD his creator was there even before his birth. It was "you," yes "you" (the opening of verse 13 is emphatic), who "formed my inward parts" (literally, "my kidneys," regarded in the Hebrew Bible as the seat of the emotions or the conscience). In 16:7 and 73:21 the NRSV translates "heart." The reference here is probably to what the psalmist regards as his inmost self, formed secretly like his "frame" (v. 15; REB: "body") within his mother's womb. The precise meaning of the words "you knit me" (v. 13) and "intricately woven" (v. 15) is a matter of dispute. The general picture, however, seems to be that of the growth of the embryo and the fetus within the womb as the work of a skilled divine embroiderer weaving in secret an intricate pattern or design, still to be unveiled. But what leads the psalmist to say, "I praise you" (v. 14)? The NRSV, like most earlier English translations, tries to stick closely to the Hebrew in its rendering "for I am fearfully and wonderfully made." The Hebrew might be more strictly rendered, "for I am fearfully wonderful." In this case, it is the very mystery and wonder of human life from its very beginning within the womb, a mystery and wonder which the psalmist acknowledges with "that I know very well," which leads to his words of praise. The REB, however, takes a lead from most of the early versions in rendering, "for you fill me with awe; wonderful you are." In this case, the contemplation of the origin of human life leads the psalmist to acknowledge the mystery and wonder of the one who is the creator of all life, and the one who knows him: "You know me through and through" (so the REB, changing the vowels in the traditional Hebrew text). The words "wonderful are your works" (see 9:1) could support either view. It is tempting to see both views as the opposite sides of one and the same coin, the mystery and wonder which is at the heart of human life being but a reflection of the mystery and wonder of God. The REB translation culminating in "You know me through and through" perhaps leads more naturally into verses 15 and 16, which speak of the LORD as the only one fully aware of what was happening to the unborn child being shaped "in the depths of the earth" (v. 15). This may be a metaphor for the womb which has distant roots in the mythology of the great Earth Mother and in the picture in Genesis 2 of the first human being as created "out of the dust of the ground," with its play on the word for "human being," 'ādām, and the word for "ground," 'ădāmâ — an "earthling" created out of the "earth" (cf. Job 10:9).

Verse 16 poses several difficult problems. The NRSV translation "my unformed substance" is a rendering of a Hebrew word which in later Hebrew can mean an embryo. This then assumes that it is the psalmist's "days" which are recorded in the LORD's book, recorded even before day one of the psalmist's life. A reordering of two letters in the Hebrew word gives the REB's rendering "deeds," and it is such deeds which are naturally recorded in the LORD's "book" (see 56:8; 69:28). Whether we follow the NRSV or the REB in this verse, there runs through it a strong sense of a purpose which shapes life and which is the expression of the will of the creator (cf. Jer. 1:5). It is small wonder, then, that the concluding verses in this section, verses 17-18, echo in different language the sense of unfathomable wonder which was expressed in verse 6 at the end of the first section. The LORD's thoughts are described by the psalmist as being incredibly "weighty," a translation of a verb which usually indicates something as being valuable or precious (cf. Eccl. 10:1). It is as if the psalmist is having difficulty taking on board all that is implied in his confession of God as his creator. The Lord's thoughts are not only "weighty" but infinitely beyond any human reckoning; compare the use of the "sand that is on the seashore" in talking about the countless descendants promised to the patriarchs in Gen. 22:17; 32:12. The second half of verse 18 is uncertain. The NRSV translation, "I come to the end" — which presumably means "to the end of my attempt to count them" — represents a different understanding of the Hebrew text, which traditionally has been rendered "I awake" and often interpreted in terms of resurrection, an interpretation which makes little sense in context. If the NRSV is correct, then this section ends with the psalmist recognizing his human limitations. He can never fully come to terms with the mystery and wonder of the God who has created him. He does, however, know one thing beyond any shadow of doubt: "I am still with you." The God he worships is no divine technocrat creating a machine and then leaving it to work according to its own internal mechanism. The creator who was there while life was being fashioned secretly in the womb is the God who is ever present and in whose presence the psalmist lives out his entire life. Sophisticated modern medical technology may reveal to us what is happening in the womb, but it hardly destroys the mystery and the wonder of emerging life. The REB's interpretation of the closing words of verse 18, "to finish the count, my years must equal yours," while possible, seems less appropriate in context.

19-22 We have seen that the psalmist is a realist about the dark experiences which overshadow his life (vv. 11-12). He is also a realist about the world in which he lives. He may say with confidence "I am still with you" (v. 18), but he knows that there are others for whom that would be a meaningless statement and who would challenge everything for which the LORD stands. There is, therefore, nothing incongruous with the spiritual sensitivity of verses 1-18 in this section. He characterizes such people as "the wicked" (see 1:1), the "bloodthirsty" (cf. 5:6), those who are malicious and arrogant (v. 20). The text in the second half of verse 20 is uncertain. The NRSV's wording "against you" is an alteration of a word which normally would mean "your cities" but which was taken by some of the early versions to mean "your adversaries" (REB), a meaning it has in Aramaic. What is clear is that the psalmist regards such people as a threat to the LORD. They are "those who hate you . . . those who rise up against you" (v. 21). And the LORD's enemies are his enemies. For the psalmist there can be no moral or spiritual neutrality. He knows whose side he is on. The translation "How I hate those who hate you" (REB) catches better the emphatic nature of the statement than the NRSV, "Do I not hate. . . ?" He looks upon those who defy the LORD with disgust (cf. 119:158, the only other occurrence in the Psalms of the verb translated "loathe"). They are, he claims, "my enemies" (v. 22), whom he hates with "perfect hatred" or with a deep, continuing hatred (REB: "undying hatred"). It is worth pondering, however, whether there may not be a closer connection between this section and what has gone before it in the psalm. The very intensity of this hatred and the maliciousness displayed by such people may have been part of the reason why the psalmist was led to explore in greater depth the reality of that other relationship from which he believed he could never be separated, his relationship with the LORD. The theological problems raised by such a bitter reaction have been discussed elsewhere (see Psalms 109, 137). The temptation to self-righteousness is only too obvious. The words with which the psalm closes provide a healthy corrective.

23-24 Verse 23 takes us back to the opening words of the Psalm. "You have searched me" (v. 1), now "search me"; you have "known me" (v. 1), now "know my heart . . . know my thoughts" (v. 23). This is a wholesome recognition by the psalmist that the world cannot simply be divided into "others," who are a threat to God, and "me," a perfect saint. He is acknowledging that he himself still needs to be scrutinized, examined, tested by God. He himself stands at the crossroads where ways divide. Faced with God, he needs to know whether he himself is involved in any "wicked way" or any way which causes God pain (REB: "any path that grieves you"). For those who read this psalm as a declaration of innocence in face of charges leveled against the psalmist, the possibility of rendering this phrase "the way of an idol" makes a good deal of sense. It is better, however, to see in these words the psalmist placing himself entirely in the hands of God, recognizing that he himself has faults and needs to see himself constantly in the searching light of God's presence. Indeed, it is possible to wonder whether he may be having doubts about the hatred he has been directing against other people. Was it purely a defense of the ways of God, or was there in it an element of gloating satisfaction? His last words are not directed against those he has accused of defying God but are a prayer for himself — "lead me in the way everlasting" (v. 24). The phrase "the way everlasting" occurs only here in the Hebrew Bible. Since the word translated "everlasting" can mean the past, this could be a reference to the good old ways, the traditional ways of faith and obedience which had shaped the life of the community. Equally, however, the word can refer to time which begins in the past and goes on into the future to embrace the whole of human experience. So "the way everlasting" may point to the continuing way which lies ahead, a way which will be characterized by that enriching presence of God which has been and is the psalmist's experience. We will not go far wrong if we take the same way, following the spiritual pilgrimage outlined in this psalm.

Psalm 140
THE ANTIDOTE TO VENOM

This is a psalm of lament on the lips of someone who is aware of being on the receiving end of venomous slander. He lays his plight before the LORD, whom he confesses as "my God" (v. 6). He prays that those who plot his downfall will meet with richly deserved retribution (vv. 8-11) and concludes on a note of confident faith. Traditionally, this and the three following psalms have been linked with the difficulties David faced during his lifetime, and in particular during the revolt led by his son Absalom (2 Samuel 15–18). Most modern scholars tend to place these psalms in the postexilic period, though there is little in them to point to any precise dating.

1-5 The psalm falls naturally into five sections, with the liturgical marker *Selah* at the end of the first three sections (for *Selah,* see Psalm 3). The first two sections, verses 1-3 and verses 4-5, begin with the urgent appeal characteristic of such psalms: "Deliver me [cf. 7:1] . . . protect me [v. 1; cf. 64:1]" and "Guard me . . . protect me [v. 4; cf. 12:7]." They then describe those whose venom is being directed against the psalmist, switching back and forth between the singular and the plural. Thus in verse 1 "evildoers" is literally "an evil person" and "those who are violent" is "a man of violent deeds," while verses 2-3 speak throughout of "they." Against the background of words which convey a wide variety of possible meanings, the language becomes more precise. As in 120:7 the war metaphor (v. 2) is used to indicate verbal attacks. This is then further spelled out in two graphic pictures.

In verse 3 the picture is that of the sharp fangs and the deadly venom of a poisonous snake. The word translated "vipers" occurs only here in the Hebrew Bible and has been understood to mean "spider," but the parallel with "snake" makes "viper" or "cobra" a more likely translation. The second half of this verse is one of a series of passages from the Psalms used by Paul in Rom. 3:10-18 to illustrate the universality and the deadly power of sin.

In verse 5 the picture is that of a trapper or hunter setting hidden snares or "nets" to catch the prey (cf. 9:15-16; 10:8-9). The text in verse 5 is uncertain. The REB is probably correct in rendering in the second line "villains spread their nets." This involves merely a change in the vowels of the word which the NRSV translates "cords."

Both pictures stress the deadly seriousness of the situation the psalmist faces at the hands of those who are secretly out to get him. They are people who "plan evil things in their minds" (v. 2) and are determined to ensure his "downfall" (v. 4). Behind this word "downfall" there is a Hebrew verb which means "to push hard" (cf. 118:13). The psalmist is being pushed to the limits.

6-8 With venomous hostility staring him in the face, the psalmist in verses 6-8 turns to the LORD. He begins by confessing his faith in words of transparent simplicity, "You are my God" (see 31:14). On that basis he humbly makes his appeal to the LORD to listen to his prayer (v. 6; cf. 86:6). It is an appeal made in confidence, because it is made to "my strong deliverer," literally, "the strength of my salvation," a phrase found only here in the Hebrew Bible, but one which weaves together two aspects of the character of God to which the Psalms repeatedly bear witness: "strength" and "salvation" (see 3:8; cf. 21:1). The psalmist knows this to be true because he has experienced it: "you have covered my head in the day of battle" (v. 7). The word here translated "battle" normally refers to weaponry. It is likely that this expression depicts God as providing the psalmist with the necessary equipment (e.g., shield and helmet) with which to go into battle. We may compare the use made of this picture of the whole armor of God as essential to the Christian life in Eph. 6:10-17. Knowing himself to be thus equipped, it is natural for the psalmist to pray that the plans of his enemies will be frustrated (v. 8). The ending of verse 8 and the beginning of verse 9 pose problems of interpretation. As the NRSV footnote indicates, after the words "do not further their evil plot" the Hebrew reads "they are exalted." This is retained in the NIV with the words "or they will become proud," confirming as it were the arrogance (v. 5) which lay behind their attacks, and thus providing a reasonable climax to this section. Both the NRSV and the REB, however, follow the Greek (LXX) tradition and transfer "they are exalted" to the beginning of verse 9 to give the translation "lift up their heads." This is neither necessary nor convincing. It may well be that there is a deeper corruption in the text at this point. If so, the end of verse 8 could read "As for their plots, O God, tear them to pieces."

9-11 Verses 6-8 prepare the way for the two remaining sections of the psalm, with verses 9-11 developing the thought of verses 3-5 and 8, and verses 12-13 returning to the theme of verses 6-7. Verses 9-11 focus upon the inevitable punishment which will overtake the psalmist's slanderers. Since the attack on the psalmist has been compared to the venom of vipers (v. 3), it is likely that the word translated "head" in verse 9 should be rendered "poison" (cf. Job 20:16). The verse would then read, "As for the poison of those who surround me — may the mischief of their lips overwhelm them." Let the venom with which they sought to destroy the psalmist do its deadly work in their own lives. The "burning coals" in verse 10 may be a reference to the story of the destruction of Sodom and Gomorrah (see 11:6 and Genesis 19), a destruction which the inhabitants of these cities brought upon themselves. The word "pits," a word found only here in the Hebrew Bible, may mean "floods," destructive floods engulfing everything in their path, with possible echoes of the waters of chaos and their mythological association with death. Verse 11 returns to the picture of the hunter in verse 5. Now there is to be a role reversal. Those who hunted the psalmist are themselves to be hunted down by the very evil they sought to inflict upon the psalmist. By their slanders they sought to have him debarred from the community, his rights to hold property in the land annulled; now that is to be their fate. Throughout this whole section there runs the theme vigorously expressed in other psalms that evil signs its own death warrant (e.g., 7:14-16; 9:15-16). The recurring tragedy in life is that those who traffic in such evil, not least in slander, seldom recognize this until it is too late.

12-13 There is, however, an antidote to such venom. This is the note on which the psalm ends in verses 12-13. The psalmist first expresses the certainty he has — "I know" (cf. 56:9) — a certainty rooted in God as a dependable judge who "maintains" or "will give" (REB) the "needy" their rights and uphold the cause of the "poor." It is as one identified with the "needy" and the "poor" (see 9:12), with those who suffer any form of oppression, that the psalmist comes to the LORD. He belongs to "the righteous" (see Psalm 1) and "the upright" (see 11:7), to those who are committed to live as God's people. Life may be harsh, but for them there is a "Yes, but" (see Psalm 73), which means that they will yet have cause to give thanks to the "name" of the LORD (see 5:11) for all that he is and does. They will have that plus in life which is denied to all who traffic in evil, the joy of living in "your presence." This would certainly mean for the psalmist having the privilege of worshipping God in the temple and of continuing to live in the land which was God's gift to his people. Ultimately neither temple nor land could contain or prove essential to the living experience of the presence of God. For Christian spirituality that presence centers on a person and on the word with which Matthew's Gospel ends, "I will be with you always, to the end of time" (Matt. 28:20).

Psalm 141
FACING TEMPTATION

This psalm has some of the characteristic marks of the wisdom teaching as we saw that teaching laid out in Psalm 1. There is the contrast between the wicked (vv. 4, 10) and the righteous (v. 5). There is the need to say "No" to the company of the wicked (v. 4) and "Yes" to a life focused on God (v. 8). But this psalm is an individual lament which stresses that life often does not fall into two neatly defined categories or ways. You may belong to the righteous, may be committed to God, yet feel only too keenly the temptations which the wicked dangle before you. This is a psalm of someone who has faced such temptation and is aware that he needs help. He is fighting an inner battle from which he believes he can emerge victorious only with the help of the LORD. Who this psalmist was we do not know. There have been many attempts to deduce from the text a precise setting and date for the psalm. Theories range all the way from the time of David, following the psalm heading, to a Jew who lived seven or eight hundred years later in the Diaspora. Part of the difficulty is that the text, particularly in verses 5-7, is beset by serious problems. The general meaning of the psalm, however, is reasonably clear. It speaks of an experience with which it is easy to identify.

1-2   The psalm begins, as so many such psalms do, with an appeal to the LORD expressed in the twofold occurrence of the verb to "call" or to "cry" in verse 1 (cf. 130:1). The urgency of the cry is underlined by the words "come quickly to me" (cf. 70:5). His appeal takes the form of a prayer offered to the LORD in the temple precincts. The word translated "incense" in verse 2 can refer either to the smoke which rises from the sacrifice of the burnt offering (cf. 66:15) or to the incense which was burned while the sacrifice was being offered (cf. Lev. 16:13). It is probably the latter here. As the incense accompanying the "evening sacrifice" (Hebrew *minḥāh;* see 40:6) rises, the sign of its acceptance by the LORD, so in faith the psalmist offers his prayer with "uplifted hands" (see 28:2), asking that his appeal may be accepted by the LORD. Some have argued that verse 2 presupposes that the psalmist is far from the temple and that his prayers are being offered as a substitute for the sacrifice he is unable to offer. In context, however, this seems unlikely, unless we date the psalm late and see it coming out of the experience of exile or of a Jew of the Diaspora who lived far from Jerusalem. That it could be so interpreted by a faithful Jew in such situations is but witness to the way in which liturgical language is capable of being adapted to changing circumstances and needs. Thus the reference to the "evening sacrifice" ensured that in early Christian tradition this psalm was regarded as an appropriate evening hymn.

3-4   Verses 3-4 lay bare the urgency of the appeal. His loyalty to the LORD was being severely tested by the evil which was prevalent in society around him. There were people trafficking in nefarious deeds, "evildoers" (see 5:5) actively encouraging others to join their club, to share their "delicacies" (v. 4) or delights. This word occurs only here in the Hebrew Bible, but it is paralleled in inscriptions. It may refer to banquets, though not necessarily, as some have argued, to banquets associated with the worship of other gods. Indeed, the world in which this psalmist was living is very like that described in 73:3, 12, where the wicked prospered and enjoyed the fruits of high society living. In Psalm 73 the psalmist was led to question whether his faith was worth holding on to. Here the psalmist seems to have been on the verge of joining the ranks of the unscrupulous highfliers. He may indeed have yielded to this temptation, but he is now having second thoughts. Verse 3 finds its parallel in the words of Jesus ben Sirach: "Who will set a guard over my mouth, and an effective seal upon my lips, so that I may not fall because of them, and my tongue may not destroy me?" (Sir. 22:27; cf. Ps. 34:13). Conscious that he has said things he regrets, things that may have met with the approval of the wicked with their false sense of values, the psalmist asks the LORD to do just this, to set a "guard" and a "watch over the door of my lips" (v. 3). But more than his words are at stake. His "heart" — his conscience, his will, his inmost thoughts — is in danger of being corrupted by association with evil, so he pleads, "Do not turn my heart to any evil" (v. 4). These words have been described as "a remarkable expression of divine control over the mind" (L. C.

Allen). They are perhaps better seen as the psalmist's confession of his total dependence upon God and a recognition that without the grace of God he may be exposed to situations in which he would be powerless to resist temptation. Thus we pray, "Do not put us to the test" (Matt. 6:13, REB). Both the NRSV and the REB assume that the "evil" referred to in verse 4 implies some evil actions, but the Hebrew might equally well be translated "evil word," that is, evil speaking, and thus be the climax to verse 3. Whatever meaning we give to evil in this context, the psalmist is conscious that he is vulnerable, living on the edge, his thoughts, words, and deeds pulling him either towards evil company or back to God. In 1 Cor. 15:33 Paul quotes the words of a Greek dramatist, "Bad company ruins good character" (REB). Often people fail to realize this until it is too late; not so the psalmist.

5-6 In verses 5-6, the details of which are far from clear, the psalmist insists that at heart he is against such corrupting influences. In verse 5 he asserts that he is willing to accept needed discipline. Both the NRSV and the REB assume minor alterations to the Hebrew text in the first line of verse 5. It might be translated, "May the righteous strike me in steadfast love and correct me," that is, "May those who are truly committed to the LORD show their loyalty by pointing out to me the error of my ways and by redirecting my steps." Thus the psalmist is acknowledging that there are two circles to which he may belong, the company of the wicked or the company of the LORD's faithful people. He knows that they point him in different directions. The NRSV and the REB then follow the Greek (LXX) text in the translation, "Never let the oil of the wicked anoint my head." Since oil was often used to anoint the head of a welcome, distinguished guest, this is tantamount to saying, "I do not wish to be an honorary member in Club Wicked." Far from it, his constant prayer is directed against the evil they cultivate, "their wicked deeds," words which point up the dilemma, the inner struggle, he faces. His prayers do not necessarily coincide with the way he acts. He, and we, may pray to be rid of temptation yet still in weakness yield to it. The different translations of the first half of verse 6 in the NRSV and the REB underline the difficulties in the text. It might also be translated, "When they fall [literally, "drop"] into the hands of the Rock, their judge," with "Rock" being a well-known title for God (see 18:2). Whatever translation we follow, the verse points up the fate which awaits the wicked. When that happens, says the psalmist, "they shall learn that my words were pleasant." That does not mean that they will necessarily repent of their evil ways. He is simply declaring that, faced with inevitable judgment, they will recognize that there is a graciousness in life (for "pleasant," see 27:4; 133:1) to which the psalmist has struggled to bear witness but which has eluded them.

7-10 The concluding section of the psalm takes us back to its beginning. The urgency of the psalmist's initial plea arises out of a situation which he knows he is not alone in facing. The NRSV "their bones" (v. 7) is a needless alteration of the Hebrew "our bones." Its only justification is the belief that verse 7 should be taken along with verse 6 as a further description of the judgment which is to befall the wicked. But verse 7 is best taken as the introduction to the final section of the psalm. Just as plowing breaks up the soil (cf. REB), so the psalmist and others in the community have been broken by what he vividly portrays as Death, the Monster who chews up his victims and leaves their bones strewn on the ground at the entrance to his abode, Sheol (see 6:5; compare the picture of Sheol as a ravening monster in Isa. 5:14). This leads the psalmist to turn again to the LORD, this time using visual imagery: "But my eyes are turned toward you, O God, my Lord" (v. 8; cf. 25:15). He seeks "refuge" in the LORD (see 2:11), refuge from what he sees as his naked defenselessness. In language similar to that in 140:5, 11 he seeks protection from those who are hunting him down and pleads that such people will meet their rightful end by becoming the victims of their own malicious intentions, trapped in the nets they prepared for the psalmist (vv. 9-10). The closing words "while I alone escape" or "pass on my way" (REB) leave us with a picture of the psalmist declaring his faith that, successfully surviving all attempts to hunt him down, he will continue along the path where his eyes are firmly fixed on the LORD. He has faced temptation, he knows its power, but he believes that it can be conquered, not in his own strength but with the help of the LORD who is his refuge. The letter to the Hebrews looks at this theology against the background of its picture of Jesus, the one and only high priest, and remints it in memorable words: "For we do not have a high priest who is unable to sympathize with our weakness, but we have one who in every respect has been tested as we are, yet without sin. Let us therefore approach the throne of grace with boldness, so that we may receive mercy and find grace in time of need" (Heb. 4:15-16).

Psalm 142
A CRY OF DISTRESS

The heading of this psalm is similar to that of Psalm 57. This tells us how the psalm was interpreted and linked with the life of David at a certain point in Jewish tradition. It is difficult, however, to fit the psalm easily into the cave incidents in David's life as they have come down to us in 1 Samuel 22 and 24. Much depends for the interpretation of the psalm on the meaning we give to the word "prison" in verse 7, a Hebrew word which only occurs here in the Psalms. It has been argued that "prison" here is a synonym for death or the abode of the dead. In this case the psalm may be read as a deathbed lament. The introductory appeal in verses 1-2 then leads into the content of the lament proper in verses 3-7, verses which should be placed in quotation marks. That the psalm would have a certain appropriateness in such a setting need not be doubted. When Francis of Assisi was dying, some of the psalms were recited by his friends gathered round his deathbed. Francis responded in particular to the opening words of this psalm. Much of the language traditionally associated with death in the Hebrew Bible, however, does not appear in this psalm. To view it simply as a deathbed psalm is unduly to restrict it. The word "prison" may, of course, be taken quite literally. If so, this is a psalm of someone who is in prison awaiting trial, through which, by due legal process, probably carried out at the temple, the LORD's verdict will be made known (cf. Lev. 24:12; Num. 15:34). What the charges are is not clear, nor do we know the identity of those bringing the charges. The psalmist describes them simply as "my persecutors" (v. 6). If this is the situation, we are listening to a prisoner who is conscious of serious charges hanging over his head and who is appealing to the LORD, the one person he fully trusts to vindicate him. Some of the most moving prayers and statements of faith have come out of just such situations, from some of Paul's letters through John Bunyan's *Pilgrim's Progress* to Dietrich Bonhoeffer's *Letters and Papers from Prison*.

Prison, however, may be used in a metaphorical sense, as in Isa. 42:7, where it is a way of talking about the exile in Babylon. It is a usage with which we are familiar in everyday language. We talk about someone being imprisoned in needless fears or frustrations. In this case "prison" is the psalmist's way of talking about the oppressive, crippling situation he faces and from which he wishes to be set free to resume his rightful place as a member of the worshipping community. This seems the best approach to the psalm, even if we cannot be sure precisely what difficulties he was facing. Nor is there any evidence which would lead us with confidence to assign a date to the psalm.

1-3a The opening section of the psalm contains an urgent appeal to the LORD. The psalmist is unable to contain his distress. He needs help, and he cries out for it. Notice the emphatic and reiterated "with my voice" (v. 1; REB: "aloud"). Even if the psalmist believed that the LORD knew what was happening to him, he still needed to put it into words, which enabled him to bring out into the open his deepest need. The verb translated "I cry" (v. 1) is a different verb from the one we saw at the opening of Psalm 141. It usually points to a plea for help in oppressive circumstances (cf. 77:1). We hear it again in verse 5. It is a plea which takes the form of the psalmist making "supplication" to the LORD (see 30:8). The REB catches the flavor of this word when it translates, "I plead . . . for mercy." The psalmist is not claiming any right to the LORD's help; there is nothing he can offer but his own weakness and vulnerability (v. 6). He can but appeal to the LORD to be true to his own gracious nature.

"I pour out my complaint" (v. 2). The word translated "complaint" is a word which in other contexts is translated "meditation" (e.g., 104:34 and frequently in Psalm 119). It is a word which speaks of what is going on inside a person. "Complaint" is perhaps a loaded translation; "inner turmoil" might provide a better parallel here to "my trouble" (see 22:11). The same phrase is translated "Let my cry come to you" in 102:1, leaving open what kind of cry from the heart that is. "When my spirit is faint" (v. 3) is an expression which may refer to anything physical (cf. 107:5) or spiritual which undermines a person's vitality (for "spirit," see 51:10-12) and leaves that person weak and vulnerable. Here it is probably pointing to the "dark night of the soul" with which the psalmist is struggling to come to terms. He is sure of only one thing. "You know my way" (v. 3), words which in Hebrew place strong emphasis on "you." The REB's paraphrase, "You are there to watch over my steps," is possible but unduly restrictive in meaning. The words underline the psalmist's conviction that the LORD knows what has happened to him in the past, what is happening to him now, and what will happen in what lies ahead (for "way," see 1:6).

3b-4 Verses 3b-4 spell out the crisis in the psalmist's life. He knows that there are people only too willing to hunt him down (cf. 140:5). His problem is aggravated by a profound sense of loneliness and friendlessness. The REB's translation "I look" at the beginning of verse 4 is better than the NRSV's "Look." "I look" where I might have expected to find help, "on my right hand," the right hand being the place where a counselor or defense witness would stand (cf. 109:31), but I look in vain; "there is no one who takes notice of me" (v. 4). The best illustration of this expression is to be found in the book of Ruth. Ruth responds to Boaz's kindness to her by asking "Why have I found favor in your eyes, that you should take notice of me when I am a foreigner?" (Ruth 2:10), words later echoed by her mother-in-law in 2:19. The word translated "take notice" implies that someone is prepared to take a friendly interest in another person, the kind of friendliness which the psalmist finds totally lacking in his hour of need. He knows of "no refuge" (REB: "way of escape"), no place to which he could flee to escape danger (cf. 59:16). It is a pity that the NRSV uses the word "refuge" here, because it is a different word from that translated "refuge" in verse 5. He feels "no one cares for me," a use of the verb to "seek" similar to that in Deut. 11:12 and Jer. 30:17. He feels an outcast, denied the help he desperately needs.

5-7 In the closing verses the psalmist renews his appeal to the only one who, he believes, must care. "I cry to you, O LORD . . . my refuge" (see 2:11; 73:28; 94:22) and "my portion" (cf. 16:5; 73:26) — "in the land of the living," that is, "as long as I live" (v. 5). Sustained by such a faith, he spells out his request. The words "Give heed to my cry" (v. 6) are familiar from other psalms (e.g., 17:1). Here again most English translations fail to preserve the rich variety of words used in the Hebrew. Behind the translation "my cry" is a Hebrew word which is close to our English word "shout." It is frequently used in the Psalms to indicate a shout of praise. It lies behind the translation "sing for joy" in 5:11 and is rendered "shouts of joy" in 126:2. Equally it can mean a shout of distress (cf.

106:44). It is the natural response to a situation which is screaming out to be redressed. It is as if the psalmist is hammering at the LORD's door, beseeching him to come out and to rescue someone who is near the end of his tether (for "brought . . . low," see 79:8; 116:6). The second half of verse 6 echoes the language of 7:1. The psalmist feels he is at the mercy of people who are out to destroy him, "my persecutors" or pursuers. The REB's translation "those who harass me" is helpful in context in keeping options open, since we have no means of knowing what kind of persecution is implied. All we know is that this is a harassment before which the psalmist feels helpless. They are "too strong for me."

The closing verse of the psalm looks to the future. Its plea "Bring me out of prison" looks to a future which will make good all the deprivation from which the psalmist now suffers. It will enable him to "give thanks to your name" (cf. 140:13) and to take his place once more in the worshipping community of God's people, "the righteous" who "will surround me." This translation follows the use of the same verb in Hab. 1:4, where "the wicked surround the righteous." The REB's rendering "place a crown on me" follows a Jewish tradition which links the verb with a Hebrew word for "crown," a word which appears in the Hebrew Bible only in the book of Esther (e.g., Esth. 1:11). This might be taken to mean that they give him a right royal welcome or acknowledge that he has won his case (compare the NEB: "crown him with garlands"). Whatever translation we follow, the picture is that of a joyful welcome which may equally be conveyed by the word "surround," as in "surround him to congratulate him." Here again we see what we have noted repeatedly in the Psalms, the way in which the experience and faith of the individual find their context in and contribute to the faith of the community. The psalm ends by noting that the desired outcome will come as the LORD's gift. The only possible reason for it happening is that "you will deal bountifully with me" (cf. 13:6; 119:58). There will be a newfound freedom in which he and the community will rejoice. It is a freedom to which he bears witness as a debtor to grace. For the psalmist that is the secret of new life and cause for thanksgiving. It still is!

Psalm 143
IN GOD'S HANDS

This is the last of the seven psalms which Christian tradition has regarded as penitential psalms (see comment on Psalm 6). Strictly speaking, only verse 2 makes any reference to penitence. The rest of the psalm is a typical lament in which the psalmist appeals to the LORD for help in the face of attacks by enemies (vv. 3, 9, 12). Much of the language and thought in this psalm is closely paralleled in other such psalms, not least in the immediately preceding one. Thus "my supplications" echoes "supplication" in 142:1, and "my spirit faints within me" (v. 4) virtually repeats 142:3a. Yet this psalm is no mere pastiche of material from other psalms; it has its own character and structure. After an introductory appeal to the LORD in verses 1-2, the crisis in the psalmist's life and the profound effect it had upon him are described in verses 3-6. This leads naturally into the petitions which dominate the second half of the psalm in verses 7-12.

1-2   The opening appeal to the LORD uses language with which we are familiar from other similar psalms — "Hear my prayer" (cf. 102:1), "give ear" (cf. 5:1; 17:1), "answer me" (cf. 27:7; 108:6). It is an appeal characterized as "my supplications." The psalmist is throwing himself upon the LORD, whom he believes to be gracious (see 141:1). It is an appeal which makes sense in the light of two fundamental attributes of the LORD, "your faithfulness" (cf. 89:1) and "your righteousness." Both words point to what lies at the heart of the covenant relationship between the LORD and his people and to what makes the covenant lasting even in the midst of bitter experiences which seem to call it into question. The "righteousness" of God for the psalmist is not coldly stern morality. Calvin in this context well describes it as "God's goodness which leads him to defend his people." In the closing verse of the psalm, "your righteousness" stands together with "your steadfast love" (see 5:7), as it frequently does in other psalms (e.g., 36:10, where the NRSV translates "salvation"; cf. 103:17). "Faithfulness," "righteousness," and "steadfast love" all describe what Israel believed to be true to the essential nature of God, a God who cared for his people and would never let them go. Yet the psalmist is aware that he can make no claims upon this God. If the LORD were to act like a human judge and go by the strict letter of the law, no one would emerge from such a trial innocent or acquitted, "for no one living is righteous [or "in the right"] before you" (v. 2). This is the only place in the Hebrew Bible where such a sweeping verdict on human life is made (but cf. 130:3). It is the psalmist's way of taking with total seriousness the fact that he shares in the evil which infects all human life and leads to the inevitable judgment of God. It is not surprising that, in both Gal. 2:16 and Rom. 3:20, Paul uses the Greek (LXX) text of these words to illustrate his argument that neither Jews nor Gentiles can put themselves in the right with God, an essential premise for his proclamation of the good news of God's gracious acceptance of us in Christ. The psalmist's only status in the eyes of the LORD is that of being "your servant," a status repeated in the closing words of the psalm: "for I am your servant" (v. 12). This is the psalmist's acknowledgment that he is wholly dependent upon the LORD and that his life must be characterized by commitment to the LORD (cf. 116:16).

3-6   These verses describe the crisis in the psalmist's life. It focuses on "the enemy," probably a collective noun here, since verses 9 and 12 speak of "my enemies." The enemy has "pursued" him (cf. 142:6), "crushing my life to the ground," trampling him, as it were, under foot, leaving him sitting "in darkness like those long dead" (v. 3). Lamentations 3:6 uses similar language to describe the appalling tragedy which had befallen Jerusalem, a tragedy which it describes in a variety of images which hover around the theme of death (cf. 88:7, 19; 139:11-12). The psalmist is thinking of himself as almost as good as dead, like "those long dead," the memory of whom has faded (cf. v. 7). Verse 4 repeats the opening words of 142:3 and adds words which underscore his sense of being totally devastated (cf. 79:7, where the verb here translated "appalled" is rendered "laid waste"). It adds up to a picture of someone who is psychologically and spiritually broken and at the end of his tether. His crisis deepens when he reflects upon the tradition of faith in which he had been nurtured. "I remember . . . I think about [cf. 1:2, where this verb is translated "meditate"] . . . I meditate" (see 142:2) on a past which bears eloquent witness to the LORD in action, a past characterized by "your deeds . . . the work of your hands" (v. 5), all that you have done for your people in the course of their history. But where is the evidence of this God in action now (cf. 44:1-8 and 9-12)? The psalmist can only "stretch out" his hands (v. 6; cf. 44:20), a phrase parallel to the "lifting up of my hands" in 141:2, reaching out desperately to the LORD. The second half of verse 6 employs a vivid image which in another form we met with in 63:1. There the psalmist thought of himself as being like a weary, thirst-crazed traveler, crossing an arid landscape, desperately looking for water. Here the psalmist compares himself to the parched, cracked earth urgently in need of revitalizing rain. Since he is aware that his only hope for renewed vitality lies in the LORD, the rest of the psalm is dominated by reiterated and increasingly urgent petitions to the LORD.

7-12 Words which we have heard on the lips of other psalmists in similar crisis situations come tumbling out: "Answer me quickly. . . . Do not hide your face from me" (v. 7; cf. 10:1; 13:1; 69:17; 102:2). The need is urgent: "my spirit fails," a phrase whose nearest parallel is 84:2, "my soul . . . faints." There, however, the context is that of a psalmist overwhelmed by joy. Here these are the words of someone struggling to come to terms with what has happened to him, overwhelmed by harassment which has taken him to the very threshold of death. The closing words of verse 7 repeat part of 28:1. He needs reassurance, and he needs it spelled out for him. Verse 8 probably implies that he is waiting to hear the declaration of the LORD's "steadfast love" on the lips of a cultic official during the morning liturgy in the temple. Sometimes there are things which we know in our heart of hearts, things we have been brought up to believe, but things we need to hear again if they are to motivate our lives. Worship, which assumes a continuing trust in the LORD (see 4:5; 78:22), provides the context for such a hearing. True worship, which shines through the words "to you I lift up my soul" (cf. 25:1; 86:4), must give direction to the way in which we live day by day, so the psalmist says, "Teach me the way I should go" (cf. 142:3).

The petitions in verses 7-8 are echoed in different language in verses 9-10. "Save me [cf. 142:6]. . . . Teach me. . . . Let your good spirit lead me." In terms of his own need the psalmist is neatly encapsulating successive stages in the spiritual life. It is rooted in an experience of "salvation," of what God gives to us and does for us. But that is only the beginning of a new life which must be brought into line with God's "will," a Hebrew word which indicates what is acceptable or pleasing to God (cf. 40:8; 103:20). Such a life, however, is only possible with the help of God, so the psalmist prays, "Let your good spirit lead me." The phrase "your good spirit" is only found again in the Hebrew Bible in Neh. 9:20. It probably indicates the benign, guiding presence of God which we can unquestioningly trust to lead us on "a level path" (v. 10). This NRSV translation involves a needless alteration to the main Hebrew textual tradition, which reads "on level ground" (REB), a phrase used in Deut. 4:43 to describe the flat tableland east of the Jordan belonging to the tribe of Reuben. It is used here to indicate a secure future, with the ground level or firm under the psalmist's feet (cf. 26:12).

The psalm ends in verses 11-12 with a dramatic contrast which has its roots in the blessings and curses which are spelled out in, for example, Deuteronomy 27 and 28 as being built into the terms of the covenant which binds the LORD and his people. To be loyally part of the covenant people ensures blessing. This is what the psalmist is claiming for himself in the words "you are my God" (v. 10) and "I am your servant" (v. 12). So the psalmist prays, in words which reflect the character and purposes of the LORD, "preserve my life." This is a plea not merely for physical survival, but for a revitalized life, no longer a prey to the "trouble" (cf. 142:2) which threatens to mar it (cf. 30:3; 119:25). The psalmist's "enemies," however, since they have threatened all that the psalmist as God's servant cherishes, stand under a curse which means their extermination (v. 12).

This may strike us as a harsh note on which to end. It is one which confronts us in several psalms (see 5:10 and Psalm 109). We may struggle to reconcile this with the words of one who himself took "the form of a slave [servant]" (Phil. 2:7) and from the cross said, "Father, forgive them; they do not know what they are doing" (Luke 23:34). But this same Jesus knew that there were issues which separated people and that there were consequences which followed from the decisions they made, and the actions which flowed or did not flow from these decisions. In the parable of the judgment of the nations in Matt. 25:31-46, the criteria for separating the sheep and the goats may go far beyond what the psalmist envisaged, but the sheep end up with the verdict "blessed," while the goats are "accursed," facing eternal punishment. The psalmist does not invoke this eternal dimension. He has to hold on to what he believes to be the way in which God works within the horizons of this world. Within these horizons he believes, since this is God's world, that evil must be taken seriously and must face irrevocably God's verdict, "No!"

Psalm 144
THE SECRET OF NATIONAL PROSPERITY

This psalm falls clearly into two parts: verses 1-11, a royal psalm centering on the king's plea for deliverance "from the hand of aliens" (v. 7); and verses 12-15, a prayer for a benediction on the nation. The two parts are so different in content, style, and language that many scholars have argued that they are in fact two quite separate psalms, with verses 12-15 probably a fragment which has strayed in from some other psalm. This is unnecessary.

We have had occasion to note at several points the close links which bind together, for good and for ill, king and people (see, e.g., Psalm 72). The concluding section provides the clue to understanding the whole psalm. It seems clear from some of the language used in verses 12-15 that these verses come to us out of the experience of the postexilic community. The phrase translated "of every kind" (v. 13), more literally "from kind to kind," uses a word which elsewhere is found only in 2 Chron. 16:14 and is generally recognized as a Persian loanword. These verses probably come from a community facing hard times. They are looking for a renewal of the nation's life consistent with its relationship with the LORD. Verses 1-11 consequently look back to that relationship and national well-being in the time prior to the exile, when the Davidic king was central to the nation's life and guaranteed the nation's security and prosperity. The heading to the psalm in the Greek (LXX) text adds the words "against Goliath" after David, with Jewish tradition identifying the "cruel sword" of verse 11 with the sword of Goliath (cf. 1 Sam. 17:45). Verses 1-11 draw heavily upon earlier liturgical and royal material, notably the "Thanksgiving of a Warrior King" which is Psalm 18. It reshapes that material to make it relevant to the life of the later community. It speaks of the LORD, "who rescues his servant David" (v. 10; cf. 89:3, 35, 39 and the heading to Psalm 18). Here the psalm may be keeping alive the hope of the postexilic community for the coming of a future Davidic king, or it may be that the community, as in Isa. 55:3-5, sees itself as the heir to the promises rooted in the LORD's "steadfast, sure love for David" (Isa. 55:3). If this approach to the psalm is correct, then we are seeing here what religious communities, Jewish and Christian, have done with the Psalms across the centuries — reinterpreted them to speak to the particular need of those who gather for worship, sometimes by weaving together verses from different psalms to achieve that end.

1-11 As we have seen, verses 1-11 draw heavily upon liturgical material found elsewhere in the Psalms. Where this occurs, we shall simply draw attention to the discussion in these other psalms. Although the building bricks of these verses are, therefore, to be found elsewhere, particularly in Psalm 18, they have been used and fitted together to make a psalm which has its own distinctive character. It is natural to think of the opening words of this section as coming originally from the lips of the king. Verses 1-2 celebrate in hymnic style the LORD, who is the mainstay of the king's life. The language "my rock," "my fortress," "my stronghold," "my deliverer," "my shield," the God "in whom I trust" is the language of 18:1-2. The specific skill bestowed upon the king by the LORD, "who trains my hands for war," echoes 18:34, with its meaning underscored by the parallel "and my fingers for battle." These are the words of a warrior king who draws strength from and puts his trust in the LORD. The NRSV translation "my rock" in verse 2, although it follows 18:2 and the parallel passage in 2 Sam. 22:2, involves a change to the Hebrew text which the REB legitimately renders as "my unfailing help," my *ḥesed* (see 5:7), the one on whom I can totally depend. In the closing words of verse 2, the mainstream Hebrew tradition reads "my people" instead of "peoples." If this is correct, then it must refer to the king's crushing of internal dissent and revolt (cf. Absalom's revolt against David, 2 Samuel 15–18). However, the plural "peoples" (REB: "nations") has some textual support and seems more likely in context (cf. 18:47).

Side by side with the celebration of the dependable power and supporting strength of the LORD, verses 3-4 place the insignificance, the fragility, and the transitoriness of all human life. The language of verse 3 recalls 8:4, though the verbs are different; "regard" is literally "know" (cf. 139:1), and "think of them" is the verb translated "takes thought of me" in 40:17. The emphasis upon human fragility and transitoriness in verse 4 draws upon 39:5, 11, where everyone is "mere breath," and upon 109:23, where the psalmist says, "I am gone like a shadow at evening." These verses, which have no parallel in Psalm 18, probably give us a glimpse into the mind of the community from which the psalm in its present form has come. It is a community conscious of its own fragility and vulnerability, conscious that even the monarchy, which had once been the glory of Israel, had bitten the dust. It is a community reaching out to the LORD in whom alone it can find refuge.

In verses 5-8 we hear the words of the warrior-king appealing to the LORD to make his presence known and to rescue his royal protégé from all the forces which threaten to overwhelm him. Verses 5-6 draw upon and indeed quote material in 18:7-14, but with a significant difference. Whereas Psalm 18 celebrates what the LORD has done and is doing, here the same words are formed into a prayer. The recollection "He bowed the heavens and came down" (18:9) becomes the prayer, "Bow your heavens, O LORD, and come down" (v. 5). The statement "he sent out his arrows and scattered them; he flashed forth lightnings and routed them" (18:14) becomes the request "Make the lightning flash and scatter them; send out arrows and rout them" (v. 6). Likewise, compare 18:16 with verse 7. This is prayer in the midst of crisis, not thanksgiving for deliverance from it.

Verses 7-8 throw some light on the nature of the crisis. The "mighty waters," symbolic of all that threatens life (cf. 18:16; 29:3), are defined in terms of "aliens" (cf. 18:44, 45, where this word is translated "foreigners," and 137:4), "whose mouths speak lies, and whose right hands are false" (vv. 8, 11). These words probably point to people who had entered into solemn treaties with the king but who had no intention of keeping them. In their eyes such treaties were mere scraps of paper to be ignored or torn up when it suited them. What they publicly said bore no relationship to what they were prepared to do (cf. 12:2). Political doublespeak has a long history.

Having made his prayerful appeal to the LORD, the king now turns in verses 9-10 to offer a vow of thanksgiving in words which draw upon 33:2-3. He will sing "a new song" which will reflect the "victory" ("salvation," see 3:8) which lies in the hands of the LORD, a victory he will give to "his servant David" (cf. 89:39, 50). The first section of the psalm then closes in verse 11 by reinforcing the nature of the crisis faced, by repeating with slight variation verses 7 and 8, the "cruel sword" graphically describing those who threaten the future of the king and his people.

12-15   The second section of the psalm may be in the form of a prayer (NRSV) or a benediction (REB). Unless we alter the text, it is introduced abruptly in Hebrew by a word (*'ăšer*) which occurs at the beginning of the third line of the previous verse and is there translated "whose." Perhaps it is being deliberately used in a slightly different sense to point up the contrast between "*their* mouths" and "*our* sons." "Think," says the psalmist, "of a community whose human and material resources find their true fulfillment." The youth on whom the community depends for the future fulfill their potential. Sons are thriving and sturdy, like well-nourished plants; daughters are strong, graceful, and elegant, "like sculptured corner pillars of a palace" (REB, v. 12) or a temple. There is thriving agriculture, abundant harvests. Fields in the open countryside teem with sheep (v. 13). Verse 14 is capable of different interpretations, clearly indicated by the differences in the NRSV and REB renderings. If the Hebrew word which means "heavy" or laden in verse 14 suggests "heavy with young," then it would be better to continue this picture into the next line and translate with the REB "there will be no miscarriage or untimely birth" (literally, "no break and no going out"). The closing line of the verse may then be translated "nor bellowing in our broad meadows" (so Allen), no cattle crying in distress. The Greek (LXX) text, however, renders the word "heavy" as "stout," and this lies behind the REB's rendering "fat and sleek." The picture may then switch, as in the NRSV, from the cattle to the citizens who will never be forced to go into exile, out through the broken walls that once guarded their city. Amos uses very similar language in his ironic picture of the once pampered society belles of Samaria going into captivity: "Through breaches in the walls you shall leave" (Amos 4:3). In such a scenario it is natural to think of cries of distress in the streets. Whatever the precise picture, verse 14 is describing life unmarred by all that causes pain and distress.

Twice in the final verse we hear the "Happy are . . ." formula (see 1:1).

The translation "to whom such blessings fall" is a legitimate paraphrase of the Hebrew, which says "a people for whom it is like this." The second "happy are . . ." formula stresses that such a prospering, revitalized community owes everything to its relationship with the LORD. It is as if the psalmist's final word is to say, "Yes, you may look forward to such a prosperous future as the LORD's gift, but never forget the giver. Your relationship with him is more important than the gift." It was only such a faith which enabled the community to respond both to good times and to bad times. It is the basis of Job's initial response when disasters struck: "the LORD gave, and the LORD has taken away; blessed be the name of the LORD" (Job 1:21). We may see in God the source of all that is creative and enriching in life, but we must never worship God only for what he *gives,* but for what he *is:* the LORD who in the mystery of love chose Israel as his people (cf. Deut. 7:7) and called them to worship him and him alone.

Psalm 145
GOOD REASONS TO PRAISE GOD

This is the last example of an acrostic psalm (cf. Psalms 9–10; 119). It has only twenty-one verses; one letter of the Hebrew alphabet is missing, the letter corresponding to *n*. However, one Hebrew manuscript, the Greek (LXX), and the Syriac add a line beginning with the missing letter. That is now confirmed in the form in which the psalm appears among the Dead Sea Scrolls. Both the NRSV and the REB include this line. Although the NRSV includes it as part of verse 13, "The LORD is faithful . . . ," it agrees with the REB in linking it with what follows in verse 14. The Dead Sea Scrolls version of the psalm adds after each verse the refrain, "Blessed be the LORD, and blessed be his holy name," a pointer to the way in which the psalm was then being used in congregational worship (cf. Psalm 136). The psalm is a hymn of praise. Although it has been argued that we are listening to one solo voice throughout the psalm, it is more likely that the solo voice is leading and eliciting from the congregation a celebration of the goodness of the LORD. It is the only psalm in which the word "Praise" appears in the heading. As such, it may be preparing the way for the great Songs of Praise, the hallelujah chorus, which follow in Psalms 146–150. It stands in a rich liturgical tradition and draws on that tradition in its language and imagery, but it weaves its own distinctive pattern.

1-3   In the opening verses we listen to the words of the psalmist who is leading worship. For the opening words, "I will extol you," see 30:1. It would be equally possible to translate "Let me extol you" and then "let me bless your name." The psalmist addresses one whom he describes as "my God and King" (see 5:2). Words associated with kingship are heard across this psalm, and in verses 11-13 the word "kingdom" occurs four times. Before the psalm launches into this kingdom of the LORD, it is careful to spell out clearly what kind of king this is. For the reiterated use of the word "bless" in verses 1-2, compare Psalm 103 and the opening of Psalm 104. That the psalmist's attitude is no momentary whim is stressed by the repeated "forever and ever" at the end of verses 1 and 2 and the "every day" at the beginning of 2. He is witnessing to the attitude and commitment of a lifetime.

In verse 3 the congregation responds by celebrating the "greatness" of the LORD in words familiar from Psalms 48:1 and 96:4. These words, however, now lead in another direction, to the acknowledgment that this greatness is "unsearchable." God may know everything about us, as Psalm 139 asserts, "O LORD, you have searched me and known me" (139:1), but we do not, and cannot, know everything about God. We bow before the mystery of one whose greatness we but dimly understand (cf. Isa. 40:8). All authentic worship must contain this sense of the transcendence of God. Here is the divine King, great beyond all human understanding.

4-7 The psalmist draws the congregation's attention to the activity of this transcendent LORD. Words describing the LORD in action keep tumbling out: "your works" (v. 4; cf. 103:22; 104:24), "your mighty acts" (v. 4; cf. 106:2), "the glorious splendor of your majesty" (vv. 5, 12; cf. 8:1, 6), "your wondrous works" (v. 5; cf. 9:2; 98:1), and "your awesome deeds" (v. 6; cf. 139:14). This is the story of the LORD's greatness which, handed down from generation to generation, now occupies the psalmist's thoughts (for "meditate" in v. 5, cf. 1:2; 119:15) and which he gladly proclaims to the congregation. The greatness that they are invited to "celebrate" (v. 7; literally, "pour forth") in song — a greatness to which all the activities of the LORD bear witness — is the greatness of "your abundant goodness" and "your righteousness," that generous concern of the LORD for his people which expresses itself in his being present to defend his people and to right all wrongs done to them (cf. 143:1; for "goodness," see 25:7). It is not surprising that the congregation's response in verses 8-9 begins by recalling, as other psalms do (cf. 103:8), the credal confession of Exod. 34:6-7 and proceeds to spell out the LORD's goodness in terms of his "compassion" (see 25:6; cf. 40:11; 103:4). This is a divine king whose compassion reaches out to embrace the whole of his creation (v. 9).

10-12 The psalmist now develops themes from the congregation's response. If this is the LORD who has "compassion over all that he has made" (v. 9), that compassion should evoke "thanks" from "all your works" (v. 10); and that "steadfast love" so abundantly displayed by God (v. 8) should lead to a heartfelt response from his "faithful" people (for the link between "steadfast love" and "faithful," see 4:3). The theme of such a response must be "the glory of your kingdom" (see 3:3). The word translated "kingdom," which occurs four times in verses 11-13, occurs again in the Psalms only in 103:19 and elsewhere in the Hebrew Bible only in late books (Chronicles, Esther, and Daniel). It is a kingdom characterized by "power" (v. 11), the singular of the word translated "mighty acts" in verse 5. Verse 12 continues this theme by picking up the language of verse 5.

13-20 The congregation now celebrates this kingdom of the LORD. Verse 13 occurs again in slightly varied form on the lips of Nebuchadnezzar (Dan. 4:3, 34). All human power and dominion pale into insignificance in the light of this kingdom. But for the congregation this is not naked power, but power which expresses itself in compassion. This compassionate power is celebrated in two sections, each beginning with a statement about the essential nature of the LORD.

If in the second half of verse 13 the missing *n* line is correctly rendered in the Dead Sea Scrolls, then this is the LORD who "keeps faith with his people" (cf. Deut. 7:9 and the discussion of the word "faithfulness" at 25:5). This is the LORD, therefore, who acts to support all who stumble and to "raise up all who are bowed down" (v. 14; cf. 146:8, the only other place in the Hebrew Bible where the words translated "raise up" and "bowed down" occur). It is as if the LORD is being depicted as a caring father or mother picking up a child who has fallen, ever present to help in all the difficulties the members of the family may encounter (v. 14). Here is someone to whom the whole human family can look expectantly and in trust, a bountiful provider of food, "satisfying the desire of every living thing" (v. 16). Here and in verse 19 "desire" indicates not any old desire, but what people truly need if they are to live a fulfilled life in the LORD's world. It is noteworthy that in this section the emphasis is on the LORD's universal caring providence.

Verses 17-20 speak of the LORD who is "just" or "righteous" (REB; cf. v. 7) and "kind," a poor translation of the word which means "faithful" *(ḥasîd),* unswervingly loyal. In this section we move from universal providence to the dependable way in which the LORD meets the needs of his own people. In the background is the thought of the covenant relationship between the LORD and Israel (see 50:5). What it means to belong to the people of the LORD is spelled out in a series of descriptive phrases: "all who call upon him [cf. 116:4, 13, 17] in truth" or faithfulness (v. 18; see 25:5); "all who fear him" (v. 19; cf. 34:7, 9); "all who love him" (v. 20; cf. 31:23; 97:10). Here are people characterized by a willingness to admit that they need the LORD, that they must approach him in reverence, and that they must live with a consuming passion which places God at the center of all that they are and do (cf. Deut. 6:4-5). They are people who are living in response to a God who is "near" (v. 18), accessible, aware of what is taking place in the lives of his people, a God who fulfills their "desire" (v. 19; cf. v. 16), who "hears their cry" (cf. 4:1, 3), who "saves" (v. 19; see 3:2), who "watches over" (v. 20), protects, keeps guard over his people (cf. 91:11; 121:7,

8). This is the LORD's emphatic "yes" to his people, but to the "wicked" who place themselves outside such care, there can only be an equally emphatic "no." They are on the way to destruction (cf. 141:10).

The closing verse, verse 21, takes us back to the beginning of the psalm. It echoes the words "praise," "bless," and "name forever and ever" (v. 1) and joins together the psalmist who leads worship with the congregation, symbol of that greater company of God's people, as if to remind us that the true worship and praise of God must come from the whole created world. We are thus being prepared to tune in to the final triumphant "Hallelujah Chorus" in Psalms 146–150.

PSALMS 146–150

The last five psalms begin and end with *halĕlû-yāh,* "Praise the LORD!" They provide a fitting theological climax to the entire collection. Much that we have heard in other psalms now fades into the background. Here there are no urgent questions — no "Why?"'s or "How long?"'s, no puzzling doubts, no talk of threats from enemies, no wrestling with what authentic worship means. There remain only "Songs of Praise" which put everything else in perspective. If we cannot lift up our hearts in songs of praise for what we believe God to be and to have done, then our faith has no solid foundation. These songs provide us with a series of variations on some of the central certainties of Israel's faith. They have thus had an assured place in the morning service in the synagogue. Their mood is reflected in the prayer of St. Augustine, "Great art Thou, O Lord, and greatly to be praised. Great is Thy power, and Thy wisdom is infinite. Thee would we praise without ceasing. Thou callest us to delight in Thy praise, for Thou hast made us for Thyself, and our hearts find no rest until we rest in Thee."

Psalm 146
PRAISE THE LORD, WORTHY OF TRUST

The opening ascription of praise in verses 1-2 parallels the opening and closing words of Psalms 103 and 104. This, claims the psalmist, is no passing mood but a song of praise which will be on his lips as long as he lives. It springs out of a tested relationship of trust, which means that he comes to one whom he calls "my God" (v. 2; cf. 22:10). Such a relationship means saying firmly "No" to certain other values in life which are deceptive and illusory. "Do not put your trust in princes" (v. 3; see 118:9). Who such "princes" are in this context is not clear. They may be foreign overlords. This would fit in with the Greek (LXX) headings to this and the following psalm, which link them with Haggai and Zechariah in the postexilic period when national independence was but a dream. Equally they could be anyone holding positions of power and influence in the community. Political leaders, press and media barons, and multinational corporations of our own day could be classified as "princes," concerning whom we may rightly at times be cynical (for "trust," see 4:5). Indeed, "princes" here are singled out as being no more than "mortals" (literally, "son of man"; see 8:4), by very definition transitory. Their "breath" (Hebrew *ruaḥ;* see 51:10-12), the gift of life which comes to them from God, departs to return to the God who gave it. The moving poem on the inevitability of death in Ecclesiastes 12 ends, recalling the creation story in Gen. 2:7, "and the dust returns to the earth as it was, and the breath returns to God who gave it" (Eccl. 12:7).

3-5 These verses similarly recall Gen. 2:7 in their deliberate play on the words "mortals" and "earth" (Hebrew *'ādām* and *'ădāmāh*). The earthling comes from the earth and at the end of his life span returns to the earth. His "plans" or projects — an Aramaic word occurring only here in the Hebrew Bible — perish with him (v. 4). There is, therefore, no "help" (v. 3; REB: "power to save"; see 3:8) to be found in anyone who shares this human frailty (cf. Psalm 90). Verses 3-4, therefore, act as a foil against which the rest of the psalm spells out and celebrates the one in whom alone true security can be found, the LORD who is the "God of Jacob" (see 20:1). For the last time, we hear at the beginning of verse 5 the "Happy are . . ." formula (see 1:1). True fulfillment in life comes to those who place their "help" and their "hope" in this God. The word translated "help" (v. 5) is not the same word as that translated "help" in verse 3 in the NRSV. It is found in the Psalms as a title of the LORD (cf. 33:20) and indicates strength and security (cf. 121:1, 2). The word translated "hope" occurs only here and in 119:116, but elsewhere the verb is translated by the NRSV as "look to you" (104:27; 145:15). It points in this context to people who refuse to be dazzled by human power but keep their eye firmly and expectantly fixed on the LORD.

6-10 The next section spells out the character of the LORD in words familiar from other psalms. He is the creator of the universe (v. 6), of "heaven and earth" (cf. 121:2) and "the sea" (cf. 95:5), with all the associations the sea had in ancient Near Eastern mythology as representative of the forces of chaos (see Psalm 29). He is a dependable creator who "keeps faith forever" (see 25:5), the one who never changes no matter what else may change in our experience of life. He is, however, no distant or remote deity, but the one who is compassionate, concerned for those who are most at risk from oppression and exploitation. Verse 8 echoes the language of 145:14, with the surrounding verses and words putting flesh, as it were, on those who are "bowed down." This is the God who "executes justice for the oppressed" (v. 7; see 10:14, 18); "gives food to the hungry" (v. 7; cf. 107:36-38); "sets the prisoners free" (v. 7; cf.

102:20); "opens the eyes of the blind" (v. 8; cf. Isa. 42:7); "loves the righteous" (v. 8; see 11:7); and protects "the strangers . . . the orphan and the widow" (v. 9; cf. 94:6). Over against this open outreach to those in need, the section ends, as does 145:20, with the door being firmly closed against the wicked. Celebration of a compassionate God, however, is only meaningful on the lips of those who show a like compassion in their lives (cf. Deut. 24:19-22). When Jesus in the synagogue in Nazareth read very similar words from Isaiah 61 and declared "Today this scripture has been fulfilled in your hearing" (Luke 4:18-19), he was affirming that the same divine compassion was to be the basis of his ministry (cf. Luke 7:18-23).

The psalm ends by underlining the traditional link between the community's celebration of the LORD and the Jerusalem temple on Mt. Zion (see 2:6). There at the temple, in the great religious festivals of the year, the LORD was acknowledged as king over his people and over the whole world, a king who "will reign forever" (v. 10). To such a God there can only be one lasting response of faith: "Praise the LORD!" We listen to these words echoing across the ultimate vision of the fulfillment of all God's purposes in Revelation: "Hallelujah!" (Rev. 19:3) and "Hallelujah! For the LORD our God, the Almighty reigns. Let us rejoice and exult and give him the glory" (Rev. 19:6). Within Christian hymnology, Ps. 146:2 appears in Isaac Watts's memorable version, "I'll praise my maker, while I've breath . . . my days of praise shall never pass while life and thought and being last."

Psalm 147
PRAISE THE LORD —
GOD OF NATURE, GOD OF HIS PEOPLE

This psalm falls clearly into three sections, verses 1-6, verses 7-11, and verses 12-20. Each section begins with an invocation, "Praise the LORD!" (v. 1); 'Sing to the Lord with thanksgiving" (v. 7); and "Praise the LORD, O Jerusalem!" (v. 12). The Greek (LXX) text treats verses 12-20 as a separate psalm, thus enabling it to come in line again with the traditional Hebrew numbering of the Psalms, having fallen one behind since it counted Psalms 9 and 10 as one psalm. This division, however, is highly unlikely. There are many linguistic features holding together the three sections of the psalm. This psalm would find its natural setting in one of the great religious festivals in the postexilic period. The phrase "the outcasts of Israel" (v. 2) is one which occurs again in Neh. 1:9 and most naturally refers to Jews banished from their homeland during the exile or later scattered across the world. There are, moreover, some interesting links with the thought and language of Isaiah 40–55, as well as with other psalms, notably Psalm 33.

1-6 The psalm begins where the previous psalm ends, by focusing upon worship in the Jerusalem temple, and weaves together its themes of compassion and creation. After the opening "Praise the LORD!" it is best to follow the REB and take the rest of verse 1 to refer to the pleasure and appropriateness (cf. 33:1) involved in singing the LORD's praise (see 135:3 for a discussion of the word the NRSV renders "gracious"). It is so because the LORD is showing his compassion to his people by building up Jerusalem and bringing home its scattered exiles who have been through experiences which have left them broken and scarred (vv. 2-3). The LORD's healing touch is at work. The "downtrodden," the afflicted or the humble (see 9:18), are being upheld, while the wicked who are out to destroy them are being thwarted (v. 6). The reference to the building up of Jerusalem (v. 2) need not imply any specific incident, such as the mission of Nehemiah. It may point to the continuing process in the postexilic period of restoring the city and welcoming home Jews from the Dispersion. Within this framework of compassion, there are two verses, 4 and 5, which recall the theology of the great prophet of the exile, Isaiah 40–55. He too has a word of compassion, of coming deliverance, to speak to his broken people (cf. Isa. 40:1-2). It is a message which he knows some of his people may find hard to believe. In a series of rhetorical questions, he challenges them to draw strength from the fact that the God with whom they are dealing is the all-powerful LORD in whose hands lies the whole created universe. In 40:26 he calls upon them to look up into the sky with its myriad stars: "Who created these? He who brings out their host and numbers them, calling them all by name." This is the all-powerful God, he claims, whose "understanding is unsearchable." The question of Isa. 40:26 is converted in this psalm into a ringing declaration of the awesome power of the LORD, the God whose understanding or wisdom is "beyond measure" or, as the REB neatly puts it, "beyond all telling" (see 145:3; cf. 139:18). Such is the God who "heals the brokenhearted" (v. 3). Who can stop him from doing it?

7-11 With song and musical accompaniment, the congregation is now invited to express its "thanksgiving" (see 50:14; cf. Psalm 100) to the LORD. His graciousness is seen in the natural world, in his sending the rain which clothes with grass what would otherwise be a parched hillside (v. 8), and in his providing food for "the animals," probably domestic cattle, and even for the "young ravens" (v. 9). The "young ravens" may be singled out from among the birds since there was a popular, if unfounded, belief that ravens left their young to fend for themselves. Their croaking was thought to be a sign of their being neglected (cf. Job 38:41). But the LORD provides even for them. Jesus uses the ravens, whom God feeds, to stress to his disciples how much more valuable they are to God than the birds (Luke 12:24). This is the God, claims the psalmist, whose values are not our values, who remains singularly indifferent to what we often regard as important, be it "the strength of the horse," that is, a war steed (cf. 33:16-17, the ancient equivalent of the tank or the stealth bomber) or "the speed of a runner" (v. 10; literally, "the legs of a man"). Here the reference is probably not to what we would call athletic prowess, but to the stamina of the infantry. Indifferent to human power the LORD may be, but he is not indifferent to "those who fear him" and "those who hope in his steadfast love" (v. 11; see 33:18).

12-20 These verses invite Jerusalem to sing and to praise the LORD for his providential care. It is hard to see why the NRSV uses the word "praise" twice in verse 12, since the Hebrew uses two different words, the first of which is rendered "extol" in Psalm 117. This providential care expresses itself in a variety of ways. It guarantees the city's security and ensures a thriving population within it (v. 13; for the "bars" which held in place the city gates, cf. Lam. 2:9). It grants *shalom* (see 4:9) to the whole land, a land blessed with the finest agricultural produce (v. 14). It controls the forces of nature. The language of verse 15 — "He sends out his command . . ." — recalls the creation story in Genesis 1, where "God said . . . and it was so" (Gen. 1:9, 10, 11, 14). This is a word which "runs swiftly," which nothing can thwart (cf. Isa. 45:23; 55:11). Graphic illustration of this is now provided as the psalmist describes what happens rarely, but with dramatic effect, in his native land. Severe winter weather brings the snowstorm which seems to wrap the land in a blanket of white wool. Frost is sprinkled like white "ashes" over the landscape (cf. Exod. 16:14, where this simile is used in connection with the manna). Hail or ice particles (cf. Job 37:10; 38:29) litter the ground, and water is frozen. The REB translation of verse 17b — "he sends the cold, and the water stands frozen" — involves a simple and widely followed emendation of the Hebrew text. It certainly provides a better contrast to the "waters flow" in verse 18 than the question which the NRSV retains. Then comes the thaw. The warm wind blows, and the frozen water begins to flow again. All this, says the psalmist, is the LORD's doing, the effect of his word.

God's providential care also finds expression in the covenant relationship between the Lord and his people. There is another word, the word given to Jacob/Israel (see 20:1), which means that his people live under his "statutes and ordinances" (v. 19; cf. 119:5-8). The words "He has not dealt thus with any other nation; they do not know his ordinances" (v. 20) point to the particular privilege which was given to Israel. It would be wrong, however, to read into these words any sense of religious triumphalism. The reference to "statutes" and the twice-repeated "ordinances" stress rather that this is a privilege which places Israel under the obligation to be obedient to the revelation which it has received. There may be an excuse for other nations flouting the ordinances of the LORD, but there is no such excuse for Israel.

The words "Praise the LORD!" are meaningless except on the lips of those who are responding to the grace of God in a life of obedient commitment. As Amos forcibly reminded the people in the name of God: "You only have I known

of all the families of the earth; therefore I will punish you for all your iniquities"
(Amos 3:2).

Psalm 148
PRAISE THE LORD —
THE UNIVERSE IN CHORUS

No other psalm witnesses more clearly to the breathtaking comprehensiveness of
Israel's faith. Here is a choir, not of temple singers nor of the chosen few but of
the whole created universe, lifting its voice in an uninhibited song of praise. The
psalm divides into two parallel sections. Verses 1-6 begin with "Praise the LORD
from the heavens"; verses 7-14 with "Praise the LORD from the earth." Towards
the end of each section we hear the words "Let them praise the name of the
LORD" (vv. 5 and 13), on each occasion backed up by the reasons for so doing,
introduced by the word "for."

1-6   The psalm begins not in the limited horizons of earth, but in the highest and
outermost sphere of creation: "Praise the LORD from the heavens" (v. 1), you
"highest heavens" (v. 4; literally, "heaven of heavens"), probably here an emphatic way of saying "heaven itself." Six times the word "praise" is heard in
these verses. The heavenly song of praise is heard first on the lips of "all his
angels . . . all his host" (v. 2; see 24:10; 34:7; cf. 103:20-22). The various heavenly
bodies then join in: "sun and moon . . . shining stars" (v. 3), as do "the waters
above the heavens" (v. 4; cf. Gen. 1:7). There are echoes here of the creation
hymn in Genesis 1, not least in the theological stance of the psalmist. In some of
the pantheons of the ancient Near East, the celestial bodies had a prominent role.
They were worshipped. Astrology was concerned to unravel the influence they
exercised over human affairs. All this, as in Genesis 1, is swept into the theological
wastepaper basket. There is only one God, the LORD. Everything else exists in
finitude, solely to praise him. The heavenly bodies are aware of his awesome
character, his name (v. 5; see 5:11), "for he commanded and they were created"
(v. 5; cf. Genesis 1). They remain secure in their place for all time, as the LORD
ordained. The REB's translation in verse 6, "by an ordinance which will never
pass away," is preferable to the NRSV's rendering, "he fixed their bounds, which
cannot be passed." Just as Israel's life was determined by the "statutes and
ordinances" given to them by the LORD (cf. 147:19), so the life of the whole
created world moves within the orbit of a divine ordinance or decree (cf. Job
28:26).

7-14   An earthly antiphon now responds to the heavenly choir. The earthly chorus
includes the "sea monsters and all deeps." This may be no more than a reference

to the teeming life in the seas, including the gigantic whales (cf. Gen. 1:21), but lurking behind these words there may still be echoes of the forces of chaos which, from time immemorial, were regarded as a threat to the order the LORD had established (see 74:13). Nature joins in the antiphon: "fire and hail, snow and frost" (v. 8). "Frost" is the reading of the early versions, but the Hebrew text has "smoke." This should be retained. It gives a line in which fire and smoke are paired together, as are hail and snow in an *ab-ba* pattern. Both pairs point to awesome forces in nature, volcanic activity on the one hand and exceptionally severe winters on the other (cf. 147:16-17). Just like the "storm winds," they may seem beyond human control, but they simply act in obedience to the LORD's word or command. The panorama continues with the towering mountains, the fruit trees, the majestic cedars, the animals of the wild, domestic cattle, the creatures that crawl on the earth, and the birds that fly in the sky (vv. 9-10; cf. Gen. 1:20-25). Last but not least, the human race brings its songs of praise — all peoples and the most powerful of rulers and potentates, everyone irrespective of sex or of age. They come to acknowledge that it is the LORD's "name" (cf. v. 5), and the LORD's name alone, which is "exalted," peerless (cf. Isa. 12:4), just as his glory towers above all creation (see 8:1), above "earth and heaven" (v. 13).

The anthem, however, is not yet finished. Another voice is still to be heard, a distinctive voice, that of his covenant people, his "faithful" (see 4:3) — the "Israel who are close to him," those who know in a special way his presence in their midst (cf. Lev. 10:3). They have their own reason for praising the LORD. For them, "he has raised up a horn," that symbol of strength (see 75:5; cf. 92:10; 112:9), which his people discovered anew in the midst of their changing, tempestuous history. Although the REB may be right in taking "praise" in verse 14b as the second object of "raise up," thus translating, "and crowned with praise his loyal servants," the thought of Israel as receiving praise does not fit in well with the overall theme of the psalm. It is better to assume that the strength that the LORD gave to Israel ensured that the life of his faithful people would be characterized by praise, praise to the LORD who guaranteed that this would be a people "close to him."

This is a psalm which in varied forms has echoed across history. In an expanded form it provides the basis for "The Song of the Three Jews" in the Apocrypha, a song intended to be inserted between Dan. 3:23 and 24. As such it provides a remarkable testimony to the vitality of a faith which would enter the fiery furnace, not in fear or despair, but with such a song of praise to the LORD. It continues to hold its place in Jewish liturgical tradition in the weekday morning service. For St. Francis it became the model for his "Canticle to the Sun," which in turn has provided the basis for the hymn "All Creatures of Our God and King." This hymn begins with Psalm 148 and ends by identifying "all his faithful" and the Israel "close to him" with the Church, capping the psalm with a distinctively Christian song of praise:

And thou, most kind and gentle death,
Waiting to hush our latest breath,
   O praise him, Alleluia!
Thou leadest home the child of God,
And Christ our Lord the way hath trod.
   O praise him, O praise him, Alleluia!
      Alleluia! Alleluia!

There is no more vigorous and inspiring version of this psalm for congregational singing, however, than the Scottish Metrical Version, which begins:

The Lord of heaven confess,
On high his glory raise.
Him let all angels bless,
Him all his armies praise.
   Him glorify
   Sun, moon and stars;
   Ye higher spheres,
   And cloudy sky.

Psalm 149
A VICTORY HYMN

All approaches to this psalm are attempts to explain its two dominant and (in many people's eyes) jarring features: the unrestrained joy of God's people in verses 1-5 and the execution of vengeance on their enemies in verses 6-9. Its origins have been sought in the celebration of the kingship of God and his triumph over all enemies, dramatically enacted in one of the great festivals of the religious year in the Jerusalem temple (see Psalms 47; 93, 95–99). More particularly it has been described as "a hymn sung and performed in the religious assembly on the eve of battle against heathen nations" (Dahood). Others have stressed the eschatological orientation of the psalm, pointing forward to that final victory for which God's people live in hope. Equally uncertain is the date of the psalm. Traditionally there has been a tendency to associate it with the Maccabean revolt against Seleucid domination in the second century BCE. There are, however, no specific features in the language or the imagery of the psalm to point clearly in this direction, nor indeed in any other direction. Even a postexilic date, though likely in view of the numerous linguistic links with Isaiah 60 and 61, is far from certain.

The language of the psalm has unfortunately led to its being used to justify the call to arms and subsequent bloodshed in the name of religion. Thus for the Protestant Thomas Münzer it became the battle hymn of the bloody Peasants' Revolt in the sixteenth century, while for Caspar Schopp it provided a call to arms for

Roman Catholic princes in the Thirty Years' War which was to ravage Europe. More sensitive Christians have sought to "transform the letter of the psalm into the spirit of the New Covenant" (Delitzsch). Thus the "two-edged swords" (v. 6) have become "the sword of the Spirit which is the word of God" (Eph. 6:17), and God's people are here "encouraged to eschew despair and to look for the dawn of a new day when justice would be seen to be done" (Allen). *Siddur Lev Chadash* omits this psalm from its daily services, while retaining Psalms 148 and 150. The theological problems this psalm raises, however, are no greater and no less than those we have seen in many other psalms, where religious sensitivity goes hand in hand with the cry for vengeance against enemies, whether national or personal (see, e.g., Psalms 109 and 137). The psalmist speaks to us out of his own situation. He rejoices in the "Yes" which the LORD says to his own people, and in the emphatic "No" said to all who oppose the LORD's purposes. The military language in verses 6-9 probably goes back to the concept of holy war rooted in the traditions surrounding the conquest of Canaan, with its demand for the total elimination of all other peoples (cf. Deut. 7:1-6). Whatever the limitation of this concept, it provided Israel with a robust faith rooted in the conviction that her enemies were God's enemies and that such enemies would fall under God's judgment and reap their deserved reward.

1-5 The opening words of this hymn echo the closing verse of Psalm 148. The scene is "the assembly of his faithful" (cf. 148:14), where the people of Israel, "the children of Zion" (see 2:6), gather to praise and to rejoice in the LORD, whom they acknowledge as their "Maker" (see 100:3) and their "King." They are summoned to "sing to the LORD a new song" (see 33:3; cf. 96:1), in a joyful act of worship in which voices blend with dancing and the musical accompaniment of tambourine and lyre (v. 3). To this we may compare the festival procession of 81:1-3 and the way in which Miriam, according to Exod. 15:20-21, led the celebration of the deliverance at the Reed Sea. Verse 4 then spells out the reason for this joyful celebration. They are worshipping the LORD who "takes pleasure in his people" (cf. 147:1), the God whose grace has been with them, the God who "adorns [or will adorn] the humble with victory" (see 3:2). This is the only place in the Psalms where the verb translated "adorns" occurs. The corresponding noun often has royal associations, hence the REB's rendering, "he crowns" (cf. 71:8; 89:17, where the noun is translated "glory"). What other response can "the faithful" make to such a God than one of unrestrained rejoicing? The concluding words of verse 5, "on their couches," is something of a puzzle. Calvin believed that this pointed to the daily rest that the people would enjoy under the LORD's protection. This at least has the merit of taking seriously the word "couch," which usually means a bed (cf. 36.4). That it can mean something like a prayer mat (cf. REB: "as they prostrate themselves") is doubtful. The suggested emendation "according to their families" (cf. Num. 1:18) would provide a picture of the community gathered for worship in their traditional family groups.

6-9 Victory, deliverance for the people of God, means defeat for their enemies. The praises raised on high to the LORD presuppose the doom of all who oppose his purposes. Voices are raised in praise, but in their hands are "two-edged swords" (literally, "a sword of mouths" or edges; cf. Prov. 5:4, where a similar phrase describes the adulteress or loose woman). These are sharp swords used to "execute vengeance on the nations" (v. 6; cf. 94:1). Their kings and nobles suffer the expected fate consequent upon national defeat. They are dragged off in "fetters" and "chains of iron" (cf. 105:18). This is no chance fate. It is the result of "the judgment decreed" (literally, "written"). This may be a reference to the LORD's book in which he was believed to record all that happened or was destined to happen for good and for ill (cf. 56:8; 69:28). It is just possible, however, that the reference is to earlier prophecies of judgment against the nations (e.g., Amos 1:3–2:3). Whatever precise significance we give to this phrase, one thing is clear: this is the LORD's doing, and it redounds to the "glory" (Hebrew *hādar;* see 8:1) of his "faithful ones" (v. 9), the third time this word has appeared in the psalm (cf. vv. 1, 5). What is at stake is not merely nationalistic triumphalism, but the true status of the people of God in a world under his control.

Although we may hesitate to use some of the language of this psalm, we give voice to the same faith and the same hope when we pray "Your kingdom come, your will be done on earth as in heaven" (Matt. 6:10). In the face of so much that seems to call into question that kingdom and that will in the world in which we live, we dare to pick up the closing words of the psalm — "Praise the LORD!" — and look forward to the final judgment and rejoicing which the vision in Revelation 19 proclaims.

Psalm 150
THE FINAL SONG OF PRAISE

This is the last of the Songs of Praise which began with Psalm 145. But it is more than that. The first four books in the present Psalter end with a doxology (41:13; 72:18-19; 89:52; 106:48). Psalm 150 is an extended doxology which sets the seal on the entire collection. There is no mistaking its purpose. It begins and ends, as the previous four psalms do, with "Praise the LORD!" and in between the opening and closing words the word "praise" occurs no less than ten times. It is as if this psalm is saying to us, "Whatever else you may forget about the Psalms, never forget that central to authentic faith is the praise of God. Forget that and you will undermine the foundations of everything else."

1-2 Verse 1 confronts us with an open question. There is no doubt that "his mighty firmament," that vault which according to Gen. 1:6 arches over the earth, signifies the heavens; but what is meant by "his sanctuary"? If it is intended to be parallel in thought to the "mighty firmament," then it must mean God's heavenly sanctuary (see 11:4). If, on the other hand, it is being used in contrast to the "mighty firmament," it will refer to the earthly sanctuary, the temple in Jerusalem with its courts which rang with the people's praise. In this case we have here in reverse order the call to praise the LORD in Psalm 148, first "from the heavens" (v. 1), then "from the earth" (v. 7). Now praise is to be heard first "in his sanctuary," then "in the heavens." It could be that both heavenly and earthly sanctuary are meant, since the earthly sanctuary was considered to be a reflection of the heavenly temple, the throne of God transcendent. As we have seen in the previous psalm, the call to praise the LORD is backed up by a statement of the reasons which make such an appeal fitting and necessary. The reasons are briefly stated in verse 2 in general terms which the worshippers could fill out on the basis of their own experience. They center on "his mighty deeds" (cf. 145:4) and on his "surpassing [REB: "immeasurable"] greatness" (cf. 79:11). Both speak of that power beyond human comprehension which Israel knew went hand in hand with compassion, as previous psalms have repeatedly stressed.

3-5 In verses 3-5 the temple orchestra is invited to make its contribution to the Songs of Praise: trumpets, which called the people to worship on festal occasions (cf. 81:3); "lyre and harp" (v. 3; the NRSV's rendering, "lute," is misleading; cf. 81:3) and "strings" (cf. 45:8, the only other occurrence of this word); percussion, "tambourines" accompanying the dance (v. 4) and "clashing cymbals" (v. 5); and the "pipe" (v. 4) or flute, a word nowhere else found among the temple instruments in the Hebrew Bible, but used in joyful family celebrations (cf. Job 21:12; 30:31).

But no music or musical instruments, however inspiring they may be, can adequately express the praise of God. They must be joined "by everything that breathes" (v. 6), all animate life. The "breath of life" comes to every living thing, according to Gen. 7:22 (cf. Gen. 2:7) as God's gift. It is a gift which must evoke from everyone and everything a response of praise. The true hallelujah chorus must be a universal chorus.

So the last chord of the Psalms dies away, only to be picked up and sent echoing around the world in Jewish and Christian communities across the centuries. "Praise the LORD!" — nothing more needs to be said but "Amen" (see 41:13), as we affirm our commitment to join in that universal hallelujah chorus.

SELECTED BIBLIOGRAPHY

Commentaries

Allen, L. C. *Psalms 101–150.* Word Biblical Commentary 21. Waco, Tex.: Word Books, 1983.

Anderson, A. A. *Psalms.* New Century Bible. 2 vols. London: Oliphants, 1972.

Anderson, G. W. *The Psalms.* Peake's Commentary on the Bible. London: Thomas Nelson and Sons, 1962.

Augustine. *The Book of Psalms.* 6 vols. Library of the Fathers. Oxford: J. H. Parker, 1847-57.

Barnes, W. E. *The Psalms.* 2 vols. Westminster Commentaries. London: Methuen & Co., 1931.

Braude, W. G. *The Midrash on the Psalms.* 2 vols. New Haven: Yale University Press, 1959.

Briggs, C. A., and E. G. Briggs. *A Critical and Exegetical Commentary on the Book of Psalms.* 2 vols. International Critical Commentary. Edinburgh: T & T Clark, 1906.

Buttenweiser, M. *The Psalms.* Library of Biblical Studies. New York: Ktav Publishing House, 1969.

Calvin, J. *Commentary on the Book of Psalms.* 4 vols. Translated by J. A. Anderson. Edinburgh: Calvin Translation Society, 1845-47.

Cassiodorus, F. M. A. *Explanation of the Psalms.* Translated and annotated by P. G. Walsh. New York: Paulist Press, 1990-91.

Craigie, P. C. *Psalms 1–50.* Word Biblical Commentary 19. Waco, Tex.: Word Books, 1983.

Dahood, M. *Psalms.* 3 vols. Anchor Bible 16, 17, 17a. Garden City, N.Y.: Doubleday, 1966, 1968, 1970.

Delitzsch, F. *Biblical Commentary on the Psalms.* Translated by F. Bolton. 3 vols. 2d ed. Reprint, Grand Rapids: Eerdmans, 1952.

Durham, J. I. *Psalms.* Broadman Bible Commentary 4. Nashville: Broadman Press, 1971.

Eaton, J. H. *Psalms: Introduction and Commentary.* Torch Bible Commentaries. London: SCM Press, 1967.

Eerdmans, B. D. *The Hebrew Book of Psalms.* Leiden: Brill, 1947.

Gunkel, H. *Die Psalmen.* Handkommentar zum Alten Testament. Göttingen: Vandenhoeck & Ruprecht, 1929, 1968.

Kidner, D. *Psalms.* 2 vols. Tyndale Old Testament Commentaries. London: Inter-Varsity Press, 1973, 1975.

Kirkpatrick, A. F. *The Book of Psalms.* The Cambridge Bible for Schools and Colleges. Cambridge: Cambridge University Press, 1902; reprint, 1951.

Kissane, E. J. *The Book of Psalms.* 2 vols. Dublin: Browne & Nolan, 1953-54.

Knight, G. A. F. *Psalms.* 2 vols. Daily Study Bible Series. Edinburgh: St. Andrew Press, 1982-83.

Kraus, H.-J. *Psalms.* 2 vols. Translated by H. C. Oswald. Minneapolis: Augsburg, 1988-89.

Leslie, E. A. *Psalms: Translated and Interpreted in the Light of Hebrew Worship.* Nashville: Abingdon Press, 1949.

Luther, M. *First Lectures on the Psalms.* Luther's Works, vols. 10, 11. Edited by H. C. Oswald. St. Louis: Concordia Publishing House, 1974.

————. *Selected Psalms.* Luther's Works, vols. 12, 13, 14. Edited by J. Pelican. St. Louis: Concordia Publishing House, 1955.

Oesterley, W. O. E. *The Psalms.* London: SPCK, 1939, 1959.

Podechard, E. *Le Psautier.* 2 vols. Lyon: Facultes Catholiques, 1949, 1954.

Rhodes, A. B. *Psalms.* Layman's Bible Commentaries. London: SCM, 1964.

Rogerson, J. W., and J. W. McKay. *Psalms.* 2 vols. The Cambridge Bible Commentary. Cambridge: Cambridge University Press, 1977.

Sabourin, L. *The Psalms: Their Origin and Meaning.* New York: Alba House, 1974.

Spurgeon, C. H. *The Treasury of David.* 3 vols. Grand Rapids: Zondervan, 1966.

Stuhlmueller, C. *Psalms.* Old Testament Message 21, 22. Wilmington, Del.: Glazier, 1983.

Tate, M. E. *Psalms 51–100.* Word Biblical Commentary 20. Waco, Tex.: Word Books, 1990.

Weiser, A. *The Psalms: A Commentary.* Translated by H. Hartwell. The Old Testament Library. London: SCM, 1962.

Other Studies

Anderson, B. W. *Out of the Depths: The Psalms Speak for Us Today*. Philadelphia: Westminster, 1983.

Broyles, C. C. *The Conflict of Faith and Experience in the Psalms*. JSOT Supplement Series 52. Sheffield: JSOT Press, 1989.

Brueggemann, W. *Israel's Praise: Doxology against Idolatry and Ideology*. Philadelphia: Fortress Press, 1988.

————. *The Message of the Psalms: A Theological Commentary*. Minneapolis: Augsburg, 1989.

Buber, M. *Right and Wrong: An Interpretation of Some Psalms*. London: SCM, 1952.

Clements, R. E. *One Hundred Years of Old Testament Interpretation*. Philadelphia: Westminster, 1976.

Clines, D. "Psalm Research since 1955: 1. The Psalms and the Cult." *Tyndale Bulletin* 17 (1966): 103-26.

————. "Psalm Research since 1955: 2. The Literary Genres." *Tyndale Bulletin* 20 (1969): 105-25.

Culley, R. C. *Oral Formulaic Language in the Biblical Psalms*. Toronto: University of Toronto Press, 1967.

Davidson, R. *The Courage to Doubt*. London: SCM, 1983.

————. *Wisdom and Worship*. London: SCM, 1990.

Day, J. *Psalms*. Old Testament Guides. Sheffield: JSOT Press, 1990.

Drijvers, P. *The Psalms: Their Structure and Meaning*. New York: Herder and Herder, 1964.

Eaton, J. H. *Kingship and the Psalms*. Studies in Biblical Theology. London: SCM, 1976.

————. *Psalms of the Way and the Kingdom: A Conference with the Commentators*. JSOT Supplement Series 199. Sheffield: JSOT Press, 1996.

Gerstenberger, E. S. *Psalms*. Part 1. The Forms of Old Testament Literature. Grand Rapids: Eerdmans, 1988.

Goulder, M. *The Prayers of David: Psalms 51–72*. JSOT Supplement Series 102. Sheffield: JSOT Press, 1990.

————. *The Psalms of the Sons of Korah*. JSOT Supplement Series 20. Sheffield: JSOT Press, 1982.

Gunkel, H. *The Psalms: A Form-Critical Introduction*. Philadelphia: Fortress, 1967.

Guthrie, H. H. *Israel's Sacred Songs: A Study of Dominant Themes*. New York: Seabury, 1996.

Johnson, A. R. *The Cultic Prophet in Ancient Israel*. 2d ed. Cardiff: University of Wales Press, 1962.

————. *The Cultic Prophet and Israel's Psalmody.* Cardiff: University of Wales Press, 1979.

Kraus, H. J. *Theology of the Psalms.* Translated by K. R. Crim. Minneapolis: Augsburg, 1986.

Lamb, J. A. *The Psalms in Christian Worship.* London: Faith Press, 1962.

Levine, H. J. *Sing unto God a New Song.* Bloomington and Indianapolis: Indiana University Press, 1995.

Miller, P. D. *Interpreting the Psalms.* Philadelphia: Fortress Press, 1986.

————. *They Cried to the Lord: The Form and Theology of Biblical Prayer.* Minneapolis: Fortress Press, 1994.

Mitchell, D. C. *The Message of the Psalter: An Eschatological Programme in the Book of Psalms.* JSOT Supplement Series 252. Sheffield: JSOT Press, 1997.

Mowinckel, S. *The Psalms in Israel's Worship.* 2 vols. Translated by D. R. Ap-Thomas. Oxford: Basil Blackwell, 1962.

Raabe, P. R. *Psalm Structures: A Study of Psalms with Refrains.* JSOT Supplement Series 104. Sheffield: JSOT Press, 1990.

Rayner, J. D., and C. Stern, eds. *Siddur Lev Chadash.* London, 1995.

Seybold, K. *Introducing the Psalms.* Edinburgh: T & T Clark, 1990.

Shepherd, M. H. *The Psalms in Christian Worship: A Practical Guide.* Minneapolis: Augsburg, 1976.

Westermann, C. *The Living Psalms.* Translated by J. R. Porter. Grand Rapids: Eerdmans, 1984; Edinburgh: T & T Clark, 1990.

————. *Praise and Lament in the Psalms.* Translated by K. R. Crim and R. N. Soulen. Atlanta: John Knox Press, 1981.

————. *The Praise of God in the Psalms.* Translated by K. R. Crim. Richmond: John Knox Press, 1965.

————. *The Psalms: Structure, Content, and Message.* Translated by R. D. Gehrke. Minneapolis: Augsburg, 1980.